W9-BCA-024

Agile Business Rule Development

Jérôme Boyer • Hafedh Mili

Agile
Business Rule
Development

Process, Architecture, and JRules Examples

 Springer

Mr. Jérôme Boyer
IBM
4400 North First Street
San Jose, CA, 95134
USA
boyerje@us.ibm.com

Prof. Hafedh Mili
Université du Québec á Montréal
Dépt. Informatique
C.P. 8888
Succursale centre-ville
Montréal Québec H3C 3P8
Canada
hafedh.mili@uqam.ca

ISBN 978-3-642-19040-7   e-ISBN 978-3-642-19041-4
DOI 10.1007/978-3-642-19041-4
Springer Heidelberg Dordrecht London New York

ACM Computing Classification (1998): J.1., H.3.5, I.2, D.2

Library of Congress Control Number: 2011924779

Cover design: KuenkelLopka GmbH

Printed on acid-free paper

Springer is part of Springer Science+Business Media (www.springer.com)

To my family and friends who support my day to day work and humor

To Amel, Haroun and Khalil, for giving a meaning to what I do

To Aicha, Taieb, Faouzi, Ali, Kamel, Fatma, Hedia, Seloua,
Sadok and Nebiha, for being there when it matters

To Lal-Melika and in memory of Si El Moncef

Foreword I

We all make a huge variety of decisions every day. For the vast majority of our daily chores we make those decisions based on the set of experiences and philosophies that we have developed and evolved over time. It is that combination of experience that makes us who we are—and that ensures that we are uniquely qualified to perform our jobs. The problem is that all too often the things that make us unique will lead us to making different decisions from everyone else in the organization. Those differences may be acceptable for a large class of the decisions we make. However, that can also be detrimental to the organization when it comes to certain *core* business processes.

Businesses that are able to capture the criteria by which they make business decisions are able to drive better business results. By capturing those criteria you can reason about their effectiveness. You can combine the best of everyone's experience to ensure you are able to respond to the most comprehensive set of circumstances. You can communicate those criteria across the organization and thus ensure that decisions are being made consistently. You can publish those criteria and use them as a benchmark against which to measure the effectiveness of decisions made in different parts of your organization. You can evolve those criteria in a systematic fashion—testing the effectiveness of decisions and evolving them over time to improve the performance of your business.

And what is the codification of those criteria? By any other name we refer to them as "business rules". Business rules are an independent representation of how the business should behave—the principles and expectations that go into business decisions.

Business rules capture decision criteria in a way that can be applied coherently, comprehensively and consistently across the organization. Further, they enable us to automate the execution of those decisions in our business processes. And by separating the business rules from the technical plumbing of the application we can update automated decision criteria, adjusting those rules as often as new experiences, changes in the environment, or *changes in philosophy* dictate. We can update how our business behaves at the speed of change in our marketplaces.

This book is about Business Rules. It opens by reasoning about the power of separating business rules from the technical infrastructure of our applications. It outlines methods for creating and maintaining business rules. It covers approaches to integrating business rules into our business processes, and for monitoring results and driving improvements to the rules, that in turn, drive improvements in business outcomes. It does so by discussing architectural issues, proposing general solution patterns, and illustrating those patterns for the case of IBM's business rule management system, WebSphere ILOG JRules. Most importantly, it explains how to *manage* rules like you would any other valuable *business asset*.

Quite possibly this will be the most important and comprehensive book you will ever read on the topic of business rules. I highly encourage you to read it from cover to cover and use it to guide your business process and application development activities. Having done so, I'm convinced that you will be in a better position to drive significant improvements to how we leverage Information Technology as a competitive weapon in our business markets.

Rob High, Jr.
IBM Fellow
IBM SOA Foundation, Chief Architect

Foreword II

I first met Jerome and Hafedh at an ILOG event in 2008 when ILOG, then an independent software company focused on business rules, had just donated its work on an Agile Business Rules Development (ABRD) methodology to the open source community. I had heard of this methodology while I was working on Decision Management at FICO, another business rules vendor, but had not had a chance to work with it. I was immediately impressed with both ABRD and the Eclipse Process Framework in which it was presented. I had worked on Ernst & Young's methodology and its automation in the 90s and I understood both the work involved and the value of managing the methodology—not just writing it. ABRD was clearly a well thought out methodology, embodying many best practices for business rules-based development, that could help organizations adopt Decision Management and business rules management systems.

Decision Management is an approach that focusses on automating and improving operational business decisions, including the many micro-decisions that impact a single customer or a single claim. It requires a solid platform for managing decision-making logic—a business rules management system (BRMS)—and a methodology for effectively finding and automating this logic. The combination of business rules and a Decision Management approach results in systems and processes that are simpler, more agile, more aligned with the business and fundamentally smarter. Effective management of the decision logic has improved decision accuracy, compliance and consistency.

Some companies make the mistake of assuming that decision management and business rules can be adopted by an IT department without changing existing governance and development approaches. Others assume that they can handle business rules as part of modeling and managing business processes. In fact, new approaches and techniques are required. Best practices already call for developers to separate the data, user interface and process definitions from applications. Decision Management takes this one step further and separates decision-making logic from the remainder of the technical implementation. Further, it empowers business users and analysts to collaborate effectively with their IT teams and even to control some of the logic themselves. But extracting decision-making logic as business rules and managing those business rules over time requires new skills, new techniques and new best practices, i.e. a new development methodology.

Among rule development methodologies, ABRD is unique in that it promotes iteration and the early use of a business rules management system. Focussing on incremental and iterative development, it has been specifically developed to handle new artifacts like business rules, decision points and more. It applies the key tenets of the agile manifesto and takes advantage of the power of business rules management systems to deliver on those tenets. Its approach to rule elicitation values "Individuals and interactions over processes and tools". It prototypes early to ensure "Working software over comprehensive documentation". It leverages the ability of non-technical business people to understand and even edit business rules to deliver "Customer collaboration over contract negotiation". Finally, it relies on the faster update and deployment cycles of a business rules management system to ensure projects put "Responding to change over following a plan".

I have helped several companies adopt business rules, using ABRD and the ILOG business rules management system, now part of the IBM WebSphere product suite. These companies have seen tremendous improvements in business agility and in business/IT alignment. Their use of a business rules management system played a big part in these improvements. To be truly successful, however, these companies have also had to adapt and change their approach to systems development and maintenance. Whether they were using agile methods or not for their traditional development, the need for a new approach to effectively apply agile techniques to business rules was clear. ABRD delivered what these companies needed to be successful.

A book on ABRD, then, is both timely and necessary. With this book, Jerome and Hafedh have written more than just a complete guide to ABRD. This book provides an introduction to business rules and to the ABRD methodology. It discusses key ABRD cycles and activities. It outlines key design patterns and covers critical issues in everything from rule authoring to deployment and testing. Rule performance, rule governance and detailed descriptions of how to do all this with IBM's flagship business rules management systems round out a thorough and complete book. If you plan to use business rules to extend and manage the decisions in your operational environment, something I highly recommend, this book will show you how to use an agile approach to do so.

James Taylor

James is CEO and Principal Consultant, Decision Management Solutions and is based in Palo Alto, CA. He is the author, with Neil Raden, of Smart (Enough) Systems (Prentice Hall, 2007) and of numerous chapters on decision management and business rules. He is an active consultant helping companies all over the world implement business rules, and can be reached at james@decisionmanagementsolutions.com.

Preface

Why Business Rules

According to Wordnet, a rule is "a principle or condition that customarily governs behavior" or "a prescribed guide for conduct or action." Businesses, and organizations in general, operate under a number of rules: rules about what services to offer and to whom; rules about how much to charge for those services; rules about how to handle service recipient requests; rules about hiring employees, promoting them, firing them, reimbursing their travel expenses, and paid leave rules; customer relationship management rules; web portal layout rules; salary scales and overtime rules; opening hours rules; emergency behavior guidelines; promotional campaign targeting rules; cross-selling rules, up-selling rules, meeting conduct rules; document disposal recycling and security rules; and so forth. Business rules are everywhere. Every bit of process, task, activity, or function, is governed by rules.

Thus, the question is not *why* business rules, but rather, *how* business rules? Currently, some of the business rules are implicit and thus poorly enforced; those should minimally be written (formalized), if not enforced. Others are written and not enforced. Others yet are poorly written and obscurely enforced. Some are even written and should not – but that is a different story ☺.

The *business rule approach* looks for ways to (1) *write* (elicit, communicate, manage) the important *business rules* in a way that all stakeholders can understand, and (2) *enforce* those business rules *within* the IT infrastructure in a way that supports their traceability and facilitates their maintenance.

The *business rules approach* is no longer the exotic paradigm it was at the turn of the century. Banks are doing it, insurance companies are doing it, phone companies are doing it, retailers are doing it, manufactures are doing it, and government agencies are doing it. This book is not about convincing you of the merits of the business rules approach – it is about helping you adopt it effectively.

Why an *Agile* Business Rule Development Methodology

Business rule pioneers have long recognized that we need a *distinct* development methodology for business rules, one that is different from traditional development methodologies (see justification in Chap. 1). That much we know. But how about *agile*?

Business rules embody *functional requirements*. The business rules approach emphasizes the elicitation, analysis, documentation, and management of such requirements. In fact, rule discovery, discussed in Chap. 4, borrows many techniques from requirements engineering. Thus, "*agile* business rule development" may sound like an oxymoron – how can an approach that puts so much emphasis on requirements be agile?

True. Agility is not a *defining* characteristic of business rule development, except perhaps for the rule maintenance phase, where *IT agility* is achieved through separate authoring and deployment of business rules. To the contrary, most business rule development methodologies put a heavy emphasis on up-front business modeling and analysis. Further, many experts consider business rules within the broader context of enterprise architecture, business–IT alignment, business process reengineering and management, service-oriented everything, or some other intimidating and long-drawn-out are-we-there-yet kind of IT/business transformation that requires deliberate, strategic planning, an unshakeable faith in the outcome, a lot of patience, and deep pockets – in short anything *but* agile.

That is exactly our point. Because agility is not a *given* with business rule development, we need to *engineer* it within business rule development methodologies, and *that is* what *agile business rule development* (ABRD) is about. If we think of a methodology as a pentad of *processes, deliverables, roles, techniques*, and *best practices*, ABRD differs from other business rule methodologies mainly along the *processes* and *best practices* dimensions and, to a lesser extent, on the emphasis (or lack thereof) we put on some of the deliverables. Indeed, ABRD borrows *many* of the business rule–specific techniques and deliverables from other, *rule development* methodologies, including Barbara von Halle's STEP methodology (see von Halle 2002). The *agility* of ABRD, on the other hand, is borrowed from agile methodologies and development principles such as OpenUp, and test-driven development. In particular, ABRD is (1) incremental, (2) iterative, and (3) test-driven. Rather than spending weeks and months discovering and analyzing rules for a complete business function, ABRD puts the emphasis on producing executable, tested – though partial – rulesets since the first few weeks of a project, and *strives* to do that without jeopardizing the quality, perennity, and foresight of the end result.

Our experience in the field shows that ABRD is valuable, feasible, effective, and perfectible! We more than welcome your feedback on the customization and use of ABRD, through personal communication or via the public companion Web site we have set up for the book (http://www.agilebrdevelopment.com) to share comments, criticisms, experiences, information, and insights!

Why This Book

While we think that the ABRD methodology is a story worth telling, it alone does not justify writing – or reading – a book!

Successful adoption of the business rules approach requires four ingredients:

1. *Foundations*, to understand what business rules are (and are not), why you should use the *business rules approach*, and what it can do for you.
2. *Methodology*, to understand *how* to apply the business rules approach, from a *process* point of view, to your business.
3. *Architecture*, to understand how *rule automation*, i.e., how the separate packaging, deployment, and execution of business rules impacts your application.
4. *Implementation*, to actually deliver the technical solution within the context of a particular *business rule management system* (BRMS).

We have long felt that the available business rules literature did not address these four ingredients in an integrated way. There are a number of excellent *foundational* books – most of them are cited in this book – including Ron Ross's *Principles of the Business Rules Approach* (Addison Wesley, 2003) and Tony Morgan's *Business Rules and Information Systems: Aligning IT with Business Goals* (Addison Wesley, 2002). While these books present some business rule–related techniques – some of which are used in this book – they do not provide a step-by-step methodology and do not delve far enough into architecture, let alone implementation. On the methodology front, a number of authors have done a great job, including Barbara von Halle, from whom we gratefully borrow many of the techniques and deliverables of her STEP methodology (see *Business Rules Applied: Building Better Systems Using the Business Rules Approach*, John Wiley & Sons, 2001). However, the book did not (could not) focus on architecture or implementation. James Taylor and Neil Raden's *Smart (Enough) Systems: How to Deliver Competitive Advance by Automating the Hidden Decisions in Your Business* (Prentice-Hall, 2007) focused on how business rules are part of an overall approach to managing and automating decisions but only touched on methodology and the software development life cycle.

From the tool end of the spectrum, we have a number of great books with practical and immediately applicable know-how around specific – typically open-source – rule engines (e.g., JESS) and *budding* business rule management systems (BRMSs, e.g., JBOSS Drools); however, many such books are *definitely* short on methodology (not their focus), short on architecture, and say little about rule management, and governance issues and functionalities.

Hence, the idea of writing this book, which covers all four aspects in significant detail: the *foundations*, in Chaps. 1, 2, and 6; *methodology*, in Chaps. 3, 4, 5, and 16; *architecture and design*, in Chaps. 7, 9, 12, and 14; and *implementation* in Chaps. 8, 10, 11, 13, 15, and 17. We use an insurance case study that deals with *claim processing*. We highlight the major issues in the book text and provide excerpts from the various deliverables. The full versions of the deliverables are available through the companion web portal http://www.agilebrddevelopment.com.

Why JRules

First of all, let us reiterate why we think going to implementation is important. Implementation shows how some design solutions and patterns are *operationalized* within the context of a particular technology. This not only helps the readers to implement the solutions within the chosen technology, but it also helps them in adapting/adopting the solutions to other technologies. The Gang of Four patterns book would not have been the same without the C++ and Smalltalk examples, and that, whether you are implementing in C++, Smalltalk, Java, or C#.

Having decided to go all the way to implementation, we had to pick a business rule management system ... or two ... or more. If we were to pick one, it had to be JRules, for several reasons. First of all, it is the one business rule management system (BRMS) that we know best: we have a cumulative experience of 25 years, going through several generations of JRules, and have witnessed major shifts in the industry, in terms of architecture and functionalities. JRules also happens to be a market leader and a mature product, both in terms of deployment architecture and rule management functionality. Our biases notwithstanding, we believe that JRules benefited from great product management, often anticipating and leading market trends.

If we were to pick a second BRMS, which one would it be? Our choice would probably go to JBoss DROOLS, the leading BRMS in open-source tools, both in terms of user community and in terms of entry cost. Including DROOLS would have significantly lengthened this book (another 200 pages) – and the time to write it. And besides, if we pick two, why not pick a third BRMS?

Throughout this book, we strove to identify and separate product/vendor-independent issues, from product-specific features and limitations. This is certainly true for the methodology part, where the contents and semantics of the various work products and deliverables are the same, regardless of the technology. It is also true for rule authoring (a constraint is a constraint, regardless of which BRMS you use), for rule integration (embed rule engines or implement rule execution as a service), for rule testing (unit testing, test scenarios, regression testing, performance tuning, etc.), and for rule governance (rule life cycle, change management, etc.). Out of 18 chapters, only a third (6) are JRules specific.

What happens now *as* JRules evolves? There are three levels of evolution: (1) features, (2) API, and (3) architecture. Features evolve constantly, as menu actions are added here and others are removed from there. That is inevitable, and of no consequence to us: the JRules-specific parts of the book are *not* a product tutorial, anyway; they simply show how to implement some general solution patterns with JRules. As for changes to the API, they seldom break old code. The ones that are *not* related to architecture often consist of limited scope refactorings. With the exception of *Decision Validation Services*, whose *packaging* is fairly recent,[1] the APIs referred to in this book (for ruleset packaging, deployment, execution, performance

---

[1]By contrast, the core functionality underlying DVS is fairly mature.

tuning, execution server integration, and rule governance) are fairly mature and stable. Changes to the architecture can be more problematic to the shelf life of the material in this book. However, the current architecture uses proven state-of-the-art technologies that are beyond the turbulence of the first years. The portal http://www. agilebrdevelopment.com will maintain information about consequential product updates and will update our operationalization of solution patterns accordingly.

How to Read This Book

This book consists of 18 chapters, organized in eight parts:

Part I, "Introduction," introduces the business rules approach (Chap. 1) and provides example application areas for business rules (Chap. 2).

Part II, "Methodology," focuses on methodology. The *agile business rule development* (ABRD) methodology is presented in Chap. 3. The *rule harvesting cycle* is introduced in Chap. 4, where we talk about rule discovery and analysis, and the *prototyping cycle* (phase) is discussed in Chap. 5.

Part III, "Foundations," covers the basics/main ingredients. Chapter 6 introduces rule engine technology, by going over its history, and explains the inner workings of rule engines, in general, and the JRules rule engine, in particular. Chapter 7 explores the design space for business rule applications and for rule management in the early phases of the rule life cycle. Chapter 8 introduces the JRules BRMS.

Part IV, "Rule Authoring," deals with rule authoring. Chapter 9 explores rule authoring design issues in a technology/vendor-independent way. Chapter 10 discusses JRules artifacts and functionalities for setting up the rule development infrastructure (project structure, business object model) and proposes best practices for it. Chapter 11 discusses rule authoring per se, where we introduce the JRules rule languages and artifacts, and rule execution orchestration.

Part V, "Rule Deployment," deals with ruleset deployment and execution; Chap. 12 discusses deployment and execution issues, in general, whereas Chap. 13 explores deployment and execution options in JRules.

Part VI, "Rule Testing," deals with testing. Chapter 14 discusses rule testing and validation issues, in general, whereas Chap. 15 explores JRules functionality for rule testing, tracing, and performance monitoring.

Part VII, "Rule Governance," deals with rule governance. Chapter 16 introduces rule governance and discusses the main process and design issues. Chapter 17 explores JRules support for rule governance.

Part VIII, "Epilogue," concludes this book with a short epilogue.

Clearly, by choosing to address *foundations, methodology, architecture,* and *implementation*, this book caters to five different audiences:

- *Project managers* will find a pragmatic, proven methodology for delivering and maintaining business rule applications.

- *Business analysts* will find a methodology that they can use for rule discovery and analysis, and a number of guidelines and best practices for rule authoring, and for structuring rules during development.
- *Rule authors* will find a number of guidelines and best practices for rule authoring, in general, and detailed explanations about rule artifacts and rule authoring languages in JRules.
- *Application and software architects* will find an exploration of the design space for business rule applications, and a number or proven architectural and design patterns, in general, and for the case of JRules.
- *Developers* will find practical design and coding guidelines for implementing design choices, in general, and using JRules.

Incidentally, CTOs and product/business line managers will also find some value in this book; thanks to our explanation of the business rules approach, to the example application areas, and to a discussion of rule governance issues, but they are probably better off with other foundational books such as those mentioned earlier.

The following table shows reading paths for the different audiences:

Target audience	Should-read chapters/parts	Optional chapters
Project manager	Parts I and II: Chaps. 1–5, Chaps. 8, 16, and 18	Chaps. 7 and 14
Application architect	Parts I and II: Chaps. 1–5, Chaps. 8, 12, 14, 16, and 18	
Software architect	Part I: Chaps. 1–2, Chap. 3; Part III: Chaps. 6–8; Part V: Chaps. 12–13; Part VI: Chaps. 14–15; Part VII: Chaps. 16–17); and Part VIII: Chap. 18	Chaps. 4 and 5
Business analyst	Part I: Chaps. 1–2, Chaps. 3, 4, 8, 9, 14, 16, and 18	Chap. 7
Rule author	Part I: Chaps. 1–2, Chaps. 3, 8; Part IV: Chaps. 9–11, Chap. 16; Part VIII: Chap. 18	
Developer	Part I: Chaps. 1–2, Chaps. 3 and 5; Part III: Chaps. 6–8, Chap. 10; Part V: Chaps. 12–13; Part VI: Chaps. 14–15; Part VII: Chaps. 16–17; and Part VIII: Chap. 18	

Acknowledgments

This book has been an on-and-off project for many years. Vilas Tulachan, an independent J2EE consultant and author, and a JRules consultant and trainer, has revived an earlier incarnation of this book project, which, while it did not materialize in its earlier form, kept us talking about it above the noise level, until a concrete book proposal was submitted to Ralf Gerstner, our indefatigable Springer editor, in the fall of 2007.

We wish to thank Ralf for his legendary patience with us through many (self-imposed) missed time targets. Thanks to ABRD, we are much better at delivering business rule solutions than we have been at delivering this book!

ABRD is the open-source descendant of the proprietary ILOG ISIS (ILOG Solution Implementation Standard) methodology. Our thanks to the members of the ISIS team, namely, Pierre Berlandier, who has written extensively about rule governance, and Jean Pommier, who supported the development of ABRD, its open publication – and the writing of this book!

Our sincerest thanks go to Tonya Teyssier, a conscientious, patient, and generous JRules curriculum developer from IBM WebSphere Education, who sacrificed many evenings and weekends to help us write – and think – clearly the first chapters of the book. She has become a master of euphemisms in "constructively criticizing" some of the earlier drafts.

Eric Charpentier, a JRules consultant extraordinaire, who excels at everything he does, provided us with very valuable and timely feedback on *all* the chapters of the book. He certainly helped us a great deal in improving the organization and pedagogy of many chapters of the book. Eric blogs about topics ranging from scorecards to rule governance (see http://www.primatek.ca/blog).

James Taylor, a leading authority on decision management, including business rules, and analytics, and an independent consultant, speaker, and author, volunteered to read a complete draft of the book, and provided us with valuable, timely, concise, to the point (and witty) feedback, James-style! He blogs extensively about decision management (check JT on EDM, at http://jtonedm.com/), and has authored, with Neil Raden, *Smart Enough Systems: How to Deliver Competitive*

Advantage by Automating Hidden Decisions (Prentice-Hall, 2007), which is becoming a classic on decision management.

We both wish to thank our respective families who, like families of all authors, have to put up with absentee – or absent-minded – father/partner for a never-ending book project. Are we there yet? Yes, we are . . . till the next book ☺.

December 2010   Hafedh Mili and Jérôme Boyer

Contents

Part II   Methodology

Part IV   Rule Authoring

Part I
Introduction

Chapter 1
Introduction to Business Rules

Target audience
- *All*

In this chapter you learn
- *What are business rules*
- *What are the motivations behind the business rules approach*
- *In what ways do business applications with business rules differ from traditional applications*
- *Why do we need a different development methodology*

Key points
- *A business rule is a statement that defines or constrains some aspect of the business. Business rules have a business motivation and an enforcement regime.*
- *The business rules approach enables, (a) a better alignment between information systems and business, and (b) a greater business agility.*
- *Business rule applications externalize business logic and separate it from the underlying computational infrastructure where it can be managed by business.*
- *Business rule development differs from traditional application development in many ways: (1) it is business requirements-centric, (2) enterprise-level ownership – and management – of business logic, and (3) business-led implementation and maintenance of business logic.*

1.1 What Are Business Rules?

An on-line store might not accept a next-day delivery order if the order is received after 3:00 p.m.

J. Boyer and H. Mili, *Agile Business Rule Development*,
DOI 10.1007/978-3-642-19041-4_1, © Springer-Verlag Berlin Heidelberg 2011

My bank will not lend me money if my debt-over-income ratio[1] exceeds 37%

Section 152 of the US tax code defines a dependent as a person who is either a "qualifying child" or a "qualifying relative." A taxpayer's qualifying child for any taxable year is a person who:

- Is the taxpayer's child, sibling, step-sibling, or a descendant of any such relative
- Has the same principal residence as the taxpayer for at least half the taxable year
- Is younger than 19 at the end of the taxable year, or is a student who is younger than 24 at the close of the year, or is a student with disability – regardless of age
- Has provided for no more than half of her or his support for the taxable year

A *qualifying relative*, on the other hand.

My health insurance does not reimburse medical expenses incurred abroad if the claim is presented more than 1 year after the expenses had been incurred, or if the claimant has spent more than 182 days abroad within the past year.

Passengers with frequent flyer status Silver, Gold, Platinum, Super Platinum, and Super Elite Platinum may board at their leisure.

My car insurance does not cover drivers who have been convicted of driving while intoxicated (DWI) within the past 2 years; they are referred to a public no-fault insurance.

Fannie Mae will only underwrite mortgages on properties that have hazards insurance that protects against loss or damage from fire and other hazards covered by the standard extended coverage endorsement. The policy should provide for claims to be settled on a replacement cost basis. The amount of coverage should at least equal the minimum of:

- 100% of the insurable value of the improvements[2]
- The principal balance of the mortgage (as long as it exceeds the minimum amount – typically 80% – required to compensate for damage or loss on a replacement cost basis)

---

[1]The debt over income ratio is the ratio between total (monthly or yearly) debt obligations over gross income for the same period (monthly or yearly).

[2]For example, if a property is worth $200,000, $80,000 for land and $120,000 for the building, then the value of the improvements is $120,000.

> Periodic interest payments made to the accounts of foreign entities who filed IRSform W-9 are subject to 28% backup withholding and need to be reported to the IRS in form 1099, with the box number 3 checked.

> Citizens of NAFTA countries who travel into the USA by road need only show proof of citizenship.[3]

> When mailing out monthly account statements, include marketing materials that match the customer profile.

> Plane tickets purchased with Amex/Visa Gold/<insert your favorite card here> have built-in trip cancellation insurance.

> If two alarms are issued by the same network node within 30 s of each other with the same alarm code, then group them under the same umbrella alarm.

> If a wheel shows two consecutive temperature readings higher than 558°, then check for sticking brakes.

These are just a sampling of the types of rules that we have come across in our practice. Application areas include customer relationship management, marketing campaigns, the mortgage industry (retailers, mortgage insurance, secondary market), banking (credit cards, loans), car insurance, health insurance, loyalty programs, tax law, compliance, e-government, telecommunications, engineering, transportation, manufacturing, etc.

So, what *is* a *business rule*? If we break down the term "business rule" we get a *rule* of the *business*. Wordnet defines a *rule* as, among other things, "a principle or condition that customarily governs behavior," or "a prescribed guide for conduct or action." A rule of the *business* means that this principle or prescription is in the *business domain*, that is, it is part of the *requirements* (the *problem domain*), as opposed to a prescription dictated by a particular technological choice (the *solution domain*).

Business rule authors have proposed a number of definitions for business rules. Tony Morgan defines a business rule informally as "a compact statement about an aspect of the business . . . It is a constraint in the sense that a business rule lays down

---

[3]NAFTA: North American Free Trade Agreement, binding Canada, Mexico, and the USA.

what must or must not be the case" (Morgan 2002, p. 5). Ronald Ross defines a business rule as "a directive intended to influence or guide business behavior" (Ross 2003, p. 3). Barbara von Halle would like us to think of business rules as "the set of conditions that govern a business event so that it occurs in a way that is acceptable to the business" (von Halle 2001, p. 28).

The Object Management Group (OMG) defines a *rule* as a "proposition that is a claim of obligation or of necessity," and a *business rule* as a rule that is under business jurisdiction (OMG 2008). The *Business Rules Group*, which is an independent non-commercial peer group of business rule specialists, has produced a number of documents about the business rules approach, and has contributed to OMG's work on business process management and business rules. The Business Rules Group considers business rules from two perspectives, the business perspective, and the information systems perspective, defined as follows:

- From the business perspective: ". . . a business rule is guidance that there is an obligation concerning conduct, action, practice or procedure within a particular activity or sphere. Two important characteristics of a business rule: (1) there ought to be an explicit motivation for it, and (2) it should have an enforcement regime stating what the consequences would be if the rule were broken" (BRG 2008).[4]
- From the information system perspective: ". . . a business rule is a statement that defines or constrains some aspect of the business. It is intended to assert business structure, or to control or influence the behavior of the business" (BRG 2008).

This distinction between the two perspectives is needed to account for the fact that a business process typically involves human actors and an information system, and business rules guide both. From the information system perspective, the rules talk about the data that is captured by the information system about the real world entities involved in the business process such as customers, products, or transactions. For example, in the insurance domain, a number of on-line quotation systems have three outcomes. In addition to "accept" and "decline" responses for clear-cut requests, borderline cases may receive a "manual referral" response so the request can be reviewed by a human underwriter. The human underwriter operates under a slightly different set of business rules from the ones automated in the information system. Such business rules would typically be captured in underwriting manuals.

While the bulk of this book is about the information system perspective, the early chapters address both perspectives.

Two characteristics of business rules stand out from the above definitions: (1) business rules are about business, and (2) business rules concern both the *structure* and the *behavior* of the business. We will elaborate these two characteristics further below.

---

[4]The Business Rule Group web site: http://www.businessrulesgroup.org/defnbrg.shtml.

1.1.1 Business Rules Are About the Business

Indeed, in the examples given, there is a *business motivation* behind the rule. To illustrate this point, consider our first rule about next-day delivery and the 3:00 p.m. deadline. Why would an on-line store put in place such a restrictive rule, and risk losing business as a consequence? A plausible justification could be that it *may* take more than 4 h to, (a) find a free warehouse clerk to fulfill the order, and for the assigned warehouse clerk to (b) locate the book in the warehouse, (c) prepare a package for delivery, and (d) deliver the package to the nearest Federal Express or UPS branch. Notice that the same *rule* would apply if the customer called by *phone* to place the order. Similarly, the rule about rejecting drivers with recent DUI convictions: the obvious business motivation is that such drivers present a high risk of causing accidents, and would cost the insurance too much money.

Von Halle says that "business rules are the ultimate levers with which business management is able to guide and control the business. In fact, the business's rules are the means by which an organization implements competitive strategy, promotes policy, and complies with legal obligations" (von Halle 2006). The Business Rules Group (BRG) has proposed a *Business Motivation Model* that attempts to formalize the link between business rules and business objectives (BRG 2007); the OMG's *Business Motivation Model Specification* is based on (BRG 2007). Roughly speaking, business rules are seen within the context of business plans: a business plan includes *ends* (business objectives) and *means* to achieve the *ends*. Business rules are part of the *means* that businesses deploy to achieve their goals (profitability, market share, customer loyalty, etc.); we will say more about the business motivation model in Chap. 4.

1.1.2 Business Rules Concern Both the Structure and the Behavior of the Business

This distinction is evident in the information systems perspective of the *business rules group* definition, and somewhat in the OMG definition, which distinguishes between *structural* or *definitional rules* and *operative* or *behavioral rules*. Roughly speaking, *structural rules* define the business information model. The statement "a sale record includes the buyer, the product, the quantity, the price, and any applicable discount" is a structural business rule. We can think of it as the definition of the **Sale** entity (or class). Similarly, the statement "an order can include one or several line items, one per product, indicating number of units and price" is also a structural business rule, which can be seen as defining the **Order** entity. A *behavioral rule*, on the other hand, is about how the business reacts to business events. Most of the example rules shown above are actually *behavioral rules*. The first rule (3:00 p.m. deadline) is relevant to *order entry*. The debt-over-income ratio is about loan application underwriting. The health insurance rule is relevant to the processing of claims. And so forth. Generally speaking, *behavioral rules* kick in when something happens at the boundaries of the system. This distinction and others are described in more detail in Chap. 4.

1.2   Motivations for the Business Rules Approach

Before we talk about the business rules approach, let us talk about the "nonbusiness rules approach."

The sample of rules shown above has, *for the most part*, been successfully implemented in working information systems by people who have never heard of the business rules approach. So what is the hoopla about the business rules approach?

The next few real-life examples will illustrate three *major* issues that are adequately addressed by the business rules approach. We will present the examples first, and then identify the dominant issues:

- A company is in the natural gas business. It sells natural gas to public utilities. It draw 8–9 figure contracts with these public utilities, whose prices depend on the total volume (a certain volume of natural gas over the duration of the contract), throughput (a certain volume per hour), options to request a 10% (or 15% or 20%) increase of throughput within 6 h to accommodate consumption peaks, the possibility of storing the gas for low usage periods, etc. Beyond the raw volume (x cubic tons of gas), each one of these "options" has an infrastructure cost – and thus a price associated with it. The company's top management looks at the yearly numbers and figures two things: (1) given the volume that it sells, it should be making more money, and (2) overall, its customers are having a good deal, relative to the competition, and some customers have *very* good deals, but neither the company nor its lucky customers know it. We need to capture those pricing rules precisely so that (1) we can fine-tune the rules to make more money and yet remain competitive and (2) we can tell customers, precisely, how good a deal they are getting. As it turned out, those pricing rules walked out the door every day between 4:00 and 7:00 p.m., got stuck in traffic on most days, and called in sick some of the time – not to mention the occasional vacation. Not only that, but they took on separate lives in separate spreadsheets on the contract officers' laptops.
- A US state manages a number of social benefits (welfare) programs for people with disabilities, senior people, low-income people, single mothers, back-to-school single mothers, back-to-work programs for long-term unemployed people, food stamps, etc. Each one of these programs has eligibility guidelines, the contours of which have been defined by the laws that created those programs. Applications to the various programs are dispatched to "case workers" who assess the eligibility of the applicants and determine the benefits level. Case workers were overwhelmed, and their determinations were uncomfortably inconsistent.

Managers asked a couple of questions: (1) exactly *what* rules were being used, (2) how to ensure that those rules are used *consistently*, and (3) why processing times for straightforward cases were the same as for complex borderline cases.

These were but two of many examples of organizations that did not know precisely the rules under which they were operating, and consequently, operated under different – and often conflicting – sets of rules. Hence:

Issue 1: Organizations need to know which business rules they are using, and whether they are using them consistently.

- A phone company's core business is local phone service. The company was getting in the long-distance service. The local *public utility commission*[5] wants to ensure that phone companies with a monopoly on local phone service offer the same quality of service between customers who use them for long-distance service, and customers who use other carriers. Thus, "our" phone company has to file a report every month that shows quality of service statistics for *its* long-distance customers, and for the long-distance customers of other carriers. Because heavy penalties are levied when statistics show that the company gives preferential treatment to its long-distance customers,[6] an important part of the report filed with the PUC is the method of calculation. And, in the case of audit, our phone company has to be able to show that it *has, indeed, used those calculations to produce the report.*
- The *n*th user acceptance testing postmortem meeting. The customer complaints: "the system still does not do what it is supposed to." Technical lead: "Perhaps not, but it does what you told us to do." The customer: "I never told you to underwrite loans for customers with FICO score lower than 600." Technical lead: "You never told us the contrary either: you said underwriting decisions are based on our risk assessment score, not on FICO score alone." Customer: "yeah, but isn't the FICO score a big component of the risk assessment score." Technical lead, getting tired with all this fuzziness: "Define big." Customer: "Well, big as in 80%, perhaps more?" Technical lead turns to developer, whispers something, developer opens Eclipse on his laptop, and starts looking frantically through code, then his face illuminates: "well, we have it set at 90%." Customer, after doing calculations by hand, is adamant now: "Can't be! Show me." Developer looks at technical lead for a cue, and technical lead responds:

---

[5]In the USA, Public Utility Commissions (PUCs) are statewide regulatory commissions with a mandate to balance the needs of consumers and utilities (electricity, natural gas, water, telecommunications, etc.) to ensure safe and reliable utility service at reasonable, competitive rates.

[6]For example, both Jane and Joe have their local service with our company – they have no choice – but Jane chose our company for long-distance service, whereas Joe chose a competitor. If both Jane and Joe make a service call, say to report a problem with the line, the PUC wants to know if Joe's calls are handled as diligently as Jane's (how fast it takes customer service reps to get back to Jane vs. Joe, how many calls it takes to resolve the issue, what is the elapsed time between opening the case and closing it, etc.).

"Show them the code!" The developer starts looking for a cable to connect his laptop to the overhead projector. He does not find one, walks out of the room. The project manager, who called the meeting, asks "do we have to do this now? Because we have ..." The technical lead and customer answer emphatically: "Yes!" The developer comes back with a cable, and puts up the method addFactor from the prosaically named **RAStrategyDataProxy** class on the screen:

```
public void addFactor(float v, HashMap<Interval,Float> penalties) {
    Iterator<Interval> intervals = penalties.keys();
    float pen = 0;
    while (intervals.hasNext()) {
        Interval next = intervals.next();
        if (next.contains(v)) {
            pen = (penalties.get(next)).floatValue();
            break;
        }
    }
    raScore = WEIGHT* raScore + (1-WEIGHT)*pen;
}
```

The technical lead is happy with how intimidating this must look to the customer, and looks at her defiantly, as if taunting her "Ok, so what are you going to do with it?" The customer, unfazed, wastes no time throwing the curve ball back at him: "Don't look at me like that! Translate!"

Now it is *his* problem again: explain classes, methods, generics, hashmaps, and iterators to a business person! Luckily, this business person is a very smart lady who was once a programmer ... 30 years ago ... in COBOL. Lo and behold, after explanations about what the penalties hashmap represents, and through many detours through the code, for example, to find where the constant WEIGHT is defined, what raScore means, how it is initialized, and how it gets updated, they actually find the bug. True, WEIGHT is set to 90%, and the risk assessment score is initialized to the FICO score, but each time a new factor is taken into account, the underlying weight of the FICO score is actually decreased by 10%. This explains the discrepancy between the customer's hand calculations and the output of the program. It is 6:30 p.m., the tension has subsided, the meeting is finished, and as everybody walks out, the project manager sighs "There's gotta be a better way!"

This story ended well because the customer was smart, stubborn, no pushover, and was once a programmer. How many business customers are like that? Further, in this case, we were able to pull out a single Java method that enforces the business rule, and inspect it. We are seldom that lucky. Indeed, the business logic will often be scattered in many places: context-sensitive interaction screens based on customer profile or location, configuration data in external files, limited validation functionality in input screens, control logic in functions, database integrity constraints, SQL code, and the nightmarish stored procedures. Hence:

Issue 2: Organizations need to describe the business rules that are embodied in their information systems in a way that all stakeholders can understand, and need a way of ensuring traceability between those rule descriptions and the actual implementations of the rules.

- An insurance company sells all kinds of policies to individuals and corporations. Its marketing department regularly evaluates its underwriting rules to assess the profitability of the various market segments. For example, assume that the insurance company covers drivers who are as young as 18 years old. Given that young drivers are more accident prone, one may ask whether the 18- to 19-year-old market segment makes money for the insurance. To this end, the marketing department compares the total claims paid out in the past 6 months, on policies held by drivers between the ages of 18 and 19, to the total value of premiums collected for that market segment. If the company collects more in premiums than it pays out in claims, then that market segment is cost effective. Else, it needs to make its rules more stringent to weed out the statistically losing market segment. All is good. The marketing department performs these simulations every month, on the data for the previous 6 months, and makes recommendations for new underwriting rules. IT takes a minimum of 4 months to implement such changes with the current technology. Hence, the company cannot react as rapidly to changing market conditions. Its reaction is always 4 months behind, and when IT is doing the final testing, everyone knows that the rules that are being tested are already 3 months obsolete.
- The mortgage division of a financial services and insurance company has reacted quickly to the sub-prime mortgage market crisis by tightening the eligibility requirements for mortgages as soon as the first signs of the crisis started showing on the radar, that is, in the late spring of 2007. By mid-July, new eligibility requirements were published internally and sent out to retail branches. By late fall, the online mortgage application system was still using the old eligibility criteria. Potential customers with shaky credit, who had been hearing about tightening credit from the 6 o'clock news, started believing in Santa Claus when the online system replied "Congratulations. Your application has been pre-qualified. A mortgage specialist will be in touch with you soon." Which specialist sometimes had the un-CRM task of calling the customer to say "we apologize: our on-line system still operates under the old eligibility rules." Not cool.
- An investment company buys and sells (trades) securities on behalf of its customers. For each trade, it chooses the best exchange market on which to execute the trade based on (1) the types of security (bonds, equities, etc.), (2) the actual security (e.g., Microsoft stock), (3) the volume (e.g., ten versus ten million), (4) the commission charged by the exchange market on such trades, (5) any contractual agreements between the investment company and the exchange, (6) any contractual agreements between the exchange and the

customer on behalf of which the trade is being made, and (7) the market conditions. Trade execution routing is automated through an application. The investment company would like the application to be responsive to changes in the various factors. However, the frequency of these changes goes from once in a lifetime (e.g., the emergence of a new exchange market or of a brokerage house) to the minute (market conditions), to anything in-between (weekly, monthly, etc.).

These are just three real-life examples of situations where the IT infrastructure of a company becomes an *impediment* to evolution, as opposed to an *enabler*. Hence:

Issue 3: Organizations need an agile development infrastructure/paradigm that enables them to react to the changing environment in a timely manner.

Having accepted that business rules should, and do, for the most part,drive our business information systems (Sect. 1.1), the several *real* examples showed a number of problems with the way business rules are typically implemented – or not, as for the case of the natural gas company – in information systems. The *business rules approach* addresses all of these problems. So what is it? Barbara von Halle defines the business rules approach as "a <u>formal way</u> of <u>managing</u> and <u>automating</u> an organization's business rules so that the business <u>behaves</u> and <u>evolves</u> as its leaders <u>intended</u>" (von Halle 2001). We like this definition because we feel that it captures the essence of the business rules approach in a single sentence:

- It is *a formal approach*: This means clearly defined processes, tasks, roles, and work products, that is, a methodology.
- *Managing* and *automating* business rules: Management and automation are related but separate concerns. *Management* includes collecting, recording, validating (for accuracy), assessing (for business worth), publishing, and evolving the business rules. This needs to be done – and can be done – whether those business rules are automated or not: as our natural gas supplier example showed, important rules of the business were not defined precisely and consistently across the enterprise. As for *rule automation*, it means making those rules *operational*, that is, come up with a <language, interpreter> pair so that enterprise applications can reference them.
- [The business] *behaves* and *evolves* as [. . .] *intended*: As our mortgage underwriting example duel between business and IT showed, language barriers between business and IT can make the first goal – *behave* as *intended* – difficult to achieve, and equally difficult to verify. As the last three examples showed, traditional development techniques *cannot* possibly meet the pace of change of the business environment.

We can think of this definition as a set of *requirements*. In the next section, we look at how typical *implementations* of the business rules approach look like.

1.3   How Do Business Rule Applications Differ from Traditional Business Applications?

What does a business application developed with the business rules approach look like? We know how a business rule application *should not* look like: it should *not* look like the rule-based systems that were developed in the 1980s: (1) custom *(from the ground up)* development methodologies with esoteric terminologies; (2) their own programming language – or at least one not used in business applications; (3) their own data storage (persistence) mechanisms; (4) poor scalability; and (5) little or no connectivity to any of the existing business systems. No wonder the technology failed to penetrate business information systems back then!

To understand what business applications developed under the business rules approach look like, we have to understand what the business rule approach entails. A *full implementation* of the business rules approach has three components:

1. A methodology for rule management, that is, collecting, recording, validating, assessing, publishing, and evolving the business rules
2. One or several more or less formal languages for expressing business rules at different stages of their life cycle and for different audiences (business, IT, and computer)
3. A tool set for managing and executing the rules, a *Business Rule Management System* (BRMS)

The three components are interrelated:

- The BRMS supports the methodology to various degrees through a shared repository for rule artifacts, workflow/process management functionalities, an enforcement of roles through access control, and so forth.
- The management functionalities of the BRMS support the creation and modification of rules expressed in the rule languages, and the translation of rules between the various languages.
- The rule automation (execution) functionalities of the BRMS support the execution of rules in one or several of the supported rule languages.

Some authors consider the provision of an executable rule language, as distinct from the application programming language, and the provision of rule execution functionalities by the BRMS as a highly desirable but not a necessary aspect of the business rules approach. We agree that it is highly desirable, and if we consider agility as an essential aspect of the business rules approach, then we will have to consider it *necessary*.

Figure 1.1 shows the three components of a *business rules approach implementation* and their dependencies. Part II of this book (Chaps. 3, 4, and 5) will deal with process. We introduce BRMS in general and JRules in particular, in Part III (Chaps. 6, 7, and 8). Rule authoring and rule languages are discussed in Part IV (Chaps. 9, 10, and 11). Rule execution is discussed in Part V (deployment, Chaps. 12 and 13)

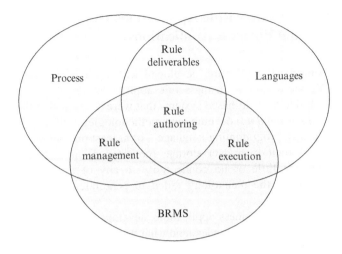

Fig. 1.1 The three components of a business rules approach and their interrelationships

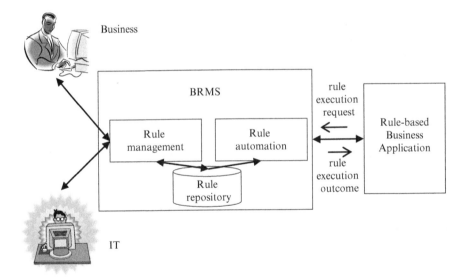

Fig. 1.2 The role of a BRMS in a business rule implementation

and Part VI (testing, Chaps. 14 and 15). Rule management is discussed in Part VII (rule governance, Chaps. 16 and 17).

Figure 1.2 shows the BRMS within the context of its operational environment. The BRMS has two components, a management component and an execution component, sharing a common repository of rules. The rule repository is read and modified by management functionalities, but read-only by automation (execution) functionalities. The rule repository may contain different representations of the same business rules, depending on lifecycle stage and on audience. Figure 1.2 shows that both business and IT access the management functionalities. We will not try to be more precise at this point; Chap. 3 presents the different roles in more detail.

According to this scenario, the rules relevant to business applications are executed *outside* of the business applications: the rule automation component of the BRMS acts as a rule execution service on behalf of business applications. This is the most typical scenario for full-functionality BRMSs and shows one way that business applications developed with the business rules approach differ from traditional development methods. However, it is not the only way of executing rules; this and other issues will be discussed at length in Part III of this book.

In this context, business applications developed with the business rules approach – or business rule applications, in short – differ from traditional applications in four ways: (1) the code itself, (2) deployment, (3) run-time behavior, and (4) maintenance. We will discuss the four aspects in turn.

The code. A good application design with the business rules approach should exhibit very few code-level differences with *good* nonbusiness rule applications. The only difference is in the way control-intensive domain functionality is implemented. A good object-oriented design would typically assign each domain-specific function to a *facade* or *controller* method, which in turn would coordinate domain objects to produce the result. Take the property insurance coverage for mortgages rule (third example presented in Sect. 1.1). A good object-oriented application would have a method called "`checkPropertyHazardInsuranceCoverage()`" defined for the class **MortgageApplication**, or for some **PropertyAssessmentService** class, which returns `true` if the coverage is adequate, and `false` otherwise. In a nonbusiness rule-oriented application, the method would implement the business logic described by the rule in the implementation language (java or C# or Object Cobol!) with loops, **if**s, **then**s, and **else**s. A business rule application would, instead, code the business decision logic in a rule language and delegate its execution to the rule execution component of the BRMS, as illustrated in Fig. 1.2. Other than that, the code should look identical! In fact, we consider it *good practice* to circumscribe the parts of a business application that are "aware" of business rules, and that interact with a BRMS.

Deployment. With regard to deployment, a business rule application differs from a traditional application in that application logic is broken into two pieces: (1) business rules that are managed and executed by a BRMS and (2) a computational infrastructure that is responsible for everything else (materializing application objects and managing them, managing the application workflow, architectural services, etc.). These two pieces are packaged separately, and deployed separately, and often asynchronously; we will say more when we talk about maintenance.

Run-time. In terms of run-time behavior, we should see no difference between the *functional behavior* of a business rule application and that of a traditional one: they are supposed to be both implementing the same business rules, and thus we should get the same outcomes for the same inputs! In fact, this is one way that we can validate a business rule application that is a reengineered version of a legacy application – as most rule projects are. In terms of run-time architecture, an implementation scenario such as Fig. 1.2 means that our business rule application needs to invoke an external service, although we could also embed a rule interpreter (called *rule engine*) in the business application in the same executable/run-time image.

Maintenance. Maintenance is probably the one aspect of a business rule applications that is most different from traditional applications. As we saw in Sect. 1.2, one of the key motivators for the business rules approach is the need for agility so that business rule applications can evolve as fast as the business needs it. Several factors make maintenance easier and faster:

1. *Understandability by business*. Business rules are expressed in languages that business users can understand, enabling them to either specify the rules themselves or to easily validate them.
2. *Separate deployment*. Because business rules are deployed separately from the code base of applications, we can have a rule maintenance and release cycle that is separate from – and hence much lighter-weight than – your average application maintenance and release cycle.
3. *Separate execution*. As a corollary of separate deployment, and based on the scenario shown in Fig. 1.2, business rules are executed by the BRMS, on demand from business applications. This means that we can have *hot deployment* of new business rules, without shutting down the business application. In fact, the Websphere ILOG JRules BRMS – JRules, in short – enables us to run *different versions* of business rules *simultaneously*. We will introduce JRules in Chap. 8 and talk about situations where we might need several versions of rules in Chap. 13.

Figure 1.3 illustrates the different release and maintenance cycles for the core of business applications and for the business rules.

The lower part of the figure shows the maintenance and release cycle for the application code, which should be fairly stable. After the first release of an application, we may have an update release or two within the first year, but after that, the pace of change slows down even further – often once a year or less, for back-office systems. With regard to the rules, we can have many smaller updates as frequently as needed, including daily, or even hourly, if quality assurance can follow!

1.4 Why Do We Need a New Methodology?

The business rules approach makes business rules explicit, separates them from other application requirements and development artifacts, and manages their development, their deployment, and their execution. The way that we develop the basic application infrastructure, however, need not change significantly. If you have been

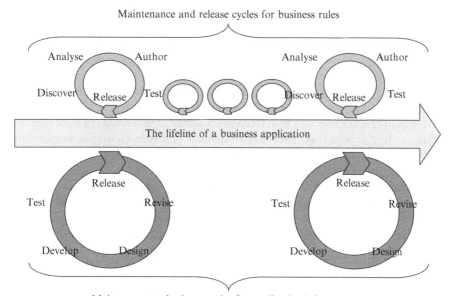

Fig. 1.3 Maintenance and release cycles for application core versus business rules

using some homegrown version of the Unified Process (UP), or some agile method, or flavorful combinations of the two such as OpenUp,[7] you need not change the way that you develop your application infrastructure: (1) you still use use cases or business process description (or whatever it is that you use) to capture functional requirements, (2) you still use object models to represent the business domain and the way it is captured in the software, and (3) you still design your architecture using the same criteria (distribution, scalability, performance, and security) and the same solutions. However, we need well-defined processes, roles, and deliverables to handle business rules, and their relationship to the application infrastructure. In the remainder of this section, we will discuss the ways in which the *process* of developing a business rule application differs from traditional application development. Part II of this book will go over our own methodology, *Agile Business Rule Development* (ABRD); in this section, we will content ourselves with highlighting the issues.

Synchronous versus asynchronous rule management. Before we start talking about various development activities, we need to make a distinction between two ways of developing and managing business rules, which have different methodological implications:

---

[7]OpenUP is an Eclipse project that uses the *Eclipse Process Framework* (http://www.eclipse.org/epf) to specify an agile version of the Unified Process.

- We can develop business rules as a separate activity, independent of specific business application projects, and project schedules. We can think of business rule management as part of a broader *knowledge management* practice within the organization. This means, among other things, the existence of a rule management organization within the enterprise, which can serve various business applications. The rule management organization is then responsible for collecting, codifying, validating, and publishing the business rules. The application project organizations will then reference a subset of those rules in their applications. In this case, we have a well-defined producer–consumer relationship between the rule management organization and the application project organizations. Figure 1.4 illustrates this scenario.
- We can also develop business rules as a by-product of specific business applications. In this case, the rules will be developed incrementally, and always within the context of a specific application project. However, the rules will be stored and managed in a shared repository. Figure 1.5 illustrates this scenario.

Which approach works best? Each of the two approaches has its advantages and disadvantages. The first approach may be more appropriate for a large and *mature* organization which will have a dedicated team of business analysts whose job is to create and manage business rules for the enterprise. This approach requires top-level management commitment since it requires significant up-front investment costs in human resources that are not easily linked to operational priorities. One of the methodological challenges that such teams would face is the scoping of their activities. Indeed, without any specific mandate at hand, they need to identify and prioritize the business areas that they need to address. Also, the chances are that in the first few months or years of operation, many project organizations will not find in the repository everything that they need. The advantages of this structure include

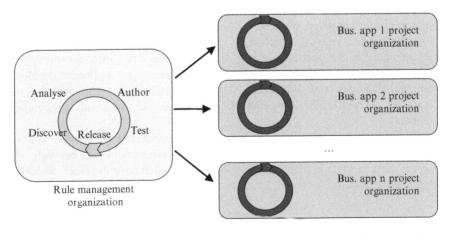

Fig. 1.4 Rule management is the responsibility of an independent organization that produces rules consumed by different project organizations

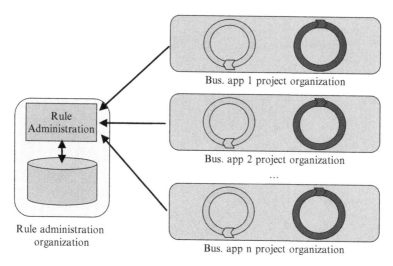

Fig. 1.5 Each project team develops and manages the business rules it needs for the application it is building

a de facto enterprise-wide visibility of rules, a more coherent rule repository, and a more consistent application of rules across business applications.

The second approach does not require substantial up-front investments that are hard to justify, will not suffer from "analysis paralysis" since rules will be collected within the context of specific applications, and each business application will have all the rules it needs by the time it is done. However, it has two major disadvantages: (1) a duplication of effort between various project teams, especially if several projects are running in parallel and (2) having to manage multiple sets of rules with a potential proliferation of variations on the same rules, or worse yet, conflicting versions of rules. Figure 1.5 shows this scenario. In this case, we have an enterprise-wide lightweight *rule administration* function, in terms of a shared repository and centralized access control, but each business application project team is responsible for managing its rules, from discovery to execution.

In practice, enterprises would use an organization that is between these two extremes, depending on its maturity level. An enterprise that is making its first foray into the business rules approach should use the organization shown in Fig. 1.5, for the first couple of pilots, typically in sequence. It is more likely in this case that the same people involved in the business rule component of the first application will also be involved in the second application, both to perfect their techniques and to act as *seeds* for other teams. As they get involved in more projects, these pioneers will also start developing a global view of the business rules, and start seeing opportunities for sharing and reusing rules between applications, and across business functions. They may eventually get integrated into an enterprise-wide *business rules expertise center* that includes expertise in business rules methodology, business rule implementation technology, and business knowledge. Some of these pioneers may be loaned to specific project teams, while others focus

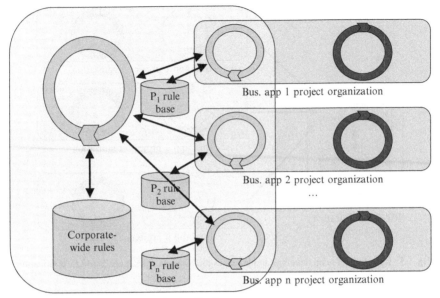

Rule management organization / business
rule expertise center

Fig. 1.6 An intermediary organization that combines the agility of synchronous development while leveraging common expertise and corporate-wide rules

on corporate-wide rules. Figure 1.6 illustrates such an organization, which we have seen operate successfully in some of the more mature organizations. Figure 1.6 shows that there is two-way communication between project-specific rule activities and corporate-wide rule activities. Indeed, project-specific rule teams will use the corporate-wide rule base as a potential source of rules relevant to the application at hand. Also, in the process of collecting rules for a specific application, they may find that some rules are generally applicable, and include them – or ask that they be included – in the corporate-wide rule base.

The methodology presented in this book, ABRD, is based on the synchronous model – Fig. 1.5.

New application development versus reengineering existing applications. Many of our engagements with customers dealt with new applications aiming at automating previously manual, decision-intensive business processes. Such projects have the necessary business focus from the beginning, and provide an opportunity to apply the principles of the business rules approach, almost by the book. However, *many more* engagements consisted of reengineering existing applications. The scope and depth of the reengineering effort determine the extent of freedom that the project team will have in implementing the new system, and the number of painful compromises that need to be made to accommodate the legacy system. Figure 1.7 shows different reengineering scopes in relation to a layered system

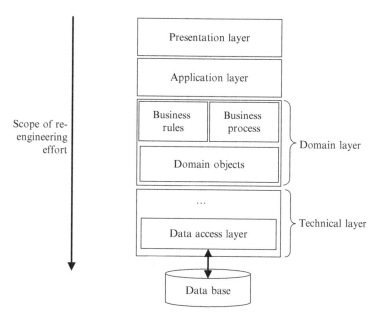

Fig. 1.7 The implications of the business rules approach depend on the scope of the reengineering project

architecture. We will comment on a few points in this space that correspond to the most typical situations.

A common scenario consists of introducing new technologies into a legacy system to make it more scalable, agile, modifiable, etc. In this case, business rules technology is introduced along with a mix of other technologies, including an object-oriented domain layer, a web-based presentation layer, a business process workflow engine, etc. In this case, the only thing that is salvaged from the legacy system is often limited to the legacy database (or EIS layer); anything from the data access layer up to the presentation layer is built from scratch. With the appropriate discipline (e.g., business focus), these projects may be managed – and feel like – new application development (*forward engineering*), with few constraints and compromises.

Another common scenario consists of reengineering the top layers of the application, going from the presentation layer down to, and excluding, the domain objects layer. This means that the domain objects are already built in Java or C#, and that we need "only" to reengineer the way the business rules are implemented and executed in the application. This scenario is not trivial as the existing domain object implementation may not readily lend itself to the expression and execution of business rules according to the business rules approach. The gap needs to be bridged through a combination of methodology and technology.

Figure 1.8 shows a methodology matrix that illustrates the methodological variants of the business rules approach. The STEP methodology (von Halle 2001)

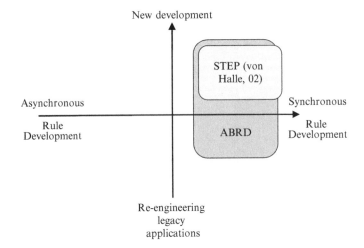

Fig. 1.8 A business rules methodology matrix

is an essentially synchronous, forward-engineering methodology for new applications built under the business rules approach, and addresses both the infrastructure of the application and the business rules component in the same framework. ABRD focuses on the business rules component and its interface with the application infrastructure, of which it is fairly independent.

We now turn our attention to the various development *activities* and see how they are affected by business rule methodologies, depending on where they fit in this matrix. For the sake of discussion, we will consider (a) requirements capture, (b) analysis and design, (c) coding/authoring, (d) testing, and (e) maintenance; the changes brought upon by the business rules approach are fairly independent from the actual *process* along which these activities are organized.

Requirements capture. In the synchronous mode, for new developments, we elicit the business rules as part of the requirements capture. However, the business rules are gathered in separate deliverables, which cross-reference other requirements deliverables such as domain models and business use cases. Further, there is an explicit emphasis on business rationale (business policies and motivations behind them), as opposed to focusing on the business actions that derive from such rationale. Accordingly, we need specific processes, roles, techniques, and deliverables to handle business rules. The processes and techniques for eliciting business rules, and the intermediary deliverables, depend on the requirements capture technique traditionally used by the organization. For example, if an organization relies on *use cases* for capturing functional requirements, the business rules will be captured in the context of *decision steps* within those use cases [see, e.g., the *use-case rule discovery roadmap* of the *STEP* methodology (von Halle 2001)]. If we have a reengineering project, the legacy system and its documentation are usually used as a potential source – seldom the only one – for business requirements in general, and business rules in particular. In this case, the process and techniques for rule discovery are adapted accordingly.

In the asynchronous mode, we clearly need separate processes, roles, techniques, and deliverables for the discovery of enterprise business rules, independently of requirements capture for specific business applications.

Analysis and design. The analysis and design of the *infrastructure* of a business application are marginally affected by the adoption of the business rules approach, except for a more explicit business focus, and the reliance on a BRMS for performing business decisions (see, e.g., Fig. 1.2). However, there are lots of new things to analyze and design on the decision/business rule side of the application. There is such a thing as *rule analysis*, which deals with things such as breaking complex business rules into several simpler more atomic ones, detecting redundancies, overlaps or contradictions between rules, documenting the business motivations of rules, and so forth (see Chap. 4). Further, we need to package rules into coherent units of testing, deployment, and execution – called *rulesets* – depending on the underlying business process and on application design considerations (Chap. 9). We also need to specify and design the management component of the BRMS, including the structure of the rule repository (Chap. 9), the rule metadata, the enforcement of the rule change processes, etc. (Chaps. 16 and 17). Finally, we need to design the way in which the business application will interact with the BRMS for executing the business rules (Chaps. 7, 12 and 13).

Coding/authoring. The coding of the application infrastructure is not affected by the use of the business rules approach. However, decision logic is now coded separately as business rules through a BRMS system, and we need a new set of processes, techniques, skills, roles, and tools for *rule authoring*. One of the major consequences of this separation is that the two aspects of the application are decoupled and can progress independently. We have been involved in projects where the application infrastructure was completed before the first business rule was coded and tested. An incredulous CIO protested "how could you send half the development team home when you are still capturing requirements." We have also been to projects where all of the business rules have been coded, and many were tested, before a single domain Java class was coded. Rule authoring issues and solution patterns are fairly independent of where we stand in the methodology matrix (Fig. 1.8). Part IV of this book (Chaps. 9, 10, and 11) is dedicated to rule authoring.

Testing. In traditional system development, *functional testing* can only start after large chunks of an application have already been implemented. Further, *black box* functional testing provides little to no help in diagnosing an application's business logic, whereas *white box* functional testing requires us to identify and analyze logical paths within complex execution traces. With the business rules approach, we can test *individual* business rules, with *little infrastructure code*. This is like performing *functional unit testing* where we are able to identify, trace, and modify individual logical paths through the application code. The testability of individual rules is a powerful verification and validation tool. Part VI of this book (Chaps. 14 and 15) deals with rule testing.

Maintenance. In traditional system development, maintenance requests follow a similar implementation path, whether the request concerns business logic or infrastructure code: once a manager has signed off on a maintenance request, it falls into the hands of IT who implement it, test it, and deploy it. With the business rules approach, because business rules (decision logic) are developed and maintained separately, we have different processes in place that recognize the *business* nature of *business rule maintenance*, and that take advantage of the lighter deployment mechanisms for business rules. Business rule maintenance is part of a wider set of rule management activities that we refer to as *rule governance*. Rule governance processes depend heavily on the business rule approach variant along the synchronous versus asynchronous development dimension (see Figs. 1.4 to 1.6). Rule governance is discussed in Chaps. 16 and 17.

1.5   Summary and Conclusions

Organizations develop business information systems to support their business processes. These information systems should behave in a way that is consistent with the organization's business objectives and policies. They do so by enforcing *business rules*. Put another way, business rules embody the business soul of business applications. Both business and IT need to know what those rules are, and sometimes customers and regulators do too. The rules need to be expressed in a language that all the stakeholders can understand, and implemented in a way that enables us to change them at the speed of business, as opposed to the speed of IT. These are the motivations behind the so-called business rules approach.

The business rules approach consists of three interrelated components:

1. A methodology for creating and managing the business rules
2. One or more languages for expressing them at different stages of their life cycle and for different audiences
3. A tool set for managing and executing them on behalf of business applications

We saw in Sect. 1.4 that business rules methodologies come in different flavors, depending on the maturity of the organization with the business rules approach and on the nature of the project, that is, a new development versus a reengineering project. We also saw how the adoption of the business rules approach affects traditional development tasks such as requirements capture, analysis, design, coding, testing, and maintenance. The remainder of this book addresses all of these activities within the context of the Agile Business Rule Development methodology and the IBM Websphere ILOG JRules business rule management systems (BRMSs) – JRules in short.

So, is it an evolution or a revolution? We do not like revolutions. Revolutions start with destruction – destroying legacies – lead to initial chaos – even if temporary – and are often run by quasi-religious zealots. And the outcome is often unpredictable. The ingredients for the business rules approach have been around for more than 20 years. It is their combination, in their current mature form, which gives the approach its revolutionary power.

In this chapter, we strove to focus on the basics, which does not necessarily do justice to the complex technological landscape of today's enterprise applications. More detail and nuances will be presented in the next 17 chapters of the book!

1.6 Further Reading

There are a number of resources about the business rules approach that the reader can consult to complement the information provided in the chapter.

- A book by Ronald Ross titled *Principles of the Business Rules Approach*, published by Addison Wesley, February 2003, Addison Wesley. As the title suggests, this is a foundational book. It talks about the essence of business rules, how they relate to business events, and proposes an extensive classification of rules. This book says very little about implementation, and does not present a step by step methodology for building business rule applications – nor was it its intent.
- The book *Business Rules and Information Systems: Aligning IT with Business Goals*, by Tony Morgan, Addison Wesley, March 2002. This is another foundational book – a *great one, nonetheless*. It presents the essence of the business rules approach by explaining what business rules are, what they are about, and attempts a rigorous approach to rule capture and analysis. There is little in terms of a step-by-step methodology and *very* little in terms of technology.
- Barbara von Halle's book, *Business Rules Applied: Building Better Systems Using the Business Rules Approach*, published by John Wiley & Sons, in 2001. This book presents the STEP methodology (*Separate, Trace, Externalize*, and *Position* rules for change). It does an excellent job of presenting methodology but is a bit short on design and very short on implementation.
- The business rules group web site (http://www.businessrulesgroup.org) contains links to the various papers published by its members. Topics addressed include the definition of business rules (see Sect. 1.1), the business rule motivation model, and the business rule maturity model.
- The Object Management Group (http://www.omg.org) has a number of active standards related to business rules, a number of which are based on (more readable) submissions of the business rules group.
- The *business rules forum* (http://www.businessrulesforum.com) is an annual conference for people interested in the business rules approach, and is a good opportunity for learning about new product features and cutting-edge thinking.

Chapter 2
Business Rules in Practice

Target audience
- *All*

In this chapter you will learn
- *Typical applications areas for the business rules approach*
- *The case study used throughout this book*

Key points
- *The business rules approach applies to all kinds of industries and spheres of activities.*
- *The business rules approach applies to all organization sizes, from the smallest of enterprises to the biggest fortune 100 companies.*
- *The business rules approach has been successfully used to automate all sorts of business processes, from back-office processes to front-end processes.*

2.1 Introduction

Recall von Halle's definition of the business rules approach, "a formal way of managing and automating an organization's business rules so that the business behaves and evolves as its leaders intended" (von Halle 2001). This definition is fairly broad and can apply to any type of organization, be it a for-profit organization (an enterprise), a not-for-profit public organization, or a government. It can also apply to any type of "business," whether it is financial services, health, insurance, telecommunications, manufacturing, transportation, or customs and border control!

Historically, the business rules approach has started in engineering domains, due to its *expert systems* lineage (see Chap. 6). Roughly speaking, expert systems are computer programs that attempt to capture *human expertise* in areas where the expertise is rare and heuristic in nature to solve problems. By heuristic we mean that it calls for the *human judgment* of *experts* as opposed to being mechanical from first

J. Boyer and H. Mili, *Agile Business Rule Development*,
DOI 10.1007/978-3-642-19041-4_2, © Springer-Verlag Berlin Heidelberg 2011

principles. This is generally the case in domains where the relevant knowledge is complex (many interrelationships), extensive (volume-wise), and incomplete (some missing links). The expert systems approach has thus typically been applied to areas in medical diagnosis and engineering design. Example medical applications include the pioneering *Internist* system, which was used to diagnose internal medicine problems (ref), and the DENDRAL system, which was used to classify substances based on their spectrometer readings (ref). Example engineering applications include the [vax design expert system], which was used to design the architecture of Digital Equipment Corporation's[1] VAX family of computers.

The *business rules approach* has a much broader scope than the expert systems approach. The issue is not so much to codify complex decision processes, the kind that require a 12-year postsecondary education – Internist, for example. As we showed in Chap. 1, the issue is one of capturing the business's policies, whatever they are, being able to share them with the various stakeholders, operationalizing them, and being able to evolve them at the speed of business. In fact, most of the rules shown in Sect. 1.1 are quite simple.

In the remainder of this chapter, we will go over some general application areas. The business rules approach has been applied to many different industries, from manufacturing, to financial services, to insurance, to e-government. In each one of these industries, it has been used to support both core vertical processes (e.g., loan underwriting, insurance claim processing), as well as support, horizontal processes (e.g., accounting, human resources, CRM). Space limitations do not allow us to present examples from all the industries that we were personally involved in, and all of the business processes that we supported. To get an idea about the range of industries and processes that used the business rules approach, the reader can check the list of customers of the various tool vendors or look at the technical program of the latest edition of the business rules forum.[2]

In this chapter, we will talk about three major areas: engineering (Sect. 2.2), financial services (Sect. 2.3), and insurance (Sect. 2.4). For each industry, we will give two example applications. The case study used throughout this book is from the insurance domain and will thus be presented in Sect. 2.4. We conclude in Sect. 2.5.

2.2 Engineering Applications

In this section, we present two example applications from the engineering domain. These examples are not meant to be either exhaustive or representative, but illustrate the broad range of problems that call for the business rules approach.

---

[1]Digital Equipment Corporation was a manufacturer of mid-size time-sharing mainframes that was purchased by Compaq in 1998, which in turn merged with HP in 2002. The VAX family of computers was its flagship product line.

[2]Check http://www.businessrulesforum.com/

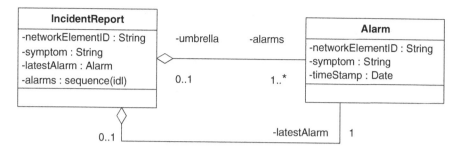

Fig. 2.1 A simplified object model for alarm filtering and correlation

2.2.1 Alarm Filtering and Correlation

Telecommunication companies operate and manage networks. Roughly speaking, a telecommunications network consists of a network whose nodes consist of network equipment and whose edges consist of links – different kinds of cables. Typical networks include tens of thousands of nodes and span thousands of miles. Companies manage their networks remotely whereby each piece of equipment emits regular messages – sometimes referred to as heartbeats – related to their working status. These messages are routed to operators' consoles. Operators monitor the status of the network by analyzing the inflow of messages and are called upon regularly to diagnose eventual problems with network nodes or links, and when warranted, dispatch repair crews to fix the problem. Messages that indicate abnormal function – called *alarms* – are the ones that operators focus on. While alarms represent a small fraction of the volume of messages sent by network elements, we are still talking about millions of alarms of different severities that operators need to sift through daily. However, given the way that alarms are generated, the number of *alarms* that operators need to focus on can be reduced considerably.

First, consider this: a single malfunction will generate a stream of alarms with a given time regularity. As any Unix user knows, if you unplug the network cable from your workstation, you will receive a series of annoying "network cable problems?" messages on the Unix console. If you re-plug the cable, the messages stop. You unplug again, the messages (alarms) start again. We need rules that will tell us that (a) the first stream is related to a single incident and (b) the first and second streams are related to two different incidents. What the operator should see on their console is two incident reports, instead of hundreds or thousands of "network cable problem?" alarms. Intuitively, a rule might say:

> If we have two alarms originating from the same network element with the same problem, within 5 seconds of each other, then they are related to the same malfunction.

Consider the following data model (Fig. 2.1). The **Alarm** class represents the raw alarms emitted by the network elements. **IncidentReport** represents the corresponding incident report that we are able to *infer* from the individual alarms.

Thus, an **IncidentReport** will point to all of the relevant alarms through the "alarms" association – implemented with the "alarms" data member. An **Incident Report** will also point to the *latest* alarm related to the incident – the "latestAlarm" data member. Both **Alarm** and **IncidentReport** refer to the ID of the network element that raised the alarm and include a description of the problem – the "symptom" data member. The "timeStamp" attribute of **Alarm** refers to the time of occurrence.

We can operationalize the above intuitive rule with the following two rules, one that creates a new incident report from an alarm, and one that groups an alarm into an existing incident report as shown in Fig. 2.2.

Other examples of alarm filtering and correlation take into account the effects of a malfunction on one network element on neighboring network elements.

```
RULE   'new incident report'
  if    an Alarm AL is received and
        there is no IncidentReport IR such that
                AL and IR are about the same network element and
                AL and IR have the same symptom and
                AL occurred within 5 s of the latest alarm of IR

  then
        create an IncidentReport IR_new suchz that
                IR_new.latestAlarm ← AL
                IR_new.networkElementID  ← AL.networkElementID
                IR_new.symptom ← AL.symptom
                add AL to IR_new.alarms


RULE   'add to existing incident report'
  if    an Alarm AL is received and
        there is a IncidentReport IR such that
                AL and IR are about the same network element and
                AL and IR have the same symptom and
                AL occurred within 5 s of the latest alarm of IR
  then
                IR.latestAlarm ← AL
                add AL to IR.alarms
```

Fig. 2.2 Sample rules for alarm correlation

For example, a node that is downstream from a broken link will report the absence of upstream activity, whereas nodes upstream from that link will fail to give a sign of life.

2.2.2 Train Cars Preventive Maintenance

Trains constitute one of the most efficient modes of transportation for both people and merchandise. Freight trains, however, have the bad habit of derailing, much more so than passenger trains, for a combination of technological and economic reasons.[3] A common cause of derailment is unstable train cars which can jump over the tracks at "high" speeds, or displace the tracks themselves, with a similar result. What makes cars unstable? What train conductors refer to as *flat wheels*, i.e., when the steel wheels of a train car lose their perfect circular shape (see Fig. 2.3c). What creates those flat spots? To simplify and caricaturize a bit, the answer is, extended hard braking: in the same way that hard breaking with rubber tires consumes the

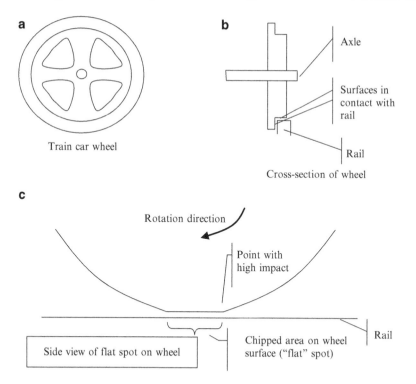

Fig. 2.3 The "flat wheel" problem with train cars

_____

[3]Safety can almost *always* be framed in economic terms, i.e., costs versus benefits.

rubber (those skid marks), extended hard breaking with trains will either cause the wheels to lock and grind against the rail, or, even if they don't lock, they will heat to such high temperatures that, eventually, the surface will chip and break to a similar effect. And why would a train conductor push the brakes hard for an extended period of time? Well, not on purpose: the brake shoes around the wheel can get stuck, even after the conductor releases the pressure. Indeed, freight trains use nineteenth-century braking technology: air (pneumatic) braking system, which can get stuck. With over five million cars in circulation aged 0–120 years, it is not economically or logistically feasible to upgrade them all at once – as we would have to, considering how air brakes work ...

Railroad companies have been trying to detect sticking brakes in running trains so as to prevent "flat wheels" and ultimately, derailments. For this, they use a definitely twentieth-century technology: they place infrared temperature readers along the tracks that measure the temperature of the wheels on passing trains. Such detectors can be placed at regular intervals, e.g., every 20 miles. A wheel temperature reading above 558°F is considered suspicious and is sent to an operator console at the railroad control center. If 20 miles down the track, the next temperature reader registers another reading above 558, then a control center operator will notify the train conductor. The train conductor may choose to ignore the warning if coincidentally he had pushed the brakes at both spots. He may also stop at the next station – or right away – to inspect the suspicious car.[4]

Naturally, not all consecutive high temperature readings are suspicious. There may be cases where a train would be braking for a long distance such as the span between two temperature readers: if a train is climbing down a mountain, the conductor would push the brakes for the entire descent. Thus, readings for *descending* trains on specific track segments would be ignored. Further, not all hot temperatures point to sticking brakes: both wheels (left and right) of the same axle need to be hot, since their braking shoes are connected via a bar, etc. Clearly, there is a nontrivial engineering knowledge that is needed to capture and interpret problematic situations.

In addition to capturing and standardizing engineering rules used by Rail Traffic & Control (RTC) operators and conductors to detect sticking brakes, we can use historical data about cars to perform preventive maintenance. While a single instance of a sticking brake for a car may not suggest a problem with the breaking system, repeated instances may suggest a – costly and time consuming – repair of the car. Further, a car that experienced a number of sticking brakes incidents may need to have its wheels replaced, or minimally, thoroughly inspected. Each inspection and repair has a cost associated with it, but the benefits are considerable. Not only does the cost of an accident, regardless how minor, ranges anywhere from a

---

[4]Interestingly, with current technology (pre-RFID), the control operator can only "guess" what car the hot wheel belongs to, based on its position in the train, but cannot be sure because trains can exchange cars (drop some, acquire others) at different stations, and the positions – and cars – will keep shifting. Some railroad operators have a policy of *not* telling conductors which car has the hot wheel, as added security, and let them find out by walking along the train – which could be miles long – to find out on their own.

few to a few dozen million dollars,[5] but there is a more substantial business cost: the unreliability of delivery leads to a pricing model that is well below trucking, even though, on the average, trains can deliver merchandise across the North American continent as fast as trucks do.

2.3 Financial Services

Through our combined 20 year experience with the business rules approach, we can confidently say that the overwhelming majority of the important players in the banking and mortgage sector have adopted the business rules approach for some of their core processes, most notably, for managing their loan and credit products, including consumption loans, student loans, mortgage loans, credit cards, and so forth. All of these products share an important characteristic: they involve giving money (or making it available) to a customer, for a fee (interest), with an expectation of repayment of capital and interest. For these products to make money for the financial company, the customer has to be *able* and *willing* to repay the capital and interest. Ability deals mostly with income. Willingness is more behavioral and deals with the propensity of the customer to pay back debt. It is usually assessed based on a track record of the customer with debt. Banks, mortgage banks, and credit card companies use a whole set of business rules to assess the ability and willingness of prospective customers to repay back their debt. We will discuss a simple mortgage underwriting example. Our second example deals with tax reporting. The US tax system is notorious for its complexity. It takes us into the wonderful world of tax law and gives the reader a glimpse of what lies out there in terms of business rules.

2.3.1 Mortgage Underwriting

A *mortgage loan* is a loan that is guaranteed or *secured* by a property. A borrower needs an X amount of money that they commit to repaying over a period of time according to some repayment schedule, typically over a period going from 10 to 30 years. Because X tends to be large, the lender requires a property (house, apartment, building, piece of land) in guarantee that it can take possession of and sell, if the borrower *defaults*, i.e., is no longer able to pay. More often than not, the borrower contracts a mortgage loan to *purchase* the property they are giving as guarantee.

---

[5]The costs of an accident include (1) replacing equipment, (2) repairing tracks, (3) insurance deductibles for lost merchandise, (4) costs of cleaning up spills, (5) costs of evacuations, (6) compensation to other users of the track, (7) penalties paid to local authorities and regulatory agencies, (8) costs to any litigation resulting from the accident, etc.

Other reasons include renovating the property, sending the kids to college, buying a new car, consolidating debt,[6] or taking a dream vacation!

Mortgage lenders will apply a number of business rules to assess the potential borrower's willingness and ability to pay. Roughly speaking, the rules may be seen as falling into three categories:

1. *Eligibility rules.* These are pass/fail kinds of rules that determine whether the mortgage loan application is even worth looking at. Failing an eligibility rule is "fatal" to a loan application. But passing it does not guarantee acceptance: more analysis (*underwriting*) is required to make a determination. An example of an eligibility rule concerns the age of the borrower: they must be old enough for a mortgage note to be enforceable in the jurisdiction where the property is located.
2. Detailed assessment rules (*underwriting*), which are applied against *eligible* loan applications, to determine whether the loan should be granted or not.
3. Computation rules, which determine (compute) the parameters of the loan, such as the interest rate, the repayment schedule, the level of insurance required, etc., based on the loan amount, the financial situation of the borrower, and their credit history.

In fact, these rules are typically applied in sequence: only *eligible* applications are analyzed/put through underwriting, and we compute the loan parameters only for those applications that are deemed to have acceptably risk.[7] Figure 2.4 illustrates this process in an activity diagram notation.

The eligibility rules are fairly standard across the industry, and they concern the loan itself, the borrower, and the property. An example of an eligibility rule for the loan itself is about the down payment of the borrower. A typical[8] rule might say:

The borrower must put minimum cash down of 5%. The 5% must come from the borrower's savings or other liquid assets. The remainder of a larger down payment may come from other sources such as gifts.

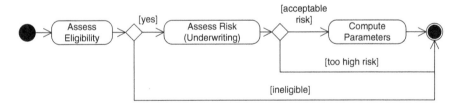

Fig. 2.4 A simplified process for evaluating a mortgage application

---

[6]If the borrower has a number of outstanding loans, including credit card debt, they can borrow money from their bank to pay back their other debts.

[7]In actual applications, there is a third outcome which sends the loan application to a loan officer for "manual underwriting," who may ask for more information before making a final determination.

[8]The rules illustrated in this section come from *Fannie Mae's underwriting guidelines*, which set the industry standard for investment-quality mortgages – not the subprime type.

Other constraints may concern the so-called loan-to-value (LTV) ratio: a borrower cannot borrow more than some threshold percentage of the value of the property that they are purchasing. For example, a bank might require that the loan does not exceed 75% of the value of the property. Thus, for a property that is worth $100,000, the bank cannot lend more than $75,000. Said another way, the borrower must put a down payment that is at least 25% of the value of the property – $25,000 in this case. In practice, this threshold itself depends on several factors, including:

- *The intended usage of the property.* If the mortgaged property is the principal residence, a bank will tolerate a higher LTV ratio (up to 95%) because it figures that borrowers will do their utmost to avoid defaulting on the loan – and risking eviction. If the mortgaged property is an investment property, then the bank's tolerance is much lower and it may put the threshold at 70%.
- *The intended usage of the loaned money.* If the money is borrowed to *purchase* the property, the bank will tolerate higher LTVs, but if the borrower wants to spend the money on a Hawaiian cruise vacation, say, then the bank will be less tolerant.

Rules about the borrowers concern their age, their residency status, and their debt load. A US mortgage banker will only lend money to US citizens, or permanent residents of the USA, or legal foreigners, provided that they (intend to) live in the property and that the LTV is less than 75%, or ... Regarding the debt load, banks will not loan you money if the repayment of that loan, plus your other recurring payments, exceed some threshold portion of your income – typically 37%. In case several borrowers apply for the loan jointly, it is their combined debt over their combined income that has to be over 37% ... nevertheless, the debt over income ratio of each borrower alone must be less than 43%, etc.

Then there are eligibility rules about the property itself, including location and construction type. A US mortgage banker will not want to mortgage a Canadian or French property, and vice versa. Also, you cannot mortgage mobile homes, whose values depreciate more like that of a car, as opposed to appreciating more like that of a fixed building.

And this is just to determine if we should bother analyzing the mortgage application (*underwriting*) or not. A whole other set of rules will look at credit reports, including single scores (e.g., FICO score) as well as credit history (bankruptcy or not, and how far back, number of late payments of bills, how much, how many, how late, and how long ago), cash reserves, and so on and so forth.

And this is just for your run of the mill mortgage. Then there are a number of special products aimed at different segments of society to help promote home ownership and to compensate for all sorts of disadvantages, including socio-economic and geographical ones. Some of the criteria may be tightened or relaxed, in which case some government agencies or government mandated institutions may shoulder some of the risk. The parameters can also be adapted for special real estate markets, which are either too high priced, or shielded from cyclical market trends, or in flood or earthquake zones, etc. Before you know it, we are talking about hundreds and thousands of business rules.

Historically, the better organized mortgage institutions developed underwriting manuals, with rules and tables and all, and provided training to their underwriters. When new rules were added or existing ones were modified, memos, change notices, updates, or whatever they were called, were sent around the enterprise to inform the underwriters of the changes, and occasionally, remedial training was offered to explain the changes. In some ways, these organizations had a very partial implementation of the business rules approach: they managed – more or less effectively – the business rules of the enterprise. However, they did not automate them. Indeed, all of the decision making was performed manually; information systems were used simply to record information and the decisions reached by the human underwriters. Further, their way of managing the business rules did not facilitate their evolution. Most often, the carefully crafted glossy color manuals became obsolete by the time they were distributed.

With the first generation of automated underwriting systems, IT had to implement the business rules based on the (obsolete) underwriting manuals, the notes, memos, meeting minutes, e-mails, and other records of the organization's memory. Omissions were frequent, misunderstandings galore, and making changes took a whole lot of time. As we illustrated in Chap. 1, one of our clients's web underwriting application lagged behind the policy changes implemented by the enterprise since the subprime meltdown, leading to an embarrassing problem for customer relations.

It should come as no surprise that the majority of the major mortgage institutions have adopted the full business rules approach (management, automation, evolution), some as far back as 15 years ago – and even before, if you count the kind of ad-hoc rough-edged custom "rule engines" that the more creative ones have implemented.

2.3.2   Tax Reporting and Withholding

Resident companies and individuals in the USA file their income tax forms every year, the former, soon after the closing date of their financial year, and the latter, on April 15th. Employers are requested to collect income taxes on their regular employees' salaries every month and send them to the Internal Revenue Service (IRS). Employers compute the monthly deductions based on the information they have about their employees (marital status, number of dependents, etc.) in such a way that the taxes collected during the year come as close the final tax bill as possible. During the year, the IRS does not get details about who paid which taxes: they receive a bulk payment from each employer for all their employees for the period (month, trimester). At the end of year, employers send their employees a summary of their income and all of the deductions during the year, including taxes collected. Copies of those summaries are also sent to the IRS. A similar scheme is used for corporations: corporations *can* make provisional income tax payments during a given fiscal year based on the previous year's income. When they file for taxes at the end of the fiscal year, they compute actual taxes owed based on *actual* income for the fiscal year and then make the necessary adjustments consisting of additional taxes to be paid, if not enough taxes were collected during the year, or a tax refund, otherwise.

When a US company makes out a payment to another resident company for products or services rendered, or a nonsalary payment to a resident person, it is the responsibility of the receiver of the payment – the resident company or resident person – to declare (*report*) the payment at the end of the year and to pay taxes on it. What happens when the receiver is *not* a resident? Because the IRS cannot run around the globe collecting taxes from foreign entities that had had a US income, it requires *the payers* to preemptively withhold taxes on *each payment* and *report it* to the IRS. For example, a Spanish person opens an investment account with a US brokerage house and buys some stock. If they later sell the stock at a higher price, the *capital gains* they made are taxable. The brokerage house should *withhold* taxes on the capital gains and deposit the remainder of the proceeds from the stock sale.

The general, default rule says: withhold 30% on income made by foreign entities. The explanations and exceptions to this rule take 58 pages of three-column dense IRS prose that, in turn, refers to a bunch of other IRS publications . . . and that is the simplified version for small businesses ☺. What takes so long?

- We need to define "foreign" entities and "nonresident alien," for the purpose of this tax law. This is usually ascertained by the documentation that the entity or person filed when they opened their brokerage account. There are a bunch of forms (W-8, W-9), and variations within those forms (W-8BEN, W-8ECI, W-8EXP, W-8IMY). And then, it depends on which boxes were checked or filled out in each form.
- Not all foreign entities are subject to withholding. For example, foreign governments and international charities are exempt. Again, this is a question of which form was filed by the brokerage account holder, which boxes were checked or unchecked, which fields were filled, and what was written in them.
- The withholding tax rate (30%) depends on the type of payment! First of all, not all payments correspond to income. If you buy 50 shares of some company at $10 and sell them for $9, the proceeds of the sale ($450) are *not* a taxable gain. And then, it depends on the income type: you have interest, dividends, capital gains, each of which is subject to a different tax – and thus withholding rate.
- Then there are tax treaties with individual countries. So our Spanish investor would be subject to a 10% withholding rate on interest income, whereas a Turkish investor, say, would be subject to a 15% withholding rate on interest income. People and companies from countries that do not have tax treaties with the USA will pay 30%, across the board, for all income types.
- Then there is the case when the foreign entity is a *flow-through entity*. Intuitively, a flow-through entity is a partnership through which money simply flows to the individual partners. For tax purposes, we allocate the gains back to the individual partners and withhold tax in accordance with each partner's nationality. Thus, if we make a $200 interest payment to a flow-through 40–60 partnership between a

Spanish and a Turkish, we treat it as an $80 interest payment to the Spanish, subject to 10% withholding, and a $120 interest payment to a Turkish, subject to 15% withholding.

And once we figure out all of this, we need to figure out which form to use to report the income and submit the withheld tax, and in which box or column to report which amount.

And you thought that your business rules were complex!

An investment bank used the business rules approach to implement these tax reporting and withholding rules. This bank executes anywhere from hundreds of thousands to millions of transactions per day. Transactions typically include information about the type of payment (interest, dividend, etc.), the amount, and the customer account (payee). Each transaction coming into the system was first submitted to the reporting and withholding module, which applied the business rules to figure out whether the payment was subject to reporting, withholding, and how much. Then, based on the outcome, the appropriate deposits were performed on the appropriate accounts, and the information recorded in a reporting module. The application was delivered in a record time, and the project schedule was followed to the *hour*. This was due to a combination of a *disciplined* use of *agile* methods and the business rules approach. The latter meant, among other things, that our customer's accountants were still sorting out the business rules with IRS accountants, while IT was putting the final touches on the application infrastructure. This was a textbook case of the decoupling between the application development cycle and the business rules development cycle illustrated in Fig. 1.3.

2.4 Insurance

The insurance industry is another big consumer of business rules technology, and insurance companies have been among the early adopters. The business rules approach has been used for both its core processes (policy underwriting, claim processing), as well as support processes such as accounting, CRM, and marketing. In this section, we will present two examples, one for policy underwriting, for regular insurance, and another for claim processing, looks at an example from health insurance. The case study used throughout this book is in claim processing.

2.4.1 Policy Underwriting

Let us take a representative sample of a thousand (1,000) drivers between the ages of 30 and 40, and see how many of them get into accidents over the period of 1 year, and tally up the costs of these accidents in terms of vehicle repair, medical bills, income support during work stoppage or due to disability, and god forbid, death. Assume that all of this adds up to $600,000. Let us figure out how much it would cost to insure these 1,000 drivers so that (a) all of the costs are covered by the insurer and (b) the insurer makes money – after it has paid its staff, its buildings, the various services it uses, its utility bills, and the tax man. Let us say that those extra costs add up to $400,000. If the insurer wants to make money, it should charge at least $1,000/year. An insured would be more than willing to pay that insurance premium, because even though the *expected* (mathematical average) cost to each insured is $600/year, most will incur no cost during that year, but the unlucky ones who get into an accident can go bankrupt.

Let us now throw in some competition. A competitor figures that *women* between the ages of 30 and 40 get into much fewer accidents than men, with perhaps an expected yearly cost (in terms of claims) of $350, per driver per year. Having figured that, the competitor will offer insurance to women at a much lower cost, while possibly jacking up the prices for men to reflect their true cost. If women flock to the competitor, they deprive the first insurer of his lower-cost customers, and so he too needs to *segment* the market and price the coverage accordingly. Once they have segmented based on age and gender, then they get into driving habits, e.g., occasional drivers versus drivers who use their car to commute to work, rural versus city driving, etc. Then they look at the driving record considering DUI convictions, accidents, moving violations, and so forth.

Insurance companies typically have large marketing departments full of statisticians, actuaries, and marketers who peer over market data, demographic data, and all sorts of statistics (accident statistics, for auto insurance, epidemiological studies, for medical insurance, etc.) to identify the level of risk associated with different segments of the market. The result of these studies is a bunch of rules that help determine (a) which potential customers to underwrite (accept) at all, and (b) for those that are accepted, how to price the insurance contract to them in such a way that the insurer beats the competition and makes money.

Figure 2.5 shows a simplified version of what an automated underwriting process might look like. An insurance broker fills out an electronic form based on data supplied by a potential customer. The system first validates the data, i.e., things such as the social security number,[9] the zip code, or the driver license number. If the

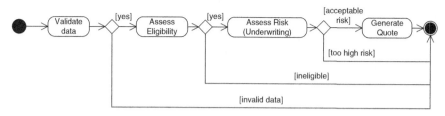

Fig. 2.5 A simplified process for insurance policy quote generation

---

[9]There are two possible levels of verification: we could either check that the social security is well formed or further check that it belongs to the potential customer.

data is invalid, the insurance policy is rejected. If the data is valid, we look at eligibility criteria. For auto insurance, these include things such as the age of the driver, the driver license (jurisdiction, expiration date, possible suspension). If the policy is eligible, then we go into pricing and generate a quote. Else, we produce a rejection report explaining while the policy was rejected. Each one of the steps of this process will involve a bunch of business rules.

Actual processes used in policy underwriting systems are far more complex. When a potential customer calls an insurer's call center, they do not typically know what insurance product they want: the insurance agent has to ask a number of questions, to identify the insurance type, and each insurance type can have its own eligibility and risk assessment criteria. To say that you want to insure a car is not enough: is it a personal car for personal use, or a company car, or a rental car. Second, the data that you supply depends on the type of insurance. If you say that you want to insure a company car, we will ask about the company: what is its yearly income, how many employees, how long it has been in business, etc. Insurance agents will usually navigate through a sequence of input screens where the next input screen to pop-up depends on the data entered so far. Further, some data fields are usually validated on the fly, while others are performed once the data entry is complete. Further, the risk assessment phase is usually done in several stages. The first stages typically consist of computing one or several scores. In the last stage, we make a decision based on where the score(s) fall: between 50 and 150, between 150 and 250, and above 250. Finally, the last stage will typically have three outcomes, instead of the binary yes/no: we have "may be" for borderline cases, in which case the policy is sent for *manual referral* to a human underwriter. Typically, the underwriter would talk to the customer to seek additional information before making a final decision.[10]

Full-service insurance companies will offer insurance products to individuals – *personal lines* – and corporations – *commercial lines*. Within personal lines, we have auto insurance, homeowners insurance, renters insurance, flood protection, valuable items, boat insurance, umbrella, etc. For commercial lines, we have auto insurance, workers' compensation, as well as insurance packages, which may be customized to company sizes (small, medium, large) and industries (restaurants, garages, stores, professional services offices, manufacturers, etc.). Each one of these products will have its own business rules, but many products will share some business rules. For example, data validation rules can be shared across many products. Eligibility rules may also be common to several products. This raises a number of rule management challenges, which we will discuss in Chap. 7.

---

[10]We have seen insurers who have a policy of referring high-risk customers to a competitor, when they know that the competitor does have an insurance product appropriate for their profile.

2.4.2   Claim Processing

People buy insurance so that when something happens, they get covered. A health insurance customer who pays for a medical service will file a *claim* to get reimbursed for the corresponding expenses. Similarly, a car insurance customer who gets into an accident and has to pay for car repairs will also file a *claim* to get the car repairs paid for.

There are different payment modalities, depending on the type – and level – of coverage, the cost of the services rendered, the kind of agreement that may exist between the service provider (doctor, hospital, or garage) and the insurer, or the level of integration of their information systems. In some cases, the insured pays first for the services rendered (medical or car repair) and then asks the insurer to be reimbursed. In other instances, the service provider is the one who files the claim *before* performing the service, to get a decision regarding coverage, and then, depending on the answer of the insurance company, will bill the insurance company and the insured accordingly. In yet other instances, the insured pays for the services, the service provider fails a claim with the insurance, and the insured receives payment.

Regardless of the payment modality, the various claim processing processes share a common subprocess, which starts with the input or electronic reception of a claim form – regardless of who is filing it – along with invoices for services rendered (or estimates for services to be rendered). The claim is then validated (data fields). Next, we match a claim to the coverage to figure out which of the services rendered are covered by the policy. Finally, we determine the amount of the payment; this is called *claim adjudication*. Figure 2.6 shows a simplified claim processing process.

The tasks of the "happy path" involve a large number of business rules. Claim validation deals with the validation of the various data fields of the claim, such as the name of the insured, their social security number, the policy number, the identification of the service provider, the various dates, etc. The process of Fig. 2.6 shows that invalid claims are routed out of the system, after we prepare a validation report that describes the things that are wrong with the claim. In some systems, the validation report is sent to a human claim handler who follows up with the insured or with the service provider to complete or correct the information.

Claims that are found to be data-valid are submitted to a process that determines their eligibility under the coverages of the insurance policy. This decision is ripe with hundreds if not thousands of rules, regarding the identity of the insured and

Fig. 2.6 A simplified claim processing process

their affiliation/relation to the policy holder,[11] the date at which the accident/sinister occurred, relative to the effectiveness period of the policy – and any default extensions thereof – and the duration of the association of the insured to the policyholder, the location of the accident/sinister, the cause of the accident/sinister, the nature of the damage, the nature of the service rendered to fix the damage, the location (distance *and* jurisdiction), affiliation, certification, or identity of the service provider, the time that separates the service delivery from the accident/sinister, the time that separates the service delivery from the claim submission, etc. Then you look at corroboration. For example, in car insurance, an assessor will examine the accidented vehicle to assess the damage, and the type – and cost – of repair to be performed. With health insurance, medical doctors peer over medical records to assess the necessity of the recommended treatment, and the absence of less expensive alternatives; in rare cases, a health insurer will require that insured seek second opinions from other specialists – or ones that are affiliated with them, etc. A number of these rules are coverage-specific. For example, coverage C_1 covers procedures P_1 and P_2 performed by any qualified <whatever>, whereas coverage C_2 covers only procedure P_1 with a yearly cap of X amount of dollars, if performed by an affiliated <whatever>, etc.

Once we determine the *eligibility* of a claim, then we need to determine the level of coverage to determine how much the insurer will pay versus how much the insured will pay. Here again, we have hundreds and possibly thousands of rules, depending on the complexity of the products offered by the insurer. First, we have the notion of deductibles (the insured pays the first X dollars, or the first $X\%$ dollars), then you have caps, which can be per insured, or per policy, or per procedure/service, per year or over the life of policy, or a combination thereof. Then you have reimbursements that depend on the location at which the service is rendered. For example, the health insurance of one of the authors will pay a flat rate for a "semi-private bed" for hospitalization (i.e., two patients to a room), regardless of which option I choose (private, i.e., one bed per room, or semi-private, or shared, with four to six beds in one hospital room), and when I submit a claim, I get reimbursed for the minimum of actual expenses incurred and the price of a semi-private room. However, the price of a semi-private room depends on where the hospitalization occurs: anywhere in Canada versus in the USA, versus Europe, etc.

In this presentation, we simplified the underlying business process by clearly separating claim data validation, from claim eligibility, from claim adjudication. Some business rules might be considered borderline between two areas, and some reasonable people might disagree.[12] Without getting into the various issues

---

[11]The insured could be the policy holder, or a dependent or the spouse of the policy holder, e.g., for health or personal car insurance, or working for the policy holder, in case of a commercial insurance, etc.

[12]My health insurance puts a $500 yearly cap on physiotherapy. Assume that I reach the cap within a particular year and that I submit another claim for physiotherapy for an extra $100. Should I consider my claim as eligible but adjudicated to zero, or should I consider it as not eligible since I will not get a single penny in reimbursement and does it make a difference?

involved, let us just say that (a) the distinction is important for several reasons, including legal ones and (b) we found it useful to always push customers for crisp business process definitions because it helps them sharpen their understanding of their business and simplify their business rules by breaking them into "atomic" parts (see Chap. 4).

Much like with the policy underwriting rules, the rules for claim processing need to evolve frequently to accommodate the following changes:

- Changes in the insurance products, with the addition of new types of coverage
- Changes in the costs for performing various procedures/services
- Changes in diagnostic and treatment/repair techniques
- Changes in demographics or other trend-setting phenomena[13] that can affect the revenue versus expense relationship
- Pressure from competitors, etc.

For this reason, most of the large insurance companies that we know are at different stages of adoption of the business rules approach for their claim processing, going from looking into the technology and building proofs of concepts to actually maintaining production business rule applications. Some customers we worked with have started introducing the approach to some of their product lines and are generalizing to other product lines. One particular customer has an enterprise-level business rules competency center, which is responsible, among other things, for implementing and maintaining a fairly sophisticated business rule management system.

The case study used throughout this book is based on claim processing. We will elaborate on the process shown in Fig. 2.6 as the need arises in the subsequent chapters.

2.5 Conclusion

In this chapter, we presented a sample of six application areas for the business rules approach, addressing both core business processes and support processes, in telecommunications, railroad operations, mortgage underwriting, tax reporting and withholding, insurance policy underwriting, and insurance claim processing, which is the case study used throughout the book. This is but a small sample of the range of application areas. Business rules have been used for a broad range of e-government services, from managing student loans, to managing welfare programs, to customs, to taxation, to managing various compliance programs. It has

---

[13]For example, in the health insurance business, population aging increases the incidence of chronic age-related diseases which require different business models. Similarly, advances in medicine on one hand and changes in diet and lifestyle on the other, change the profile of medical conditions (what they are and their preponderance in the general population) that insurers have to deal with.

also been used for various aspects of customer relationship management (trade promotions, web personalization, recommender systems, loyalty programs, product configuration, and others), manufacturing (planning, manufacturing shop controls), marketing, and others. We have also been involved with customers ranging in size from a start-up with a staff of four (including the CEO) to fortune 100 companies, with tens, or hundreds, of thousands of employees. Perhaps more to the point, we have applied the approach to $300,000 software projects as well as to 30 or 100 million dollar projects.

So what makes a software application or a company appropriate for the business rules approach? In Sect. 1.2, we identified three issues that cry out for the business rules approach: (1) the need for eliciting and sharing the business rules under which an organization operates (in short, the need for rule management), (2) the need for expressing executable business rules in a way that all stakeholders can understand, or conversely, the need to make the shared expression of business rules executable (in short, the need for rule automation), and (3) the need for development infra-structure/paradigm that supports timely rule maintenance (in short, the need for agile rule maintenance). The question then becomes, which kinds of applications face these issues? To use a Jeff Foxworthy[14] pattern:

- The need for rule management:
  - If your business operates processes with nontrivial policies and rules that are common to your industry, then, you might need the business rules approach. Indeed, this is the case of voluntary "codes of conduct" one might find within a particular industry, or imposed by regulatory agencies.
  - If your business draws competitive advantage from the way it does things, then you might need the business rules approach. Indeed, business policies and rules can *differentiate* players within the same industry (underwriting rules which might be more permissive to a particular market segment, etc.), and it is important to capture and manage those rules throughout the enterprise.

  Another way of stating the above is, "if parts of your business are knowledge-intensive, regardless of whether that knowledge is external or home-grown, then you might need the business rules approach."
- The need for rule automation:
  - If your business software *automates* some of the decision making of your business processes, as opposed to simply *records* the decisions made by human actors, then you might need the business rules approach.
  - If your business needs to *show* the business rules under which its processes operate, then you might need the business rules approach.

  Indeed, business rule automation buys you three things: (1) ease of implementa-tion of the business rules, thanks to a rule language that is more appropriate for expressing business rules than a procedural (or object-oriented) programming

---

[14]Jeff Foxworthy is a stand-up comedian, who has written a number of sketches that consist of sentences along the pattern "if <some condition is true>, then you might be a <some quality>."

language, (2) ease of deployment, thanks a separation between the business rules and the rest of the code, and (3) ease of traceability to requirements, because more often than not, the rule authoring language, or some translation thereof, is also the rule execution language.

- The need for agile rule maintenance:
  - If your business rules evolve *at all*, then you might need the business rules approach.

Indeed, rule maintenance is *always* faster with the business rules approach than with a procedural (or object-oriented) approach: (1) it is easier to *understand the change* since requirements are given as business rules, (2) it is easier to identify the *artifact* that needs to change – typically a well-identified business rule, (3) it is easier to *validate* the changed version, because it is expressed in a language close to requirements, and (4) it is easier to *deploy* the changed version, since business rules are considered as data. This advantage of the business rules approach becomes more overwhelming, as the frequency of changes increases. In fact, with traditional methods, if the business rules change more than once every 4–10 weeks – depending on the type and scope of change – then IT is simply *not* able to respond.

2.6   Further Reading

Interested readers can find out about some business rules case studies in many of the business rules publications and conferences. The annual business rules forum (http://www.businessrulesforum.com) and its more technically oriented younger sibling, October Rule Fest (http://www.rulefest.org), feature a number of speakers from industry who report on lessons learned from real projects. Experience reports in the more academically oriented conferences (IJCAI, ICTAI, etc.). A number of on-line or dual-media magazines occasionally publish essays, state of the practice surveys, case studies, or product reviews, including *Information Week*, *Information Management*, *KMWorld*, *BPTrends*, and others. Books may contain descriptions of some case studies, although project details might be hard to come by because of the proprietary nature of the underlying information. Some companies might not even want their competition to know that they are using the approach for a particular business function, because they consider the adoption of the business rules approach, *in and of itself*, as a competitive advantage.

Part II
Methodology

Chapter 3
Agile Business Rule Development

Target audience

- *All; nontechnical audiences can skip Sects. 3.3 and 3.4*

In this chapter you will learn

- *What is the Agile Business Rule Development (ABRD) methodology, and what are its core principles.*
- *Why develop business rule applications using an agile and iterative approach.*
- *How you can leverage the Eclipse Process Framework (EPF) Composer and OpenUp to customize ABRD to your enterprise environment and projects.*

Key points

- *An Agile methodology promotes iterations and early use of tools, which is the most appropriate approach to develop business application leveraging BPM and BRM technologies.*
- *The goal of executable rules over comprehensive rule description is supported by the strongly iterative approach of ABRD.*

3.1 Introduction

Business rule management systems (BRMS) introduce great flexibility to the IT architecture, enabling developers to quickly and easily change the behavior of an application and the decisions it produces. To best leverage the inherent agility of BRMS components, the application development process must also be agile, with developers, architects, and project managers working iteratively and incrementally. The integration of BRMS, Business Process Management (BPM), Business

J. Boyer and H. Mili, *Agile Business Rule Development*,
DOI 10.1007/978-3-642-19041-4_3, © Springer-Verlag Berlin Heidelberg 2011

Process Execution Language (BPEL)[1] engines, and MDM[2] in a service-oriented architecture (SOA) enforces the need for an agile method of developing new systems.

Agile methodologies, such as eXtreme Programming, SCRUM, and more recently, OpenUp, have provided an excellent foundation from which we can start to address the particularities of developing business application using business rules. What are these specificities?

Here are some typical questions from our client's business analysts, project managers, or enterprise architects:

- How do I discover the business rules?
- Can all rules be implemented with a BRMS?
- How can a BRMS be integrated with BPM products or fit into a service-oriented architecture?
- How do I represent and manage the data used by the rules?
- How do I manage the rule life cycle from requirements to testing, deployment, and retirement?

Recognizing that such concerns needed to be addressed in the context of a methodology, we began developing the Agile Business Rule Development (ABRD) methodology in 2003. The ABRD methodology includes a description of all the different BRMS actors, the activities involved, the work deliverables to produce, and the best practices or guidelines to follow. A rigid methodology has no real chance of adoption if it cannot be adapted to your own approach of developing software. Our goal, therefore, was to enable the methodology as content that could be managed through a tool that allowed users to reuse, tune, and enhance it according to their needs. The ABRD methodology was given to the Open Source community so as to capitalize on the excellent work done in Eclipse Process Framework Composer and OpenUp content and is now present as a plug-in of the OpenUp library within http://www.eclipse.org/epf.

This chapter outlines the core principles of Agile Business Rule Development and its strongly iterative approach to develop business processes and business rules. You will also be introduced to OpenUp and Eclipse Process Framework Composer tools that you can use to tailor the methodology to your organization.

3.2   Core Principles of the ABRD Methodology

The Agile Business Rule Development methodology is an incremental and iterative software development process that takes into account the new concepts required to deploy BRMS, BRE, BPEL, and BPM components into business applications.

---

[1]Business Process Execution Language is an OASIS standard executable language for specifying interactions with web services (http://www.oasis-open.org/committees/tc_home.php?wg_abbrev= wsbpel).

[2]Master Data Management is a set of processes and tools that defines and manages the reference data and nontransactional data of an organization.

The ABRD methodology is adapted to the software and business challenges of developing decision support systems and provides a better collaboration framework between IT and business than traditional waterfall software development life cycle (SDLC). Traditional software development models, such as the waterfall or the V-model, while they may be interesting to support the development of mission-critical projects, are notorious for producing over-budget, late-to-market solutions that do not match initial business expectations for fast-paced projects where requirements are evolving frequently. Such approaches leave business users with little ownership of the solution, and implementing changes can easily take months. As a result, business policy owners are uncomfortable with change – which translates into loss of agility to respond competitively. In addition to the latency between submitting change requirements to IT and the actual deployment of new rules, policy managers have no guarantee that their changes were implemented according to the business needs. Business users can only hope that all possible test cases were covered during testing.

In contrast to such development models, ABRD leverages the following principles presented by the Agile Alliance manifesto (Fig. 3.1).

The Agile development values are particularly relevant to the implementation of a rule set using the ABRD approach:

- *Individuals and interactions over processes and tools*. The rule discovery, analysis, and validation activities require active and efficient communication between the rule developer, subject matter experts (SME), and business users. Such processes are defined as lightly as possible.
- *Working software over comprehensive documentation*. Each iteration produces a working, tested set of rules that can be executed, which has far more business value than a rule description manual. While all project stakeholders benefit from such a principle, business users in particular are then sure that what they see (the rules, the business process) is what gets executed in the deployed system.
- *Customer collaboration over contract negotiation*. Subject matter experts who define the business policies and the business rules are strongly involved in the development process. As the customers of the final system and owners of the policies, they are conveniently collocated with the development team during the project. There is no specification document thrown above a wall waiting for the IT to develop the system.

Individuals and interactions over processes and tools
Working software over comprehensive documentation
Customer collaboration over contract negotiation
Responding to change over following a plan

Fig. 3.1 Manifesto for Agile Software Development (http://www.agilemanifesto.org)

- *Responding to change over following a plan.* Business rules evolve more often and faster than other standard pieces of software. This is actually one of the key values of the business rule approach. For this fundamental reason, the methodology to support the rule set development must be tailored to such rapid life cycle and include the appropriate activities, processes, best practices, and work products to support such changes efficiently.

The ABRD addresses the following goals in more detail:

- Separate rules as manageable artifacts using discovery, analysis and authoring activities, and their related work products
- Trace rules during their full life cycle from requirement to deployment and maintenance
- Link rules to business context and motivation
- Develop the rule description using business terms and high-level rule language
- Prepare the logical data model for the rule engine using object-oriented analysis and design
- Prepare the rule set implementation and deployment as decision services in an SOA
- Validate the rule set quality using a test-driven approach with continuous integration and testing once the development team develops the rules, and the business user maintains them
- Articulate the rule governance processes

Two fundamental drivers govern successful rule set development:

- The unforgiving honesty of executable rules
- The effectiveness of people working together with goodwill, shared vision, and common interests (the business user and the development team)

Executable or working rules demonstrate to the developers and the subject matter experts what they really do, as opposed to promises of a paper-based design or specification.

ABRD extends OpenUP to avoid redefining standard roles, tasks, work products, guidelines, and processes that are also relevant to rule development. As an EPF plug-in, development teams can tailor it to the specific context of their own project, leveraging the EPF Process Composer.

3.2.1 A Cycle Approach

The ABRD approach groups activities into cycles that enable iterative development. ABRD activities include:

- Rule discovery
- Rule analysis
- Rule design

- Rule authoring
- Rule validation
- Rule deployment

Figure 3.2 represents how these activities can be executed in loops or cycles.

Working in short cycles allows you to ensure that the outcomes of these iterations match the business expectations as the rule set grows.

The first cycle loops over rule discovery and analysis activities to harvest the business policies and rules. The second loop is to prototype the executable rules by looping of the rule discovery, analysis, design, and authoring activities. The third cycle, called building includes multiples potential loops adapted by what needs to be done: a pure focus on rule implementation loops between rule authoring and validation, but when SMEs advises are needed the loop can go back to the discovery and analysis activities. Finally the last cycle is to enhance the ruleset quality, by adding new tests, new rules, and deploy it to the integrated business application.

3.2.2 Cycle 1: Harvesting

The goal of this first cycle is to understand the business entities and document just enough rules so you can begin implementation.

During this first cycle, which may fit into the inception phase (see OpenUP for more information), the project team performs business modeling activities, which aim to describe the business process and decisions applied within the scope of the business application. This phase also helps identify and evaluate potential rule patterns (Fig. 3.3).

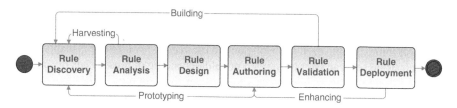

Fig. 3.2 Rule set development life cycle

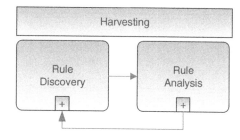

Fig. 3.3 Rule harvesting activities

To get started, the development team splits the day into two parts. The morning is spent in a *discovery workshop*, which is a 2–3 h session of harvesting the rules from rule sources. The team harvests the rules from the business process description, interviews with subject matter experts, use cases descriptions, and any other sources. The rest of the day is spent performing some analysis and documentation of the discovery results. Depending on the number and complexity of the rules, the team iterates on these two steps for 2–5 days.

One of the documents produced during this modeling phase is the *decision point table* (DPT), which describes the points in the process (tasks, activities, transitions) where there are a lot of business decisions involved (test conditions and actions). These decision points represent potential candidates for rule sets.

3.2.3   Cycle 2: Prototyping

The prototyping cycle involves preparing the structure of the project and outlining how rules are organized into a rule set. Once a certain level of discovery is done, the development team can start implementing the structure of the rule set and can begin rule authoring, while discovery and analysis activities continue (Fig. 3.4).

Starting rule authoring using the tools – typically and integrated development environment (IDE) – as soon as possible allows you to uncover possible analysis and design issues early on. Indeed, the rules may look good on paper but, just as with classical software development, the real issues arise during implementation and testing. Issues found during prototyping are communicated back to the business team during the following morning discovery workshop. This feedback loop approach provides an efficient mechanism to build a pragmatic, adequate, and business-relevant executable rule set.

To ensure that the development team understands the rule set, they can work from the *decision point table* produced during the harvesting cycle. As a starting point for initial design, each decision point in the *decision point table* is mapped to a rule set. (Rule sets can later be merged or split depending of reuse needs or service-oriented design.) The architect needs to consider the data model, the flow of rule execution (or *rule flow*), how errors and exceptions will be reported, input and

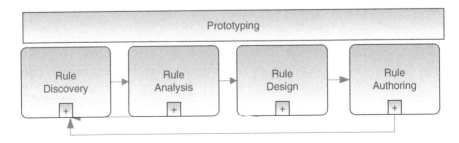

Fig. 3.4 Prototyping activities

output parameters used by the rule engine for each candidate rule set, and how decision results will be reported back to the calling client.

Chapter 5 will provide more details about prototyping activities. In particular, we will look at some BRMS-neutral best practices for project design and rule set design.

3.2.4 Cycle 3: Building

In harmony with the Test-Driven Development (TDD) approach, the goal of the building phase is to implement a set of unit test cases with real (or realistic) data, write the rules being tested, and test the rules within their corresponding rule sets and their targeted execution context.

As learned through our experiences during implementations of decision-support systems, executable rules are more important than those defined "on paper" or in some nonexecutable form. The "unforgiving honesty of executable rules" has a strong value to show project progress and acceptance of those new technologies. This agile statement is at the core of this cycle (Fig. 3.5).

This 3–4-week cycle includes daily authoring activities, which can be seen as a set of little steps involving test case implementation, writing and executing rules, and doing some validation with the team members. The short daily loops include:

- Loop on authoring and validation to develop test cases and rules.
- Loop on analysis, design, authoring, and validation to author executable rules, complete the analysis, do some unit testing and address or resolve issues. This is an improvement loop. The design is linked to enhance the data model and the rule set structure (local variables, rule flow changes, and so on).
- Loop on a bi-daily basis on discovery, analysis, authoring, and validation. The discovery will be used to complete the scope of the rule set and to address the issues identified during implementation.

By the end of this cycle, the data model used by the rules in the context of this rule set should be at least 90% complete, the project structure should be finalized,

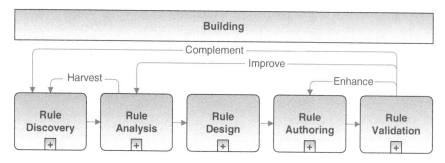

Fig. 3.5 Building activities

and a rule set should be deployed for testing so you can start testing the business application with the decision service. The rule set may only be 40–60% complete, but business users or rule writers can then elaborate and complete it in a later cycle, Cycle 5: Enhancing (Sect. 3.2.6).

If the rule set is too large to be 40% complete by the end of 3 weeks, you can execute this cycle multiple times. However, we recommend keeping this cycle to 3 weeks so you can deliver a concrete build to the Quality Assurance or validation team for review and execution, before embarking on another build cycle.

3.2.5 *Cycle 4: Integrating*

The goal of this cycle is to deploy the rule set under construction to an execution server to test it with an end-to-end testing scenario.

The integration of the decision service and the domain data model is an important task. Data coming from the real data source is sent to the rule engine to fire rules and infer decisions. During the previous phases, the development team develops a set of test scenarios with realistic or real data which triggers rule execution. Those test scenarios are executed during the integration phase to support end to end testing. They can later serve as a nonregression test suite. If the test framework is well designed, some of the data set can be used for unit testing on the rule set and also to perform higher level functional verification tests (Fig. 3.6).

3.2.6 *Cycle 5: Enhancing*

Cycle 5 may be seen as a maturing phase where the goal is to complete and maintain the rule set. This cycle includes authoring, validation, and deployment, but may still require some short face-to-face discovery activities with subject matter experts (SMEs) to address and wrap-up issues and questions (Fig. 3.7).

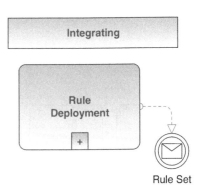

Fig. 3.6 Deployment
activities

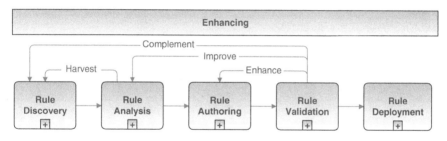

Fig. 3.7 Rule set enhancing activities

The actors responsible for completing the rule set may be different from those involved in the initial cycles. The members of this team are more business-oriented and are the owners of the rule set and business policies. Once the core infrastructure is implemented by the development team, they can complete the rule set at their own pace. Even during a development phase, the business users can start their work of completing the rule set.

Enhancements may also be required for the object model or physical data model, such as adding new facts, attributes, or entities. Such modifications can follow the standard software build management process of the core business application.

Do not expect the business team to discover and implement 100% of the rules during the development of the rule set. The scope of a decision evolves over time. The purpose of cycle 5 is to enhance the quality and completeness of the rule set. However, the rule architect must design the rule set so that when no decision can be taken for a given set of data, a default decision is enforced and that data can be identified for future analysis.

3.3 Eclipse Process Framework

As a framework, EPF provides tools for software process engineering to develop methodologies and share best practices. EPF comes with knowledge content organized in a library, and with a tool (EPF Composer see Fig. 3.8) that enables process engineers to implement, deploy, and maintain processes for organizations or individual projects.

The goal of EPF is to deliver a platform for producing software development practices, how-to, common definitions and vocabulary, and processes with tasks, roles, work products, and guidelines definitions. Libraries are physical containers for knowledge content, process configuration, and other parameters to publish the content as a set of web pages. The library is organized in method plug-ins. According to the EPF documentation, a method plug-in is "a container of content used to describe what is to be produced, the necessary skills required" and "the step-by-step explanations describing how specific development goals are achieved." Plug-ins can reference other plug-ins to extend existing content.

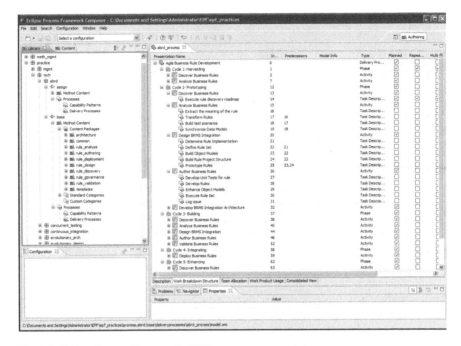

Fig. 3.8 Eclipse Process Framework (EPF) composer screenshot

Processes describe the development life cycle for a given project or team. Processes order the method content elements according to sequences/dependencies that depend on the specific types of projects and determine when specific work products can (no earlier than) or should (no later than) be performed.

As shown in Fig. 3.8, ABRD is subdivided into multiple method plug-ins:

- practice.tech.abrd.base includes all the content to describe tasks, work products, and guidance.
- practice.tech.abrd.assign includes the roles description and the assignment tasks.
- process.abrd.base includes the delivery process and capability pattern definitions for a typical rule set implementation.
- publish.abrd.base includes the view definition to export the content as HTML pages.

One way to view the methodology is to use a *Work Breakdown Structure* (WBS) to list the activities of ABRD. We define roles, tasks, work products, and guidance in a hierarchy of folders named Content Packages. All content can be published to HTML and deployed to web servers for distributed usage. Finally, process engineers and project managers can select, tailor, and rapidly assemble processes for their concrete development projects. Processes can be organized into reusable building blocks, called capability patterns, which represent best development practices for specific disciplines, technologies, or management styles.

Using EPF Composer, practice libraries, and the ABRD plug-in, you will have the tools and the base content to develop your own methodology to develop business applications in the context of a first project or within a rule deployment at the enterprise level.

For details and a download of the latest framework go to http://www.eclipse.org/epf.

3.3.1 OpenUp

OpenUP is a light Unified Process[3] that uses an iterative, incremental, and collaborative approach to development and can be extended to address a broad variety of project types. For example, you might use daily stand-up meetings for team members to discuss project status or issues. Team members include the stakeholders, developers, architects, project manager, and testers. The objective is to reduce risk by identifying issues early in the life cycle and implementing mitigation strategies.

OpenUP tries to balance agility and discipline. It measures individual progress in **micro-increments**, which represent short units of work that produce a steady, measurable bits of project progress. The process encourages team members to be self-disciplined and organized in order to facilitate collaboration as the system is incrementally developed. OpenUP divides a project into iterations that are measured in weeks, not months. Each iteration aims at delivering a measurable increment to stakeholders. For each iteration, the plan (including task asignment) is geared towards producing a deliverable at the end.

The OpenUP **project life cycle** includes four phases: Inception, Elaboration, Construction, and Transition. This life cycle is defined by a project plan. Stakeholders and team members have visibility throughout the project, which enables effective project management and allows you to make "go or no-go" decisions at appropriate times.

Agile Business Rule Development leverages all the concepts described in OpenUp and applies them for the purpose of developing business applications using rule engines, BPEL and BPM technologies.

3.3.2 ABRD Structure

Once the practice.tech.abrd.base plug-in is open, you can navigate to the Content Packages hierarchy. The structure may look like as shown in Fig. 3.9.

---

[3]See http://en.wikipedia.org/wiki/Unified_Process for detail on UP and the book "*The Unified Software Development Process*" (ISBN 0-201-57169-2) by Ivar Jacobson, Grady Booch, and James Rumbaugh.

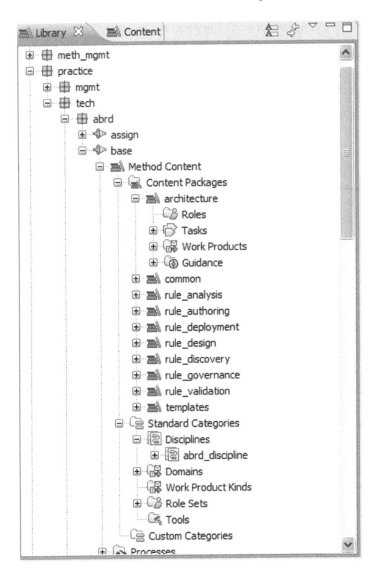

Fig. 3.9 ABRD base plug-in structure

Content is organized in a hierarchy of folders, which are mapped to the major phases of the methodology: architecture, rule discovery, analysis, authoring, testing, deployment, and governance. A common package includes the term definitions, like business rules, rule engine, the introduction, and the cycle approach explanation. When you are managing content, you need to be able to quickly develop reusable templates, so the Templates folder groups these documents all in one place. Any elements of the content can be categorized for quick navigation. Categories are defined in the Standard Categories folder.

3.3.3 ABRD Roles

ABRD role definitions were developed based on consulting engagements and on reflection over "standard" definitions. The full list of predefined roles can be found in the **practice.tech.abrd.assign > role assignments** content package. The role descriptions include:

- Business analyst
- Rule analyst
- Rule architect
- Rule writer
- Rule administrator
- Subject matter expert

3.3.3.1 Business Analyst

The *business analyst* extends the definition of Analyst as described in OpenUP. The business analyst, who is a major actor within the IT and business landscape, acts as a bridge between the two organizations, with a good understanding of the business goal, metrics, business process, and also with IT analysis skill set. In the scope of a business rule application, business analysts help move corporate policy from definition to execution inside a software application. Business analysts must translate policy into a formal specification acceptable to developers and must validate the formal specification with policy managers who may not understand the language of the specification. The typical work products the business analyst is responsible for are the business process definition, the decision point table, and glossary of term and some time the entity model or logical data model.

3.3.3.2 Rule Analyst

Another important role is the *rule analyst*, which is a specialized business analyst with a strong knowledge of how a business rule application runs, how a rule engine works, how to design a logical data model, and how to do the rule discovery and analysis activities. In rule-based project, the rule analyst is directly involved in these activities:

- Create rule templates for rule authors to use
- Analyze rules for completeness and correctness, and apply logical optimization of the rule structure
- Identify the use of rules in processes that implement business policies
- Ensure the quality of the business rules in term of documentation, meta-data, and coverage
- Ensure that consistent terminology is used in the business rules in order to build a common vocabulary and a domain data model

- Analyze business rules to identify conflicts, redundancies
- Ensure consistency of business rules across functions, geographies, and systems
- Conduct impact analysis for revision or replacement of business rules
- Integrate new or revised rules into existing rule sets
- Make recommendations for business rule changes based on business knowledge
- Facilitate resolution of business rules issues
- Act as consultant for the project team
- Act as a liaison between business and IT

The rule analyst is responsible for the discovery roadmap and detailed workshop itinerary. Rule analysts may be considered as *knowledge engineers* as they need to assess the problem to solve, structure the knowledge around the business decision, acquire, and structure the information to prepare for the implementation. Rule analysts should be involved in testing and validating the outcomes of the different decision services the business application is using. Figure 3.10 illustrates the relationship between the tasks performed and work products that the rule analyst produces or manages.

3.3.3.3 Rule Architect

The *Rule architect* is an extension of the concept of software architect. The rule architect is responsible for defining and maintaining the structure of the rule-based application. A rule architect helps the team work together in an agile fashion and understands the iterative approach and how to design the application to deliver value for each iteration. The rule architect jointly owns the solution and has strong communication skills to interface with other parts of the organization. The rule architect defines the structure and organization of the rule-based system. Outside of the standard activities, skills, roles, and responsibilities of a software architect, this role extends to:

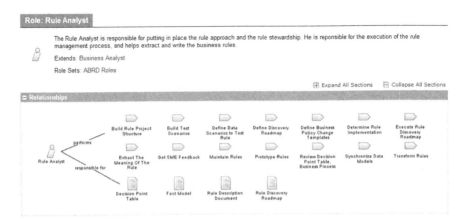

Fig. 3.10 Rule analyst role in Agile Business Rule Development (ABRD)

- Selecting the technology to ensure performance of the rule execution and usability of the BRMS platform
- Designing the infrastructure necessary for editing rules
- Producing one or several rule sets
- Building the structure of rule projects and the dependencies on the executable domain object model

If the deployment of the application is part of a service-oriented architecture, the rule architect participates in defining the various decision services that will use the rule engine. The rule architect focuses on ensuring that the overall deployment and organization of the rules makes sense from an application segmentation perspective, keeping in mind reuse, not only of decision services, but also at a lower granularity, reuse of rules.

During the analysis activity, the rule architect designs the structure of the rule repository, defining the required metadata to manage the rules, and possibly implementing the structure personally to quickly prototype and get feedback from the business team. Metadata attached to the rule is used to establish traceability for rules from business motivation to the technical implementation and used to manage the rule life cycle.

Once a first project is successfully finished, the architect has to design and deploy the BRMS capability at the enterprise level. He leads the development of the processes around repository management, rule life cycle, rule set life cycle, and rule governance.

3.3.3.4   Rule Writer

ABRD specifies a dedicated role for writing rules. We observed various approaches for this, from remote outsourcing at low cost labor to highly skilled business analysts working closely with the business users. The range of approaches may be led by the business goals and the type of business application. For example in the subprime lending market where competition is intense, the loan processing application needs to be changed quickly to adapt to new product definitions, new regulation, or new risk management. In that case, local teams need to act quickly on the rules, writes new rules or update existing ones, apply regression testing, and run simulation tests before deploying the rules. Rule writers are involved during the first phases of the business rule development, so in the agile approach, rule writers are part of the team, participating in the discovery and analysis tasks.

Off-shoring rule development is an antinomy for the agile business rule approach where business and IT work closely together and should be avoided for the sake of efficiency and long-term maintenance purposes. The business has ownership of the rules, not a remote team. To be successful, communication between the business and the rule writer has to be strong, co-located at best, and each team has to trust the other to deliver what was agreed on. *Business rules are a company asset delivering competitive advantages, which makes giving the implementation to an outside group more risky.*

Other roles involved in the application development are more standard, and we do not need to describe them in the context of this book.

3.3.3.5 Subject Matter Expert

The Subject Matter Expert (SME) is responsible for defining the business processes, the business policies, and the application requirements. He leads the business rules acquisition activities as a domain expert and uses the Rules Management Application as reviewer.

3.3.3.6 Rule Administrator

The Rule Administrator manages the rule authoring and deployment. He executes the business rule management process and ensures the integrity of the rule set by using the rule life cycle and rule set life cycle.

3.3.4 ABRD Work Products

Work products are outcomes of tasks in EPF. We grouped the work products per main area of concern like architecture, discovery, analysis, validation, and rule governance. Each major work product is detailed in the corresponding chapter below. There are some work products that serve as input to the application of ABRD. As defined in OpenUP and other Unified Processes, the project starts by an inception phase, where some business modeling activities are started. Part of these activities ABRD leverages at least the following work products:

- The business process description in the format of text or process map. Process Maps are well described using the graphical notation as specified by the Business Process Modeling Notation. For more information, visit http://www.bpmn.org. From a process modeling point of view the level 3 of process decomposition is a good source to identify decision points.
- Another type will be the use cases description of the business application. Here, we need to focus on the end user use cases which are processing business data and the ones involving business decisions. Technical or IT related use cases may not be in scope of rule discovery and analysis.

From the use case description and the business process definition, it is possible to extract a list of the candidate decision points. A decision point is an anchor into one of the activity or step of the business process or use case where a set of knowledge-driven decisions are done on the data or documents under process. Those decision points are rule rich and will be most likely implemented using BRMS technology. So building a Decision Point Table (DPT) at the earliest phases of the project will help to drive the business rule development.

3.4   Usage Scenario for ABRD

ABRD as an EPF plug-in can be extended for your own needs such as adding new content, tuning the existing processes, developing best practices for a given BRMS tool or organization, adding BPM activities and roles, etc. As an open source contribution, ABRD is evolving at each release of the EPF practice library. We recommend developing your own plug-in as an extension of ABRD. Using the EPF Composer, you should create your own plug-in referencing **practice.tech.abrd** using the New Method Plug-in wizard as shown in Fig. 3.11.

From there you can add any element as an extension of an existing element defined in the hierarchy of the selected plug-ins. Figure 3.12 shows the various EPF elements and concepts involved in a plug-in and their containment organization. It is important to note that the entities whose name starts with a lowercase letter are element instances, created by the plug-in author, while entities whose name starts

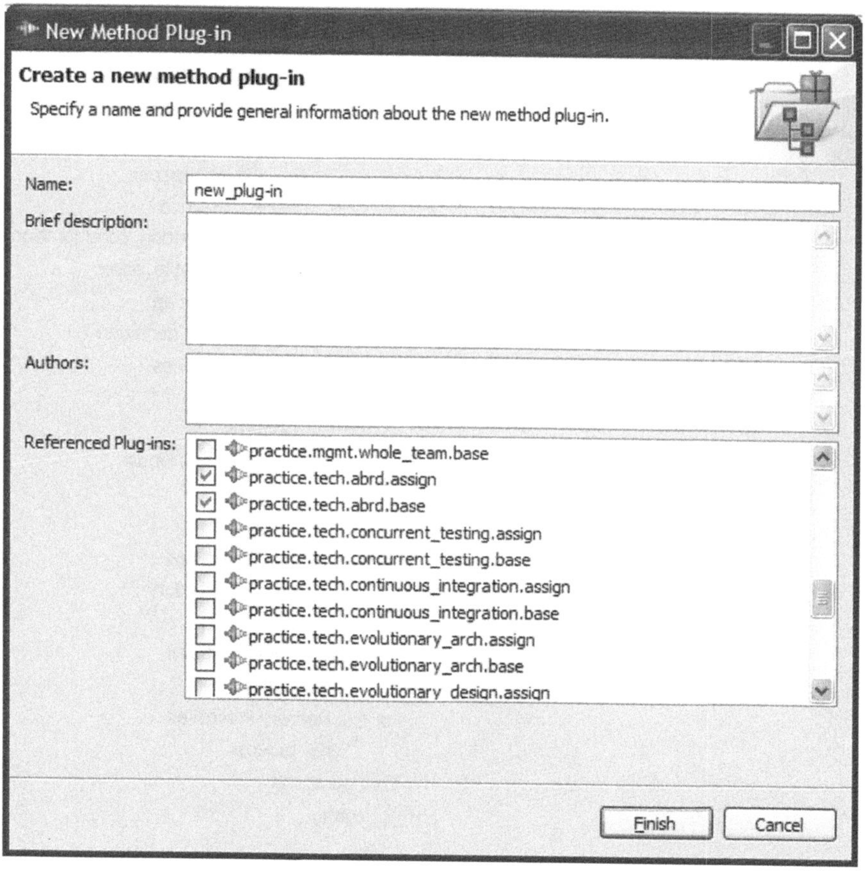

Fig. 3.11 Create your own content plug-in

Fig. 3.12 Eclipse Process
Framework (EPF) library
elements

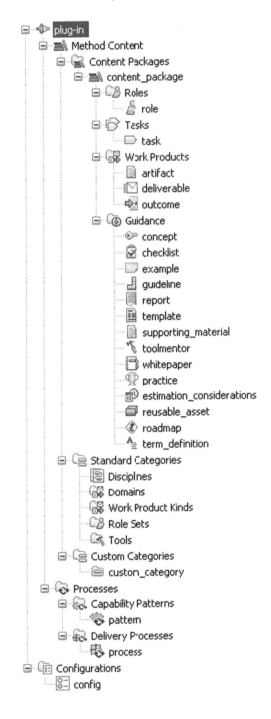

with a capital letter are structuring concepts provided by EPF. We recommend using a naming convention for the elements created. The EPF practice is to use lower case and to separate words using an underscore ("_").

Let us take an example of adding a task for an architect to design and prototype a business process using a BPEL engine. The EPF Method content developer needs to follow at least the following steps:

1. Create the *Method Content Package* with role, work product, guidance, and then task: For example, add a Architecture Package, with a bpm_architect role who will develop a bpel_process work product during the activity of design_ prototype_bpel_process as shown in Fig. 3.13.
   When creating those elements, it is interesting to note that the task may leverage work products or roles defined in other plug-ins. The business_process_ map and use_case model are coming from the *abrd* and *core* plug-ins.
2. Once we have created all the *work products*, we may need to update the role for the responsibility link to the work product. Going to the bpel_architect we can add bpel_process as a work product he is responsible for.
3. It is possible to add *guidance* like a "how to guide" describing how to use a BPEL designer. This guidance can be linked to a task or a work product.
4. Optionally create within each task some *step* which the main performer will have to complete for this task.

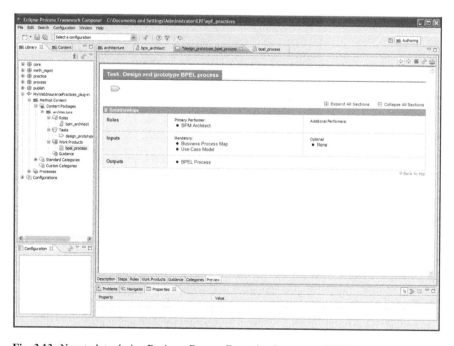

Fig. 3.13 New task to design Business Process Execution Language (BPEL) process

5. Create *categories* to classify the content elements: modify roles, work products, guidance, and tasks accordingly. Method Content elements are organized into logical categories. The categories can appear in your final, published website as views. The following table shows sample categories adapted from the typical EPF categories.

Standard categories	Description	Example
Disciplines	Disciplines are a collection of tasks that are related to a major area of concern within the overall IT environment	Perform certain requirements tasks in close coordination with analysis and design tasks
Domains	A domain is a refineable, logical, hierarchy of related Work products grouped together based on timing, resources, or relationships	Architecture domain to capture WP related to architecture
	A work product belongs to only one domain	Requirements, project management, risk management, etc.
		Customer lending is a candidate domain
Work product kinds	Work product kind is another category for grouping work products. A work product can have many work product kinds	Specification, plan, model, assessment
Role sets	A role set is used to group roles with certain commonalities	The analyst role set could be used to group together roles such as business process analyst, system analyst, and requirements developer
		BRMS role set could be used to group rule analyst, rule admin
		. . .
Tools	Tools is a container for tool mentors which provides guidance on how to use a specific tool	Clearcase mentors user guides

For example, we can define a new category of work products to include any elements related to BPEL and then attach the bpel_process to this category (Fig. 3.14).

Another example of a useful category is to group roles by specialty or domain area, or from an organization point of view (e.g., customer vs supplier, various departments). Role sets should be created as soon as there are several specific roles in a plug-in, to simplify views and allow them to be consistent.

Using the same mechanism, we can create one architecture *discipline* to group all the tasks related to the application architecture.

6. Define *configuration* for the publishing step. The ultimate output of the EPF Composer is a published website with method guidance and processes that can be used by a project team. A Method Configuration is a selection of Content Packages across different Method Plug-ins containing the method and process

```
📄 *bpel_process ⊠                                                                    ▭
```
Work Product (Artifact): bpel_process

▼ Categories
Manage the categories :o which this work product belongs.

Domain:

	Select...
	Clear

Work product kinds:

🔳 bpel_wp_kind, ycur_plugin/Categories/WP Types	Add...
	Remove

Fig. 3.14 Grouping work products together

content that will be included in the published website. So under the Configurations node in the Library View, we can create a "MyPlugin" configuration,
and then we need to specify the plug-ins we may reuse.

7. Create *Capability Pattern*. A Capability pattern is a special process that
describes a reusable cluster of activities in a general process area that provides
a consistent development approach to common problems. Capability patterns
can be used as building blocks to assemble delivery processes or larger
capability patterns. Under the Processes-Capability Patterns node in myPlugin,
we can add the "architecturePattern." Once created, we can open the Work
Breakdown Structure (WBS) to add some tasks by drag and drop from the
configuration panel. The WBS may look like:

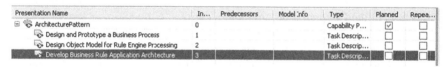

Presentation Name	In...	Predecessors	Model Info	Type	Planned	Repea...
⊟ 🐾 ArchitecturePattern	0			Capability P...	☑	☐
🔖 Design and Prototype a Business Process	1			Task Descrip...	☐	☐
🔖 Design Object Model for Rule Engine Processing	2			Task Descrip...	☐	☐
🐾 Develop Business Rule Application Archtecture	3			Task Descrip...	☐	☐

8. Create *Delivery Process*. A Delivery Process describes a complete and
integrated approach for performing a specific type of project. We add a
Delivery Process named "myDeliveryProcesses" under the Processes/Delivery
Processes node and drag and drop our "ArchitecturePattern" from the configuration view. The process WBS will look like:

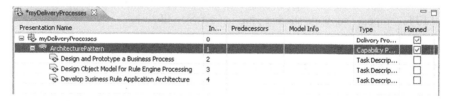

Presentation Name	In...	Predecessors	Model Info	Type	Planned
⊟ 🐾 myDeliveryProcesses	0			Delivery Pro...	☑
⊟ 🐾 ArchitecturePattern	1			Capability P...	☑
🔖 Design and Prototype a Business Process	2			Task Descrip...	☐
🔖 Design Object Model for Rule Engine Processing	3			Task Descrip...	☐
🔖 Develop Business Rule Application Architecture	4			Task Descrip...	☐

Doing this kind of method, we can add as many capabilities as needed to tune
our processes for our project or group or company.

Fig. 3.15 Published content of "MyPlugin"

9. Create *View*. Custom categories can be used to compose publishable views, providing a means to organize method content prior to publishing. Under the Custom Categories node of "myPlugin," we can create a custom category name "my_plugin_views," then within the Assign table can add any elements content like an introduction, the architecture discipline, and our process.

To complete our configuration we need to add the newly created view in the Views of the Configuration: myPlugin_cfg.

10. The last step is to publish our content in static or web application. The content of several plug-ins can be mixed into one published view. Each view corresponds to a tab in the tree view of the portal. Using the top menu Configuration/Publish, we can export the Configuration named "myPlugin_cfg" and get a web page like as shown in Fig. 3.15.

The left side offers a navigation tree to access content pages displayed on the right side. HTML-based content links allow for easy navigation into the content.

Using these techniques, it is also possible to integrate ABRD and your own plug-in with other agile methods such as SCRUM, XP, and RUP. The import/export facility of EPF composer supports sharing plug-ins between libraries.

3.5 Summary and Conclusions

Agility is a must for business rule application development. Regardless of the BRMS product you use, ABRD provides a starting point for developing your own best practices and method content. ABRD supports a simple cycle approach to

implementing decision points within a business process and has already demon-
strated its effectiveness through its successful use during consulting engagements
and JRules deployments all over the world.

ABRD is the first open-source methodology and is supported by the Eclipse
Process Framework, which offers the tools, content, and methodology to help your
organization tailor the contents of ABRD to your needs and to create reusable
practices for efficient development.

Chapter 4 will explore the harvesting cycle in detail. In particular, we will
discuss rule analysis in detail. Chapter 5 will discuss the prototyping cycle, where
we highlight the major design issues facing application architects, and the rule
architect. The remaining cycles, that is, *Building*, *Integration*, and *Enhancing*, start
with the same activities as *Prototyping*, continuing on with rule validation, and rule
deployment. The duration and scope of the iterations change, and the focus shifts
away from discovery and analysis to authoring, validation, and deployment. We
explore the rule deployment design space in Chap. 12 and discuss JRules' deployment options in Chap. 13. We will also explore rule testing issues in Chap. 14 and
discuss JRules's features for testing in Chap. 15.

3.6 Further Reading

Agile Business Rule Development draws on a number of best practices in software
development, general software development methodologies (e.g., RUP and
OpenUP), rule-specific methodologies, and a number of technologies.

The reader can find more information about:

- Eclipse Process Framework at http://www.eclipse.org/epf.
- A publish version of Open Unified Process can be accessed at epf.eclipse.org/
  wikis/openup/ and in the practice library http://www.eclipse.org/epf/downloads/
  praclib/praclib_downloads.php, with ABRD and SCRUM.
- ABRD content is published at http://epf.eclipse.org/wikis/epfpractices/ going
  under practices > Additional practices > Agile Business Rule Development.
- The book *"The Unified Software Development Process"* (ISBN 0-201-57169-2)
  by Ivar Jacobson, Grady Booch, and James Rumbaugh – Publisher: Addison-
  Wesley Professional presents the unified process methodology using UML
  artifacts to develop efficient software application.
- The agile eXtreme Programming methodology is introduced at http://www.
  extremeprogramming.org/ with detailed explanation of the XP rules.
- One of the most used agile and iterative methodology, SCRUM, has its own
  portal at http://www.scrumalliance.org/.
- An introduction to the Master Data Management can be found on Wikipedia at
  http://en.wikipedia.org/wiki/Master_data_management.
- The agile manifesto is presented at http://www.agilemanifesto.org.
- An introduction to the test-driven development may be read at http://en.wikipedia.
  org/wiki/Test-driven_development.

Chapter 4
Rule Harvesting

Target audience

- *(Must) business analyst; (optional) project manager, application architect, rule author*

In this chapter you will learn

- *What are the different types of rules, and why it is important to understand them*
- *How to set in place the rule harvesting process according to the source of rules and the team structure*
- *How to extract a data model for the rules from the rule description*
- *How to prepare the rules for implementation*
- *How to put into practice these techniques with a claim processing application*

Key points

- *Start by a decision point that is simple but still brings business value to the stakeholders.*
- *Describe rules using the business domain vocabulary, and future map it to a logical data model.*

4.1 Introduction

Rule harvesting includes the two main activities of rule discovery and analysis, with the goal to understand the business entities (conceptual data model [CDM]) within the scope of the application and to identify and extract the rules. A key activity in the rule harvesting phase is to formalize the decisions made during the execution of the business process by defining the different decision point candidates for business rule implementation.

Agile Business Rule Development (ABRD) puts the emphasis on developing the system through short iterations. Each iteration produces a working set of rules.

J. Boyer and H. Mili, *Agile Business Rule Development*,
DOI 10.1007/978-3-642-19041-4_4, © Springer-Verlag Berlin Heidelberg 2011

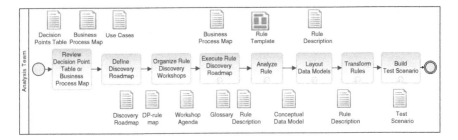

Fig. 4.1 Rule harvesting activities

Feedback from the harvesting and prototyping phases forces the subject matter experts (SMEs) to better understand their own business processes and help them to adapt those processes for more efficiency. Rule harvesting is a short project activity executed for each decision point in scope for implementation. The process flow may look like in Fig. 4.1.

Section 4.2 will discuss rule discovery. First, we start by identifying the different kinds of rules, then we describe the discovery activities. There are different ways of conducting rule discovery, depending mostly on rule sources, i.e., where we are going to discover the rules from, and the organization's modeling and requirements tradition (e.g., using use case, or process maps, or business event analysis, etc.). Thus, as Barbara von Halle suggests, part of rule discovery activities is . . . figuring out how to discover rules, i.e., *defining the rule discovery roadmap*. Section 4.2 will discuss common activities (e.g., review decision point table, define discovery roadmap, gather documents, document rules), as well as roadmap specific activities (e.g., discover rules from SMEs, discover rules from documents, discover rules from code). Section 4.3 shows rule discovery for our case study.

Rule analysis is discussed in Sect. 4.4; many of the techniques presented are based on vonHalle's STEP methodology. Analysis activities include (1) reviewing rule descriptions and fact models (Sect. 4.1), (2) transforming rules to obtain unambiguous, atomic, nonredundant, and consistent rules (Sect. 4.2), (3) building test scenarios (Sect. 4.3), and (4) verifying the rules against the data model (Sect. 4.4). Section 4.5 shows rule analysis for our case study. We conclude in Sect. 4.6.

4.2 Rule Discovery

Rule discovery, also called Business Rules Modeling in the industry, aims to develop simple modeling artifacts like rule descriptions, business entity diagrams, and business process maps. As described in Chap. 3, the development team executes this activity on a regular basis during the development of the business application. Rule discovery is an iterative process that will identify a subset of rules and document them as opposed to spending months figuring out all the rules up front and producing a huge document.

Business rule discovery techniques are similar to those used for traditional requirements elicitation, with one main difference: focus on those special needs that support decisions on how the business is executed in the company. From the inception phase the project team gets a set of work products that are used during rule discovery. These artifacts include:

1. A high-level description of the business process
2. A high-level description of the current and future architectures
3. A list of data sources and data models
4. The decision points table

The decision points table, in particular, helps define where to find the rules (rule sources) and which method to use for rule harvesting. The rule discovery process changes according to the sources used. For example, working from a legal document implies a different discovery process from the discovery based on interviewing subject matter experts.

4.2.1 Classification of Business Rules

Before deciding how to write rules and where to implement them, you first need to understand which types of rules your team will be harvesting. In early 2008, the Object Management Group (OMG) finalized a specification for documenting the semantics of business vocabularies and business rules, entitled *Semantics of Business Vocabulary and Business Rules (SBVR)*.

The specification describes SBVR as part of the OMG's Model Driven Architecture (MDA). Its purpose is to capture specifications in natural language and to represent them formally to facilitate automation. SBVR includes two specialized vocabularies:

- One to define business terms and meanings from the perspective of the business teams. It is named in the SBVR specification as *Business Vocabulary*.
- One used to describe business rules in an unambiguous way leveraging the business vocabulary.

The *meaning* is what someone understands or intends to express. The meanings are derived into concepts, questions and propositions. A phrase such as "We deny the invoice if the medical treatment was done after one year of the accident" has a clear meaning for a claim processor (CP) within a car insurance company. Analysts need to logically transform this meaning into concepts that have a unique interpretation so that we can represent the business knowledge within a comprehensive vocabulary. Concepts include a unique combination of characteristics or properties.

Within the Business Motivation Model (BMM),[1] the OMG has also defined the relation between business policies, directives, business processes, and business rules. This work is very important to clearly classify each of those concepts. The OMG definition of business policy is: "A non-actionable directive whose purpose is to govern or guide the enterprise. Business policies govern business processes." A Business rule is – "A directive, intended to govern, guide, or influence business behavior, in support of business policy that has been formulated in response to an opportunity, threat, strength, or weakness. It is a single directive that does not require additional interpretation to undertake strategies or tactics. Often, a business rule is derived from business policy. Business rules guide a business process." For the purpose of rule harvesting, keep in mind that business rules are actionable, unambiguous, and derived from the business policy. Considering rules as semantically meaningful, rather than business policies, is key to making them executable.

The OMG BMM reuses some classifications from the SBVR: business rules are separated into two possible classes:

- Structural (definitional) business rules which are describing the structure of the business entities used by the line of business organization. Such rules describe constraints on the model, like possible value, or mandatory inclusion or associations.
- Operational (behavioral) business rules are developed to enforce business policies, seen as obligations to execute efficiently the business. When considering operational business rules it is important to look at the level of enforcement and where the rule enforcement occurs.

In SBVR, rules are always constructed by documenting conditions to business entities defined in the *business vocabulary*. A fact is a relationship between two or more concepts.

Another approach to define facts is to use the Ontology Web Language (OWL) and Resource Description Framework (RDF). Developed to specify semantic web,[2] OWL and RDF can be used to model the enterprise ontology. The ontology is the source for data models used by the rules as an alternate to traditional Object-Oriented Analysis (OOA) and SBVR. OWL and RDF implement an object-relational model allowing creation of a directed graph, a network of objects and relationships describing data.

Using a mix of the SBVR classification for business rules, OWL–RDF to describe the domain and an older rule classification model which we have used for years in consulting engagements, the different types of business rules can be presented as shown in Fig. 4.2.

---

[1]*Business Motivation Model V 1.1,* Object Management Group at http://www.omg.org/spec/BMM/1.1/.

[2]From Wikipedia, semantic web is defined as an extension to the WWW in which the meaning of information and services on the web is defined, making it possible for the web to "understand" and satisfy the requests of people and machines to use the web content.

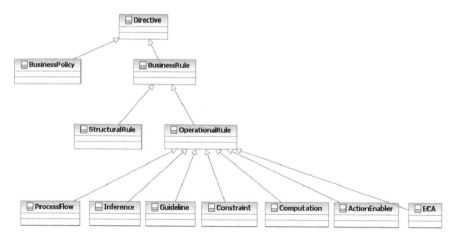

Fig. 4.2 Business rule schema

This schema represents the different types of rules that are relevant to the business, including structural and operational rules. Structural rules define the terms used by the business in expressing their business rules and the relationships (facts) among those terms. These include the vocabulary used in rule authoring. As an example a statement like: *An insurance policy includes a set of coverage. The policy is effective at a given date and needs to be renewed every six months.* Transforming this statement implies defining a structure in the insurance domain, where an insurance policy entity has an effective date, expiration date, and a list of coverages.

Operational rules are the rules that implement business decision logic. When a business decision is made (e.g., whether to sell a given insurance policy, whether to accept or reject a claim), the business rules are the individual statements of business logic that are evaluated by the rule engine to determine the decision result.

The following table is adapted from the work by Barbara Von Halle and is a simplified view of the business rules group classification. It details those categories:

Rule classification	Explanation
Mandatory constraints	Rules that reject the attempted business transaction. Grammar to use during rule documentation not implementation. <term> MUST HAVE <at least, at most, exactly n of> <term>; <term> MUST BE IN LIST <a,b,c>; SBVR expression: **it is [not] necessary that <fact>**
Guidelines	Rules that does not reject the transaction; they merely warn about an undesirable circumstance. Usually translates to warning messages. <term> SHOULD HAVE <at least, at most, exactly n of> <term>; <term> SHOULD BE IN LIST <a,b,c> SBVR expression: **it is [not] possible that < fact >** **It is possible but not necessary < fact >**

(continued)

Rule classification	Explanation
Action-enablers	Rules that tests conditions and upon finding them true, initiate another business event, message, business process, or other activity
	IF <condition> THEN action
Computations	Rules that create new information from existing information based on mathematical computation
	<term> IS COMPUTED AS <formula>
Inferences	Rules that create new information from existing information. The result is a piece of knowledge used as a new fact for the rule engine to consider
	IF <term> <operator> <term> THEN <term> <operator> <term>
Event Condition Action (ECA)	Rules where the condition is evaluated once the occurrence of an event is found. Most ECA rules use temporal operators to search events related to their timestamp of creation or occurrence
	On <event> when <condition> then <action>

To implement guidelines and constraints, you need to consider what happens when they are violated. Most of the time, the action raises an exception or a high priority issue to be managed later in the business process, which may reject the business event. The rule needs to report clearly on the selected decision so that a human can understand and act on the business transaction.

A guideline written as: *The date of loss should be before the expiration date of the policy* may translate to the following rule: *if the date of loss is after the expiration date of the policy, then create a warning ticket for the claim processor to handle.* This implementation allows the insurer to make allowances for an insured person who has a history of regularly renewing the policy but for some reason forgot to renew on time.

A constraint written as: *The borrower must put a minimum cash down of 5%* translates to this rule: *if the minimum cash is below 5% then reject the loan application with the reason "The borrower must put minimum cash down of 5%."*

Action enabler rules modify, create, or delete terms or association between terms, or execute methods, which can be web service. For example, a rule like: *if a driver has made one or more at-fault claims in the current year, decrease the discount rate by 3%* changes an attribute ("discount rate") of an object.

Computation rules implement mathematical equations and assign values to variables according to a set of given criteria. For example, a risk factor variable can be computed according to the age of the driver. It is important to note that management of computation rules may require managing the entire ruleset together if there are rules that are required to be managed prior to those calculations and at the terms of the calculation.

Process flow routing rules direct the movement through a process flow or workflow. Process flow rules are distinct from business logic rules. It may be helpful to distinguish process flow rules from the business logic rules that determine the values of the parameters on which the process flow is directed as such rules are more often complex and numerous than routing rules. Routing rules may be written as: *if there is at least one exception in previous activity of the process goes to this task if not continue on the main path.* The business logic to define if there is an exception is made within a rule engine with a lot of rules to evaluate and execute.

Inference rules use syntax similar to action enabler rules, but they create new objects or facts which may bring the engine to re-evaluate some other rule's eligibility. During discovery, it is important to understand the execution context as seen by the business user and be able to answer questions like: "If executing this rule modifies the state of the claim, will the eligibility rules that have already executed need to be reevaluated?" For example, an insurance policy underwriting rule that says *if the age of the driving license is below 3, add a risk factor of 50 and reevaluate the total risk score* modifies the risk scoring variables, which requires that other rules be reevaluated.

It is possible to continue the decomposition of those rules. For example, transformation rules in ETL (Extract Transform Load) are often considered separate from other business rules; although in pattern, they are essentially inference rules and computation rules. Data transformation rules, while important to the business, are a side effect of system implementation rather than a reflection of core business logic. For implementation, the decision to use a rule engine for data transformation rules depends on whether the rules are static, dynamic, or business driven. Some implementations use a rule engine to easily implement transformation rules between two data models instead of using a complex scripting language when the transformations have to be maintained by business users.

Recently, a new subcategory of ECA rule appeared within the IT horizon: the Complex Event Processing (CEP) statements (or rules) which support a category of business rules related to real-time event filtering, event aggregation and correlation, and applying pattern matching conditions on attributes of events. CEP applies business rules to a stream of data. A business rule to detect fraud on banking cards may be written as: *Raise a warning alarm if more than one transaction for an amount over $100 is received from the same merchant on the same card number within the last 15-minutes.* According to the preceding rule classifications, this rule would be considered a mix of ECA and inference rules. However, one important dimension of this type of rule is the time window constraint on which the rules apply and the type of language used to write the rule. Today most of those languages are based on SQL and include operators to look at time window. The action part of the rule creates new events (called the complex events), which are managed by a downstream application. The convergence of a CEP engine with a BRMS platform starts to happen, as rule engines excel in pattern matching, and can apply more complex decisions on already aggregated and filtered events. In fact, alarm filtering and correlation applications in telecommunications network management are examples of complex event processing implemented with a BRMS (see Sect. 2.2.1).

In addition to industry standards, here are other rule patterns commonly found in business applications:

Rule classification	Type of application
Compliance rules	Rules that reject the attempted business transaction
	Yes/no result but completed with reason code and explanation
	Underwriting
	Fraud detection
	Data and form validation
	Example: *Whoever receives a commission paid by an insurance company for the sale of an insurance policy needs an insurance license*
Rating	Strongly interrelated rules that compute metrics for a complex object model
	Scoring and rating
	Contracts and allocation
	Pure calculations on an object providing a final value (or rating)
	Example: *if the driver is between 16 and 22 years old the risk is set to 400 If the driver is between 23 and 27 the risk is set to 300 . . ..*
Correlation	Strongly interrelated rules that correlate information from a set of objects to Compute some complex metrics
	Billing and cost estimation
	Complement by inserting information
	Example: *if the medical bill references a patient, and the patient is not declared in the related claim then there is an issue on the claim description or the invoice is not related to a patient covered*
Stateful	Strongly interrelated rules that correlate events in a stateful way. Stateful in this context means the internal states of the engine are maintained between rule execution invocations
	Alarm filtering and correlation
	Web page navigation
	GUI customization
	Example: *if there is an alarm L1 on network element A and an alarm L2 on network element B and a direct link exists between A and B then the alarm L1 is linked to L2, remove alarm L2*

Classifying rules facilitates the design cycle, which focuses on deciding the best implementation for a given rule. Inference and action enabler rules are good candidates for a rule engine. Pure computation will most likely be implemented in code unless computation rules are subject to frequent changes in the criteria of applicability or are linked to others business rules. The classification also helps to evaluate the complexity of the rules and the workload to implement it.

4.2.2 Discovery Activities

The discovery phase contains some preparation tasks, such as reviewing the decision point table, the use case model or the business process, defining the discovery roadmap, and organizing the elicitation workshops. Some activities are recurring such as executing the discovery itself. These are basic steps, which you can extend to your own project needs (see Fig. 4.1). The remaining subsections detail some of those activities. The work products listed in this process are part of ABRD EPF plug-in.

The discovery activities are conducted during the elaboration phase of the project, but the same process is conducted even after the system has gone into production when there is a new business event, or when there is a need to modify some decision or some business policy. Companies have been operating with business rules for many years, but the form of these rules is not externalized and managed as standalone artefact. Capturing business rules relies on a combination of eliciting business requirements, reverse engineering existing applications, and expert's knowledge. Business rules are not just requirements: they specify how a business process is executed, how decisions are made, and how domain knowledge is structured. When using a business rule approach for business requirements elicitation, we are working at the business process and policies and procedures level to understand the constraints and the behaviours of the process.

The most unique aspect of the rules discovery phase is the perception of a business event as a set of decision-rich activities. We unfold the processing of a business event as a set of decisions and policies. We then dissect the decisions and policies into executable and precise business rules that guide the business event in a predictable and desirable manner. We will detail these concepts in Sect. 4.4.

There are two dimensions to consider when preparing the rule discovery activities or roadmap.[3]

- The source of rule, which can be:
  - The *documentation* which includes all sorts of documents (business plans, deliverables of earlier projects, legislation, regulations, standards, and business requirements for the current project)
  - The tacit *know-how*: the unwritten "way we do things", embodied as a collective way of doing things (organizational intelligence), or as individual expertise
  - The *legacy system*, which includes an operational system that implements some of the business logic (code mining)
  - The *Business records* as the way particular customer requirements have been satisfied, pricing formulas used in previous contracts
- The type of analysis techniques used by the project team:
  - Business event analysis
  - Use case elaboration
  - Business process modeling
  - Business mission and strategy analysis
  - Data analysis

Obviously the *know-how* discovery is the most difficult elicitation task to execute and the one that usually takes the longest time. We will provide details later in this section on how to conduct such an elicitation workshop.

---

[3]The term "rule discovery" roadmap is also used in the industry to present the journey the analysts go through.

The following table is giving the different possible starting points for the discovery activities based on the analysis method used:

Starting point	Analysis description
Business events	Start with the business events listed in the inception artifacts. Some example can be: a claim or invoice is received, the loan application is submitted, the call data record is posted ... Each business event is processed by a set of activities that can be described in document or business process. This approach is rarely used
Use case	Analyze use case description to find decision points and then rules. Preferred approach, for teams familiar with use cases, or user stories
Business process – workflow	Evaluate individual process steps and tasks to define the decision behind activity and then the rules. Used when the organization uses process decomposition for the requirements gathering and analysis phase. We group workflow in this category
Data analysis	Used in case of data change-oriented rules project. The project team looks at the life cycle of the major business objects and extracts the processes and decisions used to change the state of the data. It can start with the logical data model and how the business entities are created, updated, deleted and what their states are. One example of such an approach is to look at the states of an insurance policy, and how, who, when changes are made
Business mission and strategy	Based on a top-down rules and business policies approach. Rules sources are high-level manager, decision makers, legal documentation ...

It is important to set the expectation among the stakeholders that not all the rules will be discovered during this phase. The goal is to complete the rule discovery up to 40–60% so we can have some tangible decisions on standard business events to process. The rule writers and the development team will increase the amount of rules in scope during future iterations of the implementation.

4.2.2.1 Review Decision Point Table or Business Process Map

When the business modeling activity of the Inception phase is completed, the project team should have a decision point table document as a source for the rule discovery phase. If not, it is still possible to build it from the description of the business process. There are different ways to extract the decision points table.

Use Case Approach

If the project team uses use cases approach to document requirements, the rule discovery team can study the use case descriptions to identify those tasks or activities where the system makes a nontrivial decision. In her book "Business Rule Applied", Barbara Von Halle suggests looking for verbal cues in task/activity descriptions that might suggest a nontrivial decision making. For example, verbs such as check, qualify, compute, calculate, estimate, evaluate, determine, assess, compare, verify, validate, confirm, decide, diagnose, or process may hint at some "intelligent" processing. Behind these verbs lurk lots of business knowledge and business rules.

Here is an example of a use case description for a basic loan underwriting process:

Use case name	Check mortgage eligibility	Version	0.9
Problem domain	Handling mortgage applications	**Author**	
Purpose	A **Borrower** has submitted a mortgage application, along with supporting documentation. A **loan officer/clerk** has verified the supporting documentation, and input the application into the system. The data of the application has been validated. We check three sets of criteria, in this order: (mortgage) loan eligibility, borrower eligibility, and property eligibility. When one of them fails, we exit the use case.		
Actors	**Mortgage Loan Officer** (or clerk), on behalf of **Borrower**		
Trigger events	The data of a mortgage application has passed validation, and is now submitted through eligibility		

System response	Decision
Start the eligibility verification	
Verify the eligibility of the loan	• Check the type of loan
	• Check the transaction type
	• Check the loan amount
	• Check the down payment
	• Check the term of the loan
	• Check the loan to value ratio
The loan is eligible.	• Check the age of the borrower
Verify the eligibility of the borrower	• Check the immigration/citizenship status of the borrower
	• Check the financial situation of the borrower
	• Check the number of mortgages

This use case template includes a decision column used to drive the discussion during the rule discovery.

Business Process Modeling Approach

Business process modeling involves the same approach and should include at least the following activities:

- Define the actors of the process – by roles. Clearly list the different human actors of the process and classify them by role.
- Design the as-is process with tasks and dependencies. Do not attempt to analyze the full process in one shot, instead, use an incremental approach. Use BPMS editor to design the process and simulate it. BPMS includes some simulation tool that helps to verify the process being analyzed.
- Identify branch points in the process which lead to different subpaths from the current point. The decisions to route to one of the sub branches can be considered as business rules: in Fig. 4.2, those routing rules are simply expressed in the process model as a set of conditions leading to different branches. The simplest response will be providing a binary response, but it is possible to define responses

as a set of predefined values of an enumeration such as {good, average, bad}, {gold, silver, and platinum} .... From our experience we do not recommend having a lot of branches coming out of a conditional node in a process map. A typical process will have from 2 to 6–8 branches.

With a business process modeling approach, the analysis team looks at task descriptions to search for mental thinking verbs, the same. Then the analyst works with the subject matter experts to understand how the decisions on those activities are made. If there are decisions based on business practices and decisions, we need to log in a table format the task reference, what are the sources for rule, who is the owner, etc. Each row of the table forms a decision point. Once decision points are identified, a review of each decision point is needed. This review should take less than half a day to conduct. This session allows stakeholders to review the decision points and to set the priority for rule harvesting at each decision point level. To complete this task, you may need to get answers to at least the following questions:

- What is the current process to define, document, implement, test, and update the business rules?
- Who owns the rules and the business policy definitions within the business organization?
- Are there any classifications such as country/geography or product category with some specific rules we need to take care of? Is the same team defining them? We were working on projects where at the beginning of the project we were dealing with the core business team, but a lot of rules were overridden by the branch offices in the different countries, so the elicitation process has to be adapted to get such information.
- What is the number of rules for each decision point?
- What are examples of actual rules?
- Is there a rule sharing policy?

A good practice is to start with a simple, well-understood decision point, to help train the team on the elicitation practices, but keep in mind that the management will want to see the business value of what the team is working on. So a decision point which brings a lot of business value should be at the top of the list. With the iterative approach of ABRD, we can develop an executable ruleset in one time boxed iteration of 20–25 days. This is important to show the value of the approach with tangible results.

The purpose of this activity is to preset the roadmap definition phase and to verify that we have the important information on the business process and the related decision points.

4.2.2.2 Define Discovery Roadmap

The definition of the discovery roadmap is an important step to understand how the analyst team will extract the rules from the different kind of sources. The selection of the type of roadmap is linked to the rule source. Tony Morgan in his book

"Business Rules and Information Systems: Aligning IT with Business Goals" proposes the following discovery processes:

- The *static analysis* process uses reading and highlighting the rules within documentation, which can be legal, internal policies, procedure. The team has to gather all the related documents with the reference on version, date of creation, and validity. The elicitation is based on reading sessions completed with Question/Answer workshop sessions.
- *Interactive* involves working sessions with subject matter experts who have the knowledge of the business process and the decisions within a process task. Also a person doing the day-to-day activity is a very good source to understand how decisions are made and how exceptions to the main business process are handled. The process to elicit rules from people will be accomplished by using elicitation workshop.
- *Automated* involve using a computer and special applications to search for rule statement within procedure code, SQL procedures, code listing, and so forth. When using rule mining technology, we have to be careful to not lose the context of execution in which the if-then-else statement was implemented. Therefore, code review should always be complemented by workshop sessions for Q&A.

Code mining is one activity our customers or prospects request quite often, but which ends up being less efficient than expected. Care needs to be taken on that matter as responding and addressing the following items can be time consuming:

- Who has the knowledge of the current code? Is this person still in the company?
- Should the current business context use the same business rules as 15 or 20 years ago? If those rules are still valuable and valid they should be well known by the company and no code mining is required.
- Not all "If-then-else" statements in legacy code represent business rules, sometimes procedures, functions, and algorithms may be an implementation of business rules. The context of execution is a very important dimension to understand before reusing a coded (business) rule as-is.
- Variable names were often limited to eight characters in a flat data model. There is no need to keep it that way. You may want to think about designing an efficient object-oriented model.
- Most of the time automatic translation of badly coded business rules will generate bad business rules in the new environment.
- Business rules implemented for a business rule engine have a different structure than procedural code. They should be more atomic and isolated[4] (see also Concept: Atomic Rule in a later section), and the rule writer may leverage the inference capacity of the engine. Therefore, the automatic translation will produce poor results.

---

[4]A business rule is said to be "atomic" in that it cannot be broken down or decomposed further into more detailed business rules. If reduced any further, there would be loss of important information about the business (Source: http://www. businessrulesgroup .org/first_paper/br01c3.htm).

The following table summarizes the different techniques classified per type of source, based on Morgan (2002):

Source	Static analysis	Interactive	Automated
Documentation	Very good fit	As a complement of static analysis	Not yet possible
Know-how	Not applicable	Unique solution	Not applicable
Code	Efficient	As a complement of the other processes	Gives good result
Business record	Depends on the source	Moderate or a complement	Depends on the source (may be impossible)

When the source of the business rules is people, individual interviews are required to get the core of the knowledge and then followed up with workshops to resolve outstanding issues and process exception paths with the team.

Once we understand the type of elicitation roadmap, we can move to the preparation and execution of the rule discovery activities.

4.2.2.3 Gather the Related Documents

For rule discovery based on documentation or code, the project team must gather all the applicable documents and add (and version) them in a central document repository for traceability purpose. The more information the team can gather at the beginning of the discovery the easier the elicitation job is. There is a common pattern of human thinking that the system is working a certain way, but no document or even code can prove it really works as expected.

4.2.2.4 Studying Decision Point

It is a good practice to automate, with rule processing, the decision points of the business process, leaving the exceptions to humans. Over time some exception handling can be added to the rules. A typical case can be seen in loan underwriting rules: An expert may quickly extract the main rules to support the loan application (the loan to value should be under 85%), but over time, market conditions, regulations, new legislations, and competition may enforce the line of business to define exceptions to the core rules. Those exceptions are added to the ruleset as new rules.

From the decision point table extracted in the previous activity, it is important to complete its description by specifying the list of decisions required at this point of the process. This table may be completed by logging the outcomes of conversations with the different experts or by reading legal documents.

4.2.2.5 Organize Rule Discovery

To make a better use of the development and business teams' time, it is important to plan in advance the workshop sessions and to clearly state what is in the agenda. We recommend organizing the day in two parts:

- Use the morning for discovery workshops using elicitation techniques with the project stakeholders and subject matter experts. During the rule harvesting cycle of ABRD, the analyst team may want to use the rule template document to enter the rule description and use some simple diagramming techniques to define the business entities as conceptual data model[5] (A good tool to use is a UML class diagram editor, by adding entities as class and attributes and omitting the details of the methods and the associations). Ensure the tool, notation used are clearly understood by team members.
- Use the second part of the day to perform the analysis activities.

As explained in the previous chapter, the discovery workshops are executed using different frequency of occurrence. In ABRD harvesting and prototyping cycles, the workshops can be set every morning, but when starting with the implementation cycle, they could occur only every 2 days or more, but never more than a week apart to keep the team focused and enforce feedbacks.

The team should have access to a dedicated meeting room with white boards, pencils, paper, post it notes, and potentially a UML tool to quickly develop diagrams. To organize the sessions, the project team may need to name a moderator responsible for managing the meetings and keeping the team on track. The moderator role is to:

- Establish a professional and objective tone to the meetings
- Start and end the meetings on time
- Establish and enforce the "rules of conduct" of the meetings
- Introduce the goals and agenda for the meetings
- Facilitate a process of decision and consensus making, but avoid participating in the content
- Make certain that all stakeholders participate and have their input heard
- Control disruptive or unproductive behavior
- Gather "Open Points" and follow up actions between sessions (use a simple Excel sheet for instance or "Meeting Minutes" template document)

To organize the workshop, the project manager has to set a strict agenda inviting all the domain experts who will help to formalize the rules. Gather the required documents and explain how the meetings will be managed. The agenda may have at least the following information:

---

[5]A conceptual data model defines the meaning of the things in an organization and includes business entities and their associations.

- Which decision point is being discussed in this meeting
- Which documents to use
  - Rule template
  - Glossary of terms document
  - Business process map or use case documents
  - Conceptual data model
  - Any additional helpful documents/resources
- The meeting room and the schedule
- The name of the moderator
- The high-level rules to follow during the meeting like:
  - Be on time: you will have one "joker" for one time late. A fee of $5 will be taken after that towards a conclusion party
  - In each session all the members should participate
  - We will use brainstorming techniques
  - The moderator controls the time
  - Everyone can have their opinion
  - No criticism

The session should not last more than 2 h, typically from 9 to 11. This can be scheduled for 2 or more consecutive days.

4.2.2.6   Execute Rule Discovery Roadmap

This activity supports the three types of rule discovery: business users and experts workshop session, document study, and legacy code mining. Even if the main sources of rules are documents or code, it is still important to come back to an SME to get feedback on what the team discovered. Note that access to SMEs is quite often challenging because they are typically engaged in other production projects. To reduce this impact to a minimum, it is very important to do a lot of preparation work to optimize the meeting time.

Rule elicitation is an *ongoing* activity you perform throughout the project. *Collaboration* with your stakeholders is critical. They will change their minds as the project proceeds and that's perfectly fine.

It is important at this stage to remember that there are different types of languages for expressing business rules:

- Natural language
- Restricted Language
- Formal expression using a specific grammar

The natural language is initially used during business conversations to describe the rules, informally, without trying to impose any structure, for example with people sitting around a table. At this stage, we do not have any templates or guidelines for structure that we need to abide to. Using this language, we may have redundancy and inconstancy in the rule expressions and in the business terms used.

A second evolution is using a restricted language, still consumable by both analysts and developers, but where we have imposed some structure and grammar to the language so we can express rule statements with proper form. SBVR proposes the *restricted English* for this purpose. The statement may not be correct semantically (redundancy, consistency, etc.), but we can formalize the business term and glossary of terms. Templates such as the one below can be used to also define some meta-data attached to the rule:

Business Activity: use case # decision		
Decision:		
Policies:		
Owner	*Person or team owner of the business policies*	
Candidate rule project	*Used later during the prototyping and building phases*	
Candidate Package	*Sometimes a decision point will be mapped to a group called package and be part of a decision service. A decision service will have multiple packages with the orchestration of execution handled by a rule flow*	
History		
Rule Name	***Rule***	***Comment***
Accident Prone Customer	*Use the raw natural language of the business conversation. Later we may need to use a more strict language like the restricted English of SBVR.* A customer who had an accident report in the past is marked as accident prone	*Use comment for example to describe the type of rule* **inference**
R2	It is necessary that only one deductible be attached to a coverage	
R3		
Business entities referenced	*List the business entities used, this will help to build the conceptual data model*	
Who can change the rules?	*Can be filled during analysis, it helps to understand the velocity of the rule and prepare in the design of the ruleset and the rule governance process*	
When the change can occur?	*Same comment as above.*	

The third type of language is precise and there are no ambiguities: the rule refers exactly to information system objects. This language is parseable and nonambiguous and can be executed by a computer.

A formal language features sentences which have a clear and unambiguous interpretation. There are different kinds of formal languages:

- Predicate logic using syntax like: ($\forall$ X,Y) [Claim(X) Λ MedicalInvoice(Y) Λ Relation(X,Y) => (claimRefNumber(Y) = claimNumber(X))]
- Object Constraint Language (OCL): is an addition to UML to express constraints between objects that must be satisfied
- Truth tables or decision table which present rule as row and columns representing conditions and actions
- Semantics of Business Vocabulary and Business Rules or SBVR which defines structural and operational rules as well a vocabulary to define business concepts
- JRules Technical Rule Language executable by a rule engine
- JRules Business Action Language, high-level language close to English, which is formal as it is using a unique interpretation and unique translation. Rule writers pick among a set of predefined sentences

4.2.2.7 Discovering Rules from SMEs

Interviews and analysis workshops are the two types of interaction used with subject matter expert. For interviews, the typical number of people in the same room is around two or three and for workshops six to ten people are involved. Workshops can last several days. Interviews are used at the beginning of the discovery phase and will most likely address one area of the business process. The analysis workshop is perhaps the most powerful technique for eliciting a lot of requirements. It gathers all key stakeholders together for a short but intensely focused period. The use of a facilitator experienced in requirements management can ensure the success of the workshop. Brainstorming is the most efficient technique used during the sessions.

Brainstorming involves both idea generation and idea reduction. Voting techniques may be used to prioritize the ideas created during a brainstorming session. The workshop facilitator should enforce some rules of conduct during these workshops:

- Do not "attack" other members.
- Do not come back late from a break, even if *key* stakeholders may be late returning because they have other things to do. The sessions are short so they should be able to do other activities during the day.
- Avoid domineering position.

Some authors have suggested the following to improve the process:

- Facilitator keeps a timer for all breaks and fines anyone that is late, everyone gets one free pass.
- Facilitator encourages everyone to use 5-min position statement.
- In case of a long discussion without reaching a firm conclusion or an agreement it is good to use the business concerns to drive the elicitation.

- If a rule is not clear, then it is a good idea to try it out/prototype it.
- Use concrete scenarios to illustrate some rules. These scenarios can later be leveraged for tests.

The following table lists the standard questions the analyst team may ask during the workshop, depending of the source:

Type of input document	Questions	Type of artifacts impacted
Use case or business process map	In this activity, what kind of control the worker is responsible to perform the task? What kind of decisions? On this use case step, the person assess the application, what kind of assessment is he doing? Is there a standard check list?	Use case or BPM Rule description document
Rule description Conceptual data model	What do you mean by .... (a business term to clearly define) How does it relate to .... (other business term)	Conceptual data model
Rule statement	What about the other ranges of possible values for this condition? How often does this condition change? Do you have some other cases?	Business Entities Diagram Rule description document

Between sessions, verify that business terms are well defined and the rules make sense and do not have logical conflicts. Log all the questions related to this analysis in an issue tracking document (Open Points).

4.2.2.8 Discovering Rules from Documents

This approach is used when Governmental Administration or policy group issues legal documents. We did observe this work requires courage and rigor. When using electronic documents, we used the following practices:

- Annotate the document on anything that needs some future discussion
- Copy and paste the business policy declared in the document to the rule template to clearly isolate it for future analysis
- Work in a consistent/systematic way to ensure a good coverage
- Check for agreement with the current business model as you go along
- Investigate discrepancies and log them
- Focus on stakeholder understanding (communication is key) and insist to clarify how a legal rule is interpreted by the line of business

One risk with this approach is that the reader is making his own interpretation of the context, and the document may not include all the cases and criteria leading to interpretations. It is sometimes difficult to get the business motivation behind a written policy. We recommend applying a rigorous method to be able to achieve the following goals:

- Get an exhaustive list of the business events under scope: log them in a table
- Get the activities, tasks, and processes that support the processing of those business events
- Identify where the business rules could be enforced in the process
- Get the business motivation behind the rules
- Get explanation on rules if they are unclear, ambiguous
- Try to extract the object model under scope, domain values by looking at the terms used by the rules ...

We should still apply agile modeling by involving the SMEs to get feedbacks on the findings, assumptions, and issues. Use simple diagrams to communicate with the project stakeholders.

4.2.2.9 Discovering Rules from Code

Discovering rules from application code is time consuming and does not lead to great results. The analyst needs to study a lot of lines of code and procedures to find the conditional operators which are linked to business decisions. Depending on the design and code structure of the application, this work can be very time consuming. It is important to remember the context of execution when the "if statement" is executed, some variables may change the context of this "business rules." With some languages using limited length to define variable names it is more difficult to relate such variables to business entities. A variable in one procedure can have a different name but the same meaning. Code mining tools exist on the market and help to extract business rules and the variables meanings. It is important to keep in mind that rules written in the past may not be relevant any more. Lastly, as stated previously, most of the rules implemented as procedural function need a deep refactoring before deployment to a rule engine.

Code mining is commonly requested by people as it reassures the business team that the rule harvesting starts by the existing behavior of the legacy code. Code mining is usually better used to confirm behavior of some litigious points identified from using other techniques than to try to extract all of the rules as a whole. Rule discovery with SME, using workshop sessions, may conduct to ambiguities or misconceptions. Trying to understand how the rules are implemented in the current system helps to resolve such situations.

4.2.2.10 Documenting the Business Rules

We suggest that a template as presented above should be used for documenting rule details during the harvesting phase. To document the rule, try to use the language of the business ("problem domain") rather than the language of the technology ("solution domain"). The following rule is as stated by a business user in a car rental industry:

A driver authorized to drive a car of group K must be over 29

A rule developer may think to document the rule as:

If the age of the driver is less than 29 and the requested group of the reservation is K, modify the authorized attribute of the driver accordingly.

As stated above it is important to identify the different languages used to document the rule. The rule statements may evolve with time. We use different templates for documenting rules, depending of the type of discovery roadmap. ABRD includes different templates you can leverage.

4.3 Rule Discovery: Case Study

To illustrate all the concepts described in this book, we use a simplified business process for the claim processing application in a fictional insurance property and casualty company named MyWebInsurance. Currently, the claim processing application is using a mix of a legacy COBOL application, which has been doing an excellent job during recent years using a data processing approach, and packaged applications, which are not easily adaptable to support new requirements. In the last few months, an increase in the number of claims to process has led the business executives to address the following business problems:

* Supporting better user experience by giving clear information on the claim processing state
* Supporting a dramatic increase of the demands: more claims to process without hiring more staff
* Supporting new regulatory rules or financial audit policies that force, for example, to pay a claim within 30 days or to be able to re-play an old processed claim for audit purposes

As business grows, customer quality concerns arise because the legacy application could not easily and quickly be modified to support new demands and changes to the process. We can imagine many more drivers for the change but those important business requirements force the enterprise architect of MyWebInsurance to work on the future evolution of this claim processing application, based on agile technologies such as BPM, BRMS, MDM, ESB, and leveraging a Service Oriented Architecture.

The current business process starts with an *insured person* sending a *claim* or a *medical service provider* sending a *medical invoice* to the company. The following actors or stakeholders are part of the process. Each actor is accessing the current legacy application using different menus depending on his role.

Actor	Role	Type of interface
Claimant	The insured person	Use standard paper forms to fill the claim
Patient	The person related to the insured person who receives medical treatments after an accident	May mail medical invoice
Medical service provider	The medical provider or other service provider who can invoice.	Enter information on a legal paper form.
Mail processor (MP)	The claim or bill request is received by mail, so the mail processor enters some information in the system. The system returns the claim number and the claim processor candidate to handle this claim. The paper form is routed internally to the claim processor	Legacy text-based screen – claim entry
Claim processor (CP)	Responsible to complete the data entry, to make first level of investigation, to pay simple claim, and additionally, some are responsible to analyze customer records and determine if the billed level of service is appropriate	Legacy text-based screen – claim processor access
Claim adjuster (CA)	Responsible for coverage, liability, and damage investigations. The CA authorizes payments for both indemnity and expense payments and is responsible for providing the direction to bring claims to a timely and accurate conclusion	Legacy text-based screen – adjuster access
Branch manager	Manage the claim processing employees within a branch. He is involved in specific claim reviews typically with invoices above a certain dollar amount	Legacy text-based screen – manager access

The process below is a simplified version of a real insurance claim application, but illustrates the major activities we need to consider for our case study. The analyst is using the current application main user menu to initiate the process modeling task.

When MyWebInsurance receives the paper documents, a *Mail Processor* starts the process by looking at the paper sent and by assigning the document to a *Claim Processor*. He assigns a claim number at this moment by using a legacy system to get new claim number. Then the medical invoice or the claim follows a set of activities to assess the customer eligibility, the coverage as defined in the policy and to evaluate the amount of money to pay. The set of issues found by the different applications and by the people are resolved during the life cycle of the claim. This process can take a lot of time and it is possible that the bill may not get paid on time and to get penalties.

The claim validation and coverage verification are completed partially manually by the claim processor visiting a set of screens and data fields to verify if coding is entered correctly. There are some communication protocols, using mail to route the work item to a different person in the process. The file moves from an input basket to the output basket of the claim processor. The process is hard coded

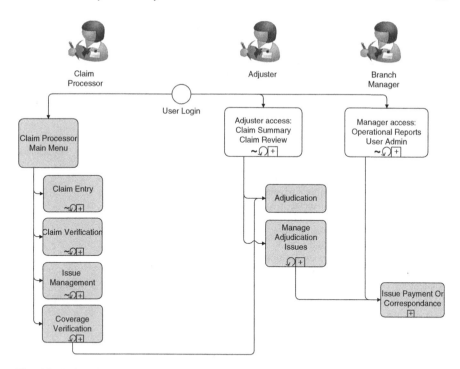

Fig. 4.3 As-is claim process as described by claim processor

in the application. Changes are difficult to make and take a long time to release. Some functions are already revamped with a web interface to reduce the cost of maintenance. When the claim is verified successfully, the adjudication can be calculated by one of the adjusters. The process in our case ends with the payment. In fact all the issues are well managed by the application, and correspondence is generated to ask questions to service providers or claimants to get more information. All correspondence is persisted in a legacy data store and can be retrieved from the screen to see the progress of the claim within the process and what information we are waiting for. Figure 4.3 was used to present this process.

We will not spend too much time describing the process in detail, but from this process the analysis team members can define the following *decision point table*:

Decision point name	Description	Source for rule discovery	Current state of automation	Rule owner – SME
Claim verification	Validate that the claim or medical invoice entered in the system contains valid data	Interview SME and insurance legal document and policies like the one related to UB92 legal form	Manual	Adjuster department

(continued)

Decision point name	Description	Source for rule discovery	Current state of automation	Rule owner – SME
Coverage verification	The system needs to verify what coverage and deductible apply to the given claim	Interview SME, query the policy data base for coverage and deductible types	Manual	Adjuster department
Adjudication	Claims adjudication in health insurance refers to the determination of a member's payment, or financial responsibility, after a medical claim is applied to the member's insurance benefits	Interview and legal rule	Manual	Adjuster department
Route issue	If there is an issue in the automated process, it will create an issue that needs to be handled manually. Decisions on who to route this issue can be made. Claims can follow at least three paths: • Automatic processing • Exception-issues to be resolved by claim processor • Exception-issues to be resolved by claim manager	Interview claim operator manager	Manual	Management department

We will focus on two decision points: claim validation and claim adjudication. For the claim processing application, the development team decided to apply a rule discovery process based on a business process analysis roadmap. Sources for the rules are divided between expert know-how and some legal documentation and forms. The execution of rule discovery workshops with the different claim processors and managers provided the following important information:

• Claims and medical invoices are received by mail. A "mail processor" (human) assigns a unique claim number and then routes the claim to a claim processor (a person). This data is manually written on the claim. The claim processor enters the claim in the system. The description is based on a simplified version of the UB92 (or HCFA1450) American standard form. In this example, we keep the

simplest version so that the process can easily be adapted to other countries. We
do not aim to develop a real business application.

Patient control number: xxxxx		Statement covers period From Through		Admission Date Hour Type Src				Patient name	
Type of bill									
Patient's Birthday		Sex	Patient's Address						
Conditions codes:									
RCC	description	Rate	Unit	Serv.date		Total Charge		Non-covered	
Payer name				Est. amount due				Due from patient	
Provider no.		Provider address							
Insured's name		Insurance company ref		Employer name				Employer location	
Treatment authorization codes		Principal procedure Code Date		Other procedure Code Date				Other proc. Code Date	
remarks				Provider signature				Date	

- Certain types of claims are either calculated manually or processed through
  stand-alone software applications. A small minority of claims are paid in full,
  requiring no adjudication.

Here is an example of a rule from a legal statements at the back page of the UB92
form: *If the patient has indicated that other health insurance or a state medical
assistance agency will pay part of his/her medical expenses and he/she wants
information about his/her claim released to them upon their request, necessary
authorization is on file.* This rule may land behind the claim validation decision
service. Some business terms like patient, other health insurance, claim information, release authorization, need to be integrated in the conceptual data model and
somewhere the process needs to include a notification activity to exchange correspondence with the other health insurance party. Studying the UB 92 form leads us
to extract the following business entities:

- This form represents a medical bill: MedicalBill. A code supports the type of bill. This code is a legal reference number and can be retrieved from a reference data source.
- Provider name, address, and telephone number are required; the minimum entry is the provider's name, city, state, and ZIP code.
- The patient's unique alphanumeric number assigned by the provider to facilitate retrieval of individual financial records and posting of payment.
- The type of bill is a three-digit alphanumeric, with the first digit specifying the type of facility:
  - 1 – Hospital
  - 2 – Skilled nursing
  - 3 – Home health
  - 4 – Religious nonmedical (hospital)
  - 5 – Religious nonmedical (extended care)
  - 6 – Intermediate care
  - 7 – Clinic or hospital-based renal dialysis facility (requires special information in second digit)
  - 8 – Special facility or hospital ASC surgery (requires special information in second digit below)
  - 9 – Reserved for national assignment

The second digit is for classification outside of a clinic, and the third digit is for frequency.

- The medical bill includes the patient information, like control number (required number assigned by the provider), name, address, and his status related to the insurance policy; patient sex is M or F. The month, day, and year of birth is shown numerically as MMDDYYYY.
- The coverage period: beginning and ending dates of the period of the injury.
- The admission type to identify if this is an emergency (severe, life threatening, or potentially disabling conditions), urgent, elective, or NA.
- The conditions code: codes identifying medical conditions related to this bill which may affect processing.
- The line item includes a medical procedure code, revenue description, a rate, service data ... The medical procedure code is a very important element to identify the type of invoice. A large portion of the rules will have conditions that look at this code.

The claim verification step is started once the claim data entry is completed. The following business policies are extracted from interactions with the different claim processors of the company (Table 4.1):

For the purpose of this sample, we are not developing a complete application. Claim processing represents one of the most difficult applications in the insurance industry. The rules above should help to support the analysis and development of our first ruleset and not support a real-life claim processing application. It is also

Table 4.1 Claim verification rule description

Process step:	Called after the claim or medical invoice is entered in the system.	
Validate claim or medical invoice	Business motivation: Any violation of the following rules will be a rejection of the claim or the medical bill. The claimant needs to provide accurate data. The sooner we can extract data inconsistency the lower will be the cost of processing.	
Rule id	Raw description of the rule	Comment – rule classification
VC01	The Claim should be initiated within 30 working days after the accident	Guidance. We may need to specify a range of possible days when the Claim must be rejected. We can propose 45 days and never after 1 year. Also the number of days could come from the policy
VC02	We need to verify that the accident location is one supported by the policy. For a given product, MyWebInsurance defines different states where the policy applies. But as the customer may want to change this coverage, the list of possible states is attached to the policy	Constraint. The list of supported states is variable. Rejection generates issue
VC03	Verify that the person state of residency is one supported by the policy	Constraint. Rejection generates issue.
VC04	The customer insurance policy has a set of coverage with coverage code, which needs to be different from 05 and a business code not equal to 45	Very specific – Constraint. Rejection generates issue
VC05	The claim must be issued before the expiration date of the policy.	Constraint Rejection generates issue
VC06	The date of loss should be before the expiration date of the policy and after the effective date	Guidance. We may need to specify a range of possible days when the Claim must be rejected according to the federal and local laws
VC07	The claim applies on a property covered by the policy (a car, a bicycle)	Constraint
VC08	The billing invoice is always linked to a claim. It includes a reference to a patient and a list of billing item. Each billing item has a procedure code, a quantity, a service data, total charges, and noncovered charges. If any procedure code is unknown raise an issue	Constraint
VC09	When the medical invoice is the first received for a given claim, we need to verify that the date of the earliest service has to be within 1 year after the date of loss, and the invoice should be received before this 1 year delay	
VC10	The first medical treatment should be within 90 days after the date of loss	
VC11	A policy applies to one or more listed drivers. Listed drivers mean the first name and last name provided by the insured person. A claim must come from one of the listed drivers	

Table 4.2 Adjudication rule description

Business Activity: adjudication of medical invoice
Decision:
Policies:

Owner	Adjudication department – Adjudicator director	
Candidate rule project	adjudicateClaimRules	•
History		
Rule name	Rule description	Comment
Verify Treatment needs independent medical evaluation	Evaluate if one of the treatments in the medical bill needs an IME by looking at the medical procedure code in table "IMEevaluationNeeded." We want to add some criteria on the invoice amount and later on the service provider	This may be implemented with a decision table to look for each line item the procedure code and the action is to set some IME needed or not with a type of IME request. This resolution will include information such as: Need peer review, need potential peer review, and need claim processor's review The invoice is put on hold, and the action is wait for IME results
Review IME results	If the invoice needs IME, verify we have all the IME results. If not continue to keep invoice on hold and create issue for each missing IME result	
Missed Medical Evaluation Appointments	When there are two or more missing Independent Medical Evaluation appointments, the invoice is set to "grounds for non-cooperation." This should force denial of the entire claim Create an issue for the claim processor to contact the person with the number of appointments missed	
Identify Medical Procedure excluded from Expert Treatment evaluation	Deny any invoice with medical procedure (s) not supported by our expert evaluation	The IME result has Treatments. So we need to verify for each line item of the invoice; the procedure code is the same as the treatment code *This can be accomplished in java or SQL with a join between two collections*
ReviewByLicensed chiropractic	The chiropractic claim must be reviewed by a licensed chiropractor. Procedure code start by "CHIR"	
GoodStanding Chiropractic	The chiropractic consultant must be in good standing and have a current license in the state in which the review is performed with no current license term violations	

Table 4.2 (continued)

Business Activity: adjudication of medical invoice
Decision:
Policies:

Owner	Adjudication department – Adjudicator director
Candidate rule project	adjudicateClaimRules

History

Rule name	Rule description	Comment
Emergency Treatment after date of loss	Create an audit review if there is a medical treatment given in the emergency room later than 5 days after the accident	ER Treatment after DOL
Ambulance after date of loss	Create an audit review if there is a ambulance transport not on the same day as the accident	Ambulance Treatment not on DOL
Too late medical treatment	If the earliest medical service date of any treatment invoiced is after 1 year of the accident deny the entire invoice and report an issue	Reason is: "First Date of Service is one year past Date of Loss"
Gap in treatments	If there is at least more than 100 days between the earliest medical service date of any treatment invoiced and the last date of medical service on previous invoice, then deny the entire invoice	
Late treatment	Create an issue when the earliest medical service is given 90 days after the date of loss	Reason is: "First Date of Service is a late treatment"
Late invoice	Create an issue when the received date of the medical invoice is 1 year after the date of loss	Reason is "Receipt date of invoice one year past Date of Loss"
Bill not timely	We are rejecting the invoice if there is any line item with a date of service older than 90 days from the date of invoice	
Outpatient reimbursement	The covered outpatient services include the following services, emergency room, ambulatory room, medically necessary outpatient hospital and clinic, radiology, and medical imaging	
	When the invoice is from an hospital and related to an outpatient service, the revenue code needs to be 490 and bill type 83X; any surgical procedure listed in CPT code will be reimbursed accordingly	
	Reimburse the service at the outpatient OMB rate	
	Otherwise claims are reimbursed by multiplying covered charges by the statewide outpatient cost-to-charge ratio	

important to note that those rules are not in their final state, we will transform them using a more formal representation during the analysis phase.

In insurance, claim adjudication refers to the determination of an insured person's payment, or financial responsibility, after a medical claim is applied to the insured's insurance benefits. Most of the time the insurance company will initiate some *expert audit*, called *Independent Medical Evaluation*, to complete the diagnostic of the patient and evaluate the appropriateness of the given treatment. An *Adjustment* is the calculation of the amounts to be made paid by the insurance company. For the "adjudicate claim" decision point, the rule discovery aims to develop the business rules as in Table 4.2 which presents a second type of template.

4.4   Rule Analysis

The goal of the rule analysis activity is to understand the meaning of the rule as stated by the business person and subject matter experts and to remove any ambiguity and semantic issue. The objective is to prepare the rules for the future implementation. As mentioned in the Chap. 3, rule analysis can start as soon as the team has some rule descriptions which are agreed upon by the subject matter experts. The rule analysis phase includes activities such as "analyze the rule description and fact models", "transform the rule", "build test scenario", "design the data model used by the rules", and "synchronize with current logical or physical data models." The flow may look like in Fig. 4.4.

4.4.1   Analyze Rule Descriptions and Fact Models

The first activity focuses on analyzing the rule descriptions to extract the business entities and terms used. During the elicitation activity, the raw description of the

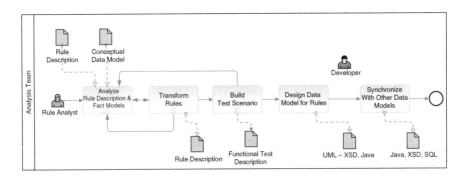

Fig. 4.4 Rule analysis activities

rule uses business terms as used in a common language, used by the people. We are at the expression level used to communicate between humans. At this level, terms have lot of ambiguities. To be able to remove those ambiguities, we need to define the meaning of the concepts used and link them by formal propositions.

W3C has produced important specifications to define semantic models which could be used to define the data model used by the rules. As mentioned earlier, OWL (Ontology Web Language) helps to define the enterprise domain model or ontology. The ontology describes the concepts in the domain and the relationships between them. It can vary from taxonomy to conceptual model. OWL leverages W3C-RDF, the Resource Description Framework, to persist the semantics of the things to be described in XML format. A reasoning engine can check the internal consistency of the statements and definitions in the ontology. It can also *classify* concepts by finding the definitions/categories under which they fit. Many companies interested in business rules are also considering developing an enterprise ontology with OWL-RDF. The adoption of such standards and emerging tools will help to develop the complete semantics needed for enterprise data models.

Using a more traditional approach, Object-Oriented Analysis (OOA) describes *what* the system is by using a set of models of the system as a group of interacting objects. Each object represents some entity of interest and is defined with a Class. A class includes attributes and behaviors as methods. OOA models are typically represented with UML use case diagrams, UML class diagrams, and a number of UML interaction diagrams. Using an OOA approach, we can model the concepts used by the business in static class diagrams to use a formal notation. At this stage of the methodology, we may have the following possible data models in our hands:

- A conceptual data model
- A logical data model
- A physical data model
- Some reference data which describes static list, enumerated value, classifications, and the like

Those models are not finalized, and they are enhanced and transformed during future iterations of the harvesting and prototyping phases. Most projects have already some data models, and database analysts contribute to explain how some business concepts are mapped to physical data model elements. When using a rule approach, it makes sense to start by the rule description and define the data model from there and *not* to start from an existing physical data model. We need a view of the current data model and a clear definition of the terms used by the rules; we do not need a complex data model to express the rules. Rule analysts have to extract the business terms from the rule statement and build a business glossary. We did observe that this glossary brings a lot of value to the line of business as terms are defined without ambiguity and interpretation. Business terms and their relationships can be represented in a conceptual data model (CDM) or entities diagram. The steps to perform the analysis are:

- Highlight the nouns used in each rule description. We are talking about Terms, as referring to a business concept used in daily business operations. It can be one or more words and nouns. They are often differences found in between departments, and each department may refer to the same business concept but defines it using different perspective and hence different words. These are actually synonyms. Examples of term are: a taxpayer, a taxpayer obligation, a loan, a claim, a legal entity, an application, a customer, a product, etc.
- Analyze facts: A fact is a statement that connects terms into a business-relevant relationship. Some examples of facts: A taxpayer files a tax return form; the customer could have only one purchase order at a time; a medical invoice is linked to one claim. The fact has to be analyzed to understand how the application will support it. It can be through use case implementation, business rule, or the relation between objects.
- Build the facts declaration to define the used terms. It is possible at this level to represent entities in a model using a diagram such as a UML class diagram (see Figs. 4.5 and 4.6).
- Map it within a conceptual data model diagrams.

A term may describe a business concept which will be mapped to a Class, a characteristic of a business entity which will be mapped to an attribute of a class, and sometimes a term may describe the way a business object behaves. In that last case, it will be mapped within a method of a finite state machine. As an example we can take the following rule description:

Adjusters reject the invoice if any line item has a date of service older than 90 days from the date of invoice.

From this rule statement, an analyst can build the following facts:

- Adjuster is an employee of the insurance company.
- Invoice is a medical invoice.
- A medical invoice has a date of invoice.
- A medical invoice has at least one line item.
- A line item describes a medical treatment.
- A medical treatment has a date of service.
- A medical treatment must have one unique procedure code, a quantity which is at least one (and most likely a price but we do not know yet).

The creation of facts may generate new rules. Here we can add the following business rules into the scope:

- If the claim is related to a loss, the date of loss has to be provided.
- The insured person must have a residency in the USA.
- The patient name, address, and status must be on the medical invoice.

It is clear that we can add a lot of facts to link terms in our model. And we can spend months of documentation doing so. In Agile Business Rule Development, we prefer having working rules and light documentation. Such facts can be presented by a set of diagrams, which will help us communicate with business users. Those diagrams evolve later to class diagrams from which we can generate code. Diagrams are always a good vehicle for communication. It is also important to make different diagrams for different audiences, but to also maintain them in synchronous manner. We propose to keep the conceptual model as a set of diagrams to communicate to the business user. These diagrams evolve with the rule harvesting phase.

It is important to note that not all the rules can be implemented and deployed into a software component. Some rules may end in a procedure manual delivered to the worker to enforce a good business practice as defined by corporate policies.

4.4.2 Transforming Rules

The activity "Transform Rules" leads to modifying rule declarations so that they become formal, atomic, and standalone elements. This is needed for understandability and ease of implementation and maintenance. This activity also includes understanding the rule patterns, eventually removing redundant rules, or resolving overlaps among rules. This activity is also conducted during the implementation of the rules, but it is started during the analysis, so we are detailing the approach in this context. The key concept is to transform rules to an atomic level as much as possible.

Concept: **Atomic Rule**

A rule is atomic if it cannot be further decomposed without losing meaning. Atomicity is desired for understandability, ease of maintenance and execution efficiency.

The following rule statement can be decomposed into two rules. From

> *The insurance does not reimburse medical expenses incurred abroad if the claim is presented more than one year after the expenses had been incurred, or if the claimant has spent more than 182 days abroad within the past year.*

to

- *When the date of creation of the claim is more than one year after the date of treatment of the medical expense then reject the medical expense.*
- *When the claimant spend more than 182 days abroad within the past year then reject the claim.*

Rule conditions are true or false and should lead to one result. The rule analyst has to clearly understand the Boolean logic.

Concept: **Boolean Logic Summary**[6]

AND/Conjunction

The conjunction of two propositions is true when both propositions are true. The truth table is:

AND B	A	True	False
True		*True*	*False*
False		*False*	*False*

Another notation is using the dot operator for AND so A.B is equivalent to A AND B.

OR/Disjunction

Disjunction of two propositions is false when both propositions are false.

OR B	A	True	False
True		*True*	*True*
False		*True*	*False*

Another notation for disjunction is using the operator + for A OR B like A + B.

NOT/Negation

A	NOT A
True	*False*
False	*True*

Implication

A→B, implication is a binary operation which is false when A is true and B is false. A→B can be expressed as NOT A OR B.

A→B B	A	True	False
True		*True*	*True*
False		*False*	*False*

XOR or exclusive OR

Exclusive OR of two propositions is true just when exactly one of the propositions is true:

XOR B	A	True	False
True		*False*	*True*
False		*True*	*False*

---

[6]See also http://en.wikipedia.org/wiki/Introduction_to_Boolean_algebra; http://www.internettu-torials.net/boolean.asp.

> **De Morgan's Law**
>
> De Morgan's law represents rules in formal logic relating pairs of dual logical operators in a systematic manner expressed in terms of negation:
>
> NOT (A AND B) = NOT A OR NOT B
>
> NOT (A OR B) = NOT A AND NOT B
>
> De Morgan's law can be used to improve rules during the rule transformation activity.

To refine rules to the atomic level, the rule analyst has to apply some transformation patterns. For example, when a rule is an inference or an action enabler, it may be important to consider separating expressions linked with ANDs within the action part of the rule (also named the right hand side).

> A pattern of criteria organized such as:
>   IF condition_A THEN do (B) AND do(C) may be rewritten as two rules to make them atomic
>
> IF A THEN do (B)
> IF A THEN do (C).

This is due to the fact that a change in the data used as part of the conditions of a rule may force the reevaluation of all rules using such data. We will detail the rule engine's RETE algorithm in Chap. 6. In the first schema nothing happens before the end of the action. So if the action B makes the condition A false, C is executed when it really should not.

When expressing an inference rule or an action enabler, do not allow ORs on the left hand side of the rule (the condition part); break the rule.

> A pattern like:
>   IF A OR B THEN do(C) can be rewritten as two rules to make them atomic
>
> IF A THEN do(C)
> IF B THEN do(C).
>
> This is a good practice when the conditions A and B are complex. A simple condition like the age is 18 or 21 does not need to be separated into two rules. Also the semantic of the OR has always to be assessed. It could be that the subject matter expert means an exclusive OR. In that last case the rules are:
>   If A and Not B then do(C)
>   If B and Not A then do (C)

When expressing constraints (must, have to) and guidelines (should), try to remove ANDs between conditions and clearly separate them in different rules.

A business policy like:
A driver must be 25 years old or older AND must have good credit rating
May be split into two constraints like:

Rule 1: A driver must be at least 25 years old
Rule 2: A driver must have good credit rating

The goal is to clearly separate the constraints. The action part of the rule will most likely raise an issue. It may be more efficient to have all the issues the business transaction is violating. Here we want to see the issues reported about a bad credit and a young driver.

Make sure that each rule contains only necessary conditions; do not over-constrain the rule applicability. The rule analyst has also to look for redundant rules and try to remove them. Redundant rules are duplicated rules, duplicated through some transformations (renaming, inversion of conditions, etc.), and redundancies among rules that create a common data value or a common truth value, or initiate a common action.

Removing redundancy is simpler if rules are atomic, otherwise analyst may get lost in the equivalence of complex logical formulas (e.g., If NOT (A AND B) is equivalent to IF (NOT A) OR (NOT B)). There are subtle forms of redundancy: IF A AND B THEN C is equivalent to IF (NOT C) THEN (NOT A) OR (NOT B). Sometimes changing the order of conditions can help highlight identical rules: IF A AND B THEN C is the same as IF B AND A THEN C. This looks obvious as written like a mathematical expression, but depending on the rule language it may be difficult to see at first reading.

Another step of the analysis is to remove inconsistent rules. Overlapping rules are partially redundant because they are not semantically equivalent but they point to problems: one rule may say IF A AND B THEN C, the other says IF A THEN C. The question will be: is B really needed to infer C? One of the two rules should be eliminated or modified to fix the inconsistency.

It is also possible to get semantically equivalent conditions with contradictory conclusions: two rules like IF A THEN B; and IF A THEN NOT(B) are two conflicting rules, probably due to two different sources of information for documenting the decisions. Typically, this is symptomatic of the fact that we are missing some necessary conditions in either rule (or both, e.g., IF A AND C THEN B; IF A AND D THEN NOT(B)).

Another pitfall are rules that lead to the same conclusion based on contradictory conditions: rules like IF A THEN B and IF NOT (A) THEN B. Logically, this means that the conclusions should always be true. This is symptomatic of the fact that the condition is not really relevant to the conclusion.

The analysis has to ensure the completeness of the rules. We may consider three kinds of completeness:

- Make sure that all the possibilities are covered for a given rule pattern. If you have a rule that says "loans for value greater than $250,000 should be approved by the branch manager", it does not tell us who must/can approve loans of value less than $250,000.
- Make sure that all derived data in the object model has corresponding computation or inference rules. This involves computed attributes, qualifications (e.g., customer status, account type, etc.).
- Make sure that integrity and cardinality constraints are somehow represented. Either in the object model or in rules.

The analysis phase is a good time to ask the business user how often the rule will change, we call this rule volatility. Rules about risk computation, eligibility, underwriting, or configuration may change over time. We notice that when a user does not anticipate the rule changing, rules unplanned at the beginning are added over time. Some rules may not change often but other rules in the same ruleset may. Moving the "non changing" rules outside of the ruleset may have bad impacts on the ruleset integrity. When looking at rule volatility, it is important to assess which factors trigger rule changes and how new rules are defined for a given decision point.

Lastly, the rule analyst needs to understand the rule dependencies and rule sharing goals. A rule R1 depends on a rule R2 if the enforcement of R2 results into a situation where R1 is relevant (or needs to be enforced). A simple example is a rule R2 which is creating new data or is modifying existing data that is tested by R1.

Rule sharing is a more complex concept to implement and may be linked to the BRMS capability. The goal is to avoid to copy and paste the same logic across rulesets. One ruleset can include a set of rules that are common to multiple ruleset. For example, testing the age of a customer can be put in a common rulesets. The other rulesets are referencing the common one, and rules are shared. A possible side effect of rule sharing is rule overriding: a specific rule in one ruleset takes precedence over another rule in a common ruleset. The overriding enforcement is most likely done using some meta-properties attached to the rule.

Understanding dependencies help determine the likely "execution" sequence of rules. The execution sequence is useful for rule analysis to detect undesirable dependencies. For the implementation, the execution sequence is useful to understand what the results will look like: some rule engine determines that sequence automatically and on the fly (chaining). If we implement business rules in a procedural fashion, we need to understand the execution sequence to enforce it. Some of the undesirable dependencies include circular dependencies leading to infinite loops.

4.4.3 Building Test Scenarios

Developing software without testing makes no sense in today's world (we hope!). Developing rules deployed in a rule engine helps developers to efficiently support a Test Driven Development (TDD) approach. Writing tests before authoring the rule makes testing part of a validation feedback loop. During the harvesting phase, the analysis team needs to develop test scenarios and data elements to support the future rule writing and testing. The development of concrete scenarios leads to the clarification of ambiguities, finds holes in the decision processing, enhances rules decision coverage, and the overall quality. Implemented rules are software elements like methods and classes in object-oriented development: we may define tests for each rule. Concrete scenarios may be written as a story board. Start by a simple case and then add more data elements to cover specific rule.

Here is an example of user story: *Jack Bee living in California and customer of WebInsurance for 3 years as a good driver. He filed a claim for a minor car accident where his friend Mark, located on the right seat, was slightly injured at the neck. Mark went to the hospital one day after the accident and he follows up with his medical provider. The hospital and the medical provider are sending invoices to Webinsurance. One medical invoice includes neck massage with a date of treatment six months after the date of the accident. The invoice should be rejected.*

With Test Driven Development (TDD) we write a single test before writing the rule which fulfills that test. Basically, the rule writer executes the following steps:

- Add test by specifying the data and expected results
- Run the tests to ensure that the new test does in fact fail
- Create or update the rule or rules so that they pass the new test
- Run the test suite again to verify the test now succeeds

The advantage of TDD is to write rules by small increments, which is safer than writing a complete ruleset without testing. Another advantage is that it helps design the code, the rules, and how exceptions are reported.

4.4.4 Verify Rules Against the Data Models

The rule analyst needs to continuously verify that business terms used in rule statements are part of the logical data model as classes or attributes. The model exposed to the rules needs to get data from data sources. If a concept is not in the data, it has to be quickly handled and managed by the application architect. So this activity of synchronizing the work done at the model level with the different existing data models is a very important task of any business rule project. Most of the time a concept has different names, but sometimes a new concept may force adding a new column in a table.

4.5 Case Study: Rule Analysis

Back to the WebInsurance claim processing application, the rules in Tables 4.1 and 4.2 are analyzed and completed after discussions with the SMEs. The following facts are added:

- The claim must reference one insurance policy.
- The insurance policy has at least one insured person.
- A patient is also called an involved party.
- An involved party is a legal entity involved in a loss; he could be the insured person.
- An accident is a loss.
- A policy is an insurance policy.
- An insurance policy lists a set of coverage.
- A coverage has a unique coverage code.
- Coverage is the amount of protection against loss.
- A deductible is the amount the insured must pay when a loss occurs.
- An insurance policy has one effective date and one expiration date.
- Claim has a date of creation.
- The insured person has one or more properties covered by one policy.
- A medical invoice includes code to define the type of bill.
- A medical bill is synonymous as a medical invoice.
- A medical bill includes the patient information.
- A medical bill includes a control number (required number assigned by the provider).
- A medical invoice is issued by one medical provider.
- A medical invoice includes a cover period.
- The cover period has beginning and ending dates of the period included in the bill.

From these facts, we can build the following conceptual data model. This model is closed to a UML class diagram, but is used as a tool to communicate the business concepts with the SMEs and the IT team. This is important to use this artifact to present the data model used by the rules (Fig. 4.5).

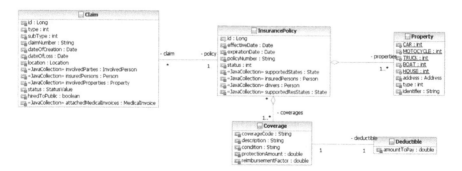

Fig. 4.5 Claim conceptual data model (CDM)

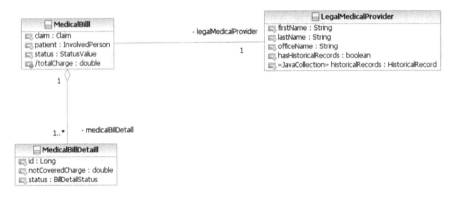

Fig. 4.6 Invoice conceptual data model (CDM)

For the medical invoice or medical bill, the model looks like as shown in Fig. 4.6.

These diagrams are not complete, but we have enough elements to prototype some rules. All these model artifacts help us build a common vocabulary with a structure and syntax we can quickly leverage for our implementation.

4.6 Summary

Rule discovery should not be performed in one long session running for weeks to produce only documentation. Rule harvesting starts at the beginning of the project but is supported with the rule analysis and rule authoring, so that the work produces executable rules and nonexecutable rules. There are cases where the business rules have to be coded in the core application, in the data model structure, or in components other than a rule engine. The rule documentation can indicate where the rule is implemented or enforced. The rule description uses the language of the business and not a technical language.

Rule Analysis is a very important activity in the ruleset development life cycle as it prepares the rules for a successful implementation. Focusing on the data model, the rule semantics and the process flow can help to determine where to implement the business rules. Analysis should not be limited to paper work, but should also use UML tools and even the rule IDE. This should not be a long activity as we are proposing to quickly move to the next phase of rule prototyping. It is easier to find issues related to rule expressiveness or the data model by implementing rules, not by writing extensive documentation.

4.7 Further Reading

Barbara von Halle's STEP methodology, presented in her first book "*Business Rules Applied: Building Better Systems Using the Business Rules Approach*" (2001), does a great job with rule discovery and analysis, both in terms of identifying the different discovery and analysis activities and in proposing effective techniques for performing them. The techniques presented here are *largely* based on STEP.

Tony Morgan's book "Business Rules and Information Systems: Aligning IT with Business Goals" proposes three rule discovery roadmap families depending on rule sources (SMEs, documents, and code), and much of our discussion of those (sections 2.2.7, 2.2.8, and 2.2.9) is inspired from that book.

Two of the main contributors on decision management and decision service approach are James Taylor and Neil Raden with their book *"Smart Enough Systems: How to Deliver Competitive Advantage by Automating Hidden Decisions"* – Prentice Hall (2007).

The Object Management Group (http://www.omg.org) has defined the Semantic of Business Vocabulary and Rules specification, which can be read at http://www.omg.org/spec/SBVR/1.0/.

The OMG also specifies an important framework to define a business motivation model, where the specification can be read at http://www.omg.org/spec/BMM/1.1/.

Detailed about the W3 "OWL Web ontology Language" (OWL) and Resource Description Framework (RDF) can be found at http://www.w3.org/TR/owl-features/ and at http://www.w3.org/TR/2004/REC-owl-features-20040210/#ref-rdf-schema.

Conceptual data model is introduced at en.wikipedia.org/wiki/Conceptual_schema and at http://www.agiledata.org/essays/dataModeling101.html.

Chapter 5
Prototyping and Design

Target audience

- *(Must) architect, developer, (optional) project manager (high-lights)*

In this chapter you will learn

- *How to prepare the rules for the implementation*
- *How to use an evaluation framework to decide where to implement the business rules*
- *How to build the object models used by the rules*
- *How to design the project structure and the related rule elements*
- *How to implement some rules to validate the analysis, find issues, and communicate to the SME*
- *How to use some common rule design patterns to facilitate rule implementation*

Key points

- *Start quickly to prototype rules to develop both rule projects and the data model.*
- *Organize rule artifacts and think of reuse as soon as possible in the project life cycle.*
- *Maintain strong communication with SME to address issues about the model, the rule description, the rule scope, and the context of execution.*

5.1 Introduction

The purpose of the prototyping phase is to take a first complete pass through the development process, confront the main design issues, and lay the groundwork for future refinements. Prototyping is incremental and iterative: we start by "implementing" a subset of the processes – or of the decisions within a single process to try out a particular design. Subsequent prototyping cycles will refine the architecture and expand the coverage of the prototype, functionality-wise.

J. Boyer and H. Mili, *Agile Business Rule Development*,
DOI 10.1007/978-3-642-19041-4_5, © Springer-Verlag Berlin Heidelberg 2011

Note that a rule-engine execution of business rules is not a sine qua none condition for the business rules approach, even though it is a highly desirable one; for one thing, without the rule-engine execution of business rules, we lose much of the IT agility that comes with the business rules approach. Thus, the first – and probably most important – design decision to make during the prototyping phase is to decide on the rule implementation. Generally speaking, we can implement business rules in five different ways: (a) at the data model level, (b) in the application code, (c) in a process map, (d) in the graphical user interface (GUI) of the application, or (e) using a rule engine. Section 5.2 explores the five alternatives, and – surprise!! – the rule-engine solution is shown to be superior to the alternatives. The remaining prototyping activities assume that we have chosen a rule-engine implementation but are independent of the business rule management systems (BRMS) that is used for the implementation. Figure 5.1 shows the prototyping activities and their dependencies. Table 5.1 shows where each activity is discussed. In this chapter, we focus on the process and will be content to highlight the broad design issues. Chapters 7, 9, 12, and to a lesser extent, 14 and 16 will revisit these design issues in far more detail.

In Sect. 5.6, we discuss prototyping for our case study, and we conclude in Sect. 5.8.

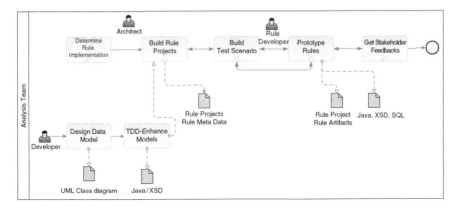

Fig. 5.1 Rule prototyping development activities

Table 5.1 Prototyping activities

Activity	Section
Determine rule implementation	5.2
Build data models	5.3
Build structures for development and execution	5.4
Develop unit tests for each rule	5.5
Author rules	5.5
Execute rules	5.5
Obtain SME feedback	5.7

5.2   Determine Rule Implementation

The purpose of this activity is to determine the best way to execute the rules. When we come out of the rule harvesting phase (see Chap. 4), it is still possible that some rules will stay on paper and will never be implemented in a software component. This includes rules used by *human decision makers* that require human judgment, or that require data that is either not recorded electronically or, data that is recorded but that is not usable. Of the ones that will be automated, there are many ways of implementing them:

- *At the data model-level.* A number of business rules *are* about the structure of the data – called *structural assertion rules*. A statement like "a mortgage application must have a single primary borrower, and may have zero or many secondary borrowers", will be embodied into two classes, **Borrower** and **Application**, and two associations. But beyond *structural* rules, we can also enforce some *behavioral* rules at the time that objects (class instances) are created or persisted, by triggering some dynamic checks (e.g., database triggers, embedded SQL code, O/R mapping code, etc.).
- *Within application code.* This is the default and most common non-rule-oriented implementation: complex decision logic is coded within functions/procedures/ subroutines, scripts, or within method bodies within the context of object-oriented applications.
- *Within business processes, within the context of a business process management (BPM) tool/system.* BPM tools address business process efficiency issues, by focusing on the fundamentals of a business process, namely, "who is involved", "when they should be involved", "what do they need to do". BPM tools support both human and automated actors. When defining a business process, typical BPM tools enable us to define/attach business/ decision logic to *tasks* within the process, to the *routing* of work items through the process flow, and to the semantics of the *business data*. In fact, a number of BPM tools do come with *some* capabilities for defining business logic *declaratively* or using some form of scripting logic. Thus, if an organization is already using BPM tools to implement and manage its business processes, it might consider implementing all of its business rules through a BRMS tool.
- *Graphical user interface.* In a number of web applications, the bulk of the business rules concern data validation and input screen navigation, i.e., deciding what screen/page to bring up next, depending on the data entered so far. Traditionally, such business rules are encoded using client-side scripting, or within (web) server-side controller classes. Performing such data validations close to the data source has its advantages, including responsiveness and avoiding unnecessary network traffic. We were hard-pressed, at times, to justify the overhead of a full-blown BRMS/rule-engine solution, and this remains a serious contender for *some* types of web applications.

- *Rule engine*. This is the case when business rules are written by business users in a declarative business-friendly language, are *interpreted* during run-time by a rule engine, and are deployed and maintained separately from the core of the application.

We argue that the rule-engine solution is the best overall *general-purpose* approach to implementing automatable business rules. However, certain *types* of rules such as *structural assertion* rules *should* be expressed within the data model. There could also be compelling *design/architectural* reasons why some of the other alternatives should be given serious considerations. An enterprise application might, legitimately, combine approaches.

Being in the software/solution space, the choice of an implementation approach should be dictated by architectural considerations/qualities. Thus, we shall assess our alternatives along the typical architectural requirements that business places on their IT architecture, namely:

- *Adaptability* corresponds to the ability to change the business logic easily. The need for adaptability may come from short deadline constraints, frequent small changes to the business logic (e.g., daily, or even hourly), or more substantial changes that may occur weekly, monthly, or quarterly.
- *Traceability* refers to the ability to *clearly* relate what was implemented to what was agreed upon between the business unit and IT. Traceability often implies that the *expression* of business logic in running applications is understandable by all parties (business and IT), *as is*, or through simple transformations.
- *Auditability* refers to the ability to trace from business motivation to execution of the policy to better understand the logic behind a decision. Good traceability is a necessary but not a sufficient condition for auditability.
- *Reusability* refers to the ability to share business logic across processes, or across applications. For example, policy holder data validation rules would apply indiscriminately to new business or policy renewal, *and* for car insurance underwriting, as well as *home* insurance underwriting.
- *Manageability* refers to the ability to manage the *life cycle* of the business logic, and in a way that is relatively independent from the life cycle of the application *core*, which tends to be more stable/evolve less often. Manageability includes issues of governance (discussed in Chaps. 16 and 17), development life cycle, and maintenance.

In the following sections, we will assess each of the five implementation choices along the five architectural qualities discussed above.

5.2.1 Implementing Rules Within the Data Model

Generally speaking, rules that *define* the structure of the data model, or that state low-level *semantic structural* constraints, such as referential integrity constraints, *should* be implemented within the data model. This means within either the *schema definition* or the object-relational (O/R) mapping, or at the level of the business entities themselves. Examples of structural rules include rules defining the structure of the business entities, like saying that attribute X applies to entity Y, or rules setting constraints on relationship, like stating that a loan application could only have two borrowers.

Table 5.2 shows how this solution measures up according to the five architectural qualities discussed in the beginning of Sect. 5.2.

Table 5.2 Rule in data model assessment

Variable	Potential assessment
Adaptability	Very static implementation. A change in the constraints placed on the object model may impact *all the layers* of the application, from the logical data model to the persistence service, and all the way up to the presentation layers. Change is managed through a full software release life cycle. Thus:
	Poor. There are some design patterns to develop a more flexible data model, including the so-called Adaptive Object Model[a] pattern, but this pattern has a number of disadvantages (e.g., type safety, consistency, performance) and is seldom used for high-volume data.
Traceability	UML class diagrams do not constitute a good communication medium with business – and cannot express/visualize many structural constraints. Business analysts prefer a simple entity model. Entity diagrams present a higher-level representation of the domain model, but force the team to maintain the link between the implementation and the business representation.
	Medium. Tools can help maintain the consistency of multiple data models and provide *some* traceability of business rules with things such as annotations, comments, or UML templates. Logical data models and physical data models are most likely *not* generated automatically from the same conceptual model. For efficiency considerations, the physical model may end up diverging more or less significantly from the conceptual model, breaking the traceability.
Auditability	*Fair.* Configuration management tools, with a strict development process and adhered to discipline in documenting any change in the model, can help trace changes to the structural rules back to the business motivation.
Reusability	*Fair.* Domain object models can be designed to be reusable. But in reality each application needs its own view of the core enterprise business object model. To avoid a lot of data transformations between applications, one approach consists of using a *canonical data model*. Each implemented application needs to design and build its own view of that model, using XML Schema (XSD), a Java data model, or any other object-oriented language. The use of a canonical object model within the context of an enterprise service bus (ESB) would require performing data conversion between models either at the service implementation level, or in the mediation layer.
Manageability	*Good.* Modern modeling tools, configuration management tools, and a strictly adhered to development process help maintain the business logic.

[a]See Joseph Yoder work at http://adaptiveobjectmodel.com/ and http://citeseerx.ist.psu.edu/viewdoc/download?doi=10.1.1.66.3382&rep=rep1&type=pdf

Concept. An Adaptive Object Model helps to add flexibility to a domain object model. The simplest version of this pattern links business concepts modeled as `Entity`. Entity has a type, modeled using `EntityType`. Entities have attributes or properties, which are implemented with the `Property` pattern. Each property has a type, called `PropertyType` and each `EntityType` can then specify the types of the properties for its entities.

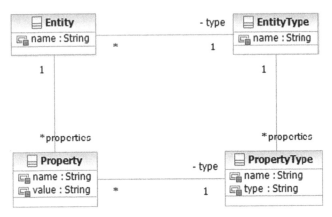

With this model a developer can add attributes to an entity easily.

```
Entity coverage = …
Property benefit = new Property("Benefit");
benefit.setValue(someValue);
coverage.getProperties().add(benefit);
```

5.2.2 Implementing Rules Within Application Code

Implementing business rules in application code is currently the most common way IT developers implement business rules. The usual justifications are performance and flexibility of the coding language, and what they perceive as a steep learning curve for business rule technology. Using hardcoded if/then/else statements is not very flexible, but in the hands of a top notch programmer it can be very efficient and arguably faster than a rule engine. When the number of rules grows to the hundreds or thousands, the code becomes complex, the business logic becomes nearly unmanageable and increasingly difficult to maintain. Using traditional software development life cycle (SDLC), changes to the business rules have to be implemented by IT developers, which means change implementation, unit testing, followed by QA testing, then promotion to production and deployment. Depending on the frequency and scope of changes, this process may be heavy and may not be agile enough for most of the business rule changes (see examples mentioned in Chap. 1).

We have often heard reluctant IT developers argue that their business rules are computation intensive, and do *not* change that often, pleading for the more efficient, and less flexible application code implementation. Consider the following business rule:

```
Verify in each item the customer bought since he is
customer with us there is at least one article of type
T so that we can propose the new product Y with X % of
discount, except if the customer is from the state of
New York or New Jersey (no discount apply).
```

We can implement this in a method which loops on the articles bought by a given customer and do the search. At a first glance, navigating a collection of objects and testing multiple conditions on them are easy to implement using the power of the programming language. The exceptions around the State can be hardcoded in the rule, or, for more flexibility, a smart developer might use some lookup table to get the list of nondiscounted states. Excluding another state from the discount offer is then as simple as adding a row in the table. "Is that (business logic) declarative/data-driven enough for you," we hear. However, if the business wants to add conditions on the product category, the customer profile, or the time of the year, the new logic requires the addition of if statements in the code, driving a code change, and so a full software development and release life cycle. This is not to say that *all* business logic should be coded within rules; dispatching, orchestration, data manipulation, and the like *are* better suited for an *imperative* (as opposed to *declarative*) implementation in application code.

Table 5.3 shows how the implementation of business rules within application code fares, relative to the five architectural qualities we mentioned earlier.

5.2.3 Implementing Rules in GUI

This is a special case of the previous one, but one that occurs often, and that merits a separate discussion. This is the case where business rules are embedded in the presentation tier. We will examine this within the context of the Model-View-Controler (MVC). Recall that, within the context of the MVC pattern, the model embodies the state of the interaction between the user and the application, and it may refer to some domain objects. The view's main responsibility is to present an up-to-date graphical view of the model. The controller is responsible for capturing user input, and translating into commands to be executed on the model. It is also responsible for view content and flow, i.e., which elements to include/display within a particular view, their data, and which view should follow/come next, after another view. In this context, the logic of the controller is often decision intensive. For example, we can have rules control the data contents of widgets within a particular view. This is useful for applications that

Table 5.3 Rules in application code assessment

Variable	Potential assessment
Adaptability	*Poor*. The need to change application code when a business rule changes is not nearly as bad as changing the underlying data model (see Sect. 5.2.1) but is still unpleasant. Indeed, while software application builds are more efficient and less costly than before, deployment remains expensive, depending on the complexity of the production environment. Changing code under time pressure usually leads to poor quality.
Traceability	*Poor*. The logic that underlies a business rule may be spread out between several methods or procedures in the application code and is not encoded in a way that *business* can understand. Strong code documentation practices and standards can help, but do not solve the problem. For example the development team may need to maintain a mapping table linking the business policy statement to the components, classes, or methods that implement the corresponding business rules.
Auditability	*Poor*. Only a disciplined use of configuration management tools with a strict development process, and an in-grained (or enforceable) change documentation practice, can ensure that code changes can be traced back to the corresponding business motivations. This is a lot of *ifs*.
Reusability	*Fair*. If the business logic is implemented in a service layer with well-defined interfaces, it may be possible to reuse the business rules.
Manageability	*Fair*. Manageability depends on the good will – and disciplines – of developers, who are expected to use configuration management tools and strictly adhere to development practices. Even when such developers can be found, one has to worry about personnel turnover, or offshore development.

involve dynamic questionnaires or product configuration. An example of such a rule is:

If the value of the selection on this page was <X> then add <Y> to the model

Similarly, a rule that controls the flow of pages could look like:

If the user visited page <X> and selected value <Y> in field <Z> then next page is <R>

Both rules may be enriched with business type conditions based on data available in the model. Many of the legacy web applications embed such (business) rules in the controller class or in scripts within the view (e.g., java script of the view). In terms of the architectural qualities discussed at the beginning of this section, this solution compares to implementing rules within application code (see Table 5.3).

Naturally, it is possible to implement controller rules using a rule engine – rule-engine implementation is discussed last. This is particularly valuable for e-commerce web sites where marketing campaign can be put in place quickly by proposing new products or new product features more dynamically. Typically, rule engines would apply a set of decisions according to previously entered data and web historical navigation. The actions of the rules could prepare some product or marketing information to display in the web page. As a rule of thumb using a rule engine in the controller is worthwhile if we need to change the logic over time, and this logic needs to take into account a lot of cross checks and complex data validations.

Our recommendation is to classify the business rules during the rule analysis, assess the rule change dimension, start to implement where it is the most efficient and makes more sense. Do not jump too quickly into the final design and conclusion. This is why the prototyping phase is important: try and catch the best implementation.

5.2.4 *Implementing Rules in Process Maps*

Business process automation (BPA) is the technology used in lieu of, or in addition to, manual processes to manage information flow within an organization. Business process automation (BPA) is supposed to lower costs, reduce risk, and increase consistency. In this context business rules embody the structure, operation, and strategy of an organization's business processes as well as the decisions within the activities of those processes. Sometimes the business process definition is itself considered as a business rule, as it embodies business decisions about how the process should be done. We do not share this view: the OMG clearly separates the business

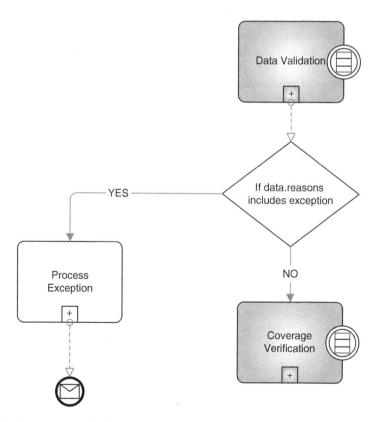

Fig. 5.2 Process map revisited

process from the business rules, where the former is driven by the latter. For a business process analyst, business rules involve routing of data, processing work items to a work queue, a task, or a sub process, which will most likely be implemented as a gateway in a process map. We have come across situations where some business rules were implemented in the process flow as a graph of gateways. A rule like:

> if a claim is for a car accident and there is no injured person then go to activity A, else if there is an injured person and the injured person is an insured person then go to activity B, else go to activity C.

Defined at the task relationship level, business rules are thus linked to the structure of the process flow. Another example, a rule like the one given below will most likely finish as a guard on a process map link.

> if there is an exception in the claim processing, we want a supervisor to study the claim and the accumulated reasons extracted by the process so far

Figure 5.2 illustrates such a process map.

In the example of Fig. 5.2, task 1 (Data validation) evaluates the data quality for the claim. This task can build a lot of issues on the data quality. If the list includes an exception or high priority issue, the process map will route to the "Process Exception" task. This task can queue the work item to a supervisor's queue with all the data needed for investigation.

If we embed the business rules directly in the *structure* of a process map, any changes to the business rules will require redefining and redeploying the process. This could be quite problematic with long-running process. Changing a business process is usually risky: we do not want to change things currently running that involve a lot of parties and stakeholders. New policies, regulations, or business strategies should affect the decision rules without having to change the core business processes.

Table 5.4 Rule in process flow assessment

Variable	Potential assessment
Adaptability	*Poor*. Hard coding business rules in process maps is not efficient, and leads to brittle and overly complex process maps.
	If we combine the business process management (BPM) with the business rule management systems (BRMS) approach, and delegate business rules to process tasks – as opposed to process structure – we achieve great adaptability.
Traceability	*Good*. if we combine BPM with BRMS, we get *excellent* traceability.
Auditability	*Good*. BPM tools typically have version control, and it is possible to trace process map changes to business requirements. When we combine BPMS and BPMS, we can take advantage of the versioning capabilities in both tools, and link process map versions to ruleset versions.
Reusability	*Fair*. Rules in a BPM map are not really reusable outside of the context of the process. However, rules defined in a task can be made reusable if they are exposed as a service. Further, a process itself can be exposed as a service.
Manageability	*Good*. Process logic will usually have a more stable life cycle, and it is managed in the BPMS.

Note, however, that there are a lot of tasks in a business process that are decision rich, with a lot of business rules to execute within the task. Those rules *can* be executed by a rule engine. The integration of BPM with BRM offers a unique set of features that support agile business processes. Table 5.4 shows how the process map implementation of business rules measures up relative to the five qualities we discussed. We will discuss both standalone BPM, and the BPM–BRM combination for decision-rich business processes.

5.2.5   Implementing Rules in a Rule Engine

Roughly speaking, a is an *interpreter* that takes two inputs, application data and business rules, and that produces a decision embodied in new data, or in new values of attributes for existing data. This is illustrated in Fig. 5.3. Chapter 6 discusses rule engines and rule-engine technology in-depth, but for the purposes of the current discussion, we will be content to illustrate the paradigm.

A key aspect of the rule-engine implementation is the fact that business rules are treated as *data* by the rule engine. This implies two things: (a) as data, they can be deployed separately from the application code, and better yet, (b) they can be *read-in during run-time*. This is the key to the *flexibility* and *adaptability* of the approach. Another key aspect of the rule-engine implementation is the fact that *the executable form* of the rules, *or a direct translation thereof*, can be understood by business. This is the key to the traceability and auditability of the approach. Table 5.5 evaluates the rule-engine implementation with regard to the five architectural qualities we discussed above.

During our consulting engagements, we have often come across some business-rules-approach-skeptics, who overplay the run-time performance argument,[1] and

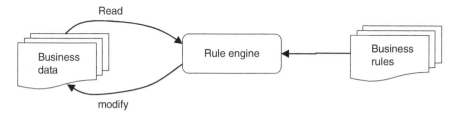

Fig. 5.3 A rule engine takes two inputs, a ruleset and business data, matches the rules to the business data, and acts on it accordingly

---

[1]The word "interprets" as in "the rule engine interprets the ruleset" can scare off many an architect. As we will see in Chap. 6, rule engines can execute tens of thousands of rules per second.

Table 5.5 Rule in rule engine

Quality	Potential assessment
Adaptability	*Excellent.* The rules can be changed quickly, off-line, and deployed, at the press of a button, often while the business application is running (a *hot deploy*). Obviously, rule governance processes need to be put in place to ensure orderly rule maintenance.
Traceability	*Excellent.* A key aspect of traceability is the fact that *most* rule engines (including JRules) support a natural language-like, domain-specific language for entering/authoring rules. This makes executable rules understandable to business. By adding rule metadata, we can capture quite a bit more about the *business context* or *motivation* of the rule.
Auditability	*Excellent.* this is made possible thanks to a number of features in commercial business rule management systems (BRMS) – including JRules, (a) powerful tracing capabilities that enables us to trace the rules that matched a specific business transaction, (b) rule reports, and (c) change management functionalities. The JRules BRMS, discussed in Chaps. 8, 10, 11, 13, 15, and 17, supports all of these, and more.
Reusability	*Very good*: Reusability is never an easy requirement to support, regardless of the technology. Good reusability results from a proper modularization of business logic along a hierarchy of decisions (decisions, and subdecisions) so that the lower-level decisions can be reused across major decision points or business processes. JRules supports a number of development and run-time rule structuring mechanisms which enable us to package rules in a way that is independent from their usage context (see Chaps. 10, 11, and 13).
Manageability	*Excellent.* By definition, business rule *management* systems (BRMS) support management functions. JRules supports a particularly rich set of management functionalities, including rule and rule set versioning, rule life cycle management, access control, and the like.

downplay the flexibility argument "our rules do not change often; we can afford to code them in application logic." For example, a rule such as the one given below may sound stable at first, with no possible variations.

If the status of the customer is gold and the product is <> then apply <> % discount.

However, discussions with the business about the meaning of "Gold customer" might identify other criteria that definitively change over time. A typical discussion may look like: "A customer who spend more than <> amount of money ... during the last 6 months ... well, except for product X where we only look at the last four months because product X has been in the market for that long ... and by the way, customers in the states A, B, and D could not be part of the gold status because ... and did we mention that a customer must be 18 years old or older ... and by the way, customers working for our company or subsidiaries cannot be part of the gold program". Before you know it, we have gone through an entire ruleset, just to capture this supposedly simple – and stable – piece of business logic.

Accordingly, our recommendation would be to use a rule engine to execute rules, or more broadly, a *business rules management system* to manage the life cycle and the execution of business rules. As shown in the previous sections, there are certain kinds of rules (e.g., structural assertion rules) or situations (e.g., the need for a responsive, client-side data validation) where the other alternatives may be given some consideration. However, by *default*, the recommendation is to use a rule-engine implementation. As we have shown in Sect. 5.2.4, rule engines can be combined with other technologies, such as business process management systems (BPMS) to get the best of both worlds.

5.3   Build Models

Having chosen a rule implementation, the next step is to implement the code infra-structure that will implement or use the rules identified during rule harvesting phase (see Chap. 4). The code infrastructure consists of two pieces: (a) the data model code, and (b) the application/service invocation code. With regard to the data model, within the context of rule applications BRMSs will distinguish between two models, (a) a *physical* or *executable* data model, implemented in the application's implementation language – Java, C#, etc. – or using XML Schema (XSD), and (b) a *business view* of the physical data model, used to author rules; Sect. 9.2.1 talks about the different requirements that we place in these languages, and how to keep them synchronized. In this section, we focus on the physical/implementation *data model*, and discuss how to build one during the prototyping cycle. However, as we show in Sect. 5.3.3, such a model needs to evolve constantly during this phase to accommodate the needs of rule authors as they write/prototype rules.

With regard to the application/service invocation code, we assume that the various decision points of our business process will be exposed as *decision services*, within the context of a service-oriented application. We will discuss some best practices regarding the packaging of such services. Chapters 12 and 13 will revisit this issue, in general, and within the context of JRules.

We start by discussing the implementation of the physical model in Java (Sect. 5.3.1). Section 5.3.2 talks about XSD specifics. Section 5.3.3 addresses model evolution during the prototyping phase.

5.3.1   Java Model

If the analysis model is available in UML format, most IDEs provide functionality to generate an implementation of the model in a number of target languages or technologies, including Java. Many IDEs will also offer the so-called round-trip engineering, where changes to the Java code are immediately reflected back to the UML model. Starting with a given UML model, it is recommended to generate the Java code in *different* projects, by applying the separation of concerns principle. For example, the data model definition should be kept separate from the definition of service/controller classes, the former being widely shared between different applications within the same domain, whereas the latter are specific to individual applications.

With regard to the application/invocation code, if we will deploy some of our services as web services using XML document/literal as the main communication style, the data model will need to be a mix of XSD and java model, with a mapping between the two. We can also generate the XML version of the Java model directly from the Java model by using the Java XML Binding API (JAXB 2.0) to annotate the business classes.

For most application implementations, we recommend to use a meet-the-middle approach for defining the web service interfaces: (a) use a bottom-up approach to define the XSD schema from the java model that was so far implemented and tested, and (b) use a top-down approach to define the web service contract (WSDL) first, and then implement some mapping objects, if needed, in the service implementation to map between the WSDL schema and the java model. For example, the WSDL interface for operations such as validateClaim, verifyCoverage and adjudicateClaim, should refer to claims through a String identifier, and then use that identifier internally to pull out the relevant data for the claim. This is preferable to having the service consumer be responsible for preparing all the data for the service provider. Not only the service consumer does not always have the "knowledge" of the required data structure, but using full objects as parameters lead to large messages. An exception to this model is when the consumer already has all the data and is delegating some of its *own* processing to another service.[2]

5.3.2 XML Schema

Using XML schema to define the data model has a number of advantages over a Java model, independent of the architecture of the application. From a data definition point of view, XSD has a richer set of constructs for expressing data extensions and refinements. For example with XSD, we can *specialize* a data type by restricting it, i.e., by constraining the set of values that the elements and attributes can take. Java has no equivalent for restriction: attributes are either inherited as is, or are hidden.[3]

Within the context of a web-services-based SOA, it makes sense to use an XSD implementation of the application data: indeed, the WSDL specification defines data types using XSDs. Idem for the general case of a message-oriented architecture: to the extent that application data will be shipped around in XML messages,

---

[2]This may sound like a common pattern, but it is not necessarily a good one from the point of view of SOA: the resulting service is not reusable and is specific/dedicated to its consumer.

[3]We can mimic restriction/specialization by redefining the setters in subclasses to make sure that only a specific subset of values is allowed. However, this would break polymorphism, and its promise of object substitutability.

we might as well define it directly in XML; this way, we will be dealing with a single data model, and we will be saving on data marshaling and un-marshaling. We have to be careful, though. There are a number of issues that we need to consider when using XSD. The first one is related to the versioning of such a schema and the complex management of version control and integrity between applications. The second issue is related to the use of industry models. Some industries have defined standard data models as set XSDs. For example, the telecommunications industry has developed the *SID Tele-Management Forum*, the real estate finance industry has developed MISMO, and the insurance industry has developed ACORD. Such models provide excellent sources for business *ontologies* and can – and should – be used as starting point for defining your own enterprise data model. However, they should not be used as is to write rules. Indeed, they typically expose an unnecessarily complex vocabulary to use for the rules, and business users will typically reject it.

The third issue raised by the use of an XSD implementation of the data model is the "decapsulation": the data elements and the business logic that manipulate them are implemented in different paradigms. This makes both reuse and testing more difficult. For example, with a Java implementation, we can easily use a unit-testing framework such as Junit to unit test our rules. This is more complicated and cumbersome with an XSD implementation. In fact, projects end up using a mix of Java and XSDs to define and manipulate data. Using JAXB2 we can generate java beans from the XML schema, and so offer also the service interface based on java objects.

5.3.3   Synchronize with the Data Models

During the prototyping phase, the data model will keep evolving. Rule authors will keep coming up with data elements that are missing from one of the many layers of data models starting with the underlying database, up the rule vocabulary. The different layers and the relations between them will be discussed in general terms in Sects. 7.6 and 9.2.1, and for the case of JRules, in Sects. 10.3 and 10.4.2. For the purposes of this discussion, it suffices to say that we need constant communication between the rule authors and IT to ensure rule author requests are handled diligently. There will be some changes, however, which have important implications and will not be resolved as quickly as everyone hopes for. For example, if a rule requires a data element that is not even available in the database, then we could have a serious problem. If the database is specific to the current application and is to be built from scratch, then we can pretty much put in it whatever we need – provided we know how to get it from external sources via other parts of the application. If the database is shared with other applications – as will often be the case – then we have a serious problem: Either the attribute is available somewhere else within the legacy systems landscape, in which case we have to figure out ways of *efficiently* pulling it out from those other sources, or it is a new data item that is not currently captured by the system, in which case we need to drop the business rule for the time being and redesign the business logic.

In addition to issues with the data *definition* (tables, attributes), we will have issues with data *Values*. Indeed, part of any business application is referential data which may include lists of codes and enumerated domain values, which rule writers use in the rules. It is important to properly design the way that data is defined and accessed by both the application and the rule-authoring environment. If the organization uses a Master Data Management (MDM) product to manage the referential data, we may need to be able to connect to the MDM from the rule-authoring environment and from the running application, using the MDM API or services.

Accessing the referential data for rule authoring can be done statically, to define the rule-authoring vocabulary – however that is defined – or dynamically, by filling out specific pull-down lists in the rule editor. A static implementation is simpler and more cost-efficient and is only appropriate when the referential data changes rarely at well-defined milestones in the life cycle of the project or application. If the referential data changes frequently, then a dynamic implementation is preferred. Depending on the BRMS product this can be easy or quite cumbersome. To access the referential data during rule execution, we should probably use a hybrid approach: reference data may be accessed dynamically, at specific times (e.g., at server start-up, or some fixed regular schedule), and remain cached in the application for rules to access them in the most efficient way; doing one or more round trips to a MDM service during a ruleset execution may not be such a good idea.

5.4 Building Structures for Rule Development and Execution

Before we start coding rules, we need to set-up the rule development infrastructure. This infrastructure has to facilitate rule development, management, and packaging/deployment, to an execution environment. Later chapters will explore all of these issues in detail. In this section, we limit ourselves to describing the process and highlighting the major issues. Section 5.4.1 will discuss the rule project structure. In Sect. 5.4.2, we look at the issue of designing/defining rule metadata. Finally, we look at orchestrating rule execution in Sect. 5.4.3.

5.4.1 Rule Project Structure

A rule project is a container for rule artifacts. Such artifacts include business and technical rules, decision tables and decision trees, functions, variables, rule flows, and ruleset parameters. Rule projects also help package and deploy rules for execution. One of the issues that we face when moving from rule analysis to prototyping is to decide how many rule projects we should have. The simplest design is to have one rule project per major decision point of the business process. It will often be the case that several decision points may share the same set of rules. To promote the reuse of those common rules, we may have to associate several projects with a single decision point. Different BRMSs might make this more or less easy. JRules's support for project dependencies, and for configurable *ruleset extractors*, gives rule architects plenty of degrees of freedom to structure rule projects to accommodate the needs of rule authors during rule authoring, and to make rule deployment and execution flexible. Rule project organization is more thoroughly discussed in Sect. 9.4, where we focus on development-time organization, in a tool-independent way, and in Sect. 10.2, where we focus on JRules's rule project organization features. For the purposes of this discussion, we will limit ourselves to some general issues, and to the relationships between rule projects, and projects related to relevant parts of the application.

The organization of rule projects and java projects follows the same pattern as traditional project organization. We partition the work to avoid concurrent updates as much as possible and define the structure to reflect business structure or technical and deployment constraints. For example, if the application uses a web tier it is important to isolate this project within a web project. Further, the services can be packaged in one java project or per major service component. The code which calls the rule engine is part of this project. Maybe one of the interesting differences with *n*-tier application structure is the fact that we are using separate projects to support the data model for the domain; it could be java classes or XML schema definitions. This project is shared between the rule projects and the application tiers and even among applications. The rule project structure should strive to isolate the rules and the subset of the business object model used by those rules in a separate rule project. Best practices for rule project organization are discussed, in general terms, in Sect. 9.4.3, and for the case in JRules, in Sect. 10.4.1.

Figure 5.4 shows an example project structure that adopts some of the basic best practices, illustrated for our case study. In this case, we have three Java/nonrule projects, which include the physical data model (the ClaimModel Java project), the claim processing service implementation (project ClaimProcessing-core), and the web application that invokes the service (project ClaimProcessing-webapp). We have three separate rule projects, each handing a nontrivial decision step of the business process, namely, validateClaim-rules, adjudicateClaim-rules, and verify-Coverage-rules.

When designing the rule project structure, an architect needs to consider the overall business context requirements. Indeed, looking at the big picture is always a good thing. At the same time, it should not jeopardize the short-term goals of getting a quick prototypical implementation, or delivery timeline for the entire project, through some sort of *analysis paralysis*. And remember, if this is your first rule project, getting the technology adopted at the enterprise level requires unmitigated success at the project level – or a very dedicated CTO. That being said, rule architects can consider some of the design drivers discussed in Sect. 9.4.

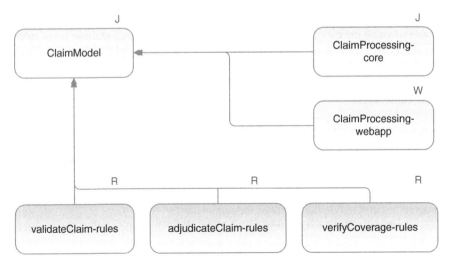

Fig. 5.4 Example of projects organization

5.4.2 Defining Rule Meta Data

During the project structure definition it makes sense to also address the life cycle of the rules under scope and to define rule properties/metadata that the business team may want to leverage during the rule management and the rule execution. The common properties we use are:

- *Rule ID, author, owner, status.* To trace the rule maintenance process. The status helps to manage the rule life cycle, for example, to avoid deploying rules under development to production. The possible values for the status can be configured and customized.
- *Expiration date, effective date.* To filter the rules according to a date and time.
- *Business motivation, policy reference, requirement reference.* To reference rules back to the requirements, the business policies, or the specifications.
- *Product reference, states, geographies.* To manage rules per type of deployment or other dimensions relevant to the business.

Properties such as rule effective date and expiration date can be used to filter out the rules that do not apply to a given business event. Another example is the geography or jurisdiction dimension, which can limit the applicability of a rule to entities (customers, properties, etc.) that fall within their jurisdiction. This filtering can happen either during ruleset packaging (e.g., effective and expiration date), or during execution (e.g., jurisdiction). The following table elaborates on the characteristics of those properties that the rule analyst can design for the future rule management:

Property name	Type	Values	Description	Nullable	Changeable	Useful for deployment or run-time?	Required
Rule ID	Int or string		Unique identifier for the rules	No	No	No	Yes
BusinessMotivation	String	""	Link the rule to the business motivation	Yes	Yes	No	No
PolicyReference	String	""	Link the rule to a business policy	Yes	Yes	No	No
Status	String	New, Defined, Deployable, Deployed, retired	Support the life cycle of the rule	No	Yes	Yes	Yes
Rule Owner	String		Department team – no named person	Yes	Yes	No	Yes
Expiration Date	Date		Date when the rule will not be extracted	Yes	Yes	Yes	No
Effective Date	Date		Date from when the rule will be extracted	Yes	Yes	Yes	No
Jurisdiction	Enumeration	For example, California, Nevada, Oregon, Arizona, Utah	List the states where the companies have branch offices and can insure person	Yes	Yes	Yes	No

As you can tell from this table, some properties may be useful for deployment or run-time. We say *may* because it depends on the BRMS being used, in general, and the underlying rule engine in particular. For example, the rule status, which indicates the status/state of a rule within its life cycle, may be useful to a deployment tool to determine which rules get deployed and which rules do not. Rule jurisdiction, effective date, and expiration date can be used during run-time to determine which rules apply to a given business event, based on its localization and occurrence date. The JRules BRMS supports a flexible and customizable ruleset extraction and deployment tool, which relies on user-defined queries to select which rules of a given project are to be extracted and deployed for a particular decision/ruleset. A number of other features enable us also to filter rule during run-time based on their properties, including so-called *dynamic rule selection*, discussed in Chap. 11, and agenda filtering (see Chap. 6).

5.4.3 Orchestrating Rule Execution

The rule project structure discussed in Sect. 5.4.1 is aimed primarily at managing rule development in a way that promotes an effective division of labor and rule reuse. In this section, we focus on the *run-time* structure of a ruleset. While the rule engines and the underlying production paradigm (see Chap. 6) do not require an internal structure to the ruleset,[4] the kinds of decisions that we map to a ruleset will often involve a series of stable and well-defined subdecisions. In that case, it makes sense to orchestrate/organize rule execution *within* the ruleset accordingly. Further, some decisions may involve hundreds or even thousands of rules. By structuring their execution within the ruleset, we ensure that only a subset of them will be evaluated at any given point in the execution of the ruleset. Hence the concept of *ruleflow*, which is supported by several BRMS, including JRules.

Rule flows typically consist of linked tasks, each of which contains a subset of rules to execute. If we think of a ruleset as a library of simple functions, a ruleflow can be thought of as a loosely structured main program. We say *loosely* structured because the rules *within a task* of the rule flow are unordered and are considered as a "bag of rules." A ruleflow typically looks like a process flow with tasks, transitions (guarded or not), starting and ending nodes, fork and join operators, and condition nodes. But the scope is different from that of a process flow: tasks can only include a set of rules, and the parameters needed to control their execution, with no external call, work queue, or work item like we have in a workflow engine. The execution of a ruleflow typically corresponds to single *synchronous* invocation of the rule engine. Depending on the BRMS, ruleflows may also help improve execution performance. In IBM WebSphere ILOG JRules, we can select different execution

---

[4]We can give a rule engine a "bag of rules" and it will sort its way through, thanks to rule dependencies and rule chaining.

algorithms for the different tasks of the ruleflow, taking advantage of the dependencies that may exist – or not – between the rules of a given task. Chapter 11 will explain JRules ruleflows, in far more detail, and will provide heuristics and best practices for designing ruleflows. For the purposes of this chapter, we will simply stress the following points:

- An initial rule flow design needs to take place during prototyping, prior to rule authoring.
- The structure of the ruleflow has to make sense from a business point of view, i.e., it has to reflect, somehow, the business structure of a (nontrivial) decision; we should not code *algorithms* using ruleflows.
- At the same time, in terms of a granularity, a ruleflow corresponds to a single invocation of the rule engine, and no heavy lifting (e.g., accessing external resources) should take place within a ruleflow.

One technique for designing a rule flow relies on the *life cycle of business objects*. Indeed, in those applications where the processing of some business objects goes through a number of discrete and identifiable stages, it helps to build a *finite state machine* (FSM) to model the evolution of the business entities through the business process. For example, a claim typically goes through several *processing stages*, from not-processed, to having its data validated (e.g., filtering out claims with null or invalid required fields), to having its coverage validated (to ensure that what is claimed is covered by the underlying policy), to being fully processed/ adjudicated. The transition from one processing stage to the next requires some checks and verifications (i.e., rules) to be performed, and a specific outcome (e.g., pass versus fail). This can be readily modeled as an FSM. This FSM can serve as the basis for designing the ruleflow.

> ***Concept*: Finite State Machine**
> In business application, FSM[5] is used to design *life cycle* of business entities, as it represents a number of *finite states* a business entity can have over time. A *state* is materialized by a node in a graph. Actions change the state. A business entity starts its life cycle on a *start* state, and then goes through transitions until it reaches an *end* state. The arrows from a node represent the different actions the business entity supports at the current state. A current *state* is determined by past states and the events received. The UML notation includes *state charts*, which are nothing but a (compact) variant of finite state machines, with things such as state generalization and state aggregation.

Within a BPM–BRM approach, the use of FSM for the important business object is a standard design approach. It is important to note, however, that FSMs are not sufficient to describe the business process. Indeed, an FSM follows a unique path whereas a business process can have multiple concurrent paths of execution.

---

[5]See also Wikipedia http://en.wikipedia.org/wiki/Finite-state_machine.

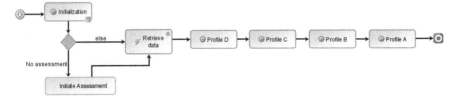

Fig. 5.5 Rule flow for a risk assessment ruleset

Figure 5.5 shows a sample – and realistic – rule flow for a risk assessment ruleset. The flow starts by making some initialization, mostly to prepare for the rule execution, and checking whether there is a risk assessment already available for this customer. If not, the rule flow triggers an assessment process by going to the left branch. If an assessment is available, it goes through a step by step evaluation of the customer risk profile, where the customer is to be classified according to one of four profiles. We start with the worse case, i.e., *Profile D. Profile* D includes rules about government blacklisted persons, or bank blacklisted customers, high-risk benefici-aries, etc. If a customer record does not match rules for profile D, they may match rules for the subsequent profile. If a customer record fails to match any of the earlier profiles, it will get assigned profile A, which is the best risk profile. This is a real-life example that illustrates the concepts presented above.

More ruleflow design guidelines will be presented in Sects. 11.3 and 11.4.

5.5   Prototyping Rules

Prototyping rules is a very important step in ABRD as it enables us to stabilize many of the design choices needed before we start tackling high-volume rule authoring in the building phase. We first describe the purpose of rule prototyping, and then discuss some rule coding patterns.

5.5.1   *Purpose of Rule Prototyping*

Rule prototyping enables us to:

1. *Validate the data models.* As mentioned in Sect. 5.3.3, regardless of how careful we were with the data model coming out of the analysis phase, as we start writing rules, we will invariably discover missing attributes – and sometimes, classes – that we needed to add.
2. *Validate the structures for rule development.* This concerns rule project struc-tures, rule metadata, and the rule flow. Indeed, by starting to input real rules, we will get an idea about whether the rule project structure makes sense/is

workable, about whether the rule metadata makes sense for all rules and, conversely, whether we need more properties. It will also help us partially validate the ruleflow by checking, among other things, if it enforces some of the rule dependencies identified during analysis.

3. *Identify and try out rule coding patterns.* Generally speaking, the rules that come out of rule analysis will map to a handful of rule types, such as *constraints*, *guidelines*, *action enablers*, and the like. They will also map to some *business decision patterns*. There are some well-documented type-specific patterns, which will be presented in Sect. 9.3, and which are true and tested. However, here we talk about *business-specific patterns*, which need to be identified, formalized, and encoded in the prototyping phase, so that they may be used on a wide scale during the building phase.

4. *Set-up a unit-testing framework.* More often than not, rule authoring starts well before the rest of the application is developed. Rule authors need a way to test rules that is independent of the full computational infrastructure of the application. A test harness needs to be set-up for this purpose, which can feed business data to a rule engine (or a rule service) for testing.

The first three goals require us to prototype a *representative subset* of the rules to be developed during the "Building" phase. If our process involves claim data validation, claim coverage verification, and claim adjudication, we should implement a representative subset of the data validation rules, another subset from the coverage verification rules, and a third subset from the adjudication rules, e.g., to tackle a particular use case. Selecting that representative subset requires a good knowledge of the business rules within the domain, and should be done with the help of business: they know which rules are more complex than others, and which ones will exercise exotic corners of the data model – and thus, uncover missing attributes or classes.

5.5.2 Some Useful Rule Patterns

In this section, we present two useful, domain-independent patterns. The first is related to collecting the results of rule firings without corrupting the business objects. The second is related to buffering rule actions until the ruleset finishes executing. The third is related to testing for data quality first, before *semantic* data validation.

5.5.2.1 Pattern 1: Providing Decision Explanations and Audits

In any ruleset making decisions or performing validations, it is a good practice to provide accumulated explanations on the issues found or the decisions taken during ruleset execution. The action part of the rule adds the issue to a collection of issues

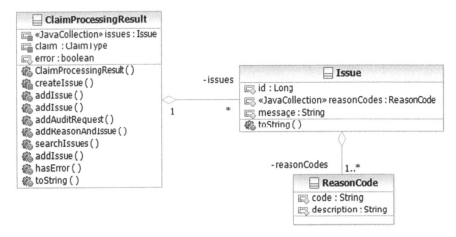

Fig. 5.6 Result data model

already found. The supporting model is simple and may look like that in Fig. 5.6, with one Result object (**ClaimProcessingResult**) associated to the main business entity – not shown in this Fig. 5.6, but assumed to be a **Claim**. The result object includes a set of *Issue*'s, and issues can use reasons (**ReasonCode**) defined in a central master data repository.

With this data model a business rule could look like:

```
if
    The day of loss of 'the claim' is before the effective date of 'the policy'
then
    add to 'the result' the issue : "claim date error" with a code "R02" and a descrip-
tion : "claim is before effective date of the policy";
```

5.5.2.2   Pattern 2: Delaying Rule Actions

There are situations when rule actions are supposed to trigger some process that we do not wish to perform immediately, for a variety of reasons, including:

- *Remoteness*. Within the context of a remote rule execution service, executing the desired actions would require remote calls.
- *Exception handling*. If any of the actions raises an exception, we want a caller-specific exception handler.
- *Transaction management and compensation*. If a block of actions fails, we may not want, or be able to perform an outright rollback: we may want to manage which steps are allowed to stand, which are rolled back, and which steps are compensated for.
- *Override*. We may want to be able to override the recommendation of the engine if it conflicts with other information.

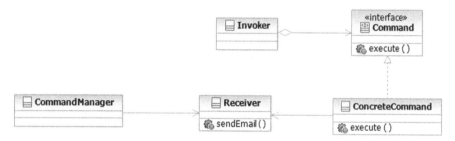

Fig. 5.7 Command pattern

For all of these reasons, the *Command* design pattern[6] may be useful within the context of rule actions. The *Command* pattern is used when the object which invokes a command is not the same object that executes it. For example, in a cross-sell business ruleset, the intent of the rules is to compute the best promotion, or actions for this given customer, customer profile, and customer history. If the action is meant to send an e-mail or an SMS, we may not want to keep sending individual SMSs for each rule that fires: we collect the messages during rule execution and then send them (or collate them) once we come out of the engine. The *command* pattern elements are shown in Fig. 5.7.

The solution is to have the rules create a ConcreteCommand by using a CommandManager in the action part of the rule. The execution of the command is postponed to a later step of the application flow by an Invoker object. Using add < > methods, the CommandManager creates instances of ConcreteCommand and sets the Receiver object for that command, which is an object that will be notified when the command is executed. The notification can be as simple as "I am done", to a full execution report. In turn, the Receiver can perform other actions to relay the information, such as sending e-mails or messages to human actors. This is useful in those cases where we have a human task in a work flow and we want the human to act on the command created by the rule engine. In this case, the e-mail would contain the relevant information the human will need, including, for example, links to confirm certain actions. A further refinement of this pattern would buffer notifications to only forward the most relevant ones, or to send an aggregated notification (e.g., e-mail) that covers all of the actions proposed by the actions of the rules.

5.5.2.3 Pattern 3: Test for Data Quality Before Business Logic

When the data that comes into the rule engine may have quality issues, it is common to prefix the business rules conditions with data quality checks to avoid null pointer exceptions or meaningless inferences. The following rule excerpts illustrate the pattern:

> if the procedure code is not null and the procedure code is equal to 55 and ....

---

[6]See detail http://en.wikipedia.org/wiki/Command_pattern.

We are likely to find the condition "the procedure code is not null" at the beginning of the action part of every rule of the current rule task of ruleset. This is somewhat awkward as it mixes "computational" conditions with business conditions, almost like saying "if the database connection is open and the credit score is higher than 650 . . .". Worse yet, it places an undue burden on rule authors to test for data quality issues in every rule they write: they will have to know which fields are nullable – legitimately – and which are not, and they have to be disciplined about writing their conditions. In such cases, the recommended practice is to separate data quality issues from business conditions that use the data. Thus, we can leverage the rule flow to address the data quality tests at the beginning and assume that these conditions are true in subsequent tasks – and in rules that go into those tasks. This solution has its disadvantages, however: it makes the rules *somewhat* contextual. As always, design is a trade-off: we have to choose our pain.

5.6 Case Study

One of the first issues that we need to address during prototyping is the data model. As explained in Sect. 5.3.3, it is in this phase that we concretely confront the data model to the rules, to identify which data is missing, and to complete it. The following table shows a sample of issues concerning the data model, and proposed ways of addressing them.

Issue	Action plan
Day of service for the bill detail is missing.	Add the date attribute to the medical invoice and to the bill detail.
Where are the medical procedure codes defined?	They are defined in an external system accessible through a data source. We need to cache them for the execution of the rules, but also for the authoring of the rules (see discussion in Sect. 5.3.3). For the time being, there are only ten codes in scope for the rules, and thus, we can handle them using a simple Java enumeration.
Claim and MedicalInvoice have nontrivial life cycles.	Need to design FSMs to support them (see Sect. 5.4.3).
The reason codes we are adding to explain the rejection of the claim or of the medical invoice should be defined in a central repository.	Implement a central reference data or use a MDM product. The reason codes can be defined during rule authoring, but later be externalized in the reference data or MDM repository. They should be accessible, programmatically, from the rule authoring and rule execution environments.
Avoid coding treatment code in the medical bill, use a treatment object that can be also populated from a predefined set of treatments.	

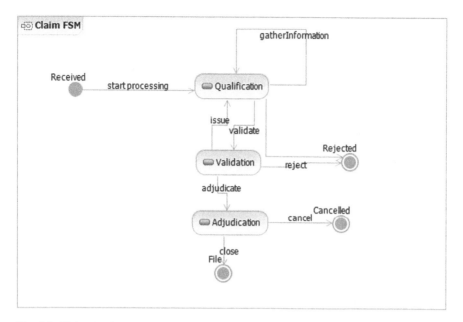

Fig. 5.8 Claim simple state machine version 1

As mentioned above, the major business entities such as **Claim** and **Medical-Invoice** have nontrivial life cycles. We propose to define the following simple FSM for the entity **Claim**, which we will enhance later in the project implementation (Fig. 5.8).

After the start of processing, the claim may be canceled at any step which is not represented in this FSM. A claim can be rejected if it has issues or during validation if it violates hard constraint rules. The completion of the adjudication step is to pay or not the claim, so the final state is to file the claim. The claimed amount and the paid amount are kept for record. This FSM can serve as the basis for the ruleflow. However, if we deem that the intermediate tasks involve lots of decisions, and that we need to access external resources between two tasks, then clearly, this FSM should not be implemented within a single ruleflow. In our particular case, qualification, validation, and adjudication can involve thousands of rules each, and represent major decisions each. Further, it is likely that adjudication will require us to pull data out of external resources as we need to look at procedure codes, payment and claim history, and the like. Hence, this is a clear-cut case where the FSM is implemented outside of the rules. There are multiple ways of implementing the FSM outside of the rules, including regular Java code, a BPEL process, or a mix of the two. Either way, it is within the context of this FSM that we would invoke a rule service to execute the rulesets appropriate for each decision.

With regard to the rule organization, a first look at the "validate claim" ruleset/decision point reveals two fairly distinct types of validations: validating the claim itself, and in case of an accident with bodily injuries, the medical invoices linked to the claim. These are clearly two different concerns, so we can design two rule projects to support the two types of validations. Further, the two validation decisions refer to two fairly distinct data models: one having to do with accident reports and equipment damage and repair and the other to bodily injuries, medical procedures, and health care providers. Thus, we can have two different Java projects to define the business objects needed by the two decisions, and two additional projects to support service definition and implementation.

5.7 Communicate Back to Business

The last step of the prototyping is to produce reports from the different rule projects, collect test execution traces, if needed, and log any issues we may have found during these steps. Showing executable rules with actual test cases to subject matter experts (SME) has a much bigger impact than well-documented policies. Concrete test scenarios and execution reports have the virtue of helping to identify issues with the ruleset, in a palpable and nonambiguous manner, and it helps the various stakeholders address these issues early on and fix them before going into the building phase (see Chap. 4), or worse, during production.

5.8 Summary

Rule prototyping is a very important phase in the ruleset development life cycle as it forces us to exercise the major design decisions early on and provides a quick value to the various stakeholders. We presented the common activities that are part of this phase, putting emphasis on (a) a data model driven by the business entities as expressed by the rules and not a data model as defined by industry standards or enterprise models (Sect. 5.3); (b) a development organization structure (Sect. 5.4) that promotes separation of concerns, an effective division of labor, and reuse; and (c) working and tested rules, understandable by the business users (Sect. 5.5). We presented some generic best practices for all of these design decisions; more best practices will be presented within the context of more in-depth discussions of the design trade-offs, in general (Chaps. 7, 9, and 12), and for the case of JRules (Chaps. 10, 11, and 13).

The deliverables of this prototyping phase are by no means throw-away artifacts: we use the term *prototyping* only as recognition of the exploratory nature of some of the design choices, and the inevitable refinement that will follow.

5.9   Further Reading

- ABRD is an Eclipse Process Framework practice plugin readers may find at http://www.eclipse.org/epf and within the practice library at http://www.eclipse.org/epf/downloads/praclib/praclib_downloads.php
- The ACORD data model can be found at http://www.acord.org
- Explanations about the *Adaptive Object Model* pattern, by Joe Yoder, are available at http://adaptiveobjectmodel.com/
- For an introductory definition of *finite state machines*, check http://en.wikipedia.org/wiki/Finite-state_machine
- The Tele-management forum is actively maintaining a rich data model, SID, as reference model for telecom service providers and vendors. Readers can see more detail and download the model at http://www.tmforum.org/Information-Framework/1684/home.html
- MISMO is accessible at http://www.mismo.org
- Test-driven development is covered in lots of books, but was developed by Ken Beck in his book: Beck, K. Test-Driven Development by Example, Addison Wesley, 2003

Part III
Foundations

Chapter 6
Rule Engine Technology

Target audience

- *Developer (must); optional for anyone wishing to look under the hood*

In this chapter you will learn

- *The history of rule-based decision making*
- *The principles of rule engines, and the implications of object-rule systems*
- *The basics of the RETE algorithm*
- *The different rule engine execution algorithms*

Key points

- *Rule-based decision making has a long history and some cognitive plausibility.*
- *Rules are treated as data processed by an interpreter – the rule engine.*
- *In the production system ideal, the "intelligence" is in the rules as opposed to the control mechanism of the engine, which should remain simple.*
- *The JRules rule engine is a Java object that "reasons about" Java application objects.*
- *The RETE algorithm makes the production system paradigm computationally efficient.*
- *Decisions that do not require rule chaining can use simpler – and an order of magnitude faster – execution algorithms.*

6.1 Introduction

In this chapter, we explain rule engines and rule-based programming. We start by briefly describing the history of rule-based programming, in Sect. 6.2. Rule-based programming belongs to the family of *production systems*, which can be thought of as

J. Boyer and H. Mili, *Agile Business Rule Development*,
DOI 10.1007/978-3-642-19041-4_6, © Springer-Verlag Berlin Heidelberg 2011

a *programming paradigm* in the same way that *object-orientation* is a programming paradigm. By the same token, we go over some of the tenets of *production systems* which find expression in some of the design guidelines for rule authoring, to be covered in Chaps. 9 and 11. In Sect. 6.3, we describe the structure of a rule engine and explain the basics of its inner workings. In particular, we go over the characteristics of production systems in general (Sect. 6.3.1), and then talk about the JRules rule engine (Sect. 6.3.2). Section 6.4 describes the three rule execution algorithms supported by JRules, namely, a simplified version of the *RETE* algorithm, which is supported by all the "modern" rule engines, the sequential algorithm, some version of which is supported by some rule engines, and the Fastpath algorithm, which is specific to the JRules rule engine. Truth be told, our (simplified) description of RETE and sequential algorithms are *also* tainted by the way JRules does it, to support our discussion of the choice of an execution algorithm in Chap. 11. We conclude in Sect. 6.5. Material for further reading is provided in section on "Further Reading."

Note that Sects. 6.2 and 6.3.1 owe much to the still current *The Origin of Rule-Based Systems in AI*, by Randall Davis and Jonathan King (1984), two rule-based system pioneers. However, any misinterpretations, inaccuracies, or gross simplifications are our own.

6.2   The History of Rule-Based Programming

Rule-based programming is part of a long tradition in computing called *production systems*. Production systems can be seen as having three distinct lineages:

1. Mathematics and theory of computation, through work of Emil Post (1897–1954) a Polish-born American logician who tried to design a universal *computation* machine, not unlike Turing's machine[1]
2. Cognitive psychology, as a way of modeling cognitive processes, including recognition and problem solving tasks
3. Artificial intelligence applications, and more specifically, knowledge-based ones, whose expertise is expressed *declaratively* as a set of if-then rules

It is not clear how much Post's work influenced the use of production systems in cognitive modeling and knowledge-based applications. However, it does provide a somewhat stylized theoretical foundation for the paradigm.

As has been the case in other areas of artificial intelligence and cognitive science, the two fields pursued two different objectives but mutually enriched each other. Cognitive psychology is concerned with understanding *human cognitive processes*. Cognitive psychologists develop *models* for such things as memory

---

[1]Post did not call his contraption a "machine," but called it "worker" or "problem solver" (see *Emil Post*, by Alasdair Urquhart, in *Handbook of the History of Logic, vol 5: Logic from Russell to Church*, eds Dov M. Gabbay and John Woods, Elsevier, Amsterdam, pp. 429–478).

(short- and long term), recall, recognition, categorization, and various types of problem-solving tasks such as planning, diagnosis, etc. Naturally, these models need to be *cognitively plausible*, that is, they need to be able to *mimic* or *explain* some *observed behavior* in psychological experiments, such as error rates or time delays in performing certain tasks. Note that here we are not concerned about *structural plausibility* of the models, that is, whether these models are good models of the actual *hardware* (the brain, neurons, etc.), although much has been made about *neural networks*, which *happen* to be biologically inspired.[2]

So what evidence do we have that our brain works like a rule engine interpreting rules? Allen Newell (1973) has been able to *model* human behavior on some cognitive tasks using a production system and task-specific rules. Further, if we compare the performance of a novice to that of an *expert*, in *any domain*, we know that novices solve problems from first-principles, whereas experts use *rules* that they have developed through their practice. These "chunks" of knowledge can typically emerge in one of two ways. First, they can emerge through repeated co-occurrences of certain events whereby we establish some sort of causality – or at least a strong correlation. For example, an *experienced* mechanic will know, with a high probability, that problem/symptom X with car model Y, or car model year Y, is due to the wear of part Z: he or she has had to investigate so many instances of the problem where part Z turned out to be the cause, that he or she can make the connection with a high level of confidence. A *very good* mechanic or a *quality engineer* will even know *why* part Z wears/breaks often (design, material, etc.), but that is a different diagnostic task. If a groundhog sees its shadow on Groundhog Day, it is going to be a long winter.[3] An insurance underwriter "knows" (statistics bore that out) that a young male driver is a high-risk one or that certain car models are more prone to theft than others.

The other way that rules can *emerge* is through what cognitive psychologists have sometimes called "chunking." One example of chunking is "short-circuiting" a long inference. What is the effect of raising interest rates on employment? Let us see: it increases the cost of borrowing for consumers, and *consequently* they refrain from borrowing to purchase stuff, and *consequently* inventory builds up, at current production levels, and *consequently* companies shed unneeded workers.[4] This may reflect the reasoning of a (bright) freshman economy student, but an economist, having gone through that inference before, will jump to the end result: *raising interest rates lowers employment*.

---

[2]Mathematically speaking, a *neural network* can be thought of as a special kind of *numerical classifier*. By varying the topology of the network and the behavior of the individual neurons/nodes, we get different mathematical behaviors (convergence, types of classes that can be identified/isolated, etc.).

[3]Check http://en.wikipedia.org/wiki/Groundhog_Day for this North American folklore.

[4]It also increases the cost of borrowing for companies, which cannot even expand in foreign markets, and it makes interest-bearing investment products more attractive than stocks, which further starves companies for capital, stunting their growth.

Let us now look at how *artificial intelligence* adopted – and adapted – this computational metaphor. Generally speaking, "artificial intelligence" applications aim at providing solutions to problems that do not have known or computationally tractable, algorithmic solutions. Traditionally, researchers have taken two general approaches to solving such problems: either devise smart algorithms or design a *knowledge-based* system that uses a general purpose problem solver that manipulates a domain-specific "knowledge base." The first generation of chess-playing programs used the first strategy: a *smart* algorithm.[5] *Knowledge-based expert systems*, on the other hand, used the second approach, which has been used to solve problems ranging from medical diagnosis (e.g., INTERNIST, MYCIN) to mineral prospection (PROSPECTOR), to chemical analysis (DENDRAL), to hardware design (X-CON), and many more application areas.

AI researchers, who were more concerned about the performance of their applications than they were about the cognitive plausibility of their creations, tweaked the *production system* paradigm to a great extent, mixing complex rule formats, with complex control and inference mechanisms, sometimes straying away from the production system "ideal" (Davis and King 1984) However, because the expert knowledge needs to be elicited from experts, and the results explained to experts and novices alike, those same AI researchers have also contributed to cognitive modeling by helping us understand how experts internalize and externalize their expertise, and by developing models, techniques, and tools for *knowledge extraction*.[6] In fact, the (business) rule discovery techniques of today are often business adaptations of the *knowledge engineering* techniques developed by AI researchers.

Naturally, the rule-based applications of today are fairly different from the AI applications of the 1980s. Traditional AI rule-based systems focused on knowledge areas where expertise was rare, expensive, or inaccessible, and hence the focus on advanced engineering and scientific domains. Rule-based business applications "borrow" the rule paradigm but for different reasons: they help externalize, share, and maintain consensus business knowledge that, more often than not, is already known and codified in the procedural code of legacy applications. Thus, both the *business* rules and the control mechanisms used to execute them tend to be rather simple. As mentioned in Chap. 1, rule-engine execution of business rules is but *one* aspect of the business rules approach, the others being business knowledge sharing and management.

In the next section, we first describe the *production system ideal*, and then describe the JRules rule engine, which is typical of rule engines operating on objects, in the OOP sense.

---

[5]It is theoretically possible to develop a chess playing program that explores *all* of the legal moves to pick ones that lead to checkmates ... the problem is there are over 10^{43} legal chess positions and it would take forever to explore them! AI researchers have developed *approximate* and *smart* search algorithms that explore only a few moves ahead (and hence, *approximate*) and that know how to focus on *promising* moves (hence *smart*). "Modern" chess playing programs also rely on a database of classical openings and end games.

[6]The term "extraction" may be evocative of *tooth extraction*. Without the appropriate techniques, the process can indeed be as painful to both the expert and the knowledge engineer.

6.3   Rule Engines

In this section, we first present the basic architecture of a production system, and discuss some of its variants. In Sect. 6.3.2, we present the JRules engine.

6.3.1   The Basics of Production Systems

A production system is typically defined in terms of three components:

1. A set of rules, or *ruleset*
2. A database
3. An interpreter

The *ruleset* is an unordered set of rules, consisting of expressions of the type *LHS* → *RHS*, where LHS and RHS stand for *left-hand side* and *right-hand side*, respectively. The database consists of a (typically) unordered set of elements, and the *interpreter* is the processor that applies the rules to the database. The process goes as follows: the *interpreter* matches the LHS parts of the *rules* of the *ruleset* against the *database*, and if a match is found for a particular *rule*, that rule is *executed*, which will typically *modify the database*. This process repeats as long as matches can be found, and terminates only when no LHS of a rule matches the current state of the database. This simple architecture belies a wide range of production systems ranging in complexity from abstract symbol manipulation machines to medical diagnosis expert systems (e.g., the MYCIN or INTERNIST family) to circuit layout designers (X-CON) to the decision component of a claim processing application or a mortgage underwriting system. What distinguishes these systems?

1. The structure of objects of the database. These can range in complexity from simple symbols (strings) to stateful, history-aware objects.
2. The structure of the rules, which can range in complexity from simple rewriting (symbol transformation) rules to having access to the full power of a modern programming language in both the LHS and RHS.
3. The functioning of the interpreter, and, more specifically, the algorithm and data structures used by the interpreter to control the evaluation and execution of the rules.

The JRules rule engine, to be discussed in Sect. 6.3.2, manipulates stateful, history-aware Java objects using the full power of the Java language in both the LHS and RHS of rules. It also supports a rich set of control structures and rule execution algorithms, to be discussed in Sect. 6.4, and again in Chap. 11, when we talk about *ruleset orchestration*. We will discuss these aspects in due time. For the purposes of this section, we explore the basic functioning of a production system using the simplest of rules and the simplest of databases.

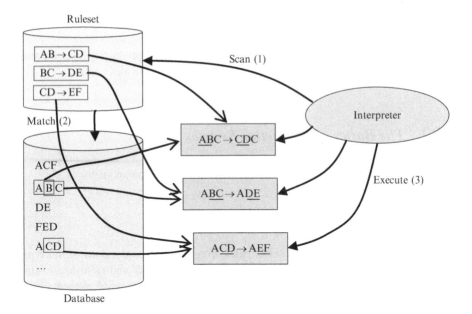

Fig. 6.1 The typical production system process cycle: (1) scan, (2) match, and (3) execute

Figure 6.1 shows a simple production system where the database consists of a set of strings (*symbols*) and the rules consist of string transformation (or rewriting) rules. In this case, the three rules match strings in the database: the (rewrite) rule AB → CD matches the string ABC (the first two letters), the rule BC → DE matches the same string ABC (the last two letters), and the rule CD → EF matches the string ACD (last two letters). The pair consisting of a rule and a matching string will be called *rule instance*. In this case, we have three *rule instances*, <AB → CD, ABC>, <BC → DE, ABC>, and < CD → EF, ACD>. To facilitate reading, we underlined the matching substring in each rule instance.

This simple example raises a number of questions about the functioning of the interpreter:

1. What order do we use to evaluate the rules on the database – and does it matter?
2. If a match is found, do we immediately execute the corresponding rule, or do we continue exploring other rule-data matches until we are through with all the rules, before we execute any rule; we refer to the latter as *batching rule execution*.
3. If we choose to batch rule execution and we identify several *rule instances*, which rule instance should we fire first – and does it matter which ordering we use?
4. If we batch rule execution, do we perform a full <ruleset, database> scan after each rule execution or do we wait until we complete executing the whole batch?

These are all *parameters* of the interpreter's *control strategy* and different production systems have used different combinations, except for the fourth question: all *true* production systems perform a full ruleset–database scan after *each* rule execution, whether rule execution is batched or not.[7]

Let us now go back to the first three questions. First, which order do we use to scan rules? This matters only if we execute *immediately* the right-hand side of a rule whose left-hand side is satisfied, that is, if we do *not* batch rules. In such a case, the end result may be different, depending on the ordering used. Indeed, because each rule changes the state of the database (by replacing a string by another), rule execution order matters: a transformation can *trigger* another rule, that is, can change the database in a way such that it matches the left-hand side of another rule, or *inhibit* another rule, by changing the database in a way that fails the LHS of another rule. Different production systems may use different scan-ordering mechanisms. In our example, the two rule instances <AB → CD, ABC> and <BC → DE, ABC> inhibit each other: if we apply the transformation AB → CD to ABC *first*, yielding the string CDC, the second one (BC → DE) is no longer applicable. Conversely, if we apply BC → DE to ABC first, yielding ADE, the rule AB → CD is no longer applicable.

With regard to the second question, that is, whether we execute a rule whose LHS is satisfied *immediately*, or whether we complete a full ruleset–database scan before we start executing rules, both strategies have been used in production systems. We also know that they produce different results since each rule execution modifies the state of the database, thereby influencing which rules match, or fail to match, the current state of the database. Notice that the JRules rule engine uses rule batching with the RETE algorithm, and immediate rule execution in the sequential algorithm; the Fastpath algorithm uses a combination of the two.

With regard to the third question (rule execution ordering), note first that this question is only relevant when we have *rule batching*, that is, when we perform a full ruleset–database scan, before we start executing any rule. If a full scan identifies several rule instances, called *conflict set,* we need an execution ordering strategy – called *conflict resolution strategy*. Further, the choice of a strategy does affect the end result. Referring back to the example of Fig. 6.1, a full ruleset–database scan identified the rule instances <AB → CD, ABD>, <BC → DE, ABC>, and <CD → EF, ACD>. The question then is which transformation to apply first; as we saw for the issue of scan ordering, the order matters, and the end result will be different.

Different ordering strategies have been used, including *rule priority*, rule *recency*, rule *condition strength*, and others. We will briefly explain them here; we discuss the JRules engine conflict resolution strategy in the next section. With rule priority, rules are assigned *priority values* which are used to order rule instances within the *conflict set*. If rule AB → CD had higher priority, it would be executed first, and the string ABC would be transformed to CDC. Note that if we

---

[7]In RETE mode, the JRules rule engine is a *true production system*. However, in Sequential and Fastpath mode, the rule engine does *not* perform a full ruleset–database scan after each rule execution. More on the algorithms in Sect. 6.4.

perform a full ruleset–database scan after this transformation (see the answer to the fourth question above), we will identify a *second* match for the rule CD → EF, and will end up with two rule instances corresponding to the same rule: <CD → EF, ACD>, which was already identified in the first scan, and <CD → EF, CDC>, which showed up as a result of executing the first rule. This is a *fundamental* feature of *true* production systems: by performing a full ruleset–database scan after *each* rule execution, we ensure that *the conflict set is always current with respect to the state of the database*. This *currency* comes at an *important cost*: that of performing a full ruleset–database scan after *each* rule execution. Thanks to his *RETE algorithm*, Charles Forgy made sure that this cost is minimal; we will talk about a simplified version of the RETE algorithm in Sect. 6.4.1.

Let us go back to our example and to the conflict resolution strategy: notice that priority *alone* does not suffice in this case, since the two rule instances/matches correspond to the same rule.[8] One criterion that is often used in rule engines – including JRules – is *recency*: If we have two rule instances in the conflict set, we pick the one that was most recently added to it. In our example, recency means that <CD → EF, CDC> is executed first, followed by <CD → EF, ACD>.

Rule condition strength is another criterion that has been used to break ties between rule instances having the same priorities: we typically pick the rule with the *strongest* condition *first*. The intuition behind this choice is to favor rules that use "more knowledge" or "more information" about the current database, as their actions are likely to be more "appropriate" to the situation at hand. Condition strength can be defined in many ways. Given two rules R_1: $LHS_1 → RHS_1$ and R_2: $LHS_2 → RHS_2$, we could say that LHS_1 is stronger than LHS_2 if the string LHS_1 contains the string LHS_2. For example, the rule ABC → <some string> has a stronger condition than either AB → <some string> or BC → <some string>.[9] The problem with such a definition is that not all rules can be ordered: for example, the rules R_1: ABC → <some string> and R_2: DE → <some string> are not *comparable*: neither string (ABC and DE) is included in the other. A weaker relation that just looks at string length may be used instead. Note finally, that this relationship does not eliminate the possibility of ties. Rule engines do need to break ties one way or another, but they may not publish all of their tie-breaking rules as we are not supposed to care – or count on a particular obscure strategy. For example, the JRules engine documentation says that we should not care beyond recency: for all practical purposes, beyond recency, we can consider the selection random.

The above discussion showed some of design dimensions for production systems, in general, and as it relates to the control strategy used by the interpreter. An important characteristic – and advantage – of the production systems paradigm is that "intelligence" is embodied in the *rules*, and to a lesser extent the database, as

---

[8]JRules supports the so-called dynamic priorities, which are *rule instance–specific* priorities. More about this in Chap. 11 (see discussion about IRL).

[9]This definition also maps nicely to logical formulas: if A, B, and C are predicates, condition strength corresponds to *logical implication*: ABC *implies* AB (ABC → AB) and BC (ABC → BC).

opposed to the interpreter: a single and simple interpreter should be able to execute rulesets in a variety of domains. Further, the "intelligence" of the rules should not be embodied in fairly complex rules or in a set of intricately dependent rules: individual rules should be simple and independent of other rules. Ideally, the "intelligence" of the ruleset should emerge from the *implicit* interactions of simple rules as they manipulate the same database.

Achieving rule set simplicity and modularity has always been a challenge, including to some of the early AI pioneers who tweaked interpreters beyond recognition to extract performance or additional inferencing behavior (see, e.g., Davis and King 1984). Closer to home, we have seen many *business rule* projects where rule authors used every bell and whistle of the JRules product to reproduce an essentially procedural decision process. We have seen rules with dozens of conditions or with conditional logic in the action part. We have also seen cases where rule authors implemented explicit and heavy-handed dependencies between rules, and/ or a very intricate orchestration (see Chap. 11).

How to avoid "overengineering" a production system, in general, and a ruleset, in particular? Some of the methodological guidelines shown in the book help. Proper rule discovery and analysis, discussed in Chaps. 3 and 4, play a *central role* by producing rules that are *business* oriented, *relevant*, properly *contextualized*, and *atomic*. Rule authoring best practices and design patterns, discussed in Chap. 9, rule entry infrastructure design, discussed in Chap. 10, and rule authoring in JRules, discussed in Chap. 11, should take care of the rest.

6.3.2 The JRules Rule Engine

In this section, we discuss the basics of the JRules rule engine. The letter J of JRules stands for Java: the rule engine itself is a Java object, instance of the class **IlrContext**, the ruleset is represented by a Java object (class **IlrRuleset**), and what we have called *database* in Sect. 6.3.1 – called *working memory* in JRules – consists of a bunch of plain old Java applications objects (POJOs). The JRules rule engine uses what we called *rule batching* in Sect. 6.3.1, and hence, it uses a data structure to hold the conflict set, called *agenda*. In this section, we will explain how the rule engine operates on Java objects. We will show just enough of the API to understand the basics: the full API will be presented in Chap. 13, which deals specifically with *deployment rules with JRules*. The supported rule engine execution algorithms will be discussed in the next section. How to select an execution algorithm and criteria for algorithm selection will be presented in Chap. 11. To better understand the inner workings of the engine, we will show rules in the *Ilog Rule Language* (IRL), which is the JRules rule execution language, and bears some resemblance to Java; IRL is discussed more thoroughly in Chap. 11.

Consider the following Java class definitions for the classes **Claim** and **Policy**; the reader can guess what the classes **PolicyHolder** and **StatusType** look like (Fig. 6.2).

```
class Policy extends … {          class Claim extends … {
private int policyNumber;         private Date claimDate;
private Date beginDate;           private Policy policy;
private Date endDate;             private float amount;
private PolicyHolder holder;      private StatusType status;
                                  private float payment;
…
// constructors                   …
public Policy(int number,         // constructors
        PolicyHolder              public Claim(Policy pcy,Date dte){…}
holder) {…}                       …
                                  // getters and setters
…                                 public Date getClaimDate() {…}
// getters and setters
public int getPolicyNumber()      …
{…}                               // utility functions
                                  public boolean filedAfter(Date dte)
…                                 {…}
                                  public boolean  filedMoreThanNumDays-
}                                 After(int numDays, Date dte){…}

                                  …
                                  }
```

Fig. 6.2 Sample class definitions

Consider now the following two IRL rules big_claim and claim_ over_90_days_past_exp_date_policy. The first rule matches claims that have an amount higher than $100,000; because of the amount involved, such claims are referred to a human claim adjudicator. The second rule rejects claims that were filed more than 90 days after the expiration of the policy. The line:

```
?myClaim: Claim(getAmount()> 100000);
```

In the rule big_claim represents the condition part of the rule. In IRL terminology, it is called a *simple class condition* and it *matches* a **Claim** object such that the result of calling getAmount() on it yields a value higher than $100,000. The condition part of the second rule is more involved but does the same thing. The action parts of the rules change the status of the matching claim (called ? myClaim in both rules) and apply the action "**update** ?claim;" that we will explain shortly (Fig. 6.3).

Roughly speaking, to apply rules to Java application objects using a JRules rule engine, we need to do the following:

1. Create the rule engine and load it with the ruleset.
2. Load up the working memory (database) of the rule engine. For the case of the JRules engine, when using the default algorithm, loading the working memory triggers an incremental scan/match of <ruleset, database>. The scan/match is incremental since the scan is "focused" on the new data; more on this in Sect. 6.4.1.
3. Perform an execute-scan-match cycle, until there are no more rules to execute.
4. Reset the rule engine for future use.

```
rule big_claim {
  when {
  ?myClaim: Claim(getAmount() > 100000);
  } then{
  ?myClaim.setStatus(StatusType.MANUAL_REFERRAL);
  update ?myClaim;
  }
```

```
rule claim_over_90_days_past_exp_date_policy {
  when {
  ?myClaim: Claim(filedMoreThanNumDaysAfter(90,
                                  getPolicy().getEndDate()));
  } then {
  ?myClaim.setStatus(StatusType.REJECTED);
  update ?myClaim;
  }
```

Fig. 6.3 Sample (Ilog Rule Language, IRL) rules

We will first show Java code that performs these four steps. Then, we will look at what happens internally inside the rule engine.

Figure 6.4 shows a typical Java code sequence for performing these steps. To simplify the first step, we will assume that the above two rules are packaged in an old-style IRL text file called "myrules.irl"; Chap. 13 will show a more up-to-date API for ruleset parsing and loading. With regard to the scan-match-execute cycle, we should mention that the scan in JRules is triggered by either changes to the working memory/database or changes to the ruleset. We change the working memory by adding objects to it, modifying them, or removing them from it; we change the ruleset by adding or removing rules, or changing their status. Finally, the scan-match-execute cycle starts with the execute step (execute-scan-match).

Figure 6.5 illustrates what happens under the hood. The left-hand side of Fig. 6.5 shows the part of the call stack that concerns the method that contains the code of Fig. 6.4.[10] The call stack includes memory locations (variables) to hold the addresses of the actual Java objects, which are allocated in the Java *heap memory*, shown on the right-hand side of Fig. 6.5. The important instructions in Fig. 6.4 have been numbered ([1]–[6]). Their effect is shown in Fig. 6.5 in terms of links created ([1]–[4]) and removed (links [5] and [6]).

The Java instruction [1] in Fig. 6.4 results into the creation of an **IlrRuleset** object in the Java heap, and the setting of reference to it from the call stack (the variable myRuleset. We will not go into the details of how the rules are organized internally, which will be covered in Sect. 6.4. The construction of the rule engine using the one-arg constructor (line [2] in Fig. 6.4) will create the rule engine with an empty working memory (a collection of null pointers), an empty agenda (a collection of null pointers), and the previously created ruleset ruleset object; the corresponding links have been labeled [2]. The instruction numbered [3] in Fig. 6.4

---

[10]Sometimes called *activation record* of the caller.

```
      // 1. Create the rule engine and load it with the ruleset

      // We need to create a ruleset object first, and then construct
      // the rule engine object with it
[1]   IlrRuleset myRuleset = new IlrRuleset();
      // begin -- old style ruleset loading and parsing
      FileInputStream fis =
               new FileInputStream(new File("myruleset.ilr"));
      if (! myRuleset.parseStream(fis)) {
          // rules/ruleset file contains syntax error(s). Exit
          System.out.println("Ruleset parsing error(s): quitting");
          return;
      }
      // end -- old style ruleset loading and parsing

      // Construct the rule engine with the ruleset object
[2]   IlrContext myEngine = new IlrContext(myRuleset);

      // 2. Load up the working memory (database) of the rule engine
      // first, get a claim object from some incoming stream
[3]   Claim myClaim = getNextClaim();
      // Next, insert myClaim into the working memory of the engine
      // This will perform a scan/match of the rules in the ruleset
[4]   myEngine.insert(myClaim);

      // 3. Perform the execute-scan-match cycle until there are no
      // more rules
[5]   myEngine.execute();

      // 4. Reset the engine
[6]   myEngine.reset();
```

Fig. 6.4 Excerpts from a Java program that uses a JRules engine

obtains a local (to the calling context) reference to some claim object. Here, we do not care how the claim object was created: the function getNextClaim() could be returning a reference to an already existing Java object, or creating a Java object itself by iterating over the results of a database query, or retrieving the next message from a queue. The important thing to stress is that the Java objects that the rule engine works on (i.e., the contents of its working memory) have an independent life cycle from the rule engine.

When we *insert* an object into a rule engine (line [4] in Fig. 6.4), we do two things: (1) add a reference to that object from the *working memory of the engine*, and (2) while we are at it, perform a <ruleset, working memory> scan/match sequence. If the newly inserted object contributes to some match, a new *rule instance*, that is, a pair <rule, data tuple>, will be added to the agenda. Figure 6.5 illustrates the case where the newly inserted claim object (myClaim) matches the rule big_claim. As a result, a new *rule instance* is added to the agenda,

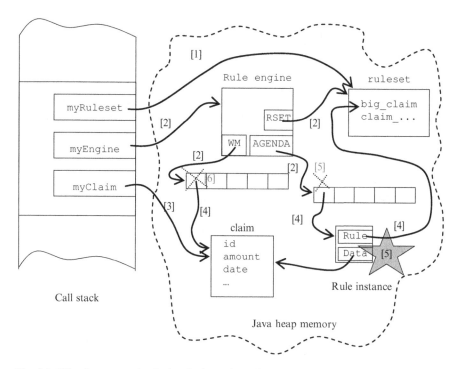

Fig. 6.5 What happens under the hood when using a Java rule engine

which can be thought of as a pair <rule, data>. The "rule" component points to big_claim and the data component points to myClaim.

The call to execute (line [5] in Fig. 6.4) triggers a loop that looks as follows:

- **while** the agenda is not empty
  - **remove** the rule instance *at the top* of the agenda
  - **execute** the action part of the corresponding rule.
  - **perform** a scan/match cycle of the <ruleset, working memory>.

Note that executing the action part of a rule can modify the working memory. Indeed, we *typically* call Java methods that modify the state of the object(s) matched by the condition part of the rule. In our example, both rules modify the status attribute of the matching **Claim** object. Thus, we need to perform a scan/match cycle after each rule execution. A consequence of this scan/match could be the addition or removal of *rule instances* to/from the agenda. In the example of Fig. 6.5, we show the effect of the execute() method as executing the action part of the top (and unique) rule instance of the agenda.

Because a <ruleset, working memory> scan/match is costly – optimizations explained in Sect. 6.4.1 notwithstanding – and because not *all* actions parts of rules modify the working memory, or modify it in a way that concerns rules, we only perform a <ruleset, working memory> scan/match when we need to. The question then is, how do we know that we need to perform a scan? Could the engine tell, by looking at the code in the action part of the rule? Alas, it cannot: we should not let the "setStatus()" name fool us: using the setter naming pattern in our code is just a coding convention . We could write a method that follows the "setter" naming pattern that does *not* change the object, and a method that changes the object that does not follow this pattern. Hence, we need to tell the engine *explicitly* that a scan is needed.[11] That is the role of the IRL action "**update** ? myClaim;" used in both rules.

The call to the method execute() returns when no rule instances remain on the agenda. This signals that no rule matches the current state of the working memory. This, in turn, means that we have "inferred" everything that could be inferred from the starting state working memory, in one or several steps. The only way then to "reload" the agenda is to insert new data into the working memory of the engine, to remove existing data from working memory,[12] or to modify existing data (e.g., myClaim) from the calling Java application, and *letting the engine know about it*.[13]

Finally, note that this behavior is specific to the RETE mode, which is the default execution behavior of JRules rule engine, and the only mode that conforms to the *production system* model described in Sect. 6.3.1; we will explain in Sect. 6.4.1 how the ruleset, working memory, and agenda are organized internally in RETE mode to make this process efficient.

The execution mode notwithstanding, the behavior presented in this section is a simplification of what will happen in your rule application:

* In the above description, application objects are provided to the engine through an explicit insertion into the engine's working memory, and the result of the rule engine execution is *implicitly* embodied in the changes performed on those objects by the action parts of rules. We will see in Chap. 11 *ruleset parameters*

---

[11]One possible alternative to having to request a scan by explicitly calling the "update" is to *instrument* the code of the classes manipulated by the engine (e.g., the class **Claim** in our case) so that the engine is notified whenever some attribute is modified. This is the technique used by *object-oriented databases*, where *persistent* classes are instrumented so that whenever an attribute of a java object is modified, the object instance is "dirtied," triggering a save at the end of the transaction. Such a solution would not work in our case for several reasons. First, this instrumentation would add processing overhead to *all* the instances of a class, whether they are manipulated by a rule engine or not. Second, it adds processing overhead to *all* object attributes, whether they have a bearing on rules or not. However, let the reader be assured: this explicit notification is transparent to business rule authors, as explained in Chap. 11.

[12]Indeed, assume we have a rule that says "if there is no claim over 1,000 then do such." If the working memory contains/references a claim worth 1,100, the rule will not match the current state of the working memory. If I remove that claim, the rule will match.

[13]The IRL instruction "**update** ?myClaim;" has a Java API equivalent, which can be called from the Java calling context as in "myEngine.update(myClaim);".

which provide a more elegant and scalable way of passing data back and forth to the rule engine.

- In the above example, the rule engine is *local* to the business application that needs it, and is manipulated *directly* through an explicit reference – the variable myEngine. We refer to this as the *embedded* mode. Most enterprise applications will access rule engine functionality *as a service* through an *abstraction layer* that provides location transparency, scalability, load balancing, run-time ruleset management (hot deployment, execution statistics, etc.), and other enterprise services. Chapter 7 will explore the design space for business rule applications in general. Chapter 12 will address the design space for *rule deployment*, in a vendor independent way, and Chap. 13 will discuss the specifics of the JRules product.

In some ways, this section provides the basic mechanics of a rule engine that refers to native Java objects. Subsequent chapters will show how this scales up for enterprise applications.

6.4   Engine Execution Algorithms

In this section, we explain the three engine algorithms supported by JRules. The RETE algorithm, explained first, is supported, in one form or another[14] by all rule engines, and fully implements the *production system* paradigm explained in Sect. 6.3.1. Some form of sequential algorithm is supported by most commercial products. The sequential algorithm does not implement the full *production system* model, but there are some classes of problems for which it produce the same result as the RETE algorithm, but an order of magnitude faster. Here, we will introduce the *JRules* sequential algorithm (Sect. 6.3.2). The sequential algorithm is applicable to only certain kinds of problems, and imposes some restrictions on the kinds of rules and rule constructs that can be used. The *JRules* Fastpath algorithm enables us to relax some of those conditions, with a performance comparable to that of sequential. The Fastpath algorithm will be discussed in Sect. 6.4.3.

6.4.1   The RETE Algorithm

We mentioned in Sect. 6.3.1 that an important aspect of production systems is the fact that we perform a full scan <ruleset, database> after each rule execution. A brute force <ruleset, working memory> scan would make rule engines too

---

[14]RETE is the name given to the original algorithm published by C. Forgy in his doctoral thesis. Subsequent enhancements, introduced by Forgy and others, have been dubbed RETE II and RETE II plus.

inefficient. The RETE algorithm proposes an organization of the ruleset and of the database (working memory) that makes such <ruleset, working memory> scans far more efficient. It does so by applying three techniques that dramatically reduce the number of tests that need to be performed:

- It builds a complex *index* of rule conditions that takes advantage of similarities between rule conditions to reduce the number of tests that need to be evaluated for the entire ruleset. This index is called the *RETE network.*
- Because a <ruleset, working memory> scan is almost always triggered by a data insertion into, or removal from, the working memory, or by the modification of an object already in working memory, the RETE algorithm is able to precisely identify those parts of the RETE network that need to be reevaluated.
- The network stores partial matches to further reduce the number of tests that need to be performed.

We explain below the structure of the RETE network and the workings of the rule engine. We will use a sample ruleset with three rules to illustrate the structure of the RETE network.

Roughly speaking, the RETE network is a hierarchy with a single entry node and several exit nodes, one per rule in the ruleset. The internal nodes of the hierarchy represent the different tests embodied in the ruleset. Each working memory event (insertion, modification, or removal of objects) is handled as a *token* entering the hierarchy from the top, and traveling down the hierarchy as far as successful tests will take it. Object insertion is treated as a *positive token*. Object removal is treated as a *negative token*. Object modification may spawn both *positive* and *negative* tokens.[15] If a *positive* token reaches a leaf node (a *rule node*), a new rule instance is added to the agenda. If a *negative token* reaches a leaf node, the corresponding rule instance is *removed* from the agenda.

We will first illustrate the structure of the network with a single rule and then show the effect of condition sharing between two rules. Figure 6.6 shows simplified class definitions[16] and Fig. 6.7 shows a sample IRL rule.

Assume now that we have inserted in working memory the following objects:

- C1 = Claim(amount = 110,000, policyNumber = 123)
- C2 = Claim(amount = 120,000, policyNumber = 456)
- C3 = Claim(amount = 1,500, policyNumber = 789)
- P1 = Policy(policyNumber = 123,   endDate = 31/1/2011,   holderSSN = 111111111)

---

[15]Actually, even object insertion can spawn negative tokens, if some rule contains a *not* condition. This will become clearer later in this chapter, and after we cover the IRL in Chap. 11.

[16]The simplification consists of (a) treating all attributes as *public* data members and (b) implementing associations between objects through "foreign keys," as opposed through direct object pointers (e.g., Claim "points" to the Policy via the data member "int policyNumber"), to illustrate more clearly joins. With regard to the public data members, we will see in Chap. 10 that JRules does indeed treat getters/setters as "bean properties."

```
class Policy extends … {            class Claim extends … {
public int policyNumber;            public Date claimDate;
public Date beginDate;              public int policyNumber;
public Date endDate;                public float amount;
public String holderSSN;            public StatusType status;
...                                 public float payment;
}                                   ...
                                    }
class PolicyHolder extends …{
public String ssn;

...

}
```

Fig. 6.6 Simplified class definitions

```
rule big_claim_holder{
  when {
  ?claim: Claim(amount > 100000; ?pNumber : policyNumber);
  ?policy: Policy(endDate.after("31/12/2010");
                        policyNumber == ?pNumber;
                        ?ssnHolder : holderSSN);
  ?holder: PolicyHolder(ssn.equals(?ssnHolder));
  } then {
    out.println(?holder + "'s high claim policy ends in 2011");

  }
```

Fig. 6.7 Sample Ilog Rule Language (IRL) rule

- P2 = Policy(policyNumber = 456,   endDate = 30/6/2011,   holderSSN = 222222222)
- P3 = Policy(policyNumber = 789,   endDate = 30/6/2010,   holderSSN = 333333333
- PH1 = PolicyHolder(ssn = 111111111)

Figure 6.8 shows the resulting RETE network. The network has a root node, which is the entry point for inserting objects into working memory. The first-level nodes are *type* nodes, where we test the type of the object. Subsequent levels correspond to single-object tests which are laid out in the same way they appear in the rule. In this case, there is only one single-object test for the classes **Claim** and **Policy**, and none for **PolicyHolder**. This part of the network is indeed a *tree* and is called the *discrimination tree*. The objects that pass these single-object tests make it to the so-called alpha nodes, which serve as inputs to the so-called network of joins. In our example, the objects C1, C2, P1, P2, and PH1 make it through the discrimination tree to the alpha nodes, while the objects C3 and P3 do not.

The *network of joins*, as its name suggests, applies the *join conditions* of the rules that are compiled into the network. A *join condition* is a condition that involves more than one object. In this case, they are "foreign key reference" type of

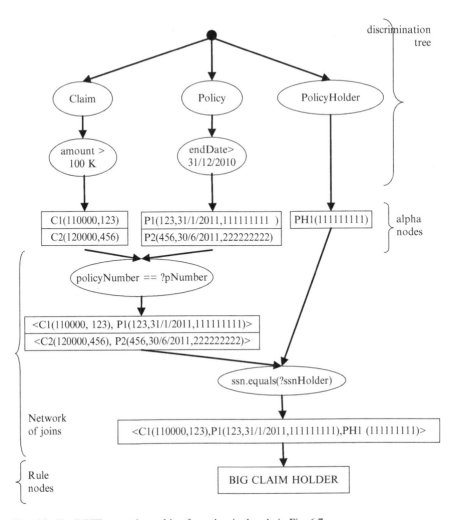

Fig. 6.8 The RETE network resulting from the single rule in Fig. 6.7

conditions, but they could be arbitrarily complex and may involve any combination of attributes. Note that join conditions are applied *only* to those objects that have passed the single-object conditions, that is, those objects that made through the discrimination tree down to the alpha nodes – C1, C2, P1, P2, and PH1, in our case.

Note also that join conditions *cascade* in the same order in which they appear in the rules.[17] For example, the condition labeled "ssn.equals(?ssnHolder)," which stands for ?holder.snn.equals(?policy.holderSSN, is only applied to those **Policy**

---

[17]The fact that "rule layout" influences the topology of the RETE network may be used to squeeze out a (tiny) bit of performance. More on this in Chap. 13.

objects *that are part of* <**Claim,Policy**> *pairs have already passed the first join test*. Thus, if we find a **PolicyHolder** object in the corresponding alpha node that matches the **Policy** component of a <**Claim, Policy**> pair, we know that we have a <**Claim, Policy, PolicyHolder**> triple that *satisfies all of the conditions of the rule*; this is the case for the triple <C1, P1, PH1> in Fig. 6.8. The alpha nodes and the outputs of the join nodes embody the ability of the RETE network to store partial matches.

Consider now what happens if we *insert* a new object in working memory. Assume that we insert a new policy holder, PH2 = PolicyHolder(ssn = 222222222). This insertion is treated as a *positive token* "dropped" from the top of the network, and works its way through the various condition nodes. Figure 6.9 shows the resulting network. Because there are no single-object conditions on **PolicyHolder**'s, PH2 goes straight to the alpha node. And because the join condition involving **PolicyHolder** is last in the network of joins, we only need to "compare" PH2 to the **Policy** components of the pairs that passed the first join condition (policyNumber == ?pNumber). Thus, the insertion of PH2 required applying a single join test (ssn.equals(?ssnHolder)) on two object pairs (<P1, PH2> and <P2,PH2>). Compare that to a brute force approach which would have generated *all possible triples* involving PH2 – nine in our case[18] – and then testing all the conditions on each triple.

We will now consider the case of an object modification. Assume that we change the amount of claim C1 from $110,000 to $11,000. Now, C1 no longer satisfies the condition (amount >100,000). Consequently, we need to pull out C1 from the corresponding alpha node, and by extension, from all the tuples in which it was involved. Because C1 was involved in a triple that satisfied all the conditions of rule BIG_CLAIM_HOLDER (<P1,C1,PH1>), the corresponding rule instance will be pulled out from the agenda (not shown in Fig. 6.9).

An object *removal* is handled in a similar fashion to the modification of C1 above: in such a case, we need not reevaluate any tests but simply pull out the object from the alpha nodes, and any nodes further down in the join network that the object (i.e., tuples containing it) may have passed.

Finally, the example in Fig. 6.9b illustrated a situation where an object state change *failed* a previously satisfied rule. Naturally, the opposite can also happen: an object that was previously "blocked" at either the discrimination tree or at some of the join tests, may now *pass* some previously failed tests and "slide down" the network, possibly leading to the creation of a new rule instance and its addition to the agenda.

Let us now turn to another important characteristic of the RETE network, which makes rule evaluation and execution: *condition sharing*. Condition sharing works as follows: if two rules share some conditions, *appearing in the same order*, those conditions/tests will appear *once* in the RETE network, and will serve both rules. Consider the following two rule excerpts:

---

[18]Namely, < any of {C1,C2,C3}, any of {P1, P2, P3}, PH2>.

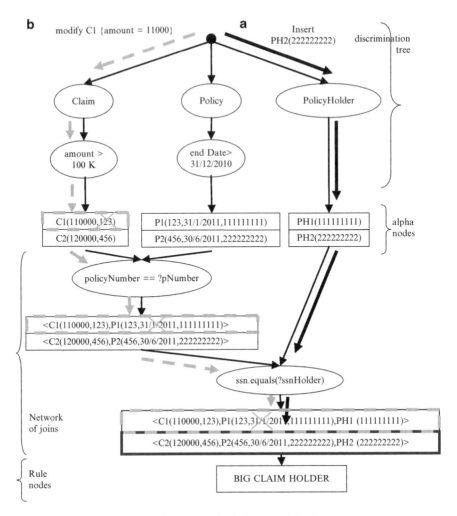

Fig. 6.9 The effect of (**a**) object insertion and (**b**) object modification

```
rule rule_one{
  when {
  ?cl: Claim(amount > 1000; payment == 0; status == IP);
  ...
}
rule rule_two{
  when {
  ?cl: Claim(amount > 1000; payment == 0; status == REJECT);
  ...
}
```

Fig. 6.10 The effect of
condition sharing between
rules on the topology of the
RETE network

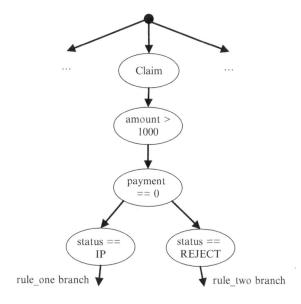

Figure 6.10 shows excerpts from the discrimination tree of the resulting RETE network. As we can see, both rules test **Claim**'s, *first* for "amount > 1000", *and then*, for "payment == 0". The two tests are then shared between the two rules. Put another way, if the ruleset parser sees a rule "**if** A and B and C **then do** X **endif**" and another "**if** A and B and D **then do** Y **endif**", it changes them into:

```
if A and B then
        if C then
                do X
        endif
        if D then
                do Y
        endif
endif
```

We finally consider the *control* or *conflict resolution* strategy of the JRules rule engine. We mentioned in Sect. 6.3.1 some of the criteria typically used by rule engines, namely, priorities, recency, and condition strength. JRules uses a hierarchy of criteria:

- *Refraction.* A rule instance that just fired is automatically removed from the agenda, *even if its condition part is still satisfied*. If the condition part becomes negative at some later point, the engine will "forget" it ever fired, and should it become satisfied again, the rule instance can get back on the agenda. This behavior actually makes sense for the majority of applications. If we want a looping behavior, of the kind "**while** COND **do** X", there is a way to override the *refraction* principle.

- *Priority*. Given several rule instances on the agenda, we pick the one that has the highest priority.
- *Recency*. In case of a tie with priorities, we look for the rule instance that involves the most recently modified object.
- *Other*. In case several same-priority instances of the agenda involve the most recently modified object, the engine will use some additional internal, nonpublic criteria.

In the early days, rule authors used to rely heavily on rule priorities to control the sequence of *rule execution*. Priorities can become hard to maintain, and lead to sloppy rule authoring.[19] JRules now offers sophisticated ruleset *orchestration* mechanisms (see Chap. 11), and the recommended practice is to stay away from priorities, and only rely on ruleflows (see Chap. 11) and on the refraction principle.

As for the other criteria, rule authors should *absolutely not* integrate the *recency* factor into their business logic, that is, they should not rely on recency to obtain the appropriate behavior. However, while tracing or debugging a ruleset, it is helpful to understand that *recency* comes into play in the ordering of the agenda. As for *other*, there is no clue in the documentation as to what those might be.[20]

While the RETE algorithm has rendered the production system paradigm computationally tractable, by being smart (selective) about the <ruleset,database> scan, there are certain types of problems where, by virtue of the nature of the rules, such a scan is not even needed. In such situations, we do not need the complexity of the RETE network or the corresponding inference algorithm. A brute force method might do a good job: that is the *sequential algorithm* discussed next.

6.4.2   The Sequential Algorithm

Assume that part of our claim processing business process, one step consists of a data validation. A ruleset for data validation would typically consist of a bunch of rules, each one of which validates a particular field or a particular combination of fields. The rules will typically follow the BAL pattern:

```
if
    <some claim field fails some condition>
then
    set the decision of 'the claim'to: "INVALID";
    add to 'the claim'validation message: <violated condition>
```

---

[19]Intellectually lazy rule authors may rely too heavily on rule priorities, as a mechanism for controlling rule execution, as opposed to relying on *logical dependencies* between rules.

[20]The *other* part used to be documented in the product. Since JRules 5, it was felt that JRules users not only should *not* rely on *other*, but they should no longer even know what *other* is ☺.

We show below an example of such a rule.

```
if
   the date of 'the claim'is more than 182 days old
then
   set the decision of 'the claim'to "INVALID";
   add to 'the claim'validation message:"Claim too old";
```

If we know that our rules are such that their action parts will *not* change the database (working memory) *in a way that affects other rules*, then *we know that a one and only <ruleset, database> scan will be needed*. Indeed, *whichever <rule, data tuple> matched on the first pass will not break after other rules have executed*, and conversely, *whichever <rule, data tuple> failed to match on the first scan, will not match after other rules executed*. If that is the case, all of the machinery for incremental <ruleset, database> scan are not needed and represent a pure overhead, with no performance gains. Indeed, for these kinds of rulesets, even RETE's *condition sharing* (see Fig. 6.10) is unlikely to provide any benefit: *typically*, different rules test on different attributes. Thus, we might as well use a brute force method for matching all rules to all applicable data tuples, and be done with it. This is the premise behind the sequential algorithm.

Figure 6.11 shows a high-level version of the sequential algorithm. It consists of two nested loops: the outer loop iterates over the data and the inner loop over the rules. Notice that we talk about *tuple* and not about *single objects*. Indeed, generally speaking, rules match *tuples* of objects. In the example of Fig. 6.7, the rule big_claim_holder matches triples <claim, policy, policy holder>. The triple <claim, policy, policy holder> is called *signature* of the rule.

While there are still data tuples to process:

1. Take the next tuple
2. While there are still rules to apply
   2.a Take the next rule
   2.b Check the condition part of the rule to the tuple
   2.c IF the condition part is satisfied THEN apply the action part

Using the initial contents of the working memory of the example in Sect. 6.4.1:

- C_1 = Claim(amount = 110,000, policyNumber = 123)
- C_2 = Claim(amount = 120,000, policyNumber = 456)
- C_3 = Claim(amount = 1,500, policyNumber = 789)

> While there are still data tuples to process
> 1 Take the next tuple
> 2 While there are still rules to apply
>   2.a Take the next rule
>   2.b Check the condition part of the rule to the tuple
>   2.c IF the condition part is satisfied THEN apply the action part

Fig. 6.11 Basic sequential algorithm

- P_1 = Policy(policyNumber = 123,   endDate = 31/1/2011,   holderSSN = 111111111)
- P_2 = Policy(policyNumber = 456,   endDate = 30/6/2011,   holderSSN = 222222222)
- P_3 = Policy(policyNumber = 789,   endDate = 30/6/2010,   holderSSN = 333333333)
- PH_1 = PolicyHolder(ssn = 111111111)
- PH_2 = PolicyHolder(ssn = 222222222)

we can get 18 different triples, corresponding to the combinations C_i, P_j, PH_k, for i = 1..3 and j = 1..3, i.e., $<C_1, P_1, PH_1>$, $<C_1, P_2, PH_1>$, $<C_1, P_3, PH_1>$, $<C_2, P_1, PH_1>$, ..., $<C_3, P_3, PH_1>$, then $<C_1, P_1, PH_2>$, ..., and $<C_3, P_3, PH_2>$. In JRules, the generation of these tuples is performed by a default *tuple generator*. Because the same tuple will be submitted to all of the rules of the ruleset (the inner loop of the algorithm of Fig. 6.11), the tuple generator needs to consider *all of the rules* of the ruleset to generate a tuple structure that can accommodate all of the rules. Naturally, the *order* of the classes in the tuple is immaterial, $<C_1, P_1, PH_1>$ represents the same data as $<P_1, C_1, PH_1>$, say. Thus, if all of the rules of the ruleset have the same signature (tuple structure), tuple generation is simple. If the rules have *different* signatures, then things get a bit more complicated.

Assume that we have three rules R1, R2, and R3, with signatures <Claim, Policy>, <Claim, Policy, PolicyHolder>, and <Claim, Policy, ServiceAct[21]>, respectively, and assume that we have on service act, SA_1. The JRules default tuple generator will generate quadruples with the signature <Claim, Policy, Policy Holder, ServiceAct>. For a given quadruple, each rule will pick the subset of elements it is interested in and apply the conditions to that subset. Thus, given a quadruple $<C_1, P_1, PH_1, SA_1>$, rule R1 will extract the pair $<C_1, P_1>$ and ignore the rest, rule R2 will see the triple $<C_1, P_1, PH_1>$, and ignore SA_1, and rule R3 will see the triple $<C_1, P_1, SA_1>$, and ignore PH_1. In other words, R1 sees it as $<C_1, P_1, *, * >$, R2 sees it as $<C_1, P_1, PH_1, * >$, and R3 sees it as $<C_1, P_1, *, SA_1>$. This behavior of the tuple generator is *customizable*, and an (*advanced*) user can replace the default tuple generator by his or her own.

Note that the inner loop in Fig. 6.11 embodies the default behavior of the sequential algorithm: we apply *all* of the rules to *each* tuple. There may be situations where, for a given tuple, we are only interested in the *first* rule that fires, after which we drop the tuple and move to the next. This is equivalent to replacing the inner loop by:

2. While there are still rules to apply *and no rule has yet fired*
   2.a Take the next rule
   2.b Check the condition part of the rule to the tuple
   2.c IF the condition part is satisfied THEN apply the action part

---

[21]ServiceAct represents an *act* (occurrence) of the service for which payment is claimed.

If the rules of the ruleset are validation rules that look for violations, and we are only interested in a pass–fail decision, then this could be appropriate. Indeed, as soon as a tuple fails a validation constraint, we drop it and move to the next. There may also be situations where we are interested in the first n rule firings, after which we drop the tuple and move to the next. Again, there may be validation applications where we care about the first n violations, after which we throw out the tuple. This again would lead to a slight change in the inner loop. As we will see in Chap. 11 when we talk about *ruleset orchestration*, these are actually *user-configurable parameters*. In fact, the whole execution algorithm selection can be set at the individual *rule flow task* level, as opposed to an entire ruleset (see Chap. 11). Thus, within a given ruleset/decision, different steps (rule flow tasks), can use different execution algorithms.

Where applicable, the sequential algorithm yields *an order of magnitude* improvement in performance. This means that the same ruleset would execute around ten times faster in sequential mode than in RETE mode. This enhancement is due, in part, to the much simpler data structures managed by the engine in sequential mode (no RETE network, no agenda), and in part, to the fact that the engine uses *Just In Time* (JIT) *bytecode generation* in sequential mode. Indeed, while the RETE mode *interprets* rule conditions and actions on the fly, in sequential mode, the first time a rule is executed (on the first tuple), the corresponding Java bytecode is generated, and executed from that point on.[22] This means that the first tuple will take a performance hit, due to the bytecode generation, but subsequent tuples will run much faster.

However, all of these niceties do not come for free. Notwithstanding the fact that the sequential algorithm works *only* for some types of problems (see above), there are some important restrictions. First, all the rule constructs that *rely* on, or assume the existence of, the working memory or the agenda, either do not work as intended or cause run-time errors, altogether. For instance, constructs that use quantifiers (**there is no**, **there exists**, **the number of**, etc.) or collections cause ruleset compilation errors. For example, a rule that includes the condition "**there is no** *claim* such that the policy holder was at fault" will cause a compilation error.[23] Idem for rules that use *dynamic priorities*, that is, priorities that are *variables* whose values will only be known once the rule condition is evaluated (see Chap. 11). Finally, more advanced rule engine functionality such as *truth maintenance* and *event processing* are not supported.

---

[22]Two comments: (1) This *JIT compilation* is to be distinguished from the *JIT* compilations of Java virtual machines whereby *Java bytecode is compiled into native machine code* if it satisfies some criteria (e.g., frequent invocation, as is the case for Sun's hotspot JVM). (2) The RETE mode *also* supports a *compiled* mode, whereby the ruleset is "parsed" off-line to generate java *bytecode*; we then talk about a *compiled ruleset*.

[23]Luckily, there is a way around that: if the "quantifier" is "scoped" on something other than the working memory, the rule is OK (more information in Chap. 11 when we talk about the IRL, and in the product documentation). Thus, whereas "**there is no** *claim* such that ..." will cause a run-time error, "**there is no** *claim* **in** *the claims of the policy* such that ..." would work.

A more annoying problem has to do with rulesets where rules have *heterogeneous* signatures, such as the three rules R1, R2, and R3 that we used above to illustrate tuple generation. The default tuple generator leads to *multiple firings of the same rule on the same data*. For example, the quadruples $<C_1, P_1, PH_1, SA_1>$ and $<C_1, P_1, PH_2, SA_1>$ will lead to *two firings* of the rule R1 on $<C_1, P_1>$, as it ignores the third and fourth components of the tuples. This is anywhere from inefficient (needlessly firing the same rule several times on the same data), to annoying (e.g., recording the same violation message, say, for a given claim, several times), to outright wrong (e.g., incrementing or decrementing a score several times for the same reason). And no customer tuple generator can fix that: however you generate your tuples, they need to have the union of the signatures, and the engine will apply all of the rules to each tuple.

The *Fastpath algorithm*, discussed next, is also targeted to problems that do not require rule chaining. It is a bit more complex, but (1) it addresses many of the weakness of the sequential algorithm and (2) it has comparable performance to the sequential algorithm – even better, on some kinds of rulesets.

6.4.3   The Fastpath Algorithm

The Fastpath algorithm is a hybrid between the RETE and the sequential algorithm. It is sequential in the sense that:

1. It does not rely on, or manipulate, an agenda.
2. There is no rescanning of rules over data, after each rule firing.

The Fastpath algorithm resembles the RETE algorithm to the extent that rules are compiled in a RETE network, and it manipulates a working memory. When an object is inserted into working memory, it is processed in the same way it is with the RETE algorithm, working its way through the network of single-object conditions (discrimination tree, see Fig. 6.8), then join conditions, down to rule nodes, if a particular tuple involving that object satisfies all of the conditions of a rule. The same process happens for all data inserted into working memory. It is the call the "execute" (see line [5] in Fig. 6.4) that distinguishes the RETE algorithm from the Fastpath algorithm. The execution loop for the Fastpath algorithm looks as follows:

1. Order the rule nodes by decreasing order of *static* priority
2. While there are still rule nodes
   2.a Take the next rule node
   2.b While there are still tuples in that rule node
       2.b.1 Take the next matching tuple
       2.b.2 Execute the rule action part on that tuple

Whereas with the RETE algorithm, we create *rule instances* for all the tuples that make it to rule nodes, and add them to the agenda, the Fastpath algorithm relies solely on the *static priority* of rules *and takes a single pass*. Indeed, we do not perform a <ruleset, working memory> scan after each rule execution (step 2.b.2). We could think of the Fastpath algorithm as a sequential, single-pass RETE algorithm.

Compared to the sequential algorithm, the Fastpath algorithm has many *advantages*:

1. It can handle rules with heterogeneous signatures, much like the RETE algorithm.
2. It can handle rules with "working memory quantifiers" such as **there is no**, **there exists**, **the number of**, and collections, *without* scoping (see footnote 26).
3. It does take advantage of shared conditions between rules, much like the RETE algorithm, to speed up rule condition evaluations.

The Fastpath algorithm also has some ***disadvantages*** compared to the sequential algorithm:

1. An up-front – albeit a one-time – cost of compiling the ruleset
2. A slower execution, on the average, than the sequential algorithm

While the Fastpath algorithm is slower, *on the average*, there are some situations where it can be *faster* than the sequential algorithm: if our ruleset contains *many* rules with shared conditions, the condition sharing that results from building the RETE network will more than offset the overhead of managing a more complex structure.

The Fastpath algorithm shares some of the same limitations as the sequential algorithm:

1. No support for rule chaining
2. No support for dynamic priorities
3. No effect (or unexpected effects) of some of the working memory manipulation *actions* such as **insert**, **update**, or **retract**
4. No support for some of the more advanced features of the rule engine, like event management and truth maintenance

Section 11.4.3 will go into criteria for selecting one algorithm over another.

6.5 Summary and Conclusions

In this chapter, we went over the history and basics of rule engine technology, in general, and for the case of JRules. We also presented the various rule execution algorithms. The RETE algorithm, developed by Charles Forgy, has greatly contributed to making the production system paradigm practical, and has been adopted, in one form or another, by commercial and open-source rule engines alike. As we showed in Sect. 6.4.2, many business decisions do *not* require rule chaining. In such cases, we do not need the machinery of the RETE network, and we can use simpler and more efficient execution algorithms. This is the case of the *sequential algorithm*. Many commercial rule engines implement *some* form or another of a sequential algorithm; we presented in Sect. 6.4.2 the JRules's implementation. This algorithm, which typically results in order of magnitude gains in execution speed, comes at a cost: a number of more or less annoying restrictions on rule language constructs and features. The kinds of decisions that do *not* require rule chaining are not likely to suffer from these restrictions, but some will. In that case, we can use the hybrid Fastpath algorithm, explained in Sect. 6.4.3.

Let us now put the issue of rule engines back into the perspective of the business rules approach and business rule management systems (BRMSs). Rule engine execution of business rules is an *important* aspect of the business rules approach, but not the *only* one – or some would say, the most important one (see Chap. 1). An organization that recognizes the rules that govern its business processes as a corporate asset that needs to be managed are able to attain most of the *business* benefits of the business rules approach. Similarly, rule engines are *important* components of *business rule management systems* (BRMSs), but not the only important ones. True, back in the early days (early 1990s), commercial BRMSs consisted of little more than rudimentary development environments and a library – in fact, some open-source tools are *still* like that. As business rules moved from engineering applications to more business-oriented applications, functionalities for rule management, testing, deployment, and monitoring became increasingly important.

How important is the rule engine execution algorithm in the general scheme of things? On some academic benchmark, the JRules rule engine can execute **tens of thousands of rules, per second, *in RETE mode***. Execution speed depends, naturally, on the complexity of the rules, the complexity of the tests performed within the rules (e.g., number comparisons versus string matching), the number of objects in working memory, the extent of condition sharing between the rules, the use of particular constructs within rules ... and the hardware on which the benchmarks ran! But rule execution speed is *seldom* an issue. In practice, materializing the data that the engine will work on (loading objects from persistent storage, pulling messages off a queue, etc.), and dematerializing the results is often the major performance bottleneck. Using the sequential algorithm, where appropriate, will divide rule execution time by ten ... but will not do much about the time to load an object from the database or pulling a message off a JMS queue. We need to keep this in mind as we consider algorithm selection in Chap. 11.

6.6 Further Reading

This already cited paper by Randall Davis and Jonathan King remains a *reference* on the origin of rule-based systems, and has been the main source for Sects. 6.2 and 6.3.1:

- Davis, R. and King, J. "The Origin of Rule-Based Systems in AI," in *Rule-Based Expert Systems: The MYCIN Experiments of the Stanford Heuristic Programming Project*, eds B. Buchanan and E. Shorliffe, Addison-Wesley, Reading, 1984, pp. 20–52

Other chapters of the same book provide an insight into the technology during its most effervescent years.

Readers with an *academic* or *historical* interest in the RETE algorithm can read Charles Forgy's original doctoral thesis on the topic:

- Charles Forgy, "On the efficient implementation of production systems." Ph.D. thesis, Carnegie-Mellon University, 1979

The Wikipedia entry for the RETE algorithm has more details about the RETE algorithm than Sect. 6.4.1. In particular, it explains how *quantifiers* (universal, existential) and *OR*ed conditions are handled, and points to additional references.

InfoWorld publishes, with some regularity, the results of some academic benchmarks using the latest versions of the best known commercial and open-source engines (http://www.infoworld.com).

The JRules documentation provides more information about the parameters of the various execution algorithms, and their customization and extension points.

Chapter 7
Issues in Designing Business Rule Applications

Target audience

- *Application architect, software architect, developer*

In this chapter you will learn

- *The major design issues for early business rule management systems*
- *An overview of the major architectural choices for a business rules application*
- *An overview of the major design issues surrounding the integration of rule engines into business applications*
- *An overview of the major design issues and best practices regarding reengineering legacy applications to introduce business rules*

Key points

- *Business rule management is about more than authoring – and managing – executable rules: we need to manage the early deliverables (rule capture and analysis) and ensure proper traceability through the various stages of ABRD.*
- *Business rule applications can come in many shapes and sizes: rules are architecture-neutral.*
- *Most BRMSs offer many rule engine deployment options.*
- *The integration of rule-based decisioning into applications depends, in part, on the architecture of the application, and in part, on rule-specific architectural requirements.*
- *There are some proven patterns to reengineer the decisioning aspect of a legacy application using rule engines.*

7.1 Introduction

In this chapter, we go over the design space for enterprise applications that adopt the business rules approach. We identify the main design dimensions, and for each dimension, we identify the general design issues and outline broad solution

J. Boyer and H. Mili, *Agile Business Rule Development*,
DOI 10.1007/978-3-642-19041-4_7, © Springer-Verlag Berlin Heidelberg 2011

strategies. We will revisit each of the dimensions in later chapters of the book to go more in depth into the design problems, and where applicable, to describe the solution patterns provided by, or made possible with, the JRules BRMS.

The first design dimension that we will consider is the Business Rules Management System space. Indeed, recall from Chap. 1 that at the core of the business rules approach is the corporate-wide management of business rules, and at the core of such a management is a business rules management system. Recall that a business rules management system (BRMS) has two major functionalities, *rule management*, and *rule automation*. Section 7.2 will focus on rule management functionalities.

Because the architectural style of the business rule application influences the way the application interacts with the rule automation component of the BRMS, Sect. 7.3 will provide a very high-level view of the major architectural metaphors for enterprise applications. Clearly, a handful of pages cannot do justice to such a broad topic about which numerous, voluminous books have been – and continue to be – written! The purpose of this section is more modest: to get some vocabulary and some points of reference that we can refer to in our subsequent discussions.

Having talked about the architecture of the business application, we then discuss the different design dimensions concerning the ways in which the business application can access the rules, in Sect. 7.4. In particular, we will talk about two general strategies for executing rules (a) by manipulating a rule engine directly, and (b) by accessing a centralized rule execution service.

A number of projects that we ran into in our practice are reengineering projects of existing applications. Minimally, such reengineering efforts involved externalizing business decisions using BRMS technology. In many cases, reengineering also involves a redesign of the presentation and application layers, adding or renovating modalities for interacting with the application. In such cases, the design is subjected to a number of constraints, and some design choices will be made for us. We will highlight the main issues and best practices in Sect. 7.5. We will summarize the key findings of this chapter in Sect. 7.6 and suggest further readings in the section on "Further Reading."

7.2   Design Dimensions for Rule Management

7.2.1   Early Versus Late BRMS Tools

We mentioned in Chap. 1 that a business rule management system (BRMS) provides functionalities for rule management and execution. While there are many commercial – and open-source – business rule management systems, none that we know of handle the entire lifecycle of rules, i.e., from rule capture all the way to rule retirement. Historically, business rule management systems have evolved from rule engine technology where the focus was on providing efficient execution of rules written in fairly formal languages (see Chap. 6), and JRules was no exception. The past decade has seen an increasing awareness of the importance of rules as *business* assets that need to be managed and shared across the organization, and management functionalities have been added to execution functionalities. However, the focus remained on rules already coded in a formal business rule language. We could call these *late BRMS* tools.

Independently, the past decade has seen the emergence of a number of *early BRMS* tools that focus on the early phases of the rule lifecycle such as business modeling, rule capture, analysis, management, vocabulary management, and so forth. Such tools include BRS RuleTrack™[1] or RuleXpress™.[2] However, we know of no product that does a good job throughout the entire rule lifecycle, i.e., from business modeling all the way to execution, maintenance, and retirement. We also know of no pair of products ("early" BRMS, "late" BRMS) that can be easily piped together to handle the entire lifecycle. Accordingly, an organization that needs to support the entire rule lifecycle will have to perform some kind of customization. Because of the complexity of the features of late BRMS tools – formal rule language parsing, translation, and execution – the recommended practice is then to *first* select the late BRMS tool among available offerings that addresses our late BRMS needs, which would be JRules in our case, and then select among the early BRMS tools the one that would require the least customization or the simplest bridge to our late BRMS tool. From our experience, what ends up happening, most of the time, is that customers custom-build the early BRMS functionalities themselves on top of early CASE[3] tools or some general office productivity tools such as spreadsheet software, shared workspaces (e.g., Lotus Notes databases), etc.

The issue that we wish to address in this section is to identify the kinds of functionalities that are needed for "early BRMS", i.e., establish a list of requirements for "early BRMS".

7.2.2 Requirements for an Early BRMS Tool

Business rules being a development artifact that results from applying a specific development process, an early BRMS tool should:

- Support the representation of "early rules", and the artifacts they depend on
- Support the processes inherent in early business rule management

---

[1]BRS RuleTrack is a product of Business Rule Solutions, http://www.BRSolutions.com.

[2]RuleXpress is a product of RuleArts, check http://www.RuleArts.com.

[3]CASE for Computer Assisted Software Engineering. Our use of the terms *early BRMS* and *late BRMS* is actually borrowed from CASE terminology, where *early CASE* refers to functionalities focusing on requirements and modeling, and *late CASE* focuses on design and coding. That distinction concerning CASE is blurring with model-driven development as we now have powerful CASE tools that can perform round-trip engineering from platform independent UML models all the way to platform-specific Java (or C#) code, and back.

Figure 7.1 shows a metamodel of rules adapted from Morgan (2002). This diagram shows the relationship between business rules, object models, process models, and business intent. We can interpret this metamodel at two levels. At the surface level, we can think of it as a way of designing *rule templates*. Figure 7.1 then tells us that a rule template must include, in addition to the name or text of the rule itself, the following pieces of information: (1) the business motivation behind the rule (business intent), (2) a list of the objects constrained by the rule, (3) the process step(s) constrained by the rule, and (4) any business events (or other process steps) triggered by the rule. Figure 7.2 shows a sample rule template.

Practically, this template can be implemented using an Excel spreadsheet, a local database form (e.g., Access), or a web form accessing a common repository. We have seen all three implementations at different customer sites.

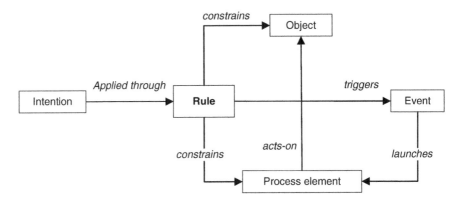

Fig. 7.1 An ontology of rules (Simplified from Morgan 2002, p. 28)

Name	AUTO_UW_Drivers_with_DUI		
Author	John Smith	*Creation date*	April 15, 2009
Rule text	Driver must not have had DUI conviction within past 7 years		
Business motiva-tion	Do not underwrite risk prone drivers	*Processes con-strained by rule*	UW/Eligibility
Objects con-strained by rule	Driver; Policy	*Business events triggered by rule*	

Fig. 7.2 A sample rule template based on the ontology of Fig. 7.1

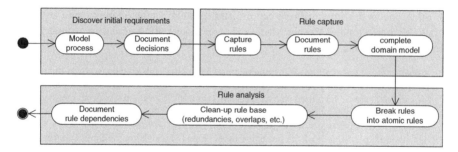

Fig. 7.3 A simplified process for rule capture and analysis

The problem with such a representation is that it is static: the things that the template refers to (objects, processes, events) can change, but their references will not. For example, after the rule is written, somebody decides to refer to all potential insurance holders as **PolicyHolder**, instead of **Driver**, **HomeOwner**, or **Tenant**. This change will not be automatically propagated to the rule description, which will then become obsolete. The solution, naturally, is to have the template refer to the actual entities (objects, processes, business events), as opposed to referring to their names. An example of such a tool is RuleXpress™ from RuleArts, which supports rule capture, and *term and fact modeling*. An alternative consists of building a bridge between a rule management tool, and a business/system modeling tool. For example, in the above template, we can imagine having automatically filled pull-down lists for the field "Objects constrained by rule". The same applies for "Processes constrained by rule" or "Business events triggered by rule".

With regard to the rule capture and analysis process, Fig. 7.3 shows a simplified process. This process, based on the STEP methodology (von Halle 2001), shows the key tasks we adopted in ABRD (see Chap. 3), without the incrementality (tackling one piece of a functional area at a time) and iteration (feedback loop). Nevertheless, the process can tell us three things:

1. The various deliverables and artifacts that are needed
2. The different *versions* of each deliverable
3. The workflow

We will discuss the early BRMS artifacts and deliverables in Sect. 7.2.2.1. The versioning and lifecycle management (workflow) of these artifacts and deliverables will be discussed in Sect. 7.2.2.2.

7.2.2.1 Early BRMS Artifacts and Deliverables

With regard to the deliverables, the ontology of Fig. 7.1 has already established the need to represent – and co-reference – process models, rules, and domain models. The main issue here is whether we need to have one or two – or more – representations of rules, one as the output of rule capture, and another, as the output of rule analysis. Consider the following Fannie Mae mortgage underwriting guideline[4] found in the underwriting manual:

> Properties must have hazards insurance that protects against loss or damage from fire and other hazards covered by the standard extended coverage endorsement. The policy should provide for claims to be settled on a replacement cost basis. The amount of coverage should at least equal the minimum of:
> a) 100% of the insurable value of the improvements.
> b) The principal balance of the mortgage (as long as it exceeds the minimum amount – typically 80% – required to compensate for damage or loss on a replacement cost basis).

If we are performing rule capture from the underwriting manual (see rule capture in Chap. 4), we would take this prose, and pretty much stuff it as is into the "Rule text" field of the rule template shown in Fig. 7.2.[5] If we put this rule through analysis, it will be broken down and will result into a bunch of rules, including:

- The property MUST HAVE a hazards insurance that protects against loss or damage from fire, flood, etc.
- The coverage amount of the hazards insurance policy of the property MUST BE GREATER THAN 100% of the insurable value of the improvements.

These are the rules that will be handed to rule authors who will code them. So now the question is, do we need both versions? We definitely need the atomic one (output of analysis), because that is the appropriate input for rule authors. We believe that it is important to keep the original version too, because that is the version closest to the original business requirement, and it is important to keep it for traceability purposes. Indeed, a policy manager who needs to *validate* – i.e., verify conformance to business intent – the result of rule analysis needs to know where the atomic rule comes from. For example, during analysis, one of the steps consists of making rules atomic, which maps a discovery-level rule into several analysis-level rules. The reverse can also happen. One of the tasks of rule analysis in STEP (von Halle 2001) is the identification of *rule patterns*. If I find several rules that use the age of the policy holder, and their credit score, to compute a risk factor, I would probably group them in a single rule artifact, i.e., a *decision table*.

This raises several issues. While the two examples above are clear-cut, rule analysis includes a number of less dramatic transformations that rules undergo. Do we always need to have two versions of each rule, one as the output of capture, and the other as the output of analysis? And if so, at what level should we perform rule maintenance? Should we maintain rules at the "capture level", and then percolate the changes down, to analysis, or, should we simply perform maintenance at the analysis level. Using our property hazards insurance example, let us say we change the requirement on the percentage of the coverage from 100% of the insurable value

---

[4]The Fannie Mae underwriting manual calls it a *guideline*, but according to the classification of rules discussed in Chap. 4, this rule represents a *constraint*, i.e., a *must-have* condition.

[5]We may massage the text using some of the *linguistic templates* described in Chap. 4.

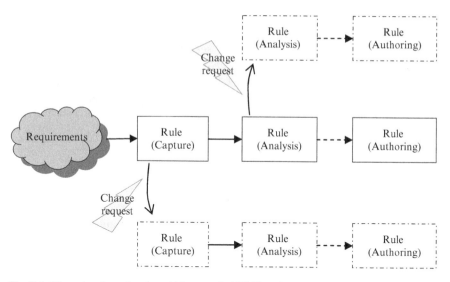

Fig. 7.4 Managing dependencies within an early BRMS tool

of the improvements to 95%. Should we update the non-atomic version – and update the atomic version accordingly – or should we update the atomic version (analysis-level) directly, leaving the non-atomic one unchanged? This depends on the type and form of the change request. If the change request concerns the entire (non-atomic) rule, then we should update the non-atomic rule, and then percolate the change down to the atomic ones. If the change request concerns only the coverage percentage, then we do not need to update the non-atomic version: it adds no value in terms of traceability. Figure 7.4 illustrates the various dependencies that would be useful to record in an early BRMS tool.

7.2.2.2 Versioning and Lifecycle Management

An important issue in maintenance, in general, is that of versioning. A naive versioning policy would create a different version each time a rule is modified. However, such a policy would lead to a proliferation of versions, with no significance to business. When first created, the attributes of a rule (fields in the rule template) will either have default values or will be empty. The various attributes may be edited at different times, and it does not make sense to treat each attribute (field) modification as a new version. At the same time, it may be useful to keep a history of the changes that took place for a given rule. Thus, a sensible versioning policy would include a combination of history management functionality, which keeps track of all changes to rules, meaningful or otherwise, and a deliberate versioning mechanism, where the user chooses to tag a specific modification as a version change.

Going back to Fig. 7.3, in addition to managing the various lifecycle deliverables, an early BRMS must also manage the workflow. Rule capture and analysis involves several tasks, each involving a set of actors playing different roles, including *policy managers, subject matter experts, rule (business) analysts, rule stewards*, etc. Chapter 16 of this book talks about rule governance in relation to authored rules. However, the same concepts apply to "early rules". In particular, an early BRMS must support role-based access control, and implement a state-driven management of rules.

7.2.3 Conclusion

In this section, we explored the kinds of functionalities that an *early BRMS* tool should support. We identified some of the things that we need to represent about rules, including their relationships to other modeling and analysis artifacts such as process models (or use cases) and domain models. We also touched upon the need to represent different lifecycle versions for rules to reflect the changes that they undergo during capture and analysis. An early BRMS tool must also support the *process* of capturing and analyzing rules, and we identified the need for managing the workflow of the various lifecycle deliverables.

None of the early BRMS tools we looked at – or know of – support all of these functionalities. Until such time that early BRMS tools support the required functionalities and integrate seamlessly with a *late BRMS* tool such as JRules, we recommend that organizations adopt and adapt existing technologies for document management. While automation is often desirable, it usually comes at a high cost in terms: (1) implementation effort and (2) reduced flexibility.

7.3 Design Options for a Business Rule Application

In this section, we explore some of the design dimensions for a business application that implements business rules using BRMS technology, but without special consideration for BRMS integration; that aspect will be treated in Sect. 7.4. Entire books have been written about application design, in general, and about specific architectures and technologies. Our goal is not to rival such treatises. Instead, we simply aim at providing the reader with some terminology corresponding to some cardinal points in the design space to anchor our discussion about rule integration (see Sect. 7.4).

The architecture of an application is influenced by many factors. The most salient of these are (1) requirements, (2) constraints, and (3) previous experience. With the regard to requirements, there is a whole bunch of them, including – fittingly called – architectural requirements, which include a variety of development-level qualities (modularity, various "abilities" such as portability, reusability, scalability, evolvability, etc.), run-time qualities (performance, fault-tolerance, recoverability, etc.), business requirements, which relate to qualities such as cost, time to market, configurability (i.e., the ability to deliver easily configurable subsets of the functionalities), organizational requirements (e.g., the ability to have components of the system developed by geographically distributed teams), etc. Constraints include things such as the obligation to adopt a particular architectural style or technology in use at the organization – or, the prohibition to use a particular technology.[6] Constraints can also include regulatory, industry-specific guidelines or requirements, and so forth.

Luckily, little architectural design is done from first principles nowadays: we draw on experiences, both our own and those of other architects, in the form of various *architectural styles* or *patterns*. It is useful to think of application architectures in terms of *architectural styles* and *technologies* that adhere to, or support, those styles.[7] For the purposes of our discussion, we will limit ourselves to the most common architectural styles, i.e., those appropriate for business applications that are typically deployed in a modern enterprise environment. In terms of technologies, we will also limit ourselves to the most commonly used technologies in an enterprise environment. Exotic, niche, or unproven architectural styles or technologies will not be considered.

Roughly speaking, when considering developing a business application, four broad categories may be considered:

- *Standalone applications.* by this we mean an application that runs on the CPU of the machine of the user that uses only those resources that are available on that machine.
- *Synchronous client–server applications.* by this we mean an enterprise application whereby the processing of business events takes place in at least two processes – which typically reside in different CPUs – and follows a synchronous call pattern, i.e., whenever a "client" tier player issues a command to a "server" tier player, the client blocks waiting for the answer from the "server". Ajax notwithstanding,[8] typical web and J2EE applications fit in this category, except for asynchronous invocation patterns, discussed next.
- *Message-oriented architectures.* this is also the case where the processing of a business event takes place in more than one process – and typically, more than one machine. The difference with the previous category is that the communication between the system's components is message-oriented and asynchronous.
- *Service-oriented architectures.* in such architectures, applications are seen as *orchestrations* of *services*. *Services* are software components that satisfy a number of properties, including the following four: (a) *loose coupling*, whereby

---

[6]We dealt with one customer who prohibited the use of J2EE technology.

[7]Some authors will talk about *architectural metaphors*. These basically mean the same thing, except that *architectural styles* have a precise meaning in the academic literature.

[8]AJAX, for Asynchronous Javascript and XML, offers limited-scope a-synchronicity between web clients and servers, and does not fit the asynchronous style discussed here.

they interact through publicly declared interfaces, with no hidden dependencies, (b) *implementation neutrality*, whereby a service can be invoked the same way, regardless of the way it is implemented, (c) *late-bound composition*, whereby services can be composed on the fly/on-demand, and (d) *coarse granularity*, whereby services implement *business-level* services.

In the remaining subsections, we look at these four families in a bit more detail. For each family, we look at five criteria: (1) simplicity of implementation, (2) performance, (3) scalability, (4) ease of deployment, and (5) ease of maintenance/ evolvability. Because the BRMS we talk about in this book – IBM WebSphere ILOG JRules – is Java based, we will consider the Java flavors of the various architectural families.

7.3.1 Standalone Applications

Within the context of the Java language, we talk about *J2SE* applications. Such applications perform all of their processing locally on the user machine, accessing local resources (a local database, the file system) for the bulk of their processing.

If you think about it, most of the applications running on your PC are standalone applications. Your file explorer, word processor, spreadsheet software, *non-web* e-mail client, or development IDE (Eclipse, NetBeans, VisualStudio) are just like that.[9] Such applications may, on occasion, access external resources. For example, a licensed desktop application may access a remote license server on start-up. An IDE may embed a version control system client which connects with the server when it is time to check-in or check-out stuff, but most of the work is done on your local workspace.[10] An antivirus software may check for updates at start-up etc.

While this architecture seems appropriate for office software or operating system utilities, is it adapted to business applications? Business applications usually access business data, which tends to be voluminous and distributed. But there are some situations where business applications can be developed as standalone, "desktop", applications. For example, a sales support application for traveling salespeople may be developed as a standalone application that accesses a local product catalog with prices schedules, and a *nearly up-to-date* inventory.[11] We have worked with insurance companies that developed desktop underwriting applications that their brokers could run on their laptops while on the road, enabling them to provide

---

[9]By the way, so is your web browser – *as an application*. Whether it is Internet Explorer, or Firefox, or Opera, or Safari, the executable is on your machine, and it executes on your machine.

[10]If the local workspace happens to reside on a remote disk, the operating system will make that transparent to the IDE.

[11]For example, the salespeople may synchronize their local inventory database (on their PC) with the corporate inventory database when they are back to their hotel at night.

quotes to potential policyholders offline without having to "wait to go back to the office". We have encountered a similar situation with mortgage brokers.

The standalone application style has one major advantage: simplicity! Standalone applications also tend to be responsive: indeed, because all resources are local, there is no network latency or database contention to deal with. *By definition*, they are not scalable, but given the type of application – i.e., a single user, in interactive mode – they often do not need to. In terms of deployment and maintenance, there are a number of tools nowadays that make the initial deployment, and the deployment of consecutive updates, relatively painless.[12]

7.3.2 *Synchronous Client–Server Architecture*

This family of architectures covers a fairly broad spectrum, from a simple, run of the mill, three-tier web application with a thin client, a web server, and a database to a full four-tier application with a thin client, a web server, an app server, and an enterprise information service (EIS) providing access to legacy data. Figure 7.5 shows a typology of J2EE-type client–server architectures.[13]

What the various flavors have in common is the client tier – web client or standalone – and the EIS tier, which stands for a database or a legacy information system that enables us to access enterprise data through an API. Between these two, we can have a direct connection (e.g., between a standalone client and the EIS resource), in which case we have a two-tier architecture, or a web container, or an application server, for a three-tier architecture, or both, for a full-fledged four-tier architecture. Naturally, if we have a (thin) web client, we minimally need a web container – and a three-tier architecture. However, it is possible to have a rich client

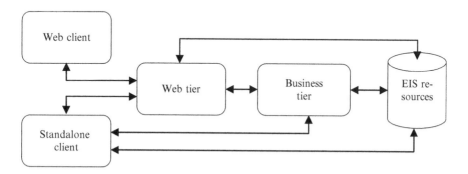

Fig. 7.5 Different client–server architectures

---

[12]Java Webstart, e.g., is about as simple as it gets.

[13]This diagram is borrowed from the J2EE literature. See for example http://java.sun.com/javaee.

connect to an application server, which, in turn, accesses data through an EIS resource. Although there are legitimate-use cases for all of the above combinations, we will focus on the most common ones: three-tier web applications, with a thin web client, a web server tier, and EIS tier, and four-tier web applications, with a business tier between the web tier and the EIS.

In a four-tier web application, we strive to separate the business logic from the presentation and interaction logic of the application. The presentation and interaction logic are embodied in the web tier, while the business logic (business entities, non-modal business functions) is embodied in the business tier. The web tier itself is commonly architected along some flavor of the *model-view-controller* pattern, first developed within the context of Smalltalk's GUI libraries, and later adapted to the web context. Indeed, most of the web-development frameworks (Struts and Struts2, Spring MVC, Ruby on Rails, Tapestry, etc.) implement some variation on the model-view-controller. Figure 7.6 illustrates the principles behind the MVC.

The view component embodies the user interface (e.g., the HTML contents of a web page) and represents (views) the current state of the model component, the controller embodies the program that captures user input, and that translates it into *commands* to be executed by the model component, and the model component represents the application logic. The plain arrows show the references between the components, while the dashed arrows represent the data and command flows between them. A key aspect of the MVC is the fact that *the model* has no explicit knowledge of the view or controller, which makes the application logic independent of the presentation technology, enabling us to offer multiple views/presentations for the same model. Another key aspect of MVC frameworks is the provision of *view* and *controller* libraries, which enable web developers to develop views and controllers by composing configurable library components, thereby enhancing the

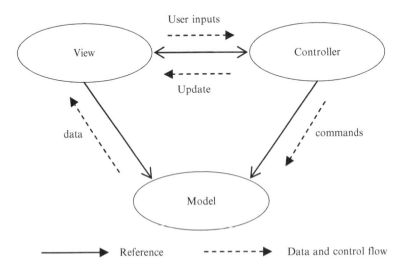

Fig. 7.6 The principles behind the MVC pattern

productivity of the presentation layer development and its quality (e.g., consistent look and feel).

Within the context of web applications, the view is typically some flavor of HTML, and the controller is a user-coded or framework-generated servlet that acts as an intermediary between the model and the view, with no direct reference or data flow between the two, as is suggested by Fig. 7.6. As for the *model* component, it is usually a *façade* for the business logic that records the current state of the application/interaction and manages the application flow. Within the context of three-tier applications, the business logic is packaged together with the model component of the web application. Within the context of four-tier applications, the business logic is packaged – and deployed – separately from the web component. In this latter case, the invocation of business services by the model component of the MVC triad may be delegated to a session bean-like interface, i.e., a proxy façade for business services. Note that, within the context of a four-tier application, the web component and the business tier component need not reside in different servers, and the communication between the two need not be remote. However, they are packaged and deployed separately.

It is beyond the scope of this section, chapter, and book, to explore the full-design space for synchronous J2EE-style client–server applications. For the purposes of the current discussion, we are interested in identifying the different places within an application that business decisions may need to be taken, and correspondingly, the different invocation sites for business rules. The latter aspects will be discussed in Sect. 7.4.2.

7.3.3 Message-Oriented Architectures

A common problem faced by IT departments is that of integrating a variety of mission critical applications developed using different technologies, running on different platforms, and that were never meant to work together in the first place. Message-Oriented Middleware (MOM) was developed to address this *enterprise application integration* problem. With MOM, instead of remote procedure calls between applications – which would be unworkable in this case – applications send each other messages that contain a description of what needs to get done, along with the data. Thus, if an online web-based order processing system wants to invoke a mainframe batch inventory management system, it can send to it a message, for every confirmed order, that contains the required inventory decrements. The mainframe batch inventory management application can process the queued messages when it kicks off at 3:00 a.m., along with the transaction logs coming from other legacy applications.

The advantages of message-oriented integration are many, including:

- *Interoperability*. Producers and consumers of messages can agree on a technology-neutral message format that abstracts the many differences that may exist in the underlying programming languages, memory models, and function call semantics.

This makes it possible to interconnect applications developed with totally different technologies. In the simple example above, the inventory management system need not even be "working" when the online order processing system "makes the call."[14]

- *Robustness*. The MOM virtually guarantees message delivery. Indeed, the messages that are sent are persisted so that if the messaging channel or the receiver fails, the messages can be recovered and put back on the queue until they are consumed by the targeted destination. By comparison, no such guarantees exist for remote procedure calls: the best a caller can do is to retry a failed call.[15]
- *Loose coupling*. The interacting applications are loosely coupled. Thus, we can replace an application by another one that does the same job, in a different location, and using a different technology. We can also add new functionality to the system on the fly by having it "listen in" on the existing message channels to consume existing messages without having to change.
- *Scalability*. In a traditional synchronous RPC call, the caller blocks until the call completes. During this idle wait, the caller uses up system resources and cannot process other business events/transactions. With MOM, an application can turn around and process other transactions as soon as it sends a request concerning the current transaction. When the receiver replies, the application can take up with that transaction where it left off.

Because of these advantages, message-oriented integration has been applied beyond its original niche of *enterprise application integration* (EAI) problems. In particular, the Java Message Service (JMS) API, which provides a standard Java API that enables Java programs to communicate with various messaging implementations, has been used to mediate interactions between Java components within the context of J2EE applications. Here, interoperability is not much of an issue,[16] but architects value loose coupling, robustness, and scalability. In particular, messaging can be used within the context of a four-tier architecture (see the previous section), either for the interactions between the web tier and the business tier (e.g., using message-driven beans) or to implement some business services on behalf of the business tier.

Again, for the purposes of this section and chapter, we will not explore the full design space for message-driven architectures. We will be content to raise the possibility of having the communication between rule "consumers" (i.e., business application components) and rule "providers" (e.g., a rule execution serve) mediated through a messaging framework or middleware.

---

[14]Contrast this with typical OO RPC calls: the caller and receiver processes need to be active for the "call to be delivered". In fact, part of CORBA's lifecycle management services consists of instantiating a server process whenever a client makes a call to a dead server object.

[15]This is often problematic because in the case of a RPC call, it is not always possible to tell when a connection exception occurred during the request or the response. Unless we use a transactional context, retrying a failed call may not be appropriate.

[16]The J2EE platform does offer other APIs to integrate with legacy EIS, e.g., JCA.

7.3.4 Service-Oriented Architectures

What is SOA? Is it a panacea that will revolutionize the way we develop software – and some say, manage our businesses – or is it yet another marketing-driven IT fad peddled by integrators and solution vendors. We believe it is neither. It is not revolutionary – you know what we think of revolutions by now – but an evolutionary convergence of advances in middleware, software architecture, and "age old" best IT practices. Like most new trends, its potential has been overhyped, and its challenges have not been well-understood. But there is real substance, and its power can be harnessed with proper methodology, reasonable expectations, and some (appropriate) technology. We first discuss the principles underlying *service-oriented computing*. Next, we discuss the historical influences of SOC. Finally, we say a few words about service-oriented *engineering*.

7.3.4.1 Service-Oriented Computing Principles

The *service-oriented computing* (SOC) paradigm views the development of business applications as the late-bound composition (*orchestration*) of loosely coupled, implementation-neutral, coarse-grained software components called *services*. Roughly speaking, a service is a collection of coherent/cohesive capabilities that can address the needs of many consumers. A flight booking service would offer *functions/operations* for searching for flights, booking flights, and canceling existing bookings. There has been much debate in the community about what constitutes a *service*. Thomas Erl (2005), an SOA pioneer, identified eight characteristics of services:

- *Standardized (service) contracts.* As software components, services define their capabilities using a standard, implementation-neutral language.
- *Loose coupling.* The services are loosely coupled, and any dependencies are explicitly stated in their service contracts.
- *Abstraction.* Whereas loose coupling refers to dependencies between services, abstraction refers to dependencies between a service provider and a service consumer. The consumer should not depend on the implementation details of the service.
- *Reusability.* Services embody reusable functionality that can service *many* consumers. In other work, we defined reusability as *usefulness* and *usability* (Mili et al. 2002). Usefulness refers to how often the provided functionality is needed while usability refers to how easy it is to use. Usability embodies many aspects, including the existence of (standardized) service contracts (see above), as well as discoverability, composability, and interoperability, discussed below.
- *Autonomy.* From the perspective of the consumer, services should be perceived as self-contained components with total control over their resources and environment. The consumer should be able to assume that the service needs no more than the parameters specified in its service contract to do its job. Naturally,

behind the scenes, a service may in turn depend on other services. For example, business services can depend on a layer of shared technical services.

- *Statelessness.* We can understand statelessness of services in two complementary ways. To be able to "service" many consumers, a service should not have to rely on implicit state information about its consumers; all of the data needed to service a particular consumer's request should be explicitly passed as parameters. The second aspect of statelessness is related to multiple interactions with the same consumer. This means that a consumer can invoke the operations of the service as many times as they want, in any order they wish, and always get the same result. In practice, of course, these two conditions are seldom attainable – and not necessarily desirable. If I am using a flight booking service, I sure hope that my interactions with the service have a lasting effect on the state of the world: the creation of a booking in the booking database. Erl writes: "Applying the principle of service statelessness requires that measures of realistically attainable statelessness be assessed, based on the adequacy of the surrounding technology architecture to provide state management delegation and deferral options".[17]
- *Discoverability.* This refers to the ability of services to document – and advertise – their capabilities so that service consumers can find them. The documentation of the capabilities of a service needs to be expressed in a domain language that is distinct from the language used to express the service contract.
- *Composability.* This refers to dual capability of services to (a) be composed at arbitrary levels of aggregation to form more complex services and (b) address many needs. This, in turn, influences two design aspects of services: (a) the modalities for interacting with the service and (b) the way the capabilities of the service are distributed among its operations.

7.3.4.2 SOC Lineage

The above characteristics embody a number of design principles that have evolved over the years, and that have found expression in a number of technologies. To name a few:

1. *Object-orientation.* From OO, we inherit the idea of a service contract (the public interface of a class), abstraction (information hiding), reusability, and to some extent, autonomy (encapsulation). However, classes do not have the appropriate granularity to form the foundation of a SOC – too small, too dependent on others.
2. Component-oriented development embodies many of the same principles that underlie OO, but at a higher level of abstraction and granularity. In component-oriented development, we have a burgeoning expression of autonomy, statelessness, and discoverability.
3. Distributed applications, in general, and message-oriented architectures, in particular, contribute remoteness, interoperability, and loose coupling. In fact,

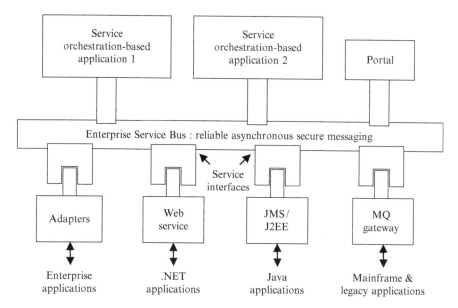

Fig. 7.7 A typical technological landscape of an SOA, using an enterprise service bus (ESB) (Adapted from Papazoglou et al. 2007)

as we will see shortly, these architectures often provide the computational backbone for SOC.

4. Business process management, which makes a clear distinction between the orchestration of a business process, and execution of the various tasks of the process by separate applications.

5. Web services, which constitute *one implementation* of SOC, and thus, not surprisingly, embody most of the above characteristics "out of the box", in part thanks to web service standards such as WSDL (service contracts) and UDDI (discoverability).

From a technological point of view, SOAs tend to be message-oriented, and an *enterprise service bus* typically constitutes its infrastructural backbone. Figure 7.7 shows a typical technological landscape of an SOA.

7.3.4.3 Service-Oriented Engineering

Now that we understand what an SOA is, and what it looks like, how do you build one? What constitutes a good service? How can I (can I?) leverage existing IT assets? And so forth. A pure *service-oriented analysis* would start from an abstract description of some business functionality and decompose it into an orchestration of *services* that satisfy the eight criteria mentioned above. To make sure that the so-identified services are *truly* reusable and composable, we need to consider *many* such business functionalities within a particular domain, i.e., we need to perform a good *domain analysis*. There are many ways to decompose business functionalities, including good old functional decomposition, process decomposition, goal-subgoal decomposition (see, e.g., Huhns and Singh (2005)), or as Zimmermann et al. (2004) have suggested, using *Feature-Oriented Domain Analysis* (FODA; Kang et al. 1990) to help with the identification of candidate services. A pure top-down approach can only be *part* of the solution: we need to take into account and leverage the existing IT assets to guide the service decomposition. Zimmermann et al. referred to this as a "meet in the middle" approach. Actually, *most* domain *engineering* methods do use a combination of *analysis* (top-down decomposition) and *synthesis* (generalizing from existing applications within the domain) to arrive at a good domain architecture (Mili et al. 2002). That being said, a number of authors and practitioners recognize that slapping a web service interface onto a legacy system does not make a good service. Indeed, legacy applications may fail many of the essential/non-packaging related criteria mentioned above (autonomy, abstraction, statelessness, and composability), and some measure of reengineering is often needed to make them good service citizens.

For the purposes of the current discussion, we will not delve any deeper into SOA. We are interested in the role that rule-based decisioning can play within service-oriented applications. Referring back to Fig. 7.7, we can see two places where rule-based decisioning might take place: (a) within the context of individual services (lower half of the diagram), or (b) within the context of the application orchestration of services (workflow routing and management). Section 7.4.2 will discuss the various rule engine deployment alternatives to accommodate these decisioning needs.

7.4   Designing the Integration of Rules into Applications

If we adopt the business rules approach, business applications will delegate the decision aspects of their processing to a rule engine (see Fig. 7.8). In this section, we look at the design space for how a business application invokes the rule engine. There are a number of design factors to consider, but the most obvious ones are: (a) what does the calling application look like and (b) how the rules are deployed, in the first place. The architecture of the calling application will typically be determined by a number of factors not having to do with the use of business rules. Section 7.3 of this chapter explored (summarily) the design space for enterprise applications; in this section, we look at how a particular point in that space influences our integration. With regard to rule engine deployment, roughly speaking, there are two broad options:

- Executing rules by manipulating rule engines directly as Java objects running within the same JVM – typically within the same thread – as the calling business application
- Executing rules by invoking a separately running – and typically remote – rule execution service

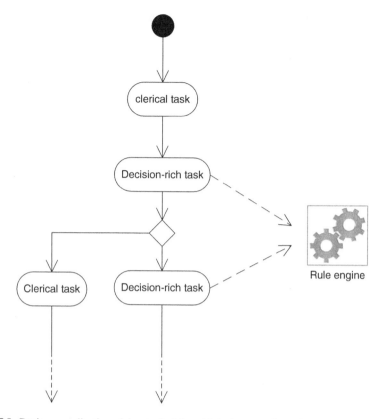

Fig. 7.8 Business applications delegate decision-rich tasks to a rule engine

A rule execution service typically offers a number of services, in addition to executing rules on behalf of business applications. Those services will be discussed in Sect. 7.4.1, and will serve for the comparison between the two deployment options. Existing BRMSs offer one, the other, or both deployment options.[17] The issue then becomes, given an application architecture, which rule engine deployment to choose? Generally speaking, we would want to use the simplest deployment option that will do the job, and that will generally plead for the option consisting of manipulating rule engines directly. However, other architectural requirements, such as scalability and hot deployment, or rule management requirements, such as versioning, might plead for a rule execution service option.

We start this section by comparing the two engine deployment options (Sect. 7.4.1). In Sect. 7.4.2, we talk about how the architecture of the calling application influences the choice of a deployment options. Section 7.4.3 provides a summary.

---

[17]JRules offers half a dozen variants of the *rule execution service* option, to be discussed in Chap. 13.

7.4.1 Rule Engine Deployment Options

Generally speaking, there are two broad options for executing rules on behalf of a
business application. In the first option, illustrated in Fig. 7.9a, the business
application manipulates a rule engine and its required resources directly. Typically,
the rule engine is written in the same language as the business application (for
example Java) and lives in the same memory space and the same thread as the

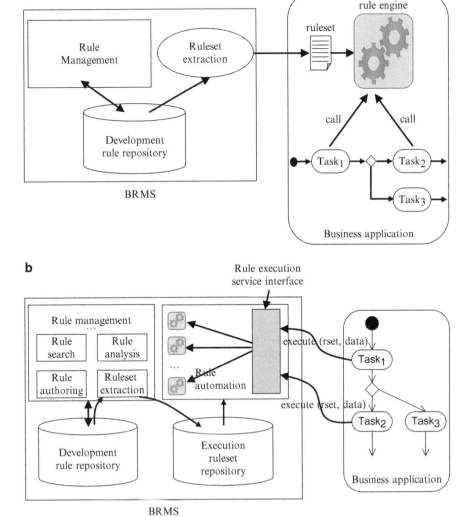

Fig. 7.9 (a) Business applications execute rules by manipulating rule engines directly. (b) Ruleset
execution as a service provided by a *rule execution server*

calling application. In this case, the execution component of the BRMS is somewhat limited to a code library that can be integrated in calling business applications, and the business application manages the lifecycle of the rule engine and its required resources – typically, the ruleset, and any reference data the ruleset needs.

In the second option, illustrated in Fig. 7.9b, rule execution is offered as a *service* to business applications offered by a *rule execution server* whereby a business application may request the execution of a particular ruleset on a specific data set, and get the result of the execution is return. In such situations, the rule execution server is responsible for managing the lifecycle of the rule engine and its required resources. The business application would use the rule execution service interface to submit a ruleset execution request. A request would have to identify the ruleset, and pass the data on which we wish to apply the rules. Typically, we would expect the rule execution server to be an independently running service. Among other things, this makes it possible to have a *remote* invocation of the rule execution service.

Note that such a rule execution service does not necessarily fit the definition of a *service* in the SOA sense (see Sect. 7.3.4.1). This aspect is thoroughly discussed in Chap. 12, which explore rule engine deployment options in far more detail.

Figure 7.9b shows a plausible implementation for such a rule execution service. We will have ample opportunity in the coming chapters to talk about JRules's own *Rule Execution Server*; in this section, we focus on what a rule execution service might entail, in general. First, it makes sense to have an execution ruleset repository that is separate from the development repository. A ruleset extraction tool generates rulesets from the development repository. As rules are modified and versioned in the development repository, new versions of the rulesets need to be created and saved in the execution repository. Some form of *ruleset versioning* is typically supported.

The rule automation component of the BRMS consists mainly of the ruleset execution service, which accesses the execution repository and relies on a pool of rule engines to service requests coming from possibly different business applications. *Scalability* is made possible by increasing the size of the rule engine pool.

The rule execution service approach (Fig. 7.9b) means that rulesets are deployed, physically separately from the business application code: to invoke a ruleset, we only need to know it by name. This means that we can update a ruleset referenced by a business application without redeploying the business application itself.[18] In mission-critical 24/7 business applications, *hot deployment* of rulesets is a must-have feature.

In summary, if we adopt the rule execution service, we can expect the following services/features:

1. *A central point of ruleset execution* for different applications
2. As a corollary, the possibility of *remote ruleset execution*

---

[18]Meaning the application code archive (in Java, it could be a *Java Archive*, or jar, a *Web Archive*, or war, or an *Enterprise Archive*, or ear).

3. *Separate physical deployment of rulesets*[19] from the executable code of business applications
4. As a corollary, *hot deployment* of executable rulesets
5. The possibility for *versioning executable rulesets*
6. The possibility for *scalability*

The vendor solutions that offer ruleset execution as a service may offer different combinations of these features. The JRules BRMS offers all of them.

Given all of these features, why would anyone bother using – or even considering – the first approach? In fact, there are many reasons to forego these services and use the simpler implementation approach. Indeed, these features come at a – sometimes substantial – cost in terms of added complexity of deployment, of implementation, and of use. For example, if a feature such as hot deployment or separate physical deployment of rulesets is not critically needed, we forego the rule execution service and choose to manipulate rule engines directly. The next two sections will explore the various design trade-offs.

It should be noted that BRMS industry players have used the Java Community Process to come up with a standard API – JSR94 – that abstracts differences between BRMS vendors. In effect, this API also abstracts away differences in deployment modes: the same API can be used whether we are manipulating a rule engine directly or interacting with a rule execution service.[20]

7.4.2 Architecture of the Calling Application

The architecture of the calling business application has a great influence over the way we integrate rule engines into the application. There are different factors to consider, including:

1. The type of application we have: standalone, synchronous client–server, message-oriented, or service-oriented
2. For client–server applications, the tier in which rules should be executed
3. Architectural requirements, e.g., application availability, connectivity to legacy systems, and must-have or cannot-have technologies

In the remainder of this section, we will go over the different criteria and discuss their impact on the choice of a deployment option.

---

[19]From, a deployment point of view, the business rules approach does enable us to treat business logic as data that is separate from program code. However, with the first deployment approach that data is often bundled with the program code in the same application code archive.

[20]As a consequence, the JSR94 API is too "verbose" in those cases where we are manipulating a rule engine directly, and too "coarse" for those instances where we are using the API to invoke a rule execution service. For example, JRules's rule engine API is more "efficient" than JSR94, and its *rule execution server* (RES) API offers finer control than JSR94.

7.4.2.1   The Types of Applications

For a standalone (desktop) application, it is hard to imagine scenarios where an architect would choose to execute rules using a rule execution service. Remote invocation would be too much of an overhead. Indeed, scalability is not an issue in this case, and there is little benefit to be gained from a central point of execution of rules – having already opted for a decentralized execution of the application itself. If hot deployment of rulesets is an important requirement, we can imagine other ways of distributing new rulesets and running different versions of rulesets. Most likely, desktop applications can run offline and do not need the rulesets to be accurate to the minute. Take the example of a traveling insurance broker who has a desktop quote generation/underwriting application on their laptop. They can connect to home base at night to load the latest version of the underwriting rules. Actually, the chances are you have a similar application running on your laptop right now. Indeed, many antivirus software packages work just this way: they work on your machine, but they check regularly with home base to load the latest virus definitions, which are nothing but *rules*, i.e., *declaratively specified patterns* of malicious code!

With client–server applications, both deployment options are plausible. Having made the decision to use a client–server type of application, using a rule execution service does not add undue complexity or overhead. The importance of features such as hot deployment, ruleset versioning, or central point of execution makes the difference. The same can be said about message-oriented architectures or service-oriented architectures: both types of architectures come at the cost of added complexity in terms of development, deployment, and execution, and executing rules through a rule execution service does not represent undue complexity or overhead.

Note that JRules's *rule execution server* (RES) supports a message-oriented execution pattern built on top of the call-and-return *rule* (execution) *sessions*, which integrates neatly with message-oriented architectures. Note also that the fact that we adopt a service-oriented architecture does not necessarily mean that (a) only a rule execution service makes sense or (b) in such an architecture, the rule execution service would be one of the published services. With regard to the latter point, SOA-type services tend to be coarse-grained business services whereas rule execution is more of a support or infrastructure service for the various business functions. Further, it is difficult to optimize properties such as autonomy and statelessness while maintaining a generic, clean service interface.

Finally, note that there are no absolutes. For every imaginable combination of <application type, rule execution type>, there is a legitimate-use case that warrants it. This is true for the application type, but also of the other criteria discussed in this section.

7.4.2.2   Which Tier, for Client–Server Applications?

Client–server applications come in many flavors, illustrated in Fig. 7.5 (see Sect. 7.3.2) and Fig. 7.10, shown below. One of the issues that designers face is

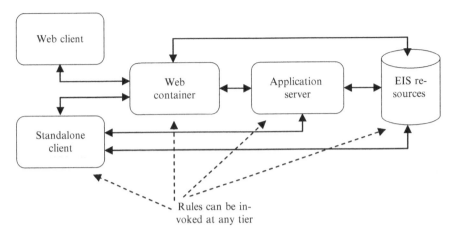

Fig. 7.10 In a client–server application, rules can be invoked at any tier

choosing the application tier at which rules can be invoked. In this section, we look at the reasons – and implications – of invoking rules at a given tier, and how that choice might influence the integration of rule execution in an application – i.e., direct engine manipulation versus rule execution service.

Business rules are part of the business logic, and the most natural place for invoking rules in a multi-tier application is the application server tier. It is also the most common one. There are situations, however, where rules may be invoked from a different tier.

Let us go back to our claim processing application, and assume that claim entry is done through a client side form. A first step in processing claims is data validation. This can take many flavors. The simplest is data format validation, i.e., ensuring that a date is a date or that a number contains no letters. This kind of validation can usually be embedded in the input field controls: the prompt for a date is a calendar! More complex validations include things such as checking the general pattern for a social security number, or a claim ID, or a policy number, prior to performing an actual lookup. Yet a more sophisticated validation will ensure that birthdates do not predate 1850,[21] say, or that a given zip code is indeed, located within the state provided. Other validations will check that the policy number is not only well formed, but also corresponds to an actual policy. And so forth.

This raises two questions. First, should the validation rules even be captured and managed by the BRMS? If so, the second question is, at what point/tier should the rules be invoked: should they be invoked at the client tier, at the web tier, the application server tier, or the database/EIS tier? With regard to the first question, the

---

[21]We have come across an insurer that was carrying a policy that was over a hundred years old. Even though the initial policyholder deceased quite a while ago, the policy was converted in some form of trust in the name of the beneficiaries.

rule classification proposed by the *business rules group* includes all of the previous validations. Indeed, *structural assertions* cover all of the "data definition rules". However, such rules are not necessarily to be captured by the BRMS: some are going to be implicit in data or class diagrams, and subsequently in database schemas or class definitions. In our example, it is clear that rules related to data syntax, such as the input format for dates and numbers, should not be captured in the BRMS. How about the well-formedness of data values? If the rules are not trivial, then they should probably be managed by the BRMS. How about referential integrity constraints?[22] Integrity constraints can be specified and enforced at the database level itself, but do we want to wait until we are about to commit a long and complex transaction? This ties into the second question, discussed below.

We are back to the question of deciding the tier at which to invoke rules. For simple validation rules, if the rules are *not* invoked at the client tier, it means that the end user could potentially be filling out a long or multi-page input form, and only finds out what is wrong after she or he submits the form for processing to the other tiers. What should we do in this case? There are three possible solutions:

1. Implement such rules at the client side using a scripting language, i.e., outside of a rule engine, or
2. Embed a rule engine on the client side, provided that the footprint of the basic rule engine API is not too heavy, or
3. Break entry forms into shorter forms that are submitted to web or app server tier to do a partial validation on the data entered on each sub-form, providing medium responsiveness of the application.

The first solution is the simplest and the most pragmatic and it should be limited to simple *semantic*[23] data validation rules. The disadvantage of this solution is the non-uniform treatment of a kind of rules both at development time – they will not be managed by the BRMS[24] – and at run-time – they will not be executed by rule engines.

The second solution strikes a balance: semantic validation rules are created and managed by the BRMS, but may use a different execution infrastructure from the rest of the rules. In this case, we need to figure out how to update the client-side rules, and the answer depends on how often rules need to be updated. Options include redeploying the client with every new version of rules, or having clients retrieve the latest version of rules from the BRMS, at start-up/initialization.

The third solution favors the uniformity of implementation: all rules are handled on the server side, and the same execution infrastructure is used everywhere. There

---

[22]The requirement that a claim refer to an actual policy is an example of a *referential integrity* constraint. In database terms, such a constraint can be specified by stating that a database table column is a *foreign key* to another table.

[23]To us, it is clear that *syntactic* data validation rules are out of scope of the BRMS.

[24]They could still be managed by the same *early* BRMS as the other rules, but not in formal// executable form.

is certainly value in such a solution, as *uniformity* is a much desired quality in architecture. But so is pragmatism.

Note that rules can *also* be invoked at the database tier. Database management systems enable us to specify and enforce *integrity constraints* that are triggered when new data is committed to the database. To the extent that a DBMS supports Java-stored procedures, we can augment the integrity constraint capabilities of DBMSs with the full power of Java-based rule description languages and execution engines. In fact, the Versata[25] BRMS started out as a back-end BRMS. The problem with embedding rules at the data tier level is that we have to wait until we commit a potentially long transaction, before we find out if there is something wrong with the data.

7.4.3   Additional Requirements

Our application may be subjected to requirements which can influence the deployment option chosen for rule engines. For example, for mission-critical 24/7 applications, we cannot shutdown the application to update the rules. This leaves us with two options:

1. *Execute rules as a service.* New versions of rules can be deployed to the rule execution service, and become available for execution immediately.
2. Embed the rule engine in the application, but figure out a way of updating rulesets while the application is running. There are many ways of achieving this. In one solution, our application can poll a given location (file system, URL, etc.) for the latest version of a ruleset, and if it finds a ruleset that is more recent than the currently running version, it loads it. We can also implement functionality that pushes a new version of a ruleset on a running business application when that version becomes available.

The embedding solution would work, but it requires custom development and adds complexity to the application. Thus, hot deployment of rules for 24/7 applications pleads for a rule execution service solution.

Another common requirement would be to run different versions of the same ruleset, simultaneously. Take our insurance claim processing example. Our insurance company may change the claim eligibility or adjudication rules at the beginning of every year. Claims for medical services received starting January 1, 2009, may use a different set of rules from that used for medical services performed before January 1, 2009. Thus two claims C_A and C_B submitted on the same day – say January 15, 2009 – will need to be processed with two different rulesets. Strictly speaking, this can be accommodated using both deployment options. As mentioned in Sect. 7.4.1, we would expect a rule execution service to support ruleset

---

[25]See http://www.versata.com.

versioning out of the box; in such a case, the calling application just needs to specify which version of a particular ruleset it wants to execute. If, instead, we choose to embed rule engines in our application, then the application needs to manage the different ruleset versions, and the different rule engines that will run them. Again, this is technically feasible, but at the cost of much added complexity to the calling business application.

We ran into situations where a customer had a "no technology X" policy, which would preclude the use of a rule execution service based on technology X. A Wall Street company we worked with had a "no J2EE" policy, period.[26] For the case of JRules, this meant that we could not use the full-fledged J2EE version of JRules's *Rule Execution Server* (RES). Lighter versions of the RES could be used, however. Chapter 13 deals specifically with deployment in JRules.

7.4.4 Summary

In this section, we summarize our analysis of the design drivers that influence the choice of a deployment option for rule engines. Table 7.1 looks at general application characteristics. As the previous discussion showed, there are no absolutes: the "+" and "−" signs should be interpreted as "tends to favor" and "tends to disfavor".

Table 7.2 looks in more detail at client–server applications. Here, we look at both the rule invocation tier and deployment option, based on the rule type.

Table 7.1 Influence of application characteristics over rule engine deployment options

Deployment option Application type	Embeddedrule engine	Rule execution service
Desktop application	+	−
Client–server	−	+
Hot deployment	−	+
Executable ruleset versioning	−	+

Table 7.2 Influence of rule type on rule invocation and deployment for client–server applications

Rule type	Invocation tier	Favored deployment option
Syntactic data validation	Client side	Outside of the BRMS. Client-side scripting
Simple semantic data validation rules	Client side	Client side embedded rule engines
Other types of rules	Application server	Rule execution service

---

[26]It is pretty much a settled debate in the Java community that EJBs are an overkill for many situations, and even more so for *entity beans*. Because there are alternatives to EJBs, even in those situations where the full EJB services are needed (persistence, transactions, security), corporate architects may be tempted by a no-exception policy. The alternative, a case by case analysis of every project, would be too energy consuming!

7.5 Reengineering Existing Applications to Externalize Business Rules

An overwhelming majority of the business rule projects we got involved in are reengineering projects. In some instances, the use of business rules is the main driver behind the reengineering effort. More often than not, business rules are introduced as part of a general modernization of a legacy system. Two factors influence the way we integrate the business rules, the *scope* of the reengineering effort and, to a lesser extent, the *driver* for the reengineering effort, i.e., business rules versus other considerations. The discussion in Sect. 7.4 was about rule engine deployment options, namely, embedding rule engines versus rule execution service, and rule invocation site, i.e., which tier for a multi-tier application, without worrying about external constraints. In this section, we look at the kinds of constraints that come from dealing with a legacy system.

Figure 7.11 shows a number of stereotypical reengineering scopes. Each scope comes with different design degrees of freedom, and a different set of constraints.

A typical scenario consists of reengineering the presentation layer, as in going from, say, a terminal-based application to a GUI application or a web client, or, going from a browser-based web application to a mobile application. In this case, the business objects remain unchanged, and so does the application/process layer. Business rules seldom get introduced in this context.[27] Another scenario will see

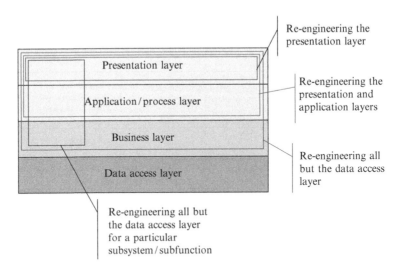

Fig. 7.11 Different reengineering scopes: different depths and breadths

---

[27]If we replace a thin client by a rich client, and introducing business rules to handle client-side validation, say, then we are changing the application flow.

both the presentation layer and the application/process layer changed, leaving the business layer and the data layer unchanged. This means that the business objects remain unchanged, but everything else above them is changed. This corresponds to reengineering *recent legacy* systems and covers many change scenarios, including introducing new modalities for invoking the application's functionality, as in going from batch to interactive, or from RPC[28] to message-oriented. It also includes more fundamental paradigm changes, as in adding a workflow or service-oriented layer on top of the existing business logic. Finally, notice that *adding* new functionality that uses the same business objects will also make changes to the application layer and to the presentation layer. Regardless of the change scenario, if we are to integrate business rules in this case, they would be introduced at the application layer.

A third scenario will have us reengineer everything above the data layer. For all practical purposes, this is similar to a new project: all of the application code is developed from scratch, from the Java entity classes all the way to the presentation layer. The only constraint here is that the new business objects will be populated by the legacy data, which can reside in databases that can be accessed directly or in other legacy systems through API.[29] In this case, ruleset execution can be invoked either from the application layer or from the business layer. Yet, a fourth scenario, not illustrated in Fig. 7.11, will have us reengineer everything, from the data layer and on up. This happens in situations where new or modified functionality requires data that is not currently captured in the legacy databases.

Naturally, in practice, reengineering scenarios are combinations of these proto-typical scenarios. We might reengineer different subsystems to different depths. When we add new functionality, we might reuse the existing infrastructure to various degrees/depths, depending on how close the existing infrastructure comes to addressing the needs of the new functionality, but also depending on the time and resources we have for the project, on the number of mission-crit al applications that use the existing infrastructure, and so on and so forth.

It is beyond the scope of this chapter – or this book – to recommend best practices for all possible situations. We will look at a couple of typical situations that we encountered, and what they mean for integrating business rules.

7.5.1 Reengineering the Application Layer

This is the case where we are reengineering a *recent legacy* system that is already implemented in object technology – typically, Java EE – to introduce business rules. In the simplest of cases, the process flow does not change: we are simply replacing programmed/in-lined business logic by a rule engine invocation. Figure 7.12 illustrates this scenario, where we assumed that we are using a rule

---

[28]RPC: remote procedure call, the way *synchronous* distributed applications work.

[29]The Java Connector Architecture (JCA) makes this distinction, *in theory*, irrelevant.

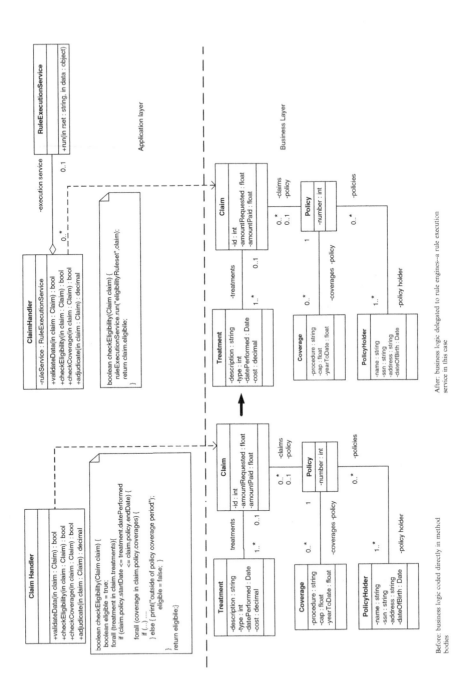

Fig. 7.12 Reengineering the application layer to introduce BRMS technology

execution service. Naturally, this is not the only deployment option: it is also possible to embed the rule engine directly in the application code, for example, as a data member of the **ClaimHandler** class, in lieu of the **RuleExecutionService** delegate. We liken this scenario to an application of the GoF[30] *strategy pattern*, which externalizes a method that can have many implementations – the method checkEligibility(Claim cl), or any of the methods of **ClaimHandler** for that matter – by delegating it to an external *strategy* object – the rule Service data member of **ClaimHandler** in this case. The difference from a classical application of the strategy pattern is that, instead of having a hierarchy of strategy classes (rule engines or rule execution services), we have a single class that is parameterized by executable rulesets.

Within the context of a multi-tier client–server application, the application layer would typically execute on the application server tier. For example, in a four tier J2EE application, the **ClaimHandler** class could be a session been invoked from within a JSP, in the web tier. In a lightweight three-tier web application, **Claim-Handler** could be a POJO (*plain old Java object*) executing in the web tier. The discussion in Sect. 7.4.3 regarding things such as hot deployment and the need to run different versions of a ruleset applies to this case.

7.5.2   Reengineering the Business Layer

This is the more common scenario where business rules are introduced along object technology to modernize or replace legacy mainframe applications. Figure 7.13 illustrates this scenario. Typically, we have an application with many functions, or a system with many subsystems, that use the same database, and the goal is to modernize one of the functions/subsystems. For that one function or subsystem, business objects will be populated by data from the common database, and saved back to that database once transactions are processed.

In this case, the new (or modified) functionality and the old one communicate through the common data access layer, i.e., common databases or by accessing the same legacy back office systems. For example, an insurance company may decide to reengineer its claim processing function, while continuing to rely on its under-writing and renewal legacy subsystems. The three subsystems may use the same policy and customer database, which becomes the common integration point between them, with no impact on either the existing databases or on the other subsystems. However, the new – or reengineered – claim processing application would create its own view of the business data and populate it from the common data store.

From a software design point of view, this scenario imposes no constraints: the fact that we are dealing with legacy databases has no bearing on the new (or

---

[30]GoF: Gang of Four, i.e., Gamma, Helm, Johnson, and Vlissides, authors of the landmark book on *Design Patterns: Elements of Reusable Design*, published by Addison-Wesley, in 1994.

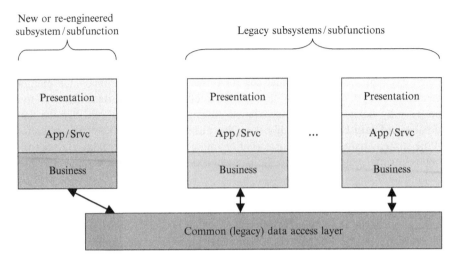

Fig. 7.13 Reengineering or adding a subsystem (subfunction) that uses the same data access layer as legacy subsystems/business functions

reengineered) application: the new business objects layer is tailored exclusively for the new business function, with no external constraints. In particular, if the integration of business rules is the main reason for the reengineering effort, we can expect the new object model to be fairly close to the *business view* of the data. Our discussion of Sects. 7.4.2 and 7.4.3 applies in this case.

This idyllic picture can break down quickly, for several reasons. First, what we represented in Fig. 7.13 as one abstract data access layer may, in fact, be a collection of separate and overlapping databases. This creates headaches both to load the new business objects from the legacy data and to save it back on those databases. Further, the new – or modified – business function may use or create new data that is not stored in the legacy databases. Assume, for example, that our health insurance company finds out one day that smoking has been causally linked to cancer or that the body mass index[31] (BMI) is a good predictor of cardiovascular health. With this new knowledge, we decide to collect this information for the underwriting process to support underwriting rules. Assume now that consumer focus groups find out that customers appreciate receiving detailed explanations about how their claims are processed, or that regulatory agencies require insurers to create an audit trail of their underwriting decisions. In either case, the new or modified function will create new data that will need to be stored.

In either case, we find ourselves reengineering the data layer, which is discussed next.

---

[31]The Body Mass Index of an adult is defined as the weight (in kilograms), divided by the square of height, in meters. A BMI of 18.5–25 is considered normal.

7.5.3 Reengineering the Data Layer

Adding data fields to existing databases is no small feat. First, at the level of the database itself, this may involve quite a bit of work. For example, adding a "smoking habit" or "BMI" field to a database means involves, minimally (a) defining a new schema, (b) copying legacy data into the new schema, and (c) figuring out which default values to use for legacy data. The latter is as much a business problem as it is a data typing problem: in the absence of the BMI, should we assume a default value of the normal range (18.5–25), or use the BMI average for a given population – or the customer database – or use value "UNKNOWN," and then make sure that the business rules know how to handle "UNKNOWN".

In a perfectly layered system/architecture, changes in the data – or data access – layer would not percolate above the adjacent layer. However, perfectly layered systems do not exist – rightfully so – and besides, what is the point of enriching the data model if the data is not exposed through the business layer to the application and presentation layers: I cannot provide values for the "smoking habit" or "BMI" attributes if no corresponding field shows up in the web form I am filling out! Thus, within the context of a shared data layer, we cannot modify the database to accommodate one subfunction, without affecting the other subfunctions.

A common solution pattern consists of building a separate database to accommodate the new data fields. This is illustrated in Fig. 7.14. For the purposes of the new subsystem or business function, we implement a new database. In this case, there are two alternative designs:

1. We could expose the legacy database to the new functionality. Database views notwithstanding, transaction processing would involve direct – and synchronous – access to both the new and old databases. Typically, we would use the new

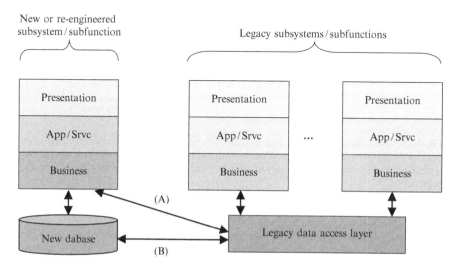

Fig. 7.14 Reengineering the data layer

database to store new entities and attributes, and keep using the old database to read and write the legacy data. This is illustrated by the connection between the new functionality and the legacy database (link labeled (A)) in Fig. 7.14.

2. We could hide the legacy database from the new functionality and embody the legacy and new data in a single new database. The new database gets its legacy data from the legacy database, and steps are taken to ensure the synchronization between the two databases. This is illustrated by the connection between the new database and the legacy data access layer (link labeled (B)).

The first approach has the advantage of a clean, sort of by-the-book design. Database views may be used to offer a unified view of the data, providing for a clean programming model. Further, the data is not duplicated, guaranteeing its currency at all times. Figure 7.15a illustrates the idea. However, this solution has major disadvantages, the most important of which is performance: an update requires synchronous updates to two or more databases, which would typically run on different servers, which could be continents apart. The problem could be made worse if the legacy data is exposed through a higher-level API[32] as opposed to raw databases.

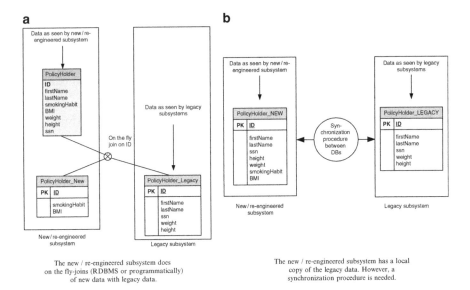

Fig. 7.15 Two strategies for integrating old data with new. (**a**) The new/reengineered subsystem does on the fly-joins (RDBMS or programmatically) of new data with legacy data. (**b**) The new/reengineered subsystem has a local copy of the legacy data. However, a synchronization procedure is needed

---

[32]Relational DBMSs (e.g., Oracle) may support joins across databases//servers, and make those reasonably efficient through built-in optimizations. Attempting to perform the join "programmatically" by first accessing the joined data sources through the JCA API, for example, would be far more problematic from both a development and run-time performance perspective.

The second approach simplifies the programming model and addresses the performance issue. However, it relies on data duplication, and we need to keep the duplicates synchronized with the master copy. The latter means developing tools and procedures to synchronize the new database with the legacy databases. This is illustrated in Fig. 7.15b. There are many architectural patterns for doing this, depending on (a) whether the legacy data is modified – as opposed to just read – by the new or reengineered subsystem, (b) on how often the legacy data is changed by either party (i.e., new versus legacy subsystems), and (c) how tolerant each party is for out of date legacy data. For example, a new or reengineered claim processing application may require all-time up-to-date information about total of claims paid against a given policy, but may tolerate a 24 h delay in propagating changes to policy holder contact information.

In practice, the second approach is often preferred, not only for performance reasons, but also to ease the migration/modernization of other subfunctions. Indeed, a key strategy in migrating a system incrementally consists of building the new data stores incrementally and have both the old and the new operate in parallel until the transition is completed, in which case we can unplug the old.

What does any of this mean to business rules? Regardless of which strategy is used to support the new data requirements (Fig. 7.15a or b), there are few constraints imposed by the legacy system on the integration of business rules: for all practical purposes, this can be treated pretty much as a new *tabula rasa* project, and the design choices discussed in Sect. 7.4 (Sects. 7.4.2 and 7.4.3) regarding the deployment model (rule engines versus rule execution service) and deployment tier still apply. We will revisit this issue when we talk about business object models in Chaps. 9 and 10.

7.6 Summary and Discussion

Your business process involves lots of business rules that evolve frequently. Your boss (or his boss) sat through a smoothly delivered keynote speech by a self-proclaimed business rule evangelist, whose fervor is matched only by his/her lack of grasp of the technology. You attended a couple of flashy product demos, which convinced you of the potential of the technology. Your organization/company has thus bought into the business rules approach as a way of managing and automating those business rules. You brought in a couple of vendors who showcased their ware, trying to sell you on the idea that their product is plug and play – as long as you purchase an additional n man-years in consulting. You brought in a couple of integrators who made a sales pitch for their agile application delivery methodology, which requires a room full of various ists and ers (business process analysts, business analysts, domain specialists, configuration management specialists, your-application-server specialists, managers, designers, developers, testers) to get anything done. Your company selected a vendor, an integrator, and a business function to implement with the business rules technology. Rule discovery and analysis teams have been assembled, trained, and may have already started collecting and capturing business rules. You are the architect, eyes turn to you, "how do we design this beast?"

The first thing to figure out is what this beast is, i.e., what is there to design? Roughly speaking, there are three areas to tackle:

1. *Designing rule management functionalities.* We referred to this as *early BRMS* functionalities (Sect. 7.2), to be distinguished from *late BRMS* functionalities, which deal with rules written in a formal executable language. We addressed three issues: (a) deciding what to represent/capture in the tool (rules, data models, process models) and how to link it to external artifacts that may be managed by external tools, (b) managing the (early phases of) rule lifecycle, and (c) versioning.
2. *Designing the business application itself.* Architectural design, at large, is beyond the scope of this book. However, for the purposes of the discussion, we presented a handful of common architectural patterns, and summarized their pros and cons (Sect. 7.3).
3. *Invoking rule engines from the business application.* There are two main design dimensions: (a) whether to embed a rule engine directly in the application or to use a rule execution service, and (b) from which tier to invoke rules. The design choices are influenced by many factors, including (a) the architecture of the calling (business) application itself, (b) the need for hot deployment of rules, and (c) the need for running different versions of rules, simultaneously. These issues were discussed in Sect. 7.4.

Because BRMS technology is often adopted within the context of a reengineering effort, our design choices for both the business application and the engine integration may be constrained by the legacy application. Those constraints depend on the *scope* of the reengineering effort. We defined the reengineering scope in terms of *depth* within the context of a layered architecture. In particular we looked at three prototypical scenarios corresponding to (a) reengineering the application layer, discussed in Sect. 7.5.1, (b) reengineering the business layer, discussed in Sect. 7.5.2, and (c) reengineering the data layer, discussed in Sect. 7.5.3. We showed, among other things, that our design choices are not much restricted if we reengineer the business layer or the data layer. We will revisit these two scenarios in Chaps. 9 and 10 when we talk about the difference – and mapping between – the application's actual implemented object model and the *business object model* against which to write rules.

7.7 Further Reading

In this chapter, we touched upon many important design dimensions. However, we barely scratched the surface.

Some of the issues discussed about early BRMS (Sect. 7.2) will find some resonance in the literature about *requirements management*, where issues of traceability and change management are of utmost importance. Actually, a number of our customers have used requirements management tools such as IBM/Rational's RequisitePro™ or MKS's Integrity™; the *International Council on Systems Engineering* maintains a survey of requirements management tools (http://www.incose.org/productspubs/products/rmsurvey.aspx).

With regard to application architecture (Sect. 7.3), we would not even know where to start. Many generalist software engineering books include a brief overview of the various architectural *styles* discussed in Sect. 7.3. Sun/Oracle's J2EE documentation should be the starting point for what we called synchronous client–server architectures (http://java.sun.com/j2ee/overview.html), to be complemented with recent J2EE patterns books. Martin Fowler's books, and his Addison Wesley's book series remain a good bet, for actionable architectural patterns that age well, including Martin Fowler's *Patterns of Enterprise Application Architecture* (Addison Wesley, 2002, ISBN 0321127420) and Gregor Hohpe and Bobby Woolf's book *Enterprise Integration Patterns* (Addison Wesley, 2003, ISBN 0321200683), which tackles message-oriented architectures. Thomas Erl's *SOA Patterns* (Prentice-Hall, 2009, ISBN 0136135161) is a good source – if a verbose one – for an effective introduction into SOA with lots of SOA best practices. IBM's developer works portal remains an excellent source for timely technical information regarding SOA and webservices – a vendor's bias notwithstanding ☺.

Finally, there are a number of web resources, too numerous to mention, that contain information about architecture. As is often the case, Wikipedia provides a more than decent entry point into related topics.

Chapter 8
IBM WebSphere ILOG JRules

Target audience

- *All*

In this chapter you will learn

- *The architecture of the JRules BRMS*
- *The concept of operations of the JRules BRMS*
- *An introduction into the various JRules rule artifacts*
- *An introduction into the various JRules modules*

Key points

- *JRules has a modular architecture, providing different components that support different tasks or cater to different users.*
- *Business users and technical users author and manage business rules using different environments, which are adapted to their tasks and skill sets.*
- *JRules provides a domain-specific language for rule authoring that has a modular/layered architecture.*
- *JRules embeds a powerful and easy to use rule unit testing framework.*
- *JRules offers a rich set of functionalities for managing rule execution.*

8.1 Introduction

This chapter presents the IBM WebSphere ILOG JRules Business Rule Management System, or *JRules* in short. JRules offers an important set of components and capabilities to enable business users and developers to manage business rules directly with various levels of implication, from limited review to complete control over the specification, creation, testing, and deployment of business rules.

The description included in this chapter is based on the JRules 7 version of the product. At the time of this writing, JRules is in its 14th year as a commercial

J. Boyer and H. Mili, *Agile Business Rule Development*,
DOI 10.1007/978-3-642-19041-4_8, © Springer-Verlag Berlin Heidelberg 2011

product. JRules was initially developed by *ILOG Corp*, a software vendor founded in 1987, and acquired by IBM in 2009. JRules is the third family of rule engine (what they were called back then)/BRMS products, starting with a Lisp implementation, followed by a C++ implementation, in 1992. JRules has gone through a number of major architectural changes around each major version number (JRules 3, around 1999–2000, JRules 4, around 2002–2003, JRules 5, in 2005, JRules 6, in 2006, and JRules 7 in 2009). One of the most significant changes occurred around JRules 6 where the old proprietary ILOG rule IDE[1] was dropped, and its functionalities split between two components, one destined for technical users, packaged as an Eclipse/RAD plug-in, and one destined for business users, packaged as a Web application. It was also starting with JRules 6 that earlier components and libraries for EJB support and rule engine pooling were packaged into a JCA-compliant *Rule Execution Server* (RES). JRules 7 shares the same basic architecture.

Section 8.2 provides a very quick overview of JRules, including the main components, the way they are meant to work together (concept of operations), and an overview of rule artifacts. Section 8.3 talks about *Rule Studio* (RS), which the JRules module aimed at technical users. We provide a brief description of the structure of rule projects, and of the various artifacts that we can create within Rule Studio projects; Chaps. 10 and 11 will go into much greater detail. We talk about *Rule Team Server* (RTS), the Web application aimed at business users, in Sect. 8.4. The *Rule Execution Server* is described in Sect. 8.5; far more detail will be provided in Chap. 13, where we talk about JRules's support for ruleset deployment and execution. We talk about *Rule Solutions for Office* (RSO) in Sect. 8.6, which consist of Microsoft Office's Word™ and Excel™ plug-ins that enable business users to edit if–then rules and *decision tables* in Word documents and Excel spreadsheets, respectively. We provide a summary in Sect. 8.7.

8.2 Business Rule Management System Main Components

The JRules BRMS platform is a collection of modules that operate in different environments while working together to provide a comprehensive Business Rule Management System. BRMS helps to manage business rule independently of the business application.

As mentioned in Chap. 1, a BRMS enables business and IT to collaborate, author, manage, and execute business rules. In addition to working on different timelines, IT and business users need to work with different tools that reflect their different skill sets and views of the application. Figure 8.1 shows the different modules provided by JRules, along with the target users and the need they help to fulfill. In the remainder of this section, we will provide a short overview of the various components.

---

[1]Integrated Development Environment.

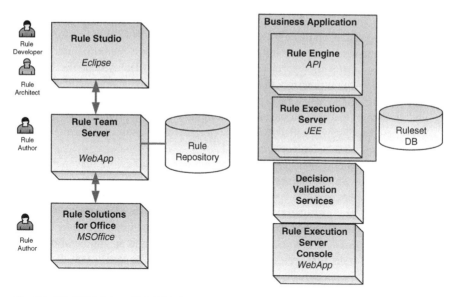

Fig. 8.1 IBM WebSphere ILOG JRules 7.1 Component View

- *Rule Studio (RS)*. Business rule application development starts in Rule Studio, an Eclipse[2]-based Integrated Development Environment (IDE). Working in Rule Studio, developers can set up the rule authoring environment, create business rules and rule templates, author more complex technical rules, and design the execution or rule flow. Rule Studio also provides tools for unit testing and deploying rules to the target execution environment. Developers can store the business rule artifacts using a source code control tool.
- *Rule Team Server (RTS)* is a Web-based application for rule authoring and management, aimed at business users. Business users can work in Rule Team Server both during application development and after the application is deployed to production, as part of the application maintenance (see ABRD cycle "Implementation and Enhancement" in Chap. 3). Rule Team Server stores rule projects in a *rule repository* which is typically persisted in a relational database.
- *Rule Solutions for Office (RSO)*. For business users and rule authors who prefer to work offline, Rule Solutions for Office supports rule authoring in Microsoft Office 2007 products. In particular, we can edit if–then rules in Microsoft Word™ documents and decision tables in Excel™ spreadsheets thanks to JRules plug-ins. We can export rule artifacts from Rule Team Server to Word™/Excel™ files, edit the Word/Excel files, and upload them back into Rule Team Server.
- *Rule Execution Server (RES)*. The rule engine module can be integrated into the core business application using a low level API, or can be deployed as a monitored

---

[2]www.eclipse.org.

component in a JEE container, the Rule Execution Server (see Sect. 7.4 for a general discussion, and Chap. 13 for JRules – specific deployment options). RES provides management, scalability, security, transaction support, and logging capabilities on top of the rule execution. Using this deployment the business application or more precisely the decision service within the application interacts with the rule engine using rule session API. RES maintains a pool of rule engines and ensures transaction propagation and security control. Coupled with RES is a Web-based application called Rule Execution Server Console, used to monitor and manage the rule sets deployed within RES.

- *Decision Validation Services (DVS)* is a unit testing framework that enables rule testing in Rule Studio and testing and simulation in Rule Team Server. Business users, developers, and QA testers can use DVS to verify the behavior of the rules in a rule set. The user can define *scenarios* in a data source such as Microsoft 2003 Excel spreadsheets. Scenarios can include the specification of expected test results (e.g., variable or object attribute values), as well as an enumeration of the rules or rule tasks that were executed in the process, to verify that the ruleset behaved as expected. Business users can also define key performance indicators (KPIs) to assess the rule set according to specific business metrics. With these capabilities a business user can perform "what–if" analyses, where a reference ("champion") ruleset is compared to the newly updated ruleset (the "challenger") during simulation testing. DVS is presented in Chap. 15.

8.2.1 The Concept of Operations

Once the first level of rule analysis is done, it is possible to quickly create rules using Rule Studio. The Rule Studio environment has all the wizards to develop object models, rule projects, rule flows, and other business rule artifacts. The object (or data) model is in fact built around two layers: the logical layer, called *Business Object Model* (BOM), is used as vocabulary for the rules, and one physical layer, called the *eXecutable Object Model* (XOM) which corresponds to the implementation of the application objects in Java or XML. XOM choices were discussed in Sect. 5.3, and will be discussed further in Chap. 13. BOM design issues were discussed *in general terms* in Sect. 9.2.1 and Sect. 10.3.

Rule Studio is used by rule developers, rule architects, software developers, and business analysts, depending on their technical skills. Note that while business analysts are not meant to be technical, it has been our experience that many business analysts have an IT background. At the very least, they are Excel specialists who can do wonders with a spreadsheet. We have also met many who are IT specialists, who are able to develop a simple database application, or even a simple Web application. For such users, an Eclipse-based environment is not an issue.

In those cases where rule authoring is performed by non-technical business analysts, developers need to *publish* rule projects created from within Rule Studio to Rule Team Server to make it available for business users to begin rule authoring.

This enables developers and business users to collaborate on the same rules while working in their separate environments. After the rule project has evolved in Rule Team Server, developers can synchronize their copy of the rules with those stored in the Rule Team Server rule repository. We recommend using this repository as the reference or master during rule maintenance, and use the synchronization to Rule Studio to work on deeper changes like the updates to object models, to the rule project structure or to the rule flow. An additional synchronization mechanism is available in Rule Team Server that allows business rules to be published as Microsoft Word or Excel documents. After working with the rules in Word™ or Excel™, rule authors can easily synchronize their updates back to the Rule Team Server rule repository.

Within Rule Team Server (RTS), business analysts manage the rule elements by using a set of capabilities to control the version, the configuration and the life cycle. In RTS all users collaborate within a shared workspace and use locking to control access to resources currently being edited. The definition of rule artifacts includes properties (metadata) like the rule *status* property, or the *effective date* to control the rule life cycle. RTS supports versioning of the various rule artifacts. Each time a rule artifact is saved, a separate version is created. RTS supports also the concept of a *baseline* which tags the current versions of all the artifacts within a rule project. Baselines freeze the state of a project at a given moment in time. They are used most often before a rule set deployment or to mark the end of a maintenance cycle.

Once the ruleset reaches a certain level of completeness, it can be deployed to a Rule Execution Server. Figure 8.2 illustrates this process.

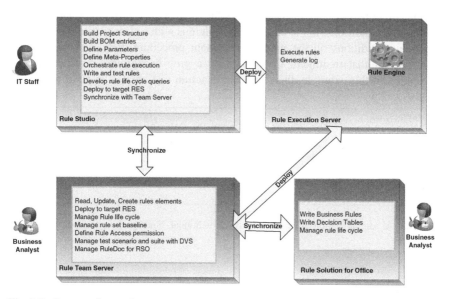

Fig. 8.2 Concept of operations

We detail later in this chapter how we build our claim validation rule projects using Rule Studio, then how rule writer can leverage the features of Rule Team Server to maintain the rule set. Let us start by looking at Rule Studio.

8.2.2 Rule Artifacts

JRules enables us to create different types of rule artifacts, depending on the complexity of the business logic, on the regularity of its structure, and on its specific use. Most business-oriented rule artifacts are based on a business-oriented, natural language-like *Business Action Language* (BAL) . The BAL and the various artifacts that use it are described at length in Sect. 11.2. For the purposes of this section and chapter, we will give a preview of two BAL-based artifacts, *action (if–then) rules,* and *decision tables.* Figure 8.3 shows an example of an *action rule.* Action rules have four parts: *definitions* part, *if* part, *then* part, and *else* part. The *Definitions* part is used to define variables local to the current business rule. The conditions of the business rule are listed in the "*if*" part, and the actions to be performed are listed in the *then* and *else* parts. As we later see (Sect. 11.2), all the parts are optional except for the *then* part. The sample rule of Fig. 8.3 has no *else* part. The meaning of this rule should be self-explanatory.

Another very useful format for representing rules is the decision table which presents all the rules with similar conditions and similar actions in a tabular format: columns represent conditions and actions, and each row represents an individual rule. Decision tables provide an efficient representation when the rules need to test ranges of possible values, enumeration values, and numerical attributes (Fig. 8.4). Among other features, the decision table editor also helps identify gaps and overlaps within rule conditions. In the table below, columns with a clear (white) background represent conditions on the medical treatment procedure code, and the amount invoiced for that treatment. Columns with a grey background represent action columns.[3] In this example, there is a single action that creates an audit request to

```
Definitions
set policy to the policy of 'the claim' where the status of this policy is not
closed;
if
  the day of loss of 'the claim' is after the expiration date of policy
then
  add to 'the result' the issue : "claim date error" with a code "R01" and a descrip-
tion : "claim is after expiration date of the policy";
  set 'the claim' has issue;
```

Fig. 8.3 A sample action rule: *definitions* <conditional binding> *if* < conditions> *then* <actions>

---

[3]The decision table editor enables us to edit the graphical attributes of condition and action columns.

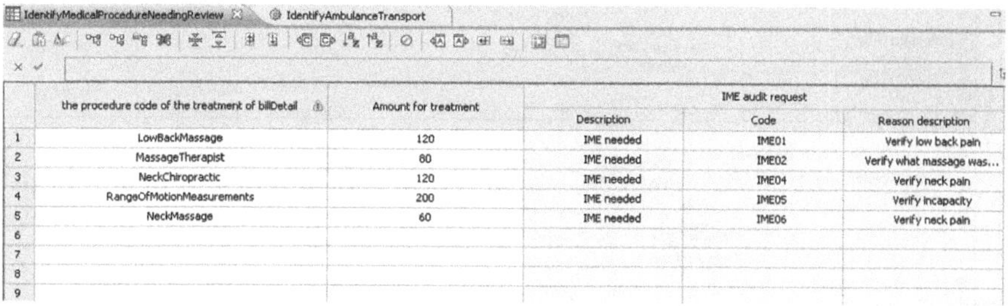

	the procedure code of the treatment of billDetail	Amount for treatment	IME audit request		
			Description	Code	Reason description
1	LowBackMassage	120	IME needed	IME01	Verify low back pain
2	MassageTherapist	80	IME needed	IME02	Verify what massage was...
3	NeckChiropractic	120	IME needed	IME04	Verify neck pain
4	RangeOfMotionMeasurements	200	IME needed	IME05	Verify incapacity
5	NeckMassage	60	IME needed	IME06	Verify neck pain
6					
7					
8					
9					

Fig. 8.4 Decision table

evaluate the accuracy for the treatment. The three action subcolumns ("Description", "Code", and "Reason description") correspond to different parameters of the audit request to be created.

The reader may have noticed a warning icon near the header of the first condition column (on procedure code of the treatment). This is warning the user that there are some values from all the enumeration of procedure codes that are not listed/tested in this table. This is a special case of a more general *gap detection* feature that decision table authors can enable or disable. A related feature also detects *overlaps* between the values listed in different rows. Depending on the business logic, this *could* be problematic and may need to be fixed. The decision table editor supports other features, discussed in Sect. 11.2.

Rules can also be expressed as *decision trees* which embody an asymmetric structure using a tree of conditions, with the leaf (bottom) nodes representing the action part. A path from the root/top of the tree to a leaf node represents a complete if–then rule. Decision trees, scorecards, and technical rules will be discussed in more detail in Chap. 11.

8.3 Rule Studio

Figure 8.5 presents the different activities and tasks each user role can execute within Rule Studio (RS) and Rule Team Server (RTS).

Rule Architects use Rule Studio to design the structure of the Rule Project. A rule project is a type of Eclipse project dedicated to the development of business rules. Designing the rule project structure includes:

- The definition of its input/output parameters
- The definition of the different data models to use, namely, the Executable Object Models (XOMs), and the Business Object Models (BOMs)
- The definition of the different queries used to search for rule elements in the current project/workspace
- The creation of the hierarchy of rule packages, and finally
- The creation of the rule flow(s)

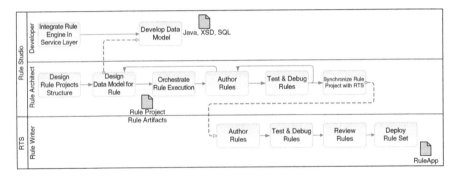

Fig. 8.5 Rule Studio and RTS rule authoring activities

As mentioned above, the XOM corresponds to the "physical" data model of the application objects manipulated by the rule engine, i.e., either Java classes (objects) or XML schemas (materialized as java objects). The Business Object Model (BOM) embodies the business view of the data, and provides the vocabulary/ domain of discourse for writing the business rules, and is constructed as a *view* of the executable object model (XOM). Chapter 9 explores the (different) requirements placed on the XOM and BOM, in general. Chapter 10 explores in depth the BOM to XOM mapping in JRules.

Figure 8.6 shows the main window of Rule Studio. On the left, the Rule Explorer view shows the different projects within the current workspace. The R above a project icon/folder indicates that it is a rule project.

Rule Studio being Eclipse-based, the center view is used to display the different editors. In this case, we have the *rule flow* editor. The view "*Rule Project Map*" at the bottom helps to guide the developer through the various activities needed to create and complete a rule project. The selectable items/links are shortcuts to various rule project actions. A greyed out link (all but "Import XOM" and "Create BOM") represents an action whose prerequisites have not been fulfilled, and reflects dependencies between the various components of a rule project. Some tasks are optional, and a rule developer/architect can take many paths through the project map.

The different rule artifacts are represented by a *definition* which can be edited in the central view, and *properties* or *metadata* used for its management. Section 5.4.3 showed examples of rule properties, and what they may be used for. Rule architects can define custom rule properties through *rule metamodel extensions*, which are defined in a two XML files.

In the remainder of this section, we will give a brief overview of the major tasks performed within Rule Studio; the underlying design *issues* and best practices will be discussed in far more detail in subsequent chapters. Specifically, we will discuss:

- *Designing the rule project structure, in Sect. 8.3.1.* This will be thoroughly discussed in Sect. 9.4, in general terms, and in Sect. 10.2, for the case of JRules.
- *Designing the business rule (meta) model, in Sect. 8.3.2.* Rule properties support many processes, including rule deployment, rule testing, and rule governance.

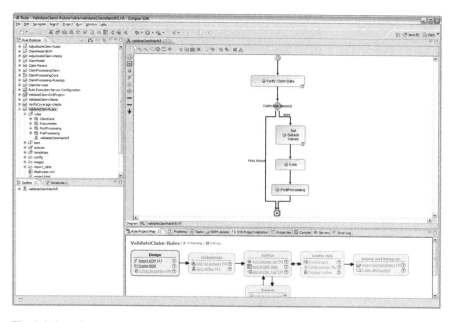

Fig. 8.6 Rule Studio with ruleflow editor

The use of these properties will be discussed in more detail in Chap. 12 (deployment issues), Chap. 14 (testing issues), and Chap. 16 (governance), in general, and for the case of JRules in particular, in Chap. 13 (deployment *with JRules*), Chap. 15 (testing *with JRules*), and Chap. 17 (rule governance *with JRules*).

- *Designing the object models, in Sect. 8.3.3.* This will be discussed in more detail in Sect. 9.2.1, in general, and in Sect. 10.3, for the case of JRules.
- *Orchestrating rule execution, in Sect. 8.3.4.* This will be discussed more thoroughly in Sects. 11.3 (fundamentals) and 11.4 (best practices).
- *Rule testing and deployment, discussed in Sect. 8.3.5.* Chapters 12 and 14 will explore deployment and testing issues, in general, and Chaps. 13 and 15 will discuss deployment and testing within the context of JRules.

8.3.1 Designing the Rule Project Structure

A rule project is a container for rule artifacts, and the artifacts needed to create them, execute them, and debug them. Section 10.2 will explore JRules rule project structure in detail, where we go over the different contents of a project. General, vendor-independent best practices for rule project organization will be discussed in Sect. 9.4. Additional best practices that take advantage of the JRules-specific

Fig. 8.7 Rule project files
and folders

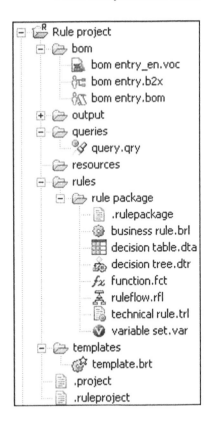

features will be presented in Sect. 10.4.1. For the purposes of this section and chapter, we will provide a brief overview of all of the above.

The various types of rule project elements are illustrated in Fig. 8.7. They include the Business Object Model (BOM), different types of rule artifacts (if–then BAL rules, decision tables, decision trees, technical rules, etc.), artifacts for rule execution orchestration (ruleset parameters, ruleflows), rule queries, and rule templates. Each element is persisted in a single file, or in a combination of files (e.g., the BOM). The elements can thus be version-controlled using a file-based version control software plugged into Eclipse (e.g., Subversion or CVS). BOM design will be briefly introduced in Sect. 8.3.3 and explored in detail in Sect. 10.3. The artifacts for rule execution orchestration will be introduced in Sect. 8.3.4 and explored in detail in Sects. 11.3 and 11.4. In the remainder of this section, we will talk briefly about the organization of rule artifacts with a rule project, give an example of rule project organization, and talk briefly about rule queries and templates.

Within a rule project, rules are organized within a hierarchy of packages. The package hierarchy is typically designed to reflect the structure of the business domain (e.g., product family, business process structure) and to accommodate the execution logic (e.g., a simple mapping to a ruleflow). As a good practice, it is recommended that rule packages include rule artifacts only at the leaf level. This has several advantages, including understandability, an easy mapping to the execution structure (rule flow, more on this in Sect. 11.3), and even more responsiveness of Rule Studio during rule authoring.[4]

Templates enable us to define fill-in-the-blank rule artifacts. Indeed, it is possible to define *rule templates* and *decision table templates* which are used to freeze some parts of a rule, or decision table, and leaving only a few prompts (or cell values) open for input/modification. Templates help enforce rule structure and rule consistency. They come in handy in those cases where the people who are tasked with rule entry and maintenance, are either non-IT savvy, or have a partial view/incomplete context of the rules.

Another important element of a rule project is the *rule query*. JRules supports a rich querying facility that uses a language similar to the *Business Action Language* (called *Business Query Language*) that enables us to search on rule *properties*, rule *definitions*, and rule *semantics*. The following query identifies the *business rules* (i.e., all kinds of rules, except *technical* rules) that have status "*Deployable*." This query can be used as part of a *ruleset extraction and deployment* process (see Sect. 13.5.2, and Chap. 17).

```
Find all business rules
  such that the status of each business rule is Deployable
```

The following query shows an example of a query on the *definition* of rules: it looks for rules that refer to a specific BOM class; rule R "is using" BOM class C, if the rule reads (definitions part, conditions part, or action parts), or modifies an object of type C (action parts). This type of query could be part of some *impact analysis*, e.g., to assess the impact of refactoring a class; more on BOM and XOM *refactoring* in Sect. 10.3.4.

```
Find all business rules
       such that each business rule is using the BOM class
  "abrd.claim.injury.Treatment"
```

As for the rule project organization, as discussed in Chap. 5, we recommend mapping one decision point to a rule set and one rule set to a rule project. Further, while a rule project is supposed to contain both *rules* and the BOM needed to write them, we recommend separating the definition of the BOM from the rules that use it so that different rule projects can refer to the same BOM. The project hierarchy below shows what the project structure might look like for our case study. The ClaimModel-BOM rule project includes the definition of the

---

[4]If the tool is configured to perform on-demand loading, this will reduce the number of rules uploaded into the developer's workspace as they navigate the project structure.

BOM used by the rules, and it depends on the "ClaimModel" Java project (XOM). The "validateClaim-rules", "validateMedicalInvoice-rules", "verify-Coverage-rules", and "adjudicateClaim-rules" rule projects contain the rules needed for the tasks "validateClaim", "validateMedicalInvoice", "verifyCover-age", and "adjudicateClaim", respectively. Sections 10.2 and 10.4 will go over the design issues and rationale in more detail.

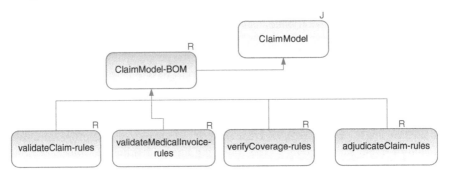

8.3.2   Designing the Business Rule Model

Rule artifacts have *definitions* (their contents), and a bunch of *properties* (metadata) attached to them. These properties can be used for rule management (mostly) but also for rule execution. The set of properties associated with rule artifacts constitute the *business rule model* – sometimes also referred to as *rule metamodel*. Out of the box, rules artifacts come with a set of predefined properties. Rule architects can *add* more properties to the default rule (meta) model. In Sect. 5.4.2 (prototyping), we presented a list of commonly useful rule properties, including properties that trace rules back to their business motivation, or that restrict their applicability (e.g., jurisdiction, effectiveness period, etc.). Rule Studio supports the *edition* of the *business rule model* using two XML files, a *business rule model extension* file (*.brmx extension), which contains the definition of the new properties (name, type, initial values, behavior upon copy, etc.), and a *data extension file* (*.brdx), which is used to provide property values, for those properties that have an enumerated set of values. Figure 8.8 below shows the Rule Studio wizard for editing the rule model extension file. The figure shows that we are adding properties to three different categories (classes), **RuleArtifact**, **Rule**, and **BusinessRule**. Properties added to **RuleArtifact** will also be added to **Rule**, which is a kind of **RuleArtifact** (the other kind being a **Function**, see Chaps. 10 and 11), and to **BusinessRule**, which is a kind of **Rule** – the other kind being **TechnicalRule**. In turn, the (metamodel) class **BusinessRule** groups *action* (**if–then**) rules, decision tables, and decision trees (see Sects. 8.2.2, and 11.2). The reader may also notice that many of the properties

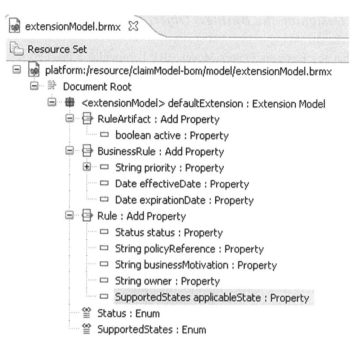

Fig. 8.8 Rule model extension

have predefined Java types (boolean, java.lang.String, java.util.Date), whereas the "status" property has type **Status** and the "applicableState" property (as in United *States* of America) has type **SupportedStates**. These two types are enumerations, and their values are defined in the *.brdx file – not shown here.

We recommend defining such properties during the prototyping phase before we embark on wholesale rule authoring, because adding property values later can be anywhere from tedious to problematic.[5] Also, it is during the prototyping phase that we start thinking of the rule lifecycle, and of the properties needed to manage it. Finally, we should take advantage of the intense and close communication between business and IT during the prototyping phase to identify and address issues in a timely fashion. Beware of the proliferation of properties, however: too many properties for rule management mean an overly complex/over-engineered rule lifecycle, and too many properties to control rule execution mean poorly contextualized rules, and brittle rule orchestration.

---

[5]For example, a property such as "author" needs to be initialized at rule creation time, and must not be modifiable. Adding it after a rule has been created can create headaches.

8.3.3 Designing the Business Object Model

Recall that the Business Object Model (BOM) provides a business view of the application object model specifically designed to write the application's business rules. The high-level language (Business Action Language) used to write the rule uses a verbalized view of the BOM, called the business *vocabulary*. The BOM is actually made of three layers that stand between the rules and the executable object model (XOM) – for example, a set of Java classes:

- The BOM data model or interface, which is the middle layer, is stored in a file with *.bom extension, contains the definition of BOM classes, with their public attributes and functions, in a Java-like syntax.
- The vocabulary, which is a verbalization of the elements of the BOM data model, puts a natural language-like coating on top of the BOM data model that stands between the BOM data model and the rules. The vocabulary is built so that rules can refer to a **MedicalInvoice** object as "a medical invoice" and to the attribute dateOfCreation of a **Claim** as "the date of creation of the claim." The vocabulary is stored in a file with extension *.voc, and can be *localized*, i.e., we can have different vocabularies associated with the same BOM data model.
- The BOM to XOM mapping (stored in a *.b2x) file, shows how elements of the BOM data model map to the underlying XOM/Java classes.

Figure 8.9 *illustrates* the three components of the BOM and their relationships to rules (on top) and to the Java classes/XOM (bottom). Truth be told, only the representation of the BOM data model is accurate. For presentation purposes, we simplified the representation of the vocabulary and of the BOM to XOM mapping to illustrate the concept. In fact, a BOM to XOM mapping such as the one represented in Fig. 8.9 is assumed by default, and *not* explicitly stored; (much) more on this in Sect. 10.3.

Rule Studio provides a BOM editor, which enables us to edit the three components (BOM model, vocabulary, and BOM to XOM mapping) in a unified and synchronized fashion. Figure 8.10 shows a partial view of the wizard (we do not see the BOM to XOM editing prompts). A thorough explanation is provided in Sect. 10.3.

There are two ways to build a BOM and to link it to a XOM:

- A *bottom-up* approach, where we start with the XOM (a Java project or a Java jar file), and build a *default* BOM from it, using a default BOM to XOM mapping. Roughly speaking, the default BOM to XOM mapping generates one BOM class for each *public* XOM class (Java class or XSD complex type), and maps all of the *public* members of the XOM class to corresponding members of the BOM class.[6] This mapping is also pretty good at coming up with reasonable verbalizations,

---

[6]With the exception of getters and setters, which are mapped by default to attributes that are read only (only getter present), write only (only setter present) or read/write (both accessors present).

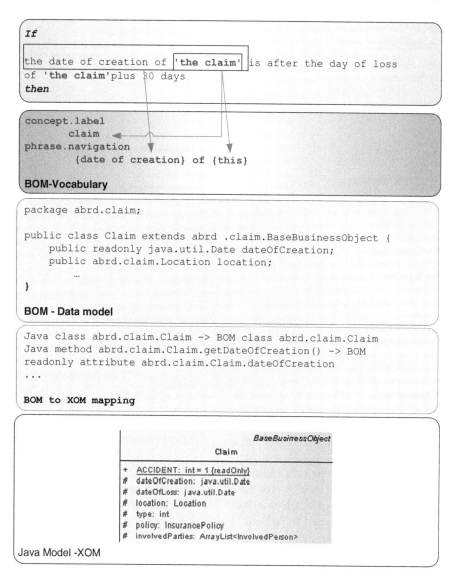

Fig. 8.9 The BOM is a three-layer structure that bridges natural language-like (BAL) rules to Java classes (XOM)

provided that developers have followed standard coding/naming practices on the Java (or XSD) side. The so-generated BOM can later be edited to modify the defaults or to add new elements.

- A *top-down* approach, whereby the rule developer constructs the BOM class by class using the BOM editor, adding data members, function members, and the like, but with no corresponding XOM. Such a BOM can be used to author rules,

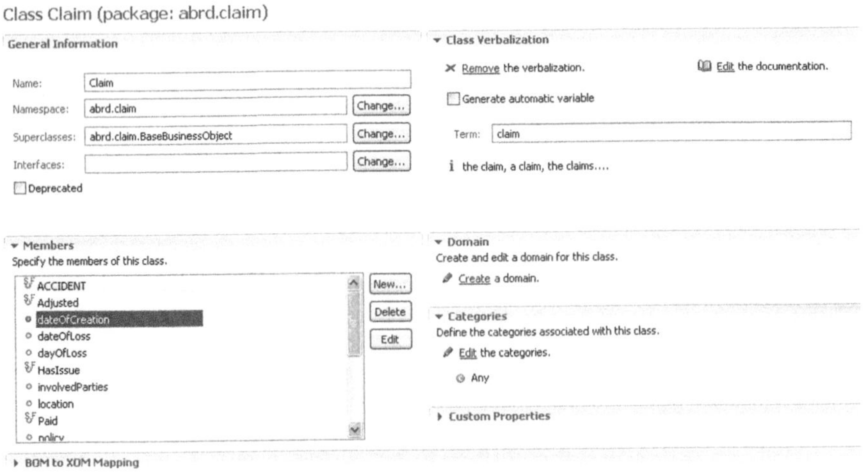

Class Claim (package: abrd.claim)

Fig. 8.10 BOM editor

but naturally, not to execute them. Once we have a XOM that we can hook up to, we can associate it with the BOM, and synchronize the two.

The bottom-up approach is the more common of the two. Indeed, in most of the projects we were involved with, the business rules approach is introduced as part of a re-engineering effort – in which case the XOM already exists. Even with new projects, it is often the case that by the time we have rules we can code, the XOM will have already been built. However, we have used the top-down approach in a number of projects where hesitant managers wanted a proof of concept/to see what rules would look like, before embarking on business rules. In general we prefer build the XOM from the conceptual data model representing the business entities and their relationships in scope for the rule expression. The XOM is built only for the rules component, in which case, the BOM *was* in some ways, the requirements for the XOM, and needed to be built first. Whichever model gets built first, both will evolve, and Rule Studio provides functionality for keeping them in sync (see Sect. 10.3).

BOM design is a critical activity in business rule development. A well-designed BOM results into an intuitive, unambiguous, and easy to use business rule vocabulary. This helps make rule authoring, rule reviewing, and rule maintenance much easier and much less error-prone. A complex BOM, one that exposes all the complexity and relationships of an enterprise model, will make rule authoring difficult and error prone. Similarly, a BOM that mirrors too closely the idiosyncrasies of the corresponding XOM will result in awkward and hard to understand rules. Chapter 10 will go into the details of BOM design, and BOM to XOM mapping and will present best practices for both.

8.3.4 Orchestrate Rule Execution

As explained in Sect. 5.4.3, whereas the rule project structure is concerned with the development time organization of rules, *rule orchestration* is concerned with the run-time execution sequence of rules. Also, while a rule engine (and the production system paradigm) can deal with a "flat" ruleset that is a "bag of rules," the decision embodied in a ruleset can often be broken into a set of more elementary, and stable sub-decisions. This is embodied in a *ruleflow*. Simply put, a ruleflow organizes rule execution in terms of a flow of *rule tasks*, with transitions between them. The transitions (flow links) can be *conditional* on some boolean expression being true. Figure 8.6 showed what the rule editor looks like. Figure 8.11 shows a basic example of a ruleflow for the data validation rule set for the Claim processing application. The ruleset execution starts a task that verifies claim data. If the claim has an issue, the processing terminates. Else, we go through three steps: (1) completing data values, (2) performing the core validation rules, and (3) performing some post-processing (e.g., preparing a validation report).

The ruleflow editor enables us to design the task flow, and to specify the task *bodies*, i.e., specify which rules execute in each task. The recommended practice is to assign one rule package to a rule task. This has several advantages, including: (1) providing execution context for the rules being authored, and (2) simplifying rule-flow maintenance. This also has an impact on the structuring of rules within packages: the mapping to executable rule tasks add one more dimension that we need to consider when we design the package structure. Section 9.4 will go into rule package organization principles and drivers. Section 11.3 will go into a far more detailed discussion of rule execution orchestration.

8.3.5 Ruleset Testing and Deployment

Continuing our process of Fig. 8.5, once the rule development infrastructure (rule projects, business rule model, BOM, and orchestration) is completed, we can start entering rules and unit-testing them. Rule testing can be performed using either Junit, or the *Decision Validation Services* (DVS) component of JRules. Chapter 14 will explore testing issues in general. Chapter 15 will explore testing functionalities of JRules, including DVS.

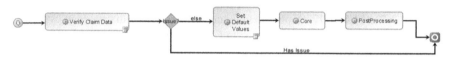

Fig. 8.11 Example of ruleflow

The last recurring activity with Rule Studio is the deployment of the rule sets to the target execution environment. Rule Studio enables us to package/extract rulesets, and deploy them. JRules supports two execution patterns for rulesets, and Rule Studio offers functionalities for both:

- *The embedded execution pattern using the rule engine API.* this is the case where the business application manages the rule engine object on its own, from creation, to population with a ruleset, to invocation, to disposal. For this execution pattern, we need to generate a *ruleset archive* by applying a *ruleset extractor* that builds the ruleset archive from the contents of a rule project.[7] The default extractor grabs all of the rules of the project, but we can develop custom extractors that use rule queries to filter which rules to include in the ruleset archive. For example, we can extract only those rules that have status *deployable*.
- *The decision service execution pattern.* In this case, rulesets are bundled within *RuleApps* and deployed to a *Rule Execution Server* that acts as a central rule execution service for various parts of an application (different decision points in a use case, different tasks of a workflow, or different activities of a BPEL process) or various applications. Rule Studio supports a number of project templates for (1) specifying ruleset bundles/RuleApps (which rulesets to include, and for each ruleset, which project and which extractor), and (2) for specifying Rule Execution Server configurations (host application server, URL, admin credentials, etc.). RuleApps/ruleset bundles can be created and deployed directly, using a live connection, to a rule execution server.

Chapter 13 will go into the details of rule deployment and execution functionalities of JRules.

8.4 Rule Team Server

Rule Team Server (RTS) is a Web-based rule management application that provides a collaborative environment for authoring, managing, validating, and deploying business rules. This is the workspace for business users with an intuitive point-and-click interface that helps support the major use cases for business rule management. Figure 8.12 shows the various activities that different user roles can perform within Rule Team Server. We will provide a brief overview of the underlying functionalities in this chapter. More details will be provided in subsequent chapters. Rule project synchronization with Rule Studio will be presented in Sect. 10.2.3. Access control and permission management within Rule Team Server will be discussed in Sect. 10.2.4 and Chap. 17. Deployment functionalities will be discussed in Chap. 13. Testing functionality will be discussed in Chap. 15. Governance functionality will be discussed in Chap. 17.

---

[7]And the rules projects it depends on ... more on this in Chaps. 10 and 13.

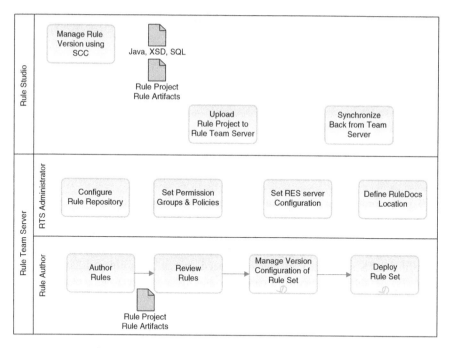

Fig. 8.12 Rule Team Server activities

Each installation of Rule Team Server manages a *rule repository*, consisting of a bunch of rule projects persisted in a relational database. Recall from Sect. 8.2.1 that rule projects are first "born" in Rule Studio and are brought into Rule Team Server through Rule Studio's publication and synchronization functionality. When we populate Rule Team Server with Rule Studio projects, it is important to respect project dependencies and publish a project before publishing the projects that refer to it. As mentioned in Sect. 8.2.1, if rule authoring is to be done by non-technical users who use Rule Team Server, its repository should be considered as the copy of record. In this case, developers should regularly synchronize their Rule Studio projects with Rule Team Server to update *their local copy*.

Upon logging into RTS, the "Home" tab presents the user with the list of projects available in the repository. The user can select a project, and explore its contents in the "Explore" tab. Figure 8.13 shows a example of the Explore tab for the "validate-Claim-rules" project. The top-level folders of the project show "Business Rules", with the package hierarchy underneath, "Ruleflows", "Templates", "Simulations", and "Test Suites", the latter two with a folder hierarchy that mirrors the rule package hierarchy.[8] The central view of the "Explore" tab shows the list of rules in the **"ClaimTiming"** package, under the **"Core"** package.

---

[8]Note that this view of a rule project is customizable and is referred to as *smart view*. RTS users can create *smart views* to present project elements in any order they want.

Fig. 8.13 Rule Team Server Explore Tab to navigate a rule project

To view or edit the contents of a rule, the user can select the rule in a table such as the one shown in the central view of Fig. 8.13, and then select the desired action in the tool bar. Alternatively, the rule table includes iconic shortcuts to viewing (magnifying glass) and editing a rule (pencil), left of the rule name in Fig. 8.13. Note that RTS supports user and role-based access control/permission management. By default, all users/roles can view and update project elements within the projects of the repositing. When we activate permission management for a given project, we can define user and role-based permissions to different users, or user roles, to create, view, edit, and delete project elements. More on this in Sect. 10.2.4.

It is important to note that some project elements cannot be edited within RTS, including *rule flows*, and the BOM, and for slightly different reasons:

- *Safety.* Both the BOM and ruleflows represent central infrastructure elements, and we should not make them modifiable by users who may not have the skill or authority to modify them.
- *Partial information.* The RTS manages a *partial* representation of the BOM.[9] Accordingly, we are not able to assess the impact of BOM changes within RTS, or to propagate them. Hence, any BOM changes need to take place within Rule Studio, where they can be synchronized with the corresponding XOM, and propagated to the vocabulary – and the rules.

This is one example of a situation where developers need to synchronize their Rule Studio project versions with those in RTS, make the needed changes and refactorings in Rule Studio, and then publish the modified project(s) back to RTS.

Figure 8.14 shows the detailed view of a rule ("claimWithin30d"), with its properties/metadata shown on the left, and its **"Content"** (definition), **"Tags"**, and **"Documentation"** shown on the right. The JRules 7 RTS offers two rule editors: a single-form editor which edits rule contents and change documentation in a single form with a "save" and "cancel" button, and a six-form wizard which enables us to change everything about a rule (including metadata/properties, and versioning policy). Note that each time the contents or the properties of a rule

---

[9]The BOM to XOM mappings needs both the BOM and ... the XOM! Which is not available in RTS.

Fig. 8.14 Rule Team Server rule details view

artifact are edited and saved, a new version of the artifact is created, according to the versioning policy; the default policy increments the minor version number, but we can force it to increment the major version number.

The Query Tab is used to create, edit, and run queries against the rule repository. Recall from, Sect. 8.3.1 that JRules supports queries on rule artifacts, which can search against the properties, contents (definition), and semantics of rules. Similar querying facilities are available within RTS. There are small differences, however, between the types of queries that we can run in RTS versus Rule Studio. For example, some rule properties are only available in RTS, including the login name of the RTS user who created or modified the rule.

Rule Team Server also supports the same ruleset deployment functionalities that are available in Rule Studio, namely:

- Ruleset extraction and archival
- RuleApp definition and generation
- Rule Execution Server configuration management
- RuleApp deployment

These functionalities are accessible to users having the role *RTS Configurator*. Regular RTS users (rule authors) can only deploy existing RuleApps to existing server configurations. Figure 8.15 shows the result screen for a successful deployment of a RuleApp to a given Rule Execution Server installation (e.g., http://localhost:8080/res).

Finally, when Decision Validation Services are installed, additional functionality is enabled in Rule Team Server to allow policy managers to run tests and simulations against their rules. Testing is based on *test scenarios*, which represent the test data and the expected results. Test scenarios can be edited by business users, as they are entered in Excel spreadsheets, where columns represent data elements (object attributes), and each row representing a test case/scenario. The format/layout of the Excel workbook is generated by DVS functionality based on the ruleset parameters. Scenarios can be combined into test suites. Users can also

Fig. 8.15 RuleApp deployment from Rule Team Server

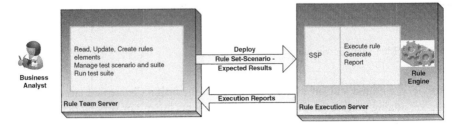

Fig. 8.16 DVS Components View

define *key performance indicators* (KPIs) that are assessed along with the expected results.

The DVS includes functionality to upload test data (Excel spreadsheet) and rulesets to an execution environment called SSP (Scenario Service Provider). The outcome of test execution is a report sent back to Rule Team Server, and displayed in HTML format for review. Figure 8.16 illustrates the process. We will show how to create test scenarios and test suites in Chap. 15.

8.5 Rule Execution Server

The Rule Execution Server (RES) is a managed, monitored execution environment for deployed rulesets. Rule Execution Server handles the creation, pooling, and management of rule sets in order to make rule invocation from the application code more scalable. It natively supports ruleset sharing and rule engine pooling, with the possibility to update rules at runtime. RES provides a management console, from which we can deploy, manage, and monitor RuleApps.

Figure 8.17 shows the architecture of Rule Execution Server (RES). RES can be thought of as two distinct components/stacks that share a database, and that communicate via JMX:

- An *execution stack*, which includes the server-side components to invoke ruleset execution (called *rule sessions*, along with factory/helper classes), an *execution unit* (XU), which knows how to load a ruleset from the database, parse it, and manage a pool engine pool to execute on behalf of business applications.

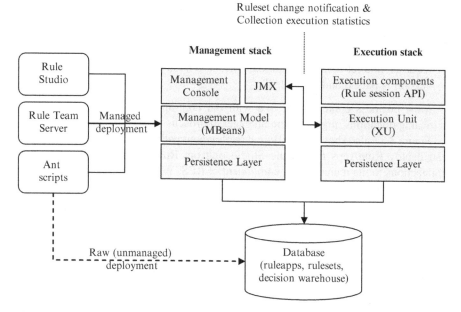

Fig. 8.17 An overview of the architecture and concept of operations of Rule Execution Server

- A management stack, which knows how to deploy rule apps/rulesets, persist them in the database, manage their versions, *and*, (a) notify the execution stack of the deployment of new or new versions of rulesets, and (b) collect execution statistics from the execution unit (XU). The management stack includes a *web console*, which enables us to perform all of these tasks, and to view management information.

The two components are fairly distinct, and are packaged as separate archives. In fact, in a cluster environment, they will not even be deployed to the same server instances: the execution units will be "clustered", whereas a single managed component is deployed on a server outside of the cluster. Further, business applications that need to execute rulesets will only interact with the execution stack via client-side *execution components* (i.e., rule sessions and rule session factories/providers), unless they need to collect management information or execution statistics.

Rule Execution Server supports *hot deployment* of rulesets. This means that we can deploy new rulesets/RuleApps, or new versions of existing rulesets/RuleApps, *while the server is running* and *executing the current version of the rulesets*, and ensure that the new versions of the rulesets will be used for subsequent calls. This is made possible thanks to the JMX communication between the management stack (the JMX box in Fig. 8.17) and the execution stack (the execution unit (XU) box in Fig. 8.17). In fact, there are two flavors of this hot deployment:

- What we might call an "eager" hot deployment, which will immediately parse new versions of rulesets, and block any *new* incoming requests for that ruleset until the new version is "installed".
- What we might call a "lazy" hot deployment, which will not block new incoming requests, and let them run with the current version of the ruleset, until the new version is parsed and "installed".

Most business contexts can live with the lazy approach, but some mission-critical applications might require an eager approach.

Figure 8.17 also shows the different deployment paths. As mentioned earlier, we can deploy RuleApps from Rule Studio or from Rule Team Server, using live connections to the management component of RES. We can also execute batch ant scripts to do the same thing. Again, there are two flavors:

- Scripts that communicate with the management model. This will ensure that proper versioning is used, and that the proper notifications are sent to the execution units.
- Scripts that access directly the database, without going through the management model. These are simpler to set-up, and more efficient to execute, but may leave the execution components in an inconsistent or out of date state.

Finally, note that there different *deployment flavors* of the Rule Execution Server. While the general architecture suggests a full-fledged J2EE deployment, we can have more lightweight configurations to accommodate the variety of execution contexts that we can encounter:

- Full J2EE deployment, including the cluster deployment mentioned above. In this case, the execution component is a full J2EE application, a JCA resource adapter, where the execution components are EJB or POJO session beans. This is the most scalable configuration, and one in which we can configure the pool size, and the like.
- Web container deployment (e.g., Tomcat 6.x), in which case, we still enjoy the services for JDBC data source management, JMX, and JNDI, and a full management stack deployed as a Web application. The execution component is using a J2SE session.
- Pure Java SE deployment in which RES executes within the same JVM as the calling application, and we need to embed a RES execution JAR within our application. The rule engine pooling is available, but no transaction support and security control.

Figure 8.18 shows the "Explorer" tab of the RES Web management console. It requires a servlet container such as Tomcat 6.0 or other JEE application server like WebSphere Application Server. The RES Console supports different user profiles like *administrator, monitor*, or RuleApp *deployer. Monitor* role can update already deployed RuleApp and access the reporting data. The RES console includes features to manage RuleApp and ruleset, to run server diagnostics, to view server logged events, and to manage reporting data in the Decision Warehouse. Decision

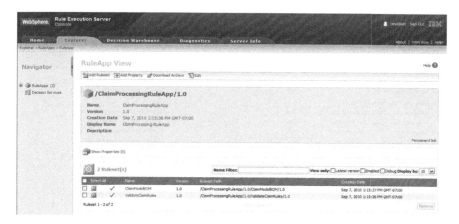

Fig. 8.18 Rule Execution Server console – exploring the deployed RuleApp

Warehouse delivers a set of features to trace, store, and view and query rule execution activities. Indeed, each ruleset execution can generate traces, which when persisted forms a decision history that can be consulted and used for auditing purposes.

Chapter 13 will go into the details of RES API and explore the different views that deployed rulesets can present to calling business applications. It will also explore in more detail the functionalities of the decision warehouse.

8.6 Rule Solutions for Office

Rule Solutions for Office, or RSO, consists of a set of functionalities that enable us to (1) publish rule artifacts from Rule Team Server to Microsoft Office 2007 Word and Excel documents, (2) edit those rule artifacts with Word and Excel, and (3) upload the new versions back into Rule Team Server to integrate them with the main editing stream within Rule Team Server. Rule Solutions for Office leverages the capabilities of the OpenXML-based file format used by Microsoft Office 2007. We will provide a brief overview of the various functionalities.

To be able to publish Rule Team Server (RTS) projects into Microsoft Office documents, an RTS administrator needs to create a so-called RuleDocs location. This location is a URL to a shared disk on a server or a local directory on user workstation. Once this is done, a rule author can publish a project to the predefined location. They do so through the "*Publish rules to RuleDocs*" action in the "Project" tab of RTS. This will prompt the user for, (a) the RuleDocs location, and (b) the (sub) set of rules to publish. By default, that set/subset consists of all of the action (if–then) rules, and all of the decision tables of the project. However, the user can select which rules to include/exclude, individually, or by specifying a query. Figure 8.19 shows the rule selection form in RTS. The user may choose to publish

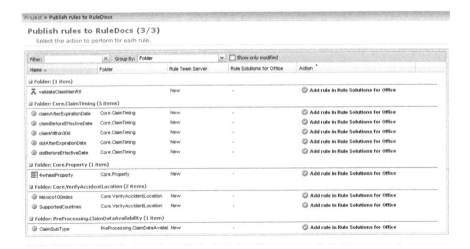

Fig. 8.19 Publish rules to RuleDocs

Fig. 8.20 RSO word *Rule Ribbon*

all of the action rules of a project to a single Word document, or to publish each *package* to a separate Word document. The same is true for decision tables and Excel documents.

The installation of RSO will modify Word and Excel, by adding new menu bar buttons, new actions, and a new behavior. Figure 8.20 shows the so-called *Rule-Ribbon* added to Word.

In Word, a *RuleDoc* includes a *Write pane* (the main editing frame in Word), a *View pane*, and a *Review pane*. The Write pane is used to insert new rules or edit existing ones. This pane supports a number of custom completions modes activated with CTRL-SPACE, SPACE, TAB, and so forth. The review pane is used to check the rules for errors and to activate or deactivate automatic syntax highlighting. The View pane is used to show or hide the RuleDoc pane and Vocabulary panel. Each business rule in a RuleDoc is stored within a *content* control that separates the contents of the business rule from the surrounding text. In Fig. 8.21, the top-level content control includes the name of the rule, its package hierarchy, while the Rule Body content control includes the text of the rule.

Content controls react to user actions and act as custom editors within Word. Completion assistants provide guidance while writing business rules by showing the applicable vocabulary terms that can be used at this particular location of the rule. This is illustrated in Fig. 8.22. They are similar to the code completion

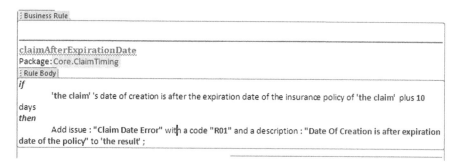

Fig. 8.21 Two content controls for one rule

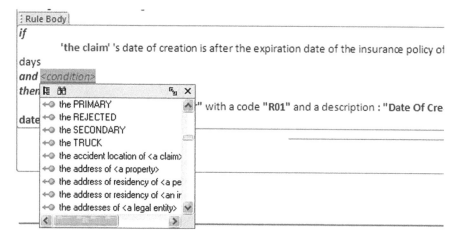

Fig. 8.22 BOM – term navigation

assistants available in Rule Studio's text-based rule editor (*Intellirule*). The content control includes also a rule syntax checker, similar to Word's standard spelling and grammar checker, that enables users to check and correct business rules.

Once authoring is done within Rule Solution for Office, the rule writer can use the Update rules from RuleDocs feature of Team Server to update RTS repository.

8.7 Summary

This chapter provided a brief overview of the IBM WebSphere ILOG JRules BRMS. We described the overall architecture of the product, the concept of operations, and then, for each component of the product, we identified the main workflows and activities supported by the component and gave a brief overview of those activities, throwing in some best practices along the way.

Many of these activities and workflows will be revisited in the subsequent chapters, namely:

- *The design of rule project structures.* General, product-neutral issues will be discussed in Chap. 9, and JRules specifics in Sect. 10.2.
- *The design of the Business Object Model (BOM).* General issues, related to the different requirements between the BOM and XOM, and relationships between them, will be discussed in general terms in Sect. 9.2.1, and for the case of JRules in Sect. 10.3.
- The rule artifacts will be presented in a product-independent way in Sect. 9.2.2; JRules rule artifacts will be presented in Sect. 11.2.
- The orchestration of rule execution, will be discussed in Sects. 11.3 (foundations) and 11.4 (best practices).
- Ruleset deployment and execution will be discussed, in general terms, in Chap. 12, and with JRules specifics, in Chap. 13.
- Rule testing will be discussed in general terms, in Chap. 14, and with JRules testing functionalities, in Chap. 15.
- Finally, everything related to rule governance will be discussed in general terms, in Chap. 16, and for the case of JRules, in Chap. 17.

This is the only chapter of the book that is product/feature driven. The remainder of the book is *activity-* or *issue-driven*, even for those chapters that deal with JRules specifics. As the product evolves, some of the actions, menus, and screens shown in this chapter may change. However, the major issues and activities should remain the same, barring a profound change in the product architecture and concept of operations.

8.8 Further Reading

This being a product-driven chapter, the reader is referred to the product documentation for more technical information and tutorials, which is now public accessible at http://publib.boulder.ibm.com/infocenter/brjrules/v7r1/index.jsp.

Part IV
Rule Authoring

Chapter 9
Issues in Rule Authoring

Target audience

- *Business analyst, rule author (skip Sect. 9.2.1)*

In this chapter you will learn

- *The major issues in setting up a domain of discourse for business rules*
- *The different languages for authoring rules*
- *Rule coding patterns for different classes of rules*
- *Principles and best practices for organizing rules during development*

Key points

- *Business rules are written against a business-oriented view of the data.*
- *High-end BRMSs offer a multitude of languages for expressing business rules; choose the one that fits the business logic.*
- *Atomic rules are easier to write, to validate, and to maintain.*
- *There are proven ways of coding certain types of rules, which rely on rules being atomic.*
- *Development-time organization of rules is a key aspect of rule management.*
- *The structure of the domain and rule reuse opportunities are key drivers for the development-time organization of rules.*

9.1 Introduction

In this chapter, we look at the general issues surrounding rule authoring in a technology-independent way. We look at three different aspects. First (Sect. 9.2), we look at rule languages. In particular, we will address two sets of issues: (1) issues related to the *business vocabulary* itself, that is, the *business object model* and (2) issues related to the rule structures. In Sect. 9.3, we look at rule coding strategies

J. Boyer and H. Mili, *Agile Business Rule Development*,
DOI 10.1007/978-3-642-19041-4_9, © Springer-Verlag Berlin Heidelberg 2011

based on a simple classification of rules. In Sect. 9.4, we deal with the organization of rules during development: how to best organize rules during development so as to reflect the structure of the domain and to optimize design time qualities such as reusability, an effective division of labor, and the like. We conclude in Sect. 9.5.

9.2   Rule Languages

During the ABRD life cycle, business rules will be expressed in a variety of languages that differ in terms of structure, formality, and vocabulary, depending on how far along we are in the process and on the target audience for the rules. Barbara von Halle talks about four different languages which correspond more or less to four different phases of the rule life cycle (von Halle 2001):

- *Business conversation language*. This is the language used for the *initial* steps of rule discovery (see, e.g., Chap. 4). This corresponds to the phrasing of rules "in their native format", that is, the way they are first extracted from their source, be it a requirements document, a regulation, meeting minutes, a procedure manual, etc. In this case, no special care is taken to structure the rules, or to disambiguate their terminology, or to validate them. Validating the terminology is one of the outcomes of rule discovery.
- *Structured natural language*. By the time we are done with rule discovery, and ready to tackle rule analysis, rules are already encoded in some sort of structured English – or whatever the language might be – using predefined *linguistic templates* that correspond to the various rule categories. Section 4.2.1 proposed a number of such templates for the various rule categories.
- *Formal rule authoring language*. This is the language used by business users to author rules in a *late BRMS*. This language has to satisfy two conflicting criteria: (1) being formal and unambiguous and (2) being intuitive and easy to use for a business person. This language should be either executable as is or mechanically translatable to a rule engine's native language.
- *Engine execution language*. This is the language understood and executed by rule engines.

Figure 9.1 places the four languages along the business rule life cycle.

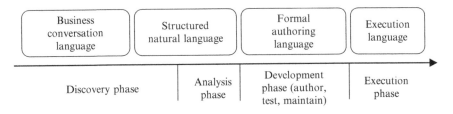

Fig. 9.1 Rule languages depending on lifecycle phase (Adapted from von Halle 2001)

Chapter 4 dealt with the business conversation language and the structured natural language. In particular, we discussed OMG's *Semantics of Business Vocabularies and Rules* (SBVR) standard for defining domain-specific vocabularies and business rules. In this chapter, we deal with the authoring and execution languages.

When we talk about languages, it is customary to talk about the *vocabulary* of the language, and the *structure* of the language, that is, the way that *sentences* are composed using elements from the *vocabulary*. With rule languages, the *vocabulary* is the *business vocabulary*, referred to as *term and fact model* in business rule methodologies. The term and fact model is often, *abusively*, equated with a class model, where terms correspond to classes and their attributes, and facts correspond to associations between entities. While this is a good approximation, there are important conceptual differences between the two. However, by the time we move into rule authoring, the term and fact model is typically implemented by an object model that embodies the business view of the data, that is, the *business object model*. In the remainder of this section, we will first talk about the *business object model* and then about the different rule languages.

9.2.1 The Domain of Discourse: Business Object Models

The business object model is an object model that reflects the business view of the data. In this section, we talk about the desirable characteristics of a business object model, ways in which it differs from the real (actually implemented) object model, and ways to bridge the two.

A *business object model* is an *object model*; it represents the world as a set of objects, having features, both structural (i.e., attributes) and behavioral (i.e., functions), and having relationships between them. This model is *business oriented* in that it reflects the point of view of a *business community*, as opposed to the point of view of IT. Like with any model, the main desirable characteristics of a business object model are:

- *Soundness*. It provides a correct rendition of the world being modeled. Practically, this means that the model has no errors. For example, if a particular kind of policy cannot have more than one insured person, it should be reflected in the model, such as in the cardinality of the association between InsurancePolicy and InsuredPerson.
- *Completeness*. In this context, the completeness of the model means that it represents every aspect of the modeled world that is relevant to the application at hand. For example, if we need to reason about medical providers to adjudicate claims, then we must have an adequate representation of medical providers in relation to claims and medical invoices.

In short, everything that we need is in the model and everything that is in the model is correct.

A *business* object model that will be used as a basis for authoring *business rules* by – potentially or ideally – *business people* needs to satisfy three additional criteria:

- *Specificity*. The terminology of the model should follow closely that used by the business community concerned by the model. If we are dealing with business rules for health insurance claim processing, then we would be talking about **MedicalInvoice**, **MedicalInvoiceLineItem**, **MedicalProcedure**, and the like. If, on the other hand, we are dealing with car repair claims for car insurance, then we would talk about **RepairShopInvoice**, **RepairShopInvoiceLineItem**, **RepairProcedure**, and the like.
- *Abstraction*. The model should represent the information at the level of abstraction that is appropriate for authoring the business rules. For example, if business rules talk about "claim amount", then the *business* object model should have an attribute amount for the class **Claim**, even if that information is to be aggregated from other data elements.
- *Relevance*. Ideally, the model should only represent the information that is relevant to a particular business function (e.g., a business process).

Note that "relevance" seems to contradict "completeness". But the combination of the two says, in essence, that our model needs to have everything I need for my business function/area, and nothing more.

More interestingly, the last three criteria seem to contradict desirable properties of a conceptual data model. Indeed, if you were a data architect tasked with the job of designing a common data store to support a bunch of applications, you would pretty much be given the opposite directives, that is,

- *Genericity*. Make sure that the model terminology abstracts the commonalities between the various functional areas that use the central data store. For example, if I am an insurance company that offers different insurance products, I would want to use the generic term **Policy** to refer to both health and auto policies, and **ServiceInvoice** to refer to invoices for both car body work, and, say, physical therapy.
- *Canonicity*. Make sure that the conceptual data model contains the minimal set of data elements from which all other data elements can be derived. Practically, this means, for example, that we should *not* represent a property amount for a **Claim**, if we can compute it from the individual service invoices.

Genericity and canonicity contradict specificity and abstraction – and to a lesser extent, relevance. We should then have two different models! The question then is how to map one to the other!

Actually, we have known how to do this for as long as we have been doing relational data modeling! To build the conceptual model, you were supposed to collect the various *views* from the various *users* of your application, normalize those views, and merge them to get the central, common data model. You can then recreate those views using the relational database view mechanism!

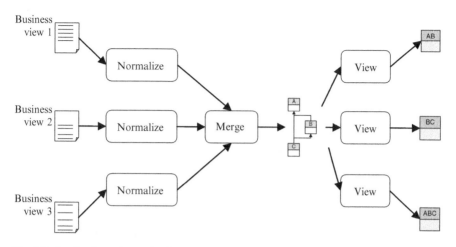

Fig. 9.2 Starting from the needs of different business (sub)communities, we derive a central data model from which the business views can be regenerated

Figure 9.2 illustrates this process. This is both a metaphor for the relationship between the business object model and the underlying application object model, and a description of some of the ways in which this mapping can work.

Let us go back to the beginning. The first generation of rule engines – then known as *expert system shells*, see Chap. 6 – used their own exotic representations of data that were inspired by *knowledge representation languages* such as *frame languages*.[1] As such, they did not integrate well with business information systems, but that was OK, because they were typically used in desktop engineering applications such as designing circuit boards for the VAX family of computers or CAD/ CAM applications. Such applications could be characterized as having high procedural expertise, high data structural complexity, but low data volume.

The specialized representation of data was a major factor in delaying the penetration of expert system shells in business applications. Second-generation expert system shells kept using their own exotic data representation languages, but were able to load their *fact base* from relational databases. This scenario is illustrated in Fig. 9.3; the reader may have noticed a similarity between this diagram and one of the reengineering scenarios mentioned in Sect. 7.5.3 (reengineering the data layer).

With this second generation of BRMSs, the integration between the BRMS and the business application is *data driven*: the two sides communicate only through shared data stores. However, rule execution could not be integrated into high-volume, end-to-end business processes. In particular, the BRMSs – called *expert system shells* – did not offer a public API that could be invoked from business

---

[1]A *frame* is data structure that represents a *class* where features are represented by *slots* which have *values* as well as a bunch of *procedures* or *demons* attached to them. Such *demons* kick in (are triggered) when a value is read, set, or modified.

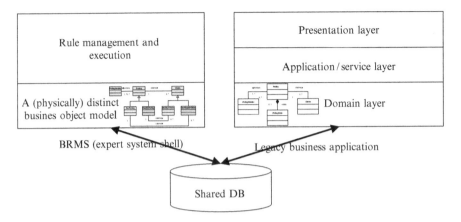

Fig. 9.3 Second-generation business rules management systems (BRMS) integrated with business applications via shared database

applications: they remained mostly desktop interactive applications that were invoked independently/asynchronously of the business applications.

The current generation of BRMSs *execute* rules directly on the native application objects, be they Java, C++ or C#. But how could they, if the rules are *authored* using the *business object model*? Well, some BRMS tools do not make that distinction: the same object model is used for authoring and execution. This is the case with most of the open-source rule engines, including JESS, OPSJ, and DROOLS.[2] The leading commercial products – including JRules and FICO's Blaze Advisor – support two distinct models. If we think of the business object model as a *business view* of the application's Java (or C++ or C#) object model, then we can translate rule references to the business object model *into* rule references to the application's object model. This translation can happen either during rule authoring or during rule execution. The two scenarios are illustrated in Fig. 9.4. Earlier versions of JRules supported authoring-time translation of rules from "rules against business object model" to "rules against application object model". Since JRules 6, this translation happens during run-time. JRules's business object model to application object model mapping is very powerful, and can accommodate substantial differences between the two models. The so-called BOM to XOM mapping[3] will be discussed in Chap. 10.

Run-time BOM to XOM mapping has a major advantage: "write rules once, execute everywhere". For example, if the BRMS at hand supports execution

---

[2]More recent versions of DROOLS support *DSL* rules which are expressed using a natural language veneer on top of the application's object model. We cannot say that it uses a *different* object model: It simply uses a different *terminology*.

[3]BOM as in *Business Object Model* and XOM as in *eXecutable Object Model*.

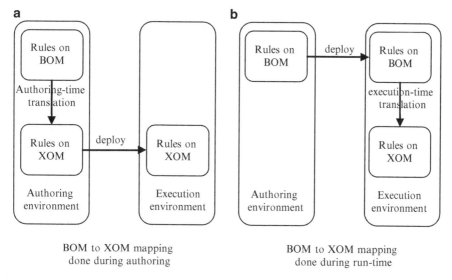

Fig. 9.4 Different business object model (BOM) to execution object model (XOM) mapping times

language–independent BOM, the same rules could be executed against Java objects or C# objects, say, which is precisely the case with JRules. More advantages will be explained in Chap. 10.

9.2.2 Flavors of Rule Authoring Languages

Business rules come in many shapes and flavors. The most common form of a business rule follows the familiar **if-then** pattern, but that is, by no means, the only one. Common formats include:

- **If-then** rules
- Decision tables
- Decision trees
- Scorecards
- Custom languages

In this section, we talk about the various flavors and the type of problems that they can accommodate.

9.2.2.1 If-Then Rules

If-then rules are the most common condition-action rules. The actual terminology may differ (e.g., **when-then** or **condition-action** or, in French **si-alors**, etc.) but the

if part represents a set of conditions on a tuple of objects, and the **then** part describes the actions to take on the elements of the tuple. Generally speaking, there are two flavors of **if-then** rules:

- So-called technical rule language, which uses syntax close to the host programming language. For example, the following is a JRules technical rule:

```
rule GoodCustomer {
    property priority = 0;
    when{
            ?customer: Customer();
            ?order: Order(amount > 1000; isRushed();
                                    customer == myCustomer);
    } then {
            System.out.println("The customer :" + ?customer
                    + " is a good customer);
    }
}
```

This rule matches a pair <?customer,?order> such that the order is worth more than 1,000, is rushed, and is made by the customer, and for each such pair, prints the description of the customer with the message shown, in the system standard output stream. In this example, the class **Order** has (public) attributes amount and customer, and the Boolean function isRushed(). OPSJ has a nearly identical syntax.[4] Other languages such as JESS have their LISP lineage still showing with the use of property-list notation for property values.

- *Business-oriented language*, what JRules calls *business action language* (BAL) or what DROOLS refers to as domain-specific language (DSL) rules. These rules use intuitive, natural language-like syntax. The same above rule written in JRules' BAL would look like:

```
Definitions
    set 'the order' to an order;
    set 'the customer' to the customer of 'an order';
If
    the amount of 'the order' is more than 1000
    and 'the order' is rushed
Then
    print "The customer: " + 'the customer' +
                        " is a good customer";
```

This syntax is more appropriate for rule authors who are business users, such as business analysts or policy managers (see Chaps. 3 and 4). Such rules are

---

[4]Unsurprisingly, considering that an earlier version of JRules is based on an earlier version of OPSJ, namely, OPS5.

typically translated by the BRMS tools into technical rules. In JRules, the *business action language* may be seen as a rule *entry language*, which is translated on the fly, by the rule editor itself, into the technical language.

Which language to use? Obviously, the business-oriented language makes rules understandable and "authorable" by business, and is much preferred to the technical rule language for business applications. However, the familiarity of the language comes at a cost: business-oriented languages tend to be less powerful. How much less? It depends. For example, in JRules, JESS or DROOLS, rule authors using the technical language can use a fairly significant subset of the Java language in the action part of rules, out of the box. With a business-oriented language, the constructs that can be used in either the condition part or the action part need to be precodified; we will show this in the context of JRules in the next chapter. Also, historically, language builders have managed, with varying degrees of success, to introduce more complex constructs into business-oriented languages in a more or less intuitive way. For example, the first versions of JRules' BAL (JRules 3.x, circa 2001–2002) were much less powerful than the technical language. The languages are now comparably powerful as far as business applications are concerned.

9.2.2.2 Decision Tables

Figure 9.5 shows an example of a decision table. The structure of the table is self-explanatory. The left two columns represent *conditions* to be tested, and the last two represent *decisions* or *actions*. The business logic described by the table could have been described by nine separate rules, one per row. The first rule might say: "**if** the driver is under 18 **then** do no underwrite". The second might say: "**if** the age of driver is between 18 and 25 *and* the number of demerit points is no more than 2 **then** underwrite and use the rate category B18-2", and so forth. Business people often represent decision logic in tables, even if they have never heard of the business rules approach. Many of our first-time customers already had some of

Age		Demerit points		Underwrite?	Rate category
Min	Max	Min	Max		
≤18		-	-	No	N/A
18	25	≤2		Yes	B18-2
		2	6	Yes	C18-8
		≥6		No	N/A
25	75	≤2		Yes	A25-2
		2	8	Yes	B25-8
		≥8		No	N/A
≥75		≤6		Yes	A75-6
		>6		No	N/A

Fig. 9.5 A sample decision table

their business rules captured in Excel spreadsheets or Word tables. With business rule methodologies, opportunities for organizing decision logic in tables arise during *rule analysis* (see Chap. 4 and von Halle 2001). During this activity, we identify recurrent patterns of rules and try to organize such rules in tables. Roughly speaking, if we have a bunch of rules that test the same data elements (age and demerit points in this example), and that take similar actions (underwrite or not, and which rate category to use), then we have an opportunity for using a decision table.

Commercial BRMS tools support decision tables: they are intuitive and easy to create, read, and maintain. JRules provides API for creating such tables programmatically from external tabular data sources, and includes Microsoft Office plug-ins to edit decision tables in Excel spreadsheets, and to synchronize them with the rule authoring environment (*Rule Team Server* or RTS, see Chap. 8); other features will be explained in the Chap. 10 .

9.2.2.3 Decision Trees

The kinds of situations that call for decision tables can also be handled by decision trees. In fact, you may find that business people think in terms of decision trees, and then express/encode the decision tree in the form of a table. A number of commercial BRMS tools – including JRules – support the specification of decision logic as decision trees. In a decision tree, each tree node represents a *decision* or test, and the branches off that node represent alternative outcomes. The decision tree for the table of Fig. 9.5 is shown below in Fig. 9.6.

Figure 9.6 shows only excerpts of the tree for the table in Fig. 9.5: it does not fit in the page. This is a major weakness of decision trees, as a way of expressing decision logic: while they may be visually appealing, they are fairly unpractical for all but the most trivial decision problems.[5]

9.2.2.4 Scorecards

The example we used for decision tables and decision trees is a typical one in applications that involve scoring actual or potential customers (applicants) to decide whether to offer them the service, and under what conditions. In *credit* scoring – and credit scorecards – the goal is to assign credit applicants a score, and then deciding, based on where that score falls, whether to grant them the credit they applied for, and if so, under what conditions. In *insurance underwriting*, we assign potential insured a risk score and underwrite based on that score.

---

[5]JRules' decision trees have a bunch of features to make the display more compact by folding/unfolding subtrees or changing the direction of the display, top to bottom or left to right. But that does not change the nature of the problem.

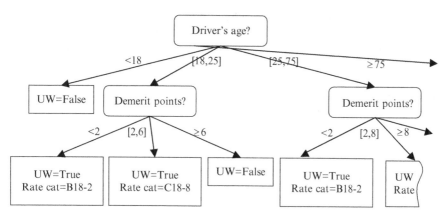

Fig. 9.6 Excerpts from the decision tree representing the decision logic in Fig. 9.5

Attribute	Value range	Score	Explanation
Age	< 18	0	Isn't insurable
	[18, 25]	30	Worst accident statistics
	[25, 75]	55	Safest age range
	≥ 75	45	Safe behavior but diminishing capacity
Demerit points	< 2	75	Safe drivers
	[2, 6]	60	A poor driver, but not a dangerous one
	≥ 6	30	A dangerous driver

Fig. 9.7 An insurance underwriting scorecard

Let us consider a variation on the decision table in Fig. 9.5. The *insurance risk* scorecard is shown in Fig. 9.7. Like in Fig. 9.5, we use two attributes, "age" and "demerit points". For each attribute, we assign a different *score* to a different value range. The final decision is based on the sum of scores assigned to an applicant. In this example, let us say that we underwrite the driver only when their cumulative score is higher than 100. Thus, a driver under 18 would not be insured, regardless of driving record. Also, any driver with more than six demerit points will not be insured, regardless of their age. Young drivers (between 18 and 25) with two to six demerit points will not be insured either, since their total score is $30 + 60 = 90$, which is less than 100.

Scorecards are convenient because a complex decision can be reduced – and explained – in terms of a single cumulative score falling into a particular range. On the surface, scorecards are similar to decision tables. However, there are important differences in terms of power and usability, which will be discussed in the next section. For the time being, let us just say that their design is part science – mostly – part art. Indeed, the parameters of the scorecards are computed using a combination of statistical analyses over historical data (the science) and usability considerations such as simplicity of the model, number of attribute ranges, etc. (Siddiqui 2006) (the art). *Some* commercial BRMSs, including JRules, support scorecards, but they are found mostly in business intelligence (BI) and analytics tools.

9.2.2.5   Custom Languages

In Chap. 4, we presented different classifications of rules. Not all classes of rules can be *conveniently* written as **if-then** rules, or variations thereof (e.g., decision tables or decision trees). We just saw one such type: scorecards. Scorecards have their own design tools and execution engines which differ from RETE rule engines (see Chap. 6). While we can turn every type of rule into an **if-then** rule – we will pretty much show how to do that in the next section – there are situations where a custom language can make rule authoring more familiar to the business users.

Assume that you are building an application for automatically filling out tax returns. The majority of tax rules are computations. Using the rule templates described in Sect. 4.2.1, a computation may be stated as:

The taxable income IS-COMPUTED -AS gross income + commissions – deductions

It would be convenient to be able to enter such a rule as is within a rule editor. In this case, the rule editor would be a *formula editor* similar to the formula editor available in Excel spreadsheets. This would be more natural than entering the rule as:

if <some trivial condition or no condition> **then** taxPayer.taxableIncome = taxPayer.grossIncome + taxPayer.commissions – taxPayer.deductions

or its business-oriented language equivalent.

Through our consulting practice, we did develop custom rule entry languages for some customers. JRules offers a rule language development framework called the *Business Rule Language Development Framework* (BRLDF), which is a java library for specifying the syntax of the custom rule language, and for translating rules written in this syntax to some target language. Note that the rule editor itself can be parameterized by the grammar of the language and its vocabulary – the business object model. Finally, instead of developing a custom rule engine for rules expressed as formulas, we translated user-entered formulas into **if-then** rules similar to the one shown above, that were never shown to business users, but that were the ones deployed. Figure 9.8 illustrates the approach.

When should you develop a custom rule language? This solution should only be considered when:

- The full rule syntax represents an unnecessary burden, and an unbearably awkward syntax for its target users.
- The cost of developing the custom rule language, the custom rule editor, and the custom rule engine was minimal.

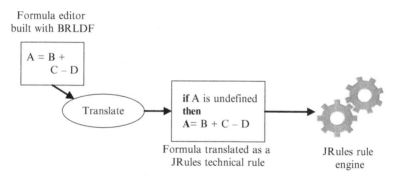

Fig. 9.8 Developing a custom rule language

• You have reasonable assurance that future evolution of the BRMS you are using
  will not invalidate your language.

Our advice, generally speaking, is to avoid customizing in all circumstances,
because your customizations can lock you into a particular version of the BRMS
product that you are using, preventing you from taking advantage of new features as
they come out. This applies to custom rule languages. If you get too creative, you may
go down toward unstable parts of the API, and find yourself, a couple of years down
the line, facing two painful choices: (1) continuing costly implementation and maintenance of custom features that have *since* become available in the BRMS product out
of the box or (2) bite the bullet and take up the costly effort of migrating your rule
assets – possibly rewriting some of them from scratch – to the new(est) version of the
product.[6] We will come back to customization issues at the end of the book.

9.3 Rule Coding Strategies and Patterns

In this section, we propose some common rule coding patterns to handle common
rule classes. Section 4.2.1 proposed the following classification of so-called decision rules, as opposed to *structural* rules and process flow rules:

• Constraints
• Guidelines
• Action enablers
• Computations
• Inferences

---

[6]The customization that we performed in this case is low risk: the custom rule language is
orthogonal to the predefined rule languages and editors, and "rules" (formulas) are translated
into the most stable part of the product, the technical rule language, which has evolved but
remained backward compatible all throughout the lifetime of the product (since 1997).

In Sect. 9.2.2, we reviewed the various languages that are typically provided by BRMSs to express rules. In particular, we saw **if-then** rules, decision tables, decision trees, scorecards, and custom languages. In this section, we look at how to express the different types of rules using the available languages (Sects. 9.3.1–9.3.4). In addition to the five categories mentioned above, we will consider risk-assessment rules and compare scorecards to decision trees (Sect. 9.3.5). We will also look into the issue of encoding business data as decision tables (Sect. 9.3.5).

9.3.1 Coding Constraints and Guidelines

Constraints express conditions that must be true for the business – or the application supporting it – to behave according to business intent. The conditions can be either on the system (or state of the business) as the whole or on individual business events or transactions that come its way. Let us take one example of each.

- A constraint for underwriting drivers for a car insurance policy, on a single driver:

  it is necessary that the driver be over 18 **and** the driver have had no DUI[7] convictions within the last 2 years **and** the driver have a credit score at least equal to 650 **and** the driver have 8 penalty points or less

- A constraint for claim processing, on the *set* of claims being handled by the system at any given point in time:

  it is necessary that for a given policy there is at most one claim being adjudicated by the system at any given moment in time.

The first constraint ensures that we only underwrite mature, safe, and financially sound drivers. The second constraint ensures that there would be no more than one claim in the system being adjudicated: this means that if a claim C_1 against policy P is being adjudicated, we cannot adjudicate another claim C_2 against the same policy P *until* C_1 is completed.[8] The difference between the two constraints is immaterial to the subsequent discussion, and so we will stick with the first kind.

The issue here is how to encode such a constraint using typical rule entry languages. A naive encoding of this constraint in a business-oriented language would go something like:

---

[7]DUI: Driving Under the Influence [of alcohol or drugs].

[8]The reason for this could be that the way we adjudicate a claim can influence the way we adjudicate subsequent claims because of things like quotas, caps, and the like, and thus we need to process each claim fully to update running tallies, etc.

if

the driver is over 18 *and* the driver has had no DUI convictions within the last 2 years *and* the driver has a credit score at least equal to 650 *and* the driver has 8 or fewer penalty points

then

mark the driver as eligible

There are at least two problems with this encoding. First, generally speaking, constraints provide *necessary* conditions (**it is necessary that**) for a business event to be processed successfully, not *sufficient* ones; in this case, there may be other conditions for eligibility which are not expressed in this constraint, such as the driver residing in a jurisdiction covered by the insurer, or not being presently incarcerated, say! Thus, it is logically/semantically wrong to say that if these conditions are satisfied, the driver is eligible.

Even if we had all of the necessary and sufficient conditions expressed into that one constraint, with this rule, I have no way of telling *which* of the several conditions a driver fails. Indeed, if the rule fails to fire for a particular driver, all we know is that the driver *either* is under 18 *or* has had DUI convictions within the last 2 years *or* has a credit score less 650 *or* has had more than eight penalty points, but I cannot say which of the above conditions she/he failed. It is important, for both auditing purposes, and for sound customer relationship management (CRM), to be able to tell why a particular transaction was rejected or a particular service was denied.

The third reason why this encoding is bad is maintenance. If we need to add a requirement, such as jurisdiction, or remove one, such as credit score, we need to modify an *existing* rule. From a maintenance point of view, that is not a good practice: to the extent that that is possible, we would like our business logic maintenance to be *conservative* (I *conserve* what I already have) and *incremental* (small changes in requirements lead to small changes in the rule base).

A key element of the problem is the expression of the constraint *in the first place*: it is not *atomic*! Recall from Sect. 4.2, a key step in rule analysis is making rules atomic. "Yeah, sure", we hear you saying, but this is where it comes to bite us. The constraint above can be expressed as four separate constraints:

it is necessary that the driver be over 18
it is necessary that the driver have had no DUI[9] convictions within the last 2 years
it is necessary that the driver have a credit score at least equal to 650
it is necessary that the driver have 8 penalty points or less

We can now encode each constraint through an **if-then** rule that identifies a *violation* of the constraint, yielding four different rules:

---

[9]DUI: Driving Under the Influence [. . . of alcohol or drugs].

if
    the driver is under 18
then
    add to driver the ineligibility condition: "Driver under 18"
if
    the driver has had a DUI conviction within the last 2 years
then
    add to driver the ineligibility condition: "DUI convinction within last 2 years"
if
    the driver has a credit score under 650
then
    add to driver the ineligibility condition: "credit score under 650"
if
    the driver has more than 8 penalty points
then
    add to driver the ineligibility condition: "more than 8 penalty points"

If we put a policy (or driver) through these rules, each condition violation will result into a rule firing, and a log that records the nature of the failure. A transaction that satisfies all of the conditions will come in and out "untouched" by the rules. This solves our problems:

1. The encoding is semantically sound: not matching these rules does not mean that the transaction will pass; it may match *other* violation rules.
2. The reasons for failure are documented/itemized.
3. From a maintenance point of view, to add a condition, we add the corresponding condition violation rule, and to remove a condition, we remove the corresponding condition violation rule!

But "our business rules are much more complex than that". Sure they are! Let us first start with a constraint that is a disjunction (**or**) as opposed to a conjunction (**and**). Consider the following simple constraint:

it is necessary that the driver be employed **or** the driver be retired with an indexed income

Mathematically speaking, this constraint is atomic: it cannot be broken any further without changing its meaning. We could encode it with the rule:

if
    the driver is **not** *employed* **and** the driver is **not** retired with an indexed income
then
    add to driver the ineligibility condition: <some message>

What would be <some message> in this case? Because failing an **or** condition means failing both of its branches, we could write "the driver is neither employed nor retired with indexed income". If we step back and think about what the constraint means, it actually means that the driver has a steady income, and there are two ways to have a steady income: either be employed or be retired with (cost-of-living)-indexed income. A less literal – and perhaps more informative – message might then say "the driver does not have a steady income". As is often the case with disjunctive (**or** 'ed constraints), the constraint expresses a *quality* and the elementary conditions express different ways/modalities in which that quality can be achieved.

Let us now consider a yet more complex example that merrily combines conjunctions (**and**'s) and disjunctions (**or**):

> **it is necessary that** (the driver has been a US resident for more than two years **and** the driver has had no DUI convictions within the last 2 years) **or** (the driver has been in the country for less than two years **and** has no moving violations)) **and** ((the driver has been a US resident for more than two years **and** the driver has a credit score at least equal to 650) **or** (the driver has been a US resident for less than two years **and** the driver has no pending collection claims))

There are two approaches to go about this one. One approach would recognize that this constraint is about two *qualities*, the driver's driving record, and the driver's credit track record. Each one of these two qualities has two modalities: one for drivers who are long-time residents and one for drivers who are recent arrivals, with no history/track record. Seeing it this way, we can change this constraint to two inferences and two elementary constraints:

> A good driving record **is defined as** (having resided in the US for more than two years **and** having no DUI convictions in the last two years) **or** (having resided in the US for less than two years **and** having no moving violation)

> A good credit record **is defined as** (having been a US resident **and** having a credit score at least equal to 650) **or** (having been a US resident for less than two years **and** having no credit history **and** having no pending collection claims)

> **It is necessary that** the driver have a good driving record

> **It is necessary that** the driver have a good credit record.

We know how to handle the last two constraints. We will show in Sect. 9.3.3 how to encode the first two inferences.

A second, more mechanical way of handling the original constraint would break it into a *disjunction of conjunctions* as in $(A_1 \text{ and } A_2. \ldots \text{ and } A_n)$ **or** $(B_1 \text{ and } B_2 \ldots$ **and** $B_n)$ **or** ..., etc. To transform any Boolean expression into a disjunction of conjunctions, we use the following transformation rules:

- **not** (A **and** B) is equivalent to (**not** A) **or** (**not** B)
- **not** (A **or** B) is equivalent to (**not** A) **and** (**not** B)
- (A **or** B) **and** C is equivalent to (A **and** C) **or** (B **and** C).

If we transform the above constraint, we get:

> **it is necessary that**
> ((the driver has been a US resident for more than two years **and** the driver has had no DUI convictions within the last 2 years) **and** (the driver has been a US resident for more than two years **and** the driver has a credit score at least equal to 650))
> **or**
> ((the driver has been a US resident for more than two years **and** the driver has had no DUI convictions within the last 2 years) **and** (the driver has been a US resident for less than two years **and** the driver has no pending collection claims))
> **or**
> ((the driver has been in the country for less than two years **and** has no moving violations) **and** (the driver has been a US resident for more than two years **and** the driver has a credit score at least equal to 650))

or
((the driver has been in the country for less than two years **and** has no moving violations) **and** ((the driver has been a US resident for less than two years **and** the driver has no pending collection claims))

The two grayed-out clauses can never be true, because they both include contradictions: the driver has been a US resident for more than 2 years and the driver has been a US resident for less than 2 years cannot both be true at the same time. Thus, our simplified constraint can now be expressed as:

it is necessary that
(the driver has been a US resident for more than two years **and** the driver has had no DUI convictions within the last 2 years **and** the driver has a credit score at least equal to 650)
or
(the driver has been in the country for less than two years **and** has no moving violations **and** the driver has no pending collection claims)

Actually, a business analyst might intuitively frame this as "we have a rule for long-time residents and a rule for recent residents", and that would be the correct interpretation, mathematically.

We can handle the last constraint in two stages. In the first stage, we check if the driver satisfies either set of constraints independently. The first batch of rules will say something like:

if
        the driver has not been a US resident for more than two years
then
        add to driver the failure condition for over 2 years: "resident less than 2 yrs"
if
        the driver has a DUI conviction with last two years
then
        add to driver the failure condition for over 2 years: "DUI conviction last 2 yrs"
if
        the driver has a credit score less than 650
then
        add to driver the failure condition for over 2 years: "low credit score"

The second batch will say:

if
        the driver has been a US resident for more than two years
then
        add to driver the failure condition for less than 2 years: "resident more than 2 yrs"
if
        the driver has a moving violation
then
        add to driver the failure condition for less than 2 years: "Moving violation"
if
        the driver has pending collection claims
then
        add to driver the failure condition for less than 2 years: "pending collection claims"

In this case, we maintain two lists of error codes: one for error codes for the case of long-time (more than 2 years) residents and the other for error codes for the case of recent (less than 2 years) residents. A seventh rule would wrap this up:

if

> the driver has error codes for more than two years **and** the driver has error codes for less than two years

then

> mark the driver as ineligible because: <some message>

In the rejection letter/report, the driver would get an explanation saying that they failed the "more-than- 2-years" rule for the reasons A and B, say, and they failed the "less-than-2-years" rule for the reasons E and F.

Let us recap: in case a constraint contains an atrocious combination of **and**'s, **or**'s, and **not**'s, which approach is better:

1. Organize the constraint as a combination (conjunction or **and**'s) of qualities, each having several modalities (disjunctions or **or**'s), or
2. Turn the constraint into a disjunction of conjunctions, and treat each conjunction as a separate constraint

It depends! If the constraint can naturally be written as a conjunction of disjunctions,[10] and each disjunction corresponds to different modalities for an obvious quality (e.g., driving record and good credit record), *and* the modalities for the various qualities are independent,[11] then the first approach is logically sound, and it yields more intuitive rules. If, on the other hand, the constraint is inscrutable, then we have no choice but to go for disjunctions of conjunctions and use the second approach suggested here.

To sum the collected wisdom of this section:

1. *Before you do anything, make your **rules** atomic*. It has been our experience that rule analysis, in general (Chap. 4), and making rules atomic, in particular, is not always/often taken seriously. But that is OK! If you do not perform rule analysis up front, you will have to do it in the process of actually coding the rules. Atomic rules are easier to understand, easier to code, and easier to maintain.
2. *To code a constraint, write rules to detect its violations, not its satisfaction*. We showed why with our first, rather simple, example of a conjunction of conditions: we are able to document the precise reasons for which a transaction failed a constraint.
3. *Beware of logical illusions*. We use the term "logical illusions" by analogy to "optical illusions". When we capture rules, we sometimes make unwritten

---

[10]Mathematically, we know that all Boolean expressions can be written as disjunctions of conjunctions, but the dual is not true: not all Boolean expressions can be written as conjunctions of disjunctions.

[11]Meaning, I could satisfy the "good driver" quality in any one of the **or**'ed ways, and I can satisfy the "good credit" quality also in any one of the **or**'ed ways.

assumptions about the world which will come back and bite us. Indeed, we could take a rule expression that looks right, transform it using logically sound (but not always intuitive) transformations, and end up with a rule that looks (and feels) wrong. What happened? Well, in many cases, it is those "unwritten" assumptions that did not get transformed along with the rest of the rule, leaving a logical hole.

Finally, everything we said about a constraint applies to a guideline. For the purposes of rule authoring, the only difference between a constraint and a guideline is what you do in case it is violated: with a constraint, a violation typically results into a failure of the current process. With a guideline, a violation typically results into logging some observation or raising a flag, but the process continues.

9.3.2   Coding Computations and Inferences

Both computations and inferences assign values to attributes, under certain conditions. With computations, the attribute is typically quantitative (numerical), and the business rule consists of a formula that derives a value of the attribute from values of other attributes and quantities. With inferences, the attribute is typically – but not always – *qualitative*, and we assign a discrete value. We will consider examples of both.

An example of a computation is our taxable income rule from Sect. 9.2.2.5:

The taxable income IS-COMPUTED-AS gross income + commissions – deductions

Unless you build a custom entry language for such formulas (see Sect. 9.2.2.5), computations are typically encoded using **if-then** rules. An encoding of this rule could be:

if <some trivial condition or no condition> **then** taxPayer.taxableIncome =
taxPayer.grossIncome + taxPayer.commissions – taxPayer.deductions

or its business-oriented language equivalent. What we referred to as <trivial conditions> could be conditions on the attributes "taxableIncome", "grossIncome", "commissions", and "deductions" being already set/computed, so that this rule kicks in only when the input quantities have been computed. Other computation rules are typically needed to compute the input quantities themselves (i.e., gross income, commissions, and deductions).

With inferences, the value of the attribute typically depends on a combination of values of other attributes, without being derivable via a mathematical formula. They can be coded in a similar fashion. They are typically used for *tiering*. The general pattern is:

if <some condition on other attributes or quantities> **then** set the value of <our attribute>
to <a constant value>

Assume that our insurance company wants to classify drivers as "high cost", "average cost", and "low cost". We would have a different rule for each value, as in:

if the driver made at most one claim in the past year, and they were not at fault **then** set
the profile to the driver to: LOW-COST

if the driver made one or two claims, and they were at fault in no more than one claim
then set the profile to the driver to: MEDIUM-COST

if the driver made three or more claims and they were at fault in at least one claim **then**
set the profile to the driver to: HIGH-COST

Inferences lend themselves nicely to decision tables, as the different values
typically depend on the *same* set of input attributes: the input attributes become
condition columns and the value of the inferred attribute makes the *action* column.
A special case of inference, *risk scoring*, will be discussed in Sect. 9.3.4.

9.3.3   Coding Action Enablers

Action enablers are defined as **if** <condition> **then** <action> rules, and so they
can readily be expressed as **if-then** rules. The only problem with action enablers is
that many other types of rules pass themselves off as action enablers. The reason is
that any of the above categories (constraints, guidelines, inferences, and computations) *can be* expressed as **if-then** rules. However, there are two main differences
between *true* action enablers, and other types of rules passing themselves off as
action enablers.[12] First, there is the type of action being performed in the action part
of the rule. With computations and inferences, the action part sets the values of an
attribute. With constraints (or guidelines), the action part typically records the
failure of a particular condition. By contrast, with action enablers, the action part
launches a *domain meaningful* process, as opposed to a value setter. The second
major difference resides in the impact of firing an action enabler, as compared to
firing a constraint, say. Typically, an action enabler launches a secondary business
process, while the main process continues. By contrast, firing a constraint violation
rule puts an end to a business process – its happy path.

9.3.4   Coding Risk-Assessment Rules

Risk assessment is a common application area for so-called decision management
technologies in general, and business rules in particular. Credit risk is perhaps the
most common – and best known – of the application areas, but companies in many

---

[12]Mistaking an inference for an action enabler is not a problem, except for purists, but mistaking a
constraint for an action enabler can be a problem as it prevents the rule author from seeing the
general pattern – and from taking advantage of some of the rule patterns presented here.

industries, including financial services, insurance, retail, and various utilities use risk scoring for a variety of purposes, including:

- *Acceptance/rejection decisions.* To decide whether to accept a customer's application for a particular product or service – called *underwriting* in insurance and financial services
- *Pricing.* To decide what premium to charge a given customer, based on the risk that they represent
- *Troubleshooting.* To identify existing accounts that are heading for trouble and that may need to have the terms revised

Risk assessment is a two-step process. The first step consists of *building a risk model* based on some historical data. The purpose of the model is to categorize a given business transaction into one of several classes/bins, each characterized by qualitatively different customer behavior. The second step of risk assessment consists of *operationalizing* the risk model by making business decisions on incoming business transactions based on the class within which they fall. In the simplest case, the model classifies incoming transactions into an *accept* bin and a *reject* bin. More complex models can have more graded answers such as going from *accept* to *accept with a higher premium*, to *accept with a higher premium and additional guarantees*, to *manual referral*,[13] or to *reject*. Different scores can also suggest different products, different terms for the same product, etc.

In Sect. 9.2.2, we saw two forms of decision models: (1) decision trees (or tables) and (2) scorecards. Scorecards assign a score to a business entity/business event, based on values of its attributes, and that score is later used to make a decision about the business entity/business event. Decision trees, on the other hand, involve a cascade of tests ultimately leading to a decision. In terms of decision power, decision trees have one major advantage over scorecards: scorecards assume that the attributes used for computing the score are independent. Consider the table in Fig. 9.7: a scorecard assumes that the age of the driver is statistically independent of the number of demerit points (penalties) that the driver has. We know that that is not the case: young drivers' temerity and lack of driving experience makes them more prone to reckless driving, and thus to traffic tickets. A decision tree model makes no such assumption: quite to the contrary, its asymmetry reflects dependencies between attributes. In the example of Fig. 9.6, the partitions for the "number of demerit points" depend on the age range; in fact, for a given age range, we do not even look at the number of demerit points.

On the minus side, decision tree models lack gradualness: a driver who is 1 day short of a pivotal date will not make it, regardless of the other qualities she/he might have which could normally compensate. This is less of a problem with scorecards.

---

[13]Manual referral refers to a situation where an automated system is not "confident enough" to make a decision on its own (based on the encoded business rules), and the application (for a loan or an insurance) is sent to a human decision maker.

Scorecards have an additional "business" advantage over decision trees: a decision can be explained in simple terms ("sorry, we require a score of more than 600, and you have only 560") without revealing the detailed mechanics of the decision itself; knowledge of the detailed mechanics of a decision may lead to ... hum ... data manipulation.[14]

There are other decision models out there, such as neural networks, which are also numerical classifiers. A major problem with neural networks is that the decisions are totally opaque ... including to the organization administering the decision! We know that they work – when they do – but we cannot characterize, in a readable, intuitive fashion, the kinds of business entities or events that belong to each category ("rejected", "accepted", etc.).

It is beyond the scope of this chapter – and book – to go into risk scoring in more depth. For our purposes, suffice to say that we have two alternatives, namely scorecards and decision trees, whose parameters are determined using statistical analyses of historical data, and they each have their own strengths and weaknesses, both in terms of predictive performance and in terms of explanation power.

9.3.5 Encoding Business Data Tables

While decision tables are useful and intuitive, not every *business data* table would make a good *rule decision table*. We have encountered many situations where customers maintain some of their reference business data in tables, and consider moving the data to decision tables. Two common examples are product configuration tables and pricing tables.

Let us say you are a local phone service company offering a variety of phone-based services, some of them are bundled, with optional features, required features, incompatible features, and the like. Figure 9.9 shows excerpts of what such a table would look like. The column "BUS or RES" refers to whether the product is available to residential versus business customers, "Pulse versus Tone dialing" specifies the type of line on which the service/product is offered (e.g., some services require a digital/tone dialing line), and "visit premises required" specifies whether a visit to the customer's premises is required to activate the service.

How would this table be used? Imagine a CRM application used by call center operators who field calls from prospective customers. Either a customer calls to order a specific feature, in which case the call center agent checks that the customer satisfies the requirements (BUS vs RES, and Pulse vs tone dialing), and either accepts or denies the order. Alternatively, the call center agent could try to convince the customer to order the required product to be able to acquire the service. For example, a customer calls to order call blocking, the agent asks them whether they have tone dialing, the customer says no, and the agent convinces the customer to switch to the

---

[14]For example, applicants "manipulating" some of their attributes for the purposes of passing the underwriting process (about income, savings, etc.).

Product code	Description	BUS or RES	Pulse vs tone dialing	Installation delay	Visit premises required
LFW	Consumer unlimited lifeline	RES	Pulse; Tone	2 business days	Yes
ZBNSY	Call blocker	RES; BUS	Tone	1 business day	No
ZBNCN	Caller ID and number	RES; BUS	Tone	2 business days	No
...	...	...	...	...	...
B1W	Business measured local service	BUS	Pulse; Tone	2 business days	Yes
...	...	...	...	...	...

Fig. 9.9 A sample product table that can be used to drive a customer relationship management (CRM) application

more expensive tone dialing to be able to receive the "call blocker" service. As for the last two columns, they may be used to inform the prospective customer and to prompt the call center agent to schedule a visit to their premises if one is required.

The question now is, should we build a decision table from the product table,[15] considering that such product tables typically run in the thousands or tens of thousands of rows/rules, one for each product, option, and feature, and combinations thereof? There are two underlying questions:

- Can the BRMS handle tables of such size?
- Is it the most efficient way of handling the creation, maintenance, and referencing the product table?

The answer to the first question depends on the BRMS. JRules has no built-in limitations on the size of decision tables, but the decision table editor, a Java GUI application may suffer with large tables. As for the second question, the answer is probably no. Forget the tools, and let us step back and think about the *tenets* of the business rules approach, as opposed to any particular implementation; if the goal is to externalize business logic in a way that business can understand and to separate it from the application code, then implementing the business logic as a database table – or Excel spreadsheet – that is referenced by the CRM application is consistent with the approach.[16] Further, the "rule maintenance" is easy and familiar to business users.

---

[15]Actually, probably two tables: the first, with columns <product code, BUS vs RES, Pulse vs Tone>, which describes the prerequisites and can be used for order selection, and the second, <product code, installation delay, visit premises> to be used for order processing.

[16]This solution has one disadvantage: the business rules of the application would not *all* be under the same roof; some business rules will be managed by the BRMS, while others will be managed by external databases. Mature organizations can develop a common portal through which they can access both a BRMS and other data sources.

Another common example is *pricing* tables. A pricing table can be thought of as a decision table, where we have one row per product variant, one condition column per product characteristic, and one action column containing the price. As with the table of Fig. 9.9, such tables will typically have *dozens* if not *hundreds* of columns, and *thousands* if not *tens of thousands* of rows, each representing a specific combination of product features and options. Within any given row, only a small fraction of columns have non-null values, corresponding to that specific product. Should we implement such tables with decision tables? Again, the answer is no, for reasons similar to the ones we mentioned for the product table in Fig. 9.9. But this begs for the question as to how tables got this big in the first place. Actually, the answer to this question often provides also an answer as to how to make such tables usable and maintainable: often they result from joining different product tables together, based on a unique product ID, leading to a multiplication of the number of rows, and an accumulation of columns most of which have empty values for any given row. By "unjoining" such tables, we are able to recover a set of smaller, and more manageable tables, which can be used in sequence to finally find the specific product combination for which a price is sought. Our experience has been that our customers loathe such an exercise in price table reengineering, because errors have an immediate impact on the top line! Yet, we often found that such an effort is necessary to make such tables manageable, regardless of which technology we choose to implement them!

9.4 Organizing Rules During Development

Now that we have gone over the ingredients for rule authoring, we look into the issue of how we organize our rules during development, that is, within the management stack of a BRMS. Why is this issue, and what choices do we have? Consider our case study of MyWebInsurance Corp., which sells a number of insurance products, including health insurance. The functional area we looked at so far deals with business rules for claim processing. Claim processing is but one of many business processes that deal with health insurance policies; underwriting and policy renewal are two other processes. Underwriting involves a number of tasks including data validation, eligibility, tiering,[17] and pricing. Policy renewal may also include eligibility, tiering and (re)pricing. The rules for renewal eligibility may be similar in some respects to the rules for underwriting eligibility, but different in others. For example, rules concerning the credit risk of the policy holder may be similar, but the rules concerning health condition will be different: MyWebInsurance may decline to underwrite a policy of a particular type for some types of existing medical conditions, the first time around, but may have no choice but to

---

[17]In this context, *tiers* are categories. For example, policy holders may be assigned a risk qualification with three *tiers* in it, *low risk*, *medium risk*, and *high risk*. Tiering, then, refers to the process of assigning a policy holder to a *tier*.

renew the policy if a condition of one such type manifests itself, or is diagnosed while the policy is in effect. Similarly, if MyWebInsurance also sells life insurance, some of the validation rules for underwriting may be similar to the ones for health insurance, for example, rules about the personal data of the policy holder, their occupation, and so forth, and different from those in health insurance regarding, for example, coverage options. The issue we deal with in this section is how to organize the various rulesets during development to manage their development effectively.

First (Sect. 9.4.1), we present the main structuring dimensions of rules during development. In Sect. 9.4.2, we discuss what we mean by "manage their development effectively", that is, we discuss a set of design criteria for a development-time organization of rules. We present best practices in Sect. 9.4.3.

9.4.1 Rule Structures

When we develop large software, the different components of the software may be divided in different *projects*. A project reflects a somewhat self-contained set of artifacts that depend on each other. For example, within the context of a client-server application, the client part may be developed in one project whereas the server part is developed in another project. When a given component is too big for a project, we can divide it in several projects that build upon each other: a first project presents the foundations of the component. Then, new projects build upon that foundation layer to implement elementary services. Then other projects implement processes that orchestrate such elementary services, and so forth. Within a project, software artifacts may be further divided into *packages*. Within a team development context, with several applications being developed in parallel, the projects related to a given application may be stored in a *repository*, and thus, a development organization might have several active repositories. Figure 9.10 shows the various development structures that we mentioned, and their relationships.

This repository → project → package structure makes sense not only for regular software, such as Java classes, but also for business rules. In fact, a number of business rules management systems – including JRules – use this hierarchy of structures to organize rules: a *rule* repository may include a number of *rule* projects, which in turn, can include a number of *rule* packages. Rule packages contain rules, and can be nested at will. Typically, rule projects will include or refer to other artifacts that may be needed to author rules, including some sort of a domain-specific

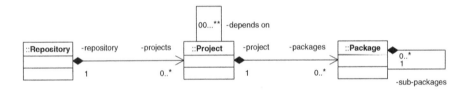

Fig. 9.10 A hierarchy of containers for regular software development artifacts

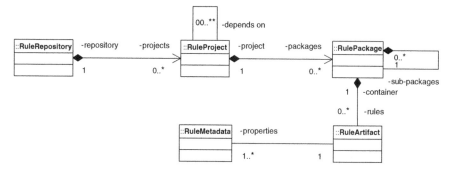

Fig. 9.11 The development-time representation of rule artifacts

language (DSL) for the functional area of the project, etc. Also, rules will have some metadata attached to them. Typical metadata might include the usual administrative properties, such as *name, author, creation date, last modification date*, or *version number*. It might also include properties related to the business aspects of the rule, such as *jurisdiction, effective date, expiration date*, and the like. Figure 9.11 illustrates this organization. The ongoing discussion will refer to this organization.

9.4.2 Design Drivers for an Effective Organization of Rules

Having defined the available structures to organize rules in the previous section (see Fig. 9.11), let us now go back to our MyWebInsurance Corp, and try to figure out how to organize the rules into repositories, projects, and packages, given its product portfolio, the various business processes that it wishes to automate, the similarities and differences between the business rules relevant to the various decisions. To make the decision/design process easier, this section looks at the various factors that have an influence on the organization of rules during development. We will propose best practices in Sect. 9.4.3.

There are two major design drivers that influence the organization of rules during development. The first – and probably strongest – driver is *the problem domain*. Indeed, we expect the structure of the product portfolio and the business processes to be reflected somehow on the way that rules are captured and managed during development. The second strongest driver for organizing rules deals with *development-time qualities* such as rule reuse, a good division of labor in the likely case where several people are authoring rules, rule maintenance, and so forth. It has been our experience that two additional drivers, albeit weaker ones, also influence the organization of rules, but only cursorily: the application landscape, in terms of how many applications will use the rules, and where they live, and run-time qualities, in terms of predictability and performance. For the purposes of this discussion, we will limit ourselves to the first two – and strongest – drivers.

9.4.2.1 The Problem Domain

MyWebInsurance, like most insurance companies, offers a wide range of insurance products. Figure 9.12 shows excerpts from its product portfolio. We expect the organization of our rules to somehow reflect the structure of the product portfolio, with AUTO insurance rules (car insurance, motorcycles, recreational vehicles, etc.) being captured, organized, and managed separately from, say, home flood insurance rules or identity theft rules!

But then, for every product, we might have several business processes to automate with business rules, such as underwriting, renewal, claim processing, and so forth. Similarly, we would expect the underwriting rules to be captured, organized, and managed as one set, distinct from, say, the claim processing rules – some of which we have seen in the previous chapters.

For a given business process, we would typically have many tasks, and the business rules relevant to each task would also be fairly distinct: for example, a number of document-processing applications start with a *data validation* step, which checks that social security numbers are well formed, that birthdates are indeed dates, that such dates are plausible (e.g., no claimant born before 1850 or in the future), and this happens before any product- or process-specific logic takes places, such as eligibility, pricing, adjudication, etc. Each one of these process steps embodies a *cohesive* set of rules that should be organized together.

Then, there is the issue of *jurisdiction*: for a given <product, process, step> combination, the business rules may also depend on the jurisdiction. Eligibility or pricing rules may depend on the jurisdiction, for example, the state/province, or county, or even zip code! Thus, we would want to group the rules for a given <product, process, step, jurisdiction> combination together! Figure 9.13 shows the full range.

A first-cut – and somewhat naive – solution would map this hierarchical structure to the hierarchy of Fig. 9.11. For example, we could map a product line to a repository,

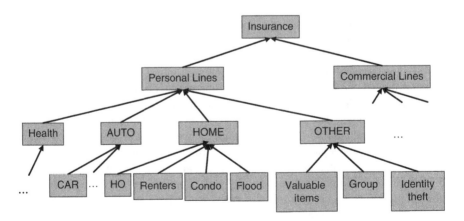

Fig. 9.12 An insurance product folio

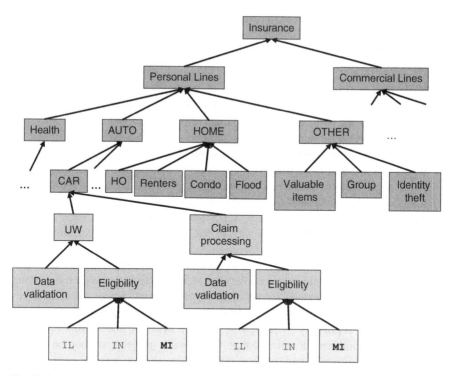

Fig. 9.13 The full range of business rule families

have one project per business process, and within each project use one top-level package for process step, and then use sub-packages to accommodate jurisdictions. In practice, this would not work very well because the product landscape tends to be more complex. First, we would have more layers in the product taxonomy. Second, products tend to consist of bundles or packages of more elementary products or features. Third, processes themselves can be fairly complex, with several nesting levels. Fourth, there might be other variability dimensions in the products, the underlying processes, or the corresponding rules, including effectiveness periods of the rules – think of it as *time jurisdiction* – customer type, and so forth.[18] Thus, with the repository →project → package structure, we quickly run out of dimensions! Not to mention the other factors that we have not talked about yet.

---

[18]Some of these variability dimensions can be handled *within the rules* themselves. For example, the rules that are applicable to Illinois (IL) can have a condition that says "and if the policy holder is a resident of Illinois". There is a tradeoff between how much context to put in the rules themselves (explicitly), how much to embody in the organization of rules (implicit). Making context explicit is "safer" and provides for a simple strategy of extracting rules for execution: "get them all", they will filter themselves out. By contrast, having the context embodied in the organization requires a more elaborate strategy for extracting the rules relevant to a particular execution. We will come back to this issue later when we talk about the way *run-time qualities* influence *development time* organization of rules.

9.4.2.2 Development-Level Qualities

In a nutshell, the organizational structure of rules should make it "easy" to work with rules during development. This means many things:

1. *Understandability of the structure.* The structure should make sense to the rule author. A rule author who needs to enter a new rule that talks about age requirements for holders of a recreational vehicle policy needs to know where the repository → project → package hierarchy she/he should insert the rule. If the structure reflects business context, it should make it that much easier to know where to add the rule – or where to find a rule that needs modification. Actually, if the organization structure of the rules follows the structure of the problem domain, as discussed above, it would provide the necessary business context. However, as mentioned above, the repository → project → package structure alone cannot handle the complexity of the problem domain, let alone other factors, to be covered next.

2. *Reusability. Some* business rules are reusable across products, across business processes, or across jurisdictions. We should be able to define such rules in one place, and then reuse them for the appropriate products, processes, or jurisdictions. This requirement means several constraints on the structure of rules. First, a hierarchical repository → project → package structure that mirrors the structure of the problem domain cannot work, since projects cannot be shared between repositories, and packages cannot be shared between projects or between higher-level packages. Second, the packaging of rules should enable us to separate reusable rules from non-reusable ones. For example, it should be possible to separate eligibility rules for policy holders for car insurance, in general, from those that are prevalent in, say, Indiana. However, the structure should still be understandable, so that the rule author who wishes to enter a rule for a particular <product, process, step, jurisdiction> combination will know where to go.

3. *An effective division of labor.* When *several* people are authoring rules – as is often the case – we need to be able to divide up the work in such a way that the rule authors can work *independently* and *consistently.* At a fairly coarse level, we know that rules for AUTO would probably end up in a different repository altogether from health insurance, say. However, we may need to have different people working on eligibility rules for home owners, for different jurisdictions – say Indiana versus Michigan. This pleads for having the Indiana rules in a different package, say, from the Michigan rules, provided that the BRMS supports package-level locking. Generally speaking, given the level of granularity of locking afforded by the BRMS, the organization of rules should make it possible to separate the things that rule authors can – or should – work on independently. The granularity of locking only ensures that different rule authors can work *independently* but does not ensure that their work will be *consistent.* For example, JRules supports rule-level locking, and so technically, it is possible to have different rule authors working on rules anywhere in the project package hierarchy.

However, it is not a good idea to have two rule authors modify rules within the same low-level package. Because the rules of a low-level package are likely to be executed together, they provide the execution context. Thus, a rule author A who is modifying rule R_a that is part of package P needs to know that the other rules of the package remain the same while he modifies his rule.

4. *A simple mapping to a rule execution structure.* Eventually, from all of the rules that we will be authoring in the development repository, we will need to pull out different subsets – referred to earlier as *rulesets* – that we will be ultimately fed to individual rule engines to implement the decision-making capability of a particular business process step. This raises two issues. First, what should be the level of granularity of the decision that we handle in a single ruleset, or equivalently, in a single rule engine invocation? Second, given a chosen level of granularity, how easy would it be to pull out the rules that make up that ruleset (or, equivalently, that are relevant to a particular decision) from the development-time organization of rules? For the time being, we are not going to worry about the first issue, because we cannot have a useful discussion that is independent of the JRules BRMS; we will revisit this issue in subsequent chapters. To illustrate the second issue, let us assume that our BRMS can only extract the contents of a rule project, in an all-or-nothing fashion. This means that any decision/rulesets would have to be implemented with one or several projects, as we cannot pick and choose the packages or rules within a project that we needed for a particular decision. If my decision is "eligibility for Indiana drivers", that means that I should have a dedicated project just for eligibility rules for Indiana drivers. And if there are eligibility rules for drivers that are applicable across jurisdictions, they should be in a separate project all by themselves. This simple example illustrates how deployment considerations can trump a number of other criteria in choosing a development-time organization for rules.[19]

In the end, the development-time structure that we adopt will be the result of all these influences. The next section will present some useful structuring patterns.

9.4.3 Best Practices

In the previous section, we identified the design drivers for a good organization of rules during development. The purpose of this section is to attempt to turn the previous analyzes toward something that will help you design your development-time organization of rules. Obviously, a lot depends on the complexity of the problem at hand. If you are a business rules expertise center for a major insurance company tasked with the job of designing the organization of rules for the entire

---

[19]Luckily, JRules has a very flexible extraction strategy for rulesets, to be discussed in later chapters, but earlier versions of the product (JRules 3, 4, and 5) had more restricted out-of-the box *ruleset extractors*, and one had to use a nontrivial API to extract the desired rules out of a project.

corporation, then you have your job cutout for you. If you are at the other end of spectrum developing your first business rule application for a particular process and a specific product variant, then your job is going to be a lot easier. The previous discussion provides you with the vocabulary to frame the problem, and that is more than half the battle. In the remainder of this section, we will present some best practices.

9.4.3.1 Think It Through

The most precious piece of advice – one whose simplicity sometimes disappoints our customers – is to actually sit down and analyze the rules landscape using the design parameters we discussed earlier.

You know your problem:

- You know how complex your business is
- You know how much of it you will need to tackle in the short, mid, and long term, and how much of that you can afford to worry about in the short term
- You know if there are opportunities for rule reuse in your business
- You know how many people will likely end up developing and maintaining the rules
- You know which BRMS you will be using, what structuring mechanisms it provides, besides the basic repository → project → package hierarchy, and what ruleset extraction strategies are supported
- Etc.

You should start by mapping out the domain first, and then bring in the other factors.

The design team should necessarily involve business people and technical people. Business people bring to the table their knowledge of the product portfolio (e.g., various types of insurance policies), of the business processes, and will know the similarities and variabilities between the rules. The technical people bring to the table their knowledge of the BRMS and its relevant features.

9.4.3.2 Package Nesting Patterns

A desirable feature of any organization – of rules or other types of artifacts – is its consistency. This manifests itself at all levels of the repository → project → package hierarchy: repositories should have similar scopes, the projects within a given repository should follow one of a handful of project types/templates, and the organization of packages should be consistent within a given project. In this paragraph, we present some package structuring patterns.

- *Specialization nesting pattern*. In this pattern, the parent package groups rules relevant to some concept, and the sub-packages group rules relevant to specializations of the concept. An example of this pattern is shown across where the specialization is based on the product. For example, if <Product X> is the product family "HOME" and <task Y> is "policy holder eligibility", we get:

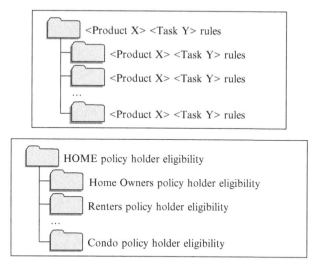

- *Process–subprocess/task nesting pattern.* In this case, the parent package groups rules relevant to a particular process or task, and the sub-packages groups rules specific to subtasks of the process.

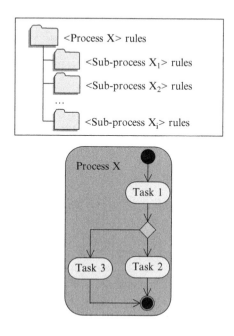

A sample instance of this pattern is shown below:

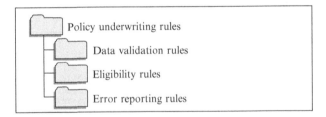

- *Jurisdiction–sub-jurisdiction pattern*. In this case, the parent package groups the rules that concern a particular jurisdiction, whereas the sub-packages group the rules for sub-jurisdictions, as shown across. An instance of this pattern from our insurance example is shown below:

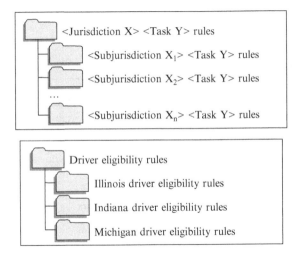

Figure 9.14 shows instances of the three patterns across the sample insurance domain discussed in Sect. 9.4.2.

9.4.3.3 Use Metadata to Supplement the Repository → Project → Package Hierarchy

Regardless of how many levels of nesting we use for rule packages, the repository → project → package has one serious limitation: it is a *hierarchy*, that is, a rule can be found in only one place. Rule metadata enables us to mesh the hierarchical dimensions with other cross-cutting dimensions. This implicitly assumes that the process of extracting rules for execution will rely on the values of rule properties to decide whether a given rule is relevant to a given decision or not. For example, we

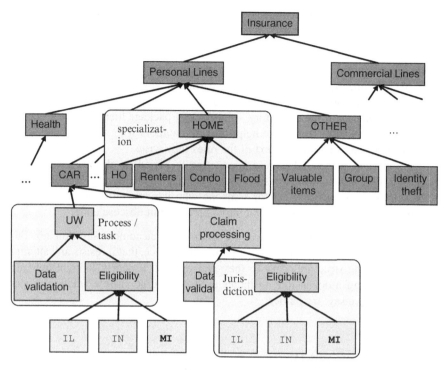

Fig. 9.14 Some package nesting patterns

could have a single rule package that contains all driver eligibility rules for car insurance, for *all jurisdictions*. However, we use a multi-valued rule property called "jurisdiction" that takes a single state (say "Michigan"), a set of states (say, "Illinois, Michigan"), or "ALL_STATES" as values. If we have a car insurance policy to underwrite, and the driver lives in "Michigan", then we can pull out all of the driver eligibility rules, those that are applicable to "Michigan".[20]

9.4.3.4 Always Favor Structure over Computation

This piece of advice is somewhat a counterweight to the previous one. Reliance on metadata to organize rules during development means more reliance on programming to extract rules out of the development repository. We have seen situations

---

[20]Should we pull out rules with "Jurisdiction" = "ALL_STATES" when the driver lives in "Michigan"? Probably, but that means that we need to have a policy about how to handle rules with different jurisdictions that conflict. For example, the "ALL_STATES" rule may require a minimum age of 20, whereas the "Michigan" rule requires a minimum age of 22. If the driver is 21, is she/he eligible or not? JRules has a mechanism for rule overriding, which we will talk about in Chap. 10.

where customers had fairly complex   and convoluted procedures – for extracting the rules that are relevant to a business decision (a *ruleset*) from the development repository. This complexity has two main disadvantages:

- It means that the development-time organization of rules bears no resemblance to the run-time organization of rules. In particular, rules that appear in the same package may not execute together, and conversely, rules that may belong to remote branches of the repository → project → package hierarchy may end up executing together. This is not helpful to rule authors who need to have some idea about the execution context of the rules they write.
- An important piece of business knowledge is buried in obscure procedures. Indeed, figuring out which business rules are relevant to which decision should be relatively straightforward for someone who is navigating the development repository; it should not be buried into – clever – but obscure code.

Through our consulting practice, we often hear customers say "oh no, our problem is more complex than that", implying, in essence, that it resists any attempt to rationalize the structure. And so they end up with a poorly thought-out rule structure, but half a dozen rule attributes used by complex rule extraction procedures. Not so, we say: try harder!

9.5   Summary and Discussion

In our practice, we are sometimes disheartened when customers assign rule authoring to the more junior members of a business rules project team. Rule authoring is important: it is a key step in the business rules approach, and is as least as critical to the success of a business rules project as any other step, from capture (Chap. 4), to analysis (Chap. 4) to integration (Chaps. 7 and 11), to testing (Chap. 13), or governance (Chap. 15). (Good) rule authoring is also hard: in order to use the technology to its fullest potential, there are a number of design dimensions to pay attention to. First, there is the problem of setting up the rule authoring environment. Roughly speaking, this involves two aspects: (1) setting up the language(s) for coding rules and (2) setting up the development-time organization of rules. Setting up rule languages is concerned with the design and implementation of a business-oriented view of our application data. We showed in Sect. 9.2.1 the relationship between the business view of the data and the actual implementation of application data. We explored in Sect. 9.2.2 the various rule artifacts that we can use to express business logic.

Having "set the table" for authoring rules, it is now time to take those rules identified and analyzed during rule capture and analysis (Chap. 4), and turn them into formal, executable rules. This transition is far from trivial. Indeed, coming out of analysis, rules are mostly *declarative*, stating *what* must be, but not *how* it comes to be. Thankfully, there are proven rule coding patterns, appropriate for each rule category identified in Chap. 4, namely, constraints, guidelines, computations, inferences, and action enablers. Patterns for these types of rules were presented in Sects. 9.3.1–9.3.3. We have also looked at two special cases of business rules, risk scoring (discussed in Sect. 9.3.4) and business data such as product tables and price tables (discussed in Sect. 9.3.5).

The organization of rules during development is a key factor in the success of a business rules effort. A good organization makes use of rule development, maintenance, and management that much easier. It can also simplify rule deployment. We saw in Sect. 9.4.2 the various design drivers for the organization of rules, and presented organization patterns and best practices in Sect. 9.4.3.

9.6 Further Reading

While fluency in Boolean logic is not required – the patterns shown in Sect. 9.3.1 should cover all you will need – interested readers can check any introductory mathematics college textbook. Alternatively, Wikipedia's entry for Boolean algebra (http://en.wikipedia.org/wiki/Introduction_to_Boolean_algebra) provides a very good and broad introduction into the topic, even including a reference to a recent introductory textbook.

As mentioned in Sects. 9.2.2.4 and 9.3.4, risk scoring is an important application area for the broader *decision management* area, which includes business rules as well as business intelligence, analytics, etc. As mentioned in Sect. 9.2.2.4, building risk-scoring models is part art part science, and the book *Credit Risk Scorecards: Developing and Implementing Intelligent Credit Scoring* by Naeem Siddiqui (Wiley, 2006, ISBN 9780471754510) presents the state of the art from a vendor (SAS Institute) that specializes in analytics, in understandable business terms.

Chapter 10
Rule Authoring Infrastructure in JRules

Target audience

- *Developer, rule author, business analyst (may skip 3.3)*

In this chapter you will learn

- *The structure of rule projects in JRules*
- *The different components of a rule project*
- *Rule project relationships and their importance in modularizing rule development*
- *The Business Object Model (BOM), which is used for rule authoring, and how to build it from the application (or executable) object model*
- *Best practices for organizes organizing rules, and the artifacts they depend on, in rule projects*
- *Best practices for the design of a stable and flexible BOM*

Key points

- *Getting the rule project structure right is an important first step in rule authoring.*
- *Rule project dependencies can be used to modularize rule development and to maximize the reuse of rule artifacts.*
- *The BOM to XOM mapping is a powerful mechanism for obtaining a vocabulary that embodies business needs from an application model geared towards IT needs.*
- *The BOM update and refactoring capabilities of Rule Studio enable us to selectively propagate some changes from the XOM to the BOM, and to shield the BOM – and rules – from the others.*

10.1 Introduction

In Chap. 9, we explored the design space for rule authoring, in a technology-independent way, and proposed patterns and best practices for authoring. In this chapter and next, we present the JRules rule authoring artifacts, languages, and

J. Boyer and H. Mili, *Agile Business Rule Development*,
DOI 10.1007/978-3-642-19041-4_10, © Springer-Verlag Berlin Heidelberg 2011

tools. This chapter focuses on the *rule authoring infrastructure*, i.e., the rule project structure, and the set-up of the rule authoring vocabulary; the next chapter focuses on the rule *authoring* per se. This chapter is by no means a user-manual into the JRules rule authoring infrastructure tools. Instead, we focus on some of the design dimensions that were discussed in Chap. 9 that relate to the business object model and to rule organization, but within the context of the JRules product. We start by presenting the concept of a *rule project* in JRules (Sect. 10.2), and the Eclipse-based project dependency relationships, which provide a powerful modularization mechanism. The *Business Object Model* is presented in Sect. 10.3. In particular, we stress the layered structure of the BOM that enables us to (a) separate the business view of the data from the implementation view – the BOM to XOM mapping, (b) separate the terminology from the semantics – the notion of *vocabulary*, and (c) shield rules from (most) refactoring in the implementation model, while propagating changes in the terminology. Best practices for project organization and BOM design are presented in Sect. 10.4. We conclude in Sect. 10.5. Material for further reading is presented in section on "Further Reading."

10.2   Rule Projects

Referring back to Sect. 9.4.1, a *rule project* contains a set of rule artifacts (if-then rules, decision tables, decision trees, etc.) grouped in rule packages, and the elements needed to define them, chief among them, the business object model (BOM). In JRules, projects are first created in Rule Studio (RS), which is an Eclipse-based rule authoring environment with the power – and extensibility – of the Eclipse platform (see Chap. 8). Typically, this is a job for developers who know JRules, as opposed to your typical business analysts or *policy managers*. Indeed, as we will show later, the definition and the customization of the business object model (BOM) requires a good knowledge of the Java language and a good knowledge of the ILOG rules technical language – or IRL – and we will explain why. In addition to setting the BOM, a *rule architect* would typically design the higher levels of the package hierarchy, create some rule templates to be used by rule authors for rule authoring, write some impact analysis or deployment queries, and design the execution behavior of the ruleset (ruleset parameters, ruleflow, etc.). We call this the *rule entry infrastructure*. Once the rule entry infrastructure is set, the developer hands the project over to a rule author for authoring the rules. Depending on a number of factors – discussed in Sect. 10.2.4 – rule authors may work with the Rule Studio environment, or within *Rule Team Server* (RTS), the web-based rule authoring environment. To make the project available to Rule Team Server (or RTS), the developer instantiates a remote connection to RTS from Rule Studio, and uploads the project to RTS. Later on, changes can be made to the project in either environment, and so the two versions will need to be synchronized. Figure 10.1 illustrates this.

We first start by discussing the structure of rule projects by going over the different artifacts that they can contain and their relationships. In particular, we

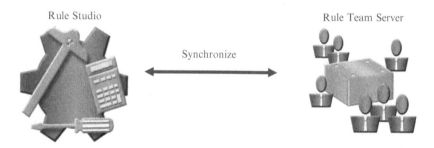

Fig. 10.1 Rule projects are first born in Rule Studio before they can be shipped to Rule Team Server

would go over the *business object model* (BOM) without delving into the details since the BOM will be discussed more thoroughly in Sect. 10.3 of this chapter. Next (Sect. 10.2.2), we talk about dependencies between rules projects. Section 10.2.3 presents best practices about organizing rules in projects. Synchronization between Rule Studio and Rule Team Server will be discussed in Sect. 10.2.4.

10.2.1 The Structure of Rule Projects in Rule Studio

Roughly speaking, a rule project contains rules grouped in packages plus a bunch of other things needed to define them. Rule projects are a special case of Eclipse projects and consist of the following components:

- *Rule artifacts*, grouped in packages
- The *Business Object Model*
- Rule queries
- Rule templates

10.2.1.1 Rule Artifacts

JRules supports all the rule artifacts discussed in Sect. 9.2.2, and more:

- *Business Action Language (BAL) rules*, which are rules written in a natural language-like format; the Business Action Language (BAL) will be discussed in Sect. 11.2.3
- *Technical rules*, which are rules written in the native execution format;[1] the technical rule language – IRL, for ILOG rule language – will be discussed in Sect. 11.2.2
- *Decision tables*, discussed in Sect. 11.2.4

---

[1]Almost. More on this later.

- *Decision trees*, discussed in Sect. 11.2.5
- *Scorecards*, discussed in Sect. 11.2.6
- *IRL Functions*, which can be thought of as IRL macros used internally by the rule engine; the IRL language is described in Sect. 11.2.1
- *Ruleflows*, which are procedural constructs used to orchestrate the evaluation and execution of rules
- *Ruleset variables*, which represent variables that can be referenced from within rules and ruleflows
- *Ruleset parameters*, which are used to pass data to the rule engine (and back) from outside applications

Ruleflows, ruleset variables, and ruleset parameters will be discussed in Sect. 11.3.

10.2.1.2 Business Object Model

With the exception of ruleset parameters, which are defined as *rule project proper-ties*, all of the rule artifacts are organized in a hierarchy of packages under the "rules" folder. The *Business Object Model* (BOM) represents the business view of the data, and it consists of a set of *Business Object Model entries* (BOM entries). Figure 10.2 shows a single BOM entry, called "claim processing BOM." Each BOM entry is associated with an *eXecution Object Model* (XOM), which is the native format for the actual objects manipulated by the rule engine. In Sect. 9.2.1, we described the relationship between the business view of the data and the physical view as analogical to that between a relational view, and the physical model view. With JRules, this analogy is a fairly accurate one; we will talk about

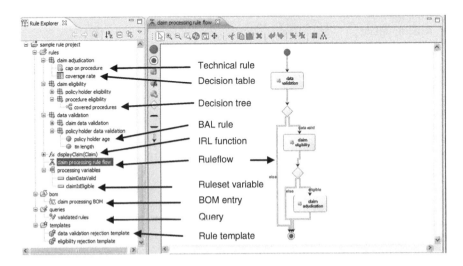

Fig. 10.2 A screenshot of a sample Rule Studio project

the BOM in Sect. 10.3 of this chapter. For the purposes of this section, suffice it to say that *typically* each BOM entry maps to – and references – an *eXecution Object Model* (XOM). Execution object models *typically* consist of the set of Java classes contained in JAR file, or the set of Java classes contained in an Eclipse Java project within the same workspace as the rule project. In the latter case, the rule project has a *project dependency* or *reference* to a Java project.

In JRules, the BOM is the *vocabulary* or *domain of discourse* for the rule artifacts mentioned above: BAL rules, technical rules, decision tables, decisions trees, ruleset variables, IRL functions, etc. Different artifacts use different *views* of the BOM. For example, technical rules and IRL functions use the "raw format" of the BOM, whereas BAL rules and decision tables, for example, use the natural language-like veneer on top the raw format; this will be discussed in Sect. 10.3.

10.2.1.3   Rule Queries

Rule projects also contain *rule queries*. One can write queries on the rules of a project[2] based on:

- *Their metadata.* Rule properties include things such as the rule name, its author, its effective date (date at which the rule comes into effect), its expiration date (date at which a rule expires), its development status (e.g., one of "new," "defined," "validated," "rejected," "deployable," and "retired"), its jurisdiction (e.g., a particular state or county), etc.[3]
- *The (business) object model elements they reference/modify.* For example, all the rules that reference the "age" attribute of the policy holder or that modify the "payment" field of the claim.
- *Their semantics.* For example, rules that might be triggered by a particular boolean condition, or that trigger another rule.

Queries have many uses in JRules, including:

- *Reporting.* Producing various reports on the contents of a project (e.g., rules authored by X).
- *Impact analysis.* For example to assess the impact of modifying or replacing a particular BOM element (a class, an attribute, an operation) by finding those rules that reference it.
- *Logical analysis.* To compute logical relationships between rules, for analysis and validation (semantic queries).

---

[2]If a rule project *depends on* another rule project, the domain of the query will be extended to include the rules included in that project. And so on (recursively). More on project dependencies in Sect. 10.2.2.

[3]JRules comes with a predefined set of rule properties, but developers can *extend* the *rule model* and add organization or application-specific metadata.

- *Ruleset deployment.* As mentioned in Chap. 8, JRules makes a clear distinction between the development-time organization of rules – rule projects – and the run-time organization of rules – rulesets. JRules provides a default mapping between the two that packages the contents of a project into a ruleset. With queries, we can filter which rules actually get deployed into the ruleset: example criteria include development status (e.g., only validated rules are deployed), jurisdiction, effective/expiration date, etc. We talk about *rule set extractors* in Chap. 12.

Rule queries are written in the *Business Query Language* (BQL), which is very similar to the *Business Action Language* (BAL).[4]

10.2.1.4   Rule Templates

Rule *templates* are fill-in-the-blank rules that rule authors can use to author rules, instead of starting with an empty rule. Figure 10.3 shows the example of a template for rules that reject claims because of invalid data. In this example, rule authors need only write the condition part, which corresponds to a data validation constraint violation; the action part is pretty much completed where only the message argument (the string "Data is invalid: ...") needs to be edited.

Rule templates are not only convenient, but they can be used as safeguards to make sure that business rule authors do not mess up the business logic. For example, our processing logic may rely on the fact that data validation rules set the value of a particular data member of class **Claim** to signal a data validation constraint violation. We have to make sure that all the rules that detect validation errors properly set that data member. Using a rule template that builds in that action

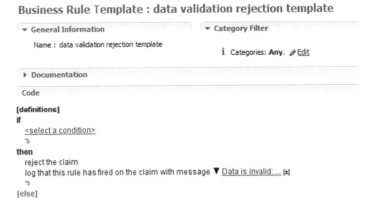

Fig. 10.3   A rule template

---

[4]On some level, a rule is like a query: the condition part 'queries' the working memory for tuples of objects satisfying some conditions, and the action part applies some actions to the result.

would do the trick. In the template of Fig. 10.3, we put into the rule action part two actions that set the appropriate data member to the appropriate data value – what the action "reject the claim" actually does behind the scenes[5] – and logs the rule firing. In this case, it so happens that those two actions are *frozen*, i.e., they cannot be removed from rules generated from the template; the rule template editor enables us to freeze or unfreeze selected parts of the rule template, down to the function argument level. In the remainder of Sect. 10.2, and the subsequent sections, we will revisit various rule project constituents that we discussed here.

While rule projects can only be *created* in Rule Studio, they can be modified in either Rule Studio, or in Rule Team Server, the web-based rule authoring environment (see Chap. 8). To edit a rule project in Rule Team Server (RTS), we need to first publish it from Rule Studio to Rule Team Server (see Sect. 10.2.4). After logging in to Rule Team Server, we can edit project elements there. We will revisit this in Sect. 10.2.3, but for the time being, we can think of the two projects (the RS version and the RTS version) as equivalent.[6]

10.2.2 Rule Project Dependencies

We mentioned in the previous section that rule projects *typically* contain the definition of a *business object model* (BOM), and that the BOM is *typically* derived from Java class definitions contained in JAR file, or in a Java project within the same workspace. JRules enables us also to define dependencies *between* rule projects. If a rule project RP_A *references* a rule project RP_B, then:

- The BOM defined in RP_B is *visible* within RP_A, meaning that we can write rules that refer to the BOM of RP_B.
- The ruleset parameters defined in RP_B are accessible within RP_A, meaning that we can refer to them in the rule artifacts of RP_A.
- The ruleset variables defined in RP_B are accessible with RP_A by using an import statement.
- The rule artifacts defined in RP_B are accessible within RP_A. In particular (a) templates defined within RP_B can be used within RP_A, (b) rule queries defined in RP_B can be used to define ruleset extractors in RP_A, (c) rule packages defined within RP_B can be assigned to rule tasks within RP_A, (d) rule flows defined within RP_B can be assigned as *flow tasks* rule tasks within RP_A, and (e) rules in RP_B can override rules that are in project RP_A.
- Queries defined in RP_B can be run on the artifacts of RP_B alone, or be extended to artifacts in RP_A.

Within Rule Studio, project dependencies are limited to the rule projects within the same workspace. They are editable through the project's *properties* under

---

[5]More about this in Sect. 10.3.

[6]Not true, but an acceptable first approximation.

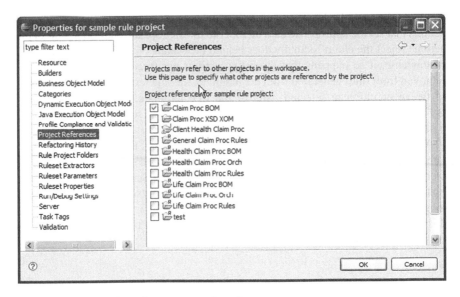

Fig. 10.4 Adding project references to a rule project

"Project references," like any Eclipse project. Figure 10.4 shows a screenshot of the corresponding property editor. In this case, we have 11 projects in this workspace, and the project "sample rule project" (our RP_B above) references project "Claim Proc BOM" (our RP_A above). Within Rule Team Server, project dependencies are limited to projects within the same repository, and only users with role "Configurator" and above can edit a project's dependencies.[7]

One of the subtle implications of rule project dependencies is the notion of *BOM path*, similar to the concept of *class path* with Java code. Indeed, because the BOM of a project RP_A is made visible to project RP_B if RP_B references RP_A, potential conflicts could arise if the same entity – a BOM class – is defined in both the BOM of RP_A and the BOM of RP_B. Hence, the notion of a *BOM path*. For each project, JRules defines a default BOM precedence, which an author can edit. The default precedence rules of BOM entries are:

- Within a single project with no external references, BOMs appear by order of definition, with the most recent BOM entry showing last.
- Within a given project, *dynamic BOM entries*, i.e., BOM entries generated from XSDs, appear *before* BOM entries that are built from Java XOMs.
- If project RP_B references project RP_A, then the BOM entries of RP_A appear *before* the locally defined BOM entries.

---

[7]This means that a regular rule author cannot edit projects' dependencies, and that is a good thing, because of the subtle implications on rule writing (BOM visibility, variable visibility, etc.).

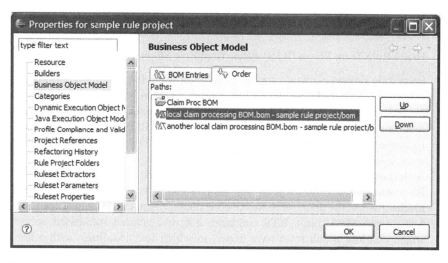

Fig. 10.5 BOM path

These rules apply recursively, to a dependency chain of any length. Users can override these defaults by moving BOM entries up and down the BOM path (see Fig. 10.5).

With the BOM path of Fig. 10.5, if some class com.mywebinsurance.model. Claim is present in both the BOM of the rule project "Claim Proc BOM," and in the locally defined "local claim processing BOM," it is the definition found in the project "Claim Proc BOM" that will be taken.[8]

Rule project dependencies enable us to modularize our rule development, and to get an effective division of labor. Section 10.4.1 will present best practices about organizing rules in different related projects.

10.2.3 Synchronizing Projects Between Rule Studio and Rule Team Server

As mentioned above, projects are first born in Rule Studio. However, Rule Studio is not an appropriate tool for your typical business rule author (*policy manager*), for three reasons:

- Its GUI metaphors are more geared towards developers, and relate little to business metaphors.
- Its computational requirements often exceed the capabilities of the desktop (or laptop) of the typical business user.

---

[8]This is counter-intuitive to inheritance, where locally defined structures and behavior prime over inherited ones.

- It is a dangerous tool to put in the hands of business users, who may inadvertently break the structure of a rule project and the underlying business logic.

Hence Rule Team Server (RTS) differs from Rule Studio (RS) in two major ways:

- Some rule project elements are *not* editable in RTS, for two main reasons: (a) safety, to maintain the integrity of the project, and (b) because the information needed to edit the element is not available RTS. Examples of (a) include *ruleflows*, *ruleset parameters*, the *business object model* (BOM), and the BOM path. Examples of (b) include the BOM, again, as well as customizable features that require Java code.
- A (far) more granular access control to the elements of a rule project. Whereas RS controls access to projects and project elements through access control mechanisms of the underlying source code management (SCM) tool (ClearCase, Subversion, MKS, etc.), RTS combines a coarse-grained role-based access, which controls which roles have access to which functionalities, with a fine-grained permission management, to manage read/write access to the rule artifacts of a project.

There are a number of other minor functional differences, some of which were explained in Chap. 8.

Implementation-wise, RS and RTS use different representations of projects and project elements:

- RS uses a file-based representation of project elements. Typically, we have one file per artifact, be it a BAL rule, a technical rule, a decision table, a decision tree, a scorecard, a rule flow, a variable set, a function, etc. Aggregate artifacts are represented a directory that includes a file that represents the aggregate metadata, and the actual contents of the aggregate, as files or subdirectories included therein. Figure 10.6 shows part of the file hierarchy for our sample project. Hence access to these artifacts is managed through the underlying source code control system.
- RTS uses database persistence. Roughly speaking, RTS uses different tables to represent different types of artifacts[9] and the relationships between them. Concurrent access to these artifacts is thus managed through the database locking mechanism.

JRules provides functionality for exporting a project from RS to RTS. This functionality makes a remote connection from RS to a running instance of RTS and either creates a fresh new project in RTS to receive the exported RS, or synchronizes the current state of the RS project with the most current state of the corresponding RTS project.

Figure 10.7 shows a screenshot of the project synchronization wizard. In this particular case, we are synchronizing our "sample rule project" between RS and the

---

[9]We don't have a table for *each* rule project element types as similar element types are represented by the same table, but have one attribute distinguish between them.

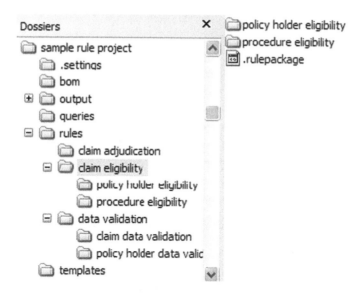

Fig. 10.6 RS represents rule projects using the file system. The right-hand side shows the contents of "claim eligibility" directory, which represents the "claim eligibility" rule package

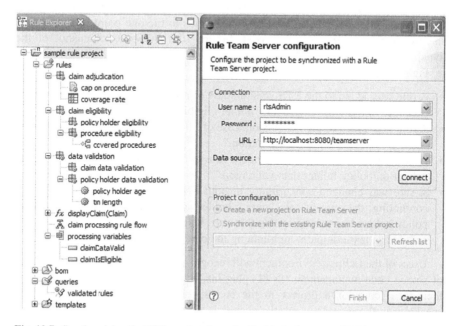

Fig. 10.7 Synchronizing the RS "sample rule project" with the instance of RTS running at http://localhost:8080/teamserver

Rule added to RTS version

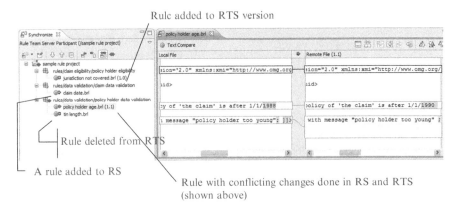

Rule deleted from RTS

A rule added to RS

Rule with conflicting changes done in RS and RTS
(shown above)

Fig. 10.8 A case where synchronization yields several changes in both RS and RTS versions

instance of RTS. To *create* a new project on RTS, we need to connect to RTS as an administrator. But to simply synchronize an RS project with an *existing* RTS project, regular user (policy manager) privileges suffice.

Having exported an RS project to RTS, the two projects will typically continue to evolve independently, and will go out of sync. When we synchronize the two versions, the synchronization functionality will perform a three-way comparison between (a) the current version of the RS project, (b) the current version of the RTS project, and (c) the initial version of the project in RTS. Indeed, the initial version of the project in RTS corresponds to the one point in time where the two versions were synchronized. Figure 10.8 shows a screenshot of the synchronization view.

Figure 10.8 illustrates cases where:

- A rule was added to the RTS version: case of rule "jurisdiction not covered," in package "claim eligibility/policy holder eligibility."
- A rule was added to the RS version: case of rule "claim date," added to package "data validation/claim data validation."
- A rule was deleted from RTS version: case of rule "tin length" in package "data validation/policy holder data validation."
- A rule was changed concurrently in both RS and RTS, and the changes are conflicting: the case of rule "policy holder age" in package "data validation/ policy holder data validation." In this case, RS puts side to side the two versions, and does a text compare, highlighting the parts that were changed.

Users of the Eclipse environment will recognize the familiar look and semantics of source code management (SCM) plug-ins, when a developer tries to check in their local copy of a project in the corresponding SCM repository. Roughly speaking, in those cases where the change is one-sided, the user has the option of either accepting the change, or rejecting it. In the case of conflict, the user can selectively combine changes coming from either side, if she/he wishes to. The example of Fig. 10.8 shows three conflicting changes within the rule "policy holder age."[10]

While JRules offers functionality to synchronize projects between RS and RTS, an organization needs to put in place a set of processes, both manual, and automated, to prevent development chaos; having to resolve conflicting changes between two versions of rules should not be a way of rule project life. The first question that we ask is: notwithstanding the initial creation of a rule project, do we really need to have projects edited in both environments. The answer lies in which environment is being used for creating and maintaining rules, which depends on who is responsible for maintaining the rules. We have encountered three typical scenarios.

Business users are responsible for creating and maintaining the rules, and they use RTS. This is the textbook scenario of usage of the tool set. In this case, developers create the project(s) in RS, export them to RTS, and let the business users edit the projects there. At first glance, there should be no reason in this scenario for the version that resides in RS to change. Thus, when developers synchronize the RS projects with the RTS versions,[11] they should not encounter any conflicts. However, even in this case, there are going to be cases where the RS projects need to be updated. First, recall that the BOM and the ruleflow are not editable in RTS. Thus, if either needs to be changed, we can only implement the change in RS. Second, there are cases where rule testing identifies a problem with a ruleset that cannot be identified through tracing. In such cases, we need debugging of the kind that is available only in RS, and a developer may have to correct the problem (i.e., edit the rule).

So what we do in those cases where we do have to change a project in RS? The safest – and coarsest – solution consists of freezing the project in RTS by making it not editable there,[12] then synchronizing RS with RTS to bring the most recent version from RTS to RS, then making the desired changes in RS, then synchronizing the projects again to export the change to RTS, then releasing the project in RTS. This solution will work in all cases. However, it makes an RTS project unavailable for editing for the time it takes the make the needed changes within RS. This may be justifiable if we are making a change to the BOM, for two reasons: (a) to take advantage of RS's refactoring functionality and (b) to prevent the business users from using the old BOM. Idem for the ruleflow, as it provides the execution context for the rules, and rule authors need it to be current.

---

[10]Actually, in this case only the one about the threshold birthdate for the policy holder is substantive. The others are due to small – non essential – differences in serialization format between the two environments.

[11]One reason we may want to do that is if deployment to the Rule Execution Server (RES) of the development, testing, QA, or production environment is performed from RS as opposed to from RTS, which is the recommended practice.

[12]We can do that by removing a user group from the groups of users who have the right to access the project. By doing so, the project no longer shows up in their project selection in RTS.

If the change that we need to make in RS concerns a single or a handful of rules, then we can make our "freezing" in RTS more selective, as opposed to freezing an entire project. An administrator can log into RTS and lock those rules that are being debugged for the duration of the debugging, to release them later, possibly with changes.

Whatever the case, to prevent conflicts between changes made in RS and RTS, we serialize those changes in time so that, at any given point in time, a project is being edited only in one environment. This is a combination of (a) JRules basic functionality (synchronization, RTS permission management, RTS locking), and (b) a human process that uses this functionality. Adherence to the human process is, naturally, crucial and is part of rule governance, to be discussed in Chaps. 15 and 16.

IT developers are responsible for creating and maintaining the rules, and they use RS. While one of the goals of the business rules approach is to have business take over the creation and maintenance of rules, the *complete take over* from rule discovery all the way to rule coding does not *always* happen, on the initial development of the business application, or in subsequent rule maintenance mode. Many customers that we encountered prefer to leave rule authoring and unit testing to IT.[13] In this case, developers use RS to author and maintain rules. However, rules are available for business to *view* within RTS, in a read-only mode. This scenario is easy to handle: developers simply synchronize the RS project with RTS whenever they have a new stable version (or "release") of the RS project to share with business.

Business is responsible for creating and maintaining the rules, and they use RS. We also encountered this scenario in many situations where business units have in their midst what we call "technical business analysts" who are, typically, ex-developers who are quite comfortable with Rule Studio's interaction metaphors. This scenario is no different from the previous one and presents no challenges.

10.2.4 Managing Multiple Users

Whether we are using RS or RTS to author and maintain rules, we need to manage multiple users creating and modifying rules within the same environment. As mentioned in the previous section, RS uses a file representation of rule project elements, and manages the different versions of rule project elements through the connectivity of RS to a source code management system. By contrast, RTS uses a database to store rule project elements, and manages concurrent access through the database. In the remainder of this section, we will first summarize the concept of operations of source code management software, and see how those apply to rule projects. We will then discuss the many access control features of RTS.

---

[13]We have also encountered situations where IT developers are transferred, administratively, from the IT department over to business units where they report to a manager within the business unit.

In Rule Studio, coordination between multiple users is managed by the underlying source code management software. There a number of source code management applications, both commercial, such as SourceSafe, ClearCase, MKS, or Perforce, as well as open source ones, such as CVS, Subversion, and others. There are two general approaches to handling multiple users, *pessimistic locking*, of the kind done by databases, where only a single user has write access to a particular resources, and *optimistic locking*, which is a euphemism for no-locking at all. This strategy is *optimistic* because it makes the optimistic hypothesis that users will work on different parts, and thus, there will be no need to lock entire projects, say, if one just wants to change a rule. If the "optimistic hypothesis" turns out to be wrong, then we deal with it with conflict resolution, as illustrated for the case of synchronization between RS and RTS.

The tools mentioned above differ in functionality, but most use optimistic locking. This model is illustrated in Fig. 10.9. Different users work on their own local copies of rule projects, which they synchronize regularly with the state of a common repository. To have access to a given rule project, a user needs to be *registered* within the SCM and be granted access to the repository containing that project. The first time they access the project, they typically *check-out* a particular version of the project from the repository, to get a local copy on their machines or private workspace. They can then work off-line from the SCM repository making as many changes as they wish. If they want to make their work available to others – or simply to back it up – they *check-in* their work. This creates a new version of the project in the repository. If other users have checked out the same version as the current user and have already checked-in their changes, then the tool performs the kind of comparisons we showed in the previous section. If a user judges that there are irreconcilable differences between the version of the project that they want

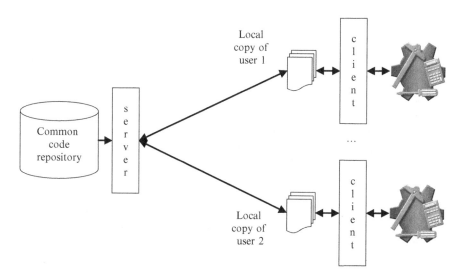

Fig. 10.9 The concept of operations of source code management software plug-ins to RS

to check in, and the latest version in the repository, they can then start a new development *branch*.

Note that the model illustrated in Fig. 10.9 applies to the case where the client component of the SCM is well-integrated with the Rule Studio, i.e., as an Eclipse plug-in. If that is not the case, then the client module and the local copy in Fig. 10.9 trade places: we can use a separate command-line SCM client interface to check-in and check-out projects, and use RS on the local copy, totally unaware of the SCM. This model is workable but is less user-friendly and more brittle.[14] However, if there are no Eclipse plug-ins – or if the existing ones are buggy – we have no alternative.

A common complaint about traditional SCMs is the lack of granularity of their access control mechanism. Some tools grant read or write access in an all-or-nothing fashion: to the entire repository, or none. Others, such as subversion, will support access control to the path level: enabling a particular group of users to access only some subdirectories of the repository in a read or write fashion. Either way, the permissions being file-based, this means two restrictions:

- We cannot grant a user or user group access to certain kinds of artifacts and not others. For example, if a user has read/write access to a rule package, they can modify everything in that package, including rules, ruleflows, functions, variable sets, and so forth.
- For a given artifact, the access is all or nothing: either the user can modify both the contents and the metadata, or they cannot modify either.

If we have business users working with RS, this can be a problem.

RTS's access control mechanism is much more fine-grained than can be afforded with RS and SCM software. First of all, RTS supports role-based access, where users belong to roles, and the roles that a user has determine what *functionality* the user has access to. The tool comes with four default roles, which can be customized to the needs of the organization:

- **rtsUser**. This role corresponds to the typical rule authors. They can browse projects, create rule folders (packages) and various rule artifacts, query projects, analyze them, produce rule reports, export/import rules and decision tables to Microsoft Office documents,[15] and (re)deploy *existing* rule apps with the most current version of the project.
- **rtsConfigurator**. In addition to **rtsUser** functionalities, this role also has access to project and environment configuration functionalities, including: (a) managing project baselines, (b) editing project dependencies, (c) generating

---

[14]SCM files deal in files: they do not know about rule projects, rule packages, and the like, and thus, performing a (text) file-based reconciliation of two rule project versions is typically tedious and error prone.

[15]JRules includes Office plug-ins that enables to edit rules in Word documents, and decision tables in Excel spreadsheets. See Chap. 8.

ruleset archives, (d) editing ruleset extractors, (e) editing RES server configurations, and (f) editing/managing ruleapps.

- **rtsAdministrator**. In addition to **rtsConfigurator** functionalities, it includes functionalities for (a) enabling and configuration of project-level security, (b) running diagnostics on the current RTS, and (c) configuring the current installation of RTS (schema, persistence locale, message file, etc.).
- **rtsInstaller**. It has access to the installation functionalities for RTS.

Any RTS user has to be a member of one of these four groups, plus, as the case may be, other site or domain-specific groups. For example, MyWebInsurance may decide to create three groups, **policyUnderwriting**, **claimProcessing**, and **tester**, where rule authors working on policy underwriting will be members of both **rtsUser** and **policyUnderwriting**, rule authors working on claim processing will be members of both **rtsUser** and **claimProcessing**, and testers will be members of both **rtsUser** and **tester**. An RTS user who creates a rule artifact can assign the artifact to one of the groups of which she or he is a member. We discuss below the use of groups.

By default, RTS does not enforce project level security: all users of all groups can access all the projects of the repository. However, an administrator (**rtsAdministrator** group) can enforce security for a specific project, and specify which groups have access to the project. Figure 10.10 shows a screenshot of the set-up form.

Having defined the groups that can access the project, we can specify what kind of access. This is done through *permissions*. A *permission* is specified through four parameters:

- *The specific action.* Create, view (read), update, delete.
- *The value.* Can be yes or no for create, and yes, group, or no for the view, update and delete.

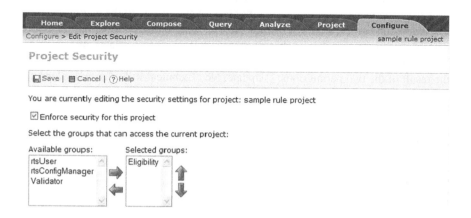

Fig. 10.10 Enforcing security for a particular project

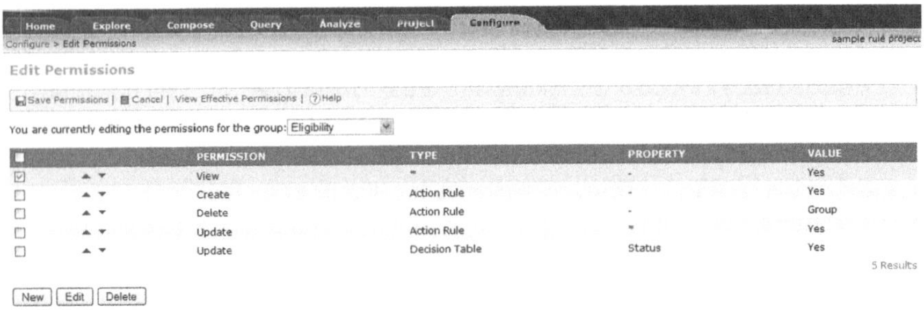

Fig. 10.11 Examples of five permissions

- *The type*. Refers to the type of project artifact for which we want to specify the permission. Types include: Action Rule, Technical Rule, Decision Table, Decision Tree, Template, etc., or the wild card ("*"), which means all types.
- *Property*. Refers to a property of the selected type, and the wildcard ("*") to mean all properties of the selected type.[16]

The last two parameters describe the *scope* of the permission. For example, to allow the viewing of all the artifacts of a project, we define the permission: <View, Yes, *, - >. To allow the update of the "status" attribute of a decision table, we define the permission <Update, Yes, Decision Table, Status>. To allow the deletion of action rules created by members of the same group, we write <delete, Group, Action Rule, – >. Figure 10.11 shows five permissions defined for the "Eligibility" group on our "sample rule project." Effectively, members of this group can view all the artifacts of the project (first permission), create action rules, delete action rules created by other members of the group, update all the aspects of an action rule (content and metadata), and update the "status" attribute of decision tables – but nothing else.

How about creating a decision table, or changing the "effective date" of a decision tree? Once we enforce security for a given project, all the actions become forbidden, unless explicitly allowed. Hence, with these permissions, it is not possible to create a decision table or to update the "effective date" of a decision tree. Further, more specific permissions override less specific ones. For example, the result of the two permissions: <Update, No, Technical Rule, *> and <Update, Yes, Technical Rule, Status> means that I cannot update any aspect of a Technical Rule, except for its status property.[17] The tool enables us to view the *effective permissions* based on the ones that were explicitly defined, where it shows all of the defaults and takes into account the overrides.

---

[16]When the selection of a property does not make sense or when "all" is implied by default, the property parameter takes the value "-."

[17]In this case, the permission <Update, No, Technical Rule, *> may not even be needed, as what is not explicitly allowed is not permitted by default . . . unless we have a more generic permission such as <Update, Yes, *, - > that we want to override for Technical Rules. And so forth.

In terms of managing *concurrent access* to project artifacts, RTS automatically *write-locks* a project element whenever a user starts editing that element. The write-lock is released when the element is saved. An RTS user can also explicitly write-lock an element, and hold the lock even after the current session terminates. The write-lock can be released by the same user or by an administrator.

10.3   The Business Object Model

The Business Object Model embodies the business view of the application data. It represents the domain of discourse for rule authoring. A lot of the *artistry* in setting up rule authoring deals with the confection of the BOM. We start with the basics of the BOM in Sect. 10.3.1. Section 10.3.2 deals with the BOM to XOM mapping in more depth. In particular, we show how to recreate a *differentiated* business object model from a generic and stripped down *execution object model* (see discussion in Sect. 9.2.1). Because execution object models will likely evolve during the development phase and lifetime of an application.

10.3.1   The Basics of the BOM

The Business Object Model embodies the domain of discourse for business rules. It represents the link or *bridge* between the implementation of the application data – what we call *eXecutable Object Model*, or XOM – and the business rules. Roughly speaking, the BOM consists of a three layers:

- The *vocabulary*, which is the collection of natural language-like expressions that we use to write rules, such as "the date of <the claim>" or "the age of <the policy holder>"
- The *business object model* itself, which is an object model defined in terms of packages, classes, attributes, methods, and associations
- The *BOM to XOM mapping*, which describes how the BOM maps to the actual XOM

Figure 10.12 illustrates the three layers and the relationships between them, and to the rules, on one end, and to the XOM, on the other. *Typically*, the starting point for building a BOM is a XOM, and the *typical* XOM is a set of Java classes packaged as a Java project, a class directory, or a JAR file. JRules has a utility that builds a *default* BOM based on the XOM, i.e., default values for the three layers mentioned above. We will explain what those defaults are when we explain the relationships between the various layers.

Let us start from the middle: the business object model looks like a regular object model, with nested packages (com.mywebinsurance.claimprocessing), a bunch of classes which, in turn, have attributes and methods. The **PolicyHolder** BOM class

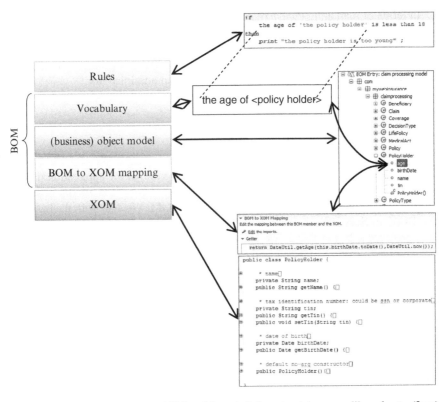

Fig. 10.12 The structure of the BOM and how it links natural language-like rules to (Java) application objects

appears to have *four* public data members, "age," "birthDate," "name," and "tin," for "tax identification number" which, for the case of individuals, consists of their social security number; we will worry about the constructor later.

In Java, to write a condition about the age of a **PolicyHolder**, one would write something like:

```
if (myPolicyHolder.age < 18) {…}
```

In the example of Fig. 10.12, we are using the JRules *Business Action Language* (BAL, see Sect. 10.4.2) which uses natural language-like "paraphrases" of the various elements of the BOM. With the BAL, the default reference to an attribute ATT of some class CLS is through a phrase "the {ATT} of {this}" where {ATT} refers to the name of the attribute, and {this} will be replaced by an object variable name of the type CLS. The collection of such phrases is called the *vocabulary* of the BOM. The vocabulary file is like a property file where the key refers to the BOM model element, and the value refers to the phrase template. The following are excerpts from the vocabulary file for our claim processing BOM:

```
...
com.mywebinsurance.claimprocessing.PolicyHolder.age#phrase.navigatio
n = {age} of {this}
...
com.mywebinsurance.claimprocessing.PolicyHolder.tin#phrase.action =
set the tin of {this} to {tin}
com.mywebinsurance.claimprocessing.PolicyHolder.tin#phrase.navigatio
n = {tin} of {this}
...
```

Note that we have a single entry for the "age" attribute, corresponding to *navigation*, i.e., to read/get the value of the attribute. Because the "tin" attribute is read/write, we have both a "navigation" phrase (getter) and an "action" phrase (setter). Generally speaking, the vocabulary file will have one or two entries for every attribute or every BOM class, which correspond to reading or writing the value of the attribute. It will also have one entry for the class itself to define the term. The good news is that JRules generates the vocabulary automatically, and does a pretty good job at it, provided that the BOM – and the XOM – use recommended naming conventions; more on this in Sect. 10.3.2.

Let us now turn to the bottom half of Fig. 10.12, i.e., the relationship between the BOM and the underlying XOM. If we look more closely at the **PolicyHolder** BOM class, and compare it to the Java class, we notice three main differences:

- In the BOM **PolicyHolder** class, the attributes "name" "birthDate" and "tin" are public whereas in the Java **PolicyHolder** class, they are private.
- The Java **PolicyHolder** class has getter/setter functions for those private attributes whereas the BOM **PolicyHolder** class has no such functions.
- The BOM **PolicyHolder** class has an "age" attribute which does not appear in the Java **PolicyHolder** class.

The first two differences are related: in the process of building a BOM class for a Java class, JRules ignores the data and function members that are *not* public. However, it assumes that the Java class uses the Java Beans naming convention, and thus, if the Java class has functions that follow either of (or both) the two patterns:

```
TypeT getSomeName();
void setSomeName(TypeT value);
```

the corresponding BOM class will have a read (or write, or read/write) attribute called someName.

The "age" attribute illustrates the power and flexibility of the BOM to XOM mapping: we can define an attribute in the BOM class that is not physically stored in the Java class, but that is *computed on the fly* based on some actual physical attribute. Hence, if business rule authors like to think in terms of age, we can provide them with an "age" attribute in the BOM **PolicyHolder** class, as long as we provide a way of computing it from the actual/physical data stored in the Java **PolicyHolder** class. That mapping is illustrated in Fig. 10.12 by the expression:

```
return DateUtil.getAge(this.birthdate.toDate(),DateUtil.now());
```

which is entered as the "BOM to XOM mapping" for the "getter" of the "age" attribute, where DateUtil is a custom Java utility class that manipulates dates. More powerful mappings will be discussed in Sect. 10.3.3.

The structure described so far corresponds to a single *BOM entry*. Each BOM entry consists of three distinct files corresponding to the three layers shown in Fig. 10.12. In the example of Fig. 10.12, we have a BOM entry called "claim processing model" consisting of three files:

- "claim processing model_en.voc". It is the vocabulary file. Notice the "_en" suffix in the file name, which represents the locale. Indeed, we can have different vocabularies associated with a BOM based on the locale.
- "claim processing model.bom". It represents the model itself represented in a java interface-like textual format. The following shows excerpts from that file. In addition to the Java signatures of the various attributes, methods, and constructors, the file may contain other BOM-specific properties such as domains and categories, to be explained in Sect. 10.3.5.

```
package com.mywebinsurance.claimprocessing;
...
public class PolicyHolder {
    public java.util.Date birthDate;
    public string name;
    public string tin;
    public PolicyHolder();
}
...
```

- "claim processing model.b2x". It groups in a single file all the *custom* BOM to XOM mappings for the current model entry. We will come back to this in Sect. 10.3.3.

A typical project BOM would consist of several *BOM entries*.
We can build a BOM entry in Rule Studio (RS) in one of two ways:

- *From scratch*, by manually adding packages, classes, data, and function members using various RS (Eclipse) wizards. In this case, we have to do everything manually (1) specify the names of the various model elements (packages, classes, attributes, methods, and constructors), (2) their Java types, where applicable, (3) generate their verbalizations, and (4) specify the BOM to XOM mappings.
- *From an existing XOM*, which can be either a Java project within the same workspace, or an external Java jar file or class directory, or an *XML schema* – referred

to as a *dynamic XOM*. In either case, Rule Studio analyzes the XOM, and then creates BOM elements from that XOM. Thanks to the BOM entry creation wizard, Rule Studio will perform 90% of the job with a few selections and clicks, using default verbalizers and default BOM to XOM mappings. A user can later edit the BOM to override some defaults or add virtual elements to the BOM, such as the "age" attribute mentioned above (more on that in Sect. 10.3.3).

Which method is preferred? Clearly, if you already have the target XOM, then you should build the BOM (entry) from the existing XOM. However, there are situations where one would want to start authoring rules before the underlying implementation code has been completed, and there one would build the BOM from scratch. These issues will be discussed in Sect. 10.4.2.

10.3.2 Verbalization

Verbalization is the process of assigning a term or phrase to a BOM model element, e.g., as in assigning the phrase "`the {age} of {this}`" to the attribute "`age`" of the BOM class **PolicyHolder**. Rule Studio has a default "verbalizer" that can verbalize the elements of an entire BOM entry, in one batch, or single BOM elements (classes, attributes, and methods), one by one. Developers can override the default verbalization for a given model element. Default verbalization follows simple rules that we explain below.

First, we look at the verbalization of identifiers. The rules are illustrated in Table 10.1.

In particular, if we adopt the Java nomenclature for spelling multi-word identifiers – capitalizing the first letter of every word, with the possible exception of the first – the verbalizer will actually separate out the individual words.

Consider now the verbalization of attributes. First, the name of the attribute is verbalized to generate what JRules calls a *subject*, which is then used to generate a *navigation phrase* (a getter expression) and an *action phrase* (a setter action). Table 10.2 illustrates the default verbalizations for non-boolean attributes.

Notice that the name of the attribute in the navigation and action phrases appears in a template form (i.e., between curly brackets) between it is editable. For example, a BOM developer may choose to use the term "date of birth" instead of "birth date," and adjust the plural to "dates of birth" (as opposed to the default "date of births"). The figure across shows the wizard for editing terms. This wizard knows a bit

Table 10.1 Verbalization of identifiers	Identifier	Its default verbalization
	lowercasename	lowercasename
	UPPERCASENAME	UPPERCASENAME
	UpperFirstLetter	upper first letter
	upperFirstLetter	upper first letter
	lowerSECOND	lower SECOND

Table 10.2 Verbalization of non-boolean attributes

Attribute	Verbalization (subject)	Navigation/action phrases	Examples
Name	name	{name} of {this}	the name of **"my policy holder"**
		set the name of {this} to {name}	set the name of **"my policy holder"** to **"John"**;
birthDate	birth date	{birth date} of {this}	the birth date of **"my policy holder"** ...
		set the birth date of {this} to {birth date}	set the birth date of **"my policy holder"** to **13/4/1991**;

about the English language so that the indefinite singular form for "age" is "an age" and not "a age," and the plural of "bankruptcy" is "bankruptcies" and not "bankruptcys."

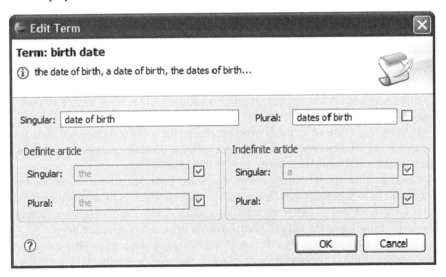

The verbalization of boolean attributes is different and is illustrated in Table 10.3. The last example shows an instance where the default verbalization does not work: both the navigation and action phrases need to be edited to get rid of the extra "is" (underlined in the table).

Finally, JRules enables us also to verbalize methods, as those may be used within conditions – those that return values – or actions of rules – those that return void. The parameters of such functions then become data prompts for the rule author. Assume that our class **PolicyHolder** has a method with signature:

```
void addAccident(Date d, Responsibility resp);
```

Table 10.3 Verbalization of boolean attributes

Attribute	Verbalization (subject)	Navigation/action phrases	Examples
`approved`	`approved`	`{this} is approved`	`"my claim" is approved`
		`make it {approved} that {this} is approved`	`make it true that "my claim" is approved;`
`isRejected`	`rejected`	`{this} is rejected`	`my claim" is rejected`
		`make it {rejected} that {this} is rejected`	`make it true that "my claim" is rejected;`
`hasBeenPaid`	`has been paid`	`{this} is has been paid`	`"my claim" is has been paid`
		`make it {has been paid} that {this} is has been paid`	`make it true that "my claim" is has been paid;`

where **Responsibility** is an enumerated type with the values AT_FAULT and NO_FAULT. The default verbalization for this method is the ugly:

```
{this}.addAccident({0},{1})
```

Notice here `{0}` and `{1}` that stand for the first and second positional parameters of the function (date and responsibility of the accident, respectively), and that become data prompts for the rule authors using this action. In a rule, this action would appear as follows:

```
'my policy holder'.addAccident(21/8/2009,"AT_FAULT");
```

Not exactly business user friendly. We can change the verbalization template to the following:

```
add a {1} accident to {this} on {0}
```

where `{1}` stands for the *second* parameter of the function,[18] i.e., the responsibility, `{this}` stands for the policy holder, and `{0}` stands for the *first* positional parameter, i.e., the date. This action will then appear in a rule as follows:

```
add a "AT_FAULT" accident to 'my policy holder' on 21/8/2009;
```

---

[18]We can all thank Java, C++, C, or the assembly language for this numbering convention, depending on how far back you want to go ☺.

This is part of the artistry that goes into setting up the verbalizations for the BOM elements, and that can make rule authoring – and reading – more intuitive and more business friendly. The person responsible for configuring the BOM (business analyst or rule developer) needs to be familiar with the "vocabulary" and phrasing used by business to mimic it as closely as possible in the BOM.

10.3.3 BOM to XOM Mapping

We introduced the BOM to XOM mapping in Sect. 10.3.1 and explained how it acts as a bridge between the business view of the data (BOM) and the actual implementation of the business data (XOM). Recall also that Rule Studio enables us to create a *BOM entry* from a XOM such as a Java project, a Java jar file, or an XML schema. The BOM creation utility uses a *default* BOM to XOM mapping, which we can override or customize. We will first talk about the default mapping, and then talk about custom BOM to XOM mappings.

Table 10.4 shows the main default mappings for a Java XOM. Anything that is not *public* does not appear in the BOM. When we build a BOM entry from a specific XOM, Rule Studio does not store these default mapping in the B2X file (BOM to XOM), which starts out empty. The B2X file is *only* used to store custom mappings.

We now explore some typical uses for the BOM to XOM mapping. Our first example of Fig. 10.12 showed one case of custom BOM to XOM mapping. In that example, we added an "age" attribute to the **PolicyHolder** BOM class, that did not exist in the Java **PolicyHolder** class, but that was *computed* from the "birthDate" attribute. Generally speaking, the Rule Studio BOM editors enables us to manually add data and function members to a BOM class that have no equivalent in the corresponding XOM, provided that we supply the BOM to XOM mapping for that

Table 10.4 Default Java XOM to BOM mappings

Java construct	BOM construct
Package	Package
Public class	Class
Public interface	Interface
public Type attName;	public Type attName;
public Type getAttName() with no corresponding setter	public readonly Type attName;
public void setAttName(Type arg) with no corresponding getter	public writeonly Type attName;
A getter/setter pair get/setAttName(Type a)	public Type attName;
A non-getter/setter public function	A similar public function
Public constructor	constructor
An "extends" relationship between Java classes or interfaces	An "extends" relationship between corresponding Java classes or interfaces
An "implements" relationship between a class and an interface	An "implements" relationship between the corresponding BOM class/interface

data or function member. We call those *virtual* data or function members. For a *virtual data member*, the BOM to XOM editor enables us to specify a "getter" and/ or a "setter" expression, depending on whether the data member is readonly, writeonly, or read/write. Below, we reproduce parts of the BOM to XOM editor for the "age" attribute, shown in Fig. 10.12. This fragment is part of the BOM class data member editor, for the attribute "age."

▼ BOM to XOM Mapping
Edit the mapping between this BOM member and the XOM.

 ✎ Edit the imports.

 ▼ Getter

```
return DateUtil.getAge(this.birthDate.toDate(),DateUtil.now());
```

In this case, because the "age" attribute is computed, it is read only, and we only specify the getter.

10.3.3.1 Virtual Functions

We can also specify *virtual* functions, i.e., functions that exist only in the BOM. If such a function returns a non-void value, it will appear in the condition part; if it returns a void, it will appear in the action part. Assume now that a claim is only eligible if it has been filed less than 180 days after the expense was incurred, for an ongoing policy, and less than 90 days after the expiration of the policy, for an expired policy. We could add a boolean function to the BOM class **Claim** with the following signature:

```
boolean filedMoreThanNDaysAfterDate(int nDays, Date aDate);
```

We can then specify how to compute such a function in the BOM to XOM mapping, as shown below. The variables nDays and aDate refer to the arguments of the function, with types int and java.util.Date, respectively. The pseudo-variable **this** refers to a **Claim**, and the dot reference this.date, to the date of the claim.[19]

---

[19]So which object model do we refer to in the BOM to XOM mapping? Logically, this should be the XOM, as we are showing how BOM elements map to XOM elements. In practice, we can refer to the BOM, *and* to any Java object model referenced in the rule project, included but not limited to the XOM. Thus to access the attribute "date" of **Claim**, I can use either "myClaim.date" or "myClaim.getDate()."

▾ **BOM to XOM Mapping**
Edit the mapping between this BOM member and the XOM.

🖉 Edit the imports.

▾ Body

```
Calendar calendar = Calendar.getInstance();
calendar.setTime(aDate);
calendar.add(Calendar.DAY_OF_YEAR,nDays);
return this.date.toDate().after(calendar.time);
```

This function can then be verbalized as follows:

```
{this} was filed more than {0} days after {1}
```

And used in a rule:

Business Rule: claim date - expiration policy

▸ General Information   ▸ Category Filter

▸ Documentation

Code

```
if
    'the claim' was filed more than 90 days after the end date of the policy of 'the claim'
then
    reject 'the claim' ;
    log that this rule has fired on 'the claim' with message "Filed more than 90 days after end of policy" ;
```

In this rule, {this} was substituted by the variable **"the claim,"** the first argument {0} was set to **90**, and the second argument {1}, which is a date, was replaced by the end date of "**the claim**." Incidentally, the second rule action (log that this rule has fired on ...) is itself a virtual function of the BOM class **Claim** with the signature:

```
void logRuleFiringWithMessage(String message)
```

The verbalization:

```
log that this rule has fired on {this} with message {0}
```

and the BOM to XOM mapping:

▾ BOM to XOM Mapping
Edit the mapping between this BOM member and the XOM.
🖉 Edit the imports.
▾ Body

```
Object[] args= {this};
String claimString = (String)context.invokeFunction("printClaim",args);
String fullMessage = "Rule ["+ ?instance.ruleName + "] fired on "+ claimString + " with message: " + message;
this.messageList.add(fullMessage);
```

This mapping is a bit more complex, and illustrates some advanced features of the BOM to XOM mapping and of the IRL language. First, rule {this} refers to a claim. In the first line, we are initializing an array of **Object**'s with {this} (the claim). In the second line, we are building the string that represents a claim by making what looks like a reflective call to some one-argument function called "printClaim" (sort of a custom `toString()` method), and that is exactly what it is: the method `invokeFunction(String functionName, Object[] args)` is an **IlrContext** (the class that represents rule engines) method that invokes an *IRL function* called `functionName` with the arguments `args`. We described IRL functions briefly in Sect. 10.2.1 as macro-like functions defined within rule projects. Such functions can be used within the action parts of IRL rules (covered in Sect. 11.2.1), function task bodies (see Sect. 11.3.2), within the initial actions and final actions of ruleflow tasks (Sect. 11.3.2), within *other* IRL functions, or within BOM to XOM mappings. In all the places *but* BOM to XOM mappings, these functions would be invoked normally, as in "`printClaim(my_claim);`." However, within the BOM to XOM mapping, they need to be invoked reflectively.[20] This code fragment shows also the use of two predefined IRL variables: `context`, which refers to the engine currently executing this piece of code, and `?instance`, which refers to the rule instance currently executing.[21] The latter enables us to access the rule name, the tuple of objects for which the rule fired, the priority of the rule instance on the agenda, etc., which makes it possible to write generic – and detailed – rule logging capabilities, as the rule above illustrates.

10.3.3.2   Virtual Classes

We now turn our attention to *virtual classes*. A *virtual class* is a class that exists only in the BOM with no direct equivalent in the XOM. As with virtual attributes and methods, we only need to specify what XOM (Java) class this BOM class maps to. First, let us explore a scenario where you would want to create a virtual class, and then we will show how to define such a virtual class.

We have shown in Sect. 9.2.1 the requirements that we place on BOM and on XOM. In particular, we identified *specificity* as a desirable property of the BOM and *genericity* as a desirable property of the XOM. Assume that our business people created the model shown in Fig. 10.13 on paper, before handing it over to IT to implement. This model distinguishes between an AUTO policy and a Health policy and makes a distinction between a medical claim and a car repair claim.

Upon closer inspection of the attributes of the various classes (not shown in this figure), an object designer, or a data architect, might find this model unnecessarily differentiated, and might decide to implement the model shown in Fig. 10.14, instead. In this model, both kinds of policies are represented by the same class

---

[20]The BOM to XOM mapping is used by the engine during run-time. Further, IRL functions can refer to BOM virtual functions. If we allow IRL functions to be called normally within the BOM to XOM mapping, we could end up with an arbitrarily long – and potentially circular – translation sequence from BOM to XOM.

[21]The Java type for `?instance` is **ilog.rules.engine.IlrRuleInstance.**

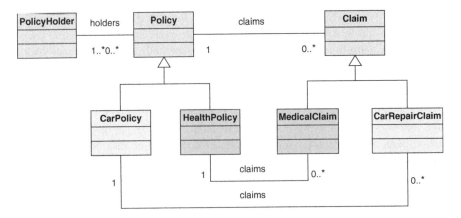

Fig. 10.13 The business view of the application data ("BOM on paper")

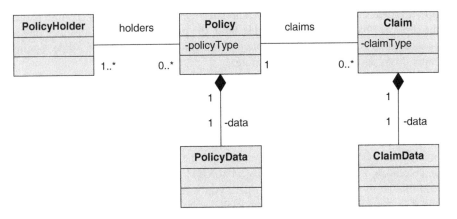

Fig. 10.14 The actual implemented XOM

Policy, which now has an attribute called `policyType`. Common policy attributes are represented in the class **Policy** itself, whereas policy type-specific attributes are represented in a **PolicyData** object. Idem for the **Claim** class.

If we create a BOM from this XOM, rule authors will not have the concept of a "health policy" or of a "car policy," but they can talk about a "policy" whose `policyType` equals "HEALTH_POLICY" or "CAR_POLICY." Virtual classes allow us to (re)create the BOM classes **HealthPolicy** and **CarPolicy** even though there is a single underlying XOM class, **Policy**. Figure 10.15 shows the BOM editor for classes. We are defining the class **HealthPolicy** as a class from the package `com.mywebinsurance.claimprocessing` and specifying its execution name (see (1) marker on figure) as `com.mywebinsurance.claimprocessing.`

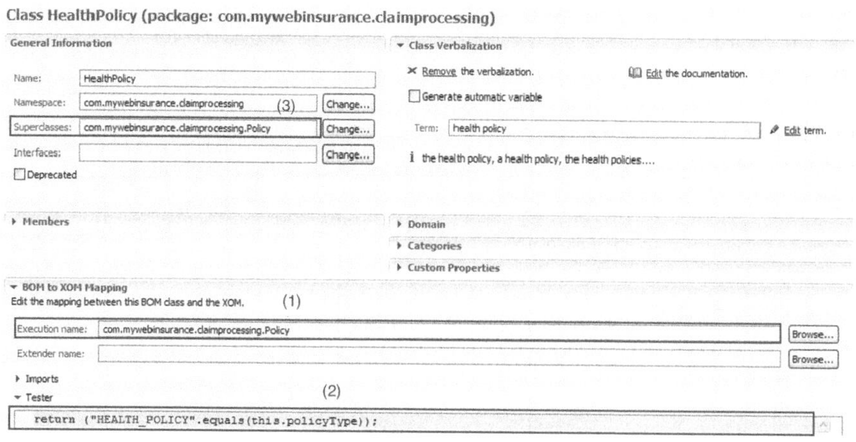

Class HealthPolicy (package: com.mywebinsurance.claimprocessing)

Fig. 10.15 BOM editor for BOM classes. To define a virtual BOM class, we need to (1) specify its execution name (i.e., corresponding XOM class), (2) specify what conditions instances of the XOM class need to satisfy (tester), and (3) specify its BOM superclasses

Policy. However, a **HealthPolicy** is not *any* **Policy**: it is a policy whose "tester" expression (see (2) marker) returns true:

```
return("HEALTH_POLICY" .equals(this.policyType));
```

where the variable `this` refers to a **Policy**.

Having defined the class **HealthPolicy**, we now wish to use it within rules, and test its data members, such as `startDate`, `endDate`, like any regular **Policy**, i.e., we wish to *inherit* the data and function members of the ... BOM class **Policy**. To do that, we need to specify the *BOM class* **Policy** as a *superclass* of **HealthPolicy** (see marker (3)). Figure 10.16 illustrates the required steps to define the virtual class **HealthPolicy**.

Note that, unlike with Java classes, BOM classes do support multiple inheritance: I can specify two or more BOM superclasses for any given BOM class. We will come back to this feature when we talk about best practices.

10.3.3.3 Dynamic XOM

Finally, we talk about *dynamic XOMs*, and more specifically, the XSD-based XOM. In short, JRules enables us to write and execute rules about XML data. This means two things:

- *At rule definition time*. The BOM is defined from an *XML schema* as opposed to a set of Java classes.
- *At rule execution time*. The rule engine can manipulate a generic and efficient run-time representation of XML data through the same object-based API that is used to access Java objects. This object-based API abstracts away the way objects are created, and their attributes read and set.

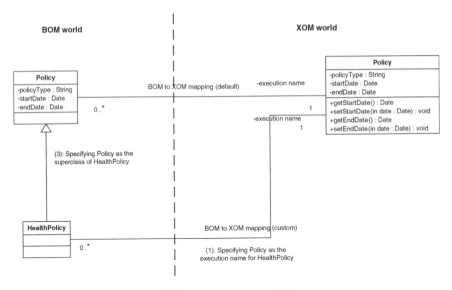

Fig. 10.16 Steps to specialize a BOM class with a virtual BOM class

Table 10.5 The basics of the XSD to BOM mapping

XSD	BOM element
Complex type	BOM class
XSD element or attribute	Read/write BOM attribute
An XSD element with maxOccurs >1	A java.util.Vector attribute with a collection domain of the element type (i.e., a multi-valued attribute)
Built-in XSD simple types	Corresponding java types
Extension and restriction	BOM class inheritance
Restricted simple types	Corresponding Java type with a literals domain

Table 10.5 shows the basics of the XSD-based BOM to XOM mapping. Roughly speaking, XSD's complex types map to classes, where the type's <element>s and attributes map to read/write BOM class data members, and the built-in XSD types map to the corresponding Java types. If an <element> has a maxOccurs higher than one, than the element is mapped to a java.util.Vector, with a BOM annotation that specifies the element type.

Table 10.6 shows excerpts from an XSD, and the corresponding excerpts from the BOM classes. For the sake of presentation, in the BOM column, the package names were omitted from the class names, with an ellipsis shown instead ("..."). The reader will notice that all BOM classes in this case inherit from the default **IlrXmlObject**, which is the actual implementation class for XML data (more on this below). The XSD types **string, float,** and **int** map to the Java types **java.lang.String**, float, and **int**, respectively. The XSD **date** type maps to the ILOG type **ilog.rules.xml.types.IlrDate**, which knows how to convert back and forth to a **java.util.Date**. Notice also how the Policy XSD

Table 10.6 The basics of the XSD to BOM mapping

Excerpts of an XSD schema	Excerpts of the corresponding BOM
| ```xml
<xs:complexType
            name="PolicyHolder">
 <xs:sequence>
  <xs:element name="name"
            type="xs:string"/>
  <xs:element name="tin"
            type="xs:string"/>
 ...
 </xs:sequence>
</xs:complexType>

<xs:complexType name="Coverage">
 <xs:sequence>
  <xs:element name="procedure"
            type="Procedure"/>
  <xs:element name="deductible"
            type="xs:float"/>
  <xs:element name="yearlyCap"
            type="xs:float"/>
  <xs:element name="totalToDate"
            type="xs:float"/>
 </xs:sequence>
</xs:complexType>

<xs:complexType name="Policy">
 <xs:sequence>
  <xs:element name="number"
            type="xs:int"/>
  <xs:element name="startDate"
            type="xs:date"/>
  <xs:element name="endDate"
            type="xs:date"/>
  <xs:element name="policyHolder"
        type="PolicyHolder"/>
   <xs:element name="insured"
        type="PolicyHolder"
        minOccurs="0"
        maxOccurs="unbounded"/>
   <xs:element name="coverage"
        type="Coverage"
        minOccurs="1"
        maxOccurs="unbounded"/>
 </xs:sequence>
</xs:complexType>
``` | ```java
public class PolicyHolder extends
       ilog.rules.xml.IlrXmlObject
   // some custom properties
   property ...
{
   ...
}

public class Coverage extends
       ilog.rules.xml.IlrXmlObject
   // some custom properties
   property ...
{
   ...
}

public class Policy extends
       ilog.rules.xml.IlrXmlObject
   // some custom properties
   property ...
{public int number
            property // custom properties

   public ...IlrDate startDate
            property // custom properties

   public ...IlrDate endDate
            property // custom properties

   public ...PolicyHolder policyHolder
            property // custom properties

   public ...Vector insuredList
            domain 0,* class ...PolicyHolder
            property // custom properties

   public ...Vector coverageList
            domain 1,* class ...Coverage
            property // custom properties

   ... // plus some other stuff
}
``` |

elements insured and coverages mapped to **java.util.Vector** instance variables, with a *domain* that is of the appropriate element type (**PolicyHolder** and **Coverage**, respectively); we will talk about *domains* in Sect. 10.3.5 of this chapter.[22]

---

[22]This feature of JRules has been around since 2002, i.e. prior to JDK 1.5 (which came out in the fall of 2004) which introduced support for genericity, and the handling of collections has remained unchanged for backward compatibility reasons.

Notice that the classes **PolicyHolder**, **Coverage**, and **Policy** exist only in the *BOM*; during run-time, the underlying XML data – that conforms to the XML schema – will be represented by instances of the **IlrXmlObject** class, regardless of the BOM class. Indeed, unlike JAX-RPC, JAXB, or JAX-WS frameworks, JRules does *not* generate Java classes for the corresponding XML schema complex types; we can think of the XSD-mapped classes as *virtual classes* with an execution class **IlrXmlObject**.

For now, suffice it to say that if your application manipulates business data that comes in an exotic, self-describing, and evolving data format, you too could develop support for your exotic format, at both rule definition time (BOM to XOM mapping) and at rule execution time.

10.3.4 Refactoring

To use a common *cliché*, the only constant in today's business applications is change. The BOM has a *pure* layered architecture where each layer depends only on the layer just below it (see Fig. 10.17). Eclipse's refactoring functionality has been extended by the JRules plug-in to propagate changes in a given layer to the layer just above it. In this section, we review the different kinds of changes, and the available functionalities to propagate them through the layered structure of Fig. 10.17.

10.3.4.1   Changes to the XOM

A stable XOM is an elusive goal in many rule projects, especially ones where both the business layer (i.e., business entities) and the business rules are within scope of the development or modernization effort. We might as well live with it, considering

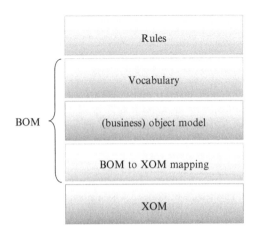

Fig. 10.17 The BOM's
layered architecture enhances
the rules' resilience to change

Fig. 10.18 An example of the "Update BOM" wizard, for BOMs created from a XOM

that Rule Studio enables us to cope with the most common situations. If we build a BOM from a XOM (see Sects. 10.3.1 and 10.3.3), whenever we change the XOM, we can ask the tool to update the BOM accordingly. This is done by selecting the corresponding BOM entry, and selecting the action "BOM Update" in the contextual menu. This will compare the current state of the XOM to the current state of the BOM, and (a) identify the differences, and (b) propose actions to bridge those differences. Figure 10.18 shows the interface of Rule Studio's BOM – XOM synchronization wizard. The top part shows, side by side, the XOM and the BOM. The class Coverage (left-hand side) has a warning sign, which indicates that it is not consistent with the corresponding BOM version. The list of differences is shown in the lower pane – here just one indicating that the attribute "description" of the XOM class Coverage could not be found in the corresponding BOM class. For each difference identified, the tool proposes one or more (generally two) actions that can be performed to bridge the difference. In this case, the tool proposes to update the BOM class – and thus, add the attribute "description" to it.

Let us now consider the typical changes to the XOM, and how they could be handled:

1. *Additions.* If we add XOM elements, when we re-synchronize the BOM with the XOM, the tool offers to propagate those additions to the BOM. This works for both the addition of XOM classes and the addition of function or data members to existing XOM classes. This will have no effect on existing BOM or rules.
2. *Removals.* If we remove a XOM element, be it a class or a member of a class, the BOM update wizard will note that the corresponding BOM element has been "orphaned" and will offer to either delete it or to "deprecate it." We could also do nothing. If we do nothing, Rule Studio will complain that the now-orphaned BOM element has no XOM corresponding element, in which case, we should use the BOM to XOM mapping to map it to *other* existing XOM elements. Deprecating it means that we set the property "deprecated" of the BOM element to true, which will flag rules that use it with "deprecated" warnings.[23] This will also stop making the element available in the pull-down lists or code completion

---

[23]You may need to "clean" the project for the warnings to show up.

feature of the rule editor. We still have to use the BOM to XOM mapping to map the orphaned BOM element to something. If we delete the BOM element . . . we better make sure that the element is not used in any rule, first.[24]

3. *Renaming*. If we rename a XOM element, depending on where it is performed, the changed can be propagated automatically throughout the BOM, or will have to be done manually:

   – *Renaming done through Eclipse's refactoring menu*. This is possible *if* the XOM is a Java project included in the same workspace as the project containing the BOM. In this case, Eclipse's refactoring functionality will propagate the renaming to (a) the BOM, by renaming the corresponding BOM element, and (b) the vocabulary, by changing the *corresponding key in the vocabulary file*, but leaving the *value*, i.e., the actual verbalization, unchanged. Figure 10.19 shows an example of rename refactoring, which is propagated all the way to the key part of the vocabulary file.

   – *Renaming done manually*. This would be the case for any XOM that is *not* a Java project within the same workspace, such as an XSD XOM, or a Java XOM supplied as a jar file, or a bunch of .class files. In this case, the "BOM Update" facility will note an addition to the XOM, corresponding to the new name, and a removal from the XOM, corresponding to the old name. We can handle it either by renaming the BOM element manually, which will propagate it to the vocabulary (see below, BOM changes), or by using the BOM to XOM mapping to map the BOM element with the old name to the XOM element with the new name.

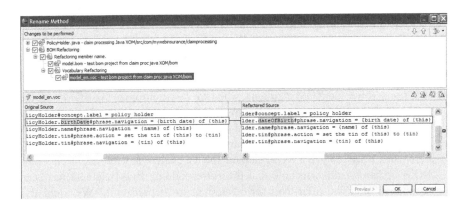

Fig. 10.19 Renaming a Java (XOM) method through Eclipse's refactor will propagate the change to the .bom and vocabulary file, without affecting the rules that use the member

---

[24]Rule queries and Eclipse search functionality enable us to ascertain that. We could also first deprecate the element then see if any rules generate "deprecated" warnings, and if none do, we could then *safely* delete it.

4. *More complex refactorings.* In this case, Eclipse's refactor menu will not do the trick, as the tool gets confused. Instead, we should use the "BOM Update" functionality to propagate some of the changes, and fix the rest manually.[25]

5. *Non-semantics preserving changes.* If we change the type signature of a method (e.g., number or types of parameters), then we use "BOM Update," and it should be treated as an addition and a removal. In some cases, it may be appropriate to map the old BOM method to the new XOM method using the BOM to XOM mapping. For example, if the new XOM method has an additional parameter, perhaps that parameter has a reasonable default value, and we can keep the old BOM method, but as a virtual method. This would need to be handled on a case-by-case basis.

The important thing to note from this analysis is that in any of the above change scenarios, the rules are shielded by the changes to the XOM, as the change is absorbed in the various intervening layers between the XOM and the rules.

10.3.4.2   Changes to the BOM

Most changes to the BOM originate from the XOM and were discussed above. The changes that do originate from the BOM correspond to the addition, modification, or removal of virtual BOM elements:

1. *Additions of virtual BOM elements.* This is, for the most part, non-problematic, except in those cases where the new BOM element has the same verbalization as an existing BOM element.

2. *Modification of a virtual BOM element.* Renamings have no effect as the vocabulary absorbs the change. As mentioned earlier and illustrated in Fig. 10.19, the vocabulary file assigns BOM element phrases that will appear in rules, in a key = value. Renaming the BOM element will only modify the key part, as illustrated in Fig. 10.19, leaving the verbalization – and the rules – unchanged. More substantial changes can break existing rules. For example, if we modify the signature of a virtual method, its verbalization will need to change to account for the additional/ fewer parameters, which will be propagated to the rules that use it (see below). This, in turn, will break those rules.

3. *Removal.* See the discussion above regarding removal, and removal versus deprecation.

---

[25]For example, if we move a data member and its accessors up the hierarchy of classes, the right thing to do would be to move the corresponding public data member up the BOM hierarchy. However, the tool cannot do that on its own: the "BOM Update" will enable us to add the member to the superclass, but will not remove it from the original class, and will not complain about it since it does have a XOM equivalent. However, if the data member is used in a rule, the rule editor will complain about an "ambiguous sentence," meaning that two data members have the same verbalization.

10.3.4.3 Changes to the Vocabulary

If we make a change to the verbalization of a BOM element, *and save* the BOM, Rule Studio will prompt the user to confirm the verbalization modification as it may affect existing rules. If the user accepts to proceed, a refactoring menu is presented to the user, showing the various rules that use that BOM element/its verbalization with the before and after text. The user has then the options of (1) rejecting the change (save), or (2) accepting it and propagating it to all concerned rules or a subset thereof.

Notice that the propagation of verbalization changes to rules *will only work if the rule is syntactically correct to start with.* If the rule is wrong, the result can be unpredictable: in the best case, the change will not be propagated and the rule will remain wrong. In the worst case, you lose parts of the rule text.

10.3.5 Enhancing the Rule Authoring Experience

JRules offers a set of bells and whistles that make life easier for rule authors. We will present two important ones, *categories* and *domains*.

10.3.5.1 Categories

Any self-respecting BOM will have dozens of classes and hundreds if not thousands of members. While editing rules, the number of drop-downs that are provided to rule authors is likely to be overwhelming. However, any given rule will typically address only one facet of the data. In our claim processing example, a rule about the *eligibility* of a given *procedure* will be concerned with coverages attached to the policy, and not about personal or credit data about the policy holder. JRules offers a way to *filter* those BOM elements that show up in rule editors based on the *categories* assigned to the BOM elements and the *categories* assigned to rules. Figure 10.20 illustrates the relationship between BOM elements, categories, and rules.

Categories are defined at the project level. By default, a rule project starts with a single category "Any," and all BOM elements and rules are assigned the category "Any." Thus, by default, rules will pull in all the BOM elements. Assume that we add the categories "Claim eligibility" and "Claim adjudication" to the project. We can then assign the category "Claim eligibility" to those BOM elements that we think are relevant to assessing the eligibility of a claim, and "Claim adjudication" to those BOM elements that we think are relevant to adjudicating the claim. Naturally, some BOM elements will be relevant to both areas, and can have both categories. In this case, the class Claim is relevant to both and will have both categories. Figure 10.21 shows the Rule Studio wizard for assigning categories to a BOM class.

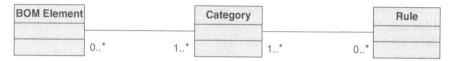

Fig. 10.20 The relationship between BOM elements, categories, and rules

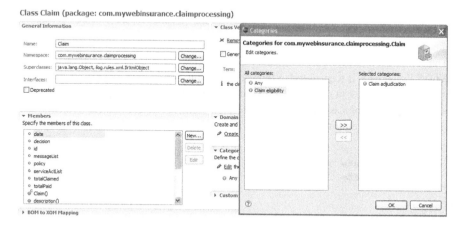

Fig. 10.21 Assigning categories to a BOM class

Table 10.7 Semantics of category filters

BOM element		BE_1	BE_2	BE_3	BE_4	BE_5
Categories		Eligibility	Adjudication	Eligibility, Adjudication	Any	
Rule	Category filter					
Rule_1	Eligibility	Visible	Not	Visible	Visible	Not
Rule_2	Adjudication	Not	Visible	Visible	Visible	Not
Rule_3	Eligibility, Adjudication	Visible	Visible	Visible	Visible	Not
Rule_4	Any	Visible	Visible	Visible	Visible	Not

When we define a rule, we can also edit its *category filter*, which uses a similar wizard to that of Fig. 10.21 to assign one or more categories to the rule. In so doing, we determine the subset of BOM elements that are selectable – and thus usable – in the rule. The default category "Any" plays the role of a wildcard: a BOM element with category "Any" is available to all rules, regardless of their category filters, and a rule with category filter "Any" will have access to the entire BOM.[26] Table 10.7 illustrates the semantics of the category filter.

---

[26]It is technically possible to assign no category to a BOM element, which makes it unavailable for rule authoring, altogether.

Notice that when we assign a category to a class, it is not "inherited" by members of the class. This may sound counter-intuitive but in the above example, while the Claim class itself is relevant to both claim eligibility and adjudication, some of its members will be relevant to only eligibility while others will be relevant to only adjudication.

10.3.5.2 Domains

The BOM uses Java types, regardless of its origin, be it a Java XOM or an XSD XOM. Pre-Java 5, if we wanted to represent the state component of a US address, say, we had two choices: (1) use the Java String type for the java attribute, but then control what values can be assigned through the input forms, or (2) use what is called the (pre-JDK 5) Java enumeration pattern with a class **State** as illustrated below.

```
public class State {
        private String stateCode;
        private String stateName;

        // getters
        ...

        private State(String code, String name){
                stateCode = code;
                stateName = name;
        }

        public final static State AL = new State("AL","ALABAMA");
        ...
        // 50 states later
        public final static State WY = new State("WY","WYMONING");
}
```

JRules enables us to restrict the set of values that a BOM attribute, a BOM function parameter, or a BOM function return value can take using *domains*. With domains, when a rule author is prompted to enter a value for that attribute/parameter/return value, they will get a dropdown list of the domain values, as illustrated in Fig. 10.22. Here, the "decision" attribute of a Claim, a String, has been restricted to the values shown using a *literal domain*, i.e., a domain whose values are explicitly enumerated.

Generally speaking, JRules enables us to define five kinds of domains:

1. *Literal domains.* In this case, the values are enumerated. This works for scalar types and for String. This will also work for actual Java 5 (and beyond) enumerations: if a BOM attribute or function parameter or return value is a Java enum, then it will have a literal domain consisting of the elements of the enumeration.

Business Rule: date eligibility

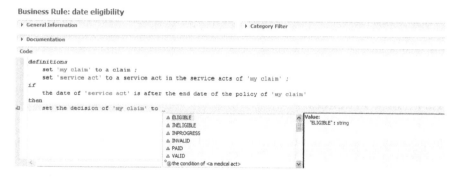

▶ General Information   ▶ Category Filter

▶ Documentation

Code

```
definitions
    set 'my claim' to a claim ;
    set 'service act' to a service act in the service acts of 'my claim' ;
if
    the date of 'service act' is after the end date of the policy of 'my claim'
then
    set the decision of 'my claim' to
```

△ ELIGIBLE	**Value:**
△ INELIGIBLE	"ELIGIBLE" : string
△ INPROGRESS	
△ INVALID	
△ PAID	
△ VALID	
@ the condition of <a medical act>	

Fig. 10.22 The "decision" attribute of Claim has type String, but with a domain {"ELIGIBLE","-INELIGIBLE","INPROGRESS","INVALID","PAID","VALID"}

2. *Bounded domains.* For numerical types, where we can specify a range of values.
3. *Static references.* This corresponds to our State example above. If our Java class uses the enumeration pattern illustrated below, Rule Studio will *automatically* create a domain that includes *all* of the public static final data members for each attribute, parameter or return value. We can later edit that domain to remove values. For example, with the State class above, any BOM attribute, parameter, or function return value will have a domain consisting of all the enumerated states. That domain can later be edited to remove or put back states.
4. *Collection domains.* If a BOM data member or a function parameter or a function return value is a Java collection (Vector, ArrayList, List, etc.), we can define a *collection domain* on that attribute/parameter/return value by specifying the *type of the elements of the collection*. For example, the class **Policy** has an attribute called coverageList, with the java type java.util.Vector, we can specify a collection domain on coverageList by stating that its *elementType* is **com.mywebinsurance. claimprocessing.Coverage**. Naturally, if your Java 5 (and beyond) class used the generic type variety for the vector, i.e., **Vector<com. mywebinsurance.claimprocessing.Coverage**>, then Rule Studio will add the collection domain automatically, with the appropriate element type. With pre-JDK 5 collections, we have to add them explicitly.
5. *Other.* We can specify custom domains in cases that do not fit the above patterns, using an esoteric notation.

Domains are useful for three reasons: (a) convenience to rule authors, (b) maintaining data value integrity, and (c) support for powerful rule constructs with the *Business Action Language*, discussed in Sect. 10.4.2.

Notice that Rule Studio supports the dynamic computation of domains. Consider a domain that enumerates the possible medical procedures. That list will likely be updated as new medical procedures are developed every day. We would want that domain to be updated automatically whenever new procedures are added so that rule authors will *automatically* get the most up-to-date list of procedures to write their rules. It is possible to set-up *dynamic domains* in both Rule Studio and Rule Team Server, which get initialized at the beginning of each session with the tool.

10.4 Best Practices

In this section, we present best practices related to the organization of rule projects, and to the design of the BOM.

10.4.1 Best Practices for Organizing Rule Projects

We just saw in Sect. 10.2.4 how JRules deals with multiple users accessing and updating the same rule projects, in both the RS and RTS environments. While both RS and RTS support multiple users concurrently accessing the same rule project, a rule project does represent an easily manageable modularization boundary, in both RS and RTS. As such, it can be used as a unit for work for an effective division of labor. However, when we are trying to divide up work between the members of a team, we need to be concerned about *both* (a) enabling team members to work separately on things that are within their exclusive jurisdiction, with no interference from others, *and* (b) enabling them to share the things that are common to their work. This is where *project dependencies*, discussed in Sect. 10.2.2, come in handy. Figure 10.23 illustrates the idea. The common rules are defined in a separate

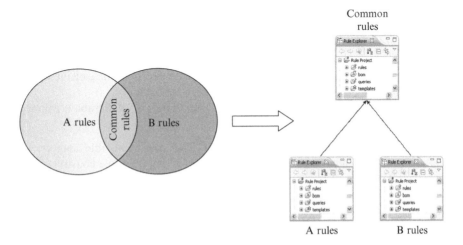

Fig. 10.23 Using project dependencies to better modularize rule projects that share some rules

project, and are thus (a) made accessible to both projects, and (b) maintained separately from them.

Project dependencies also come in handy for building and maintaining BOMs. Because different decisions/rulesets may use the same BOM, we should define the BOM in a separate project and have projects for rules that depend on that BOM refer to that project. Going one step further, we could also use project dependencies and the notion of a BOM path (see Sect. 10.2.2) to build the BOM incrementally. For example, in the case of MyWebInsurance, we use rules for new policy under-writing, rules for policy renewal, and rules for claim processing. All three decision areas refer to a **Policy** and the **PolicyHolder**'s basic data. Policy underwriting and policy renewal would *also* refer to the **PolicyHolder**'s **DrivingRecord** and **CreditProfile**. On the other hand, policy renewal and claim processing refer to **Claim**'s, past (for renewal) and present (for claim processing). We could thus a first rule project with no rules in it but just the basic common BOM, i.e., containing **Policy** and **PolicyHolder**. Other BOM-only rule projects are then created to add process-specific BOMs. And so forth. Figure 10.24 illustrates this idea.

The example of Fig. 10.24 is just another variation of Fig. 10.2: when have two or more rule projects that overlap (BOM-wise or rule-wise, or ruleflow-wise, etc.), we separate the common parts from the exclusive parts and put each in a project where the projects with the exclusive parts refer to the project with the common parts. Figure 10.25 shows the full pattern.

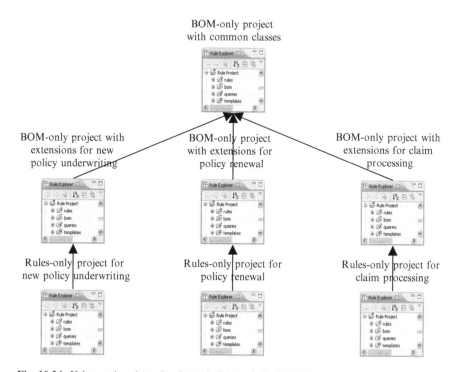

Fig. 10.24 Using project dependencies to build specialized BOM by leveraging commonalities

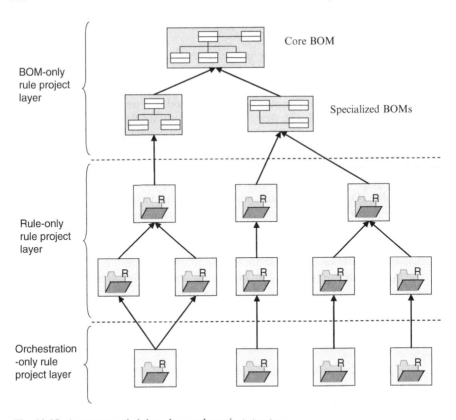

Fig. 10.25 A recommended three-layer rule project structure

We will talk about rule execution orchestration in more detail in Sect. 11.3. For the time being, suffice it to say that an orchestration-only rule project is a rule project that defines a *ruleflow*, which is a process flow for rule execution where each task of the process flow *typically* runs the rules contained within a rule package. Thus, an orchestration-only project would define a rule flow that sequences the execution of rules (rule packages) defined in the rules-only layer. This enables us to reuse the same set of rules for different processes. For example, the same policy data validation rules could be used for both new policy underwriting and for policy renewal. Thus, such rules would be defined in one rule project, which could be referenced by two orchestration-only rules that pull those rules in for both processes. We will revisit this topic briefly in Sect. 11.3.

10.4.2   Best Practices for the Design of the BOM

The clear separation that JRules draws between the actual implementation of application data (the XOM) and the business view of it (the BOM) is a very powerful feature. It provides "rule architects" with lots of degrees of freedom, and, alas, too much creativity. As with many features of the product, they should be used wisely, and we should show restraint in ringing all of the bells and blowing all of the whistles. In this section, we present some best practices.

10.4.2.1 Best Practice 1: Build Your BOM from Interfaces

If you are doing anything remotely OO or Java, there are a bazillion reasons to program to interfaces, as opposed to classes, and most authors hammer that message, and most frameworks rely on such a separation. We will give you a few more reasons to separate interfaces from implementations, by showing you the benefits of building your BOM based on interfaces, as opposed to based on the classes that implement them.

Recall that when you build a BOM from XOM, the BOM builder ignores all of the XOM elements that are *not* public: any model element that is private, protected, or package is *ignored*. Second, implementation classes will typically have *business functions*, but will also included many utility methods that provide services to the business functions, or that implement non-business infrastructural services (saving, loading, serializing, logging, etc.). Such methods will only clutter the BOM, and we know that they will not be needed to write rules. Thus, *business interfaces will contain all of the necessary and sufficient elements you will need in the BOM.*[27]

Then there is the issue of nomenclature. Business interfaces (typically/should) use implementation neutral terminology. A policy is called Policy and not Policy-Bean, or PolicyImpl or PolicyTransferObject, or PolicyDAOImpl, or PolicyDAO-BeanObserver, or PolicyDAOImplFacade. As we saw above in Sect. 10.3.2, the Rule Studio BOM builder does a pretty good job of verbalizing your classes. If you use the names used in your implementation classes, they are likely to be polluted by initials of the authors, prefixes or suffixes of the various frameworks that you are using, markers of the coolest design pattern you just read about, etc.

But the strongest argument of all is the applicability of your rules. Assume that you build your BOM from the classes shown in Fig. 10.26. Here we assume that **PersonalAutoPolicy** deals with vehicles used *exclusively* for personal activities whereas **CommercialAutoPolicy** deals with vehicles used exclusively for business activity. The BOM classes will mirror this structure. If you write a rule about a **AutoPolicy**, and you hand your rule engine an **PersonalAuto-Policy**, the rule will be evaluated on that policy and will fire if applicable. Idem for **CommercialAutoPolicy**. You would also typically have rules specific to **PersonalAutoPolicy** and others specific to **CommercialAuto-Policy**. Assume now that MyWebInsurance decides to create a novel auto insurance product that combines the features of a personal and business auto policy: we will call it **DualUseAutoPolicy**. This kind of insurance will share *some*

---

[27]Naturally, provided they are properly designed.

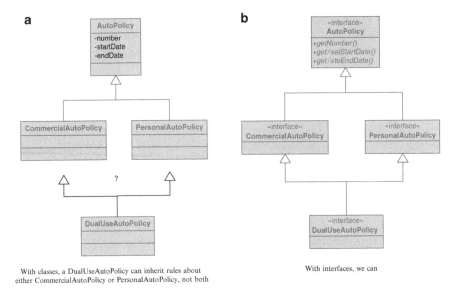

With classes, a DualUseAutoPolicy can inherit rules about
either CommercialAutoPolicy or PersonalAutoPolicy, not both

With interfaces, we can

Fig. 10.26 Building the BOM from interfaces yields more robust and more reusable rules

characteristics with **PersonalAutoPolicy** and others with **Commercial-AutoPolicy**. We would also want to *reuse* the corresponding rules about **PersonalAutoPolicy** and about **CommercialAutoPolicy**. With Java classes, this would not be possible: the **DualUseAutoPolicy** class can inherit from either **PersonalAutoPolicy** or **CommercialAutoPolicy**, but not both. And thus, we would be able to reuse either the relevant rules about **PersonalAutoPolicy** or the ones about **CommercialAutoPolicy**, but not both. With Java interfaces, we can define a java interface **DualUseAutoPolicy** that extends both **PersonalAutoPolicy** and **CommercialAutoPolicy**, the BOM classes (interfaces in this case) will mirror that structure, and rules specific to either **PersonalAutoPolicy** or **CommercialAutoPolicy**, will apply to **DualUseAutoPolicy**.[28]

10.4.2.2 Best Practice 2: Too Much of a Good Thing …

The layered architecture of the rule authoring stack of JRules provides a very clean abstraction mechanism. This enables us to limit the impact of the changes we make to the different layers (see Fig. 10.12). This is important because when we start identifying and coding rules, we frequently identify new data requirements, typically new *business* attributes or actions that rule authors need to write rules

---

[28]OK, maybe you do not want *all* of the rules that are specific to either **PersonalAutoPolicy** or **CommercialAutoPolicy** to apply to **DualUseAutoPolicy**'s and that is OK, because the tool allows you to pick and choose (see Sect. 10.5 about rule orchestration).

(e.g., new attributes). In general, if the *application* object model has been thought out thoroughly, *most* of the data and functionality will be present in the XOM in a "raw" form: then, it is just a matter of *computing* the required attributes from the existing ones (e.g., computing age from birth date), or implementing virtual functions that provide a convenient shorthand for some XOM functionality. Either way, the new data and function requirements will be defined in the BOM to XOM mapping. Naturally, there will be cases when the required data or functionality is not present in any shape of form. In that case, we need to make changes to the XOM. But as the project progresses through the various iterations of ABRD (see Chaps. 3 to 5), and as the application goes into maintenance mode, the XOM should become fairly stable.

At what point does the BOM to XOM mapping become too much of a good thing? As mentioned in Chap. 8, the BOM and the XOM need to satisfy different sets of requirements: the BOM needs to be close to the business, at the expense of some redundancy, and the XOM needs to be "canonical,"[29] at the expense of some readability.

First, by *design*, given a well-designed XOM, all of the virtual BOM elements will be more or less redundant with other elements. The convenience of having a BOM element to express *every* nuance and *relationship* between concepts comes at a price:

1. The possible confusion between close BOM concepts
2. The conceptual overhead of learning a rich vocabulary

For example, assume that some rules need to reason about service acts that cost more than some value. We could either add a virtual method to the class **Claim** that does just that:

```
Collection<ServiceAct> getServiceActsCostingMoreThan(float cost);
```

with the verbalization:

```
the service acts of {this} that cost more than {0};
```

and code the "cost filter" in the BOM to XOM mapping by iterating over the service acts of the claim, and returning those that cost more than the argument. Or, assuming that the service acts of a **Claim** are verbalized as "the service acts of {this}," we could code the "cost filter" directly in the rule language (see BAL in Sect. 10.4.2) as in:

```
set 'costly service acts' to all service acts in the service acts of
   'my claim' where the cost of each service act is at least 500;
```

---

[29]That is, it contains a minimum number of "orthogonal" concepts that can accommodate the most data or functionality needs.

Editing the BOM to accommodate new rules should be an *exceptional occurrence*, especially in rule maintenance mode; we should not have to edit the BOM – and add one virtual function – for *every* condition any business user or policy manager can think of. Alas, we have seen many customer projects where the BOM grows linearly with the rule set ...

There is another reason why one should *not* put too much in the BOM to XOM mapping. Unlike Java code, which source-code management software handles quite well (class/file-level versioning, class member granularity for merging conflicting versions, documenting changes), the BOM to XOM mappings are all lumped into a single file, with coarse-grained versioning, and little or awkward visibility to developers. This makes it into the least manageable part of your code. Of course, there are legitimate uses for virtual functions and the BOM to XOM mapping, and once an application has gone into production, we certainly do not want to deploy a new version of the application (the XOM) each time some rule needs a new computed attribute or a new convenience method. Between application/Java code releases, we should use all the tricks of the book. However, with each planned code release, we should take the time to revisit the virtual BOM elements and their BOM to XOM mappings and assess whether they should be pushed back to the XOM. *If* the virtual BOM element embodies *significant* and *generally useful* business logic, then that element and its BOM to XOM mapping should be pushed back to the XOM at the next opportunity. Computing an age from a birth date does not represent *significant* business logic – it is rather trivial. Computing the compound yearly interest rate of a loan based on the daily interest rate – or vice-versa – is significant *and* generally useful, i.e., useful to *other* parts of the business application besides the rule service.

10.4.2.3   Best Practice 3: Do Not Be Too Creative

Consistency is a highly desirable property in software: you choose an architecture, a design, a pattern, a coding style, a nomenclature, a file structure pattern, what have you, and you apply it uniformly. Consistency is desirable because it makes software understandable, maintainable, scalable, etc., and its components reusable, portable, and all around adorable. Consistency comes at a cost: whichever pattern you choose (architectural, design, coding, structuring, naming, etc.), it will *not* be *optimal* in every situation, or for every component or part of your software. If you choose your patterns carefully, they will be optimal or near optimal *most* of the time. For the remaining cases, live with the awkwardness or sub-optimality: it is a small price to pay for the resulting consistency!

This general principle applies also to the BOM and the vocabulary. Do not be too creative. Take the example of verbalization. Rule Studio generates decent to good verbalizations, 95% of the time.[30] It also knows a bit about grammar. Do not tweak

---

[30]Less if you use lousy naming patterns – or none at all – in your XOM/Java code.

verbalizations to death so that your rules will read like English: they will not and they do not need to. We are not writing poetry: the rules need to be understandable and precise, not necessarily perfectly constructed English sentences or pleasant to the ear. Consistency makes learning the BOM and the vocabulary much easier, and the resulting rules less error-prone.

10.5 Discussion

In this chapter, we discussed rule projects and the Business Object Model. Together, they provide the basics of the rule authoring infrastructure. They also play a crucial role in the quality and the manageability of the rules. A poor BOM design can lead to rules that are barely better than programming code. A poor BOM design can also lead to rules that are brittle, i.e., that are not properly shielded from non-essential changes taking place on the XOM side. A poor rule project design can lead to an inefficient and chaotic division of labor between rule developers. It can also lead to poor rule reuse and sharing and to nightmarish rule maintenance. It is critical to get those designed right before rule authoring can start. Naturally, the BOM will most likely continue to evolve during rule authoring and maintenance, but we have to get the basic *architecture* of the BOM right before we start. The design guidelines and best practices provided in this chapter should give you a head start.

The design tasks, skills, and decisions described in this chapter fall within the purview of the *rule architect*. A typical rule *writer* does not have the skill, and should not be given the responsibility, of designing rule project structure and the various BOMs. Chapter 11 will address rule writer-specific tasks and skills within the context of JRules.

10.6 Further Reading

As this chapter is JRules specific, additional sources of information can be found in the product documentation and on IBM's support site for *Websphere Ilog JRules*. More information about the rule engine execution algorithms can be found in Chap. 6 and its references. The web site http://www.agilebrdevelopment.com, which is dedicated to this book, contains complementary information.

Chapter 11
Rule Authoring in JRules

Target audience

- *Business analyst, developer, rule author*

In this chapter you will learn

- *The different rule entry languages and rule artifacts, namely, technical rules, action rules, decision tables, decision trees, and scorecards*
- *How to build your custom rule language*
- *How to orchestrate rule execution with ruleset parameters and ruleflow*
- *How to optimize rule execution by selecting the appropriate rule execution algorithm for a given rule task*

Key points

- *The Ilog Rule Language (IRL) is the foundation upon which other languages and rule artifacts are built.*
- *Action rules, decision tables, decision trees, and scorecards are translated into/executed as IRL technical rules.*
- *Be aware of the possibility to develop your own rule language (with the Business Rule Language Development Framework), but resist the temptation to.*
- *Refer to your application objects through ruleset parameters.*
- *Use ruleflows to orchestrate rule execution. They provide a high-level control mechanism and a context for rule execution.*
- *Ruleflows offer opportunities for speeding execution through run-time rule selection, and algorithm selection.*

11.1 Introduction

In Chap. 10, we explored the rule authoring *infrastructure* in JRules, where we focused on *rule projects* and *the business object model*. Rule projects and rule project dependencies enable us to modularize rule development in such a way as to facilitate the sharing and reuse of rule artifacts across different functional areas. The *business*

J. Boyer and H. Mili, *Agile Business Rule Development*,
DOI 10.1007/978-3-642-19041-4_11, © Springer-Verlag Berlin Heidelberg 2011

object model represents the business view of the application data – be it Java classes or XML data. It is defined through a powerful (*BOM to XOM*) mapping language in much the same way that relational database views are defined using the underlying database, by filtering irrelevant properties, defining computed attributes, or introducing so-called *virtual* classes that mean something to business but that are not supported in the underlying application model (Java or XSD). In particular, we saw how the architecture of the BOM and the BOM to XOM mapping is able to *absorb* a wide range of changes to the underlying application model (Java or XSD), without affecting the existing rules. If it is the rules that we want to rephrase, a *vocabulary refactoring functionality* propagates vocabulary changes to the rules that use them.

In this chapter, we first explore the different kinds of rule languages (the *ILOG Rule Language*, or IRL, and the *Business Action Language*, or BAL) and rule artifacts that use them, namely, *technical rules* (IRL), *action rules* (BAL), *decision tables* (BAL), *decision trees* (BAL), and *scorecards* (IRL). We also provide an overview of a framework for developing rule languages. In Sect. 11.3, we discuss rule execution orchestration, where the focus is on organizing the execution of rules during run-time. We will talk about ruleset variables and parameters and about *ruleflows*, which are process flows whose tasks consist of groups or rules. Ruleflows enable us, among other things, to statically select the algorithm to use to execute for a particular rule task, and to dynamically select the rules that execute within a particular task. Best practices are presented in Sect. 11.4. We conclude in Sect. 11.5.

11.2   Rule Artifacts

In this section, we give a *brief* overview of the various rule artifacts. Space limitations do not allow us to delve too deeply into any of the artifacts or languages covered; the tutorials and reference manuals included in the product documentation do a much better job at that! Our purpose is to provide the reader with a roadmap of the rule artifacts, and the relationships between them.

With this in mind, it makes sense to start with the IRL language, or *ILOG Rule Language*, which is the ancestor of all of the languages and artifacts,[1] and *technical rules* which are if-then rules written using IRL. IRL is also the only language that the rule engine understands, and every other language or artifact has to map to IRL. We then talk about the *Business Action Language*, which references the business *vocabulary* as opposed to the BOM elements directly, and *action rules* which are *if-then* rules written in BAL. We next talk about decision tables and decision trees, which are higher-level rule aggregates written using the BAL. Scorecards represent yet another high-level artifact typically used in risk assessment or credit worthiness applications. Finally, we briefly talk about the *business rule language development framework*, which is a flexible framework for developing rule languages, of which the BAL is an instance. Figure 11.1 shows the different kinds of languages, artifacts, and relations between them. Ruleflows will be discussed in Sect. 11.3 about rule execution orchestration.

---

[1]The first full-fledged ILOG Rule Language was based on the rule language OPS5 (see Chap. 6).

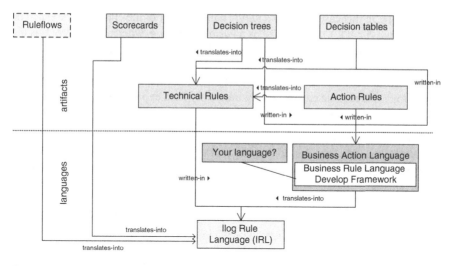

Fig. 11.1 The rule language landscape in JRules

11.2.1 IRL and Technical Rules

As shown in Fig. 11.1, the *ILOG Rule Language* is the base language for rule artifacts of JRules, including, but not limited to, if-then "technical rules". Historically, IRL was synonymous with if-then rules, and so we will start with the subset of IRL that concerns if-then rules, called *technical rules* as opposed to *action rules* which are written using the BAL. Let us first start with a simple example.

```
rule YoungDriver {
  property priority = 0;
  when {
    ?driver: Driver(age < 25);
  } then {
    System.out.println("Found a young driver:" + ?driver);
    }
}
```

A rule has a name (`YoungDriver`), some metadata/properties (**property** `priority = 0`), an if/when/condition part (**when**`{?driver: Driver (age < 25);}`), and a then/action part (**then** `{System.out. println("Found a young driver:" + ?driver);}`). This rule will fire for those instances of class `Driver` found in working memory, whose `age` attribute is smaller than 25. For each such driver, the rule will print the string "Found a young driver:" followed by the output of the `toString()` method on that object. The expression `Driver(age < 25)` is called a *class condition*, where the class name is `Driver`, and the condition is `age < 25` where age in this case refers to a *public* data member of the class $Driver$. The expression $'"?driver : ..."$ is a *variable binding*, where $?driver$ is the variable name. In this case, $?driver$ will be bound to an instance of $Driver$ that matches the condition $age < 25$, and becomes referencable in subsequent conditions or actions of the rule. The action part of the rule shows some vanilla-flavor Java. Indeed, we can use pretty much any Java expression in the action part, with the following limitations:

1. The underlying object model ("vocabulary") is the BOM and not the XOM. This means that only the classes that are part of the BOM are "referencable."[2] For example, if the underlying Java class $Driver$ has a pair of getter/setter for attribute age, in IRL, we set the value of age using the dot notation ($?driver.age = 24$), i.e., by manipulating the BOM class, as opposed to using the setter ($?driver.setAge(24)$). Further, we can refer to virtual classes and virtual class members (see Sect. 10.3.3), which do not exist in the real world (Java).
2. The definition of complex types (classes, interfaces, enums) is not supported, but who would do such a thing in the action part of a rule, anyway.
3. Some exotic expressions are not supported, e.g., the instantiation of anonymous Java classes.

Consider now this next rule:

```
rule big_claim_over_90_days_past_exp_date_policy {
  property effectiveDate = java.util.Date("1/1/2010");
  property expirationDate = java.util.Date("12/31/2010");
  property status = "development";
  when {
    ?myPolicy: Policy(?bDate: beginDate; ?eDate: endDate);
    ?claim: Claim(amount > 1000; date.before (?bDate) ||
                              date.moreThan(90,?eDate);
                              policy == ?myPolicy);
  } then {
    ?claim.status = Claim.REJECTED;
    update ?claim;
    System.out.println(?claim+ " is rejected because ..." +
                              ?myPolicy);
  }
}
```

---

[2] When we build a BOM entry from a Java project, we not only "import" the classes from that project, but we also "import" commonly useful classes from the Java library including basic types, collections, java.util.Date, java.util.Calendar, etc. These additional classes constitute what JRules calls the *boot bom*. Empty BOM entries actually are not empty: they contain the *boot bom*. The default boot bom can be changed.

More often than not, rules have *effectiveness periods* during which they are in force. Rules can expire if they are replaced by new rules, or if they embody a time-limited policy such as limited-duration promotional campaigns and such. The property status is used to assign a development status to a rule. Indeed, like other software artifacts, rules will undergo a *development lifecycle* starting with the coding of the rule (status = "development") to its testing, from which a rule can either be rejected or promoted to production. A rule that is in production may return to development, for debugging or maintenance, or retirement – if it is superseded by new rules. We will talk about rule governance in Chaps. 16 and 17.

Consider now the condition part of the rule. This rule has two *class conditions* which are considered to be ANDed. The first class condition (?myPolicy: Policy(...);) is actually no condition: It will match *any* Policy object in working memory, and will bind the values of its beginDate and endDate attributes to the variables ?bDate and ?eDate. The second class condition on **Claim** consists of three test/conditions, also considered to be ANDed: (a) a condition on the amount (amount > 1000), (b) a condition on the date of the claim, which says that the date of the claim is *either* prior to the beginning of the policy *or* is more than 90 days past ?eDate, i.e., more than 90 days past the endDate of ?myPolicy (date.before (?bDate) || date.moreThan(90,?eDate)), and (c) a condition tying ?myPolicy to ?claim. The last condition (policy == ?myPolicy) ensures that, should the working memory of the engine contain several policies and several claims, the rule only matches < ?claim,?myPolicy > pairs that are related. In JRules-speak, the last *two* conditions are called *join conditions* because they relate two objects together.

The action part of this rule shows three statements. The first and third statements look like regular Java. The second statement (**update** ?claim) tells the engine to reevaluate the rules involving the object ?claim. Indeed, the engine needs to be told explicitly which objects may have changed in a way that might match new rules, or invalidate existing ones.[3]

Let us take a first shot at the grammar for technical rules, using a mixture of EBNF[4] and regular expressions:

---

[3]Recall the discussion in Sect. 6.3.2 regarding the engine notification. The good news is that BAL rule authors do not need to worry about this, because this behavior can be configured at the BOM level. Indeed, we can set up a particular data member setter (or void function member) to automatically trigger an update when used in the action part of a rule. We will come back to this in the next section when we talk about BAL to IRL translation.

[4]EBNF stands for Extended Backus-Naur Form. People familiar with Yacc or ANTLR will recognize the syntax. Things that are supposed to appear as-is (language keywords) appear between quotes. Things that are optional appear between square brackets ([optional]). Groups of things that can appear zero or more times appear as (...)*.

- TECHNICAL RULE ::= "**rule**" RULE_NAME "{" (RULE_PROPERTY)*
  "**when** {" CONDITIONS "} then {" ACTIONS "}}"
- RULE_PROPERTY ::= "**property**" PROP_NAME "=" PROP_VALUE ";"
- CONDITIONS ::= CONDITION (CONDITION)*
- CONDITION ::= CLASS_CONDITION | EXISTS_COND | NOT_COND |
  COLLECTION_COND | EVALUATE_COND | WAIT_COND
- CLASS_CONDITION ::= [VAR_NAME ":"] SIMPLE_CLASS_COND ";"
- SIMPLE_CLASS_COND ::= CLASS_NAME "(" TEST_BIND_LIST ")"
  [SCOPE_EXPRESSION]
- SCOPE_EXPRESSION ::= "**from**" SINGLE_OBJ_EXPRESSION | "**in**"
  COLLECTION_OBJ_EXPRESSION
- TEST_BIND_LIST ::= TEST_OR_BINDING (";" TEST_OR_BINDING)*
- TEST_OR_BINDING::= TEST | BINDING
- NOT_COND ::= "**not**" SIMPLE_CLASS_COND ";"
- EXISTS_COND ::= "**exists**" SIMPLE_CLASS_COND ";"
- EVAL_COND ::= "**evaluate(**" TEST_BIND_LIST ");"
- COLLECTION_COND ::= [VAR_NAME ":"] "**collect**"
  SIMPLE_CLASS_COND ["**where(**" TEST_BIND_LIST ")"] ";"

- ACTIONS ::= ACTION (ACTION)*

We will say a few words about the different types of conditions. This will help us understand the BAL to IRL translations, to be discussed in the next section. Consider the following condition:

```
rule no_expensive_claims_in_WM {
  when {not Claim(amount > 1000);}
  then {System.out.println("No expensive claims in WM");}
}
```

The condition part is satisfied if there are no claims in working memory worth more than 1,000. Similary, the rule:

```
rule there_are_expensive_claims_in_WM {
  when {exists Claim(amount > 1000);}
  then {System.out.println("there are expensive claims in
WM");}
}
```

will fire *once* if there exist claims worth more than 1,000. In particular, if there are one or a hundred such claims, the rule will still fire only once. Contrast that with

```
rule found_an_expensive_claims_in_WM {
  when {Claim(amount > 1000);}
  then {System.out.println("found expensive claim in WM");}
}
```

which will fire for *every* claim in working memory that is worth more than 1,000.

Consider now the following rule:

```
rule policy_with_no_expensive_claims {
  when {
    ?myPolicy: Policy();
    not Claim(amount > 1000) in ?myPolicy.getClaims();
    } then {
    System.out.println("Policy with expensive claims");
    }
}
```

In this case, we look for a policy in working memory, and check that there are *no* claims, *for that policy* (**in** ?myPolicy.getClaims()) that are worth more than 1,000. The expression "**in** ?myPolicy.getClaims()" corresponds to what we referred to in the grammar as SCOPE_EXPRESSION. We use **in** when the scope is a collection (?myPolicy.getClaims()) and **from** when the scope is a single object.

Let us now illustrate an example of COLLECTION_CONDITION. Consider the following rule:

```
rule policy_with_more_than_3_at_fault_claims {
  when {
    ?myPolicy: Policy();
    ?claims: collect Claim(amount > 1000;
     responsibility == AT_FAULT) in ?myPolicy.getClaims()
                          where (size() > 3);
  } then {
  System.out.println(?myPolicy + " had more than 3 " +
                     "at-fault claims worth more than 1000");
  }

}
```

In this case, the variable ?claims will contain a collection[5] of the claims of ?myPolicy that are worth more than 1,000, with AT_FAULT responsibility. The "**where**" clause indicates conditions on the collection, in this case (size() > 3).

We conclude our overview of IRL by an illustration of the **evaluate** condition. The **evaluate** condition is a convenience construct that enables us to group variable bindings and tests outside of a class condition. For example, the rule big_claim_over_90_days_past_exp_date_policy shown above can be written as follows using an **evaluate**:

---

[5]The exact type is ilog.rules.engine.IlrCollection, which is a *dynamic collection* in the sense that objects will be automatically removed from the collection as soon as they no longer satisfy the conditions that got them in.

```
rule big_claim_over_90_days_past_exp_date_policy {
  property effectiveDate = java.util.Date("1/1/2010");
  property expirationDate = java.util.Date("12/31/2010");
  property status = "development";
  when {
    ?myPolicy: Policy();
    ?claim: Claim();
    evaluate(?bDate: ?myPolicy.beginDate;
             ?eDate : ?myPolicy.endDate;
             ?claim.amount > 1000;
             ?claim.date.before(?bDate) ||
             ?claim.date.moreThan(90,?eDate);
             ?claim.policy == ?myPolicy);
  } then {
    ...
  }
}
```

In other words, we took all of the bindings and tests out of the class conditions, and grouped them in the (external) **evaluate** condition. The Boolean value of an **evaluate** is the conjunction of the individual tests contained within. In fact, the technical rules generated from BAL rules look like this (more about the BAL to IRL translation in the next section). Note that, considering that the conditions clauses of a rule are ANDed, the **evaluate** enables us to write disjunctions between tests that are part of different class conditions.

In this section, we skimmed the surface of the IRL language. There are a number of rule-specific constructs that can be used within the condition and action parts of a rule that we did not talk about:

1. Constructs for event management: The IRL (and the JRules rule engine) enables us to reason about time and events. For example, we can write a rule that says "if event A occurred, wait 5 s for event B to occur, if it does, do X, if you time out, do Y."

2. Constructs for truth maintenance: There are situations where rules create objects from within their action parts when their condition part is satisfied. Consider the e xample of a monitoring application that creates an **Alarm** or a **ServiceRequest** object when some parameter of the system or device being monitored goes out of range. With normal rules, if the parameter in question returns to its normal range, the **Alarm** or **ServiceRequest** remains in working memory and will be processed. If we want the **Alarm** or **ServiceRequest** to be retracted if the conditions return to normal, we use specific constructs within the rule.[6]

---

[6]Called *logical conditions* and *logical assert*. The system maintains some sort of a reference-count of *justifications* for Alarm (or ServiceRequest) objects, and we need to redefine the equals method on the class Alarm (or ServiceRequest) accordingly. More can be found in the product documentation.

3. Constructs for working memory management within the action part of rules. Actually, we saw one: the **update** keyword. There is the **insert**, **retract**, **modify**, and **update refresh**. All of these have equivalent methods in the **IlrContext** class. More about these constructs can be found in the product documentation.
4. The **else** clause in rules. Indeed, IRL rules can have an **else** clause, but with a special meaning: the "**else** action part" is executed when all the conditions but the last **evaluate** statement yield true.[7]

Finally, as mentioned above, the IRL is not just for writing technical rules: It is also used to write *functions* and ruleflows. We will talk about ruleflows in Sect. 11.3.2.

11.2.2 BAL and Action Rules

When we deliver trainings, we lose developers at about this point. They tune out and start playing with IRL exploring the limits of the language, raising their heads only to ask questions. Alas, for all its power – we have only scratched the surface – the IRL is not appropriate for business consumption. Business cannot understand IRL rules, cannot relate them to business logic, and cannot own them, by taking over rule development and maintenance; if we code business rules in IRL, we defeat the major tenets of the business rules approach. The *Business Action Language* (BAL) enables all of the above.

The basic structure of a BAL action rule is illustrated below. A *typical* BAL rule has three parts:

1. A *definitions* part, to declare *rule variables* to be referenced in the condition part, the action part, or subsequent definitions
2. An *if* part, which consists of a Boolean expression that typically uses the variables of the rule
3. A *then* part, consisting of one or several actions that typically use the variables of the rule, ending with a semi colon (";")

Business Rule: claim date

▸ General Information	▸ Category Filter
▸ Documentation	

```
Code
    definitions
        set 'current claim' to a claim ;
    if
        'current claim' was filed more than 90 days after the start date of the policy of 'current claim'
    then
        set the decision of 'current claim' to "INELIGIBLE" ;
        log that this rule has fired on 'current claim' with message "Claim filed too late" ;
```

[7]We would not explain it any further, especially that we strongly recommend *not* using else, because it makes rules error prone and the ruleset hard to maintain.

As mentioned earlier, when we talked about the BOM, BAL rules, much like IRL rules, refer to elements of the BOM. However, whereas IRL rules refer *directly* to the BOM elements using a Java-like object notation, BAL rules refer to BOM elements through their *verbalizations*. We show below the corresponding IRL translation.[8]

```
rule claim_date {
    property status = "new";
    when {
        current_claim: Claim();
        evaluate (current_claim.fileMoreThanXDaysAfter(90,
            current_claim.policy.startDate.toDate()));
    } then {
        current_claim.decision = "INELIGIBLE";
        update current_claim;
        current_claim.logRuleFiringWithMessage("Claim filed
too late");
    }
}
```

The BAL definition of the variable "**current claim**" yielded the simple class condition, with an object binding:

```
current_claim: com….Claim();
```

and the condition of the *if* part ended up in a single **evaluate** statement. This is the general translation pattern from BAL to IRL. Lest we oversimplify:
1. *definitions* become simple class conditions.
2. The conditions of the *if* part get lumped into a single **evaluate** statement.
3. The BAL *then* part maps to the (IRL) **then** when part.

Two points are worth noting. First, the reader may have noticed the "**update** current_claim;" action shown in the IRL translation. This action was inserted in the action part of the rule *after* the assignment of a new value to the decision attribute of the BOM class **Claim**, because that attribute had the "Update object state" option checked. Second, the BAL to IRL translator replaced the white space in the variable name ("**current claim**") by an underscore (current_claim) to make the variable name IRL/Java compliant.

In the remaining paragraphs, we will talk briefly about definitions and variables, the condition part, and the action part. Before we do that, we will present the high-level structure of the language in a similar notation to the grammar of the IRL shown in the previous section:

---

[8]In this and subsequent IRL translations, we omitted class package names for presentation purposes. Just be aware that the *real* IRL code shows fully qualified class names in class conditions.

- BAL_RULE ::= [DEFINITION_PART]   [CONDITION_PART]
  ACTION_PART [ELSE_PART]
- DEFINITION_PART ::= "**definitions**" DEFINITION ";"
  (DEFINITION";")*
- CONDITION_PART ::= "**if**" CONDITION ((**and** | **or**)
  CONDITION)*
- ACTION_PART ::= "**then**" ACTION";"(ACTION ";")*
- ELSE_PART ::= "**else**" ACTION";"(ACTION ";")*

Notice that:

1. *Only* the action part is required in a BAL rule; everything else is optional. Thus, the following is a valid BAL rule.

Business Rule: minimal rule

▶ General Information	▶ Category Filter

▶ Documentation

Code

```
then
print "Hello world";
```

2. A BAL rule can have an **else** part. As with the case of IRL, we discourage the use of the **else**, and for similar reasons.
3. The conditions of the condition part can be combined freely using the logical operators **and** and **or**.

We will further expand on the different components as we talk about them.

Definitions and variables. To write conditions and actions on objects, we need to refer to them through *variables*. In BAL (and IRL), there are three different kinds of variables:

1. *Rule variables.* These are variables defined in the rule itself through the DEFI-NITIONS part of the rule. Such variables have rule-scope: They are only visible within the rule, and only live while the rule is being executed.[9] In particular, the names of these variables need only be unique within the context of a single rule; several rules can use the same variable name (e.g., "**current claim**").
2. *Ruleset variables.* These are variables that are defined at the rule project level. They are visible within all of the rules of a project, and they live during one ruleset execution.
3. *Ruleset parameters.* These variables are also defined at the rule project level, and are visible within all of the rules of a project. They are used to pass data in and out of the engine during ruleset execution.

The difference between ruleset *variables* and rule *parameters* is like that between the *local variables* and *parameters* of a function.

---

[9]The lifetime issue is a bit more complex: It spans the evaluation of the condition part and the lifetime of the rule instance, if one is created. See Chap. 6.

We will talk about ruleset variables and parameters in Sect. 11.5. Here we focus on rule variables. The syntax for a rule variable definition can be described as follows:

- DEFINITION ::= "set" VAR_NAME "to"VAR_VALUE ["where" BOOLEAN_EXPRESSION]
- VAR_VALUE ::= CONSTANT | REFERENCED_VAL| ANON_OBJ_VALUE | ANON_OBJ_COLL
- REFERENCED_VAL ::= VAR_NAME | ATTRIBUTE REFERENCED_VAL
- ANON_OBJ_VALUE ::= BOM_TYPE [SCOPE]
- ANON_OBJ_COLL ::= "all" BOM_TYPE [SCOPE]

The following illustrates the first three types of definitions:

```
definitions
    set 'THRESHOLD EXPENSIVE ACT' to 1000 ;
    set 'current claim' to a claim ;
    set 'claimed service act' to a service act in the service acts of 'current claim' ;
    set 'expensive service act' to a service act in the service acts of 'current claim'
            where the cost of this service act is at least 'THRESHOLD EXPENSIVE ACT' ;
    set 'expensive service act cost' to the cost of 'expensive service act' ;
    set 'current policy' to the policy of 'current claim' ;
    set 'young policy holder' to the policy holder of 'current policy'
            where the birth date of this policy holder is after 1/1/1990 ;
then
    print "Illustrating definitions" ;
```

The first definition corresponds to setting a variable to a constant. The next three correspond to setting a variable to an anonymous object value (ANON_OBJ_VALUE), with three variants: (a) simplest, (b) with scope, and (c) with scope and test. The last three definitions correspond to REFERENCED_VAL . The first ('expensive service act cost') illustrates the case where we create a variable to hold the value of a *scalar* attribute. The last two ('current policy' and 'young policy holder') show the case of a variable that holds the value of an attribute that is a domain object, without and with a condition. The following shows the IRL translation for the first five definitions:

```
evaluate (THRESHOLD_EXPENSIVE_ACT : 1000);
current_claim: Claim();
claimed_service_act: ServiceAct() in
                        current_claim.serviceActList;
expensive_service_act: ServiceAct(?this.cost >= (float)
THRESHOLD_EXPENSIVE_ACT ) in current_claim.serviceActList;
evaluate (expensive_service_act_cost :
                        expensive_service_act.cost);
```

The reader will notice that variables that are of scalar type are defined using a binding (VAR_NAME ":" VAR_VALUE) embedded within an **evaluate**. The middle three are defined using simple class conditions, with or without embedded tests, and with or without scope (**in** current_claim.some-Attribute).

We now illustrate the definition of collection variables:

```
definitions
    set 'some claim' to a claim ;
    set 'all claims in WM' to all claims ;
    set 'some claim service acts' to all service acts in the service acts of 'some claim' ;
    set 'expensive service acts' to all service acts in the service acts of 'some claim'
                where the cost of each service act is at least 1000 ;
then
    print "illustrating collections" ;
```

And we show below the resulting IRL:

```
some_claim: Claim();
all_claims_in_WM: collect Claim();
some_claim_service_acts: collect ServiceAct() in
                                some_claim.serviceActList;
expensive_service_acts: collect
                ServiceAct(?this.cost >= 1000) in
                                some_claim.serviceActList;
```

What can you do with collections? You can test the contents of a collection or its size, in the condition part, or iterate over its elements to apply a bunch of actions, in the action part. We will illustrate both uses in the subsequent discussion.

The condition part. Roughly speaking, the condition part of a rule consists of a logical combination of individual conditions using the logical operators **and** and **or**. In turn, each "top-level" condition can itself be a single Boolean term or a logical formula, with operators **and**'s, **or**'s, and parentheses. This is embodied in the next four grammar productions (rules).

- CONDITION_PART ::= "**if**" CONDITION ((**and** | **or**) CONDITION) *
- CONDITION ::= BOOLEAN_TERM | BOOLEAN_TERM (**and** | **or**) CONDITION
- BOOLEAN_TERM ::= BOOLEAN_TEST | "(" CONDITION ")"
- BOOLEAN_TEST ::= COMPARISON | PREDICATE | SET_MEMBERSHIP | COLLECTION_TEST |

Next, we will show examples of the various Boolean tests.[10]

```
definitions                          Set membership
    set 'current claim' to a claim ;
    set 'service act' to a service act in the service acts of 'current claim' ;    comparisons
if
    the total claimed of 'current claim' is more than 1000
    and the decision of 'current claim' is not one of { "VALID" , "ELIGIBLE" }
    and ( the birth date of the policy holder of the policy of 'current claim' is after 1/1/1980
    or ( 'current claim' was filed more than 90 days after the end date of the policy of 'current claim'
    or the date of 'current claim' is before the start date of the policy of 'current claim' )
    or there are at least 5 coverages in the coverages of the policy of 'current claim'
            where the percent cap used up of each coverage is at least 95 ,
    or there is no coverage in the coverages of the policy of 'current claim'
            where the procedure of this coverage is the procedure of 'service act' , )
then
    set the decision of 'current claim' to "INELIGIBLE" ;
    print "illustrating conditions" ;                    Collection conditions

Predicate
```

---

[10]*Please* do not write rules like this one at home ☺: This rule breaks every rule writing guideline we mentioned in Chap. 9. It is only meant to illustrate various syntactic constructs.

With the exception of collection conditions (COLLECTION_TEST), which we will address shortly, we build Boolean tests by selecting an object (a variable) or the attribute of an object, then a comparison operator (or a predicate) appropriate for that object, and then an operand of the appropriate type. In the rule above (which is utterly non-sensical), we show three comparisons. The first compares a numerical data member (total claimed of **'current claim'**) to a constant (1,000). The second compares a date attribute (the birth date of the policy holder of the policy of **'current claim'**) to a constant date (1/1/1990), while the third compares a date attribute (the date of **'current claim'**) to *another* date attribute (the start date of the policy of **'current claim'**). The case of a predicate is illustrated by the condition **'current claim'** was filed more than 90 days after <some date>. The SET_MEMBERSHIP case is illustrated by the condition the decision of **'current claim'** is not one of {**"VALID"**, **"ELIGIBLE"**}. Set membership tests (is not one of and is one of) are available for all types (simple types, object types) and the values of the set can be enumerated *literally*, as in this example, or given as a collection variable.

Let us look now at the collection conditions. The BAL offers several types of conditions on collections, which may be described using the following grammar:

- COLLECTION_TEST   ::=   QUANTIFIED_COLLECTION_TEST |
  COLLECTION_SIZE_TEST | COLLECTION_CONTENT_TEST
- QUANTIFIED_COLLECTION_TEST ::= QUANTIFIER [NUMBER]
  OBJ_TYPE [scope] ["where" COLLECTION_ELEMENT_TEST]
- QUANTIFIER::= **"there are"** | **"there are at least"** | **"there
  are at most"** | **"there are more than"** | **"there are less
  than"** | **"there is no"** | **"there is at least one"** | **"there
  is one"** | **"there is at most one"**
- COLLECTION_SIZE_TEST ::= **"the number of"** OBJ_TYPE [scope]
  ["where" COLLECTION_ELEMENT_TEST] COMP_OPERATOR NUMBER
- COLLECTION_CONTENT_TEST ::= COLLECTION_NAME (**"contain"** |
  "does not contain") OBJECT

Behind the scenes (IRL), all of these conditions map to an IRL COLLECTION_CONDITION, but with different tests on the collection size (QUANTIFIED_COLLECTION_TEST and COLLECTION_SIZE_TEST) and collection contents (COLLECTION_CONTENT_TEST). The rule above shows two examples, using the "**there are at least**" and "**there is no**" forms. The following shows the IRL equivalent[11]:

---

[11]We simplified the underlying IRL to make it more readable, by: (a) removing class package names, (b) reducing the number of extraneous parentheses, and (c) simplifying/faking the way Date constants are handled.

```
when {
  current_claim: Claim();
  service_act: ServiceAct() in current_claim.serviceActList;
  var$_$0: collect Coverage(?this.percentCapUsedUp >= 95) in
                           current_claim.policy.coverageList;
  var$_$1: collect
    Coverage(?this.procedure.equals(service_act.procedure))
                    in current_claim.policy.coverageList;
  evaluate (
    current_claim.totalClaimed > 1000
    && current_claim.decision !in {"VALID","ELIGIBLE"}
    && (current_claim.policy.policyHolder.birth-
           Date.compareTo(new IlrDate(1990,1,1)) > 0
      || (current_claim.fileMoreThanXDaysAfter(90,
                 current_claim.policy.endDate)
        || current_claim.date.compareTo(
                 current_claim.policy.startDate) < 0
          )
        || var$_$0.size() >= 5
        || var$_$1.size() == 0
      )
      );
  } then {
      ...
      }
```

The reader will notice that all of the conditions of the *if* part of the BAL rule ended up in the single **evaluate** statement.

There is more to BAL conditions than what we just covered. Our goal in this section is to show the "philosophy" of the BAL language. The full language reference is available in the product documentation.

BAL Actions. BAL actions are fairly straightforward. They can be of five different types:

- ACTION ::= SIMPLE_ACTION | FOREACH_COMPOUND_ACTION
- SIMPLE_ACTION ::= ATTRIBUTE_SETTER | VOID_FUNCTION_ACTION | VARIABLE_SETTER | SYSTEM_ACTION
- ATTRIBUTE_SETTER ::= "set" ATTRIBUTE_EXPRESSION "to" ATTRIBUTE_VALUE
- VARIABLE_SETTER ::= "set" VAR_NAME "to" VAR_VALUE
- FOR_EACH_COMPOUND_ACTION ::= "for each" OBJ_TYPE ["called" VAR_NAME ","] in COLLECTION ":" "-" SIMPLE_ACTION ("-" SIMPLE_ACTION)*

The previous rule examples illustrated ATTRIBUTE_SETTER (e.g., "set the decision of 'current claim' to "INELIGIBLE";"), SYSTEM_ACTION (e.g., "*print* "illustrating conditions";"), and VOID_FUNCTION_ACTION (e.g., "log that this rule has fired on 'current claim' with message "Claim filed too late";"). The next rule illustrates the compound statement.

```
definitions
    set 'current claim' to a claim where the decision of this claim is "ELIGIBLE";
    set 'service acts' to the service acts of 'current claim' ;
then
    for each service act called 'my service act' , in 'service acts'   :
    - set the payment of 'my service act' to the cost of 'my service act'
    - print "the procedure" + the procedure of 'my service act' + " was paid in full" ;
    set the decision of 'current claim' to "PAID";
    print "illustrating for each" ;
```

and the (simplified) IRL equivalent:

```
when {
    current_claim: Claim(?this.decision.equals("ELIGIBLE"));
    service_acts: collect ServiceAct() in
                                current_claim.serviceActList;}
then {
    foreach (ServiceAct my_service_act in service_acts) {
        my_service_act.payment = my_service_act.cost;
        printMessage("the procedure"+ my_service_act.procedure +
                                    "was paid in full"));
    }
    current_claim.decision = "PAID";
    update current_claim;
    printMessage("illustrating for each");
}
```

The BAL is used in many other places, besides *action rules*. It is used to write preconditions, condition and action columns in decision tables (to be discussed next), preconditions, node conditions and actions in decision trees (Sect. 11.2.4), as well as in many places in ruleflows (function tasks, initial and final actions in all ruleflow tasks, transition guards, and rule selection, see Sect. 11.3.2).

11.2.3   Decision Tables

As mentioned in Sect. 9.2.2.2, when we have several rules whose conditions test on the same set of attributes and whose actions perform the same actions (modulo some parameter values), it pays to organize those rules in a *decision table*, both during rule analysis (see Chap. 4) and during rule authoring. JRules supports decision tables, like most BRMS. Figure 11.2 shows a decision table that sets the parameters of a coverage (deductible and yearly cap), based on the procedure covered, and on the type of policy (individual versus group policy). This table has four columns, two *conditions columns*, labeled "Covered Procedure" and "Policy Type", and two *action columns*, labeled "Deductible" and "Yearly Cap". Each line of the table corresponds to a rule. Here, we selected the line number 6, which corresponds to the case where the procedure is ECG (Electro-CardioGram), the policy type is "GROUP". In this case, the deductible is $20, and the yearly cap is $125 (per insured). As shown in the screenshot, by selecting a particular row of the

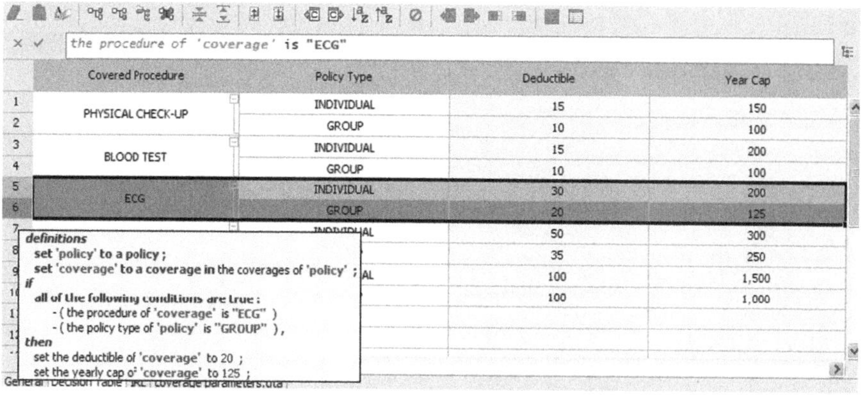

Fig. 11.2 A sample decision table

decision table, Rule Studio brings up a tool tip consisting of the BAL equivalent of the rule represented by that row.

Let us first get some vocabulary. Notice that for each value of "Covered Procedure", we have two possible values of "Policy Type". Each value of "Policy Type" is considered as a *branch* of the corresponding value of "Covered Procedure". The set of covered procedures {"PHYSICAL CHECK-UP", "BLOOD TEST", ECG, "X-RAY", and "CAT SCAN"} is said to represent a *partition* of the domain of procedures. Similarly, the set {INDIVIDUAL, GROUP} is said to represent a *partition* of the domain of the attribute "policyType" of the class Coverage. This table is called *symmetrical* because the same *partition* of "Policy Type" is used for all the values of "Covered Procedure". We now show how the table is defined.

Figure 11.3a shows the wizard for defining condition columns. A condition column enables us to enter a Boolean condition similar to the kinds of conditions we enter in a BAL action rule. The condition should be fully specified except for one (or several) value(s), which needs to be specified in the cells of the columns. In this case, the condition is "the procedure of `coverage` is <a procedure>", and we need only specify <a procedure> in the cells of the column. The column has an editable title. We can also specify conditions that column cell values must satisfy – in addition to being of the appropriate type, which is guaranteed by the table editor. Similarly, for the second condition column, the test is "the policy type of `policy` is <a policy type>."

Figure 11.3b shows the wizard for defining action columns. The action corresponds to any valid action we can insert in the action part of a rule (see previous section), with the exception of FOR_EACH_COMPOUND_ACTION (see previous section). Depending on the parameters of the action, the action column can have two or more subcolumns. In this case, the action is a setter that takes a single value. The second action column is defined in a similar way: The action is "set the yearly cap of `coverage` to <a number>." Notice that we can specify a *default value* for an action parameter. We can also specify additional

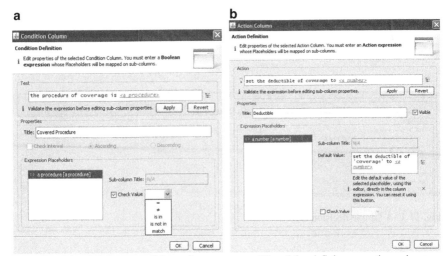

Wizard for defining a condition column   Wizard for defining an action column

Fig. 11.3 Wizards for defining condition and action columns. (**a**) Wizard for defining a condition column and (**b**) wizard for defining an action column

constraints on the cell values, in a way similar to values in condition columns. Finally, we can make an action column invisible.[12]

The reader may wonder where the variables that are referenced in the condition and action columns (**coverage** and **policy**) come from. The answer is: *preconditions* of the table. Generally speaking, preconditions are used to define variables and to enter conditions that hold true for all of the columns of the table. Figure 11.4 shows a screenshot of the *tab* used to define preconditions.

We will not discuss all of the wizardry of the decision table editor. However, a few features are worth mentioning:

- JRules performs different kinds of verifications and analyses on decision tables, and the results of these analyses can be presented as "Info", "Warning", or "Error":
  - *Symmetry.* A table is said to be symmetrical if for each condition column i, the same *partition* of values for that column is used consistently for all the values of column $i-1$. As mentioned above, the table shown in Fig. 11.2 is symmetrical because the same partition {"INDIVIDUAL", "GROUP"} for "Policy Type" is used for the values of "Covered Procedure."
  - *Overlap.* This refers to the case where the values "within a partition" overlap.[13] In the table of Fig. 11.2, we would have had an overlap if, for

---

[12]This is useful in those situations where (a) all the cells have the same value, or (b) the action takes no arguments – and thus no values to enter – or (c) the action represents a non-business tasks that business rule authors should not care about.

[13]This is a misnomer because mathematically speaking, the *partition* of a set S is a set of *non-overlapping* subsets of S whose union equals S.

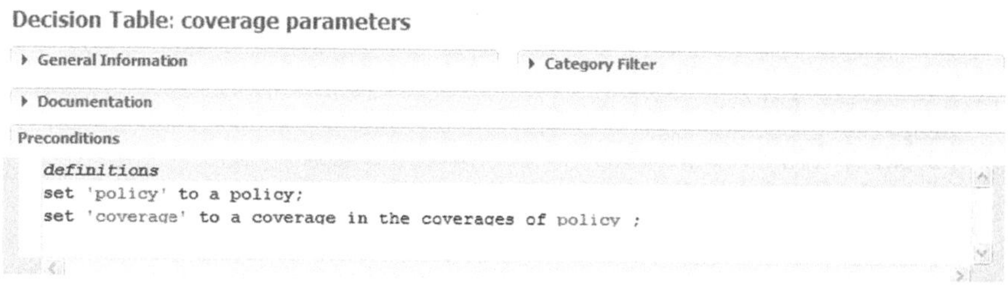

Decision Table: coverage parameters

Fig. 11.4 Defining preconditions for a table

example, row 5 had both "INDIVIDUAL" and "GROUP", and row 6 had "GROUP". If that were the case, when procedure="ECG" and policy type = "GROUP", we would hit both rows 5 and 6 of the table. This is not a *logical* error, but more often than not, overlaps result from data entry errors.

- *Gaps.* Gaps are best illustrated with a numerical (range) condition column (not used here). Assume that we have a condition column based on age ranges. If our condition had age ranges [0,18], [18,30], and [65,100], then one might wonder about the age range [30,65]: What happens in such situations? Again, this is not a *definite logical* error per se, but, more often than not, indicative of a data entry error.
- JRules can enforce *locking* different aspects of the table:
  - *Preconditions.* Making sure that the preconditions part is not editable.
  - *Number of* columns. We can prevent the addition and removal of condition columns, action columns, or both.
  - *Condition column contents.* For each condition column, we can selectively lock the *tests* (preventing users from changing the column test, or column cell overrides), the *partitions*, i.e., how many different values in the partition, or the *values* themselves. In our case, if we lock the *partition* of column "Policy Type", it means that we can have *exactly* two cells/branches for every procedure, but the table author can select which values to enter in each cell. If we lock the *values* for the column, it means that values themselves are not editable, i.e., nothing about the column can be changed.
  - *Action column contents.* With action columns, we can lock the *action*, the *status*, or the *values*.
- JRules supports the graphical customization of the table. Indeed, we can change the background color, text color, text font, text style, and text size, for column headers, condition columns, and action columns (separately).

JRules supports a bunch of other features for data entry (e.g., splitting cells, merging cells, inserting the values of a *BOM domain*, etc.) that make life easier for table authors.

Looking under the hood, decision tables are actually encoded as ... a bunch of IRL rules, one per row! The following shows the beginning of the IRL file for the table of Fig. 11.2. The rule `coverage_parameters_0` represents the first row of the table, i.e., row 0. There are 10 such rules, each one corresponding to a different combination of procedure and policyType values.

```
// begin DT coverage parameters
// -- begin rule 'coverage parameters 0'
rule coverage_parameters_0 {
    property ilog.rules.dt = "coverage parameters";
    property ilog.rules.group = "coverage_parameters";
    property status = "new";
    when {
        policy: com.mywebinsurance.claimprocessing.Policy();
        coverage: com.mywebinsurance.claimprocessing.Coverage()
in policy.coverageList;
        evaluate ((((coverage.procedure.equals("PHYSICAL CHECK-
UP"))) && ((policy.policyType.equals("INDIVIDUAL"))))));
    } then {
        coverage.deductible = 15;
        coverage.yearlyCap = 150;
    }
}

// -- end rule 'coverage parameters 0'
// -- begin rule 'coverage parameters 1'
rule coverage_parameters_1 {
...
```

At first glance, this may not sound like the most efficient implementation. Indeed, the table format "leads us to believe" that conditions are shared between different rows and the tests are performed only once. For example, the first and second rows of the table share the same value for procedure, i.e., "PHYSICAL CHECK-UP", but if each row is represented by a separate rule, then we lose the condition sharing. Actually, not so! Recall from Chap. 6 that the RETE algorithm ensures that if two rules start with the same condition, that condition will be shared and it will be evaluated only once for both of them. Hence, once the ruleset containing this table is parsed and the RETE network is built from it, conditions will be shared, as suggested by the table.

As mentioned in Chap. 9, JRules provides API for creating decision tables and decision trees – to be discussed next – from tabular data,[14] including csv (comma-separated values) files, Excel spreadsheets, and relational data bases. A few years back (2005), in one project for a Wall Street financial services company, we used decision tables to encode rules that figure out which kinds of financial transactions for specific types of foreign customers were subject to IRS reporting and withholding.[15] Our input from "business" was a bunch of Excel spreadsheets

---

[14]Check root package ilog.rules.dt, and more specifically, ilog.rules.dt.model.

[15]The Internal Revue Service expects all US entities (corporations, individuals) to file for taxes every year, and it has the necessary authority and ... hum ... leverage to make sure they comply. With foreign entities, because it lacks such "leverage", it requires that a percentage of their gains on *each transaction* be preemptively withheld (typically 30%, but sometimes 15% or 10%) or reported ... unless, of course ... (a few hundred rules and exceptions based on type of entity, country of origin, existence of treaties, type of transaction, etc.).

prepared by tax accountants. After a minor clean-up, we were actually able to load up the spreadsheets using the API, saving countless hours of data entry, but more importantly, getting rid of a major source of errors. Since JRules 7.x, there is out of the box functionality (*Rule Solutions for Office*) to *export* decision tables from Rule Team Server (RTS) as Excel 2007 spreadsheets, and to *import* them back after editing.

11.2.4 Decision Trees

The same kinds of situations that call for decision tables can also be handled by decision trees. As mentioned in Chap. 9, you may find that business people actually think in terms of decision trees, but encode the decision tree in the form of a table. With JRules decision trees, they can encode them the way they see them. However, there are situations where decision tables would be too rigid. Going back to our example decision table, it may the case that, (a) for *some* procedures, we actually do not care about the type of policy as the same deductible and yearly cap apply whether the policy is INDIVIDUAL or GROUP, and (b) for some others, the deductible and yearly cap do not only depend on the type of policy, but also depends on the number of insured. To encode such a situation with a decision table, we will need three condition columns but some columns will have empty values. Here, a *decision tree* comes in handy as different *branches* of the three can have different *tests* and different *depths*. Further, a decision tree allows different rule/action nodes to have different sets of actions; doing the same with decision tables would require some acrobatics. Figure 11.5 shows such a decision tree where we have branches of depth 1, 2, and 3. Each leaf node (box) represents the action part of a rule whose condition part consists of the path leading to that node. As was the case with decision tables, behind the scenes, decision trees are actually encoded as

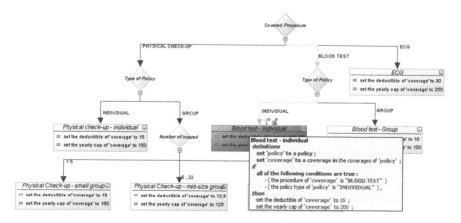

Fig. 11.5 A sample decision tree for computing coverage parameters

separate IRL rules. With regard to condition sharing, as explained for the case of decision tables, because of the structure of the RETE network (see Chap. 6), common conditions will indeed be shared between the different rules. In fact, the encoding of the rules of the decision tree in the RETE network mirrors the decision tree!

As is the case with decision tables, JRules enables us to check for gaps and overlaps between the different branches of the tree. In terms of GUI wizardry to create decision trees, the reader is referred to the product documentation. We will mention, however, that the decision tree editor enables us to fold rule nodes or entire tree branches, and to turn the tree sideways, with the root on the left side of the panel, and the branches going rightward. Both of these tricks enable us to somehow manage the expansive nature of decision trees: more often than not, the decision table format is much more compact than the decision tree format. However, business users love the visuals: They fit nicely in PowerPoint presentations☺.

11.2.5 *Score Cards*

In the insurance and financial services sector, an important rule-rich business process is *underwriting*. Simply speaking, underwriting consists of assessing the eligibility of an actual or potential customer to receive a product or service. An important aspect of underwriting is *risk scoring*. You use risk scoring when the underwriting is a multi-criteria decision – as it often is. In such a case, no single criterion is eliminatory, but the accumulation of factors, positive or negative, can tip the balance one way or the other. With risk scoring, you assign a single score to the (potential) customer based on a set of criteria. If the score falls below a certain threshold, the product or service is denied. Else, it is granted.

JRules supports *scorecards* through a product add-on called *Scorecard Modeler*. Figure 11.6 shows an example of a scorecard for *policy underwriting*. In this fictitious example, we assign a score to a (potential) policy holder based on four criteria: (a) the age, (b) the number of claims when the policy holder was at-fault in the past 3 years, (c) the number of claims of the policy holder in the past 3 years, *regardless* of responsibility, and (d) the number of years of driving experience. The higher the score, the better (i.e., lower) the risk. The first three columns assign the score per se. The last two are used to customize what is called *reasoning strategy*, to be discussed below. For the driver's age, we assign different scores to different age ranges: the highest the risk, the lower the score. Drivers between the ages of 25 and 75 are considered to possess the best mix of qualities (e.g., sobriety, reflexes). With regard to the number of claims, at-fault or in general, the smaller the number of claims, the higher the score. With regard to the driving experience, the longer the experience, the higher the score. With this scorecard, a driver who is 30 years old, with one at-fault claim and one not at-fault claim, and 11 years of driving experience,

Attribute	Range	Score	Expected Score	Reason Code
Driver age	< 18	0	50.0	YOUNG DRIVER (LT 18)
	18 ≤ Driver age < 25	20	50.0	YOUNG DRIVER LT 25
	25 ≤ Driver age < 75	50	50.0	
	≥ 75	30	50.0	SENIOR DRIVER
At fault claims last 3 years	< 1	100	100.0	NO AT FAULT CLAIMS
	1 ≤ At fault claims last 3 years < 3	40	100.0	
	≥ 3	0	100.0	WRECK ON WHEELS
Claims last 3 years	< 1	100	70.0	
	1 ≤ Claims last 3 years < 3	60	70.0	
	≥ 3	0	70.0	WRECK ON WHEELS
Years driving experience	< 1	0	40.0	NOVICE DRIVER
	1 ≤ Years driving experience < 3	20	40.0	MODERATE EXPERIENCE
	3 ≤ Years driving experience < 10	30	40.0	
	≥ 10	50	40.0	

General | Scorecard | IRL | riskScoring.sct

Fig. 11.6 A sample scorecard

would get a total score of: 50 (for age) + 40 (at-fault claims) + 60 (claims in general) + 50 (driving experience), for a total of 200. A 23-year-old driver, with no claims, and 5 years of driving experience would get: 20 (for age) + 100 (at-fault claims) + 100 (claims) + 30 (driving experience), for a total of 250.

Which driver to accept (or reject), if any? As mentioned in Chap. 9, all of the parameters of the scorecard, including which attributes to use for scoring, how many ranges to use for each attribute, what are the bounds for each range, what score to use for each range, how to compute the overall score (simple sum versus weighted sum), and *what the decision threshold should be*, are determined by statistical models.[16] For example, MyWebInsurance may have a policy to under- write only those drivers who have less than 5% chance of making a claim worth more than $5,000 within the first year. Statistical score models will tell, among the many things mentioned above, what the threshold score should be.

With regard to the *reasoning*, Scorecards make it possible to not only return an overall score, but to also return *reason codes* to explain a particular score. Scorecard Modeler maintains lists of reason codes that can be used within a particular scorecard. In the most trivial approach, we could use one reason code *per row* of the scorecard, and ask that *all* reason codes be returned. Most business applications do not care about *that* level of precision. Instead, business may find it useful to identify those attributes that have unusually (or damningly) low scores.

Scorecard Modeler offers a number of "knobs" to tune the *reasoning strategy*: We can specify a maximum number of reason codes, and doing so, we need to specify criteria for determining which reason codes to return in case we have

---

[16]As is the case with statistical models, it is part science (mostly), part art. Note that the JRules Scorecard Modeler does not support those statistical analyses: They need to be done using other tools such as the SAS Enterprise Miner™.

more candidates than the maximum, and how to order them. Possible criteria for figuring out which reason codes to include: (a) reason code priority (they have one), (b) deviation relative to maximum score, (c) deviation based on expected score, or (d) custom reasoning strategy. For deviation, we can take positive deviation, or negative deviation or both. In the example of Fig. 11.6, we used *negative deviation* relative to *expected score*, meaning that we return reason codes for the attributes ranges that are farthest below the expected score. The fourth column of the scorecard shows the expected score. With regard to the ordering, we can start with reason codes corresponding to the highest deviation (i.e., worst outliers) or smallest. There are also rules for handling duplicates. And so forth.

If we look under the hood of a Scorecard, we find four IRL rules, one per attribute, that look like the rule below.[17] This rule, which is not meant for human consumption, sets the reasoning parameters in the action part, and assigned scores for the different ranges of the attribute in the action part using "**if**" statements.

```
// -- begin rule 'riskScoring_1'
rule riskScoring_1 {
  property ilog.rules.group = "riskScoring";
  property status = "new";
  when {
      scorecard: Scorecard() from riskScoring;
      PolicyHolder() from theClaim.policy.policyHolder;
      evaluate (scorecard.rejection == null);
  } then {
      scorecard.name = "riskScoring";
      scorecard.scoringStrategy = "Sum";
      scorecard.reasoningStrategy = "Deviation based on ex-
pected score";
      scorecard.reasonOrderBy = "Descending deviation";
      scorecard.reasonFilterBy = "Negative deviation";
      // -- other reasoning strategy parameters
      ...
      if(theClaim.policy.policyHolder.numberAtFaultClaimsLas
tThreeYears < 1) {
          scorecard.setScore("numberAtFaultClaimsLastThree-
                                        Years", 100);
          scorecard.setReasonCode("numberAtFaultClaimsLast-
              ThreeYears","NO AT FAULT CLAIMS");
      }
      if(theClaim.policy.policyHolder.numberAtFaultClaimsLas
tThreeYears in [1, 3[) {
          scorecard.setScore("numberAtFaultClaimsLastThree-
                                        Years", 40);
      }
      ...
```

[17]We greatly simplified the actual IRL to make it readable. The actual IRL has more actions, and some of the functions have more parameters.

The business logic implemented by Scorecard can easily be implemented by individual (business-friendly) BAL action rules, one per attribute, per range, such as the following:

```
definitions
    set 'my policy' to a policy ;
    set 'my policy holder' to the policy holder of 'my policy' ;
if
    the number at fault claims in the last three years of 'my policy holder' is 0
then
    add 100 to the score of 'my policy' ;
    add the reason code "NO AT FAULT CLAIMS" to 'my policy' ;
```

We could also use one decision table per attribute. The scorecard solution has the advantage of conveniently grouping the various scoring rules into one place, and presenting them in a visually intuitive/appealing fashion. It also enables us to conveniently customize the scoring calculation and manipulate reason codes.

11.2.6 The Business Rules Language Development Framework

In Chap. 4, we presented different classifications of rules. Not all classes of rules can be *conveniently* written as **if-then** rules. While we can turn every type of rule into an **if-then** rule, there are situations where a custom language can make rule authoring more familiar to the business users. Let us revisit the example we mentioned in Sect. 9.2.2.5. Assume that you are building an application for filling out tax returns. The majority of tax rules are computations. Using the rule templates described in Sect. 4.1, a computation may be stated as:

The taxable income IS-COMPUTED-AS gross income + commission–s deductions

It would be convenient to be able to enter such a rule as is within a rule editor. In this case, the rule editor would be a *formula editor* similar to the formula editor available in Excel spreadsheets. This would be more natural than entering the rule as:

if <some trivial condition or no condition> **then** taxPayer.taxableIncome = taxPayer.grossIncome + taxPayer.commission–s taxPayer.deductions

or its business-oriented language equivalent.

JRules offers a rule language development framework called the *Business Rule Language Development Framework* (BRLDF), which is a java framework for specifying the syntax of the custom rule language, and for translating rules written in this syntax to some target language. If the target language is JRules IRL, then we can reuse the entire rule development and execution infrastructure for our new language. Figure 11.7 illustrates the approach.

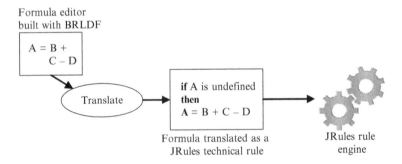

Fig. 11.7 Developing a custom rule language

In Chap. 9, we discussed situations under which it is justifiable to build a custom rule language. In this section, we provide a high-level description of how to do it with the JRules BRLDF. In the BRLDF, a rule language is defined by three components:

1. An *abstract syntax*. This syntax defines the structure of the language in a notation similar to the EBNF-like notation we used to describe the IRL and the BAL. In this case, the syntax is defined in an XML schema. We show below excerpts of the abstract syntax for our formula editor. The types prefixed with namespace "brl" are ones reused from the definition of the BAL.

```
<complexType name="T-equation">
  <sequence>
    <element name="left-hand-var" type="brl:T-local-var"/>
    <element name="right-hand-side"type="T-formula"/>
  </sequence>
</complexType>
<complexType name="T-formula">
  <choice>
    <element name="value" type="brl:T-local-var"/>
    <element name="expression" type="T-operation"/>
  </choice>
</complexType>
<complexType name="T-operation">
  <sequence>
    <element name="left-op" type="T-local-var"/>
    <element name="operator" type="brl:T-operator"/>
    <element name="right-op" type="T-expression"/>
  </sequence>
</complexType>
# etc
```

2. A *concrete syntax*. This syntax defines the *graphical properties* of the constructs of our language. This is where we specify the textual patterns (actual *tokens*), the text styles, the tool tips, prompts, whether there is a newline after a particular element, etc. We also specify the classes that process our language (see the next element). The concrete syntax is given in a *properties* file format. We illustrate the format in the excerpts below.

```
# Define the text pattern of 'if-then-else'
<T-equation>.text = <left-hand-side>=<right-hand-side>
<T-equation>.style = keyword
# Specify the parser/translator (see below) IRL
<T-equation>.translatorClass = MyTranslator
<T-equation>.codeGeneratorExtender.irl = MyCodeGenerator
# Specify graphical properties of elements
<T-equation>.<left-hand-var>.toolTip = Pick a variable
<T-equation>.<left-hand-var>.label = left-hand-side
...
```

3. *Parsers/translators*, which parse sentences of our language into an intermediate form and then translate/generate a target language. These are Java classes built using the *parsing and translation framework* that is part of the BRLDF. As mentioned above, to be able to reuse the rule deployment and execution infrastructure, it is a good idea to translate rules written using our custom language into IRL. In the above example, the class **MyTranslator** parses rules and generates the abstract syntax tree, whereas the class **MyCodeGenerator** reads such a tree and generates IRL.

Having defined the language, we now need to integrate it into the authoring environments, i.e., Rule Studio and Rule Team Server. This, in turn, involves three things:

1. Defining a new *rule class* that represents the new type of rules within these development environments. This is the class that defines which properties such rules can have. This is done through the *rule extension model*, in both RS and RTS.
2. Making sure that the language definition is available to the environment: that includes the files used to define the abstract syntax and the concrete syntax, and the Java classes that implement the parser and IRL translator. In RS, this is done through a specific plug-in.[18] In RTS, the whole thing is packaged in a jar file, and the RTS archive is repackaged to include the language jar file.
3. Customize the rule editors (Guided Editor and Intellirule) to handle the new language. Luckily, the rule editors are *parameterized* by the rule language, and thus, not much needs to be done for the customization.

Notice that the BAL language *itself* is developed using the BRLDF. In fact, the files that contain the abstract syntax and the concrete syntax are public and editable. Further, the parsers and translators for the BAL are part of the public API. This means three things:

1. If all you need is to change the ordering of BAL constructs or some of keywords, then you could simply edit the abstract syntax and concrete syntax files, with no programming involved.

---

[18]If you must know, we need to create an Eclipse plug-in project using the extension point `ilog.rules.studio.brl.languages`.

2. If you need to add a new kind of definition, condition, or action, then all you
   need to do is to define the abstract and concrete syntax for the new construct in
   the corresponding files, and code the corresponding parser and translator for
   abstract syntax tree nodes that represent the new construct.
3. If your language is too different from the BAL, you could still reuse many of the
   artifacts used to build the BAL, which have been conveniently modularized: (a)
   a component that handles bindings (variable definitions), (b) a component that
   handles conditions, and (c) a component that handles actions.

In our experience, developing a custom rule language is *rarely* justified, in terms
of business need, development cost, and maintenance risk. Luckily, thanks to the
incremental approach of the BRLDF, we can often address the most pressing BAL
irritants/shortcomings using low-cost, low-impact modifications of the BAL.

11.3   Rule Execution Orchestration

In Chap. 6, we presented the principles behind rule engines and rule engine
execution. Recall from Chap. 6 that an engine maintains three memory areas: (a)
a *ruleset* consisting of a set of rules that embody a computation, decision, or action
that the engine implements, (b) a *working memory*, containing (or referring to) the
objects that the ruleset will be applied to, and (c) an *agenda* that maintains a list of
so-called *rule instances*, which are candidate rules for firing. We saw earlier in this
chapter the development infrastructure in JRules, namely, rule projects and the
BOM, and we just covered the different rule artifacts.

What we know from Chap. 5 (prototyping) and Chap. 8 (an introduction to JRules)
is that, simply speaking, a rule project – a development artifact – is mapped to a *ruleset* –
a run-time concept. What we know from Chap. 6 is that the rules of a ruleset are treated
as an indiscriminate "bag of rules" where all of the rules are evaluated on all of the
objects in working memory with no underlying structuring or sequencing, except for the
ordering on the agenda. This leaves a couple of key questions to address:

1. How to get data into the rule engine – and its working memory – in the first
   place, especially within the context of a *rule execution service*, as we discussed
   in Sect. 7.5.1. This introduces the notion of a *ruleset signature*, and more
   specifically, the notion of *ruleset parameters*.
2. How to structure the execution of rules within a ruleset. While each ruleset is
   meant to implement a single business decision, such a decision will typically be
   broken down into a set of sub-decisions that need to be executed in a particular
   sequence. In fact, the structure of these sub-decisions may be a guiding principle
   in the organization of rules *during* development, as illustrated in Sects. 7.4.2 and
   7.4.3. This is the notion of *ruleflow* that we hinted at in many places in the
   previous chapters (Chaps. 5, 6, 7, and 8).

We can think of these two aspects as the *execution infrastructure* of a rule project.

In this section, we address these two aspects in detail. First, we talk about ruleset parameters: What they are, how to create them, and how to use them, both inside and outside the rule engine. Incidentally, we will also talk about *ruleset variables*. Section 11.5.2 introduces the basics of ruleflows: what they are, and how to create them. Section 11.5.3 will discuss advanced ruleflow concepts, namely, run-time selection of the contents of rule tasks, and algorithm selection.

11.3.1 Ruleset Parameters and Variables

If we think of ruleset as a *function*, ruleset parameters are parameters of that function:

1. They have a name and a type.
2. They have a direction: *in*, *out*, or *inout*.
3. They are *visible* anywhere within the "function", and can be referenced by name.
4. Their lifetime depends on the calling scope.

While this is a fairly accurate analogy, some qualifications are in order. Of course, in Java, methods have a single *out* parameter, which is the return value,[19] and all of their parameters are *inout* because Java passes variables by reference. With rulesets, the distinction between *in* and *inout* parameters makes sense within the context of a *remote invocation* of the rule engine. Let us first show how to define ruleset parameters, and then show how they can be referenced *within* the rules of a project, at rule development time, and by the rule engine calling application, at rule execution time.

To the extent that rule projects map to rulesets, ruleset parameters are defined at the *rule project* level. Figure 11.8 shows a screenshot of the wizard for defining

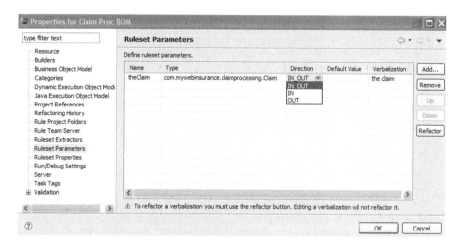

Fig. 11.8 Wizard for defining ruleset parameters

---

[19]Of course, we *could* have several out parameters in Java ... if we aggregate them in a single return object.

ruleset parameters. In this case, we have a single parameter, which is the Claim object, and it is inout. Incidentally, that is the only *in* object we need because it is the root of an object hierarchy that contains the various service acts, and the policy, which in turn points to the policy holder, its coverages, etc. It is the only *out* object we need because the decision and the total payment are stored in the claim object itself, and the itemized payment amounts are stored in the ServiceAct objects. Note that a ruleset parameter has a *verbalization* which enables us to refer to it in rules.

First, we look at how data is passed to the engine using ruleset parameters, as opposed to through the working memory; the full API will be discussed in Chap. 13. The following shows how data is passed through insertion into working memory, and how the result of rule execution is retrieved.

```
// initialize the rule engine (load and compile ruleset:
// see chapter 12 for details
IlrContext myEngine = …;
// get next claim object and insert into working memory
Claim myClaim = fetchNextClaim();
myEngine.insert(myClaim);
// Execute the rules. See chapter 6 for details
myEngine.execute();
// Check the outcome by examining the decision attribute
String decision = myClaim.getDecision();
if ("PAID".equals(decision))
   System.out.println("The Claim "+myClaim+" was paid in
the amount " + myClaim.getTotalPaid());
```

Now with the ruleset parameter:

```
// initialize the rule engine (same as above)
IlrContext myEngine = …;
// get next claim object and pass as parameter value
Claim myClaim = fetchNextClaim();
IlrParameterMap inputs = new IlrParameterMap();
inputs.setPatameterValue("theClaim",myClaim);
myEngine.setParameters(inputs);
// Execute the rules, and collect the inout/out params
IlrParameterMap outputs = myEngine.execute();
Claim modClaim =(Claim)outputs.getObjectValue("theClaim");
// Check the outcome by examining the decision attribute
String decision = modClaim.getDecision();
if ("PAID".equals(decision))
   System.out.println("The Claim "+modClaim+" was paid in
the amount " + modClaim.getTotalPaid());
```

There are a couple of subtle differences between the two "data passing" modes. In the first case, the calling application relies on the fact that the engine lives in the same JVM, and hence the variable myClaim stays current: Upon returning from the call "myEngine.execute();" the variable myClaim will reflect whichever changes were made by the rules. With the parameters, the calling application does *not* rely on the fact that the engine lives in the same JVM, and will retrieve the modified value of myClaim into a separate variable modClaim. This makes the second approach more scalable in the sense of being *remotable*. In fact, the Rule Execution Server (RES) API, to be discussed in Chap. 13, relies on ruleset parameters to pass data back and forth.[20]

We now look at how ruleset parameters are referenced in rules. As mentioned above, ruleset parameters are visible within all the rule of the project, and can thus be referenced within rules. Going back to our "claim date" BAL rule from Sect. 11.2.2, we can now write the rule without a ***definitions*** part:

```
if
    'the claim' was filed more than 90 days after the start date of the policy of 'the claim'
then
    set the decision of 'the claim' to "INELIGIBLE" ;
    log that this rule has fired on 'the claim' with message "Claim filed too late" ;
```

And if we look at the IRL:

```
rule claim_date {
  property status = "new";
  when {
      com.mywebinsurance.claimprocessing.Claim() from theClaim;
      evaluate (theClaim.fileMoreThanXDaysAfter(90,
                        theClaim.policy.startDate.toDate()));
  } then {
    theClaim.decision = "INELIGIBLE";
    ?context.updateContext();
    theClaim.logRuleFiringWithMessage("Claim filed too late");
  }
}
```

If we compare this IRL to that produced for the original rule (Sect. 11.2.2), we see a couple of differences:

1. In the earlier rule (Sect. 11.2.2), we looked for the claim object in working memory, whereas, here, the claim object is *scoped* within the ruleset parameter.
2. If we look at the action part, the rule in Sect. 11.2.2 includes an update on the claim object, namely: '**update** current_claim;' whereas the above rule does an update on the rule engine itself ("?context.update-Context()").

---

[20]This is a somewhat abusive simplification, but it will do for now: (1) the API for manipulating XML data (XML XOM) is slightly different, for both working memory insertion, and parameter passing, (2) with *inout* parameters, for the case of local invocation (same JVM, as in the example above) the variable passed as inout *will* reflect the changes made by rule execution (no need to fetch the new value from outputs), and (3) the RES API does enable us to pass data that is to be inserted in working memory.

Recall that '**update** some_object;' causes the rule engine to reevaluate all of the rules relevant to some_object, which is the mechanism that underlies rule chaining. However, what if the object is *not* in working memory, as is the case with ruleset parameters? Technically, ruleset parameters are treated as data members of the rule engine object itself[21] and thus, whenever a ruleset parameter is modified, the BAL to IRL translator throws in '?context.update Context()' whose effect is to reevaluate all of the rules that concern ... the ruleset parameters!

Finally, note that passing a data object as a ruleset parameter does *not* insert it into working memory. Thus, the original form of the rule "claim date", where we defined a rule variable in the *definitions* part, would not work. Indeed, the class condition:

```
...
current_claim: Claim();
...
```

Would fail because there would *not* be any **Claim** object in working memory! So what do we do? We have three alternatives:

1. Rewrite the rule ... naah!
2. Find a way of inserting ruleset parameters into working memory so that "working memory-style" rules continue to work. There are several more or less elegant techniques of doing this that *do not* involve the Java code; we will see one such technique when we talk about ruleflows (Sects. 11.5.2 and 11.5.3).
3. Design the signature of the ruleset (i.e., the ruleset parameters) *before* we start writing rules, and then write rules that refer to those parameters. This is the recommended practice. We will come back to this and other practices in section on "Further Readings".

We now talk about *ruleset variables*. If *ruleset parameters* are to *rulesets* what *function parameters* are to *functions*, then *ruleset variables* are to rulesets what *function-scope local variables* are to functions: they are visible everywhere in the ruleset/rule project, and they *keep their values* during the invocation of the ruleset; we could not say "their lifetime spans a ruleset invocation", because ruleset variables actually survive a ruleset invocation, and even keep their values from one invocation t o the next... unless we clean them using "myEngine.cleanRuleset Variables();", or the more drastic "myEngine.reset();".

Like with ruleset parameters, ruleset variables can be referenced in both rule conditions and rule actions. We typically use ruleset variables to hold intermediary results of the "reasoning" of the rule engine that we wish to pass from one rule to another, with no other place to store them. A fairly common use is to implement routing logic with ruleflows, to be discussed next. For the time being, we simply show the mechanics of defining ruleset variables. Figure 11.9 shows the wizard for

---

[21]And in a distant past (Rules C++), they were.

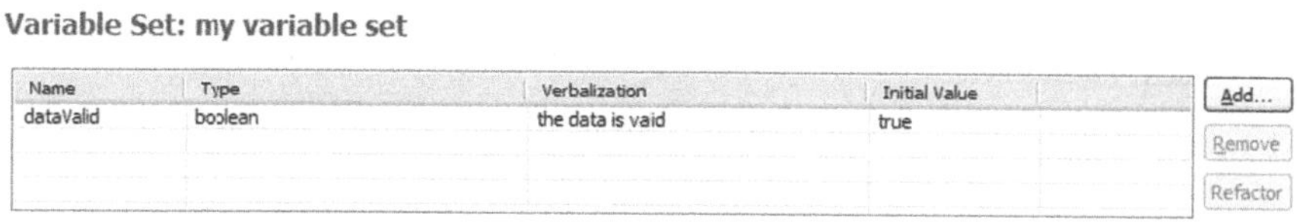

Variable Set: my variable set

Name	Type	Verbalization	Initial Value	
dataValid	boolean	the data is vaid	true	Add...
				Remove
				Refactor

Fig. 11.9 Wizard for defining ruleset variables

defining ruleset variables. Ruleset variables are defined through *variable sets*. We can have several variables sets within the same project, but only one per package. However, the variables are accessible in all the packages of the project.

11.3.2 Ruleflows: Basics

A ruleflow is a way of organizing the execution of the rules of a rule project/ruleset in terms of groups of related rules. It is a *process* flow whose *tasks* consist – *mostly* – of the execution of groups of related rules. As mentioned in the introduction of this section, while a ruleset is meant to implement a single business decision, that decision is typically complex enough that it can be broken down into more elementary decisions. This breakdown was actually presented as one of the criteria for organizing rules during development (Sects. 7.4.2 and 7.4.3). The basic idea is that the rules of a ruleset are broken down into subsets distributed among the tasks of the ruleflow, and they will be evaluated in the sequence embodied in the ruleflow. Another way of putting it: the ruleflow becomes sort of the "main program" of the ruleset.

Figure 11.10 shows the different types of components of a ruleflow. Much like a Java function, a ruleflow has a single entry point and one or more end points. There are three types of tasks in a ruleflow:

1. *Function tasks*, which include some *imperative* IRL or BAL code to execute, i.e., the kind of code we would find in the action part of a rule (IRL or BAL) or in IRL functions. Function tasks are typically used as the starting tasks of a ruleflow to perform required initializations. For example, we could use a function task to insert ruleset parameters in working memory!
2. *(Simple) rule tasks*, which contain a bunch of rules and rule packages that will be evaluated – and fired, if applicable – when the processing reaches that particular task.
3. *Flow tasks*, which consist of the execution of a *nested* ruleflow. Indeed, some complex decisions may require two or more levels of decomposition, and some tasks of the *main* ruleflow may consist of executing *another* ruleflow.

The three types of tasks can have *initial actions* and *final actions*, which consist of imperative IRL or BAL code to be executed upon entering or exiting the task. Ruleflow tasks are linked to each other and to the start and end nodes using *transitions*. Transitions can be *guarded*, i.e., they can be crossed only when certain *conditions* are satisfied. Those conditions are *Boolean* expressions that can reference variables that have *rule project (ruleset) scope*, i.e., either global Java

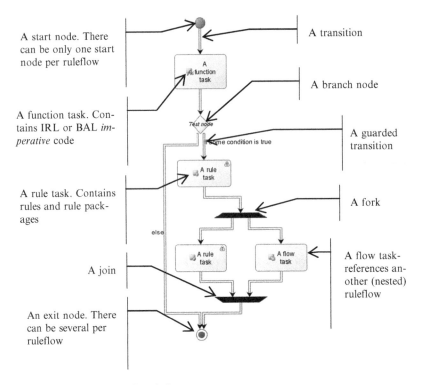

A start node. There can be only one start node per ruleflow

A transition

A branch node

A function task. Contains IRL or BAL *imperative* code

A guarded transition

A rule task. Contains rules and rule packages

A fork

A join

A flow task-references another (nested) ruleflow

An exit node. There can be several per ruleflow

Fig. 11.10 The components of a ruleflow

variables,[22] ruleset variables or ruleset parameters. We can have several transitions coming out of the same task. If we have *n* transitions, $n - 1$ should be guarded, and the *n*th should be tagged with the *else*. When several transitions come out of a task, we can use a *branch node* for better visuals, even though it is not strictly necessary. Ruleflows can have *forks* and *joins*. Because there is no *parallel* execution of ruleflows, forks simply tell that there is no precedence between the branches of the fork. However, under the hood, the branches are serialized.

Figure 11.11 shows what a claim processing ruleflow might look like. The initialization function task does, indeed, insert the ruleset parameter theClaim into working memory so that rules that refer to a claim in working memory (i.e., non-scoped class condition) would still work. Both the data validation step and the eligibility step are complex and require ruleflows of their own. Hence, the claim processing ruleflow (Fig. 11.11a) references a data validation ruleflow (not shown) and the claim eligibility ruleflow (Fig. 11.11b).

In this ruleflow, we only check the eligibility of the claim if the data is valid, and we only adjudicate if the claim is eligible. This need not be the case. For example, we could choose to check eligibility even if some data fields are erroneous or do not

---

[22]For example, public static class data members.

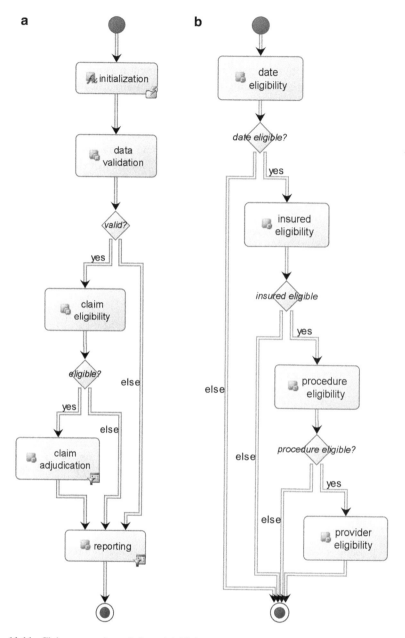

Fig. 11.11 Claim processing ruleflow. (**a**) Claim processing main flow and (**b**) claim eligibility ruleflow

make sense. Deciding which way to go is often a combination of computational constraints and business considerations. For example, in an automated system where throughput is important, we may decide to throw out a claim as soon as it fails any of the data validation tests or any of the eligibility criteria. If there are problems past the first failure point, we will not know. However, a claims service representative may need to provide a complete diagnosis for a rejected claim for legal reasons, or for customer relationship management reasons: Tell the customer what to fix for their corrected submission, once and for all, instead of asking for yet another piece of documentation as the claim passes the various eligibility criteria.

For the sake of brevity, we will not show the Rule Studio wizards for creating and editing ruleflows. However, we discuss the corresponding IRL (Fig. 11.12).

We will comment the structure of the IRL, here displayed in multi-column format for compactness. The top pane shows the definition of the main ruleflow,

```
1    use claim_eligibility;
2    use data_validation;
3    flowtask claim_processing {
4      property mainflowtask = true;
5      body {
6        claim_processing#data_initialization;
7        claim_processing#data$_$validation;
8        if (data_validation.dataValid) {
9          claim_processing#claim$_$eligibility;
10         if ((theClaim.decision.equals("ELIGIBLE"))) {
11           claim_processing#claim_adjudication;
12           goto _node_5;
13         } else { goto _node_5; }
14       } else {
15         _node_5 : claim_processing#reporting;
16       }
17     }
18   };
```

```
19   functiontask                      ruletask
     claim_processing#data_initiali     claim_processing#claim_adjudic
     zation {                           ation {
20     body {                             algorithm = default;
21       insert theClaim;                 ordering = dynamic;
22     }                                  body {
23   };                                     claim_adjudication.*
                                          }
24   flowtask                          };
     claim_processing#data$_$valida
     tion {                            flowtask
25     body {                          claim_processing#claim$_$eligi
26       data_validation;              bility {
27     }                                 body {
28   };                                    claim_eligibility;
                                         }
30   ruletask                          };
     claim_processing#reporting {
31     algorithm = default;
32     ordering = dynamic;
33     body {
34       reporting.*
35     }
36   };
```

Fig. 11.12 The IRL equivalent to the "claim processing" main ruleflow "claim processing." The IRL construct for ruleflows is *flowtask* (line 3). A ruleflow/flowtask has a bunch of properties (line 4) and a body (lines 5–17). The body looks like any good old main program, even using a GOTO! Each statement in the body references a task, including the (function) task "data initialization" (line 6), the (flow) task "data_validation" (line 7), etc. Transition guards show up as simple if-then-else statements. The first transition (line 8) tests on a *ruleset variable* called "data_valid" defined within the rule package "data validation." The second guarded transition (line 10) tests on the value of the decision attribute of the ruleset parameter "theClaim."

Now that we have looked at the "main program", let us look at the "subroutines", i.e., the definitions of the various tasks. Lines 19–23 show the definition of the function "data_initialization": It consists of a single IRL statement: "insert theClaim." In turn, the flowtask "claim_processing#data$_$validation"[23] is defined as invoking "data_validation" in its body, which is the name of the nested ruleflow. This externally defined entity is actually declared in line 2, with the statement "**use** data_validation." The flowtask "claim_processing # claim$_$eligibility" (shown in second column) is defined in a similar fashion.

Consider now the ruletasks "claim_processing#reporting" (lines 30–36) and "claim_processing#claim_adjudication" (shown in second column). Their bodies are supposed to contain names of rules or rule packages. The notation "reporting.*" is similar to Java's import convention: The "*" means all of the contents of the package "reporting", including rules, and subpackages. The act of determining the body contents of a rule task is called *rule selection*, as in selecting the rules that will be evaluated and executed within the rule task. For these two cases, we talk about *static rule selection*, meaning that the *body* of a rule task is determined statically, at ruleflow development time. We can also have *run-time rule selection*, to be discussed in the next section.

Rule tasks also show two properties, "**algorithm**" and "**ordering.**" Within a ruleflow, we can *use a different rule execution algorithm for each task*. In fact, a ruleset that contains a ruleflow *behaves as* different rulesets, one per task, and the rule engine behaves as a bunch of rule engines, each with its own ruleset and agenda, but they share working memory.[24] We will discuss algorithm selection in the next section, and best practices for algorithm selection in section on "Further Reading".

---

[23]JRules enables us to use variable names that contain spaces. However, internally, it replaces spaces by "_" . . . and "_" by "$_$".

[24]We insist on the term *behaves as* because internally, it *is* the same ruleset object and the same rule engine, except that different subsets of the ruleset will be activated as we move from one rule task to another.

11.3.3 Ruleflows: Advanced Concepts

In this section, we talk about two features of ruleflows, *run-time rule selection*, and *algorithm selection*. *Rule selection* deals with the selection of the rule contents of a rule task. This selection is typically done at ruleflow development time where we pick a set of rules or packages to execute in the rule task. JRules enables us to compute the body of a rule task at run-time, and we will show how. As mentioned above, within a ruleflow, we can select a different rule execution algorithm for each rule task, and for each algorithm, we can specify additional parameters. We will show how to do that, and discuss situations where each algorithm is appropriate.

11.3.3.1 Run-Time Rule Selection

Figure 11.13 shows the Rule Studio wizard for selecting rules. From the property sheet of a rule task, we can select the "Rule Selection" which shows two panels. The top panel shows the list of rules and rule packages in the rule task. Initially empty, we can edit it by pressing the "Edit . . ." button which brings up the wizard shown on the left of Fig. 11.13. In the "Select Rules" wizard, we get, on the left hand side, the list of all rules and rule packages included in the current project *and in the projects that the current project depends on*. We can move rules and packages from the left to the right, and back, using the familiar $>$, $\gg$, $<$, and $\ll$ buttons. Once we press the "OK" button, the contents of the right list become the body of the rule task.

If we leave it at that, that is going to be the body of the rule task. In the example of Fig. 11.13, we are looking at the rule task "claim adjudication" from the "claim processing" ruleflow (see Fig. 11.11a). Here, we selected the rule package called "claim adjudication." Note that this does not mean that *all* of the rules of the package "claim adjudication" will be evaluated/executed in this ruletask: Indeed, the ruleset extractor might actually filter out some rules from that package based on development status (e.g., only validated rules) or based on effective and expiration date. Thus, during run-time, this task will have all of the rules of the package "claim adjudication" *that were extracted by the ruleset extractor.*

Fig. 11.13 The Rule Studio wizard for rule selection

As we mentioned above, we can also make *run-time rule selection*, which acts as an additional rule filter. Let us first consider a business scenario that requires run-time rule selection. Business policies and rules change regularly – one of the motivations for using the business rules approach! Insurance companies will update their rules regularly based on market trends, marketing studies, new actuarial studies, changing regulations, etc. When new rules come into effect, they usually have an effective date. If they are meant to replace older rules, the older rules will be made to expire on that date. However, new rules will generally apply *only* to new business. Existing contracts *will* continue to be honored according to the old rules. For example, if we decide to change the yearly cap on a particular procedure, the new cap will apply to *new* policies, or to existing policies *at renewal time* but will not apply retroactively to existing policies that are still in effect. So how do we handle that? One solution would have us use *different* rulesets, one per effectiveness period. When a claim comes in, we check the start and expiration dates of the policy, and select the ruleset to use accordingly. The yearly cap for procedure X is updated on January 20. The yearly cap for procedure Y is updated on February 18. The list of approved providers is updated on March 5 ... you get the idea: We will end up with *numerous* rulesets, and a cumbersome and error-prone ruleset dispatching mechanism. This is the business case for *run-time rule selection*: Our rule packages may contain rules with different effectiveness periods. However, for a given claim, we will select which of those rules to use, based on the effectiveness period of the policy of the claim.

Figure 11.14 shows the corresponding *run-time rule selection filter*. The BAL expression compares the "effective date" and "expiration date" of the rule to the "start date" and "end date" of the policy of the claim. Naturally, we can use any *run-time* property of a rule[25] and any property of the business data manipulated by the ruleset. Because the set of rule properties (metadata) is extensible, the possibilities are endless. For example, thanks to so-called *hierarchical properties* (properties whose values fit in a hierarchy), we can imagine filters based on the *jurisdiction of the rule*, and the place of

Fig. 11.14 The *dynamic run-time rule selection* filter

---

[25]The *properties* of a rule can be either *extractable*, in which case they are available in the *run-time* representation of rules, or *non-extractable*, in which case they are development time-only properties. The extractability of a rule property is a true/false attribute than can be set in *rule model extensions*. See Chap. 17 for more information about extending the rule *metamodel*.

```
ruletask claim_processing#claim_adjudication {
  algorithm = default;
  ordering = dynamic;
  scope {
    claim_adjudication.*,
  }
  body = dynamicselect (?rule) {
    return ((?rule.?effectiveDate.compareTo(
                  theClaim.policy.endDate.toDate()) < 0
            && ?rule.?expirationDate.compareTo(
                  theClaim.policy.startDate.toDate()) > 0));
  }
};
```

Fig. 11.15 IRL for a rule task with a dynamic run-time rule selection

residence of the policy holder. For example, California and US-wide rules will apply to a policy held by a San Francisco resident, whereas Michigan rules will not.

Figure 11.14 above shows a radio button labeled "Static BAL". So what is *static BAL run-time rule selection* filter? A *dynamic BAL run-time rule selection* filter is run *each time* the control flow reaches the rule task, i.e., each time the rule task is executed. In our case, that is the behavior we want, because our ruleset will be run with a *different* claim each time. By contrast, a *static BAL run-time rule selection* filter is applied *only* the *first time* the rule task is executed and the body of the task will remain constant throughout the lifetime of the ruleset object. There are not that many use cases where a *static BAL run-time rule selection* filter is appropriate.

Figure 11.15 shows the IRL for the rule task "claim adjudication". By comparing it with the IRL in Fig. 11.12, the reader may notice that the package "`claim_adjudication.*`" now represents the *scope* of the rule task, and the body consists of the filter. The filter is like a Boolean function that takes a rule as an argument, and return true if the rule should be included, and false otherwise. The *scope* determines the set of rules over which this filter will be applied?

Had we picked the *static BAL* button (Fig. 11.14) instead, the keyword `dynamicselect` would be replaced by the keyword `select`. And had we picked the button "IRL" (Fig. 11.14), we would have had to enter the body block, and would have had the leisure to pick either `dynamicselect` or `select`. We could even have used a different *signature* for the filter (static or dynamic) which takes no arguments and returns an array of rules to include in the rule task, in one shot, which makes the computation of the body more efficient. Indeed, dynamic run-time rule selection does have a performance cost, and if we are not careful, we can make it *prohibitively* costly.

11.3.3.2 Algorithm Selection

As mentioned above, we can select a different execution algorithm for each task within a ruleflow. JRules offers three execution algorithms, discussed in Chap. 6:

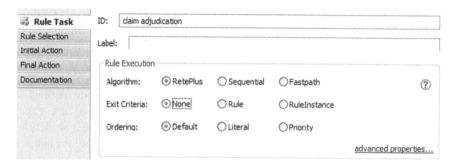

Fig. 11.16 The rule task algorithm selection wizard

1. The *RETE* algorithm, which is the default algorithm. This is the most powerful of the three, and it supports *rule* chaining (see Chap. 6).
2. The *sequential algorithm*, which applies the rules of a ruleset/task to the data of the working memory *sequentially*. Thus, for a given object tuple $<$object$_1$, object$_2$, ... ,object$_n>$, each rule is evaluated only once, if at all. This leads to a more efficient execution, but does not support rule chaining and has other limitations, to be discussed later.
3. The *fastpath* algorithm, which combines characteristics of the RETE algorithm and of the sequential algorithm. It does *not* support rule chaining, but it does not have many of the sequential algorithm limitations.

Figure 11.16 shows the algorithm selection wizard. In addition to the algorithm selection, we have two additional properties, with three potential values each:

1. *Exit criteria*, which defaults to "None" but can take the value "Rule" or "RuleInstance." None means that we let the engine fire all of the rules that are satisfied. With RuleInstance, as soon as the engine fires *any* rule instance, we stop the execution and exit. With Rule, we let the engine fire all of the instances of *highest priority* rule, and then exit.
2. *Ordering*, which defaults to ... "Default" but which can take the values "Literal" or "Priority." Default refers to the use of *dynamic priorities* to order the execution of rules. Priority means that rules are executed according to their static priorities, and Literal means that rules are executed according to their order of appearance in the task body (yuk!).

We can also enter some advanced properties in a textual format. One such property is firinglimit which can take any positive integer value, to mean how many rules of a particular task can fire before the task is terminated. A firinglimit=0 means no limit, i.e., we let the algorithm run its course to the end. Generally speaking, the value None for "Exit Criteria" means firinglimit=0, and the value RuleInstance or Rule (depending on the execution algorithm) means firinglimit=1.

Note that not all combinations of values are legal. For example, Default ordering is not legal for the sequential algorithm, because the sequential algorithm does not support dynamic priorities: we will get a ruleset parsing error.[26] Further, not all the legal combinations make sense. For example, the combinations <Algorithm=RetePlus, Ordering=Literal or Priority, Exit Criteria = anything> are legal but would yield a RETE algorithm with no agenda or rule chaining. Why bother? We will discuss below the legal combinations that do make sense. The reader can consult the product documentation for the more exotic combinations.

For the RETE algorithm. As mentioned above, only the Default value makes sense here. With regard to the exit criteria, if we use "None", we let the "while agenda not empty" loop discussed in Chap. 6 run its course until the agenda is empty. If "Exit Criteria" is RuleInstance, the "while agenda not empty" loop actually stops after the first rule instance is executed. This exit criterion might be needed for a rule task that contains rules that detect violations of eligibility or validation constraints: If all we are interested in is the pass/fail decision, then we can exit at the first violation, i.e., the first rule instance. With "Exit Criteria" equal to Rule, we take the first rule instance (i.e., the top of the agenda), and fire *it* and *all* of the other instances of the same rule that are on the agenda. Often, all of the other instances of the same rule will have the same priority as the first one, and will be "right behind" on the agenda. But there are situations where that would not be the case: For example, when that rule uses dynamic priorities – and thus, different instances will have different priorities – or when there are other rules on the agenda with the same priority – in which case other criteria such as recency (see Chap. 6) come into play.

For the sequential algorithm. As mentioned above, the Ordering property can be either Literal or Priority in this case. With Literal, for each data tuple, the rules are applied in the other in which they (or the packages that contain them) are listed in the rule task body. With Priority, the rules are applied according to their static priority. Regarding the Exit Criteria property, None means that all of the rules will be applied, RuleInstance does not make sense (because we have no agenda), and Rule means that as soon as a rule is fired, we drop the current data tuple, and take the next one.

For the fastpath algorithm. Because this algorithm does not rely on an agenda, the Ordering property can be either Literal or Priority, with the same behavior as with the sequential algorithm. Regarding the Exit Criteria property, None means that all of the rules will be applied. Using RuleInstance means that as soon as a rule instance is fired, we end the task. With Rule, we execute all of the instances of the first rule, based on the ordering property, and then we exit the task.

In this section, we discussed algorithm selection, and discussed the various parameters. We will discuss criteria for selecting one algorithm versus the other in Sect. 11.6.3.

---

[26]We will be able to *extract* the ruleset, but when we load it into a ruleset object, we get a ruleset parsing error.

11.4 Best Practices

In this section, we review some best practices regarding rule authoring and rule execution orchestration.

11.4.1 Best Practice 1: Design the Signature First

We saw in Sect. 11.5.1 how the use of ruleset parameters can change the way rules reference application objects, and ultimately, where rules will fire on not. Adding ruleset parameters *after* people have written rules can require some acrobatics:

1. Rewriting rules so that they now refer to the ruleset parameters
2. Add rules or ruletasks to insert ruleset parameters in working memory

It is better to start right, from the beginning. We will talk shortly about how to pick the correct signature.

The same is true with ruleflows: It is better to start designing the structure of the ruleflow *before* rule authoring starts. Indeed, we recommend that the rule architect design the high-level package structure of the rule project (see Sect. 9.4.3 for some design patterns) and the ruleflow, before rule authors start writing rules. This way, rule authors will write rules within the context of a predefined and carefully designed development structure (rule package hierarchy), and that structure is pre-mapped to the execution structure (ruleflow) through rule task rule selection. Indeed, when we write a rule, it *helps* to know the context under which the rule will be executed, i.e., the point in the process, what things are already assumed to be true, etc.

Regarding the ruleset signature, which data items should I pass back and forth between the calling application, and the rule engine? Actually, there are two aspects to this question, the *business* data contents, and the *computational* data structure. With regard to the *business* contents of the parameters ... business knows! Policy analysts know which information they need for policy underwriting, policy renewal, or for claim processing. For each one of these processes, there is, naturally, the main document or transaction (e.g., policy application, claim), but also a bunch of ancillary or supporting data (see Fig. 11.17).

For example, for policy underwriting, we would want to know about the policy (which risks are to be covered, deductibles, restrictions), but we may also want to know about the (potential) policy holder credit file. For claim processing, in addition to the claim itself, we may want to get the policy itself, to see which coverages are included, but perhaps also some historical data about past claims, etc. Only business knows the sources of information they draw upon to make decisions.

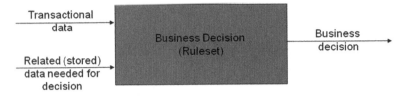

Fig. 11.17 The *business* signature of a ruleset

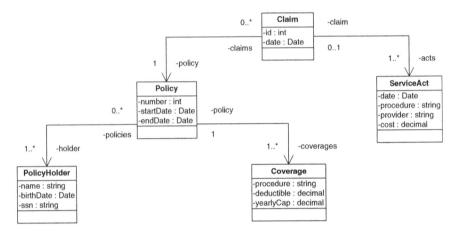

Fig. 11.18 A model of the data needed to make a decision

Having decided on the business contents of the data, the question now is how to structure it to pass it back and forth. We illustrate the issue with the model in Fig. 11.18. In this particular case, from the `Claim` object, we can access all of the information about the service acts, the policy, the coverages, and the policy holder. Hence, passing the `Claim` object is enough: The policy can be accessed as "`the policy of the claim`", the service acts can be accessed as "`a service act in the service acts of the claim`", etc. If we need the past claims, then we have several alternatives:

1. If we need the aggregated data from the past claims (e.g., total amount, number over a three year period, etc.), then those can be stored at the `Policy` object as attributes.
2. If we need the actual individual claims, then, either the `Policy` object points back to the claims made against it, in which case the main `Claim` object suffices, or we need to pass the set of past claims, separately, as a ruleset parameter.

Similar issues will arise regarding the decision output. Generally speaking, if the "rule team" has some control over the XOM, we can custom tailor the XOM (e.g., adding collection attributes to point from a `Policy` to past claims) to make the ruleset signature simpler.

11.4.2   Best Practice 2: Rulesets and Ruleflows

One of the design issues that will come up has to do with the granularity of the ruleflow. At the highest level, we have a business process that involves a number of decisions. At the lowest level, we have individual business rules. JRules provides with rulesets and ruleflows as a way of structuring rule executions. The question then becomes:

1. What should be the granularity of a ruleset?
2. Having chosen a ruleset granularity, how far down should we decompose the decision implemented by a ruleset using ruleflows?

Let us answer the ruleset question first, and then we will tackle ruleflows.

Chapters 3 and 4 argued that *decision points* within a business process are candidates for a ruleset. However, we did not talk about the granularity of the business process. Because business processes can themselves be nested, we had not answered the question entirely. Let us consider our case study. Figure 11.19 shows claim processing, at three levels of detail. At the highest level, we have the entire business process from the reception of the claim in paper format to actual payment. Starting with the process in the left, the first task consists of entering the claim data into the system, possibly scanning and archive receipts, etc. The next task consists

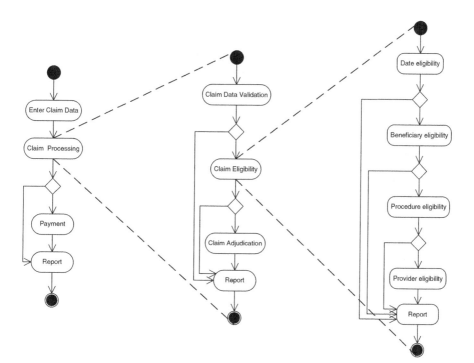

Fig. 11.19 The claim processing, at three levels of detail

of processing the claim, and if the claim is deemed payable, then we go through payment, and then report. The claim processing task itself can be broken down into data validation, eligibility, and adjudication. In turn, claim eligibility can be broken down into data eligibility, beneficiary eligibility, procedure eligibility, and provider eligibility.

So the question is which of the three processes should be a ruleset, if any? Generally speaking, a process or task should be a candidate for a ruleset if it satisfies two sets of criteria:

1. *Business criteria*:

   – The process or task should be *decision intensive*, i.e., it should involve business rules.
   – The process or task should embody a *cohesive decision*, i.e., have a single identifiable, business meaningful outcome.

2. *Computational criteria*:

   – The process or task should represent a *short-lived, synchronous* activity.
   – The process or task should not involve any *heavy-lifting*, e.g., accessing a legacy EIS, or making a remote connection.

The business criteria are self-explanatory. The computational criteria are justified by the fact that ruleset execution requires a single, synchronous rule engine invocation (the method $execute()$). Indeed, we would not want a rule engine invocation to last minutes, hours, or days, and lock the resources (claim object, policy object, etc.) while the engine is running. Second, we would not want to be dealing with exceptions raised by the external resources (e.g., a SQL exception, a database connection timeout, a deadlock, a remote method invocation timeout, etc.) within a ruleset execution because they are at worst, unrecoverable, and at best, leave the engine in an inconsistent state, making the entire rule engine invocation suspect.

Going back to our example (Fig. 11.19), *both* the claim processing process (middle one) and the claim eligibility process (right one) satisfy *all* the criteria, and are potential candidates for a ruleset. However, the top-level process does not:

- It is debatable whether we could call it *decision* intensive: Two tasks out of three are clerical and do not involve decisions (data entry and payment).
- It fails *both* computational criteria: It is *not* a short-lived process as it involves an external manual task (data entry, archiving), and it *does involve* accessing external resources, for both data entry and payment.[27]

Having eliminated the top process as a candidate for a ruleset, we can now worry about the next two.

---

[27]Data entry typically involves saving the data entered in the database, but also, pulling out the policy object from the database. Payment requires either printing checks or making automatic transfers by accessing a banking system.

If we choose to make "claim processing" a ruleset – as we have assumed in this chapter – then the internal process will be implemented using a ruleflow. One could also imagine deciding otherwise. In real life, the process labeled "claim processing" will likely require thousands of rules. Further, while data validation is generally relatively simple (e.g., checking individual property values), claim eligibility will involve lots of rules, and lots of data. If a claim fails data validation, we would have loaded all of the business data (policy, policy holder, past claims, etc.) for nothing. An architect might then choose to implement the "claim processing" process (middle of Fig. 11.19) in Java – or in BPEL or in some workflow engine – and then implement data validation, claim eligibility, and claim adjudication as separate rulesets.

Having decided on the granularity of the ruleset, now the question becomes: How fine-grained should be our ruleflows? Considering that a ruleflow is a piece of *hardcoded procedural logic*, the procedural logic needs to be *business-oriented*, so that it makes sense to the people writing rules, and it should be *stable* so that we do not have to frequently redesign the ruleflow. Indeed, the high-level package structure of a rule project and the ruleflow embody the *architecture* of the rule project and of the corresponding ruleset. We should *not* implement computational algorithms or replicate procedural code using ruleflows: We should let the engine do its job with the built-in inference mechanisms. For example, you know that you have gone too far if each rule task contains a handful of rules.

11.4.3 Best Practice 3: My Kingdom for an Algorithm

Chap. 6 explained the various rule engine execution algorithms. Section 11.5.3.2 of this chapter explained the different parameters of the various rule task execution algorithms, and how to set them. In this section, we present criteria for selecting an execution algorithm and its associated parameters for a particular task.

If you do nothing, the default execution algorithm for rule tasks is the RETE algorithm. As mentioned earlier, this is the most powerful of the three execution algorithms, and it supports all of the IRL constructs, including **exists**, **not**, truth maintenance, and event-based reasoning. This execution mode supports rule *chaining*. In the context of a ruleflow, rule chaining for a rule task means that the firing of a rule within that task can trigger the firing of another rule within the same task. Let us first refresh our memory about what rule chaining means. Consider the "procedure eligibility" task, in Fig. 11.19. A procedure is considered eligible if (a) it is covered by the policy and (b) it is *justified*. Assume that this is written using two rules as follows:[28]

---

[28]Note that the current BOM does not support these rules. They are used for illustration purposes.

```
   Rule 1 - coverage:
definitions
   set 'a service act' to a service act in the service acts
      of 'the claim';
if
   there exists a coverage in the coverages of the policy of
      'the claim' where the procedure of this coverage
      is the procedure of 'a service act' ,
then
   set the status of 'a service act' to "COVERED" ;


   Rule 2 - justification:
definitions
   set 'a service act' to a service act in the service acts
      of 'the claim' where the status of this service act is
      "COVERED";
if
   there exists a prescription in the documents of
      'the claim' where the procedure of this prescription
      is the procedure of 'a service act' ,
then
   set the status of ' a service act' to "JUSTIFIED" ;
```

The justification rule (Rule 2) will only be triggered for those service acts that have the status "**COVERED.**" If Rule 1 and Rule 2 are in the same task, only the RETE algorithm will ensure that if Rule 1 is executed for a particular service act, then Rule 2 will be evaluated and potentially triggered. Indeed, both the sequential algorithm and the fastpath algorithm will take a *single* pass at the rules, and if Rule 2 happens to be looked at before Rule 1 (see discussion in Chap. 6, and the rule ordering parameter in Sect. 11.5.3.2), we will never be able to establish that a service act is eligible!

Because the RETE algorithm is the least efficient of the three algorithms, we have to consider whether we need it for a particular task. Two sets of reasons would compel us to use the RETE algorithm:

1. *The decision logic.* The above example illustrated a case where rule chaining was needed for the proper execution of rules. Other cases include truth maintenance and event-based reasoning, which also require the RETE algorithm.
2. *The use of or reliance on working memory or agenda constructs in rules.* This means constructs like dynamic priorities, which are not supported in either sequential or fastpath. It also means *unscoped*[29] **exists**, **not** and collections, and their BAL equivalents, which are not supported by the sequential algorithm, and **insert**, **update** and **retract**, which will have unexpected or unpredictable behavior[30] in sequential and fastpath.

---

[29]That is, without the **in/from** constructs.

[30]For example, in RETE mode, when an object is **insert**'ed, *all* of the rules that concern it will be evaluated. In sequential and fastpath mode, the new object *may* or *may not* be considered

The two factors are not independent: business logic can also dictate the kind of IRL construct we use. For example, while we can refrain from using unscoped **exists** or **not** – by scoping them using **in/from** constructs!—it may be far more awkward, for a particular application, to implement the business logic without **insert** or **retract**, say.

If you have established that, *for a particular task*, the business logic does *not* require the RETE algorithm, and if the rules that do go into that task do not use the IRL constructs mentioned above, then we should aim for the more efficient alternatives, the sequential or fastpath algorithm. Which one should you use? As it turns out, this is not only a question of efficiency, but it is also a question of correctness. Indeed, if the rules within a rule task do not have a *homogeneous signature*, the sequential algorithm will not behave correctly.

Informally, the *signature* of a rule is the *tuple* of objects on which the rule applies. Formally, the *signature* of an IRL rule is the set of *simple class conditions* of the rule. At the BAL level, it is the set of *object* variables of the rule – including *object* ruleset parameters, *object* ruleset variables, and *object* local variables.[31] In the example above, the rules Rule 1 (coverage) and Rule 2 (justification) have the same signature: {**Claim**, **ServiceAct**}. By contrast, the signature of the following rule is {**Claim**, **PolicyHolder**, **ServiceAct**}.

```
Rule 3 - different signature:
definitions
    set 'a service act' to a service act in the service acts
of 'the claim;
    set 'a policy holder' to apolicy holder in the insureds
        of the policy of 'the claim;
if
    ...
```

Recall from Chap. 6 that the default tuple generator used by the sequential algorithm (see Chap. 6) takes the *union* of the signatures of the rules within the task to generate the tuples. Thus, if Rule 3 were in the same rule task as Rule 1 and Rule 2, the tuple generator will use the signature {**Claim**, **PolicyHolder**, **ServiceAct**} as the structure for the tuples. Given the objects $claim\_1$, $serviceAct\_1$, $serviceAct\_2$, $policyHolder\_1$, $policyHolder\_2$, the tuple generator will generate the tuples: $T_1 = $ <$claim\_1$, $policyHolder\_1$, $serviceAct\_1$>, $T_2 = $ <$claim\_1$, $policyHolder\_1$, $serviceAct\_2$>, $T_3 = $

---

depending on the tuple enumerator used by the sequential algorithm or the rule ordering algorithm used by fastpath.

[31]*Object* local variables are variables defined using the form "set <var name>to a <object type> [scope expression]." A variable that represents the *value* of an attribute (regardless of its type) is not mapped to an IRL class condition.

<claim_1, policyHolder_2, serviceAct_1>, and $T_4 =$ <claim_1, policyHolder_2, serviceAct_2>. For each tuple, we will apply Rule 1, Rule 2, and Rule 3, sequentially; if a rule has a smaller signature than the tuple, we "project" the tuple on the signature of the rule, meaning that the extra objects are ignored. This means that Rule 1, for example, will be evaluated *twice* on the pair <claim_1, serviceAct_1>, first while we process T_1 and a second time while we process the tuple T_3. The same is true for the pair <claim_1, serviceAct_2>, which will be evaluated twice by Rule 1, once for T_2 and a second time for T_4. The same is true for Rule 2. Having a rule execute several times on the same tuple of objects within a single run can be anywhere from inefficient to outright wrong. Hence, if the rules within a task do not have the same signature, the sequential algorithm should not be considered.

If the rules within a task *do* have the same signature, then it becomes a matter of performance. Recall that the fastpath algorithm does build a RETE network from the rules; it is just that takes a single pass at the rules. Compiling the rules of the task into a RETE network does have a cost. The benefit is the underlying condition sharing. Thus, if the rules of the task have numerous randomly ordered conditions, the fastpath algorithm will incur the RETE network construction costs, without the benefit of condition sharing: We should use the sequential algorithm. If the rules share some conditions, then the fastpath algorithm is preferred.

We summarize our *preliminary* discussion in the decision process of Fig. 11.20. This decision process needs to be qualified. In particular, the need for the RETE algorithm and for WM or agenda constructs can, in some cases, be eliminated, or reduced in scope. This is illustrated with a couple of examples below.

Most underwriting decisions – be they for mortgage or insurance – involve two distinct phases: (a) a *risk assessment* phase, which assigns a risk score to the customer application (for a loan or an insurance policy) and (b) a decision phase, which consists of assigning a recommendation (typically, accept, reject, or send for manual referral) based on that score. The underwriting decision itself *does* require rule chaining between risk assessment rules and decision rules. *However*, if we break the underwriting decision into two tasks, then the ruleflow built-in control flow will enforce that rule chaining. This is illustrated in Fig. 11.21. With this decomposition, instead of selecting a single algorithm for the task "Policy under-writing" (left ruleflow), we can now select different algorithms for the rule tasks "Risk scoring" and "Decision". Typically, risk scoring rules compare attributes to predefined ranges and increment or decrement a cumulative score, and they do not require rule chaining. The same is true for decision rules which typically compare a single risk value, or a set of score, to predefined thresholds and assign a decision with justifications. Thus, we should be able to use the sequential or fastpath algorithm for each of the two tasks taken separately – provided that the IRL/BAL constructs that are used in the rules allow it!

While this is a useful heuristic, it should be used *sparingly*: We should resist the temptation of slicing business decisions into finely granular, sequential decisions,

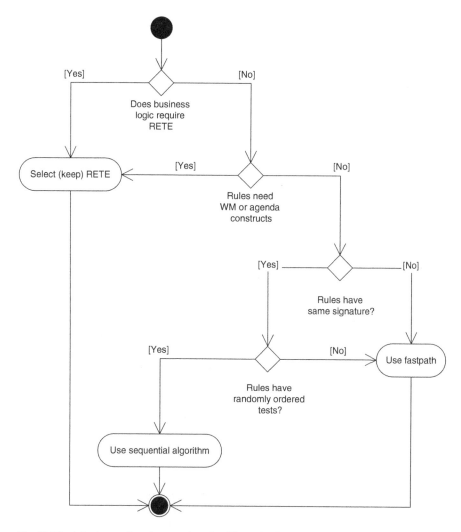

Fig. 11.20 A first-cut rule task execution algorithm selection process

just to get rid of rule chaining. Do not lose from sight the guidelines provided in Sect. 11.4.2 regarding the granularity of ruleflows.

With regard to the IRL or BAL constructs that are problematic or forbidden in sequential/fastapath, by adhering to a few stylistic guidelines, we can live without *most* of them – and never miss them again. For example, we can refrain from using unscoped **exists**, **not**, and collections in IRL, or their BAL equivalents. In particular, by using ruleset parameters to communicate business data to the engine and by refraining from inserting objects in working memory – as is the recommended practice, see Sects. 11.3.1 and 11.4.1 – we have no choice but to use the *scoped* versions of **exists**, **not**, and collections: Rules would *not* work otherwise, regardless of the execution algorithm!

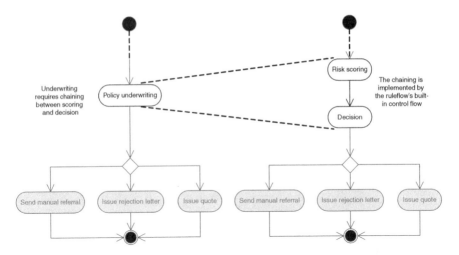

Fig. 11.21 By breaking a decision into two, we *may* obviate the need for rule chaining

This discussion raises two issues. First, *technically*, it *is always possible* to write the business rules so that they can execute in sequential or fastpath ... as it is possible to write them in Java or assembly language! The question is: ***How much of a price are we willing to pay for efficiency***. Keep in mind that business rules are supposed to become the communication language between business and IT. If that language is tweaked to the point that the business logic is no longer recognizable by a business person, be it a mortgage specialist, for a mortgage underwriting application, or a network operator, for an alarm filtering and correlation application, then we defeated the purpose of the business rules approach.

The second issue is related to the interplay between rule authoring and algorithm selection. If we design the ruleflow before we write the rules – as is the recommended practice, see Sects. 11.4.1 and 11.4.2 – then we will not know which algorithm to use for each rule task, until the rules are written. This erodes, a bit further, the separation of concerns between the *development time concerns* surrounding rule authoring and the *run-time concerns*. In particular, it raises the question of how much a rule author needs to know about the execution context of the rule that she or he is writing, for that rule to execute *correctly* and *efficiently*. This is a valid concern, but as we showed for the case of problematic IRL/BAL constructs, we can achieve quite a bit with a good preliminary design (Sects. 11.4.1 and 11.4.2), and a few stylistic guidelines, which can be enforced through the use of rule templates.

11.4.4   Best Practice 4: Do You Really Need a Custom Language?

We showed in Sect. 11.4.6 the JRules *Business Rules Language Development Framework* or *BRLDF* for short, a framework for developing custom rule authoring languages. The BRLDF, which has evolved over a dozen or so years, has a nice modular design, and provides a nice separation between the *abstract syntax* of a language from its *concrete syntax*. It also provides a clean separation between *parsing* and *code generation*. The BRLDF also enables us to build a language *incrementally* by modifying an existing language. This provides for localized and low-cost customization of existing languages. This makes it particularly easy to customize or extend the BAL, which is built using the BRLDF.

That being the case, do you really need a separate rule language? Now? The answer is probably no, and almost certainly not now. In Chap. 9, we argued that a new rule language is justified only when the following conditions, reframed within the context of JRules, are satisfied:

- The BAL syntax represents an unnecessary burden, and an unbearably awkward syntax for the rule authors.
- The cost of developing the custom rule language, the custom rule editor, and the custom rule engine was minimal.
- You have reasonable assurance that future evolution of JRules will not invalidate your language.

With regard to the second condition, the BRLDF design ensures that the cost of developing the language is indeed minimal, if we build it by extending or reusing parts of the BAL. However, how could we have a reasonable assurance that future evolution of the product will not invalidate your custom rule language? And if so, for how long? JRules is one of the most mature – if not *most* mature – BRMSs on the market. And yet, historically, it underwent major modernizations every few years. A case in point is the change between JRules 5 and JRules 6, which came out in late 2005/early 2006. In JRules 5, BAL rules are persisted in the form of their abstract syntax trees, serialized in XML format. In JRules 6, BAL rules are persisted in BAL text format. JRules 6.x and 7.x include utilities that know how to read the old representation format (XML-based abstract syntax trees) and how to convert them to the new format. However, these utilities understand, out of the box, only the *standard* BAL syntax.[32] This means a set of painful choices:

1. Refrain from upgrading to the newest product version, thereby foregoing valuable additional functionalities, bug fixes, or architectural enhancements.
2. Manually migrate your existing rules into the new version of JRules.
3. Develop your own migration utilities.

Note that both choice two and three imply that you upgrade your implementation of the custom language into the new version of JRules/BRLDF.

Different customer circumstances have at one point or another dictated each of the three choices. We can certify that they were all painful, and we do not recall a case where it was *candidly* felt that the customization added-value was, with hindsight, worth the initial language development effort (minimal) *and* the

---

[32]Well. They can also handle simple extensions like specifying value editors or specializing tokens of the language, but they cannot handle different grammatical structures.

migration pain (major). So how do customers get talked – or talk themselves – into building risky custom languages? Two reasons: (a) uneducated or unreasonable user requirements, and (b) an eager development organization. Indeed, if JRules is brought into an organization to replace another niche BRMS-like product, business users may insist on (and get) keeping every single nicety – or idiosyncracy – of the niche-product it is replacing, even when there are better or cleaner way of doing it in the generalist JRules. This could mean recreating an idiosyncratic rule entry language.[33] Second, developers are often eager to please because developers … love to develop: Any opportunity to delve into the more exotic parts of the API is a welcome relief from the often repetitive development tasks. Project managers and technical leads should know when to call off the party and say no.

As for the timing, while we believe that there is seldom a good time to develop a custom rule entry language, doing it on your first major rule project is definitely the *wrong* time. Project teams have enough to deal with on the first release of a rule-based application; they should not overburden themselves with "cosmetic" or nice-to-have features. And besides, the requirements for such a language can only be determined through practice.

11.5   Discussion

There is a lot more to what we collectively referred to as "rule authoring" than actually coding individual rules. Rule execution orchestration involves a number of complex design decisions that impact rule authoring, rule deployment, and rule execution. In this chapter, we identified these design decisions, described the design space, and discussed some best practices.

Designing rule execution orchestration falls within the purview of the *rule architect* and is of no concern to rule *writers*. As illustrated for the case of algorithm selection, the rule architect needs a deep understanding of the business logic, a deep understanding of the BAL, IRL, and an understanding of rule engine mechanics. Similarly, ruleset signature requires good business logic knowledge and software architecture knowledge.

As this chapter and last showed, the rule architect has a central role in rule authoring, management, and execution. He also needs a variety of skills straddling three different areas: business, java, and JRules. From our experience, customers often misunderstand this role and assign its tasks to individuals who lack one – and sometimes two – skill sets, or worse yet, assign different tasks to different individuals. This typically leads to suboptimal or incoherent designs.

Our experience has also been that customers underestimate the skill level required of rule writers. In most projects, we have been to where IT is responsible for authoring and maintaining rules, it was often the most junior members of the

---

[33]We can call it a *domain-specific language* to make it more acceptable ☺.

team that got to write rules. That is a shame because good rule authoring requires a deep understanding of the business logic, an awareness of the rule coding patterns discussed in Chap. 9, and a mastery of the business action language (BAL) and its derivatives. A junior *IT* person would typically lack at least one of the skill sets.

As with any other technology, quality is *not inevitable*. Get the wrong people, and you get the wrong results. If this is your first business rules project, get the wrong people, and not only do you get the wrong results, but you also learn the wrong lesson – and set back business rule adoption in your organization by a few years.

11.6   Further Reading

As this chapter is JRules specific, additional sources of information can be found in the product documentation and on IBM's support site for *Websphere Ilog JRules* at http:/publib.boulder.ibm.com/infocenter/brjrules/v7r1/index.jsp.

More information about the rule engine execution algorithms can be found in Chap. 6 and its references. The Web site www.agilebrdevelopment.com, which is dedicated to this book, contains complementary information.

Part V
Rule Deployment

Chapter 12
Issues in Deploying Rules

Target audience

- *Application architect, developer, business analyst*

In this chapter you will learn

- *Technology and deployment issues to consider when planning your integration, like transaction support, scalability, data access, ruleset deployment*
- *How to manage the ruleset life cycle*
- *How to implement rule execution as a decision service using web service, SCA and JMS*

Key points

- *Access to the data model used by the rules can impact performance and should be part of the decision service implementation not the ruleset.*
- *Data model definitions are different: there is one for messaging and service contract level; one for the rule execution, and one for persistence in the database.*
- *Parallel processing of rule execution is a common implementation in business application to support scalability and hot deployment.*
- *Ruleset parameters should not be exposed as generic service, but behind a service interface which specify the business intent of the different decision service operations.*

12.1   Introduction

In this chapter, we present the common issues around rule deployment, the ruleset packaging and life cycle, and the decision service integration. We start, in Sect. 12.2, by looking at the major deployment and integration considerations an application architect is considering when looking at rule engine technology: transaction support, scalability, data access, and rule hot deployment. The main reason

J. Boyer and H. Mili, *Agile Business Rule Development*,
DOI 10.1007/978-3-642-19041-4_12, © Springer-Verlag Berlin Heidelberg 2011

for that comes from the fact that business rule applications are transactional, processing business data under performance constraints: care and strong architecture are needed. In Sect. 12.3, we describe the concept of decision service, covering details on the different integration technology to use to support the implementation and the communication with such business services. Communication between the application and the rule engine can be implemented in a variety of ways; using standard or proprietary API, we present the Java Specification Request 94 (JSR94) API, which defines how a Java program can access a rule engine without using a proprietary API.

Section 12.4 reviews the design and the management of the ruleset life cycle and how to deploy ruleset to the different physical environments. Deployment includes packaging the rules in an executable format and making them available to the rule engine in the target environment. A ruleset is a set of rules that can be executed by the rule engine to produce decisions. The questions to consider are how to select the rules as part of the ruleset and how to support a life cycle that controls the quality of this piece of code. We conclude in Sect. 12.5.

12.2 Integration and Deployment Considerations

When defining and designing the rule engine integration as well as the rules deployments, the architect has to study at least the following requirements: transaction support, scalability, data access, and ruleset hot deployment. We present in this section those requirements in more details.

12.2.1 Transaction Support

Most of business applications using a rule engine are transforming the business data exposed to the rule engine by modifying attributes of business entities, adding new entities, etc. This processing may be done as part of a transaction. The rule engine has to be a good citizen in the support of transactions. Transactions are a means of guaranteeing that changes made to a data source are completed accurately, respecting the ACID[1] properties:

---

[1] A is for ATOMICITY, C for CONSISTENCY, I for ISOLATION, and finally D for DURABILITY.

Concept: The ACID Properties	
ATOMICITY	The transaction should be completed or rolled-back completely and unambiguously. In the event of a failure of any operation, effects of all operations that make up the transaction should be undone, and data should be rolled back to its previous state.
CONSISTENCY	A transaction should preserve all the invariant properties (such as integrity constraints) defined on the data. Upon completion of a successful transaction, the data should be in a consistent state.
ISOLATION	Each transaction should appear to execute independently of other transactions that may be executing concurrently in the same environment.
DURABILITY	The effects of a completed transaction should always be persistent.

For a rule-based application, the action part of a rule can modify any object within the graph of objects in its working memory. Those objects may come from a data source. The architect needs to take into account if the call to the rule execution is in the context of a transaction or not and consider if modified data objects must be persisted back to the data source by the ruleset. We recommend that transactions should not be started within a rule or rule flow. It is better to let the calling client create a transaction and propagate the changes when the rule execution is completed. The client code makes the decision of rolling back or committing the transaction, depending on the rule execution results. Managing transactions within the ruleset is more complex because it requires that the rule flow include an initial action to start any transactions, separate tasks to manage exceptions and trigger rollbacks, and final steps to commit the transaction. Transaction support should be provided by the application server and be transparent to the rule engine and rules. The transaction manager allows resource enlistment and may conduct the two-phase commit or recovery protocol with the resource managers.

Concept: There are two types of transactions:

- Distributed transactions, which support multiple resources in a coordinated manner
- Local transactions, which begin and commit transactions to a single resource manager

Two-phase commits ensure that the resource manager parts of the transaction either commit all or abort all changes made.

The business method, which uses a rule session, can be part of an existing transaction. Depending on the type of deployment, it may be possible to specify the value of the transaction attribute within some deployment descriptor. The value specifies how the method call should react to the transaction: from never (the method must not be called with a transactional context) to mandatory (the method requires a transaction). Modern application servers make it easier to define and work with transactions, but do not eliminate the activity of designing which components handle transaction origination and completion. In some extreme cases, rule engines may execute rules with a longer processing time than other method calls, so it is important to specify the maximum duration for the transaction timeout depending on the time required to process the rules. It is good practice to constantly monitor the time for rule execution so you can tune the transaction timeouts or evaluate the impact of newly deployed rules.

12.2.2 Scalability

The second architecture assessment and design consideration is related to scalability. Scalability is the property of the application or the system to support a growing amount of transaction to process without impacting dramatically the performance. When looking at business applications, which use rule engines, there are various factors which can impact performance: the number of objects used in the fact model, the number of rules, the number of concurrent callers, the type of access to external data sources, the type of objects used to present the data, and so on. From the rule execution point of view, some business applications may use rulesets with a large number of rules (around 20,000 rules) and need to fire rules with an average of 100 ms. Scalability can be achieved by looking at the data access, the hardware configuration, the rule engine deployment, and the design of the application. One of the most important factors for rule execution is the data access, which we will detail in the next section.

Adding hardware can improve scalability. There are two models of extension: vertical, by adding resource such as CPU or memory to the current server, or horizontal by adding new servers. Vertical extension involves using multiple rule engines in parallel ready to serve the next transaction. Rule engine pooling is a design pattern used to support creating rule engines and rulesets in advance, managed in a pool and used on demand. Globally speaking, designing a scalable architecture can be achieved through resource pooling and parallel execution for CPU-intense activities. When the rule engine fires rules, it consumes CPU resources, so we may want to execute them in parallel by using different threads of execution. Pooling is efficient to manage a regular flow of requests with little change in the number of requests. When a "spike" in requests occurs, some requests may be put on hold waiting to get access to a rule engine ready for processing. This may not be an issue to run the application for 95% of the time. In the other cases more hardware resources may be required to avoid issues when a spike occurs.

Ruleset parsing costs time, so caching already created ruleset objects is mandatory when performance is important. Executable rules have a large memory footprint of around 6 KB per rule, so vertical scaling may quickly reach the limitation of the underlying CPU architecture. For example, on a 32-bit CPU, the size of the ruleset is constrained to 4 GB of memory.

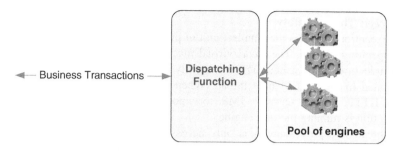

Fig. 12.1 Dispatching function in front of rule engine selection

Leveraging a multi-core or multi-CPU architecture helps to support a mix of vertical and horizontal extension and improve the rule engine pooling execution. Pooling specifies a maximum number of rule engines (linked to the number of cores), which can serve client requests in parallel. Ruleset pooling is an important implementation to support enterprise application, and most of the BRMS vendors provide such support. Some open source solutions have a big weakness in this domain. If you choose to use JSR94 to interact with your rule engine, verify that the vendor's JSR94 implementation supports ruleset pooling and hot deployment. You could implement your own pooling mechanism using the open source project, "Apache Commons Pool API.[2]" Basically, the goal is to keep the ruleset object, which is costly to create, in the pool as a keyed generic object. But there are some design and implementation constraints to carefully address which can take a lot of time to fine tune.

When a lot of business objects must be processed in a short period of time, the design to separate the processing between engines works well. The dispatching of the business transaction can be driven by type of data where each data type is processed with a different rule engine by using a dispatcher function to route the objects to the appropriate ruleset (Fig. 12.1).

When designing the business application, it is important to evaluate what data elements can be dispatched to different rule engines. The idea is to find a discriminator attribute and then partition the data accordingly. Most of the time, business transactions are independent of each other, but there are still design considerations to look at: a shared collection of reference data can represent a challenge when dealing with multiple threads. The results may be unpredictable if not implemented properly. Most rule engines and ruleset objects on the market are thread safe, but the data elements accessed by the rules must also be thread safe. This is more a design and implementation constraint on the data model when concurrent and parallel executions are important.

---

[2]See the apache project at http://commons.apache.org/pool/.

Concept: **Thread Safety**

An execution thread is the smallest unit of processing that can be scheduled by an operating system. The Java[3] virtual machine allows an application to run multiple threads of execution concurrently. On the server side, a servlet is executed in the context of a thread. When using EJB, Web services, SOAP over HTTP, Restful services, JMS, to expose a decision service, a thread of execution is running the rule engine.

Thread-safe programming is only necessary if you have data that can be modified by more than one thread at a time. Normally, if two threads try to change shared data, developer should not hope that the first thread is able to finish with the data before the second one begins to modify it. This situation is called *racing*. Most stateless implementations of decision service using rule engine do not share data. Reference data are exceptions, they could be updated in parallel of rule engine processing, if the data in the data source is changed. Most of rule applications use a rich data graph; therefore, the architect needs to assess the data model against thread safety requirements.

Horizontal extension is accomplished by adding servers. Still there is a need to dispatch the transactions to different server depending on the current server payload. Detailing such architecture is out of scope of this book. This is a complex problem to tackle, and software and hardware vendors propose different solutions to support scalability at the server level.

The scalability support has to be considered at the design phase; the different deployment strategies have to be evaluated at the early phase of the development. The architect needs to consider how each deployed decision service (see Sect. 12.4) performs when the load increases. We recommend conducting systematic tests to evaluate the service when the load is light, medium, heavy and when load varies over time. The tests measure the response time and throughput for the different test scenarios. The tools used are basic: count the number of requests sent to the engine over time and the time to respond. The graphs of response time or throughput against the selected parameters present some inflexion points within the curve. At this level, the application has reached resource conflicts that require some attention and tuning. By using a few rules, you can simulate the behavior of a ruleset containing thousands of rules before rule authoring is completed. Still the best load testing is to use actual rules and actual data. The performance results are directly linked to the type of data and rules used. So the closer we are to the production data set the better.

---

[3]See Java Thread API at http://download-llnw.oracle.com/javase/6/docs/api/packagejava.lang.

12.2.3 Data Access

Data access represents the real, recurring issue to consider when developing business rule application. Recall from Chap. 6 that a rule engine is accessing a data graph within the condition and action parts of each rule. In this section, we try to present the different problems of data access, loading the data, and changing the structure definition of the data, and present some possible solutions.

A Java rule engine manipulates Java objects. These objects are referenced within the working memory, are read within the condition part of the rule, and are modified in the action part. Loading the data means transforming data read in a database into Java objects (or Java beans). In a worst case scenario, the engine may need to load the data elements from a data store, deployed somewhere, at each condition evaluation. In reality, we will use proven technology to support loading, caching, and mapping the data to Java Objects. The Java Persistence API, JPA,[4] is such technology, for example. Still, poor performance of the object to data mapping layer can dramatically impact rule processing. During the authoring step, we assume the data elements are present, but in the deployment environment there are cases where it may not be true. Lazy data loading is such a case. For example, if we test on a coverage code for a given policy with conditions such as: *if the coverage of the policy is code 32 <...> then <action>*. When the policy is loaded from a data source but not the Coverages (lazy loading), the rule condition does not match or the rule engine may need to wait for the data to come depending on the O/R mapping implementation and configuration.

Even in pure XML document processing, the data model may need to be completed by loading some reference data before calling the rule execution. Those reference data are mapped in Java object and cached locally to the rule engine.

A solution is to load all the related data before calling the rule execution. This is a common pattern when using a rule engine. One of the advantages of this approach is to efficiently manage any exception, which may happen when loading data, outside of the rule execution. It may be difficult and complex to manage the load data issue and recovery in the context of the rule. Also the rule processing performance will be better as the data are ready for the rules; there is no wait time to get the data from data sources at the rule level.

There are cases where the amount of data to load is important but only valid for 10% of the business transaction to process. We may not want to penalize all transactions for the sake of making 10% efficient. This is a common case on reference data, like medical procedure codes or other business related codes. The worst implementation loads the data at each business event. So caching of such reference data may be a better choice. In that case, we have to be sure the reference data graph is thread safe. This problem of data loading is not exclusive to databases, it also applies when accessing legacy application content on mainframe using a

---

[4]See specification at Java Persistence API: http://www.jcp.org/en/jsr/detail?id=317.

message-oriented middleware, or accessing a web service. As JEE design encourages the use of local objects as much as possible, the same pattern applies here: the rule engine performs far better if its fact model is local. Latency can come from different sources: Network latency for remote method invocation, complex computations on the service side to return the data to the caller, database response time, and any combination of the three. Overall we need to be sure that any data referenced in the condition part of a rule is present for rule evaluation. If we do not consider this carefully, the performance for the rule processing may degenerate and the rules may not fire.

The second issue is related to the change to the data definition. In Java, class definitions must be loaded in the classpath to be available to the engine, which means any change to the data model forces a deployment of new JARs. Even if rules are hot deployed, when a change in the rule is linked to a change in the data model, the data model JAR must be redeployed first and then the rules. Otherwise, rule execution will generate exceptions or not process as expected.

To support the two previous issues, a solution is to use XML documents for getting data to the rule engine and XSD to define the structure of the data. XSDs are more flexible to change. They can be deployed to a central server and accessed with a unique URL. If the client code sends a noncompliant XML document, the XML parser detects it. Otherwise the rule using the new attribute will not fire, which may cause a functional problem. Using an XML binding approach, the deployment is linked to the BRMS product used and may offer the advantage of a pure dynamic data model definition if the XML binding is used to define the fact model for authoring the rules and also used during rule execution to map XML document to Java objects. There is no need to use an external static binding. The performance may be less optimized, but, as of today, there are many business applications that are using this approach.

Another solution is to leverage the Service Data Object (SDO)[5] specification to access dynamic data objects from heterogeneous, loosely coupled data sources (Fig. 12.2). SDO is an interesting solution when considerable variation in data amounts and data definitions are expected. Data definition generates tedious rule refactoring, so any solution where the rules can leverage a stable data model has to be privileged. The decision service and the rules use the SDO API to access the data. The access point is the DataObject, which provides flexible graph data structures to navigate to the objects needed by the rules. DataObject includes properties that can be simple type, one-to-one, or one-to-many references to other DataObject. SDO can read data from databases, XML, and any other resources depending of the implementation used. This implementation is the role of the Data Access Service component (DAS). The client code, like a rule-based decision service, accesses the data using the SDO context which manages the data graph and the change summary graph. The change summary graph highlights the changes

---

[5]See SDO specification at http://www.osoa.org/display/main/service+data+objects+home.

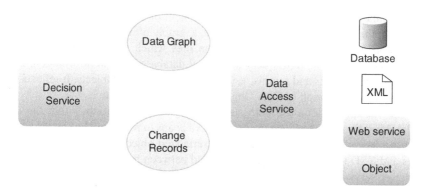

Fig. 12.2 SDO components

made on the data objects, which is persisted back by the DAS. This feature is interesting when the data loaded relies on optimistic concurrency.

Apache Tuscany SDO[6] is an open source implementation for the SDO specification. There are also commercial products that support this API. The type definition can be set by APIs or come from an XSD. Within an SOA deployment, business objects are usually defined using XSDs. The XSD can be used to set the SDO data types. Below is an example for the Claim type, which has one Policy, and one-to-many InvolvedPerson. The definition comes from the claim-model.xsd. The code to access the claim and other related object looks like:

```
// First get a SDO context using Tuscany SDOUtil implementation
HelperContext scope = SDOUtil.createHelperContext();
// get the types definition for our model using XSD
loadTypesFromXMLSchemaFile(scope, "claim-model.xsd");
// use a factory to create DataObject
DataFactory dataFactory = scope.getDataFactory();
// create our first data object: the claim using the type as define in the claim mod-
el.xsd, using the same namespace
DataObject claim = dataFactory.create("http://abrd.claim","Claim");
// set some attributes on the claim using the API
claim.setInt("id",305);
claim.setDate("dateOfLoss",new Date());
// create a one to one relationship between claim and policy
DataObject policy = dataFactory.create("http://abrd.claim","InsurancePolicy");
policy.setString("policyNumber","P012345");
claim.setDataObject("policy", policy);
```

Each DataObject has a type that can be defined, as in the example above, using XSD, or as static Java class or dynamically using the SDO API. Once we get a SDO context, we can load the type definitions from a XSD, and use the data factory to create an instance of the data object. The association between objects is managed using a containment relationship. In every data graph, a data object has a unique parent which is a container: for example, the property "policy" within the Claim is a container, used to traverse the graph of objects.

---

[6]http://tuscany.apache.org/.

The Data Access Service is a major component of SDO as it is responsible for accessing the data source and to provide a graph of DataObject to the client application. DAS works with configuration files which supplies information for data source connection, SQL query to use and database schema information. DAS executes SQL Queries and returns results as a graph of Data Objects. It reflects any changes made to a graph of Data Objects back to the data source.

Classical applications use both static and dynamic definition within the data model. Most likely an architect uses static Java beans to represent data coming from local database, RMI communication with serialized objects between Java components and XSD to define messages exchanged between heterogeneous applications using web service or JMS as communication vehicle. Tuscany SDO[7] or SDO vendors provide tools to generate Java interface, implementation class, and factory from the type defined in a XSD. The framework authorizes in that case a mix of static and dynamic management of the data model.

12.2.4 Ruleset Hot Deployment

One of the goals for adopting a BRMS is to be able to deploy the rules without stopping the business application (operation known as "hot deployment"). The rules are provided to the application as data. For example in the case of a Java application, rules are not part of the classpath and loaded as other JAR[8] files at application start-up. The rules are treated as external data parsed and loaded into the server memory. This capability sometime scares architects and production operation managers; this is why we want to elaborate on this capability.

The BRMS can use a database or a file system in the rule execution environment to store the executable ruleset. In Java SE you can use the file system, but in Java EE, a database is a more likely choice to comply with security standards. The ruleset is loaded from the data source and parsed so that the engine can execute the rules. Rulesets can be cached and shared between engines. Parsing the ruleset consumes CPU time, because the rule engine builds the RETE Network from the rule declarations. The larger the number of rules, the greater the time to parse. The integration of the rule engine into the application server has to take into account ruleset caching and support a listening mechanism to get new events when a new version of a given ruleset is available within the data source. Multiple rulesets can be deployed to the same rule execution server. Hot deployment can be an efficient feature when the engine processes business transactions in a stateless mode. The engine uses the latest version of the rules. This is mostly the case for data validation ruleset. It becomes more sensitive on underwriting or eligibility rules when audits may occur asking for reasons why the system refused or accepted any given business

---

[7]See SDO Apache project in http://tuscany.apache.org/sdo-overview.html.

[8]Java Archive: based on the zip compression format a Java archive groups all the java artifacts needed to a java application. At start-up, a java application load a set of jars files so it can execute.

transaction. In that case the audit function may need to replay the transaction with an old version of the ruleset.

Hot deployment can be an issue when there are a lot of business transactions to process in parallel. It may be interesting to evaluate when the business application is less demanding and schedule the ruleset update within that time window. The only possible deployment, without impacting dramatically the response time to process a business transaction, is to use parallel execution, with at least two rule engines serving the same business service. The loading and parsing of the ruleset has to be done in a separate thread of execution with a lower priority than the rule engine threads. The parsing of rules takes more time than rule execution, so between the start of the loading and parsing tasks the rule engine will process many business transactions. When the new ruleset is ready, the next call to get a rule engine from the pool is linking the new ruleset to the engine. This is true when the processing is in stateless mode as each rule invocation does not maintain any engine internal states, and so can reset the engine or create a new engine instance. For stateful processing, it is more complex since the service needs to understand when the rule execution is completed, and cleans the rule engine states, before getting a new engine linked to the new ruleset. This can take longer if the stateful conversation requires multiple interactions. The conversation needs to maintain some context of execution; to be sure the next call is using the same "old" ruleset and not the new one.

A few BRMS products on market have this capability. The database used in execution environment has to be different than the one managing the rule authoring environment. The ruleset life cycle is different than the rule life cycle. The two repositories have different purpose.

Some BRMS, like IBM WebSphere JRules, propose using a second database as a rule repository to store versions and configuration management elements as well as rule artifacts. At a high level, the deployment involves the following components (Fig. 12.3).

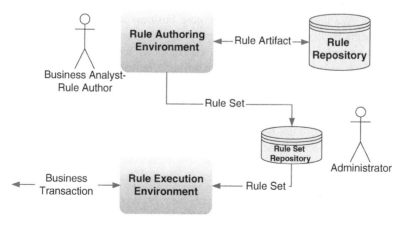

Fig. 12.3 Deployment components

- Rule authoring environment to support rules development activities
- Rule repository to store the rule artifacts
- Ruleset repository to save a packaged rules to the execution environment
- A server to execute the rules and host the rule engines

Deployment may be driven by business analysts, but controlled by production administrators. The BRMS supports the tagging of rules and rulesets to control the deployed entities. Some security and role enforcement may also be necessary when rules are deployed in sensitive environments or to control access to each ruleset.

12.3   Decision Service Integration

In this section, we present why the decision service approach is important and how to support its integration in the IT architecture. SOA is about exposing reusable business services, and implementing some of these services with BRMS technology brings agility within the IT architecture. The business service taking decision is named in the industry "decision service." In a broader way, James Taylor[9] is presenting a lot of best practices on his blog[10] about decision management. The design of a decision service should follow the same SOA best practices for business services implementation; one of these is the definition of the request/response data structure, or service contract, which represents a partial view of the fact model used by the rule engine. It is frequent to consider the objects inserted in the working memory of the rule engine to infer decision,[11] as input parameter to the operation exposed in the service contract, but in fact this approach has some major drawbacks. The major one is to ask the consumer of the rule service to send all the data, which may not be feasible, and violate the loosely coupled argument of SOA: adding new elements in the fact model involves changing the service contract (data definition), which by side effect enforces changing all the client applications. Better to design coarse grained business interface, and let the service responsible to load its data set. We think this is better to expose business interface and then use rule engine for the implementation without exposing any ruleset signature to the calling processes or application code. Business interfaces are more stable, coarse grained, and loosely coupled, all important characteristics for a sustainable SOA and leveraging best practices for SOA. Another common issue is related to the need of getting access to internal utility objects: most of rule processing needs some helper classes to facilitate writing efficient rules, those helper classes or internal technical service classes should not be exposed to the external world as part of the service definition, but be added in the working memory or parameter of the rule engine. For

---

[9]http://www.smartenoughsystems.com/ and the book from James Taylor and Neil Raden, *"Smart Enough Systems: How to Deliver Competitive Advantage by Automating Hidden Decisions."*

[10]http://jtonedm.com/.

[11]See Chap. 6 for detail on those concepts.

example, some utility classes can be required to simplify the access to the data model by the business analyst: a complex enterprise model can include hundreds of classes, with thousands of attributes, which deliver the vocabulary to write rules against. The more complex the vocabulary, the less effective is the rule authoring task. Helper classes help to abstract some concepts and offer a more accessible vocabulary.

One of the real problems of interface design resides in the data model and parameters the service operation needs to receive. There are a lot of best practices in the industry on how to design web services and the data model: top-down starting by the WSDL and XSDs, bottom-up starting by existing Java interface or classes, and a mix of the two called *meet in the middle*. We will not detail yet another approach, but what is important to note is that rule engines, in the Java world, use Java classes as a data model. The real value of Java against XSD is that we can use good programming practices to enforce the use of immutable objects as part of our data model, add behavioral methods to the Java class to support complex computation and all classical object-oriented programming practices. We can use the Java Annotations to generate mapping to persistence layer, web services definition, and XSD/XML document from our data model. Developers have full control on the functions to add to class. Most of the time a data model in Java is easier to unit test, and with an IDE such as Eclipse, the refactoring of classes is a real benefit as it is almost impossible to design a good data model to be used as rule fact model upfront. Using a pure XSD approach, when executing the development cycle XSD to Java back to XSD does not generate the same code and schemas. So refactoring may be more cumbersome.

For the service definition we will, most likely, have two models: one using simple types and the minimum data definition so that client code can reuse the service more easily. This data model is part of the request–response structure. Client code does not have to load the data for a service. For example, in the claim processing, the client caller sends a claim identifier and other important data like policy number, insured person identifier ... then the business service takes care to prepare the data for the rule engine by loading all the necessary related data. Another important consideration is to look at the reference data, and other business objects not provided by the caller, but still required by the rule engine. Such data can come as enumerations or more complex data graphs and may have a more static definition. By static we mean that it does not change often within the scope of the ruleset life cycle. Loading such data is accomplished within the implementation of the business operation using some Data Access Object,[12] or Data Access Service or other patterns. Reference data like product code, medical procedure code, and decision-rejection code used by the rule are more static and are cached behind technical services. The business operation implementation is calling such services and sends the data as reference to the rule engine. A classical example is related to the reason codes used as the action part of

---

[12]See Sun Core J2EE Patterns – Data Access Object at http://java.sun.com/blueprints/corej2eepatterns/ Patterns/DataAccessObject.html.

eligibility rules. The rule accumulates issues in the result processing, and each issue
can use predefined reason code and reason description. Those codes can be defined,
as reference data, in a central repository of a Master Data Management product.

12.3.1 Service Implementation

On the service implementation side, Java developers can integrate the Rule Engine
at the API level to access rule engines. For the claim processing, we can implement
a Java interface for all the decision services we want to support on the Claim. This
interface may be defined as below:

```
package abrd.claim.services;
  import insurance.claim.Claim;
  import insurance.claim.Result;

  public interface ClaimProcessing {
    public Result validateClaim(Claim claim);
    public Result validateMedicalInvoice(MedicalInvoice medicalInvoice);

    public Result adjudicateClaim(Claim claim);
    public Result verifyCoverage(Claim claim);
  }
```

In fact this interface can be exposed as a web service using the JAX-WS annotations, which helps automatic generation of server and client codes. The service
operation defined in the interface calls one ruleset. In the claim processing example,
we have the validate claim, the adjudicate claim, or the verify coverage operations;
each operation uses a different ruleset with different parameters. When using a web
service definition, there is no difference between a decision service and another
business service: the client should not know it is using a rule engine.

In short, the algorithm of a business operation may look like: (1) get the input
parameter, (2) load complementary data, (3) prepare the ruleset parameters, (4)
execute the rules, (5) get the result from the rules execution, and (6) prepare the
output parameters and return. If the business service needs to support stateful
execution, we need to add some working memory management before calling the
rule execution as a step 3, but also offers a set of operations at the interface level
to terminate the session by the client. This is the client which manages the life
cycle of the transaction. Most business applications are not using a stateful
processing; there is no real need to keep states on the same business transaction
between different invocations. The context can be propagated between service
operations, without maintaining state at the operation level. States are part of the
context carried on.

In the case of the claim processing, the client has access to the claim number, the
policy number, and the customer name, so the business services are based on those
simple information. Our previous interface definition is using a complex model the
client needs to prepare for us. We keep the first interface definition using Claim and

MedicalInvoice Java classes for possible pure Java application integration, but we also offer web service access using a second interface using simple type and let the implementation prepare the data for the rules:

```
@WebService
public interface ClaimProcessing implements java.rmi.Remote {
 @WebMethod(operationName = "validateClaim", action = "urn:executeValidateClaim")
 public ClaimProcessingResult validateClaim(String claimNumber);

 @WebMethod(operationName = "adjudicateClaim", action = "urn:executeAdjudicateClaim")
 public ClaimProcessingResult adjudicateClaim(String claimNumber);

 ..

}
```

Using a top-down approach a developer designs the WSDL upfront by reusing existing XSDs to define the messages exchanged between clients and the service, including all the related business objects used in the message payload. When the types are more complex, it is possible to leverage a JAXB implementation and the "Java XML binding schema to Java" compiler, XJC tool, to generate the Java classes for those business objects. When designing input parameters to a business operation, it is important to be independent of the needs of a single client business process. The service has to be designed for reuse.

Rules can call web services in their action part, but it is not recommended. It is important to use synchronous RPC like communication to prevent blocking the rule execution. It is recommended to often check the performance of the web service to ensure efficient execution of rules. In most ruleset we try to avoid calling external service as the management of error, retry, and fault compensation are difficult to do in the action part of a rule.

12.3.2 Messaging Deployment

There are a lot of business applications which use message-oriented middleware (MOM) to communicate with other applications. It is the technology of choice for asynchronous processing of messages. One of the principal arguments to use asynchronous communication is when the caller or message producer does not need an immediate response from the consumer of the message. In the case of rule engine processing, the caller is expecting a direct response from the rule execution so the synchronous approach is the simplest and most common deployment. Some solution architects propose MOM and ESB as the mean to perform communication interchanges between applications. An ESB provides more features of interest for IT architecture. For a Java rule-based system, the simplest integration with a MOM or an ESB is to use the Java Message Service API. JMS defines the interfaces to create, to send, to read, and to publish messages. It supports both publish–subscribe and point-to-point messaging.

Concepts. In point to point messaging, a sender application addresses each message to a specific JMS queue, and the receiving clients extract messages from that queue. Queues retain all messages sent to them until the messages are consumed or until the messages expire. Each message has one consumer, and there is no timing dependency between the sender and receiver.

In publish/subscribe messaging, publisher applications address messages to a JMS topic, on which subscriber applications listen to messages. The JMS implementation takes care of distributing the messages arriving from a topic's multiple publishers to its multiple subscribers. Topics retain messages only as long as it takes to distribute them to the current subscribers.

The two approaches can be used when the consumer/receiver is a rule engine. It is common to use a queue communication approach when we externalize some of the mainframe core functions to a rule engine. Instead of maintaining the underwriting business rules in COBOL code, it may be interesting to use a BRMS for this function and change the legacy application to post the transactional business data to a queue so that a decision service can apply the new rules. The message payload is an XML document, which includes in its message header some ReplyTo queue reference so that the rule engine can post results to another queue. In fact it is not directly the engine which is doing the direct retrieval or sending of message but the implementation of the business service. Same approach as previous section. The XML to Java binding can be done in the implementation of this service, as well as retrieving some other reference data or business objects.

In event processing and event driven architecture, the publisher of events does not know who the consumers are. The publish–subscribe model can be used and the rule engine processes the events: a typical application is to filter events to keep only those of interest or correlate events to derive patterns or even decisions. The event publisher pushes data to subscribers which process it without any call back.

12.3.3   Service Component Architecture

Service implementation can leverage the Service Component Architecture as an efficient approach to develop and compose business applications. Every SCA application is built from one or more components. Components encapsulate business logic. Components can be combined into larger structures called composites or assemblies. An SCA composite is typically described in an associated XML configuration file called Service Component Description Language (SCDL). One of the main goals of SCA is to clearly separate the communication details from the business logic: the protocols and quality of service are wired at execution time; the developer focuses on defining reusable services supporting business functions. Figure 12.4 is an example of a simple assembly for a subparty of our claim application. The main

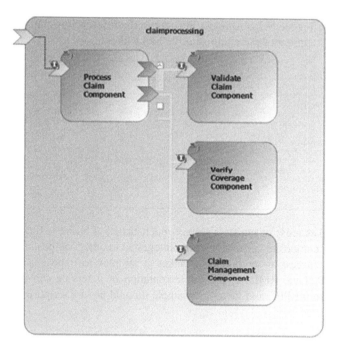

Fig. 12.4 SCA composite diagram

component is the ProcessClaimComponent, which offers a unique interface to the external "world." It has references to the three other components. From this example, we can clearly see how a rule engine through its Java Interface can be integrated as a component within a composite.

The composition of SCA component supports different language of implementation. As we focus on Java, we use the SCA Java programming model which relies on annotations to wire the application at runtime. Using @Service annotation, we expose method as a service interface by simply annotating the class. Here is an example of the main component class:

```
@Service(ProcessClaimService.class)
public class ProcessClaimImpl implements ProcessClaimService {
    private ValidateClaimService validateClaimService;
    private VerifyCoverageService verifyCoverageService;
    private ClaimManagementService claimManagement;

    public String processClaim(String claimNumber) {
        // omitted implementation
    }
    @Reference
    public void setValidateClaimService(ValidateClaimService validateClaimService) {..
```

The @Reference helps to inject at runtime the reference to the validateClaim-
Service. A fragment of the composite file looks like:

```
<sca:component name="ProcessClaimComponent">
    <sca:implementation.Java class="abrd.claimprocessing.bserv.ProcessClaimImpl"/>
    <sca:service name="ProcessClaimService">
      <sca:interface.Java interface="abrd.claimprocessing.api.ProcessClaimService"/>
    </sca:service>
    <sca:reference name="validateClaimService" target = "ValidateClaimCompo-
nent/ValidateClaimService"/>
...
  </sca:component>
  <sca:component name="ValidateClaimComponent">
    <sca:implementation.Java class="abrd.claimprocessing.bserv.ValidateClaimImpl"/>
    <sca:service name="ValidateClaimService">
      <sca:interface.Java interface = "abrd.claimprocessing.api.ValidateClaimService"/>
    </sca:service>
  </sca:component>
```

SCA makes reuse of business service much easier. A business function is implemented as a composite and can be easily integrated in other composites. The binding
mechanism (access to component) makes it simpler to expose a service using
JMS, SOAP, Java, RMI ... The implementation of a service can be in different
languages from BPEL and Java, for example it could be in a scripting language like
Ruby.

12.3.4 Embedding Rule Engines Using Low-Level Rule Engine API: JSR94

Decision service implementation can leverage a neutral API to access rule engine.
We present in this section the JSR94,[13] an industry standard that defines how Java
programs deployed in JSE or JEE can acquire and interact with a rule engine. The
goal of this specification aims to make the client code for simple rule-based
applications less dependent on rule engine vendor-specific classes. The basic
interactions with a rule engine are typically parsing the rules in scope of a ruleset,
adding object references to one engine, firing the rules, and getting results from the
engine.

JSR94 defines a ruleset as a *rule execution set* which can be loaded from external
resources like URIs, Input streams, XML streams, and readers. A rule execution set
is a collection of rules. Another important JSR94 concept is the rule session, which
is a runtime connection between a client and a rule engine. A rule session is
associated with a single rule execution set, consumes rule engine resources and
must be explicitly released when the client no longer requires it. Sessions can be
stateless or stateful.

---

[13]The JSR 94 specification can be found at http://jcp.org/aboutJava/
communityprocess/review/jsr094/index.html.

> **Concepts.** Stateless executes a rule execution set with a list of input objects in one call.
>
> Stateful is designed to maintain a long time conversation between the client and the engine and provides mechanism to assert/retract input object to the session.

The client code may run on server layer like a servlet controller, in a service tier part of an EJB or POJO, or in a standalone JSE JVM. The `Javax.rules` API divides interaction with rule engines into administrative and runtime interactions. The basic operations supported by JSR94 are:

- Acquiring a rule session for a registered rule execution set
- Deploying and un-deploying rulesets into a rule engine instance
- Querying simple metadata about a ruleset
- Executing a ruleset in either a stateful or stateless mode

The next sections provide more details for each operation.

12.3.4.1 The Client Code for Runtime Execution

From the client's point of view, the interaction with a rule engine uses rule sessions. But the first part is to get an instance of the rule engine implementation. The service provider manager helps to get a rule service provider which in turn helps to get rule runtime and rule administration implementations. Every specific implementation exposes a unique identifier for the service provider URL, below is an example using JRules service provider.

```
// Get the rule service provider from the provider manager
Class.forName(IlrRuleServiceProvider.class.getName());
RuleServiceProvider serviceProvider = RuleServiceProviderManager.getRuleServicePro
vider("ilog.rules.bres.jsr94");
```

- For the reference implementation the URL is `org.jsp.jsr94.ri. RuleServiceProvider`
- For JRules the URL is `ilog.rules.bres.jsr94.IlrRule-ServiceProvider`, and the service provider name is `ilog. rules.bres.jsr94`
- For JBoss-drools the URL is `org.drools.jsr94.rules. RuleServiceProviderImpl` and the service provider name is `http://drools.org`

The code above is used for JSE deployment, for JEE environment runtime clients should resolve the `RuleRuntime` and `RuleAdministrator` services directly using JNDI lookup.

```
Javax.naming.InitialContext initialContext = new InitialContext();
RuleRuntime ruleRuntime =
(RuleRuntime) PortableRemoveObject.narrow(
initialContext.lookup("org.jcp.jsr94.ri.RuleRuntime"),RuleRuntime.class );
```

In JSE, we can load those URL references from a properties file or a file descriptor to avoid hard coding. The next step is to get a rule engine runtime.

```
// Get a RuleRuntime and invoke the rule execution.
RuleRuntime ruleRuntime = serviceProvider.getRuleRuntime();
```

The RuleRuntime interface exposes the method to create a rule session given a previously registered `RuleExecutionSet` URI. It is possible to execute the rule engine in stateless or stateful mode using different type of rule session. We need to specify the URI for the rule execution set and the session type. The code looks like:

```
StatelessRuleSession statelessRuleSession = (StatelessRuleSession) ruleRun-
time.createRuleSession (ruleExecutionSetURI, rulesessionProper-
ties,RuleRuntime.STATELESS_SESSION_TYPE);
```

The second parameter is optional and is used to add some additional properties to the session. In JRules, it is used to give the references to the ruleset parameters and to specify if the `RuleSession` is a J2SE Plain Old Java Object (POJO[14]) rule session or a J2EE POJO rule session:

```
Map rulesessionProperties = new HashMap();
rulesessionProperties.put("claim", claim);
rulesessionProperties.put("policy", policy);
```

A stateless rules session exposes a stateless rule execution API to an underlying rules engine with two different methods to call the execution of the rule:

```
public Java.util.List executeRules(Java.util.List objects)
   throws InvalidRuleSessionException,Java.rmi.RemoteException
and
public Java.util.List executeRules(Java.util.List objects, ObjectFilter filter)throws
InvalidRuleSessionException,Java.rmi.RemoteException
```

---

[14]POJO is an acronym for Plain Old Java Object and is used to emphasize that a given object is an ordinary Java Object, not a special object like an Enterprise JavaBean.

The list of objects set as parameters will be inserted in the engine's working memory. The list returned includes all the objects created by the executed rules. The only things we can retrieve with JSR94 from an execution are the objects in the working memory. The second API uses a filter of objects the client code can supply to select those objects that should be returned from the rule engine.

12.3.4.2 Filtering Objects

To filter out objects from the list of returned objects from the rule execution call. The client code needs to provide an implementation of the ObjectFilter interface. The implementing class overwrites the filter(Object) callback methods that allow filtering out objects as desired. Here is a simple filter class that removes any claim which does not have a policy attached to it.

```
public class MyObjectFilter implements ObjectFilter {
@Override
    public Object filter(Object obj) {
        if (obj instanceof Claim) {
                Claim claim = (Claim)obj;
                if (claim.getPolicy() == null)
                    return obj;
        }
        return null;
    }
}
```

12.3.4.3 Get Rule Execution Set Meta Data

RuleRuntime can also be used to get the list of URIs that currently have rule execution set registered with them using the API:

```
List listURIs=ruleRuntime.getRegistrations();
```

The other object involved is the `RuleExecutionSetMetadata` interface which exposes metadata about a Rule Execution Set to runtime clients of a RuleSession like the name, URI, and description of the rule execution set.

```
RuleExecutionSetMetadata metadata = statelessRuleSession
            .getRuleExecutionSetMetadata();
metadata.getName();
metadata.getDescription();
metadata.getUri();
```

12.3.4.4 Stateful Session

Client code can use a stateful session to conduct long running conversation with the engine and control the working memory with new facts. Input Objects can be progressively added to the `StatefulRuleSession` through the `addObject` method. Output Objects can be progressively retrieved though the `getObject` method.

```
StatefulRuleSession statefulRuleSession = (StatefulRuleSession) getRuleRuntime()
.createRuleSession(ruleExecutionSetURI, getProperties(claim, medicalIn-
voice),RuleRuntime.STATEFUL_SESSION_TYPE);
//first call the normal execution
statefulRuleSession.executeRules();
Handle hdl = statefulRuleSession.addObject(claim);
statefulRuleSession.executeRules();
```

Objects that have been added to the `StatefulRuleSession` must be removed and updated using the `removeObject` and `updateObject` methods. A client must test for the existence of an added Object using the `containsObject` method. The `removeObject`, `updateObject`, and `containsObject` methods must all use a `Javax.rules.Handle` implementation (such as `IlrRuleSessionHandle`) instances to refer to and identify Object instances. Handles are used to ensure that `Object` instances can be unambiguously identified in the event of multiple class loaders being used or the StatefulRuleSession being serialized. The addObject method returns a Handle instance for an Object added to a StatefulRuleSession, so that it can be used in the remove API, for example.

In JRules, Ruleset parameters and objects added to the `RuleSession` when it is created are uniquely identified by an instance of the `IlrRuleSessionHandle` class.

12.3.4.5 Administrate Rule Execution Set

Administrative tasks supported by the API `Javax.rules.admin` include instantiating the rule engine and loading rules. To get the rule administrator, we use the service provider such as:

```
RuleAdministrator ruleAdministrator = serviceProvider.getRuleAd-
ministrator();
```

The RuleAdministrator allows RuleExecutionSet instances to be registered against a URI for use from the runtime API, as well as methods to retrieve a RuleExecutionSetProvider and a LocalRuleExecutionSetProvider implementation. The RuleExecutionSetProvider interface defines methods to create a RuleExecutionSet from a number of Serializable sources.

```
LocalRuleExecutionSetProvider ruleExecutionSetProvider = ruleAdministra-
tor.getLocalRuleExecutionSetProvider(null);
RuleExecutionSet ruleSet = ruleExecutionSetProvider.createRuleExecutionSet( input-
Stream, null );
ruleAdministrator.registerRuleExecutionSet( ruleSet.getName(),
    ruleSet,null );
```

The use of the local rule execution set provider is interesting to send a local execution set to a remote engine using serialization and marshaling. The API get (Local)RuleExecutionSetProvider takes an argument of type Map, which is documented as "additional properties" and used for setting the JNDI properties. The source for the rule can come from non-Serializable resources, such as binary InputStreams or character-based Readers. Registering the execution set to a URI helps to create session to an execution set. The rules registered using the rules admin API are the only rules accessible to the runtime clients.

The following code gets the name and description of the execution set deployed:

```
ruleSet.getDescription();

ruleSet.getName();
```

getName() in the case of JRules Rule Execution Server deployment returns the ruleset path. From the ruleset, we can get all the rules in a list and then for each rule its name and description.

In JRules, Rule.getName() returns a string which specify the language name and the name space for this rule, like for example "IRL/validation/max-imum_amount-brl.irl."

The rule.getDescription() returns the rule in the language of the rule engine vendor.

12.4 Ruleset Deployment

In this section, we describe the generic deployment process and ruleset life cycle, and how rulesets may be loaded into execution environment using a notification mechanism leveraging different protocols. Independent of the BRMS product used, the deployment process includes at least the following steps: (1) extract the rules in scope for the execution, (2) package the rule elements into a ruleset – a deployable artifact, (3) deploy the ruleset to the target environment, (4) notify the engine of a new ruleset, (5) let management stack inside the rule execution environment loading the ruleset, (6) trigger the engine API to parse the ruleset, and (7) send business transactions to fire the rules. Figure 12.5 illustrates this flow.

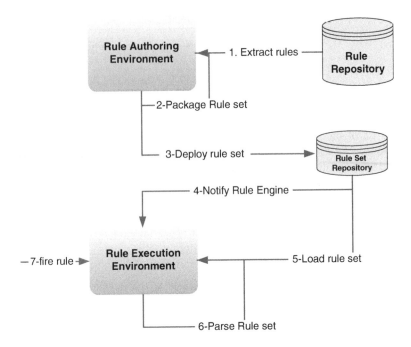

Fig. 12.5 Rule deployment process

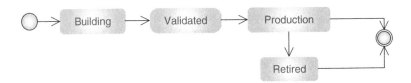

Fig. 12.6 Ruleset life cycle

12.4.1 Building the Ruleset

When the BRMS is using a rule repository supporting a meta-model, the first step of extracting the rules in scope of a ruleset is driven by using some sort of queries. In a rule repository, rules are grouped by rule project or rule group. The mapping between a ruleset and a rule project is most likely one to one. But the extraction can take care of the lower level rule life cycle to extract only the version of rule which can go in a ruleset: the ones tested successfully for example. On top of this fine grained life cycle, the development team may have to put in place some ruleset life cycle (Fig. 12.6). The main motivation is to control what goes to production and understand what version of the rules was used on a given business transaction. Depending on the application scope, this can be as simple as tagging a given set of rules with a version number or as complex as to have environments involving branching and complex version management, controlled with some formal business process. The simplest ruleset life cycle has four main consecutive stages: *Building*, *Validated*, *Production*, and *Retired*.

The *Building* stage, which is the longest and most important one, is controlled by the rule governance processes. We will detail one possible change process in Chap. 16. It is important to note that a new version of a ruleset restarts the life cycle, because we want to control it from the beginning even if a few changes occur. The existing ruleset in production may be retired when a new version is deployed. The decision to retire or not can be linked to the business requirement as sometime the rulesets have to be kept in parallel in production.

The ruleset life cycle can also be linked to the deployment strategy used by the architect. In SOA, decision services are using rulesets which need to be versioned and synchronized with the schema definitions used as model for the request–response messages. Any new version of the XML schema should enforce executing regression tests on each ruleset. This is not a major activity, but it needs to be integrated in the change process. Depending on the BRMS used, we may need to add properties to a ruleset to log the version definition of the schema used for the data model, or let the build process guaranty the integrity between the different artifacts.

Step 3 is making the physical deployment, where it is possible to use a staging approach and promote the ruleset from one platform to the others. The criteria to select the different servers can be based on the test data, the scope of processing, the decision services used, etc. The choice of target execution server can be configurable by the end user and selectable from the rule authoring environment. The list of configurable environments is based on the user profile. A traditional approach, leveraging the components as in Fig. 12.3, is to use four platforms:

- One development environment with a rule execution server is accessible by the development team and mostly used for testing, component integration tests, and nonregression tests. The rulesets are built from the rule repository using scripts and deployed on demand or deployed on a daily basis as part of the continuous integrated built process. The actors are the developers and rule authors.
- One preproduction/QA test platform – used for functional tests and system integration test (to validate the quality of the application and the rulesets deployed within the decision services). The actors are the Quality Assurance testers.
- One production platform administered with security control and tools to get rule execution reports. The actors are the production administrators with the role of rule administrator, and the rule writers responsible to maintain the rules in a controlled environment.
- One what-if simulation platform used as a mirror or partial mirror of the production platform and used by the business user to try some new policy implementation, new business intelligence partitioning, or algorithm. Ruleset can be deployed to this platform by the business users. The actors can be developers and business users.

The ruleset development flow, from extraction to deployment tasks, needs to be described with the exact involvement of the different actors, different applications, and different executable platforms. Depending on the BRMS product, some tools need to be added to automate the processing of ruleset deployment. In the development environment, the team can use continuous built process with automatic ruleset extraction and deployment to the execution server. We will detail in next chapter some tools and processes for JRules.

12.4.2 *Loading the Ruleset in Execution Server*

For the steps 4 and 5, there are different patterns to pull the ruleset from the database. The notification of step 4 can be driven by a JMX implementation where the deployment tool, a JMX console, notifies each rule engine deployed that new ruleset is deployed to the ruleset repository. On the server side, the JMX support is using an MXBean which implements a management interface. The remote methods exposed can include operations that specify which version of the ruleset is part of the data source. When a JMX console calls this method with a new version of the ruleset, the method of the MXBean implementation loads the new rulesets in background without stopping the current rule processing. Once the ruleset is parsed, the ruleset cache is updated. One other solution is based on an automatic checking by the engine to verify if there is a new ruleset in its data source to read. This implementation can use a watchdog which reads at specific time intervals a table in the data source to evaluate if there is a new ruleset to parse. Finally, we have seen some other solutions based on JMS publish–subscribe model. The decision service is a *subscriber* waiting on a predefined JMS topic to get a message about new ruleset notification. This message includes the name and version of the ruleset to load. Once the message is received, the *subscriber* loads the ruleset from the data source and refreshes its own ruleset cache. The *publisher* component, which is part of an administration application, sends the information to this topic when a new ruleset was saved to the execution server database. The use of JMS topic is interesting, as it permits to have multiple rule engines as listener to ruleset notification.

With JMS or JMX mechanisms, it is possible to hot deploy rules without stopping the core business application, which also means that the next business transaction to process is using the new version of the deployed rules.

Associated to the deployment process is the support of different version of rulesets in the execution environment and the ability to rollback. It is common to maintain different version of rulesets in the execution server. The decision service can pick up the appropriate ruleset according to meta properties attached to it, like expiration and validation dates, ruleset version number, geography location, line of business, etc. The dispatching function within the decision service looks at one of the business transaction attribute (discriminant) and selects the ruleset accordingly.

The problem of rule validity and ruleset validity is not as simple as it may look and may involve multiple different supporting implementations. Some leading BRMS offer selection of the rules at runtime, which may be a better choice than having to do it at the ruleset packaging. One rule of thumb is to evaluate the number of elements we may have to select from: the larger the number is, the worse the management will be. Over time if the number of rulesets the dispatcher needs to manage is increasing above, let say to, ten, the developer needs to reconsider the concurrent versioning and add complementary management capabilities.

Using time boxed iterations, with a clear development and scope goal, helps to drive the rule implementation. The rule authors have a short time period to execute the authoring, validation of the rules. Each rule has its own life cycle to support a fine grain control (See details in Chap. 16). When using a lower level control for the rule life cycle, each rule writer needs to "commit" his changes by promoting the rule to *Defined* status. The next steps control the rule testing and integration into the ruleset. Once ready, the ruleset is tagged with a version number and built using the rules ready for production. The rule extraction process needs to take into account previously deployed "production" rules while the authors are working on future versions of those rules: it should not take the "under authoring" rules. This is not a simple implementation and is linked to the BRMS capabilities.

12.5 Summary

We reviewed the common requirements related to rule deployment within IT architecture. BRMS provides the capability to hot deploy the business logic, the ruleset, without stopping the business application. Because the rules parsing can take time, a ruleset pooling mechanism has to be in place in the rule execution server to support scalability requirements and parallel execution. Rulesets have a different life cycle than the rules, which requires using different repositories, one for authoring and one for rule execution. The deployment process has to support the two environments to provide a simple and comprehensive platform.

Parallel execution is possible, and data analysis can partition the processing between different engines. This is a common practice used when performance is a major requirement.

The integration of a rule engine into the core application should be hidden from the client by using a business service interface. The implementation may leverage a neutral API (JSR94) to communicate with the engine, but we do not recommend it until there is a rule interchange standard to exchange rule definition between different rule vendors. The decision service design is based on business services and not on pure ruleset signature. The different technologies of deployment like web service, SCA component or JMS, are presented and represent a good solution within SOA and EDA.[15] The architect has to work on the data availability, and how

---

[15]Event Driven Architecture.

the rule engine gets access to a complete graph of object-oriented data. We presented SDO as a generic data model, adding flexibility to the data model: a good complement to the rule technology. A mix of XML document processing, with Java to XML binding technologies, are the common patterns of deployment within BPM suite and SCA implementation.

In the next chapter, we discuss how ILOG JRules supports ruleset deployment.

12.6 Further Reading

JSR94 is specified at jcp.org/en/jsr/detail?id=94.

One of the main contributors and decision management and decision service approach are James Taylor, and Neil Raden with their book "Smart Enough Systems: How to Deliver Competitive Advantage by Automating Hidden Decisions" – Prentice Hall (2007).

To know more about Service component architecture, readers can point their web browser to the Open Service Oriented Architecture collaboration website at http://www.osoa.org/pages/viewpage.action?pageId=46.

Java threading is covered in depth in Paul Hyde's book "*Java Threading Programming.*" Publisher Sams (1999).

JPA is covered by Mike Keith and Merrick Schincariol in their book: "*Pro JPA 2: Mastering the Java*^{TM} *Persistence API (Expert's Voice in Java Technology)*" – Publisher Apress (2009).

SDO specification can be read at http://www.osoa.org/display/main/service+ data+objects+home.

Chapter 13
Deploying with JRules

Target audience
- *Application architect, software architect, developer*

In this chapter you will learn
- *How rulesets are packaged as part of a RuleApp*
- *What are the ruleset versioning capabilities*
- *How to manage a RuleApp in Rule Team Server and in Rule Execution Server*
- *How to use the Rule Engine API, the JSR 94 or the Rule Execution Server rule session API to integrate rule engine processing into your application*
- *How to use a rule engine using JMS deployment*
- *The concept of Transparent Decision Service*
- *How to identify which rules executed using the Decision Warehouse capability*
- *How to develop queries to select the rules you want to have in your ruleset*

Key points
- *The main deployment unit when using the rule execution server is the RuleApp, which can be created and managed by a business user within rule team server.*
- *JRules offers a very flexible API to integrate the rule engine into the business application leveraging JEE or J2SE deployment model.*
- *Rule execution server is simple to use and delivers the rich set of features to manage a ruleset in production and scale vertically.*
- *Business users use Rule Team Server to author but also deploy rules to the different RES.*
- *Rulesets can be exposed as services, but for most business application deployed in SOA a decision service is part of reusable business services therefore better deigned with a meaningful interface and implemented using Java using the RES API.*

J. Boyer and H. Mili, *Agile Business Rule Development*,
DOI 10.1007/978-3-642-19041-4_13, © Springer-Verlag Berlin Heidelberg 2011

13.1   Introduction

In this chapter, we present the different deployment possibilities offered by IBM
WebSphere ILOG JRules. We first go over a quick review of the concepts of
operation (see also Sect. 8.2 for more details), with an emphasis on RuleApps,
which are the deployable artifacts to the rule execution server. In Sect. 13.3, we talk
about deploying rule application using the rule engine API. In particular, we review
the classes for rule engine, rulesets, and various utilities that support rule execution
tracing and debugging. In Sect. 13.4, we describe rule deployment using JRules'
Rule Execution Server (RES), whereby rulesets are deployed as services that can be
invoked by applications. Different RES configurations are discussed, depending on
the needs of the business application. We review pure Java integration, JMS, and
SCA. In Sect. 13.5, we address the deployment of Rule Team Server. We conclude
in Sect. 13.6.

13.2   Reminder on the Concepts of Operation

JRules has two authoring environments from where we can deploy rules: Rule
Studio and Rule Team Server (RTS). As seen in Chap. 5, developers use Rule
Studio to build the project structure, to develop the Business Object Model, to
organize the flow of execution, and to implement rules. From Rule Studio, they also
define the different configurations they may want to use for the ruleset deployment.
Basically, we can deploy rules to a rule engine embedded in a business application or
to a managed rule execution environment, which offers a richer set of application
management features. The choices between the two depend on the application requirements. In SOA, an architect may leverage the JEE container to support service
binding, security, transaction support, pool for connections to the different data
sources, and so forth. Therefore, the natural deployment leverages the Rule Execution
Server (RES) component, which is a Java Connector Architecture implementation.
The alternative is to use an embedded deployment in which we package the engine jars
with the application and we deploy and execute the ruleset (as ruleset archive) on a
single JVM. This last approach uses the lower level API to access the rule engine and
the ruleset archive: a packaging for the rules (see Sect. 13.3.1 later). There is a third
deployment using the RES in J2SE, which we present in Sect. 13.4.1.

Figure 13.1 illustrates the tasks a developer has to perform within Rule Studio to
prepare for an embedded integration.

The right side of Fig. 13.1 presents a potential application packaging, including
the domain data model, the application logic (business service interfaces and
implementations), the rule engine, and the ruleset. The domain data model is
most likely a Java model accessed through a data access object layer, so it can be
packaged as a standalone reusable jar: dom.jar. The business logic code uses the
rule engine and the ruleset API, which is in the jrules-engine.jar.

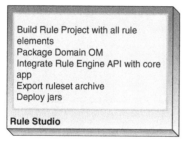

Fig. 13.1 Packaging a rule application

The embedded integration is not recommended when the requirements for management of rules and rulesets are becoming crucial. IT developers will most likely re-implement most of the features supported by the rule execution server, like database persistence for the ruleset, management stack to control the life cycle of the ruleset, rule processing statistics and logging mechanism, transaction support, security control, engines pooling, etc. When the application needs to support multiple rulesets, parallel execution, or is processing data within a transactional context, we must leverage the services of a JEE container. Rule Execution Server, deployed on an application server as a Java Connector Architecture[1] resource adapter (RA), supports transaction management, security controls, and rule engine pooling.

In RES, there are multiple patterns to invoke a ruleset: using java object (POJO), local or remote EJBs, web service protocols, or as JMS listener using a Message Driven Bean. We will detail the RES subcomponents and the activities to deploy a ruleset in Sect. 13.4.

At the lowest level, a Ruleset is packaged as a rule archive which is a jar including rule files,[2] meta data files such as the reference to BOM, the ruleset signature description, and the exported rule properties. If we use the rule engine API we have to parse the rule archive before calling the rule execution. This parsing has to be performed only at the application initialization. When using the Rule Execution Server, the rule archive is packaged within a RuleApp and transparently parsed at the first call for rule execution.

A RuleApp contains one or more rulesets. In Fig. 13.2, the ClaimProcessing-RuleApp has four rulesets with rules and one with the BOM entries.

In Rule Studio, RuleApps are managed inside projects. A RuleApp project includes XML descriptors to describe the rule project dependencies, the ruleset path, and a list of ruleset archive files. As a good design approach, a RuleApp should include rulesets that share the same domain object model and are in the

---

[1] Java Connector Architecture: http://java.sun.com/j2ee/connector/reference/industrysupport/index.html.

[2] One irl (ILOG Rule Language) file per rule. The format is a text file with IRL syntax.

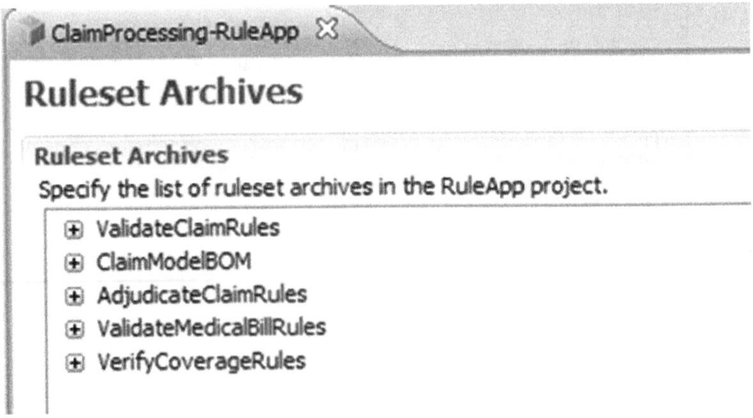

Fig. 13.2 RuleApp and Ruleset archives

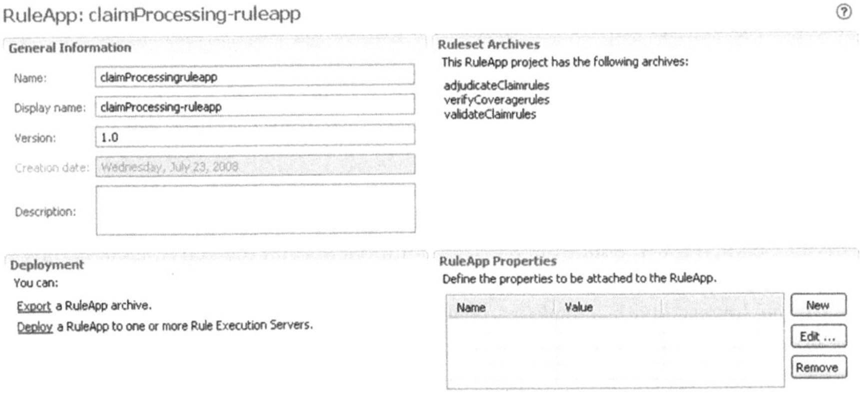

Fig. 13.3 RuleApp editor

same application context. From a RuleApp project, the developer can perform all the pure administration activities like versioning, deployment, adding management properties, export, and so forth. Figure 13.3 shows the Rule Studio RuleApp editor for the claim processing RuleApp, which includes three rulesets, "adjudicateClaimrules", "verifyCoveragerules", and "validate-Claimrules."

Each ruleset in a RuleApp can be invoked using a ruleset path. A ruleset path includes the reference of the RuleApp name and the ruleset name inside the RuleApp. The following ruleset path/ClaimProcessing-RuleApp/validateClaim-rules refers to the current version of both RuleApp and ruleset. A path such as/ ClaimProcessing-RuleApp/**1.0**/validateClaimrules/**2.1** references specific versions

Fig. 13.4 Rule App management in RTS

for both elements. Using the ruleset path it is possible to use different versions of a ruleset within the calling client code. The API supports opening a session with the rule execution server and to specify the ruleset path to use.

The following simple practice can be applied to control the version number of the ruleset:

- Increase the X of X.Y version number for each major release of the ruleset
- Increase the Y of X.Y version number to manage subversion deployment

If we change the business logic in any way in one of our rule projects, we have to upgrade the RuleApp archive to take the modifications into account. It is possible for a business analyst using Rule Team Server to author rules and to deploy RuleApps directly to a Rule Execution Server (Using the Configure Tab). In RTS, a business user can create baseline, which can be seen as a tag applied to each rule to deploy, and then he can deploy the RuleApp to the target execution environment. Figure 13.4 presents RuleApps management screen with the set of buttons to drive the deployment of a RuleApp.

It is important to use the correct RuleApp and ruleset names when defining the RuleApp in RTS: they have to be the same as the ones specified in the ruleset path as seen in previous section. If not the rule execution will not find the rulesets.

Finally, the Rule Execution Server has also a web interface used by administrator to manage the deployed ruleset archives and RuleApps. It is also possible to perform basic monitoring, to view execution statistics, and to deploy, change, and manage business rules without stopping the server. The information provided is rich as we can see the rules deployed in ILOG Rule Language format and the rules that were executed for given input data.[3] The central panel displays the content and status of a ruleset (Fig. 13.5).

We will detail the RES Console capabilities when detailing the new decision warehouse function in Sect. 13.4.4.

---

[3]A new capability called Decision Warehouse, see product documentation at http://publib.boulder. ibm.com/infocenter/brjrules/v7r1/index.jsp.

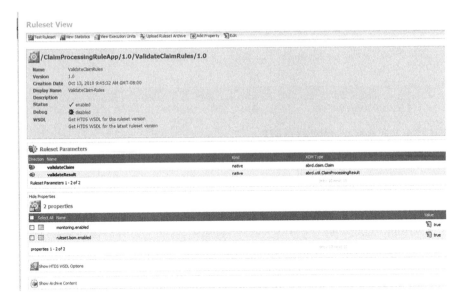

Fig. 13.5 Ruleset view as deployed in RES

13.3 Integration with JRules Engine

In this section, we cover the integration of JRules engine using the different API offered, engine and ruleset API in Sect. 13.3.1; JSR94 in Sect. 13.3.2. Using this kind of integration may be a realistic use case when none of the out of the box features supported by the rule execution server are needed by the application.

13.3.1 Deploying with the Rule Engine API

When we execute rules using the engine and ruleset API, we deploy and execute a ruleset archive in a single Java Virtual Machine. The rule engine API is packaged as jar and added to the classpath of the application. The client code using the rule engine needs to load the ruleset archive from its data source, to parse it, to instantiate a rule engine, to prepare the data as ruleset parameters or as facts inserted into the working memory, to execute the rules, and finally to process the result.

As it takes some time to build the RETE Network and other internal objects, the operation of loading and parsing the ruleset should be done only the first time the application is started. The basic API used includes the class `IlrContext` for the rule engine, `IlrRuleset` for the ruleset, plus some helper classes to load and parse ruleset archive. The following code sample presents a class called ProcessClaimImplWithJrules with a constructor preparing the rulesets by loading the archive, parsing it, and creating the `IlrRuleset` object.

```
public class ProcessClaimImplWithJrules implements ProcessClaim {
   // ruleset name...
   protected String validateClaimRsName = "validateClaim-rules.jar";
   protected static IlrRuleset validateClaimRuleset;

// constructor
public ProcessClaimImplWithJrules(){
   JarInputStream is;
   try {
      is = new JarInputStream(new FileInputStream( new File( validate-
ClaimRsName)));
      // prepare a Ruleset archive loader
      IlrRulesetArchiveLoader rulesetloader = new IlrJarArchiveLoader(is);
      // then a parser
      IlrRulesetArchiveParser rulesetparser = new IlrRulesetArchiveParser();
      validateClaimRuleset = new IlrRuleset();
      rulesetparser.setRuleset(validateClaimRuleset);
      // finally parse to create the ruleset
      rulesetparser.parseArchive(rulesetloader);
        ...
```

Parsing the ruleset archive can generate errors; it is therefore recommended to stop if an error occurs. Building `IlrRuleset` may take time so we need to avoid creating it at each rule execution call, for example, by using a factory and static variable protected with the singleton pattern. The last part of the class supports the implementation of the business methods. It needs to get an engine instance, sets the input parameters, optionally initializes the working memory, executes the rules, and finally gets the output parameters. Below is an example of code for the validateClaim operation:

```
public Result validateClaim(Claim claim) {
// Create the engine with a reference to the ruleset
ilog.rules.engine.IlrContext context = new IlrContext(validateClaimRuleset);
// Initialize the input parameters
IlrParameterMap inputs = new IlrParameterMap();
inputs.setParameter("validateClaim", claim);
   inputs.setParameter("validateResult",new Result());
   context.setParameters(inputs);
   // Initialize the working memory
    context.insert(claim.getPolicy());
   // Execute the ruleset
   IlrParameterMap outputs = context.execute();
   // Get the result
   Result rOut=(Result)outputs.getObjectValue("validateResult");
   // Clean the context
      context.retractAll();
      context.end();
      return rOut;
   }
```

The engine API is simple and is enough to support a lot of basic applications. Other transaction heavy applications should leverage the RES API, which we will detail in Sect. 13.4. But first, let us look at how JRules is supporting JSR94.

13.3.2 JSR94: JRules Specifics

As introduced in the previous chapter, the JSR 94 offers the advantage of interacting with a rule engine without any knowledge of the underlying product API. As of this writing, the value of using JSR94 is questionable until there is an agreed format to exchange rules between different engine vendors. W3C is working on defining a standard called Rule Interchange Format or RIF.[4] For more detailed explanations of the JSR94 API, see Sect. 12.3.4.

JSR-94 delegates its processing using JRules rule sessions deployed in a Java archive file named jrules-res-jsr94.jar. The JSR-94 interface is implemented with the Rule Execution Server and not with the rule engine API, which is an additional layer added on top of the engine, in order to have a common interface for J2SE and J2EE executions.

For JRules, it is not mandatory to deploy a ruleset with the JSR-94 management API to execute this ruleset. The ruleset is already being deployed to RES and the client code uses the JSR94 run time API to load object and execute rules. The Uniform Resource Identifier (URI) used should be a valid ruleset path including ruleappname/rulesetname. This also means we need to deploy a RuleApp archive to get access to the rule execution set with JSR94.

For creating a rule execution set, the input stream has to point to a XML ruleset descriptor which looks like:

```
<?xml version="1.0" encoding="UTF-8"?>
<rule-execution-set>
  <!-- The value attribute could be a valid path or a valid URL on a RuleApp ar-
chive file -->
    <location value="res_data/validateClaim-rules.jar"/>
</rule-execution-set>
```

It defines the path to your RuleApp archive file, generated by Rule Studio. The client code needs to create a service provider, which in the case of JRules should use the following URL:

```
    // Get the rule service provider from the provider manager
Class.forName(IlrRuleServiceProvider.class.getName());

RuleServiceProvider serviceProvider = RuleServiceProviderManager.getRuleServicePro
vider("ilog.rules.bres.jsr94");
```

---

[4]See detail at W3C URL: http://www.w3.org/2005/rules/wiki/RIF_Working_Group.

13.3.3 Monitoring and Tracing Rule Execution

As part of the integration there is a need to be able to trace and monitor execution of the rules. RES supports monitoring of rule execution out of the box. We will detail this in Sect. 13.4. When using the low-level API, it is still possible to attach a monitoring tool to get events from the rule engine when it processes business data. We can attach a notification observer using the engine API connectTool(engine-Observer).

```
// create a rule engine – with a ruleset
IlrContext context = new IlrContext(validateClaimRuleset);
//add the observer
context.connectTool(new EngineObserver());
```

The observer is an extension of the ilog.rules.engine.IlrToolAdapter class or an implementation of the IlrTool interface; some callback methods can be overridden to trace the execution. For example, the method notifyBeginInstance is invoked in RETE mode when the engine executes a rule, so we can log the name of the rule.

```
public class EngineObserver extends IlrToolAdapter {
....
    public void notifyBeginInstance(IlrRuleInstance instance) {
                logger.info(instance.getRuleName());
    }
```

In production environment, logging has to be designed with care. We will most likely prepare the minimum information during the rule processing and use an asynchronous call to send the message to a messaging queue for future processing done by a listener. Such heavy processing include saving the information to a database. The goal is to avoid impacting the performance of the rule engine. Asynchronous calls do not block the caller and make the receiver take care of the logging and of the persisting of the events into a data source.

13.3.4 Resource Pooling

As discussed in the previous chapter, it is possible to pool rule engines for parallel processing. JRules offers this capability out of the box using JCA connection pooling inside the RES. Even in a J2SE deployment, the JRules implementation (in jar jrules-res-execution.jar) of the JCA API is using engine pooling. The pool size can be configured using a XML descriptor file named ra.xml.

13.4   Deploying with the Rule Execution Server

In this section, we review the most important capabilities of RES in the context of application integration and ruleset deployment. We start by presenting RES architecture as a JCA resource adapter, detailing the rule engine pooling and the ruleset deployment. Then we review the RES session API to use to call for rule execution in application server or a J2SE application. We detailed the JMS deployment in Sect. 13.4.2 and the SCA deployment in Sect. 13.4.3. We present in Sect. 13.4.5 the concept of transparent decision service (TDS) as the simplest way to demonstrate smooth integration. Finally in Sect. 13.4.4 we present the decision warehouse feature, used to monitor the rule execution with RES.

RES can be deployed as a centralized service, executing multiple rulesets on the requests of multiple clients. It can also be packaged within a unique business application (WAR or EAR) and only visible by the code of this application. This packaging does not mean we cannot reuse rulesets, in fact the business services can be reused and are callable using Web Service, SCA, JMS, local Java call, or RMI depending on the communication choices. RES is based around a modular architecture that can be deployed as a set of Java Plain Old Java Objects (POJOs) running in a J2SE JVM, hosted using Apache Tomcat, or run within a full Java EE compliant application server.

RES is a resource adapter of the Java Connector Architecture. JCA is designed to provide a unified way to access external resources from Enterprise Information System (EIS), instead of having proprietary adapters for each external system. JCA enables an EIS vendor to provide a standard resource adapter for its EIS (Fig. 13.6). By plugging into an application server, the resource adapter collaborates with the

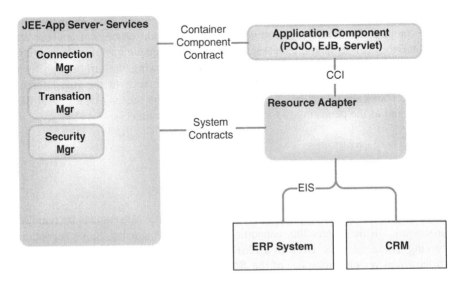

Fig. 13.6 JCA basic architecture
Source: java-sun JCA 1.5 specification

server which provides the underlying mechanisms for transactions, security, and connection pooling mechanisms.

Considering a rule engine as an EIS may look strange, at first, as a rule engine does not access EIS per say, but the goal of this implementation is to leverage the contracts provided by the JEE container such as transaction, security, and connection management without reinventing those services. Resource adapters implement two things: the Common Client Interface (CCI) used to expose the high level JCA API to the caller, and the implementation of the functionality expected using underlying EIS resource.

There are two main types of contracts that a resource adapter (RA) implements in order to get compliant with the JCA:

- The application level contract defines what the RA needs to support so components within the JEE container can communicate to the EIS.
- The system level contracts: which are connection management, transaction management, and security management.

Connection management provides a connection factory and connection interface based on the CCI. It pools the connections to the EIS to improve performance. A rule engine is attached to a connection. So rule engine pooling is linked to connection pooling. Transaction management allows EIS resources to be included in the transaction initiated by the container's transaction manager. The RA manages a set of shared EIS resources to participate in a XA or local transaction. Finally, security management secures access to the EIS through user identification, authentication, and authorization and uses communication security protocols.

The resource adapter in JRules is named eXecution Unit (XU) and aims to handle the low-level details of initializing and invoking the rule engine. It adds a management layer used to access resource adapter, resources such as connections to a ruleset data source and exposing configuration and run time data. An XU is packaged as an independently deployable unit called a resource adapter archive (RAR) .

There is only one XU deployed (.rar) per Application Server instance. Figure 13.7 illustrates a classical deployment within a JEE container. The clients are decision services, which are using the rule session factory and the rule session to access the rule engine. The implementation of a session is getting SPI connection from a pool managed by the JEE container (JCA pool).

The XU provides scalability by using context pooling and ruleset caching: Each IlrContext is linked to an SPI connection, which the application server caches within the JCA pool. In fact due to the transaction support requirement, asynchronous ruleset parsing, and hot ruleset deployment use cases, one JCA SPI connection is associated to a set of IlrContext.

The IlrRuleset is shared between engines and kept in memory until there is no more IlrContext using it (SPI connection reference). At the end of an execution, the server may decide to put the SPI connection back into the JCA pool. In this case, the associated IlrContext will be reset and ready for another execution. In the case of XML binding usage, the dynamic classes are attached to the ruleset and are therefore made available directly to the XU. For Java implementations, all the classes are passed to the XU by the rule session class

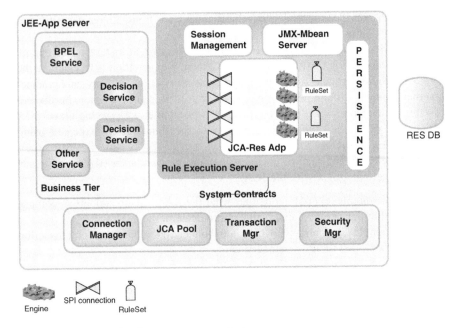

Fig. 13.7 Rule Execution Server as resource adapter

loader. In Fig. 13.7, we can imagine the decision service as packaged within a WAR or an EAR. If we deploy it in Tomcat 6 for example, we use the J2SE packaging which includes jrules-res-session.jar and the JCA API: j2ee_connector-1_5-fr.jar. The same data source must be used for the management and execution stacks. To do so we get a ra.xml file from <jrules-home>/executionserver/bin and add it to the classpath. This file will override the default_ra.xml descriptor provided in the jrules-res-execution.jar. When we use a data base to persist RuleApps we need to change some of the properties in this file, like the $\mathtt{persistenceType}$, and the $\mathtt{persistenceProperties}$.

The last important component of RES is the management model. When deploying a ruleset using the RES Console, this one saves rulesets to a data source, and signals changes to the management stack of RES using the JMX[5] protocol. The management model is based on the JMX Mbeans specification and is used to deploy, to manage, and to monitor the execution resources of Rule Execution Server. The various MBeans of the RES model are the runtime proxies of each entity within the model. There are three Mbeans deployed in each managed server:

- The $\mathtt{IlrJmxModelMBean}$ is the root of the Rule Execution Server management model. It controls every RuleApp deployed on Rule Execution Server. This MBean performs actions such as adding and removing references to the RuleApps contained within the model.

---

[5]See http://java.sun.com/javase/technologies/core/mntr-mgmt/javamanagement/ for details.

- The `IlrJmxRuleAppMBean` is a management entity that controls a deployed RuleApp. This MBean performs actions such as adding and removing references to the rulesets contained within a RuleApp.
- The `IlrJmxRulesetMBean` is the management entity that represents the execution resources for the Execution Unit (XU). This MBean exposes some runtime metrics of the execution. These metrics are computed from the various data collected on each XU in a cluster. It exposes an API to set the resources and properties that are used at execution time and provides a "hot" deployment entry point to update the rules at execution time.

The XU reads rulesets from the persistent layer whenever it needs to, that is, when the application server has removed a cache entry from the JCA connection pool, or when a new ruleset was deployed to the data source and the XU receives a JMX notification message.

13.4.1 Using RES Session API

When using a Rule Execution Server, the implementation of a business interface is leveraging the rule session object to communicate with the rule engine. Starting with JRules 6.0 rule sessions use a factory interface to allow clients to obtain management session, stateless, or stateful execution sessions. The factory represents the entry point to communicate with the RES. The code used to get a rule session factory has to specify if we use a POJO, J2EE, or J2SE sessions. Most of the time when deployed into a JEE container, it is simpler to use a Plain Old Java Object approach and create a POJO factory as a singleton within the business service implementation. We recommend defining the rule session factory as the singleton design pattern: during the first call to a ruleset, the RES creates the XU resource like the connection pool, loads the classes, and parses the ruleset. Using a singleton enforces that each subsequent call will only execute the rules and not the ruleset parsing. Using an factory instance enforces parsing the ruleset at each call.

Concept: **Singleton**
Singleton[6] is a design pattern to restrict the instantiation of a class to one unique object. In Java, this restriction applies within the classloader and uses the "static" keyword to declare the unique instance.

The factory has different implementation depending of the type of deployment. The following table summarizes each possible implementation:

---

[6]See Wikipedia detailed definition at http://en.wikipedia.org/wiki/Singleton_pattern.

Name	Description	Comment
J2SE Session Factory	Used in pure J2SE environment. It is thread safe.	The rule session implementation provided by this factory does not support transactions.
POJO Session Factory	Session used for JEE deployment. No EJB support.	Simplest interaction with the engine.
EJB3 Session Factory	Used by EJB code to get access to a rule session with JNDI lookup. The sessions are EJB session obtained from the JNDI namespace.	Pure EJB pattern, but with transparent life cycle.

Rule sessions help execute the rules in stateless or stateful mode. Most business applications are using stateless, stateful mode is rarely used. The stateful mode aims to maintain a long runtime communication model with the engine in particular to control the working memory and to keep object references at each execution call. The implementation of a stateful mode is a bit more complex as it forces developers to manage the full life cycle of the engine and its working memory. A rule session provides the class loader for the Java XOM and therefore will almost certainly be packaged in every client application. This class is dependent on the application server used. So copy the jar file from <jrules-home>/j2ee/<application-server>/jrules-res-session-<appserver>.jar and package it with your application ear.

A decision service, which uses the RES API, follows the same pattern already seen before: Get a session, set the parameters, call the rule execution, parse the results, and return the result to the caller. The session request is open using a canonical path to the ruleset under execution. The path includes the reference to the RuleApp and ruleset:

```
// Create a session request object
IlrSessionRequest sessionRequest = factory.createRequest();
sessionRequest.setRulesetPath(IlrPath.parsePath("/ClaimProcessingRuleApp/Validate
ClaimRules"));
// ... Set the input parameters for the execution of the rules
Map inputParameters = new HashMap();
inputParameters.put("validateClaim", claim);
inputParameters.put("validateResult", new Result());
sessionRequest.setInputParameters(inputParameters);
   try {
   // Create the stateless rule session.
   session = factory.createStatelessSession();
   // Execute rules
   IlrSessionResponse sessionResponse = session.execute(sessionRequest);
   // get result
   result=(Result) sessionResponse.getOutputParameters().get("validateResult");
   ...
```

This code is best written in Rule Studio using the java client for RuleApp wizard, and then integrated into the decision service implementation. If we need to use a stateful session, some care has to be taken to reuse the factory, the rule session, and other objects to avoid losing the stateful management of the working memory.

The choice of session type is linked to the deployment strategy of each decision service. When the service is deployed within the same server as the RES, a local rule session can be used. The POJO or EJB rule sessions are the possible choices to interact with the RES. The use of EJB session is relevant to support transaction propagation and security requirements. The session is coming from one of the possible session factory. Below is an example of EJB3 rule session factory to use within the decision service code:

```
IlrSessionFactory factory = new IlrEJB3SessionFactory();
// work on the session request the same way as code above …
IlrStatelessSession session = factory.createStatelessSession()
```

When the client code is remote to the RES, remote EJB can be used, or Message Driven Bean. For remote EJB, the IlrEJB3SessionFactory has a simple API to set a remote flag to get remote session. Message Driven Bean represents one of the most common deployments when we need to integrate with Enterprise Service Bus, legacy application connected with IBM WebSphere MQ or any asynchronous event architecture.

13.4.2 JMS Deployment

As detailed in the previous chapter, Message-Oriented Middleware is the technology of choice for asynchronous processing of messages. JRules Rule Execution Server delivers an out of the box Message Driven Beans (MDB) (`IlrRule ExecutionBean`) to invoke the XU within the onMessage() call using a simple session and then posts the execution results to a JMS destination. The MDB with the rule session are packaged as an EAR file and deployed in the JEE container. This implementation may be useful for event driven application or with mainframe application integration. The JMS message needs to include the ruleset path and a status property. The message body has to include the ruleset parameters using key-value pairs. The client code posting messages to a topic or a queue needs to specify the ruleset path it wants to execute. This strongly coupled integration between the client and the rule service is not a common usage of JMS. Most of the architectures which are leveraging message-oriented middleware or ESB use a loosely coupled approach where clients post messages without any knowledge of what the consumer is. So if we need to implement an Event Driven Architecture decision service which can be used with messaging communication we may need to leverage our own MDB implementation which will hide the fact we are using a rule set. The onMessage() method can do the unmarshalling of the JMS message payload into a Java data model and then can synchronously call the business service responsible to process the business objects. The outcome of the decision services can be processed by a publisher class back to the JMS layer. Queue or topic listener needs to get references to the business service

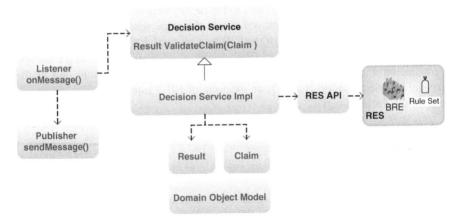

Fig. 13.8 JMS – Rule engine deployment

implementations and to the publisher so that it can send the result back to a topic for future processing. Figure 13.8 illustrates a design where the decision service implemented following the concepts presented in previous section can be re-used with the JMS communication without a lot of work.

13.4.3 SCA Component

Another interesting wizard within Rule Studio is used for generating RuleApp client code with all the needed artifacts to deploy the rule execution as a Service Component Architecture (SCA) component. One of the main goals of SCA is to clearly separate the communication details from the business logic: the protocols and quality of service are wired at execution time, the developer focuses on defining reusable services and components supporting the business functions to develop. By looking at the generated java code, there is no difference with standard RES client implementation (see Sect. 13.4.1); the only difference is coming from the composite descriptor used to define the SCA component. The component statement in the composite file may look like:

```
<component name="ClaimProcessingComponent">
 <implementation.java class="claimProcessing.server.ClaimProcessingImpl"/>
</component>
```

Before release 7.1.1 of JRules, the wizard leveraged the Apache Tuscany[7] Java runtime on client side to call the service. In later releases of JRules, the SCA

---

[7]http://tuscany.apache.org.

implementation used is the one coming from the IBM WebSphere SCA feature pack. Most likely a business application will not use the RuleApp exposed "as is" as a SCA component but will use a business service as façade for the rule execution. In that case, the generated client code can be used as a starting point for the implementation of such a business service. The caller of an SCA component needs to get a SCADomain instance by specifying the composite descriptor, then get the service reference, and finally call the business method (e.g., validateClaim).

```
// Create a Tuscany runtime
SCADomain scaDomain = SCADomain.newInstance ("ClaimProcessing.composite");
ClaimProcessing service = scaDomain.getService(
 ClaimProcessing.class,"ClaimProcessingComponent");
// prepare objects like the claim … then call the execution using the decision
service API
  service.validateClaim(theClaim);
```

For WebSphere SCA feature pack[8] the access to the service is done using the service manager like:

```
com.ibm.websphere.sca.ServiceManager.INSTANCE.locateService
("ClainProcessingComponent");
```

13.4.4 Monitoring and Decision Warehouse

When an administrator wants to monitor the rule execution, he can use the Rule Execution Server Console which is a web application deployed to a servlet container like Tomcat or WebSphere Application Server. The RES Console includes the JMX MBean server used to receive rule execution statistics. The application server needs to support JMX, JNDI, and JDBC data sources. In a J2SE deployment if we want to have the monitoring capabilities we need to have the RES Console and the RES-XU in the same JVM.

One of the first monitoring functions is to verify the server status. In the RES Console, the Diagnostic tab allows the execution of a set of predefined tests and to present color coded results. The tests address connection, resource adapter information, rule app and ruleset status, etc. (see Fig. 13.9).

In Fig. 13.9, the XU lookup and XU MBean are yellow because we did not execute a ruleset yet. The XU MBean is created when the XU connector is created. The XU connector is created when a connection is requested so a rule session opened.

---

[8]See details at http://www-01.ibm.com/software/webservers/appserv/was/featurepacks/sca/.

Fig. 13.9 Rule Execution Server diagnostic report

As part of the monitoring capabilities in JRules v7.x is a new feature called Decision Warehouse (Decision Validation Service add-on) which stores the rule execution results in a data source. The type of data persisted may vary depending on the application, but it is possible to get the list of rules fired, the rule tasks executed for a given transaction, and the content of the ruleset parameters. When the ruleset is deployed from rule team server, it is possible to get within the trace, hyperlinks back to the corresponding rule in RTS repository. This capability helps to quickly assess for a given business transaction what were the conditions which made the rule fire. Using the Decision Warehouse tab of the Rule Execution Server Console, we can search the rule execution trace by specifying search criteria. Figure 13.10 presents this capability.

It is interesting to note from Fig. 13.10 that the first rule execution took more processing time (328ms), as the RES was parsing the ruleset. The detail of the decisions made on the last claim processed gives us information about the claim sent, the path of execution within the ruleset with the rules fired. Figure 13.11 presents such results.

To configure the Decision Warehouse, we need to enable the ruleset execution monitoring by setting the `monitoring.enabled` ruleset property to `true`. It is possible to use Rule Studio, Rule Team Server, or Rule Execution server to set such property. RES offers a simple Add Property command inside the ruleset View. This command supports predefined property (Fig. 13.12).

Usually developers will want to set those properties at the rule project level in Studio by using the rule project property and the ruleset property menu. When the rule flow defines a task that uses the sequential or Fastpath algorithm, we need to

Search Decisions   Help ⑦

Enter information in one or more fields to find stored decisions: ℹ

Executed ruleset path: /ClaimProcessingRuleApp/1.0/ValidateClaimRules/1.6

Decision ID:

Rules Fired:

Tasks Executed:

Input parameters:

Output parameters:

From date:

From time: 00:00:00

To date:

To time: 00:00:00

[Search] [Clear]

3 Decision(s) found   Display by 10 ⌄

Decision ID	Date	Ruleset Version	Number of rules fired	Decision Trace	Processing Time (ms)
50de6b1f-f648-49ce-8f17-2e773cad1eac	2009-05-30 16:14:03	/ClaimProcessingRuleApp /1.0/ValidateClaimRules/1.6	1	View Decision details	16
b34c3caa-ef14-469d-bc6a-42cc9526d2d0	2009-05-30 16:13:17	/ClaimProcessingRuleApp /1.0/ValidateClaimRules/1.6	0	View Decision details	15
83d397e2-53cb-4ac5-9421-338cfca84ac3	2009-05-30 16:08:17	/ClaimProcessingRuleApp /1.0/ValidateClaimRules/1.6	1	View Decision details	328

Fig. 13.10 Search Decision Warehouse

add another ruleset property called: `sequential.trace.enabled`.
Lastly as we may want to trace what the inputs and outputs were and as such we
may need to set `ruleset.bom.enabled` property to true. If the ruleset is
based on an XSD XOM, the input/output parameters are stored as XML documents.
If the ruleset is based on a Java XOM, the toString() method of the ruleset parameter
(s) type stores the content. Using toString we can limit the information persisted to
improve the performance.

The Decision Warehouse stores its results to different data sources. It is important to properly design how to organize the data sources and partition the traces
according to the different decision services the application is supporting. It is also
possible to add our own DAO to store the information in another database;
therefore, a business user can run Business Intelligence report from it. The product
documentation details all of these and provides some customization samples.

13.4.5 Transparent Decision Service

We have seen quite often the term Decision Service in previous chapters. In a
SOA, it is a service which is making a business decision on business data. Such

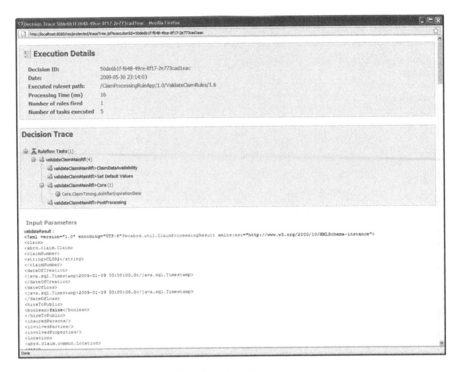

Fig. 13.11 A rule execution report from Decision Warehouse

Fig. 13.12 Ruleset properties set in RES Console

services are most often supported by a business ruleset executed by a rule engine. In IBM WebSphere JRules, there is also the concept of transparent decision service (TDS). The term transparent means we can define the decision logic externally using a rule repository without having to dig into application code to understand the rules. The Rule Execution Server can expose a ruleset automatically as a web service as soon as it uses an XSD as executable model (or is limited to using basic java types). The interface definition is based on the ruleset parameters, which are defined according to the nature of the business decisions to make, and should not be dependent on the needs of a single business process. TDS is accessed using SOAP and can offer an easy deployment within a SOA. As we explained in previous chapters, the design of reusable service consumers want to reuse enforces respecting a set of best practices like loosely coupled, coarse-grained interfaces, simple data model a client can create and send to the service provider, keep the business meaning, and the service provider responsible for his processing like loading the data. A ruleset supports one operation of a business service: service end point groups operations over a single place, an URL, over a single protocol; therefore, a ruleset has to be one operation within a packaged business service. For efficient rule processing, the data needed by the rules need to be present, a good design practice is to let the service have the responsibility of loading the data it needs and not ask the client to send the complete data set. This is truly relevant with reference data. This is not to say we need to load the data within the ruleset, but before calling the rules. Loading of the data in a ruleset may be an attractive solution but has a lot of drawbacks. In particular, when we need to support transaction initiation or propagation, the call to load the data can occur at the beginning of the rule flow; but if there are exceptions or a time out, the management of such events is more complex to support in rules than in traditional code. Finally, most of the ruleset processing needs some reference to other technical service to access them for getting reference data, or other business objects. Those services should be hidden to the caller.

There are two types of TDS in JRules: the hosted and the monitored:

- A *hosted transparent decision service* (HTDS) is a ruleset deployed as a Web service. It is installed and integrated on the same application server as the Rule Execution Server. It includes a JMX MBean and is packaged as an EAR (for example jrules-res-htds-WAS7.ear for Websphere) or as a WAR for Apache Tomcat 6 (named DecisionService.war). This web application defines some web service servlet and HTTP listeners which process SOAP requests and route the message payload (XML document) to the ruleset. Any ruleset is mapped to the following URL:

```
http://<hostname>:<httpport>/DecisionService/ws/<NameOfTheRuleApp>1.0
/<NameOfRuleSet/ 1.0?WSDL
```

The objects defined in the BOM and the ruleset parameters are used to generate the WSDL file. When the BOM was created by using XSD, HTDS is very easy to set. The WSDL binding is using SOAP over HTTP with a Document/literal style. A developer can import this WSDL and generate the client code with tool such as Apache axis wsdl2 java.

- A *monitored transparent decision service* (MTDS) resides on the same application server, but is not integrated with RES. It is generated from Rule Studio as a web app using the wizard: New > Client Project for RuleApps > Web Service. There are two projects created by this wizard. One client project which includes the client code calling the web service. And the other one the server side project

which includes the web service definition using the reference implementation of
JAX-WS so it is not supported in all application servers. MTDS manage rulesets
that use an XML schema or a Java XOM with any object types (not limited to
basic java types).

Starting with the server side generated code, the generated project includes
java files, ant script, Execution Unit configuration file (ra.xml), and other xml
descriptors to create the web service (web.xml, application server specific
deployment descriptor). Using the ant targets, we can generate a war file for
the application and deploy it to the target application server. Each rule project
part of the Rule App is exposed as a WebMethod using a signature like
`<RuleSetName>Result execute<RuleSetName> (<Rule
SetName>Request request)`. The operation results and request are
mapped to wrapper objects which include references to the ruleset parameters.
For example, the ValidateClaimRuleRequest has a reference to the Claim
(Fig. 13.13).

The implementation of the web method is using the RES API to set the parameters and to call the rule execution. The Java objects used for the data model must
respect the JavaBean specification. The generated code can be used to implement
the business services we need to code and exposed as reusable service. At the
interface definition level we are not specific to rule execution. The service method
can be renamed to better serve business operations. If we need to hook up some
reference to other services needed by the rules, we can do so in the implementation
class. The listener class can be reused to offer statistic reports in the RES Console.
The client code is also an excellent starter code to implement some simulator or
functional test framework.

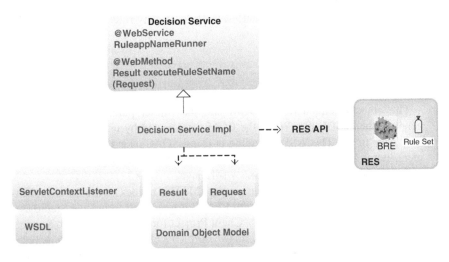

Fig. 13.13 Monitored TDS generated components

13.5 Rule Team Server

In this section, we present the deployment of rule team server web application within the IT architecture and how to leverage the data source mapping to support multiple rule repositories with one web application. Then, in Sect. 13.5.2, we briefly present the concept of queries, an element used to control the ruleset packaging.

13.5.1 Physical Deployment

As a management application, the war file does not need to be deployed on the same node and server as the rule execution server. It is better to deploy it on a different server, because it can use resources that may impact the performance of the rule processing. The deployment follows traditional Web App deployment using a database: we need to configure the JNDI data source reference and specify in the web descriptor which JNDI name to lookup. Rule team server is also delivered with an Installation Manager which helps to deploy the DB schema when the database does not exist. It is important to note that when you are using a different rule meta model the database schema is different. This is easily done by loading the XML files describing the extension model into RTS (Fig. 13.14).

All the rule projects within RTS share the same meta properties; therefore, if there is a need to have different extension model, architect may need to define different rule repository data sources. By default, the data source used is $jdbc/ilogDataSource$. If we want to specify a different data source, we have to pass it as a request parameter in the URL, for example, http://localhost:8080/teamserver?datasource=jdbc/otherteamserverds.

This capability is also used to support different development branches: one data source is used as trunk and other for other releases. We will detail that in Chap. 17. It is also possible to define one data source per group of users or line of business: finance and marketing teams may have two rule repositories clearly separated but one RTS deployed.

Configure the Rule Team Server Database

Configure the Rule Team Server database by first generating the SQL script that creates the database schema from the rule model and extensions you specify, then executing the script and initializing the database.
Warning: Make sure you have an adequate backup when using this option with existing data.

Some existing data has been found in the Rule Team Server database. What would you like to do?

◉ Generate a script that keeps my data
○ Generate a script that erases the existing data and recreates the schema

Select the extension files you want to use:

○ Default extensions ◉ Custom extensions

Model extension file: e/jextensionModel.bmx [Browse..]

Data extension file: pde\jextensionData.brdx [Browse..]

[Generate SQL] [Upload Only]

Fig. 13.14 Add custom rule properties in Rule Team Server

As part of the physical deployment is the support of "single sign on" integration for getting users information like userid, group, and password from a central directory service. RTS can be deployed in an application server and will leverage the container contract as RTS uses the JAAS API to retrieve user's data. The important configuration to complete before running RTS is the group definition and assignment of the user to one of the four groups of RTS: rtsAdministrator, rtsConfigManager, rtsUser, and rtsInstaller.

Finally as RTS is the main component to control the rule project, it is important to avoid duplicating rule repositories between multiple platforms. It is possible to manage the ruleset deployment to different RES platforms from one central deployed RTS. This is the simplest and most efficient deployment. The second pattern is to use one RTS per target platforms, as most IT environment includes at least development, test, UAT, production, we can have unnecessary deployed RTS. Rulesets are deployed to the different deployed RES. Finally, another common deployment is to use two RTS, one for all the rule authoring done by the business user, used to deploy ruleset to any execution platforms except production. And one in production managed by IT and mostly used to support rule 'hot fix', exclusively deploy to production RES. It is this last RTS instance that will be used for ruleset deployment to production server.

13.5.2   Queries

Queries are an important element of the Ruleset deployment. Using query and ruleset extractors, we can control the ruleset deployment for different purposes (e.g., test, simulation, and production) and platforms. Common dimensions used in business are the effective date and expiration date for some business entities like a product, a pricing campaign, a medicine availability, a loan eligibility, ... Business rules defining constraints on those entities have to follow the effective and expiration dates patterns. With a ruleset extractor, business users may extract only the rules valid at a given time, or can search for rules in a given status. Queries can be added to RTS repository by any type of user with the create query permission. We will detail in Chap. 17 the fine grained permission management RTS provides. Figure 13.15 presents a query developed to extract rules ready for production.

Once the queries are defined, a RTS administrator can define extractors using the feature Configure > Edit Ruleset Extractors. An extractor is defined using a name, a query, and a validator (Fig. 13.16).

Extractors are then used in the creation of the ruleset archives by specifying the extractor name. By default all the rules are extracted to the archive (Fig. 13.17).

With queries and extractors we can package rulesets as intended for the different purposes platform dependant like test, simulation, and production, or time-oriented, or any business needs.

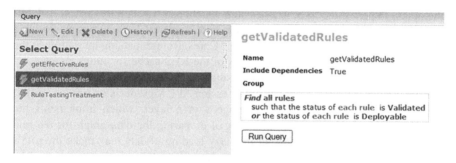

Fig. 13.15 Query to get rules ready for production

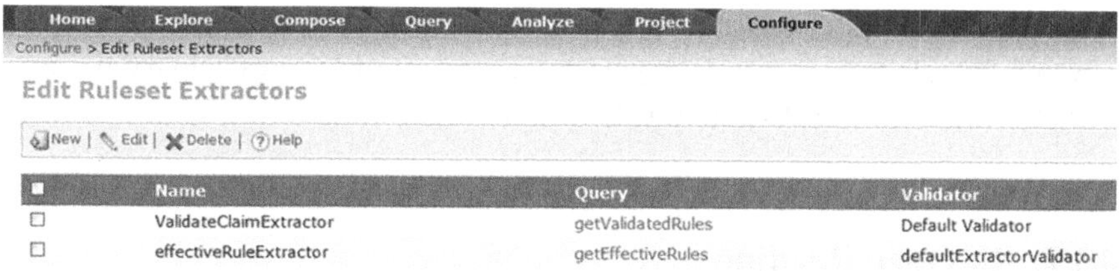

Fig. 13.16 Manage ruleset extractors in RTS

Fig. 13.17 Ruleset archives built using extractor

13.6 Summary

We reviewed the concepts of operation of JRules and detailed the RuleApp element, which includes one to many rulesets and which represents the deployable unit to the rule execution server. RES supports monitoring of rule execution, with the option to persist the trace in a decision warehouse. To support vertical scalability, the RES leverages the JCA connection pool, so parallel executions are possible as soon as the server has multiple CPUs or Cores. Ruleset parsing takes time at the first call, but once parsed a ruleset stays in the RES cache for future processing. When using a Java XOM, the ruleset parsing needs the class information as part of the classloader of the class using the rule session API. Most decision service, even if exposed as web service, should leverage a java layer, which implements the business service and completes the work of preparing the data graph for the rule processing. It is important to recall that lazy loading of data may make the rule's conditions not evaluate as true: for example, a collection of objects may not be loaded, and so a test with the *in* operator will fail. The decision service uses a stateless processing, sending all the data in one call. The deployment mode can include different patterns from JMS, for message processing, to pure POJO or EJB. As a new programming model, SCA is also supported, and SCA component implemented in Java, uses the RES API to call the rule execution. Finally, we covered the rule team server deployment, where a set of features help the business analyst to deploy the RuleApp to RES.

13.7 Further Reading

For more technical information and tutorials, the product documentation is accessible at http://publib.boulder.ibm.com/infocenter/brjrules/v7r1/index.jsp.

Service component architecture presentation can be read at IBM developerworks web site at http://www.ibm.com/developerworks/library/specification/ws-sca/, and the specification is accessible at the Open service oriented architecture portal http://www.osoa.org/display/main/service+component+architecture+home.

The rule interchange format recommendation is part of the semantic web work done at W3C. and aims to provide interoperability between rule based systems, reader can access the description of this recommendation at http://www.w3.org/blog/SW/2010/06/22/w3c_rif_recommendation_published.

The SCA support pack for WebSphere Application Server can be studied at http://www-01.ibm.com/software/webservers/appserv/was/featurepacks/sca/.

Part VI
Rule Testing

Chapter 14
Issues with Rule Testing and Performance

Target audience

- *Application architect, software architect, developer, business analyst, nontechnical audiences can skip Sect. 14.6*

In this chapter you will learn

- *The rule testing approach and how it fits into the different testing phases used in traditional software development*
- *How to use a test-driven approach to implement business rules*
- *How using SCA can help build the application and a test framework by iterations*
- *How performance could be impacted by business rules application, and what to look for during design and testing activities*
- *Testing does not end once in production, especially with rule-based applications*
- *What is rule semantic consistency checking, and what the different search patterns are*
- *The problem of tracing and logging*

Key points

- *Adopting a test-driven development helps to implement the rules by first looking at their intent. Testing business rules is about business, so the test has to be designed to prove the impact to the business.*
- *The test framework should be light and not too rigid on the assertion of the expected results, as some results are computation driven.*
- *Performance tests should measure all the potential bottlenecks, like the messaging layer, the data conversion, the data access, and the rule execution. Rule engines are optimized to run fast, and sometimes data access is the issue.*
- *As in database, join operations are costly.*

J. Boyer and H. Mili, *Agile Business Rule Development*,
DOI 10.1007/978-3-642-19041-4_14, © Springer-Verlag Berlin Heidelberg 2011

- *Testing activities remain important during the maintenance of the application.*
- *Inconsistencies in a ruleset may happen over time, but they have to be corrected as soon as possible. Some BRMS offer consistency checking features to search for rules never selected, rules that make other rules redundant, rules with equivalent conditions ...*

14.1 Introduction

In this chapter, we address rule testing, rule execution performance, continuous testing, consistency checking, and tracing. In Sect. 14.2, we first start by discussing rule testing issues, including: unit testing of rules, functional testing (FT), component testing, regression testing, and performance testing. Next in Sect. 14.3, we address one common question architects often ask about rule engine performance, and how to assess the end-to-end performance testing. We examine performance from many perspectives: issues of data creation, issues of the size of the working memory of the rule engine, and efficient rule writing. Section 14.4 presents the need for testing even after being in production as the business rules may change overtime. One of the main value proposition of a BRMS is to be able to maintain the business logic outside of the application and being able to change it as often as the business needs: this velocity does not mean we do testing only in the development phase, but we need to test during maintenance as well. In Sect. 14.5, we discuss the difficult issue of semantic consistency checking of rules. Semantic consistency checking looks at things such as rule redundancy or overlap, and distinguishing between legitimate or natural inconsistencies and overlaps, and illegitimate, i.e., erroneous ones. Next, we look at the issue of rule tracing and debugging, and we conclude in Sect. 14.7.

14.2 Rule Testing

Externalizing business rules as standalone artifacts helps to test the business logic of the application earlier than in traditional applications. We present unit testing in Sect. 14.2.1, which represents the first major testing activity started as soon as the ABRD prototyping phase. We propose to adopt a test-driven development (TDD) as, through our many years of experience, it helped us to implement code and rules the most efficient way. In Sect. 14.2.2, we explain how to leverage SCA to develop a component testing framework, which tests the ruleset with all its related components. In Sect. 14.2.3, we present how functional testing applies to rulesets and where Key Performance Indicators (KPIs) may be compared to "reasonable comfort range." Finally in Sect. 14.2.4, we present regression testing to ensure long-term quality control. Let us start by reviewing the general needs and approaches for testing.

The business rules approach enforces the definition of the data set used to test each individual rules as early as the rule harvesting phase. This data set helps to build test scenarios. The goals of a test are: first to ensure the business requirements (business policies) are supported, and second to ensure that rule updates do not cause any functional regression issues, in any part of the system. As a good practice, the test suite has to ensure that newly updated decisions are consistent and cover enough cases imagined by subject matter experts (SMEs), so that they are confident to deploy the updated business logic to production. Decisions made by the rule engine usually have a contractual value and organizations cannot afford to be wrong. Developing test cases is time consuming and often relies on the support of an SME, but it is a necessary and critical step that has to be done.

Testing with a BRMS involves helping the business users decide between different policy implementation alternatives. Business rules testing fits well into the traditional testing phases such as unit testing, component testing, functional testing, system testing, performance testing, and user acceptance testing. Any business application using the business rules approach should have a testing framework to validate the rule changes made over time. When well designed, such a framework can run automatically and can be used in simulations. Simulations represent another testing technique used by the business users to assess the performance of the rules according to business metrics or key performance indicators (KPIs). The testing framework has to be flexible enough to allow the definition of KPIs and to compare results to those metrics. This testing technique is commonly named champion/challenger technique and can rely on the use of a database (DB) of actual cases. Let us start by explaining how to unit test rules.

14.2.1 Unit Testing

Wikipedia defines Unit testing as: "Unit testing is a method by which individual units of source code are tested to determine if they are fit for use. A unit is the smallest testable part of an application. In procedural programming a unit may be an individual function or procedure."[1] In business rules programming, a unit is a single business rule, tested in the context of the ruleset, so with other rules. During the ABRD prototyping and implementation phases, the development team should adopt a Test-Driven Development (TDD)[2] approach to test the ruleset.

---

[1]See Wikipedia at http://en.wikipedia.org/wiki/Unit_testing.

[2]There is a lot of content over the web, and books on TDD, one of the first is B Kent "Test-Driven Development by Example", Addison Wesley, 2003, and obviously at http://en.wikipedia.org/wiki/Test-driven_development.

Concept: **Test-Driven Development**

Introduced by the extreme programming methodology, TDD means that the development of new functionality starts by implementing tests for that functionality before coding. The test focuses on the intent of the code, which increases the value by designing an efficient API and functionality. This concept applies well for rule authoring. As the rule is not yet coded, the test execution against an existing ruleset has to fail. Once the rule is written and the ruleset deployed to the unit testing environment, the test should succeed. A unit test is usually built with the following structure: preparing the test data, executing the rule against that data, and using assertion statements to compare the response with the expected results.

Unit testing in java is well supported by using JUnit.[3] A JUnit test case class is mapped to a rule package and then declares test methods per condition within a rule. It is also a good practice to create one java project per ruleset under test to include all the test cases and data set. Let us take as an example the implementation of the following claim adjudication policy (Fig. 14.1).

We are using the same data model as defined in the previous chapters. Starting with the test cases, we implement a JUnit class TestDolTreatmentClaim. This test method to validate the previous rule may start by creating a claim, setting some specific values to the claim and any related elements accessible from the claim, then executes the rule, and finally asserts the expected results. The code looks like as shown in Fig. 14.2.

It is good practice to start adding some mockup classes to build the basic data set to use across test cases (a class like `DataMockup.createClaimAndPolicy()`) and then overwrite the attributes needed to make the rule fire. The `assertEquals` and `validateResult` methods make the assertion of the test a success or not. To know if the test succeeded may depend on the ruleset logic. When using the decision pattern, the assertion can look at the list of decisions to see if the expected decision was created.

Concept: **Decision Pattern**

Decision pattern uses a DecisionResponse class, returned by the decision service, which includes a list of decisions done by the rules. Rule taking decision adds a Decision instance to this list. The Decision class defines all the data needed for the downstream processing. When the application uses a workflow engine, the decisions may need to be reported to a human actor. In that case the Decision includes a message, which is presented to the end user. Most of the time the Decision includes some predefined reason code, which are defined externally to the business rule, for example, in a master data management.

---

[3]See www.junit.org.

When the claim is related to a car accident the company does not reimburse for ambulance transport done at a different date of the date of loss. Any such ambulance transport in the medical invoice is waived and a notification is sent to the insurer.

Fig. 14.1 A business policy to implement

```
public void testAmbulanceTransport()   {
  Claim claim = DataMockup.createClaimAndPolicy();
  claim.setType(Claim.ACCIDENT);
  claim.setDayOfLoss(DateUtilities.makeDate(2007,11, 27));// DOL is 2007,11, 27
  MedicalBill invoice = DataMockup.createMedicalBill(claim);
  Treatment t2 = new Treatment();
  t2.setDescription("Ambulance Transport");
  t2.setProcedureCode(MedicalProcedureCode. AMBULANCE_TRANSPORT);
  MedicalBillDetail bd2 = new MedicalBillDetail(2,t2,1,  999.00,
  DateUtilities. makeDate(2007,11,28)); // not the same day as DOL
  invoice.addMedicalLineItem(bd2);

  int nbRules=executeRules(claim, invoice);
  assertEquals (StatusValue.HASISSUE,invoice.getStatus());
  validateResult("Audit Medical Bill","Ambulance Transportation after date of loss");
```

Fig. 14.2 Unit test method in JUnit

It is also possible to get the rule name or unique identifier in the execution trace of the rule to evaluate the success of the test. This is a good alternative to ease the maintenance of the unit test base by avoiding an adjustment each time the rules change. The assertion can validate that the rule has fired (or not) as expected based on its conditions, rather than checking if the expected actions have occurred. This can be achieved by analyzing the rule report. This way the successful unit test does not make assumptions on the actions induced. As time goes by, the need and frequency to change or adapt the test case becomes less frequent, since only changing the condition part of the rule can produce different test results.

Once the test is defined, we can write the rule in the rule editing environment. When the rule is complex or when this is the first time we implement such rule, we may want to add conditions one at a time to simplify rule debugging. When we already have rules with similar conditions, it is easy to copy and paste the conditions that we know are working. Here is an example of rule in JRules rule language.

```
Definitions
  set accidentClaim to aclaim from 'the claim' where the type of 'the claim'
    is Accident ;
  set billLineItemtoamedicalbilldetailinthe medical line items
    of 'the medical bill' ;
  set treatment to a treatment from the treatment of billLineItem
    where the procedure code of this treatment is AMBULANCE_TRANSPORT ;
if
  the date of service of treatment is after 'the claim's date of loss
then
  add to 'the result' an audit request : "Audit Medical Bill"with a code "R534"
  and a description : "Ambulance Transportation after date of loss" ;
  set the status of 'the medical bill' to HASISSUE ;
```

We may complete the test by adding a test method with a date of service for the ambulance transport on the same day as the Day of Loss and verify that the invoice does not have an issue (Fig. 14.3).

For unit testing, it is important to use a lightweight environment with as few dependencies as possible. Finally, each unit test class can be used for automatic regression testing. An Ant script can execute all the JUnit classes as part of the build process: this is to ensure the ruleset is still valid over time.

As we just described, unit tests are created and executed by software developers as the data model and other service layer classes are added to the system during the creation of the first rules. Later on the unit testing framework evolves to support functional testing and in that case the main actor may become the business analyst.

Leveraging Java to develop unit test cases and a unit testing framework is common even in the case of pure XML document processing. A natural approach is to develop one XML document per test method; but it may quickly evolve to a complex environment with interdependent elements. Therefore, using a pure Java implementation is often more flexible. In fact, it is possible to mix the two, using some XML documents which represent complete data set for the input requests sent to the service. These documents can be parsed to create java beans using JAXB or SDO implementation, and then the unit test method updates some of the attribute of the beans to trigger the right rules. In the code sample above, the DataMockup class can be replaced by a XML document reader, which prepares a claim, policy, and any medical invoices attached to the claim. The choice of the approach is linked to the use of an XML centric data for the application architecture or not. When the IT development team has already a set of XML documents representing real data, it makes sense to try to incorporate such a data set in the test environment. But one of the best practices around unit testing is to try making a framework as simple as possible and test as much as possible in isolation. The less we depend on complex XML documents, the better and more stable this environment will be. Using a TDD approach to develop the rules allows for a lot of refactoring on both the data model and the rules. Depending too strongly on a rigid XSD may lead to less effective rules writing and consume more development time. It is fine to start with a java model, and then generate the XSDs to expose the decision service as web service. It is also important to recall that some rules may need access to other services or logic, not accessible through the mapping in the XML document received as input to the decision service.

```java
public void testAcceptAmbulanceSameDol() {
    ..
    Treatment t2 = new Treatment();
    t2.setProcedureCode(MedicalProcedureCode.AMBULANCE_TRANSPORT);
    // the same day as DOL
    t2.setDateOfService(DateUtilities.makeXmlDate(2007,11, 27,00,00));
    ..
    int nbRules = executeRules(claim,invoice);
    assertEquals(StatusValue.RECEIVED,invoice.getStatus());
}
```

Fig. 14.3 Second test method

14.2.2   Component Testing

A ruleset by its nature is complex enough to be considered as a component. To reuse John D. McGregor's[4] ideas from his paper about component testing, the penalty of a nonworking ruleset is far greater than the cost of testing it since business rules have business impact by design. So all the unit tests we defined in the previous section are aimed to test the component as a standalone element. In this section, the ruleset is deployed in its target decision service, and the goal is to test the other components it works with. Suppose that the decision service is accessing some data source through a service layer, we now want to remove any scaffolding code we had in the unit test environment and integrate the components together to verify the rulesets are performing as expected. Using the definition used in SCA, an application is an assembly of components. A component implementation delivers some business logic exposed in one or more services. The testing framework assembly is built by using an incremental approach by adding component after component in the assembly. The component testing starts by adding the service layer that uses the ruleset, like the `ClaimProcessing-Core`, and tests at the interface level. So the test now sends `claimId` and `medicalInvoice` using the operation defined in the `ClaimProcessingInterface`. As the rules need to access data, it is still possible to use the mockup for some data elements that are not available yet and wire the appropriate service implementation when it is ready. Figure 14.4 illustrates this approach using a SCA composite diagram. The "Process Claim Component" is using the component to support the adjudicate and validate claim rules.

Some of the data set used for the unit tests can be reused in the component testing. Most likely the component testing is executed on a development server where all the components are deployed from the build server, and some specific test suites are executed on the assembly. We can still use JUnit for component testing; the difference is based on the granularity of the component interface, and the type of data used. The example below uses the primary key of the claim to get a claim stored in an external data source.

```
@Test
public void testValidateClaim(){
    // we are at the interface level now and the component implementation
    ProcessClaim pc= new ProcessClaimImpl();
    // take a claim that is after the expiration date of the policy
    ClaimProcessingResult cpr=pc.validateClaimByNumber("CL002");
```

The processClaim implementation encapsulates how data is retrieved. The test assumes the data is present and loaded from the datasource.

---

[4]See http://www.cs.clemson.edu/~johnmc/joop/col3/column3.html.

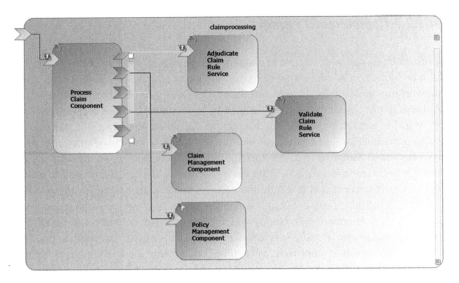

Fig. 14.4 SCA component view

14.2.3 Functional Testing

Functional testing (FT) addresses the validation of the system at its highest interfaces to verify it is compliant to the functional requirements of the application.
Functional verification attempts to answer the question "Does this proposed design
do what is intended?" without knowledge on how the system is built. With a
business rules approach we need to evaluate how the components involved after
the execution of the rules are reacting, and how the final results are exposed to the
end users. The testers need to select valid and invalid inputs to send to the system
according to the use case description or business process description. The output is
then compared to expected results. Most of the functional tests should focus on the
business requirements and how to prove the system brings value to the business. It
is the responsibility of the business team to provide test scenarios and realistic data
sets. As the business logic is externalized to a ruleset, it may be easier to see the
impact on the business key performance indicators when the logic changes. The
functional tests for the rules can be supported by a specific tooling or framework.
Functional testing occurs after some iterations of the software development. The
system needs to get enough high-level functionality to be testable. Some project
managers define functional testing as the starting step of the alpha release.

When developing functional test suites, the results of the test cases executed are
not expected to be accurate; however, they have to be within an established
"reasonable comfort range" to be qualified as passed. The definition of the "reasonable comfort range" is established by the business SMEs and is the sole pass/fail
criteria for test cases in this phase. Later on when all the functions of the application

are validated, the test cases are looking for more accurate expected results as agreed with the SMEs.

Functional tests also need to address the error cases and how the system reacts to erroneous data. The preparation of test cases can be initiated during the requirements phase and for a rule-based application during the rule harvesting phase. Functional testing uses a different execution environment with a more complete data set. Most of the time, the FT servers are deployed in a QA platform. For rule functional testing, it may be possible to design a framework where business analysts define their own data set using tool like Excel or XML document editor. The developers have to prepare this environment. The simplest framework leverages data persisted in a data base to represent the data set for the major classes of test cases: some data represent the standard customers, and some the ones with problems. This framework can leverage tools like JUnit (or extensions like HTTPUnit) to modify the data loaded from the different data sources, trigger the tests, and look at the results. Most modern applications have graphical user interfaces which are more difficult to test, but tools exist to record actions on the graphical component and user interactions so the test scenarios can be replayed. Some tools can also be used at the communication protocol level to replay the sequence of messages exchanged between the web browser and the application. The framework has to facilitate automated testing.

In the context of a BRMS deployment, it is important to notice the existence of two FT life cycles supporting both the business and IT teams working together on the rules and the application code at the same time. Indeed, rules are usually developed in parallel to the IT development activities, and are deployed multiple times during a single IT release cycle. To keep a fast development pace the FT framework should isolate the ruleset testing from the core application testing. This can also be supported by a good design of the underlying data model used by the rules. As business users are not expected to be proficient in Java or XML, the rule testing framework should provide an interface allowing them to enter the test data. Usually, the selected interface is a tool using worksheet like Microsoft Excel. Some test templates are provided as empty Excel spreadsheets requesting the author to fill data in cells corresponding to the data model. Instances of such excel files are the test cases. It is important to establish what the expected results of the tests are. At this stage, focus should not be on the detailed values of attributes, as it may not be realistic, but on the intent of the business rules. For example in a pricing computation ruleset, the combination of possible values is unrealistic to compute as an expected result. What is more important is that the premium price is set, the discount is computed as a separate value, applied to the premium, and the value outcome of the rule processing stays in a range expected by the business. For example, it does not make sense to get discount pricing above a given threshold.

Furthermore, the test base (set of all the test cases) should provide sufficient coverage of the rules to be considered complete and verify all the functions implemented through business rules. The coverage is usually expected to meet 100%, meaning that for any business rule implemented, there exists at least one test case that triggers it. The coverage analysis is conducted by consolidating all the lists of rules fired for all the test cases, compared against all the rules deployed.

14.2.4 Regression Testing

Regression testing for applications using business rules engine is a very important feature to support a continuous quality control of the ruleset. Over time, the software logic will change with the update of the rule base, so we need to ensure the application is still running as expected. Any type of testing needs to support automated testing to make the developers, business analysts, and testers more confident on the application quality, and to make them know when the application breaks. Regression testing is most likely part of the software build process, where the code is extracted from the configuration management system, compiled, packaged, and then executed in front of a set of test case suites. The suite of tests for nonregression may include all the rule unit test and functional test suites defined previously. As the testing process needs to be automatic, developers need to take care to leave the system stable at each test execution. When using JUnit, developers should leverage methods executed before and after the test to prepare and clean the environment for each test case.

As it is included in the build process, we need to ensure that the extraction of the rules from the rule repository and the packaging into a ruleset can be automated. Some BRMS products offer a headless mode to extract the rule and build a ruleset. Error reports have to be clear and accessible. One scenario is to set up automatic alarms and emails sent to the lead developers when failures occur to ensure the tests which fail are immediately investigated.

The maintenance of the regression tests can be time consuming when the changes in the ruleset are extensive. Regression tests need to compare the outcome of the current execution with the previous run. Any change may be an issue. There are cases in business rules applications where the change is expected. For example in a risk management application, changing a rule will impact the risk rating, so simply comparing the risk rating with a static value will make the test fail. Requirements change, so the tests to compare the expected value have to be modified in the test cases. When computing a complex and changeable value, it is unrealistic to test for a given risk value. The test should compare to a range of acceptable values to avoid false-failing.

14.3 Performance Testing

The performance of a decision service based on rules execution varies based on an important number of factors the application can deal with. In this section, we first review the logical steps a decision service is going through and use each step as potential measurement probe. It gives a good framework to test performance. In Sect. 14.3.1, we present the different dimensions impacting rule performance, and where traditionally bottlenecks may appear. Section 14.3.2 addresses how data are loaded before executing rules using different loading strategy, which may impact performance or ruleset result. We then present, in Sect. 14.3.3, the issues rule designer will have when loading data in the action or the condition part of a rule. Section 14.3.4 summarizes how the rule implementation itself can impact performance and how to avoid common errors. Finally in Sect. 14.3.5, we present some important rule language operators, or keyword, that may impact the inference capability of the engine and then the performance.

The main variables, impacting rule engine performance, include the number of objects used for the rule execution, the number of rules within one ruleset, the number of concurrent callers, the type of access to external data sources, the type of objects used to present the data, the possibility to run in parallel ... to list a few. The processing of a decision service, which uses a rule engine, includes the following steps:

- Prepare the data in the context of the service: this could include parsing a XML document, loading data from different data sources, or accessing cached data
- Prepare the parameters to send to the rule engine using the rule session API
- Call the rule execution
- The rule engine fires the rules until there are no more rules in its agenda
- Get and process the results
- Clean the previously loaded data, if needed, to avoid memory consumption
- Close resources
- Return the results to caller

Figure 14.5 illustrates the end-to-end flow from a client, like a process engine, calling the decision service using a web service deployment.

When assessing performance, it is important to get the metrics for the following information: the marshalling and unmarshalling of the data before sending over the

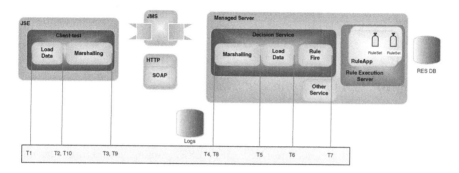

Fig. 14.5 Time stamp of a typical web service decision service

network at the client and server level, the communication time to transfer data between the two components, and then the time to execute the rules. To achieve this, we may need to use the following time stamps:

Time stamp	Description
T1	Start of the client tester. Use System.currentTimeMillis() or nano
T2	End of test data creation – can be one to n transactional data elements
T3	End of marshalling data for transmitting – sending message to the wire (e.g., a web service call using SOAP over HTTP, or a JMS send message)
T4	Time to cross the wire on the network using the communication protocol selected
T5	End of unmarshalling of the data
T6	End of ruleset parameter preparation like loading complement data set, call the rule execution
T7	End of the rule execution
T8	End of marshalling the response
T9	End of communication
T10	End of unmarshalling the response and processing it

All these time stamps can be managed in memory and persisted to log files on a shared disk at the end of the processing or managed asynchronously by another thread of execution. Logging should have a minimum impact on this overall process; 1% performance impact is the maximum a business application can tolerate. This may look obvious but all the timers need to be synchronized or there is a mechanism to "normalize" the measures by applying a delta between time stamps. The report can be presented graphically to evaluate where the system is taking the most time.

When assessing the performance, it is important to evaluate if the total rule service processing time is significant relative to overall performance goals and, if so, to determine which of the above steps are consuming significant processing time. This process helps to get the global picture, but it is always easy to isolate the rule processing and get rule performance test assessed as early as possible in the application development. Performance testing has to address the different workload patterns: stress workload when the number of business transactions is sent over the average expected workload during a long period of time, peak workload when the number of transactions increases for a short period of time, and the nominal workload.

14.3.1 Multiple Performance Dimensions

There are multiple dimensions to look at when assessing performance for an application using a rule engine: the data access, the rules implementation, the rule engine deployment architecture (J2SE, JEE, ESB, pooling, messaging), the integration, the infrastructure, and hardware. Figure 14.6 shows the potential bottlenecks. The first one may come from the using of a messaging queue and persistence

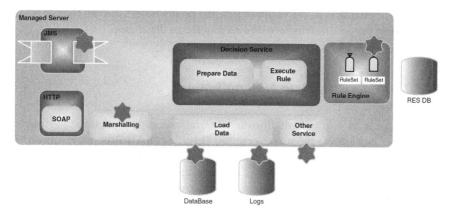

Fig. 14.6 Potential bottlenecks for decision service execution performance

of the message to support failover. The second is the marshaling or unmarshaling of the input/output parameters of the decision service. It is common to see a huge XML document sent as payload to the web service call, creating unnecessary data conversion. Loading the complementary data from a database can also expose some performance issue. A bad design of tracing and logging of the rule execution can also impact the overall performance. A call to another service may also do so. Finally, the rules by themselves can be a source for performance issue. The actual rule engine technology itself is an unlikely source of performance issues. The use of the technology by the developer is usually the culprit.

For the hardware, the always changing server capacity like increasing the memory or the CPU type and adding new server helps to increase the performance or support load increases. The network is usually less of an issue although for one of our projects, we recently had to assess why a decision service was executing slowly. After investigation, we discovered the database was not physically close to the rule execution server, but in Singapore, connected over a slow network connection. From our experience, the data access is usually the largest bottleneck among the factors affecting the performance and scalability of an application. The amount of time spent on data access is dependent on how the data is accessed. Despite the improvements on the underlying technology, database still takes a lot of time to read and process data. To try and minimize this impact, it is sometimes possible to read and cache data locally for the processing of the rules. An ESB can be used to retrieve a complete data set in the form of a message. Another source of performance issues can be located around the unmarshalling of the input and marshalling of the response. When addressing data access it is important to recall that rule conditions are applied to the data model, so the data needs to be present. To access related objects part of an association (the coverage of the policy), the rules will take more time to process if the application is doing a round trip to a data base: if the engine *needs* the policy and coverage objects to make its decision, then it would be better if both the claim object, the policy object, and all the coverage objects were materialized as java objects and fed to the engine.

14.3.2   Patterns of Data Materialization

There are at least two patterns for the materialization of data: the eager one is loading the data prior to the rule execution. This is a conservative approach which assumes that we figure out upfront which data is relevant, load it, feed it to the engine, and save it after the decision step. On the other hand, the lazy approach loads only data elements we know are mandatory (the claim), and the rules by accessing the data graph will force the loading of the rest of the data and the materialization in java objects. This last operation is performed by the O/R mapping layer, such as Hibernate or the SDO DAS (see Chap. 12). We need to take into consideration the conventional design practice used in persistence frameworks where using lazy loading is usually more efficient. When using rule engines we do not want to be accessing the DB to evaluate conditions or actions as it will impact the performance: the engine is blocked on nonessential, nonrule related tasks. In the context of a ruleset, it is also quite challenging to handle JDBC exceptions properly. It is important to know that lazy loading can lead to some strange behavior: for example, a lazy loading of Policy just loads the policy object and not its associated Coverages. A call to myPolicy.getCoverages() goes into the database, gets the Coverages, creates Java objects, and returns them. A reasonable caching strategy might cache the list of Coverages, and so a second call to getCoverages() returns the same set of objects. A simplistic cache strategy might flush the cache if the list of Coverages changes and recreates new java objects all over again. Because those new objects will have a different memory address (identity), refraction in the rules will not work, and the engine will fire the same rules that fired on the previous copies, on the new copies.

14.3.3   Accessing Data from Within the Rules

At a pure rule engine processing level, the rule execution is impacted by the number of rules and the number of objects referenced by the engine. During the implementation phase, it is possible to isolate the ruleset and perform stress tests to understand the impact of the ruleset design. The predictability of response times is important to be able to guarantee quality of service of the applications and to plan computing resources accordingly. As a starting point to any performance investigation, we recommend to clearly identifying which dependencies the ruleset has on the data loading and to external web services. It is common to have to access data from multiple sources in parallel. Does the rule access some Service Data Object using a DAS and other DAO? How are enumerated data or other master data accessed? Do the rules call web services and for what purpose? Is it a synchronous call blocking the rule to get the response? The eager design approach may be possible in most applications, but sometimes a trade off is needed to minimize impact on the ruleset performance for 10% of the cases where the data may not be present, and adapting a load on demand may be suitable. This can be done by using a first part of the ruleset (or by splitting the ruleset) to evaluate if a complement of data is needed. If not the flow of execution goes to the main stream, if yes the flow goes to an exceptional path used to load the remaining data set, and applies the appropriate business rules. Also using this approach, it is possible to avoid executing a lot of rules if data are definitively not present.

If we invoke a nontrivial service, in either the condition part or the action, we will have three issues to contend with: latency, error handling, and transactional support. Latency represents the time to execute a round trip from the caller to the receiver. Slow service calls lock engines in nonproductive cycles. This could become a serious problem if the call to the remote service is done in the rule condition where a test can be invoked very often. On the action side, the best practice is to avoid calling the service directly, but to postpone the call after the rule execution. This is possible if the action does not trigger other rules (rule chaining). The error handling in a ruleset may leave the engine in an inconsistent state. A call to a remote service can be impacted by a potential network timeout, communication error, locked resources, or an execution error on the server. Finally, handling transactions within single service invocations, or across multiple service invocations, is hard enough in general, so it is even harder from within the condition part or action part of a rule.

The action part of the rule may most likely change the states of the business objects, but we may need to avoid calling the DAO or service layer from the rule to persist the updates back to the data sources. It is preferable to leave this step until after the complete execution of the rules. The rule execution is one method part of the overall transaction. Transactions should not be initiated by the ruleset, mostly because it is not so obvious to manage a roll back, in case of exception or failure.

14.3.4 Pattern Matching Performance

A rule engine uses pattern matching to evaluate which rule conditions match the object referenced in its working memory. So the larger the number of objects in the working memory, the more time the engine spends evaluating the candidate rules. Even if the RETE algorithm was designed to handle a relatively small number of rules with a large number of objects, it takes time to process the pattern matching. When the rules share some conditions the RETE network will be able to share nodes and so will be more efficient when processing facts. At the rule level to improve performance, we can try to limit the number of conditions within a rule. Depending on the rule engine implementation, it is also possible to reduce the time to search for eligible rules by writing rules with the most discriminating condition as first test.

Concept: **Discriminating Condition**

This is a condition in a rule that tests an attribute against a constant or static value and avoids going over looking at a collection. For example, a rule which looks at a coverage with a specific procedure code on a pending claim must first assess the claim is not pending, to avoid navigating through the collection if the claim is in any state that is not *Pending*.

If

   the claim is pending and

   there is a coverage in the coverages of the policy of the claim where the procedure code is 34

   and ...

instead of

If

   there is a coverage in the coverages of the policy of the claim where the procedure code is 34

   and the claim is pending

When some conditions are processing complex evaluation, it may be interesting to split the work into different rules. Recently in one of the projects, we had to implement a complex lookup between lists of object and return a Boolean value if one element of one list was part of the other. Depending on the rules design, it may be possible to isolate this long processing search in one rule and then keep the result in a variable, so that the other rules look only at the fact that the variable was set to a given value. The underlying code of any method used in a lot of conditions needs to be optimized as much as possible. Sometimes it is possible to return a previously cached result to avoid executing the complex search for the same input parameters.

We have seen some rule implementations using test statements in the then or else part of the rule. The developer was implementing business rules like a procedure. This has to be avoided as much as possible. The left-hand side of a rule is processed much faster by the RETE than the right hand side. Actions should execute as quickly as possible. Do not perform long running tasks inside the rule engine if they can be avoided. One solution is to delegate to some service which can do their process in a separate thread asynchronously.

14.3.5   Some Guidelines on Keywords

By using some language keyword like *update, insert, retract,* or *modify* ... within the action part of the rule, one can force the reevaluation of the RETE tree. This is always a costly operation, so *update, modify, insert,* or *retract* really have to be used only when we want to infer decisions. When beginning with rule engine programming, this is a capability the developer likes to use and abuse. There is usually no real need for it. So depending on the rules there are other solutions to avoid such reevaluation. When the rule engine offers an efficient rule flow mechanism, it is possible to organize the flow of processing such that some facts are "inherited" by the previous rule tasks. This avoids duplicating conditions and avoids RETE reevaluation. For example, the beginning of the rule flow can include a task to verify that all the attributes we need later in the other rules are present by testing against null, or size greater than zero, etc. If one of such rule fires at the beginning of the ruleflow, it makes sense to stop the processing and avoid going through all rules. The remaining rules do not need to perform the same tests again, leading to improved performance.

It is recommended to avoid using the *"not"* condition as it involves looking through all the objects of a given type in the working memory. When the number of objects is important, it may take time. But as most business decision services today are processing one business event at a time, the search for objects of the same type is very limited, and using a *not* is not an issue.

In the telecom industry, there are applications which are looking at a lot of objects of the same type to evaluate the presence of an event. Examples of such application include alarm filtering and correlation, network element management, or call data record processing. In this execution pattern, the rule engine needs to leverage specific capabilities to efficiently manage this huge amount of objects to process.

Below is an example of such a rule combining a pattern matching on an alarm instance and the nonpresence of its "derived alarms":

If
    alarm1 : Alarm(status equals alive);
    Not Alarm(alarm1.ID equals parentID);
Then
    Retract alarm1;

Such a rule uses joins between facts and retraction of reference in working memory to force rule evaluation. When the number of alarms is important, this kind of rule can require a lot of time to execute. The rule engine algorithm has to be optimized to take this pattern into account. This is even truer if we add time operators like within the last minute. Then a time window has to be managed, which adds to the complexity of processing.

14.4 Continuous Testing

Part of the content presented in this section is coming from the work done by Pierre Berlandier,[5] Senior Technical Staff Member – BRMS Solution Architect at IBM, who authorized us to publish it. In traditional IT software application development,

---

[5]See one of his article at on rule repository structure http://www.ibm.com/developerworks/websphere/library/techarticles/1003_berlandier/1003_berlandier.html.

the test activity starts during the elaboration phase of the project (RUP phases) and peaks during the construction. Most of the time, once in production, application testing is reduced to a minimum, only focusing to ensure nonregression of issues fixed or added features (Fig. 14.7).

The participants to the test activity tend to be the IT QA group members and developers. They follow carefully crafted test plans that are the result of analyzing the business requirements. The business user is not usually involved. When using a rule approach, and BRMS software, the development life cycle is completed by a "change time" phase, started when the application is in production. Available for its end users, but continuously adapted to support deployment of new business policies. The new implementation of business rules needs testing, completed by the traditional nonregression test. This means the test activity remains important during the maintenance of the application as illustrated in Fig. 14.8.

The stakeholders are the same as during the rule harvesting phase and stay actively engaged during the development and the maintenance. Business people are key to the design of new test cases that should be run about new or updated policies. It is often the case that the business users are performing testing themselves.

Change management is a serious challenge to support, as each change is comparable to a mini-project that has to be executed in a short amount of time and may be triggered on short notice: we often see notice as short as 2 days before the deployment of the updated business logic. During this period, the full development cycle must be executed: from analysis to design, to implementation, and most importantly testing.

As testing of business rule is about business, it is often difficult to find test staff with the business knowledge. This is one of the most critical challenges to address when deploying efficient testing strategy. SMEs are very important to define the test data, and test cases, and to decide on the appropriate coverage required. External groups, like QA teams, may not have a clear understanding of the policy being tested. This is particularly true when the time to deploy the new business policy is short. Even sometimes the SMEs owner of the rule project may not fully understand themselves the extent of the change, or how to handle some specific cases, or conflicts

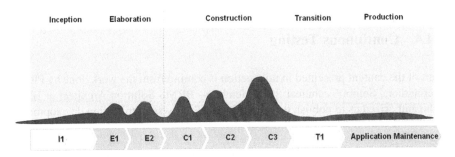

Fig. 14.7 Traditional test workload over time

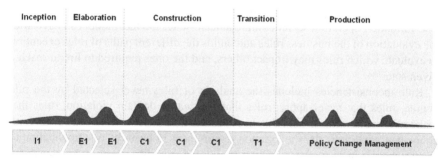

Fig. 14.8 Test activity workload with managed business rule

among decisions. As new policies get added or refined, the ruleset becomes more complex and less easy to test. Given the short time allocated to the implementation of a business policy change, there may be little time to spend on good rule design. This means, for example, not using rule templates when we should, or using ad hoc implementation such as using rule priorities, or not creating/reorganizing the proper rule packages or rule tasks in the rule flow when refactoring will help to evaluate the conflicts. This leads to testing and debugging that is harder and harder to perform. This issue can be mitigated by performing a regular rule repository refactoring exercises to keep the repository clean, documented, and understandable.

- Unit testing
- Checking the internal consistency of a rule set
  - Inspection
  - Automated tools
  - Through testing
- Regression testing

14.5 Semantic Consistency Checking

Within a ruleset, inconsistencies between rules can arise when the business users adds, updates, or deletes rules. Possible inconsistencies within business rules include redundancies, contradictions, or missing rules as well as the inability for a rule to be executable. Inconsistencies have to be corrected as early as possible to avoid quality issues. Consistency checking is a feature that verifies whether rules are semantically consistent. Inconsistencies can be found in a single rule or between rules within a ruleset. Running consistency checking analysis allows developers and subject matter experts to check the current quality of the rule under development. It is a very useful feature the development team can leverage during the ABRD phases of harvesting, prototyping, building, and enhancing. To support automatic evaluation of the inconsistencies, the business rules need to be expressed in a structured language. So only a BRMS platform with a structured rule language can support the search for inconsistencies among a large set of rules. The validation operation searches all reachable states the fact model can have after the evaluation of the business rules and builds the different paths of rules execution to evaluate which rules may impact others, and the ones required to fire to reach a given state.

Rule inconsistencies includes the analysis of rules never selected by the rule engine, rules that never apply, rules that may cause domain violation, rules that make other rules redundant, rules in conflict with others or itself, and rules with equivalent conditions. It is a common requirement in business rule application to ensure the business user is looking at all the possible cases and to evaluate conflicting decisions. The amount of permutations and tests to search for inconsistencies is a nontrivial problem. The BRMS needs to use heuristics or a dedicated search engine to support this capacity efficiently. The following table details the different inconsistencies:

Rule never selected	Rules are part of a branch of execution never reachable. For example, when using a rule flow to control the flow of execution, a rule not part of one rule task will never be selected for execution. Same logic applies if a rule task is not in a rule flow. In some BRE implementation, it may be difficult to catch this problem: the rule includes some property to define in which rule task it belongs to. The rule flow is decoupled from this semantic, and worse the application code is defining the rules part of the application. Searching for inconsistency forces looking at three different logics in different languages.
Rule never applies	When conditions are linked with the wrong operator like and/or. For example, using **and** instead of **or**: Testing if *the status of the claim is open **and** the status of the claim is rejected* ... will never be true. When conditions are inversing the value of a numerical range, like *amount is between 100.00 and 20.00*
Domain violation	If a rule contains an action that tries to assign a value that is not within the allowable domain values.
Equivalent conditions	Rules have equivalent conditions when the conditions have the same meaning and the actions may not be in conflict. This type of inconsistency may come when we add decision table with conditions testing numerical values and there is already some existing rules with such condition.
Redundant rules	Two rules are redundant if they have the same actions, and conditions of one rule are included in condition of the other. One pattern could be: R1: if C1 . C2 . C3 then A1 R2 if C1 then A1
Conflicting rules	Rules are in conflict if they are modifying the same attribute on an object with different values. R1 if C1 then O.a = v1 R2 if C2 then O.a = v2 This may be correct, but it may also generate a conflict. This is difficult to catch as this kind of assignment can be done in a complex method called by the rule.

Overlaps and gaps in conditions are two other considerations a rule analysis tool can evaluate. A gap represents a hole in a series of possible discrete values. There are two types of attributes the rule can look at: enumerations or numerical. Suppose an enumerated attribute can take the values {E1, E2, E3}. The business will often test a subset of possible values (if a == E1 ...... if a == E2 ... .) and will not take into account the other cases. This could be evaluated during the authoring of the rule by a rule developer who completes his analysis; this can easily be discovered using decision table. For numerical attribute, the gap can come from testing range of values:

$$10,000 < a < \ = 14,000$$

$$15,000 < a < \ = 20,000$$

What happens between 14,001 and 15,000?

Overlaps for numerical value can come by adding a test $13,000 < a <= 15,000$ where some values are overlapping. An efficient BRMS will identify these potential problems.

14.6 Tracing and Logging Rule Applications

The rule engine execution should support the generation of traces about the rules fired and not-fired, the execution duration, and the value of input and output facts used for the tests. The level of trace is linked to the level of testing. The business users want to understand if a rule is executed on a given set of data or want to understand why a rule did not fire. The execution can also report on the chaining between rules: The rules have dependency when the action of one rule makes the conditions of the second rule evaluated positively. Some rule engines create events when an object is asserted in the working memory, when a rule is added to the agenda, and when a rule is executed. When the engine supports ruleflows natively, it can also report on the path executed in the rule flow. Using the events or callback methods, it is easy to develop a log and trace mechanism. If the engine does not provide such capabilities, the business user may need to add a trace in the rule action, adding, for example, the rule reference to a logger. The most difficult part is to get the list of rules not fired when the engine does not send events when a rule is added to the agenda.

Logging and tracing can become a challenge when performance is important. Tracing impacts the performance. The most complex designs involve starting some thread to manage the logging outside of the main processing. At the session level, the input and output parameters are sent to this thread for filtering and processing. The output can include some specifics trace of the rules fired. The thread can be a client to another server processing the traces asynchronously so that the minimum resources are used on the rule execution server. It is important to properly design what kind of information we need to trace. A complete graph of objects is most likely irrelevant.

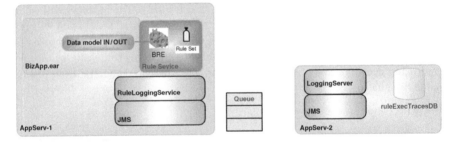

The tracing can also be done in different environments. The production environment usually is not using any trace but a preproduction environment can.

14.7 Summary

Testing is sometime not appreciated by developers, but it is a main activity which may be fun. Starting by developing the test before the rule helps to focus on the intent and expected results for the rule. Unit testing frameworks should be light and support refactoring of the data model used by the rules. In the first phase of a ruleset development, the tests ensure the ruleset keeps growing without impacting the overall business goals and the quality expected. When the ruleset reaches a certain level of development, the data model is stable enough; the business analyst can author both rules and test scenarios to validate the rulesets against a suite of data sets. His goal is to validate the functional aspect of the ruleset. The data set can include key performance indicator, so that the ruleset execution results can be compared to find the best combination of rules. All the test suites developed for unit testing, functional test, and component test can be combined to build a nonregression testing platform, used to continuously assess the ruleset quality overtime. This is a very important element to ensure the ruleset, modified on a regular basis once in production, keep the quality and intents of its design.

Performance testing helps to identify where the end-to-end decision service may have bottlenecks or performance issue. Multiple time stamps are needed to assess data conversion, data mapping, data access, and rule execution. Efficient rule authoring should be done to always think about the best possible implementation and to avoid unnecessary pattern matching or join operations.

Quality of a ruleset includes verifying on a regular basis the inconsistencies that may occur overtime. A BRMS may offer such capabilities, with for example, JRules which offers an efficient consistency checking search engine.

Finally when rules are in production, the business team wants to understand what decisions are applied on a given business transaction. The tracing and logging can include complex settings, but to be efficient should not impact the performance of the main processing but still gives efficient information. Simply putting traces in a file does not represent a long-term viable solution. Decision warehouse receiving asynchronously the main trace element, including the list of rules executed, is an elegant alternative. Chapter 15 presents testing with JRules.

14.8 Further Reading

- An introduction to the test-driven development may be read at http://en.wikipedia.org/wiki/Test-driven_development.
- Wikipedia also details the concept of unit test at http://en.wikipedia.org/wiki/Unit_testing.
- The book from B Kent "Test-Driven Development by Example", Addison Wesley, 2003.
- JUnit is one of the most used testing framework in the "Java world". The documentation and code can be found at http://www.junit.org/.
- The java architecture for XML binding specification and documentation is at http://www.oracle.com/technetwork/articles/javase/index-140168.html.
- John D McGregor at http://www.cs.clemson.edu/~johnmc/joop/col3/column3.html details the component testing, needs, and approach.
- Pierre Berlandier explores different alternatives for structuring ruleset, which can impact both performance and management. See http://www.ibm.com/developerworks/websphere/library/techarticles/1003_berlandier/1003_berlandier.html.

Chapter 15
Rule Testing with JRules

Target audience
- *Developer, software architect*

In this chapter you will learn
- *How testing is supported in ILOG JRules 7.1*
- *How to verify during authoring phase the rule consistency*
- *How to tune the rule execution performance*

Key points
- *Rule analysis uses a search engine, which helps to find inconsistencies among a ruleset, like rule never selected, wrong operator, redundant rules ...*
- *Searching for inconsistencies within a ruleset is an important capability to improve the ruleset quality.*
- *Semantic queries help to search for rules impacting others.*
- *Decision Validation Service offers the capability for the business users to test the ruleset in isolation and execute simulation: tests compared using key performance indicator.*
- *For each ruleset, assess with business users the need of using DVS.*
- *Business users use RTS and DVS together to update, rules, data set, scenarios, and to execute the suite of scenarios against a given ruleset.*
- *Performance of a rule engine is impacted by the number of rules, number of conditions in the rules, and the number of objects inserted in the working memory.*
- *Most business applications do not have performance problem. When needed, it is always possible to perform some tuning to improve performance.*

J. Boyer and H. Mili, *Agile Business Rule Development*,
DOI 10.1007/978-3-642-19041-4_15, © Springer-Verlag Berlin Heidelberg 2011

15.1   Introduction

In this chapter, we look at the rule testing and simulation capabilities of JRules, and important steps to validate the functional quality of the ruleset before deploying into a production server. As part of the quality control, there are some static analysis capabilities to assess potential rule gaps, conflicts, and inconstancies. In Sect. 15.1, we start by discussing JRules functionality for semantic consistency checking. Next, in Sect. 15.2, we present testing including unit testing and the new component called the *Decision Validation Services* (DVS), which is used by business users to define and perform functional tests. Finally in Sect. 15.3, we talk about performance tuning with JRules, using things such as (a) ruleset variables and parameters, (b) JIT compilation, (c) rule engine algorithms, and (d) automatic rule rewriting. We follow the natural flow in which those concerns arise and how they are solved by product capabilities during the ruleset development.

15.1.1   Semantic Consistency Checking

As seen in Chap. 14, the search for inconsistencies among business rules addresses the evaluation of rules that are not selectable and rules that make other rules redundant or in conflict. In Rule Studio, a dedicated "view" called "Rule Analysis" is used to perform consistency checking on a ruleset. This feature uses a dedicated search engine to generate reports which list all inconsistent or missing rules. Each report includes links to the conflicting rules; it is then easy to complete the investigation by browsing to the rules. The tool may use a custom rule extractor to consider only rules in scope for the analysis. For example, we can take into account only the rules in a given status to avoid analyzing rules still under development. The analysis can run in the background (at each rule save) or on demand. The user can select which constraints to apply to the search. The right panel in the screen of Fig. 15.1 presents the different "Analysis Options."

The report of Fig. 15.1 outlines rules never selected because they belong to rule packages that are not part of any rule task in a rule flow, rules which could not be evaluated as conditions are in conflict: the rule named BadOperator uses the AND operator instead of the OR when testing on the same attribute:

```
if
       the status of 'the claim' is CANCELED and
       the status of 'the claim' is REJECTED
then
     add the issue : "Claim Canceled or rejected" to 'the result' ;
```

Another rule assigns a value out of the range, range specified in the BOM enumerated domain:

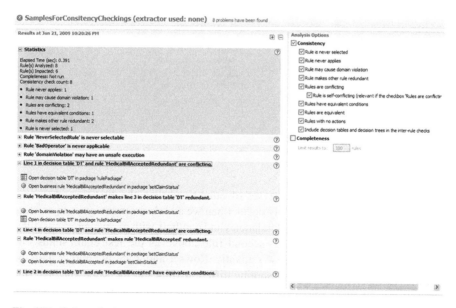

Fig. 15.1 Rule analysis report

```
if
        <some condition>
then
        set the sub type of 'the claim' to 6;  // the range was set as [1..4]
```

It is important to note that all those verifications are done on the BOM classes. Enumerated domains need to be prepared carefully to avoid wrong results. The search for redundant rules is an interesting capability. The two following rules are reported as redundant:

```
name MedicalBillAccepted
definitions
    set bill to a medical bill where the status of this medical bill
                                    is Accepted;
if
    the status of 'the claim' is ADJUSTED
then
    set the status of 'the claim' to PAID ;


name MedicalBillAcceptedRedundant
definitions
    set bill to a medical bill where the status of this medical bill
                                    is Accepted;
then
        set the status of 'the claim' to PAID ;
```

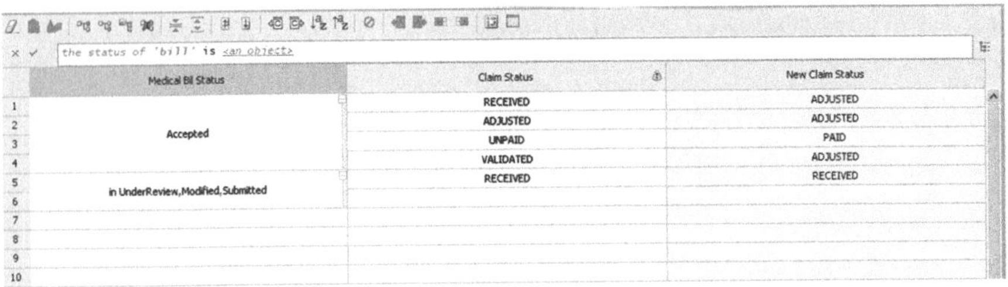

Fig. 15.2 A conflicting decision table

The second rule has a larger set of conditions than the first one making it redundant. This pattern can easily occur when we add decision tables in an existing ruleset. Figure 15.2 brings in redundancies and conflicts with our two previous rules.

Row 3 is redundant with the second rule above as the test claim.status == UNPAID does not bring any new semantic. Rows 1 and 4 are in conflict with the second rule above as they are assigning different values to the same attribute (the status of the claim) in their action part. Finally, the conditions of our first rule and the row 2 of the decision table have the exactly same conditions for different actions.

Obviously, this example is a purely academic but aims to show multiple types of conflict in one decision table. It is interesting to use this capability on real rulesets to evaluate the quality of the ruleset and maybe to reduce the number of rules. This tool helps the rule writer ask the right questions on his rule coverage. Rule Team Server (RTS) has the same capability. We recommend using all the available checks, but incrementally setting all the constraints forces the search engine to take more time to find solutions. The user can select some constraints and then updates the rules before doing a more complete run. Searching for inconsistency within a ruleset is an important capability to improve the ruleset quality. The user may decide to keep the rule as-is, ignoring the result. Also sometimes the results do not provide a valuable evaluation. It is important to remember that such capacities are still under research in the software industry. JRules is a unique product on the market to deliver such a search engine.

– Using the rule engine API
– Using the rule execution server

15.1.2 Semantic Queries

Starting with V7.0 Rule Studio offers some predefined queries to search for rules that are impacted by the execution of other rules, or rules which impact the execution of other rules. Suppose we have a rule which looks at the status of the claim like:

Fig. 15.3 Semantic query and its result

```
if
        any of the following conditions is true:
            - the status of 'the claim' is PAID
            - the status of 'the claim' is ADJUSTED
then

            add the issue : "Claim processed" to 'the result' ;
```

We want to search for rules that may enable this rule: rules that may set the status to Paid or Adjusted in their action part. We can implement the following query: *Find all rules such that each rule may enable "PreProcessing.ClaimDataAvailability.reject AlreadyProcessedClaim"* to get such rules. The returned results list one by one the rules having action enabling condition of the selected rule (Fig. 15.3).

The same applies to identify rules enabled by the one selected. The query looks like: *Find all business rules such that each business rule may be enabled by "PreProcessing.ClaimDataAvailability.rejectAlreadyProcessedClaim"*. Finally, the query: *find all ruleflows such that each ruleflow may select "Core.Claim Timing.dolBeforeEffectiveDate"* evaluates what are the ruleflows selecting a given rule. This is a useful query when we have multiple rule projects sharing rules.

15.1.3   Rule Coverage

Often IT solution architects want to understand how all the possible combinations of rule conditions are covered in the ruleset. The conditions of the rules are using a limited set of business variables or terms, which can take an integer value, enumerated value, or string. The perceived problem is to get around all possible permutations and possible assignments the variables can take to build the ruleset. Most of the time users do not want to cover all the potential conditions and let the system use default values. Obviously advanced BRMS is helping to address this problem with some gap analysis and rule analysis capabilities. We discussed the rule analysis capabilities of JRules in the previous section. The decision table editor in JRules helps to address gaps and overlaps between conditions. Figure 15.4 shows

Procedure Code	Unit		Unit Price	Net Covered Amount
	min	max		
		1	2	≥ 10,000	2,000
EMERGENCY_ROOM	3	4	≥ 8,000	3,900
HRI				0
AMBULANCE_TRANSPORT	= 1			the unit price of md * the units of the treatment of md
	Otherwise			25 * the units of the treatment of md
LOW_BACK_MASSAGE	< 2		≤ 75	25 * (the units of the treatment of md - 2)
	1	3	≤ 75	

Fig. 15.4 Decision table gaps, overlaps ...

the medical procedure code, the amount billed by the medical provider and computes the amount not covered by the insurance company.

The first column is testing against the procedure code. This attribute is constrained by an enumerated domain. The warning triangle icon on the top of the column specifies that there are some missing values not covered in the row of the decision table. This could be fine ... or not ... depending on the use case, but it is still valuable information for the rule author. The Unit column is a numerical attribute, and the warning icon specifies there are overlapping cells. On the rows 1 and 2 the zigzag graphics specify if a row has gaps or overlaps. With these capabilities, we can design and implement effective decision tables. By their structure, decision tables help address the coverage of conditions versus the possible values. The *otherwise* rule language keyword helps to assign a default value when a rule author does not want to test all possible values. It has to be used with care as it is translated as a negation of all tests in the same column, generating a complex rule to evaluate during rule execution.

Another way to ensure control over the coverage is to organize the rule package hierarchy by using business dimensions: the first level of rule package can represent some classification based on business process, or ownership, or geography ... Subdecomposition may include, for example, product definition. In that case, looking at the package hierarchy, it is easy to see the missing products.

15.2 Rule Testing

In this section we review how to support unit test and functional test with JRules. We cover in depth the Decision Validation Service component as a major feature for testing in Sects. 15.2.2 and 15.2.3.

15.2.1 Unit Test

The unit test approach was discussed in Chap. 14. JRules offers a tool to listen to events generated by the rule engine when using the RETE algorithm. The default class is IlrToolAdapter and represents a set of API used as callbacks for the engine to notify of events occurring during execution. It is possible to extend this class to process events like tracing when the engine executes a rule. The class EngineObserver does this tracing.

```
public class EngineObserver extends IlrToolAdapter {

    ...

    public void notifyBeginInstance(IlrRuleInstance instance) {
        // invoked when the engine executes a rule instance
        // with the Rete Plus algorithm
        logger.info("Engine execute rule:"+instance.getRuleName());
    }
```

This class is linked to the rule engine using the connectTool method:

```
public void buildEngine() throws IlrBadContextException, IlrToolConnectionException {
    engine = new IlrContext(ruleset);
    engine.connectTool(new EngineObserver());
}
```

Using the EngineObserver with the unit test described in Chap. 13, we get the following:

```
abrd.claim.tool.test.EngineObserver notifyBeginInstance
INFO: Engine execute rule:reviewMedicalTreatment.IdentifyAmbulanceTransport
```

The EngineObserver class can be enhanced to store the list of all rules fired; therefore, a JUnit test method can look at the list and looks up the expected rule. Looking at the name of the rule fired is helpful, but it is also important to verify the result of the rule execution on the business objects. This is true for computation rules where it is unrealistic to look at all potential computations the rules can do to search for the expected result, but it is more important to evaluate the intent of the computation and verify the results are within ranges that make sense instead of looking at a discrete value. Another pattern is to accumulate the decisions made by the rule in a list and search within the list for things expected.

Most of the details of unit testing were done in Chap. 14. JRules offers wizards to generate code to execute rules using JUnit API and an engine runner to facilitate rule debugging. To support functional testing defined by both developers and business user, JRules offers a new capability called the Decision Validation Service.

15.2.2 Decision Validation Service

Decision Validation Services (DVS) goals are to provide a set of features to test a ruleset by isolation and to offer a simulation capability business users can use to perform "what-if" analysis. As a testing tool DVS can be used in Rule Studio to test and debug rulesets. But it is also integrated into Rule Team Server and aims to verify that implemented rules lead to the expected business results. Designed as a business user tool, test scenarios are defined in Microsoft Excel worksheets, and version controlled in team server. Each scenario includes all the data needed to test rules and expected result to accept the test is successful or not. A scenario can be enhanced by defining Key Performance Indicators (KPIs) and in that case used to run simulations. Simulations aim to evaluate the rule changes against business metrics. If the metrics are better, the rules improve the business. With the same platform, it is possible to execute both quality assurance test suites and what-if simulation. Excel is one source to define test data, but it is possible to define test scenarios and data elements in an external data source such as a database. A classical use case is to leverage the historical business transactions stored in a data warehouse. For example, in a claim processing application, we may want to assess a ruleset against claims from last calendar year. Accessing such a data source is accomplished using custom code, implementing a Scenario Provider, which builds and manages scenarios (see Sect. 15.2.3.1).

The Excel worksheets set data for each input parameter using a tabular format. In fact the data model does not need to be flat. It is possible to have a graph of objects. The cell definitions in the worksheet can reference other cells in another worksheet. This is an interesting capability to define some reusable data definition like a "good" customer, a bank account, a "bad" claim .... In Fig. 15.5, there are two claims defined in a "claim" worksheet. The "claim 2" references an insurance policy named "insurance policy 1". This reference is the name in another worksheet of the insurance policy data set. This relationship between data authorize reusing data element in different scenario.

The data model has to be simple and small to be manageable. Scenario represents suites of test cases used to validate the behavior of the rules. The data structure as defined in the Excel can be a subview of the BOM as defined in the rule project: most likely the user does not need to have access to all the attributes of all the BOM classes to define the test cases. The greater the amount of data elements to define in Excel, the less usable it becomes. There is a trade off to find, and a DVS scenario definition in Excel is built by iterations, adding new scenario, new data elements, and adding new rules to the ruleset. At the beginning of the implementation, the rules may use a very limited number of conditions on a very limited dataset. The Excel can be simple. Over time, adding new rules covering more data elements, forces adding columns to each worksheet. Rule Team Server is the main front end

claim name	claim number	→ attached medical bills	date of creation	date of loss	hired to public	→ insurance policy	status
claim 1	CL000						
claim 2	CL001		9/16/2009	9/16/2009	FALSE	insurance policy 1	RECEIVED

insurance policy name	policy number	effective date
insurance policy 1	PL0001	1/1/2009

Fig. 15.5 Data entered in cells, and referencing other cell

⊞ **ValidateClaimTestSuite** *(Test Suite)*

| ⊕New | ⊕Run | ⬇Download Archive | ✎ Edit | ✖Delete | ⧉Copy | 🔒Lock | 🔓Unlock | ⊘Release lock | ⏱History | ⑦Help |

☐ **Properties**		⑦ **Documentation**
Name	ValidateClaimTestSuite	Define a set of scenario to assess all the possible case for claim data issue
Folder	/	
Group		**Rules tested**
Created By	rtsAdmin	**All rules as of the current project state**
Created On	Oct 20, 2010 9:32:36 PM CDT	**Starting Ruleflow Task:** Default
Last Changed By	rtsAdmin	
Last Changed On	Oct 20, 2010 9:32:36 PM CDT	**Scenarios**
		Format Excel (2003)
		testsuite_2.xls

Fig. 15.6 Test suite managed in rule team server (RTS)

for the business users to manage test scenarios. Once defined locally on his computer, the user can upload the Excel file in rule team server. Like any other rule artifacts, test scenarios are version managed in the rule repository (Fig. 15.6).

Before going into the details of setting up DVS, and how to customize it, there are some major considerations the project team needs to assess:

- Why business users want to test a given ruleset?
- If IT and business users are working together to develop the rules, why not IT developing test suites, and explain results to business, so rules can be updated accordingly?
- Should we use DVS for all the rulesets?
- Do we need to define scenario from existing data, in an external datasource?
- Do we need to perform simulation, what-if analysis on all the rulesets?
- At what point in the development process do we need to enforce a systematic use of DVS?
- What are the KPI for each ruleset? Are we able to define them? If there is no KPI, there is no need for simulation.

Forgetting to look at such questions may lead to a wrong usage of DVS and poor results.

15.2.2.1 Enabling DVS

There are multiple components working together to make DVS an integrated test environment. At the execution server layer, there is a server side application, called Scenario Service Provider[1] (SSP) used to execute the rules against the scenarios it received and to provide a report on the execution. The scenarios can be executed remotely from either Rule Studio or Rule Team Server. To enable remote execution the Execution Object Model (XOM) has to be packaged with the SSP and deployed on an application server. When using a pure XML binding approach, this repackaging

---

[1]See the jrules-ssp-WAS7.ear for WAS or testing.war for Tomcat in dvs/applicationservers folder.

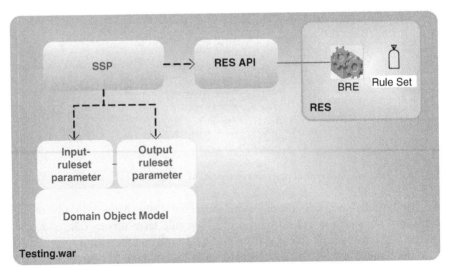

Fig. 15.7 Scenario Service Provider (SSP) packaging for Tomcat deployment

is not mandatory, as the XOM reference is part of the BOM, part of the ruleset. Figure 15.7 illustrates the integration in the "testing.war" of the ssp component, the RES session API jars, and the domain object model jar (e.g., the ClaimModel.jar).

When using an Excel-based testing environment, there are a number of steps to follow to put in place this DVS framework:

- Verify that the needed BOM classes support DVS.
- Modify any BOM constructors for classes where we want the business user to enter data for mandatory attributes. For example, we can consider the claim number as a mandatory element, so we need a claim constructor with one string argument to set the claim number.
- Generate the Excel test scenario template.
- Populate the worksheet with data which make the rule's conditions true.
- In Rule Studio verify locally the DVS execution by using dedicated eclipse "run configuration."
- Repackage the SSP (only if using a java XOM).
- From Rule Studio, verify the remote execution sending scenario to the remote SSP.
- Synchronize the rule project into RTS.
- Let business users use Rule Team Server to manage scenarios, rules and execute them remotely on the SSP.

To allow the business user to run the tests in Rule Team Server, we must enable Decision Validation Services in Rule Studio: to do so we first need to verify the BOM supports DVS: this is done by using the menu Decision Validation Scenario > check Project on the rule project to use (e.g., ValidateClaim-Rules project). A list

ID	BOM Element
⚠ RES.DVS.WARNING.30006	abrd.claim.entities.Person.Person(java.lang.String,java.lang.String)
⚠ RES.DVS.WARNING.30006	abrd.claim.common.State.State(java.lang.String,java.lang.String,int)
⚠ RES.DVS.WARNING.30009	abrd.claim.entities.InvolvedPerson.injury
⊗ RES.DVS.ERROR.30002	abrd.claim.medical.Treatment.dateOfService
⚠ RES.DVS.WARNING.30006	abrd.claim.entities.Property.Property(java.lang.String,int)
⚠ RES.DVS.WARNING.30006	abrd.claim.policy.InsurancePolicy.InsurancePolicy(java.lang.String,java.util.Date)

Tabs shown above table: BOM Update | Synchronize | Rule Project Map | DVS Project Validation

Solution Description:

attribute abrd.claim.medical.Treatment.dateOfService: cannot find the type javax.xml.datatype.XMLGregorianCalendar in the BOM.

Fig. 15.8 Decision Validation Services (DVS) project validation view. A must fix list of issues

of errors may appear in the DVS Project Validation view. Removing errors may involve changing some BOM elements or unenabling attributes in scope for DVS (Fig. 15.8).

The first common set of errors may come from the class constructor. A XOM class may have multiple constructors; therefore, in the Member tab of the BOM editor, we need to check "*DVS constructor*" check box for the constructor method we want to use during the scenario definition and rename the arguments of the constructor to give a meaningful name to column headings (see Fig. 15.9). Some warnings may come from the fact that we are using generic names for the parameters of constructor in the BOM class, renaming such parameters in the BOM constructor helps to maintain the test suite. Other errors may come from the absence of class definition in the BOM. For example, when using a java XOM created from an XML schema, using Java for XML Binding (JAXB), the data can be an XMLGregorianCalendar, it may be more suitable to use java.util.Date to support dates. As a best practice, you should limit using generated java beans as your XOM, it may be relevant for java object carry on only data element, but a more complex business entity may have his own Java class, which includes getters/setters and behavioral methods. Such business entities are really what the business user wants to write rules on and populate data for.

Third, we can generate the test suite Excel file using the menu Decision Validation Scenario > Generate Excel Scenario File Template. In one of the wizard steps, the user needs to pick up the proper DVS format (Excel 2003, Excel 2003 tabbed, . . .). Most of the time when the model is complex, the Tabbed format is needed. Each class is mapped to one worksheet. Each public attribute of a BOM class is represented in one column. It is possible using a toggle (named *Ignore for DVS*) in the attribute definition to avoid having the column generated for that attribute. Each worksheet between the scenario tab and the Expected Result tab is used to define reusable data for tests. The scenario tab includes the input parameters of the ruleset. Each row of the scenario represents one test case and must contain all the necessary data required to fire the rules. Each scenario has a unique ID and a description field to enter the intent of the test.

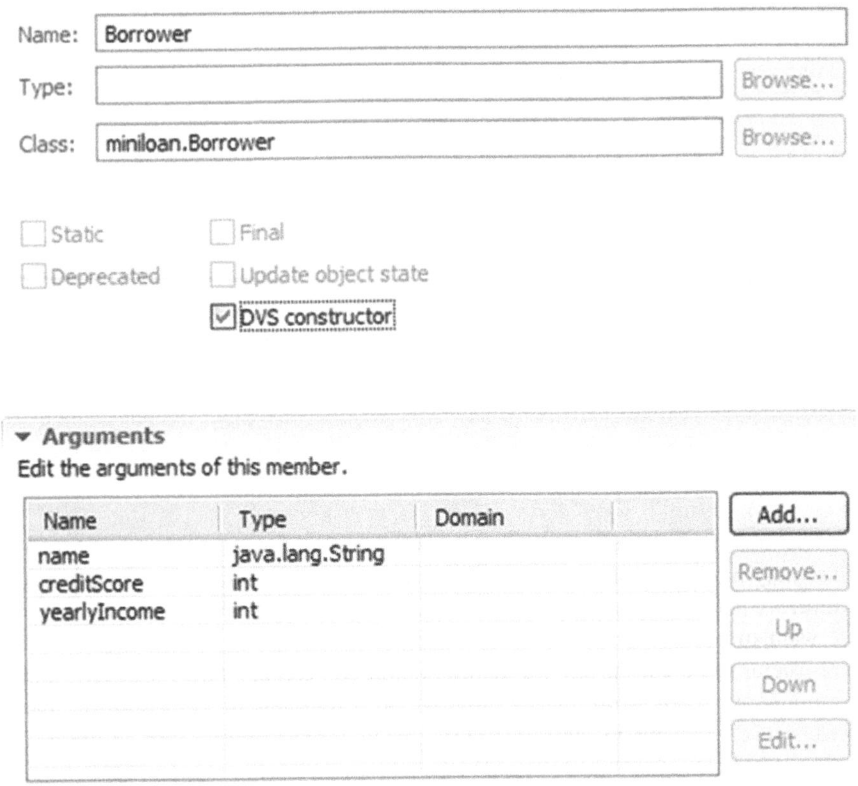

Name: | Borrower |

Type: | | Browse... |

Class: | miniloan.Borrower | Browse... |

☐ Static   ☐ Final
☐ Deprecated   ☐ Update object state
                    ☑ DVS constructor

▼ **Arguments**
Edit the arguments of this member.

Name	Type	Domain		Add...
name	java.lang.String			Remove...
creditScore	int			
yearlyIncome	int			Up
				Down
				Edit...

Fig. 15.9 Enable a BOM class constructor to be used by Decision Validation Services (DVS)

Scenario ID	the status of the claim equals	the result is error equals
Scenario 1	HASISSUE	TRUE
Scenario 2	HASISSUE	TRUE

Fig. 15.10 Expected result for each scenario

The *"expected result"* tab includes a table with columns to test the expected value for each attribute of the IN_OUT or OUT ruleset parameters. For example, we want to verify for scenario 1 the status of the claim and the error attribute of the result object (Fig. 15.10).

The link between the sheets containing the scenarios and their expected results or execution details is made by the name entered in the respective Scenario ID columns. Note that it is important to set the ruleset parameter direction properly (IN, OUT, IN_OUT): when a parameter is never modified in the rule, keep it as IN. An incorrect setting may force to set some data elements not required for the tests, and adding unnecessary complexity to the test scenario definition.

Scenario ID	the list of fired rules contains
Scenario 1	
Scenario 2	Core.ClaimTiming.dolBeforeEffectiveDate
	Core.ClaimTiming.claimBeforeEffectiveDate

Fig. 15.11 Test attribute within multiple possible values

To complete the scenario definition, there is a tab called *"Expected Execution Details"*, which can be used to specify the list of rule names expected to fire, the rule task names executed. No value in a cell enforces skipping this assertion.

It is possible to test for multiple values. Each value needs to be in the same column but in different rows. Figure 15.11 tests if the list of rules fired contains one of the possible rules: dolBeforeEffectibeDate and claimBeforeEffectiveDate.

Finally, it is important to fine-tune which data elements we want to expose in the Excel file to support efficient business scenarios. Refactoring of Excel files may involve cumbersome copy and paste. The developer needs to leverage the work done during the harvesting phase to define what the business user is expecting in terms of functional testing. The Excel format is used when the object model is simple, and the number of scenarios limited to 1,000. When the data model is more complex or the scenarios need to get historical data, it is possible to develop a scenario provide class to load those data or enrich the scenario. The DVS API is designed to support such an implementation. Also it is important to note that even with a complex BOM level, it is possible to have a simple data model for testing. When starting a project, the DVS can include a few data elements, really used within the conditions of the rules. The other elements could be ignored. This simplifies dramatically the Excel file. Getting the business user accustomed to it. The DVS ignore flag can be set to true for each BOM class/attribute we do not want to export in Excel. We propose to use an incremental approach to develop this Excel file and to add data elements over time, when new rules added to the ruleset are testing it.

15.2.2.2 Executing DVS Configuration

From Rule Studio to execute the test cases declared in the test suite, we need to create a *"Run Configuration"*. This is done using the *Run>Open Run Dialog* command and by creating a new configuration under the *DVS Excel File* node. We need to specify the rule project under test, the Excel file for the test suite, and any other parameters such as the DVS configuration (Fig. 15.12).

To run locally, developers specify the local execution in the DVS configuration tab (Fig. 15.12). Local execution means one instance of the Scenario Service Provider is created locally to parse the scenario definitions, to prepare the data for test, to execute the rules, and to generate reports. Figure 15.13 illustrates this integration of executing SSP in the Eclipse JVM.

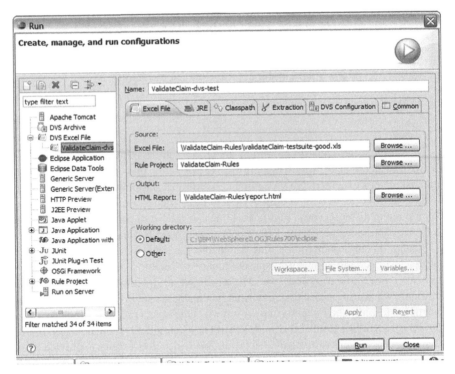

Fig. 15.12 Decision Validation Services (DVS) rule studio test using Excel file

The execution generates traces in the console view and in an external report file. This HTML report includes, for each test scenario executed, the status of the test according to the expected values set in the test suite Excel file (Fig. 15.14). From this file, it is possible to get the stack trace for exceptions generated by the DVS environment.

It is possible to debug a DVS execution in Studio. After setting some breakpoints in the rule flow or in the action part of the rule, we can use the DVS configuration in Debug mode. When using DVS some care has to be done. When the decision service implementation has some logic to prepare the data, like setting the claim reference to the result object, loading the insurance policy from a database, this logic is not part of the XOM packaged by the SSP, but even if it was, it is not called by the SSP component. Developer has to implement this logic in a custom scenario provider (see Sect. 15.2.3). It is common to use a custom scenario provider to complete the data set definition. You can also add ILR code in the initialization of the ruleset to do the binding. This problem is common and happens as soon as there is some logic in the service implementation to prepare the data for the rule execution.

To run the tests remotely from either Rule Studio or Rule Team Server, we must deploy the Execution Object Model (XOM) to the Scenario Service Provider (SSP) (Fig. 15.15).

Using Decision Validation Scenario >Repackage XOM for Remote DVS Testing wizard, we create a new DVS project to persist all the needed DVS artifacts and

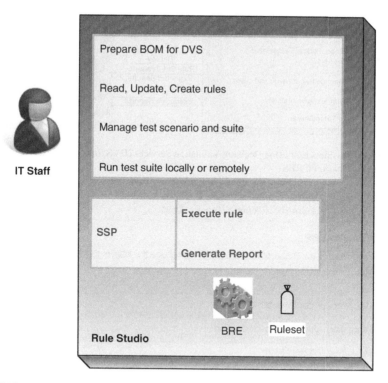

Fig. 15.13 Developer using Decision Validation Services (DVS) in studio

WebSphere. Execution Report — Sun, 2 Aug 2009 06:34:17 PDT — IBM.

Summary

Execution	Local
Decimal Precision	2 digits are used
Scenarios	1
Tests	1
Success Rate	0 %
Failures	0
Errors	1

Details for all Scenarios

Name	Success Rate	Tests	Failures	Errors	Message
Scenario 1	0 %	2	1	1	

Details by Scenario

Scenario 1

Name	Success	Failure	Error	Message
the status of the claim equals		x		the observed value **ADJUSTED** does not equal the expected value **HASISSUE**
the result is error equals			x	null

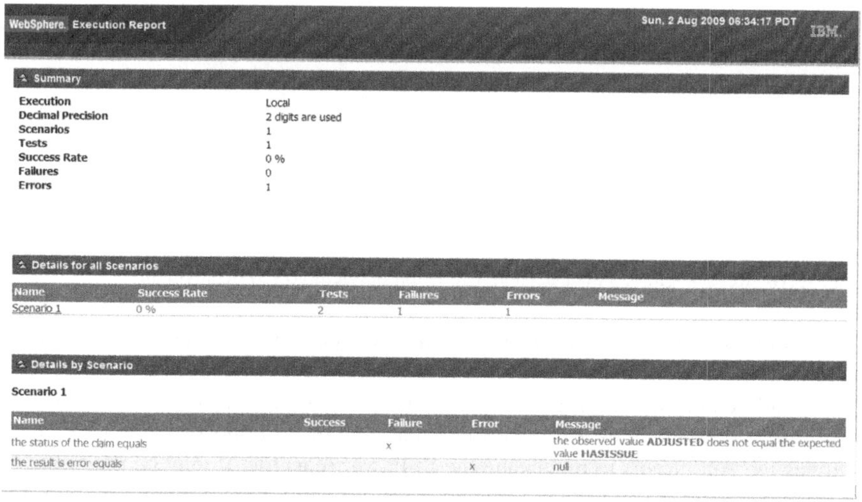

Fig. 15.14 Decision Validation Services (DVS) execution report

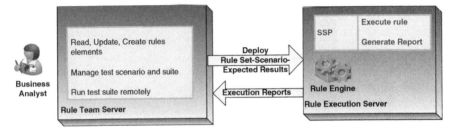

Fig. 15.15 Business user using Decision Validation Services (DVS) in rule team server (RTS) and executing scenario on RES

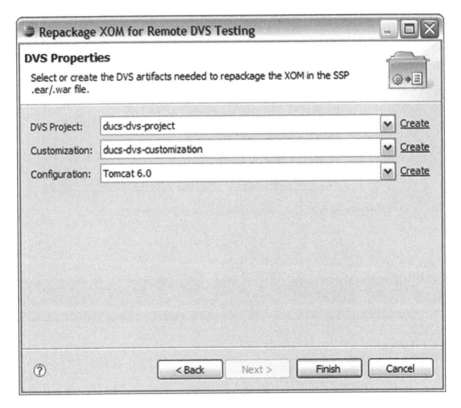

Fig. 15.16 Repackaging a new Decision Validation Services (DVS) deployment

to package and deploy new ear or war files for the target execution environment (Fig. 15.16).

A readme.html file highlights the steps to follow to deploy the new ear/war. The workspace now includes a DVS project that contains a build.xml Ant file, which defines the Ant targets to repackage the SSP .war (ear) file. It may be important to review the settings in this Ant script to avoid dragging unnecessary jars, like, for example, the asm* jars, when you do not use the sequential algorithm in your ruleset. Also ensure the latest version of the ruleset is deployed to the same RESDB as the one used by the SSP. The SSP is using a ra.xml as other RES client applications. The last step is to deploy the new generated archive to the target application server. This repackaging is needed only if there is a change in the XOM.

15.2.2.3 Business User Using RTS

The business user manages the scenario and simulation from RTS. Using *RTS Compose tab,* he/she can create new test suites or simulations. A step-by-step "wizard" drives the user to enter a set of properties, to select the rules in scope of the ruleset, to specify which type of scenario to use, and finally to enter any documentation or versioning information. As RTS is controlling versioning of rulesets and rules, it is possible to select a specific baseline for testing. When using a DVS format using Excel, the creation of the test suite uploads the Excel file and saves it into the rule repository: it becomes managed the same way as other rules artifact using (see Fig. 15.17) the edit, copy, lock, history functions....

From this panel, it is possible to execute the test suite to a remote RES/SSP server and get reports on the execution. The Run command generates the ruleset, deploys it to SSP, with the data elements defined in the Excel files, and gets the report back as an HTML page (Fig. 15.18).

Simulation has Key Performance Indicators (KPIs) to compare test executions. KPIs define how the performance of a simulation is calculated and how it is presented in the simulation report. We can use multiple KPIs for each simulation. KPIs are defined in a DVS Project, in Rule Studio, by adding class definition in a DVS Format. DVS formats are used to customize the scenario and are available both in RTS and Studio. KPIs are interesting when business users use real historical data (e.g., the claims of last calendar year). Measuring business KPI on pure test data does not bring much value. The selection of the KPIs has to be made with care as we may need to take into consideration a time dimension: for example, the number of claims adjudicated per day. This kind of metric for a claim processing application is interesting to measure the quality and efficiency of the automatic rule processing. The more claims the system can cover with accuracy, the less people

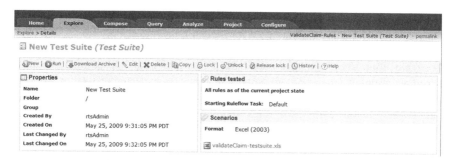

Fig. 15.17 Decision Validation Services (DVS) test suite in team server

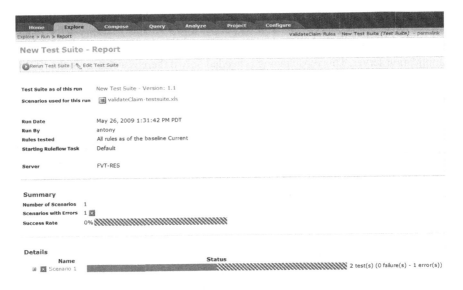

Fig. 15.18 Decision Validation Services (DVS) report in team server

are involved. The Decision Warehouse (DWH) may also be used to extract data elements for simulations. In production, KPIs are not packaged with the applications, but using decision warehouse, it is possible to design such KPI by analyzing the recent executed business transactions triggering decisions.

When a business analyst has issues and cannot figure it out by himself, he can package the DVS elements as an archive so a developer can do some debugging in Studio. The DVS archive contains the ruleset under test, the description of the DVS formats used, and the Excel scenario files if any. In Rule Studio, developers can import this archive and then defines a run configuration to analyze the issues found by the business user.

15.2.3 DVS Customization

Customization of data elements used for validating a ruleset is common in JRules deployment; even if the out of the box features based on Excel prevail. The major needs are around, accessing historical data, defining KPIs, and developing scenarios based on complex data graph or complex searches for expected results, or working on XML document as a source of data. Some decision service implementations load data eagerly before calling the rules; this logic is not available to DVS without developing code. This logic can be implemented in a Scenario Provider class, which acts as a factory of DVS scenario. Implementation of scenario providers or KPIs is done in a DVS format. DVS formats are managed in a DVS project in Rule Studio. Figure 15.19 illustrates the definition of ClaimDB format used to support the

DVS Format: ClaimDB

| Name*: | ClaimDB |

Scenario Provider

| Class*: | abrd.claim.dvs.ClaimDBScenarioProvider | ▾ Edit |

Create a new Scenario Provider   Edit properties

Rule Team Server renderer class:

| | abrd.claim.dvs.ClaimScenarioSuiteResourcesRenderer | ▾ Edit |

Launch configuration plug-in:

| | abrd.claim.dvs.custom.scenarioprovider | ▾ Edit |

Precision

○ Use all digits for decimal comparison

⊙ Use the following number of digits after decimal point

| 2 | 1E-2 |

Expected Execution Details

Select the execution details available as possible tests in the Generate Excel Scena

☐ All rules
☐ All tasks
☑ Rules fired
☐ Tasks executed
☐ Total of rules fired
☐ Total of tasks executed
☐ Total of rules not fired
☐ Total of tasks not executed
☐ Rules not fired
☐ Tasks not executed
☐ Execution duration

Select the parameters to be stored in the output values file in Rule Team Server:
☑ Input parameters
☑ Output parameters

KPI

[New ...]	Display Name	KPI Class Name	Rule Team Server Renderer Class Name
[Edit ...]	Validated Claims KPI	abrd.claim.dvs.ValidatedClaimKPI	abrd.claim.dvs.ValidateClaimKPIRenderer
[Remove]			

Fig. 15.19 Decision Validation Services (DVS) format

implementation of a scenario provider used to load the n last claims from a database, but also to define a KPI to measure the number of claims validated against the total of claim processed.

15.2.3.1 Defining a Custom Scenario Provider

When the data model used to write rules is too complex to be handled by Excel only, or when the test data already exists in an external data source such as a database, we need to implement a Custom Scenario Provider. The IlrScenarioProvider interface defines three methods to implement: one to compute the number of scenarios contained in the provider, a second one to return a scenario at a specific index, and third to close the scenario provider to clean memory. The scenario provider has also an initialize callback method used to create the scenarios and cache them in the provider. The cache includes a list of scenarios. The scenario is an implementation of the IlrScenario interface. One default implementation called IlrScenarioImpl is a simple JavaBean used to populate a scenario. The method setInputParameters(Map<string,object>) adds the ruleset parameters we can prepare for each scenario in the context of a given ruleset. This last statement implies the scenario is linked to one ruleset only. If DVS has to support multiple ruleset, there will be multiple scenario providers. It is possible to combine the use of Excel and data source to build scenarios. For example, we can load the reference of a claimId from an Excel file defined by the business user and load the complete graph of objects to contain the claim, the insurance policy, the coverage, the current medical invoices attached to the claim, and define them as the input parameters within the scenario. This logic is done in the initialization method. The get scenario by index method returns one of the scenarios cached. The scenario provider is used by the SSP to get access to the scenario, get the ruleset parameters, and use them to execute the rules. For the expected result, the scenario has a reference to an

IlrTraceTester implementation. This interface defines a test method used by the SSP
to assess if the test is successful giving the execution context, and the rule session
request and response instances. Accessing the session response object helps to get
access to the output results and to tests, for example, the status of the claim or the
list of issues created by the rules.

It is also possible to extend an existing scenario provider like the `IlrEx-`
`cel2003ScenarioProvider`, which reads a scenario suite from Micro-
soft Excel 2003 file. Extending this class helps to mix the out of the box capabilities of
DVS and add custom data management before calling the rule execution.

With a custom service provider, it is possible to mix the decision warehouse
(DWH) and DVS (see Fig. 15.20): We can trace the decisions made in production on
the main business transactions and persists them in a custom data base (ruleExec-
TraceDB). The custom DAO, dwhDao, stores the elements we want to replay and
keep statistics on. It could be the claimId, the medicalInvoiceId, and the list of the
names of the executed rules, the list of issues reported, or the list of audit reports
created by the rules. From this data base, it is possible to load back the data in the
DVS scenario provider to build DVS scenario.

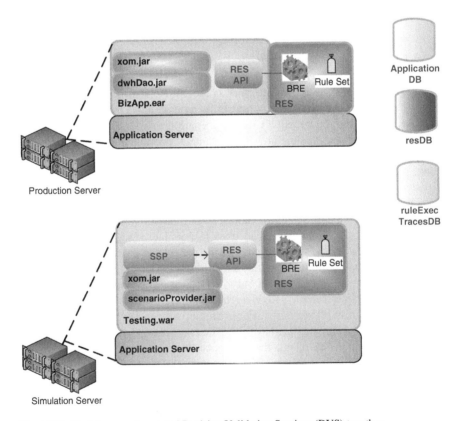

Fig. 15.20 Decision warehouse and Decision Validation Services (DVS) together

15.2.3.2 Adding KPIs

Rule Studio helps to write KPIs by generating template codes that implement the necessary Java classes. The first class is the implementation of interface IlrKPI, which defines methods called by the SSP when it runs scenario. The method helps compute custom metrics for a set of scenarios. We have one implementation of this interface per type of KPI we want to report to. The important methods are:

- Initialize, to initialize some internal data structure and attribute. The implementation received the context of execution of the tests.
- onScenarioBegin, invoked by the test runner before the ruleset is executed. This method is called for each scenario defined in the suite.
- onScenarioEnd, invoked by the runner after the ruleset has been executed. This method is called for each scenario defined in the suite.
- getKPIResult, invoked once after all scenarios have been run, it is used to prepare for the report.

The logic in ScenarioEnd is able to access the RES session request and response objects. From the response and request, we can assess what was done on our data elements and compute metrics like the number of invalid claims or claims in a given status. The code below computes the percent of claims not validated, so that this KPI can be attached to the validate claim ruleset:

```java
public class ValidatedClaimKPI implements IlrKPI {
  // keep the total number of claim processed
  protected int totalCount;
  // count count claim not validated
  protected int totalNotValidated;
  /**
   * Return the % of claims not validated.
   */
  public IlrKPIResult getKPIResult() throws IlrKPIException {
    IlrKPIResultInteger result = new IlrKPIResultInteger();
    result.setKPIClassName(this.getClass().getName());
        float percent = 0;
        if (totalCount != 0) {
          percent = totalNotValidated / (float)totalCount * 100;
        }
        result.setValue((int) percent);
        return result;
  }
  ...
    public void onScenarioEnd(IlrScenario scenario, IlrSessionRequest request,
          IlrSessionResponse response) throws IlrKPIException {
      // Get the claim as processed by rules
      Claim claim = (Claim)response.getOutputParameters().get("claim");

      if ((claim.getStatus() != StatusValue.VALIDATED)) {
          totalNotValidated++;
      }
    }
  }
  ...
```

Linked to the KPI is a renderer class to display the metrics in RTS. It is not mandatory to implement such a renderer as some default renderers exist to present numerical values. All those classes can be added to the SSP archive and to RTS archive. Some Ant tasks are predefined and generated by the rule studio wizard to help us in the repackaging.

15.3 Performance Tuning

In this section, we cover the different capabilities JRules offers to improve the rule execution. For a long time, researchers in the software industry tuned the rule execution algorithms to improve the execution performance. JRules offers an extensive set of capabilities in this area. Rule writing can improve the performance or impact it. The same applies for a data model design. We suppose here that the data elements are all present to the rule engine, and we focus in this section on the unique capabilities of JRules to improve the rule execution time.

15.3.1 Ruleset Parsing

As stated before ruleset parsing is the most costly operation in business rule application, so it has to be done at the initialization of the application. In JRules, ruleset archive includes the rule in a scripting language called IRL, the model definition within the BOM, and the potential mapping between the BOM elements and the executable model (the B2X). When deployed in RES, the parsed ruleset is kept in a cache, so that multiple calls to the rule execution do not force the parsing of the ruleset. The ruleset is also shared between different rule sessions to allow, if the hardware has multiple CPUs, parallel executions. When the number of rules is important, the time to parse becomes longer.

When hot deployment is a mandatory requirement, the parsing of the ruleset has to be done in parallel of the execution in a separate thread. In fact to respect JEE specification, the implementation code uses the JSR237 API.[2] Once the ruleset is ready, the cache of rulesets is updated to support the new rules. The Rule Execution Server offers the pooling of rule engines, but the parsing of the ruleset is done at the first call if the ruleset is not in memory. So it is recommended to call for a first execution during the initialization of the decision services. This can be done in the constructor of the service using some basic data set. JRules 7.0 offers a new API to enforce ruleset parsing at the creation of the session factory:

---

[2]JSR-237 specifies the Work Manager API, which hides the thread API, and leverage in an application server, the contract of the container to manage the pool of thread, and the thread life cycle. The Work Manager API defines Work as a unit of work, which we want to execute asynchronously, which is the case for ruleset parsing.

```
IlrSessionFactory sessionFactory = new IlrPOJOSessionFactory();
sessionFactory.createManagementSession().loadUptodateruleset (IlrPath.parsePath
("/ClaimProcessingRuleApp/ValidateClaimrules"));
```

As RES execution units leverage the JCA connection pool to pool rule engines, it is possible when the last connection referencing a ruleset is released that the ruleset itself is garbage collected. When a new call arrives on this ruleset, a new parsing occurs. To avoid this problem, the connection factory supports setting timeout parameters. The configuration is linked to the application server used. With Web-Sphere Application Server, the settings of the connection pools include the parameter Unused timeout to specify the interval in seconds after which an unused or idle connection is discarded, or the parameter Aged timeout to specify the interval in seconds before a physical connection is discarded (setting it to zero makes the active physical connection remaining in the pool indefinitely). Settings are configured using the administration console of the application server.

There is another case of possible ruleset parsing, when the number of ruleset deployed in one instance of RES is greater than the number of JCA connections configured for the execution unit. The least frequently used rulesets may be released and so need to be reparsed at the next call. The pool size can be set in the resource adapter descriptor (ra.xml).

```
<config-property>
   <config-property-name>defaultConnectionManagerProperties</config-property-name>
   <config-property-type>java.lang.String</config-property-type>
   <config-property-value>pool.maxSize=10</config-property-value>
</config-property>
```

The growing size of one ruleset may require changing these settings and even changing the physical deployment of the rulesets. As a ruleset uses a lot of memory (around 4k bytes per rule), it may be possible to reach some memory limit. In this case, it is recommended to reallocate rulesets among different servers. When one ruleset gets parsed more than once, it might be because the cached ruleset was garbage collected due to a max pool limitation, and the fact that this ruleset is rarely used.

When using hot deployment, it is possible to configure the execution unit to parse the ruleset asynchronously, letting current client applications submit business transaction while a new version of the ruleset is parsed. To set this capability, we need to modify the following parameter in the ra.xml. (The default is set to false)

```
<config-property>
   <config-property-name>asynchronousRulesetParsing</config-property-name>
   <config-property-type>java.lang.Boolean</config-property-type>
   <config-property-value>true</config-property-value>
</config-property>
```

The creation of the rule engine is also expensive as it builds the various internal structure needed by the RETE algorithm like the working memory, the agenda, the alpha nodes, and the list of tuples coming out of RETE network join nodes ... Rule engine pooling avoids redoing this processing at each invocation. In RES, the engine creation is performed at the first creation of the rule session.

To conclude this discussion, to avoid performance issue for some rule execution, the architect has to take into account the management of the ruleset to avoid unnecessary ruleset parsing, avoid blocking client requests when there is a new ruleset being parsed, and prepare the ruleset before the first call. Using the RES console, it is possible to find out how many free connections are in the pool, which rulesets are parsed, the memory allocation ... Using the Server Info tab, we need to change the Log level to debug, and then go to the execution unit to view its dump.

15.3.2   Execution Algorithms

JRules has different algorithms for the rule execution. One is an enhanced version of the RETE algorithm called the RetePlus, which is designed to optimize the evaluation of a large number of rules across a large number of objects. Tests are filtered by relevance such that irrelevant tests do not need to be evaluated. Tests can be shared between rules that use similar tests so that they do not need to be reevaluated for all the rules. As seen in Chap. 6, RETE is the algorithm of choice when the rule action is updating the state of the object in working memory or is inserting new facts in working memory. This is the case for alarm filtering and correlation, and correlation of business events applications.

When there is no need for inference, we can use a stateless processing for the pattern matching. JRules offers the sequential mode algorithm which compiles rules at initialization and processes objects using the pattern matching on basic rule condition. This algorithm is efficient when there are an important number of rules using some static priority and few objects as parameters. There is no working memory in this mode of execution. The operators *exist, not, collect* do not work in sequential mode, as they work on objects in working memory.

The third execution mode, FastPath, combines the Rete and the sequential mode to match objects against a large number of rules. It detects semantic relations between rule tests during the pattern matching process. The difference with RETE is that when a rule is evaluated for execution it is immediately executed, and its action is not propagated back to the reevaluation of the possible rules. It fits well in application processing rules in stateless mode with a very large number of rules that individually perform simple discriminations or light join tests.

The settings of the algorithm are configured in the properties of a rule task, and so apply to all rules in the task. Each task can have different algorithm (Fig. 15.21).

There are different dimensions to look at when selecting the algorithm. Compliance and validation rules are looking at few objects and generate some yes/no evaluation or compute a list of issues to process later on. FastPath or Sequential are more adapted for

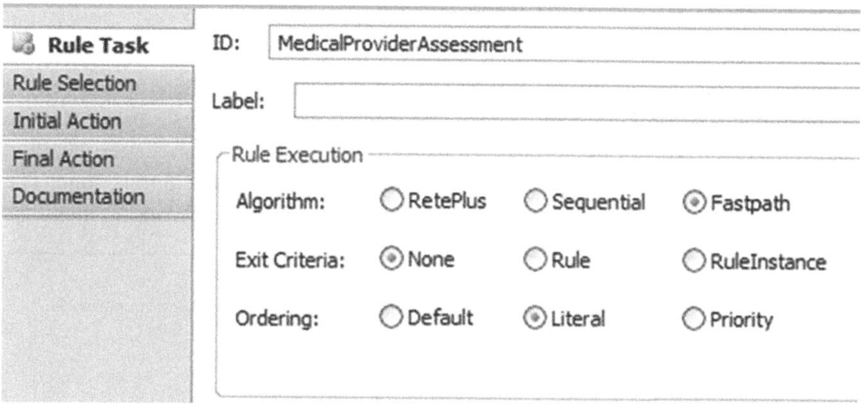

Fig. 15.21 Setting algorithm on a rule task

such applications. Applications which maintain communication with the rule engine, by inserting object reference to the working memory, require the use of RetePlus. The same choice applies if the rules are inserting/updating/retracting objects in working memory; this mode of processing is a better fit for RETE. The product documentation presents a useful table to look at the dimensions and the algorithm capability.

Regardless of the algorithm used, the number of conditions and actions in the ruleset may impact the rule execution performance. A large number of tests against a large number of objects are far slower than fewer tests. When using the RETE, a large number of conditions increase the size of the RETE network. Each node in the RETE network maintains a bunch of lists. The network's size means that any object change (insert/update/retract) will provoke many evaluations and increase memory consumption. It is often possible to avoid modifying the working memory in the rule to improve performance.

JRules supports dynamic bytecode generation to speed up the evaluation of the tests for rules in RetePlus execution mode. Rule tests can be translated directly into Java bytecode and integrated into the application to improve performance of the rules. Depending upon the rules, bytecode generation can improve processing performance of the engine by a factor ranging from 4 to more than 10 by bypassing Java introspection. The generated bytecode calls Java members directly in the rule tests, and so the more complex the rules and the more objects there are in working memory, the bigger the gain. Dynamic bytecode generation also reduces the activity of the garbage collector at run time, thereby enhancing performance. To use the JIT feature, the value of the rule engine property, ilog.rules.engine.useJIT, must be set to true. With sequential algorithm, rule actions are compiled directly into java bytecode, and so rules will execute will the same speed as native java code. For this to work, the bcel.jar needs to be part of the classpath and JRules needs to have the permission to create a class loader. Under certain environments like Java EE containers, this permission may not be granted by default, and the rule engine may throw a security exception.

15.3.3 Rule Execution Improvement

As stated in previous chapters, inserting object references into the engine working memory has a processing cost. JRules offers the concept of ruleset parameters to avoid inserting objects not needed in pattern matching. The language operators *from* and *in* reduces the number of objects on which pattern matching is done. The following rule uses a pattern matching against line item object in working memory:

```
If
  There is one line item where the status of this line item is not closed
<..>
then
  ...
```

The rule filters out the line item not closed and applies other conditions and actions on them. One rule instance per match is added to the agenda. The second rule below uses the ruleset parameters *invoice* and its collection of medicalBillLineItems. The pattern matching is local to the rule. The rule fires for each line item not closed in this collection.

```
Definitions
Set lineItem to a line item in the medical bill details of the invoice where the status of this
line item is not closed.
If
  ...
then
```

To improve rule execution performance, it is possible to modify the conditions of the rule to reduce the time to do the pattern matching. For example, we can order the test by putting the most discriminant tests at first. One recent example on processing wireless data usage illustrates this concept: there are three categories of roaming: region, domestic, and international. The data usage record is tested on a lot of attributes. The most discriminant is the roaming indicator. Putting test on it at the front of the rule avoids doing unnecessary tests:

```
If
  The roaming indicator of the data usage record is International and the data usage is above 50 and
  ...
Performs better than
If
  the data usage is above 50 and ... and The roaming indicator of the data usage record is
  International and ...
But suppose that we need to add a test on the price plan name. As price plan name has a unique value, then a condition
on such data element is more discriminant, and a rule like,
If
  The price plan is "iphone 3G 100MB" and the roaming indicator of the data usage record is
  International and the data usage is above 50 and ...
performs better than the two above.
```

Another possible improvement is to control the pattern matching used to evaluate the conditions on object. JRules proposes the concept of *finders*.

Finders allow speeding up the execution of rules by providing the engine with specific java code, which performs more efficient pattern matching. Finders are used when rules perform a lot of navigations within object relations, using language keywords such as *from*, *in*, or *collect*. The following rule fires each time there are an Account and a CashEvent in the working memory with the same accountID. As we may have hundred of CashEvents for a given account, we want to avoid putting all the cash events in the working memory and perform some costly joins.

```
when {
   account : Account(balance > 0 );
   creditcards: collect (new CashEventCollector())
                CashEvent(type equals EventType.CREDITCARD;
                          accountID equals account.ID;
                          amount < 0)
                where (size()>0);
}then {
average = -creditcards.getAverageAmount(account.currency);
```

Finders are declared in a rule engine configuration file, which is processed by the engine during its initialization.

```
node abrd.model.finance.CashEvent
{
   element useHashers = false;
   element useEquals = true;
   element useFinders = true;
   element finders =
   {
     "accurate abrd.model.finance.FinderFinancialEventImpl.findByAccountID(accountID)"
   };
};
```

The configuration above provides a list of Finders for the class CashEvent. Any reference to a CashEvent such as CashEvent(accountID equals value) in a rule condition will use the finder's method specified in this declaration. In this case, the method findByAccountID(accountID) returns a list of CashEvent where the attribute accountID is equal to the value given as parameter. The list of Finders is used to optimize the rules when the useFinders property is set to true. As a list, the value of this property is an array of string. The collect keyword is used in the condition part of a rule to create a collection of object matching the condition in the where statement: The collection object CashEventCollector stores instances of the class CashEvent that matches the conditions: *type is a creditcard and accountID is the same as the account id of the account in working memory and the amount on the cash event is negative (debit).*

The collection object is bound to a variable for the scope of the rule: `cred-itcards`. The expression in parenthesis is optional, but if provided, must return a collector object that implements three public methods: `addElement`, `updateElement`, and `removeElement`. The CashEvent-Collector subclass the IlrDefaultCollector class and adds two methods used in the action part of the rule to compute the average amount of all the CashEvent in the collection and total amount. The `collect` statement may contain a list of tests on the collection object in the `where` part of the statement. The finder mechanism is derived from the relation mechanism. This feature allows navigation through the object model using the keywords `from` and `in`. Relations are typically used for two reasons: to improve the expressiveness and readability of rules by making them using relations that are naturally defined in the object model, and to improve the performance of the rules by making the pattern matching occur only on a reduced number of objects retrieved using special lookup methods provided by the application.

The rule engine can be configured by setting properties in a file named engine. conf and by giving the path to this file in the engine configuration tab of the ruleset properties (Fig. 15.22).

Such configuration can be different per ruleset and is extracted as part of the ruleset archive. The rule engine at its instantiation reads the content of the file to set the engine's internal algorithms.

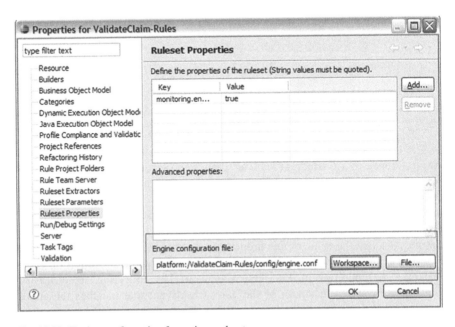

Fig. 15.22 Engine configuration for a given ruleset

15.4   Summary

Testing and performance tuning are important activities of a business rule application. Testing gives the assurance of quality before deploying new business logic, and with enhanced BRMS such capability can be used by business users. WebSphere ILOG JRules offers a comprehensive suite of features to develop test scenarios and execute them. Adding key performance indicators and the same data set can be used to perform business simulation. Finally, rule execution performance can be impacted by different variables, from the rule writing itself to the algorithm used by the engine. The data model design is also in important elements. JRules offers a lot of options to fine-tune the performance. All those capabilities explain why this product is the leader on the market.

15.5   Further Reading

For more technical information and tutorials, the product documentation is accessible at http://publib.boulder.ibm.com/infocenter/brjrules/v7r1/index.jsp.
JSR237 is about the Work Manager for Application Servers, where the specification is accessible at http://jcp.org/en/jsr/detail?id=237.
For the Just in time compiler reader can access en.wikipedia.org/wiki/Just-in-time_compilation.
J2EE Connector Architecture portal provides all the information about JCA and is accessible at http://java.sun.com/j2ee/connector/.

Part VII
Rule Governance

Chapter 16
Rule Governance

Target audience
- *All*

In this chapter you will learn
- *What are the needs for a rule governance process and how to develop it on top of a BRMS platform*
- *How to put in place a business rule management group*
- *What are the tasks, work products, and guidelines to efficiently manage rule changes*

Key points
- *Define in the early phase of the projects how the rules will be maintained*
- *Design a simple life cycle for rule artifacts and validate it with the business rule writer*
- *Design a change process to support quick deployment of business rules from elicitation to production*

16.1   Introduction

In this chapter, we present one of the most important factors of a successful BRMS deployment at the enterprise level: rule governance. We start, in Sect. 16.2, by presenting the requirements around rule governance, as they have to be considered differently because of the type of communication between business and IT, and the frequency of ruleset changes. In Sect. 16.3, we highlight a simple method to set up rule governance processes in an organization, present different rule life cycles, and detail some of the activities to define rule governance within the organization as a framework the IT team can use. In Sect. 16.4, we detail some of the potential subprocesses as part of the rule change process definition.

J. Boyer and H. Mili, *Agile Business Rule Development*,
DOI 10.1007/978-3-642-19041-4_16, © Springer-Verlag Berlin Heidelberg 2011

When a BRMS approach is introduced, the business rule management ownership moves from the IT team to the business unit team. In this context, ownership means "leading the change" since the control can still be shared between IT and business. Project teams need to develop formal processes to support this transition. Those processes are integrated in the rule governance process definition, itself integrated into the IT governance. Business rules are exposed, separated, stated in formal terms, and managed for change against formal governance processes that involve both business and IT. The traditional software maintenance methodology does not apply the same way for a BRMS approach. In the traditional approach, the IT Development–IT QA pair represents the usual bottleneck in which all the business policy updates and new business requirements have to go through. Sometimes the cycle for implementing changes is so long that it cannot be completed in a timely manner. For example, a marketing campaign defining new product bundles needs them to be available on the market quickly to beat or react to competition. A BRMS helps to reduce the bottleneck, but unregulated updates coming from different sources, with different goals and different knowledge levels of the system can alter the integrity and quality of each decision services controlled by the business rules.

The rule governance processes are keys to support the ABRD[1] cycles and especially the *Enhancing phase*. This chapter describes how to set up the rule governance processes in an organization. The next chapter addresses how to support rule governance within JRules.

16.2   Need for Governance

The main goal of rule governance is to ensure an efficient maintenance of all the decision services deployed, through an optimal collaboration between business, IT, and other stakeholders. It adds discipline to the communication and the change management of the business policies. Even when controls are put in place, the development methodology remains more agile than the traditional waterfall approach. In Sect. 16.2.1, we present where rule governance should be attached to within the organization, then continue by defining where to start from, in 16.2.2 and present, in 16.2.3, the main subprocesses defining the rule governance. Understanding such requirements help to drive the process definitions.

16.2.1   IT and Business Governance

Rule governance has to be defined in the context of IT governance, at the same level of focus as the SOA or BPM governance, but with a strong involvement of the

---

[1]See Chap. 3 on Agile Business Rule Development.

business to take ruleset ownership, initiate changes, and drive the changes. When delivering an agile architecture, IT leverages four main approaches: service oriented, central management of reference data and main business entities, externalization of the business logic, and orchestration of work and services. Each approach applies his own governance, and because IT is responsible of the production systems and a change initiated by the business may impact multiple components in the IT architecture, BPM and rule governances are allocated to this organization. In the scope of rules, there are two classes of change: one affecting a rulesets, one affecting the data model used by the rules. With a BRMS, it is easy to have the business team be able to support the change from the initiation to the deployment of the ruleset; on the other hand, the data model change may have impact on the data source, service contract, data referential, even process variables.

Deploying a service requires strict governance to avoid duplicating services or having services not really reusable. Managing reference data has been following strict data governance for a long time. Business process management improves the execution of the processes, and to support continuous measurements and improvements, needs to be controlled and governed. Finally business rule changes, which occur the most frequently in this architecture, also has to follow strict governance to avoid duplicating the business logic changes and to efficiently apply the business rule programming model.

16.2.2 How to Start Developing Rule Governance

The flexible points of a business process or of business services are supported by using the business rule approach; therefore, change management should focus on business rules more than service and process governance. The governance processes definition follows the same approach as other business process modeling efforts. It can be developed iteratively, should help facilitate the communication between the project's actors, and should help orchestrate the rule change management within a business rule management system. The idea is to start simple, involve IT and business stakeholders in the process design, define key performance indicators to measure the process efficiency, and monitor the process execution during the ruleset maintenance phase. The process definition does not include a complex set of activities, but we do expect between 10 and 15 major activities. Some steps can simply consist of documentation, while others may be an executable process supported by a workflow engine. After a first implementation, the project team can fine-tune the processes and add controls and activities. The processes can be defined in the scope of one application before being extended at the enterprise level. Once development is completed, it is important to start working on developing the best practices as they have to be incorporated in the governance.

16.2.3   What Are the Main Processes in Rule Governance?

Rule governance processes support the following subprocesses:

- Rule change process
- Rule authoring
- Rule testing
- Rule deployment
- Rule execution monitoring

Understanding the term governance is important here, as we want to clearly state how changes to the decision logic are supported, what the goals are, the actors, inputs and outputs, resources that the processes use, and demonstrate how the process is applied, and how they evolve over time to support new business constraints.

16.3   Defining Rule Governance

In this section, we detail some of the activities the team needs to follow to implement rule governance processes. We propose these activities as a framework that an organization can use to set up governance.

Organizations may not have a formal process to manage the business policies and executable business rules, or maybe they use simple steps in the standard software development methodology, which are not representative of a complete governance process. To develop the rule governance processes, we propose to follow the activities in Fig. 16.1.

In this section, we discuss how to create a rule management group, how to identify stakeholders, assigning ruleset ownership, and finally, defining the rule life cycle.

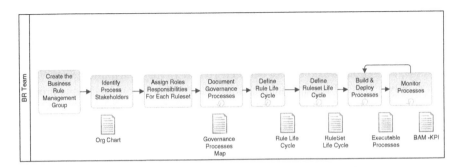

Fig. 16.1 Activities to develop rule governance processes

16.3.1   Create the Business Rules Management Group

We recommend first creating a team responsible for the definition of the governance processes. The mission of this group can be stated as follows: "Support the specification, organization, authoring and quality of the business rules to benefit the organization's business goals". To achieve this mission, the group needs to include people playing different roles, such as rule analyst, rule architect, rule author, rule tester, and rule administrator. If the company uses a business process management approach to develop its business applications, it may make sense to have the rule management team be part of a BPM center of excellence (CoE), if one exists. Business process and business rules have very different life cycles, so merging authority must be controlled. We have observed that business rule governance has to be enforced earlier than business process governance. A ruleset changes more often than the business process that call it; therefore, it makes more sense to start defining the rule governance processes earlier. Also, business process governance focuses on monitoring the process and finding some small improvements over time. Process updates may occur every 6 months up to once a year. Business rule changes can happen every day, driven by multiple factors, like competition, regulations, marketing, etc. These different impacts on the business may be better supported by having two separate governance groups: one for BPM, one for BRM.

The BRM group facilitates collaboration between the business groups who own the business processes and business policies and the IT team responsible for the operational decision logic and processes. Defining such a group requires looking at the organizational structure of the company. Dimensions such as number of business units, types, and frequencies of changes that are applied to the application, and the number of decision services may impact the structure and the size of the team and also the scope of the governance processes. The greater the number of business units involved, the stronger the need for a mediation entity.

16.3.1.1   Complexity of Changes

Changes can range from simple, like a change to a variable or a threshold, adding new conditions or actions, to more complex logic changes such as adding a new product definition or adding new rule flow within an existing decision service. Changes to the domain data model or adding new decision services are most likely considered complex as they involve a complete development cycle with more activities. The more complex the changes, the greater the need for a knowledgeable group to manage the change. The more frequent the rules changes, the stronger the need for a centralized entity that can schedule, coordinate, and prioritize the changes.

16.3.1.2 Roles

The roles found in this rule management team are:

- *Rule steward.* Develops and maintains a comprehensive management plan for the group activities and drives the definition of the rule governance processes. He leads the change management review board.
- *Rule architect.* Ensures that the overall rule management organization makes sense from an application segmentation perspective. He defines the data model for rules and the decision service definition.
- *Rule analyst.* Assists the business to define and manage the rules they own. Improves the quality of the rules by using best practices.
- *Rule author or writer.* Ensures rules are executable and with quality.
- *Rule tester.* Validates the quality of the rule implementation, as specified in the change request, and according to other quality standards established in the company.
- *Rule administrator.* Controls the deployment of the ruleset into the different executables servers and environments. He controls the versioning policy.

A more complete description of these roles, responsibilities, and competencies can be found in the Eclipse Process Framework – Agile Business Rule Development practice plug-in. It is important to consider that this group can grow from existing resources and different roles can be performed by the same person. The team can take on more responsibilities as the architecture grows to include more decision services, and more applications use these services.

16.3.2 Identify Stakeholders

When identifying stakeholders, start by documenting the current organization model with all the departments-groups exposed to the BRMS operations, such as rule definition, ownership, authoring, validation, execution, and monitoring. The groups can be internal to the company or external as partners, channels, or subsidiaries.[2]

In the past, we were exposed to projects where business rule engines are in the cashier machines deployed in each distribution shop of the company. The rules define marketing campaign and deliver local coupons to customers. The rules are defined at the corporate level but also at the local shop manager level. In this

---

[2]You can read as a complement the extensive work done on stakeholder analysis by Eric Charpentier and reported in his blog at http://www.primatek.ca/blog/2009/11/01/business-rules-governance-and-management-part-iv-stakeholders/ and the associated white paper which can be found at http://www.primatek.ca/blog/white-papers/.

scenario, strict controls of the rule authoring, ruleset quality are important dimensions to consider.

Obviously, the scope of governance processes and the organization model may not be so radical, but in a global economy it is common to work with remote teams. It is important to understand the relationship between the groups and how the information flows operate. A special focus on the decision process and escalation procedure is needed. Who owns, sponsors, and arbitrates the changes in the system. Once the organization description is completed, we can focus on adapting the organization model to support new role definitions and responsibilities with the goal to support the rule change process. Table 16.1 illustrates some possible groups that are usually impacted by the rule governance processes.

If the business rules management group does not exist as a separate entity, its members are usually associated with the IT department as they have the software development skills, which are important to manage rule change process. Some organizations have a change control board mechanism in place where change requests are reviewed and decisions are made to authorize, postpone, or reject the implementation of the changes.

To represent the organization map, we can use different models from organization charts to team–location–role diagrams. But as agile practitioners, simple diagrams are usually enough, and using a top-down view may be a good approach, including swim lanes and high-level communication flows. Figure 16.3 illustrates

Table 16.1 Rule governance group – role – process involvement

Group	Role	Process involvement
Business unit – line of business	Owner of the rules	Originates the change requests and reviews the progress along the rule development lifecycle
	Interested in rule execution metrics	Defines KPIs for process monitoring
Business rule management	Responsible for the ruleset maintenance and supports new rule initiatives	Performs the rule updates May also perform changes to the underlying object models
IT development	Responsible for the application development and maintenance	Performs major modifications to the application code, integration with rule engine, with data sources and developing the different data models
IT QA	Responsible for validating the application and ruleset. Verify that the functional and performance quality are conserved	Creates and updates test cases to adjust test coverage Executes nonregression and performance tests
IT production management	Responsible for managing the production platform	Manages the deployment process after receiving the request to deploy a ruleset Monitors the execution of the rules, and may perform some analysis to understand which rules were executed for a given business event

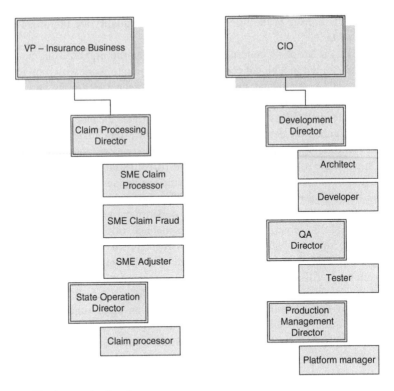

Fig. 16.2 Simple organization chart

the role mapped by swim lanes, and activities exchanging information between the lanes.[3]

As an example, our fictive insurance provider company has headquarters in California and branch offices in each state where the company insures persons and properties. We simplify the organization of an insurance company by highlighting the principal roles/stakeholders we need to support in the rule governance processes. The left side is the business hierarchy with functional and geography hierarchy. It could be a matrix organization with dotted line reporting (Fig. 16.2).

On the right side is the IT team with development, QA, and production platform management teams. As we can see, there is no official role for supporting a business rules approach. The current support is split between multiple IT responsibilities, making changes to a business rule quite long.

We propose that the business rules management group should report to the CIO and show, in Table 16.2, a set of roles played by the team members.

---

[3]For more information about swim lanes, communication flow, see the BPMN specification at http://www.bpmn.org.

Table 16.2 Team member roles and attributes

Role	Description	Attributes
Rule steward	Manage the rule management group	Years of experience in management Years of experience in BRMS
Rule analyst	Perform the analysis of rules and business terms used, and evaluate the implementation complexity and effort	Years of experience in BRMS
Rule writer	Author the rule Can be the rule analyst	Years of experience in BRMS
Rule tester	Test the rule	Years of experience in QA and test
Rule administrator	Deploy the rules and monitor rule execution	Years of experience in BRMS
Business policies owner	Business knowledge of the business policies to implement	Business knowledge, contributor to business execution and metrics
Change board manager	Team of business and IT managers responsible to support the escalation procedure for change requests involving deep changes in the application or its architecture	Escalation process, and project management competencies

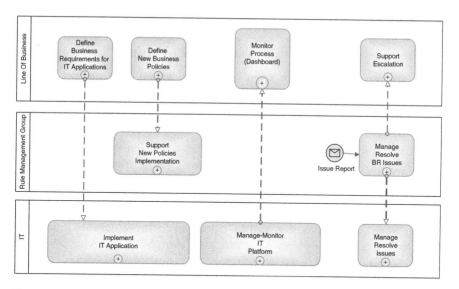

Fig. 16.3 Middle man group

Figure 16.3 illustrates how this rule management group sits between business and IT teams to support the business policy implementation. The line of business defines business requirements for applications deployed in the IT architecture.

IT implements those requirements in different applications. On the right side, the traditional issue management with business and IT addressing together the issues with a dedicated process and escalation procedures. As the business rules change cycle is different than traditional implementation, it is important to put in place this rule management group as a mediator for quick turnaround time and implementation. Finally in modern architecture, the business uses a business activity monitoring dashboard to assess the performance of the executable business processes supported by a set of applications or services within the IT architecture.

The arrows represent the communication channels. The BRM group focuses on efficiently supporting business policy implementation and associated changes. As technical and analysis competencies are needed, it makes sense for this group to report to IT.

16.3.3   Ruleset Owning Groups

In a BRMS approach, a ruleset is owned by a business unit or business department. Giving clear ownership to business is a major dimension to make rule governance work. Ownership requires allocating decision authority to the experts of the domain, which helps get the implementation right the first time without losing any information between the different translation layers used in a traditional approach. It also helps reduce the time to implement the changes in the decision logic, as the business user can make the change. The association between rulesets and owning groups may be listed in a table format so that:

- A ruleset map can be defined, to present a cartography of the difference decision services.
- Corresponding groups can be defined in the permission control mechanism within the IT servers, to manage the access permissions on the ruleset content.

In contrast to the actor and organization chart defined in the previous section, this table explicitly lists the individual owner names as the official go-to person to contact in relation with the associated ruleset. Table 16.3 represents the ruleset map for the claim processing application and is built from the decision point table developed during the earlier activities of the project. For rulesets with a large number of rules, the table may need to include an additional level of granularity lower than the decision points, in which case, you can use a hierarchy of rule packages, and define the mapping at the rule package level.

Table 16.3 Ruleset – role map

Ruleset	Responsible group	Owner	Rule analyst	Rule author	Rule reviewer
validateClaim	Claim processor	John A	John A	Mike	Antony B
validateMedicalInvoice	Claim processor	John A	Mark	Mike	Antony B
verifyCoverage	Policy team	Julie B	Julie B	Mike	Carol A
adjudicateClaim	Adjudication team	Mathew B	Mathew B	Bill	Carol A
claimFraudAssessment	Fraud team	Joe C	Mark	Mark	Carol A

16.3.4   Rule Life Cycle

The definition of the rule life cycle can range from extremely simple (such as the one presented on Fig. 16.4) to very intricate. The trade-off is between control and overhead, i.e., having a rich set of statuses to precisely track the rule during its life cycle leads to a possibly heavy and time-consuming process to move a rule from creation to deployment. Note that a complex rule life cycle implies a reasonable commitment to accurately maintain the rule statuses, and not all projects (or all teams within a project) have the bandwidth and/or the discipline to follow the maintenance process. If half of the project maintains the rule life cycle properly and the other half of the teams ignores it, the benefit is lost for all, and frictions will eventually surface in the team. The questions of whether the project and its members are committed to maintaining the rule life cycle, understanding its constraints, and viewing each of its details as valuable to the project, have to be asked candidly and answered honestly. This may lead to the adoption of different life cycles for different rulesets.

The main needs that drive the design of a rule life cycle are linked to quality control and traceability of the actions performed on the rules. The development team wants to understand the status of the rules and who the owners of the current and next actions are. Rules have to be tested and validated, after which they can be deployed to production. These are the minimum steps of this life cycle. It is also possible to manage the target environments where the rules can go. Quite often we use a staged environment with at least development, preproduction, and production platforms. In a BRMS, the rule life cycle is controlled by adding meta-property to rule elements. A common implementation is to use a *status* property and a finite state machine implementation using, for example, java code integrated into the BRMS. When change to the status drives events and activities that need to be processed by human, the use of a workflow solution may be added to the implementation. The status change triggers the execution of mini processes with human tasks, used for example to control the update to the rules is done according to quality standards.

The simple life cycle illustrated in Fig. 16.4 can be implemented with the following set of statuses:

- *New*. The rule is created and can be modified by its owner.
- *Defined*. The rule has been defined and is currently in test.
- *Deployable*. The rule can be part of a ruleset deployable and deployed in production platform.

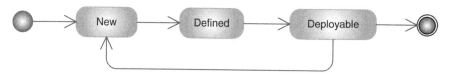

Fig. 16.4 Simple rule life cycle

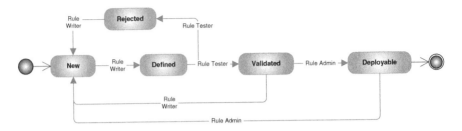

Fig. 16.5 Classical life cycle

The two main actors of this cycle are the rule writer and the rule tester. The rule writer promotes the rule from *new* to *defined* once finished with his edits. The rule tester promotes the rule to *deployable* status to authorize deployment to production. The rule tester can be a human or an automatic step in case of automatic nonregression validation. A more complete life cycle adds more control over the test state.

- *Rejected*. The rule has been tested unsuccessfully.
- *Validated*. The rule has been tested successfully.

The state diagram in Fig. 16.5 uses the following roles to control the state changes:

- *Rule Author/Writer*. End user of the BRMS application
- *Rule Admin*. Administrator of the ruleset
- *Rule Tester*. A human or an automatic process to test the rule quality

We may need to note that when a rule is created, the status is *New*. It can be reverted back to the *New* status by the rule writer for further update after it has been either *Validated*, *Rejected*, or deemed *Deployable*. To avoid complex transitions and a new state, a rule can be set *Active* or *Inactive* at any state. The implementation is done by adding an inactive property as part of the meta-model attached to the rule. Retiring a rule that was *Deployable* means the rule admin needs to set it as inactive. Once *Deployable* if the rule writer needs to change the rule, he can create a new version and change its status to *New*. The rule has to re-enter a full life cycle. For auditability reasons, a rule once promoted to *Deployable* is never deleted. It is retired or set as *Inactive*.

This life cycle can be used as a starting point for most of rule management requirements but can be adapted to fit other use cases. Within a given rule project not all rules are in the same status; therefore, there is a need to extract and build the ruleset with only relevant rules. For example: no rule in *New* state or all rules have to be in *Deployable*.

There is one issue to consider with any rule life cycle: the ruleset integrity. Suppose a user wants to change a *Deployable* rule without creating (copy and paste) a new rule by changing its status back to *New*. Any new extraction of the ruleset to production, taking into account some predefined extraction configuration, will not take any rules in *New* or *Defined* rules; therefore, the previously *Deployable* rule will not be part of the production ruleset any more, exposing the ruleset integrity. One option is to use a clever ruleset builder tool which looks up the last version of a rule that was in production and adds it to the ruleset. Another way is to have this tool forbidding deploying the ruleset in case there is a rule meeting the "back to new" state. This can also be enforced by the change process: the process can forbid extracting a new ruleset until the rule comes back to *Deployable* status.

16.4 Rule Change Process

The maintenance and modification of a rule-based system, like any other software application, should be controlled through a change management process. What makes a rule-based system unique is that the business owners of the application not only initiate the change process (in this case by identifying the need for a business policy change), but may also implement many of the changes themselves by directly updating the rules. Combining the rule life cycle and a change management process, we can finely control the rule-based application. It is important that rule governance be established, practiced, and refined during the early phases and iterations of the project so that it will be ready and refined enough for production. The entry point of the process is a change to a business policy or an update of current rules (Fig. 16.6).

The initiator can be the IT group (fixing an issue) or the line of business (change requested on an existing rule or to add new policy). We can clearly imagine the business user entering the description of the change in a web-based interface. It can be a simple entry form screen to enter the change description with other attributes such as the rule project name, rule reference in the rule repository, the target date to deploy in production, the business motivation, etc. The system stores the change request (CR) in a database, makes some data validation, and then notifies the reviewers. Any data issue is reported immediately to the user. As part of the rule management group, the rule analyst can scope the change and perform some impact analysis. There are mostly three types of outcomes from the first scope review: (1) the change is simple: proceed, (2) the change is not feasible: reject and assess with the team how to make it more simple, and (3) the change is possible, but is costly or may impact a lot of components. A deeper review has to be performed by a change management committee. The committee can accept or reject the change.

An accepted change request goes to the rule authoring, rule testing, and deployment subprocesses. The change request can be seen as a business object with state which can take one of the following values: *Submitted, Rejected, Under-estimation, Under-implementation, Under-test, Completed*, and *Cancelled*. During the process, the completion of all major activities is recorded to the change request. The change management board reviews the change request and the implementation to ensure good traceability and quality control. Part of the review is the verification that all rules and code are included in a version control repository. When the result of the review does not meet the quality standards, the development team and the rule

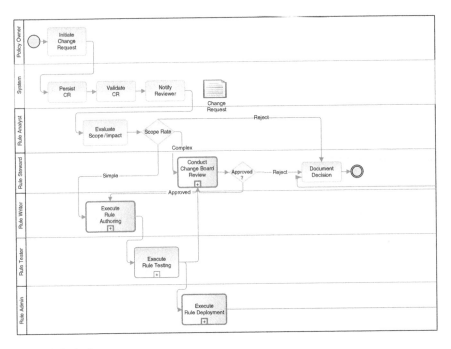

Fig. 16.6 Rule change process

management group may have to iterate over the changes. When everything is cleared, they promote the changes from the development system to the test system. This involves moving not only any modified code and possibly database table changes, but also deploying the modified rulesets to the test application server.

The responsibility of the QA testing group is to ensure that the modifications made to the rules and any associated code perform as expected and do not negatively impact the rest of the system. To this end, the QA tester verifies the test scenarios newly created by the business user and adds them to the set of nonregression tests. At the tester's discretion, unit tests, ruleset tests, and system integration tests may be added to ensure that the changes work together with the entire system. All tests that are added or modified by the QA testing group should be added to the suite of regression tests. Once all tests have been updated, the suites of tests are run and the results analyzed. If there is a problem with the changed rules or code, the tester works with the business user or developer to fix the issue.

Once the QA group has ensured that the rule and code changes satisfy the change request and do not negatively impact the rest of the system, the change request is updated and forwarded to the reviewer group. They will take the final decision to promote the ruleset and other related changes to production. The deployment to production process can be executed. This step is performed by the IT administrator group, responsible of the management of the production platform. This last group can even be part of another company, an outsourcing capability, which adds complexity to the deployment steps. As a side note, deploying BRMS within a company that uses business process or operation outsourcing can represent a real challenge and may break the value proposition of the BRMS: quick, agile change to the business logic. First the BRMS may not be accepted by the outsourcing provider, as it adds flexibility, where both the IT architecture and the provider's business model are driven by rigid change process. Second, even if the line of business team enforces the use of BPM and BRMS products to add agility to their own business, the outsourcing provider may take a lot of time and procedure to deploy the change in production; countering the productivity of such products. Governance processes should help to overcome this antinomy.

16.4.1   Scope of Change

At the ruleset level, we can anticipate three types of potential changes to a ruleset:

- Change to the rule
- Change to the data model used by the rules
- Change to the ruleset structure like the sequencing of rule flow, or the rule selection, or the ruleset parameters

A rule change includes adding rules, updating existing rules, but also, with a more dramatic impact, deleting rules. Deleting a rule that was previously in production has to be analyzed in depth. Usually, the rule will be retired, not deleted. The ruleset analysis evaluates if a rule replaces the deleted one, or if the conditions are evaluated in the context of another rule, or if the actions are generated by another rule. All those considerations can make the deletion possible or not.

The second type of change is to change the sequencing of the rules, for example, by refactoring the rule flow. This is a deeper change that needs to be evaluated with care, as some rules in a given rule task may leverage the facts that other decisions created in previous tasks of the rule flow. (For example, assigning default value, or testing the presence of fields.) Changing the order of a task can have major impacts. A rule flow structure has to be as static as possible to avoid complex rulesets that will be difficult to maintain. A decision service is used by multiple clients. The contract of the service has to describe the parameters structure, documented in a WSDL, but also the semantic description of the type of decision the service is making. Deleting a rule, rule task, or changing the sequencing of the rule flow may impact this contract. Clients could be impacted. Quite often, architects design a ruleset to manage the different types of contexts of execution by using different branches of the rule flow. Adding a different type of client may lead to add a new branch. From an SOA point of view, some practitioners use rule engines to support the variability of the service. While it is true that the capability to easily change the implementation of the logic is more easily done with business rules, it is always a good practice to ask why we have to do that. When the rule flow diagram starts to look like a bowl of spaghetti, it may be a good time to consider refactoring and splitting the services into multiple pieces.

Another type of change consists in adding a ruleset parameter or changing the type of one parameter. As the ruleset should not be exposed "as is" with a WSDL but hidden behind a business service, this change may not have a major impact in terms of SOA governance: the service contract stays the same, only the ruleset signature changes. A change to the signature of the ruleset will have an impact on the rules: the modified parameter may be directly accessed in the rule conditions. This could lead to a change in a lot of rules. Adding new parameter is less of an impact to the ruleset, as to infer decisions on the parameter, the rule writer has to write new rules, not update existing ones.

Finally, the last type of change is linked to the data model used by the rules. As mentioned before, the executable model (XSD or Java model) is maintained by the development group. Adding classes or attributes has an impact on the object, on the object-relational mapping, on the data source, and on the service contract. We do not want to detail the different patterns of how to change a data model without impacting an application, there are a many books on this subject, describing how to apply refactoring techniques to the data model. The data layer used by the rules is not more stable than a database or XML schema. It is common to add a new attribute to a class, so a rule author can write condition on this new business term. Also in a powerful BRMS, it is possible to add business concepts that are not mapped to any data element. They are used for computation or to infer new facts. A typical dynamic implementation is to add a new variable–value pair in a hash map, and then use a getter to access the value in a rule condition. In any case, a developer has to be assigned to make the change prior to the rule writer modifying the rules. The rule author, developer, and database administrator make the necessary updates to the development system to implement the change, unit test it, and report on the test results. Changes to the data model are usually made in the context of a release. It is the responsibility of the rule author to create and modify unit test cases to test the rule changes. These test cases can eventually be added to the regression tests maintained by the QA testing group.

16.4.2 Rule Authoring Subprocess

The rule writer is performing the following activities in loop: develops unit tests to assess the rule outcome, executes the tests to verify they failed, authors the rule, and executes the tests, until all tests succeed. As we are in maintenance mode, it makes sense to enforce a systematic review with the business users to ensure that the new rules accurately reflect the business intent. It may be needed to iterate on the authoring and testing of the rule until the business users are confident.

The unit tests should report if the rules with a *Defined* status were fired or not. Only rules that were fired with the expected result should be promoted to *Validated*. The ones which have not been fired should be kept in the *Defined* status or moved to the *Rejected* status. This approach works well when the rule testing coverage is good. Assessing the test suite against the list of rule fired helps to increase the coverage. All the rules part of the ruleset to be extracted should have a status of *Defined, Validated,* or *Deployable.* Once the rules are validated by tests and reviewed successfully, the status can change to *Validated.*

16.4.3   Rule Testing Subprocess

The steps of this process are simple. Once a ruleset is ready for test, the following subprocess can be executed by the QA group (Fig. 16.7).

The process includes two tasks for maintaining the rule life cycle. It is important for the QA team to take into consideration the change request description and business intent, so that testers can add functional test cases to the test suites. The ruleset has to pass successfully the previous nonregression test suites and the new functional tests added in scope of this change request. If one test fails, the rule tester needs to reject the rules that are part of the change request, and the rule author has to be notified to quickly update the problem rules.

16.4.4   Rule Deployment Subprocess

The purpose of this process is to control how a ruleset is deployed to the different servers. As described in the ruleset life cycle section above, it is common to use at least three platforms in the context of this subprocess: development, test, and production. The actors are the testers, the platform administrator, and the business analyst – rule writer. As mentioned before, the business user is not directly deploying rulesets to the production platform, only the person with rule administrator role does it. The rule deployment subprocess is seen differently depending on the actor executing it. Developers, testers, business users, and administrators do not use the same steps and tools to deploy their rules. From the rule governance point of view, we want to address the traceability and auditability requirements of the deployment phase only for the production platform. Testing and development can

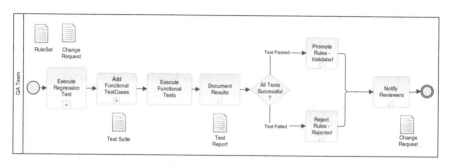

Fig. 16.7 Rule testing process

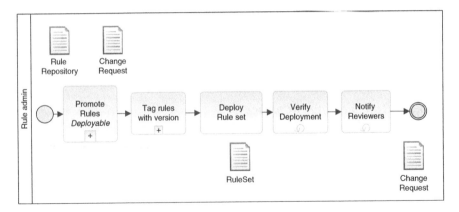

Fig. 16.8 Rule deployment process

be less restrictive. Developers and testers usually use a more ad-hoc process mostly based on their own way of managing the code integrity on their platform. The entry point is a notification received from the test group that the ruleset is ready for deployment. The rule administrator starts by promoting the rules to the *Deployable* status, then the ruleset is tagged, and versioned. Tagging and versioning is linked to the BRMS product or can be supported within a configuration management and version control tool. The other activities of the process are simple: deploy the ruleset, verify that the deployment was successful, and then notify the process stakeholders (Fig. 16.8).

The activity of verifying the deployment may include some dry test of the newly deployed ruleset. The last step is to notify through email or event to warn the business users and reviewers that the new ruleset is in production.

16.5   Summary

Rule governance is a major activity that can determine the success of a BRMS deployment within the business and IT groups. From our experience, the companies that were successful in having business users maintain the business logic of the application embraced a rule governance approach during the first or second projects using the BRMS platform. The first project proves the value proposition of a BRMS, educates the development team to implement using business rule logic, and confirms the capabilities of simple change management. By the second project or decision point implementation, the team has to leverage a common methodology and best practices found during the first project. This is the beginning of a center of excellence responsible of designing the rule governance processes. As the number of applications using business rules grows, the processes are applied systematically. The rule governance processes, the rule management group, the change board review, can be supported by a dedicated group or a community of practices. We have observed that during the first 2 years of adopting a BRMS, the rule management group is a more efficient organizational model to support the management of the different rulesets. The processes highlighted in this chapter are simple and efficient for most stakeholders and can be supported by a simple web application, with little customization of the BRMS platform. The next chapter describes how to support such rule governance processes within JRules.

16.6 Further Reading

ABRD, as a practice library, is accessible at http://www.eclipse.org/epf/downloads/praclib/praclib_downloads.php and as published version at http://epf.eclipse.org/wikis/epfpractices/ going under practices > Additional practices > Agile Business Rule Development

Business process modeling practice is covered within the BPMN specification accessible at http://www.bpmn.org

IT governance is extensively presented at http://en.wikipedia.org/wiki/Corporate_governance_of_information_technology

Reader can access a deep analysis on business rule governance, done by Eric Charpentier, an independent consultant on business rule management technology, on his blog http://www.primatek.ca/blog/2009/11/01/

Chapter 17
Rule Governance with JRules

Target audience
- *Developer, software architect*

After reading this chapter, you will be able to
- *Understand the product features relevant to the rule governance*
- *Define your own change management process using BPM product and Rule Team Server*

Key points
- *Rule Team Server is the platform of choice to support rule governance.*
- *RTS security control and behavior may be easily adapted using configuration and open API.*
- *Link the rule life cycle process to a change request management for a fine-grained control.*
- *With rule governance the business user initiates the rule change but may also perform the rule authoring and the ruleset deployment.*

17.1   Introduction

In this chapter, we describe how to apply the concepts presented in Chap. 16 using JRules components. In Sect. 17.2, we start by presenting how Rule Team Server is the component of choice to support rule governance. RTS features like the status rule property, the baseline concept, and open API to control the rule life cycle are designed to support flexible rule change management process. In Sect. 17.3, we detail how this process can be supported within RTS, using a business process approach. The choice of using Rule Team Server to support rule governance is natural, as it has all the capabilities to control rule versioning, ruleset packaging, and ruleset deployment with control. As of version 7.1, there is still some customization to add, for a company to support an end-to-end rule change management process, from change request to ruleset deployment, integrating a fine-grained rule life cycle. We explain the needs and how to support such customization.

J. Boyer and H. Mili, *Agile Business Rule Development*,
DOI 10.1007/978-3-642-19041-4_17, © Springer-Verlag Berlin Heidelberg 2011

17.2   JRules and Rule Governance

The concept of operations introduced with Rule Studio and Rule Team Server suggests a clear separation of roles and development environments to author rules: Developers use Rule Studio to create the rule project foundation and all the related elements, such as rule flows, ruleset parameters, meta-properties, BOM definition, and rule templates, and to prototype rules. The business analysts use Rule Team Server to author the rules once the project structure and the BOM are stable. The developer uses Rule Studio to perform the following activities:

* Create the rule projects
* Define the BOM, the vocabulary, and the B2X mapping
* Define ruleset parameters
* Create the main rule flow and subflows
* Implement and test technical and business rules
* Test rule execution using unit test projects
* Define the rule model extension to support some functional requirements and the rule life cycle
* Build rule templates from some rules
* Synchronize with Rule Team Server

He then completes the work by defining in rule team server the different user roles, the ruleset ownership and access control, and the rule life cycle control. Some of this work is done by doing product configuration; some need code implementation and integration. It is easy to extend capability within RTS and redeploy a new version. Rule governance is a new field and needs an agreed-upon best practices before becoming product feature, and in most cases, it is linked to the company's way to manage change in its IT: each has his own view of controlling rule change management. The first configuration is about defining roles, we detailed that in next section. In Sect. 17.2.2, we will review the rule life cycle, and how to enforce a strict control linked to the user's role. Section 17.2.3 presents how RTS supports the ruleset life cycle with the concept of baseline and presents some versioning strategy rule governance team can apply. Finally in Sect. 17.2.4, we present the parallel development of next application release when ruleset in production are in maintenance.

17.2.1   Defining Roles in Rule Team Server

Any user of Rule Team Server must belong to at least one of the groups: rtsAdministrator, rtsConfigManager, or rtsUser.[1] A rule author will be part of

---

[1]There is the rtsInstaller role, but we do not need to detail it in this book, the product documentation provides explanation on it.

rtsUser. User roles are defined in the application server configuration file or user registry. From this first setting, the set of feature a given user can access are different. All the rule authors are rtsUser, and one could be administrator to have full control on the rule repository. The configuration manager user can access any configuration features like, for example, the ruleApp management, RES server and ruleset extractor definition, the rule solution for office location definition . . ..

As a standard practice, we add to those groups at least one group per line of business, responsible of one or more rulesets. For example, for the claim processing application, each group of users responsible of a ruleset (like adjudicator, processor, and fraud) is mapped to a permission role like processor, adjudication, and fraud. We can fine-grain access control by specifying dedicated groups for pure "read only" users, using a suffix like "-ro" (e.g., validation-ro). So a given user like "Mike" (see file example below) is a rtsUser but also a member of the processor groups and has write access to rule repository elements. A person can be part of multiple groups, which may be the rule steward from the rule management group (e.g., see Carol profile below).

Using Apache Tomcat 6.0,[2] groups and users are defined in tomcat-user.xml file, and we may set the following role definitions:

```
<role rolename="adjudication "/>
<role rolename="adjudication-ro"/>
<role rolename="fraud"/>

...

<user username="bill" roles="rtsUser, adjudication, writer"/>
<user username="mike" roles="rtsUser, processor, writer"/>
<user username="carol" roles="rtsUser, validation, fraud,adjudica-
tion, tester"/>
```

When the groups are defined in the application server, a RTS administrator must first add those groups as reference in the rule repository,[3] and then enforce using security for the different rule projects of the rule repository. This operation is done using the "Edit Project Security" feature. When the security is set on the rule project, a RTS user may see in the home page only the projects he can access.

---

[2]Each application server has its own way to support security definition. JRules Rule Execution Server and Team Server are packaged for different application servers. A specific document explains how to install the components to the different app server.

[3]Use the step "Setup Group" in the installation manager (Configure > installation manager).

17.2.2   Rule Life Cycle

In Rule Studio, the rules do not need to follow a strict lifecycle or if needed only the simplest one using two first steps like New and Defined. The governance really starts to apply for maintenance of the ruleset in production. It may be sooner when the project wants to add rule governance in scope of the user acceptance test, which is making sense to ensure a more complete quality assurance. Using such a life cycle, we would recommend publishing the rules to RTS only if rules are Defined. From there, the business analysts may take the lead on the ruleset development and may use a more complex rule life cycle. In this chapter, we use the more "classical" rule life cycle presented in previous chapter.

As seen in Chap. 8, the meta properties are defined in Rule Studio and uploaded to Rule Team Server using the installation manager. The *status* property is used to control the rule like cycle. The RTS user interface does not enforce control to the modifications of the *status* property: any role with write access to the rule project may change the value of this property. To enforce fine-grained control, RTS offers the integration of custom session controller to redefine the interactive behavior of RTS. The API interface ilog.rules.team-server.model .IlrSessionController defines a set of methods to check if the current user has the permission to create, delete, or update an element of the rule repository. The session controller may filter the list of possible status values the user can choose based on his role. This is achieved by the getPossibleValues(...) method, which returns a list of values, for example as a list of String. This method has first to verify whether the input parameter is the status property, if the rule element is newly created return the possible values of *New* or *Defined*, otherwise get possible allowed status by looking at the user's role. In Fig. 17.1, a rule tester may only access the status *Rejected* and *Validated*; therefore, the list returns the two corresponding string. The code may look like as shown below and uses the session to get the detail of the selected element (the rule) and its value:

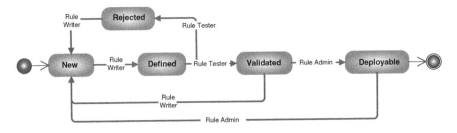

Fig. 17.1 Classical rule life cycle

```
public List<?> getPossibleValues(IlrElementHandle element,
            org.eclipse.emf.ecore.EStructuralFeature feature)
        throws IlrObjectNotFoundException {
    // we want to focus only on the status property.
    if (!isStatusPropertyCandidate(element, feature)) {
        return super.getPossibleValues(element,feature);
    }
    // Fetch the current status value
    IlrElementDetails elementDetails = session.getElementDetails
(element);
    List<String> list = new ArrayList<String>();
    // If the element is created then return the initial value for the
status
    if (element.isNew()) {
        list.add("New");
        list.add("Defined");
    } else {
        // search for possible values by looking at user role
        for (int i = 0; i < roles.length; i++) {
            String role = roles[i];
            if (session.isUserInRole(role)) {
                getStatusPossibleValuesByRole (role, elementDe-
tails.getRawValue(feature)+"",list);
            ..
        }
    }
    return list;
```

The session includes the current user's roles so it is easy to test if the roles like admin, tester, writer, or rtsAdministrator is one of the user's roles. The core of the permission logic is in the method getPossibleValueByRole, which is a list of test on current value and role:

```
private void getStatusPossibleValuesByRole (String role, String cur-
rentValue,List<String> list){
    if (currentValue == null) {
        list.add("New");
        list.add("Defined");
        return;
    }
    if (currentValue.equalsIgnoreCase("New")) { // any role
        list.add("New");
        list.add("Defined");
        return;
    }
```

```
    if (currentValue.equalsIgnoreCase("Rejected")) { // any role
        list.add("New");
        list.add("Rejected");  // stay on the same status
        return;
    }
    if (currentValue.equalsIgnoreCase("Validated")) {
        list.add("New");// any role
        list.add("Validated");
        if(role.equalsIgnoreCase("admin")) {
                list.add("Deployable");
        }
        return;
    }
    if (currentValue.equalsIgnoreCase("Defined")) {
        list.add("New");// any role
        list.add("Defined");
        if (role.equalsIgnoreCase("admin")||
role.equalsIgnoreCase("tester")) {
            list.add("Rejected");
            list.add("Deployable");
        }
        return;
    }
    if (currentValue.equalsIgnoreCase("Deployable")) {
        if (role.contains("admin")){
                list.add("New");
                list.add("Deployable");
        }….
```

Obviously, this implementation suffers from hardcoded roles and status values;
it may be more appropriate to use external file to define the transition between status
values according to role. Our goal was to present the intent and how it works.

As a good practice, it is better to subclass the default implementation (the `Ilr-DefaultSessionController`) of the interface `ilog.rules.teamserver.model.IlrSessionController`, so that we can keep the default behavior but enhance only the methods we want to change to support our own governance. When applying fine-grained permission management on rule elements, the method `checkUpdate` is called to check current permissions before committing a change to the element given as parameter. The DefaultSession-Controller has a reference to the current user session, the class is `ilog.rules.teamserver.model.IlrSession`. Any connection (remote client or web UI) to the RTS service layer creates a IlrSession instance. This is an important interface to know as soon as you want to customize RTS. There are a lot of samples in the product documentation to explain how to use the RTS public API. The session offers some capabilities to assess on which repository element the user did the last action. The code to access the status property looks like:

```
public void checkUpdate(IlrElementHandle element,
                        IlrElementDetails details,...
    details = this.session.getElementDetailsForThisHandle(element);
    //If we are checking a BusinessRule...
    if (details ! = null && details.isInstanceOf("BusinessRule")) {
    // Get the status of the rule
    String status = (String) details.getPropertyValue("status");
```

A permission management sample[4] presents in details how to limit what are the possible values a user can set to the *status* property depending of his own role. We will see later in this chapter how to use the same controller to prepare an event to notify another application, like a workflow engine, that some works are done on a business rule. The most interesting event, for example, is to report a change to a rule life cycle. For example, we want to create a work item for the tester-user work queue when the rule is set as *defined.*

17.2.3   Ruleset Baseline and Versioning

The second most important life cycle to control is the ruleset life cycle. Once a project is created within Rule Team Server, any changes to the rules are kept within the rule repository. When a project element is created, it is given the version number following a pattern like major_digit.minor_digit. The first digit is called the major version number and the second digit is called the minor version number. Major number can be used to support a release plan: each new release enforces increasing the major number. Minor number is used for update within a release. When rule authors make a modification to a project element, the minor version number is automatically increased by 1 (e.g., to version 1.1) except if he specifies that he wants to increase the major version number instead. Only the current version of an element can be edited or deleted. Previous versions can only be consulted. Previous versions can also be restored so that they become the current version. To do so the user needs to go to the History of the rule, select the version to restore, and then click the button "Restore Version."

---

[4]See WebSphere ILOG JRules BRMS V7.1 > Samples > Rule Team Server samples > Rule Team Server business rule management extension samples > Permission management sample.

Explore > Details > History   validateClaim-rules - Mexico100miles *(Action Rule)*

Q Explore Version Details | A Compare 2 Versions | Restore Version | Copy | Update Baseline(s) | ⑦ Help

Display by 10 ▾

	Version	▼ Changed By	Comment	Date	Used In Baseline
☐	1.0	rtsAdmin		11/3/08 2:07 PM	ruleset4test
☐	1.1	mike		11/11/08 9:04 PM	

2 Results

Fig. 17.2 Rule history – a rule part of a baseline

RTS uses the concept of baseline to "tag" the rules that are part of a project. This could be compared to the tagging operation done on the trunk with a conventional SCM tool. Baselines correspond to a snapshot of the state of a project at a given moment in time. A project can contain many baselines. When a baseline is frozen we cannot edit any of its project elements. Baselines are normally created and maintained by the user with the *Configuration Manager role*. Creating a baseline is simple: in the project tab, use the manage baseline section. It is recommended to follow a naming convention for the baseline name. We use name that represents the intent of the baseline, for example, specify the target platform for deployment when the baseline is for deployment. Once created it is possible to see using the history view what version of a rule is used in what baseline. This may be helpful for tracing back rules. Below the current version is 1.1, and version 1.0 is part of the ruleset4-test baseline. A baseline can only contain one version of an element (Fig. 17.2).

At any time, it is possible to display the differences between two rule versions to evaluate the changes done by the different users.

The baseline feature should support most use cases of rule management to control the ruleset integrity: any changes to the rule project that need to be deployed to the rule execution server can be part of a new baseline, used to build the ruleset. Any baseline created is frozen, which means a user cannot modify its contents by default. There are a set of features to support unfreezing an existing baseline to update the rules and then update back the baseline for future deployment. This approach works well when we can isolate the change to the rule and do not have other users modifying the rule project in parallel. This has to be the best practice, when there is a need to deliver a fix to a ruleset by applying the unfreeze-update baseline approach.

There is one important thing to avoid losing work done on the rule project after a baseline was done, and someone is trying to restore an old baseline, for example, to fix a rule in that baseline. When we restore a baseline, Rule Team Server creates a new version of all the project elements found in that baseline, which are copies of the designated version, and makes these the current state of the project.

Before the baseline restore, the repository may look like:

After the baseline restore operation, the current version of the rules are the one in the second blue rectangle, the rules in green are not easily accessible.

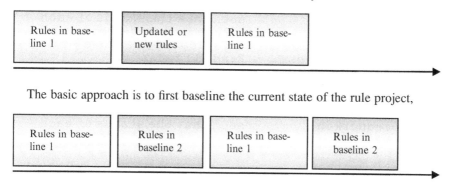

The basic approach is to first baseline the current state of the rule project,

restore the previous one, work on the rules, unfreeze-update the baseline, extract a ruleset, and deploy the hot fix. Then the last operation is to restore the last created baseline (e.g., baseline 2) so the rule repository is back to his state before the fix. The process needs to be well coordinated so that everybody is aware that, for the duration of the update, the current RTS version of the project is in fact an historical version.

A special baseline called the "recycle bin" contains project elements that are deleted from the current state of the project. This "recycle bin" is used to restore the deleted element.

When we deploy from RTS to any RES, RTS automatically adds a RuleApp property to the generated RuleApp called ilog.rules.teamserver. baseline with a value set to the deployment baseline created in RTS. An administrator can use the RES console to view this property to correlate the contents of the deployed RuleApp with a baseline in RTS. Baselines are used to control the integrity of the ruleset over the development life cycle and to provide traceability over which environment the ruleset was deployed. Before deploying to the test or production environments, the rule administrator has to create a baseline. Once agreed upon the rulesets are deployed to the production environment as well as the simulation environment if any. Recall, from Chap. 15, that business user can use a simulation environment to perform "what-if" analysis over a subset of production data, to continuously improve the quality of the ruleset, by comparing KPIs. The source of truth becomes the rule repository managed by the production RTS. The business users are executing the rule change process in this environment. The administrator of the environment deploys the ruleset on demand to the different rule execution servers of the production.

When building a baseline, it is important to consider implementing different queries to extract the rules targeted for the different environments. Table 17.1 lists the possible queries to support different ruleset extraction patterns taking into account the rule life cycle as defined in Fig. 17.1.

Table 17.1 Extraction query

Goal	Query
Extract all rules for development	Find all rules such that the status of each rule is one of { Deployable , Validated , Defined }
Extract all the rules for final testing before production	Find all rules such that the status of each rule is one of { Validated , Deployable }
Extract all rules for the production	Find all rules such that the status of each rule is one of { Deployable }

As a complement of query definition, we can develop queries to change the status of the rules. The following is an example of query changing the status property of a rule from *Defined to Validated*.

```
Find all rules
    such that the status of each rule  is Defined
Do set the status of each rule  to Validated
```

17.2.4 Deeper Changes

When the project team is working in parallel, for example, to support implementation of the next application release and the business team is working on the ruleset maintenance of current release, change management is more complex. For the next release, the development team may work on changing the underlying data model, prepare new rulesets, but most likely is not changing existing rulesets. Business user uses RTS to do so. In traditional software development, parallel development is covered by sophisticated configuration management tool using the concept of branching. A main branch (also named trunk) holds the development of next release where code elements are versioned. The maintenance of the code deployed in production is done in another branch. To avoid going too far in the detailed of SCM tool in this book, most of the time the code modified in one branch to fix a production issue, for example, may be merged back to the new code for the next application release. This is still rare, as most of the time, an issue can wait for the next release. But in the case of ruleset maintenance, the updated rules are not to fix issues, but to adapt the business logic, so merging has to happen.

There is no concept of branches in RTS, so any merging operation needs to be performed manually. In fact those merging operation are linked to the modification of the BOM and the XOM. A BOM refactoring may impact existing rules. The practice is having the developer synchronizing from RTS to Studio before doing the BOM update and then once rules are modified, synchronized back to RTS. The side effect is to not have any person modifying the rules in RTS rule repository during these operations because the rules use the old BOM and may not work with the modified BOM. Any change to the BOM can only take minutes, so it should be easy to apply such practices without impacting the overall team. This is the "out of the box" experience and works well in most case. Still there are requests, sometime, to support a multiple branches approach as we do in classical software development using a SCM tool.

As of today, RTS rule repository does not support managing different branches, but there are some approaches the team can use. The simplest mechanism, to manage multiple branches of a same project both in Rule Studio and RTS, is to use one distinct RTS data source per project branch, as illustrated in Fig. 17.3.

The developer starts by creating the different project branches using the source code control system, for example, release-2.0 and release-1.0. Then he imports the rule projects on each branch in Rule Studio in separate Eclipse workspaces so that there is no conflict in the rule UUIDs. The next step is to configure RTS and create different data sources per branch; this is done using the installation manager of RTS and using different database URL. The last operation is an export of each project from Rule Studio to the appropriate RTS data source (URL_1 and URL2). Business users and developers work as usual on the selected branch by choosing the appropriate data source for RTS (different URL). When there is a need to integrate all the change done on a branch, the RTS rule project corresponding to the branch should be synchronized back with the Rule Studio project, and the SCM should be used to perform the merge with the trunk. The main advantage of this solution is that there is no need for product customization, either on RTS or Rule Studio. All the

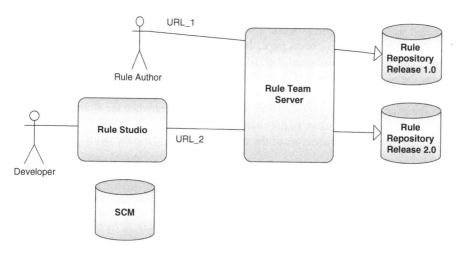

Fig. 17.3 Two data sources for two branches

features needed are available out of the box. The process can support complex
cases involving BOM and rule flow changes, and it keeps the integrity of JRules'
concept of operations: business users keep performing their work using RTS only
while IT supports major project updates (BOM, rule flow) through Rule Studio. The
disadvantages involve having multiple RTS database for each branch that needs
concurrent development, and users need to be careful about using the proper data
source or workspace that corresponds to the project branch they intend to work on.
A little discipline overcomes this issue.

Another mechanism to support branching is to use different rule projects for the
same decision service: the team is working on adjudicateClaim-rulesR2 in parallel
of the business team working on adjudicateClaim-rulesR1. When the merge operation is triggered, the developer can synchronize the previous release back from RTS
to Rule studio and use SCM and diff tools ("Team Synchronize" perspective in
eclipse) to evaluate and report the changes to the next release. Once merged the
ruleset is propagated back to RTS. This approach can be error prone and need some
care when merging the changes.

17.3 The Rule Change Management Process

In this section, we propose to make the rule change process, outlined in the
previous chapter,[5] actionable using JRules and a BPM product. We are not
presenting a specific BPM product; we rather present how to leverage the two
technologies to implement the process and we highlight some of the implementation pattern for the integration between Rule Team Server and BPM product.
The choice to combine the two types of product is driven by the fact that the rule
change process includes a set of human activities like the ruleset update, the
change review, the rule testing, and the ruleset deployment, which could be automated by an executable process.

When starting from a blank page, designing a business process starts by looking at
the main business entities and their life cycle. In this case, the main business object
may be a change request (`ChangeRequestBO`) to let the business user,
initiator of the change, logs all the information about the intent, business motivation
of the change, the rule project name, and any rule name when the change applies to
existing rule. The structure of the change request is defined to handle the parameters
entered by the different actors of the process. We could use the definition as shown
in Fig. 17.4.

We can use a basic life cycle for the change request including the following
states: *initiated, under review, under implementation, under test, deployable,
closed, canceled, and rejected.* The rule change process should have activities

---

[5]See Sect. 17.3 – Fig. 17.6.

ChangeRequestType
id [1..1] int
initiatorName [0..1] string
title [0..1] string
intent [1..1] string
businessMotivation [1..1] string
ruleProjectName [1..1] string
existingRules [0..*]
scopeAnalysis [0..*] string
status [1..1] string
creationDate [1..1] dateTime
newRule [1..1] boolean

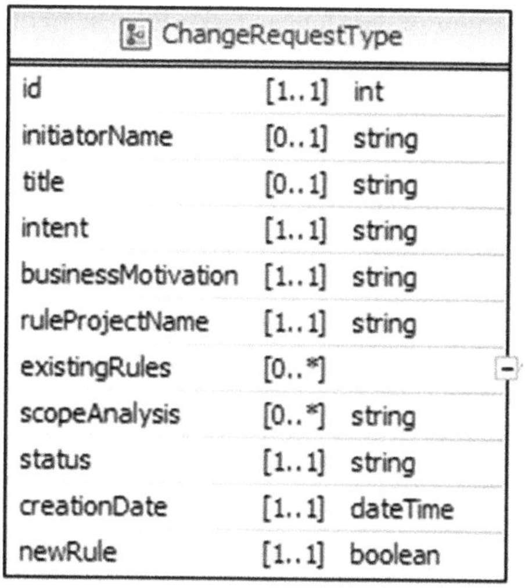

Fig. 17.4 Change request business entity

Policy Owner
Rule Analyst
Rule Author
Enter Change Request
Assess Scope/ Impact
Scope Decision
Reject
Proceed
Execute Rule Authoring

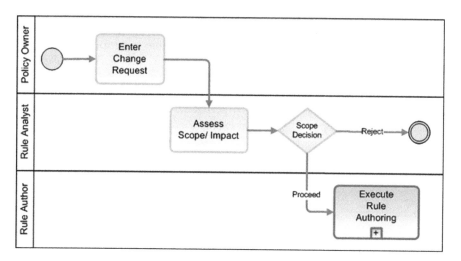

Fig. 17.5 Beginning of the executable rule change management process

which support this life cycle. Figure 17.5 presents the beginning of the executable process. It is incomplete, but we use it to present the main concepts of this section.

17.3.1 Process Implementation

There are multiple ways to implement the rule change process using a BPM product: a pure human centric process, where the change request progresses in

the flow of pure human tasks. Each actor of the process receives a work assignment, performs the work using the needed tool(s), like rule team server, and then comes back to the work queue to notify the running process that his work is completed. The implementation can support custom screens to drive the information gathering and the communication with the user. Such communication can include description of the rule analysis, the explanation of the work done on the rule repository, the test report, and the status of the deployment to production. There is no integration with rule team server. This could be a first version of the process as it has no integration.

The second type of process uses a more integrated approach where the rule life cycle is coupled with the change request life cycle. RTS may send events when the rule changes state. The process can correlate such events to assess if the activity is completed, so it can continue the process flow. We will detail how RTS can send event in Sect. 17.3.3.

For any process approach, the business policy owner may use a web-based user interface to initiate the process, by clicking on "Create business rule change request" link within one page of the enterprise portal. Basically, each time a rule change process is started a process instance is created and exists until reaching a termination node. The process is long-running process, and so process instances are persisted in process data store. When the process is started and is waiting for a human action, the user, responsible to perform the activity, will receive a work item assigned to his work queue. The work queue is also accessible using a web UI and offers a set of actions to complete the task. In the rule change process, each actor of the process receives the request in his "My tasks" area and performs the expected activities: author rules, review change request, review test report, etc. ... An example of such an entry form is shown in Fig. 17.6.

The information about the change request may even include the reference to the rule in the rule repository. Rule Team Server uses the concept of *permanent link* to

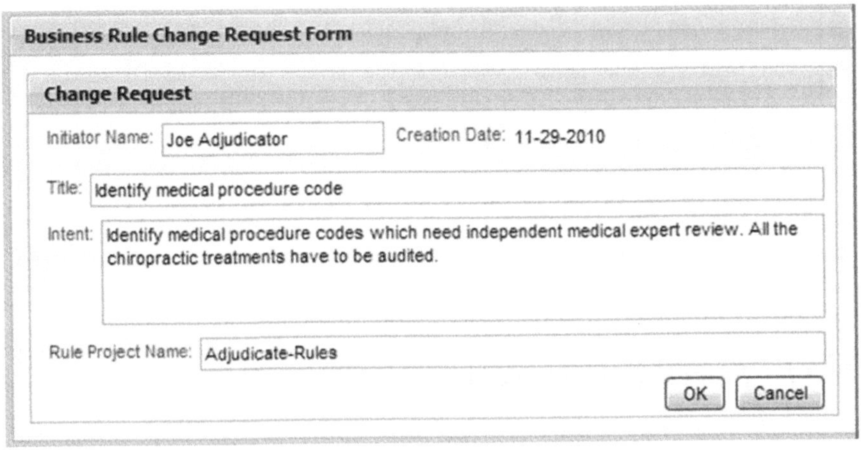

Business Rule Change Request Form

Change Request

Initiator Name: Joe Adjudicator   Creation Date: 11-29-2010

Title: Identify medical procedure code

Intent: Identify medical procedure codes which need independent medical expert review. All the chiropractic treatments have to be audited.

Rule Project Name: Adjudicate-Rules

OK   Cancel

Fig. 17.6 Enter change request

uniquely reference rule element in the rule repository. This capability is accessible using helper classes,[6] and the links may be exposed within a custom user interface, for example, coupled with the change request form: the list of rules, the user may select, comes from RTS (see Sect. 17.3.3). As an alternate, the simplest UI will have a rule name entry field, which the user will manually fill.

Once initiated the change request needs to be analyzed to assess the scope of the change and to evaluate the cost of the implementation. In the case of the business rule application, normally the impact is very limited, and the analysis should not take long. Nevertheless the change request information should include all the needed information so the assessment activity can be done quickly. The business analyst role should document the assessment as part of the change request, by editing the potential impact. The scope assessment task below is showing the different paths (proceed, reject, and cancel) the rule analyst can take. Using an agile approach, aiming to use minimal documentation, if the change is obvious, just referencing the impacted rules should be sufficient as of documentation (Fig. 17.7).

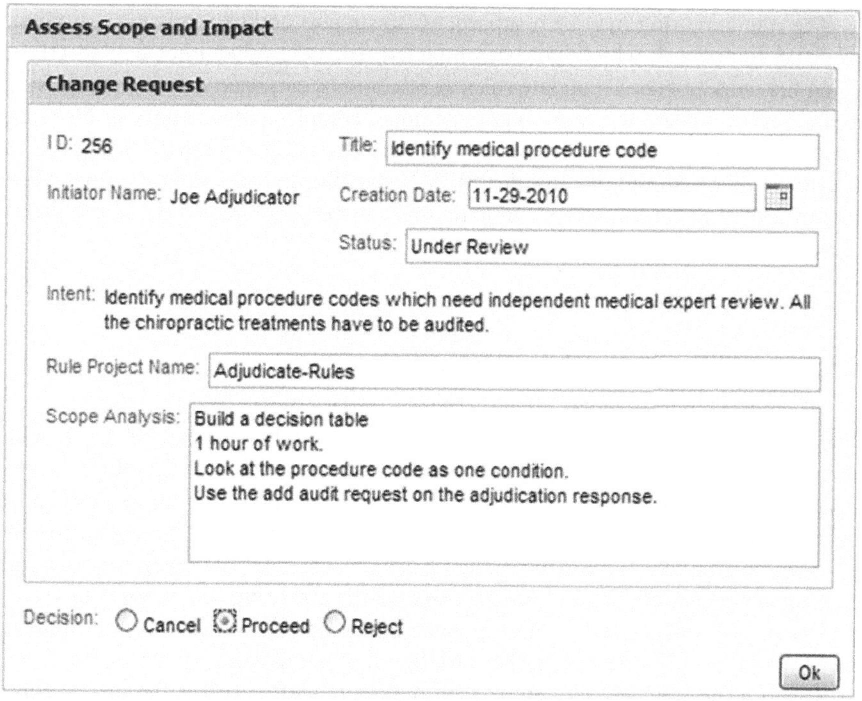

Fig. 17.7 Assess scope task

---

[6]See JRules API documentation class IlrPermanentLinkHelper.

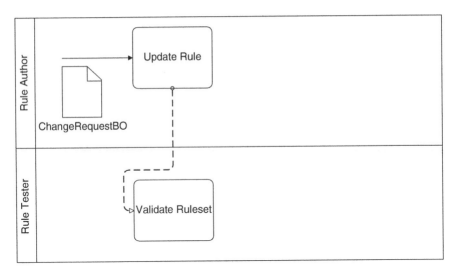

Fig. 17.8 Extract from the rule change process map

The rule authoring may be a subprocess to support complex process definition, or just a human task which will be completed when the rule author will specify it using his work queue. To update rules, a rule author can open a session with Rule Team Server, update the rules, and once done, completes his activity in his work queue so that the process instance continues to the next activity. Figure 17.8 illustrates this chaining of activities. BPMN specifies to use a message flow when the process is going through swim lane: this can be illustrated as the rule tester is receiving a message on his work queue.

17.3.2   RTS and Workflow Integration

What is interesting is to integrate the rule life cycle and the ruleset life cycle with the process activities. For example, when a rule author once completing his rule update, changes the rule status to *Defined* the process instance can be notified of such event. When all the rules listed in the change requests are implemented, the process can continue to route the change request to the next performer, for example, a rule tester. If not all the rules are yet *Defined*, the authoring task is not completed, and the process may trigger timer to generate message or escalation procedure to wake up the person supposed to perform the rule modification.

The "update rule" activity ends when the rule author specifies the task is completed. In our integration, we want to control that all the rules listed as part of the change request are in *Defined* state. Rule Team Server is then an event generator, consumed by the workflow engine. The event includes information about the rule and its status. A simple components view may look like as shown in Fig. 17.9.

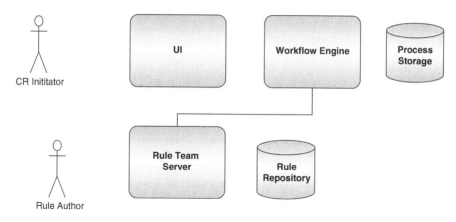

Fig. 17.9 Integration RTS – BPM – component view

17.3.3 Getting Rule Status Modification Event from RTS

The purpose of this section is to present how RTS can generate event when, for example, the rule status property changes. This capability can be use to generate intermediate events the business process engine may listen. RTS provides an extension point to customize the behavior of the user interaction with the repository, with the class `IlrDefaultSessionControler`. This class offers a set of operations we can override. To create an event when the status property is changed we want to look at two methods, `onCommitElement` and `elementCommitted`. There are code samples in the product documentation with explanation of the API.

The `onCommitElement` method is called before committing an element to the repository, so we can use it to get the previous status. The `elementCommitted` is called just after an element has been committed to the rule repository and can be used to get the updated status and to prepare and send an event. Both methods need to use their parameters to access the element committed and have access to the RTS session (teamserver.model.IlrSession), which allows connecting to RTS service layer with all the information on the current user. The session is an important object to understand as it is used to connect to RTS and provides all the information on the current project, baseline, and element under work. The elements of the rule repository are represented using a meta model, which is based on Eclipse Model Framework EMF. Without going too much into the detail, each method needs to access the element committed and use both the session and the meta model to access to the element property like a "status" property. As the session has information on the name of the rule, the name of the project, it is easy to build an event from this information. For the fun, here is an example of code with inline comments to explain the code intent:

```
public void elementCommitted(
    IlrCommitableObject cobject,
    IlrElementHandle newHandle) throws IlrObjectNotFoundException {
  // initialization code not shown
  MyEventClass anEvent = ….
  // start by verifying we are working with element as defined in team
server model
    Object detail = session.getElementDetails(newHandle);
    if (!(detail instance of IlrModelElement)) return;
    // the element needs to be a business rule - use the session for that
    EClass eclass = newHandle.eClass();
    if (!session.getBrmPackage().getBRLRule().isSuperTypeOf(eclass))
        return ;
    IlrModelElement element = (IlrModelElement) detail;
    //retrieve information from this element likename, uuid
    anEvent.setCommitterName(element.getLastChangedBy());
    anEvent.setCommittedElementName(element.getName());
    anEvent.setCommittedElementUUID(element.getUuid());
    //The project name comes from the session
    IlrRuleProject project = session.getWorkingBaseline().getProject();
    anEvent.setProjectName(project.getName());
```

The last piece of code is used to access the "status" property.

```
EClass eClass = (EClass) element.eClass();
EStructuralFeature f;
// Retrieve all properties for the class and search for the 'status'
EList<?> eAllStructuralFeatures = eClass.getEAllStructuralFeatures();
for (int j = 0; j < eAllStructuralFeatures.size(); j++) {
        f = eClass.getEStructuralFeature(j);
        if ("status".equalsIgnoreCase(f.getName())) {
            break;
        }
}
// get the value of the status property
Object object = elementDetails.getRawValue(f);
anEvent.setValueOfStatusProperty(object.toString());
```

The last part of the code could send the event to a JMS queue or topic so a consumer or subscriber can process it.

17.3.4 Getting the List of Rules from RTS

The session is interesting as it can be used to remote connect to RTS. So any java code can connect to RTS to access rule repository information. For example, a Web

UI can get the list of rules in a rule project so the user can populate fine-grained information in the change request. In this section, we propose a basic code to do so. The code uses a remote session created from a factory using the server URL, the jdbc datasource used for the rule repository, the userid and password to connect to team server. This code could have different input parameter, like the project name, and is returning a list of strings, representing each unique rule name.

```
// Connect to Rule Team Server
IlrSessionFactory factory = new IlrRemoteSessionFactory();
factory.connect(login, password, serverUrl, datasource);
session = factory.getSession();
// Get the project by name
IlrRuleProject ruleProject = (IlrRuleProject) IlrSession-
Helper.getProjectNamed(session, projectName);
// Open the current baseline
baseline = IlrSessionHelper.getCurrentBaseline(session, ruleProject);
session.setWorkingBaseline(baseline);
```

Then to search for an element in the repository, there is a helpful function on the session object called findElements. This method uses some search criteria which is based on the Business Query Language (BQL), we saw in previous chapters and in Sect. 17.2.3. So getting the list of business rules is using two lines of code:

```
IlrSearchCriteria criteria = new IlrDefaultSearchCriteria("Find all busi-
ness rules");
List listOfRules = session.findElements(
                   criteria,
                   IlrModelConstants.ELEMENT_DETAILS);
```

The objects within the list are IlrElementSummary, which includes methods to access name and properties of the element:

```
IlrElementSummary ruleSummary = (IlrElementSummary) listO-
fRules.get(i);
String ruleName = ruleSummary.getName();
String status=(String)ruleSummary.getPropertyValue("status");
String[]paths=IlrSessionHelper.getPath(session, ruleSummary,
baseline);
```

The IlrSessionHelper is a utility class, which helps to access elements within the session. Here we get the path to the rule, so that we can build a string including the rule package path and the rule name like VerifyAccidentLocation/SupportedCountries. The API is rich and permits to do interesting things for fine controlling the rule governance processes. We do not see a lot of teams doing so, as rule governance is still a new practice in the field.

17.4   Summary

Rule governance is easily supported with the JRules components such as rule team
server using existing features. Sometimes light configuration or customization
needs to be done when the IT wants to enforce control over the rule life cycle.
We also presented a potential integration with a workflow engine using a lightweight version using only human activities, and one using a light integration with
rule team server to receive event when the rule status change. Using BPM to define
an executable rule change process makes perfectly sense when company has both
products in their portfolio. The justification to start a big project on that may be
difficult to justify, when IT budgets are under constraints, but with human centric
product it is a question of days to put in place such process.

17.5   Further Reading

For more technical information and tutorials, the product documentation is accessible at http://publib.boulder.ibm.com/infocenter/brjrules/v7r1/index.jsp

Part VIII
Epilogue

Chapter 18
Epilogue

18.1 It Is About People, Process, and Technology

To borrow a much-used IT cliché, successful business rule application development relies on a combination of people, process, and technology.

- *It is about people*. Sure it is! Software development gurus have been saying it for decades. But what do they mean? It is about people as in *knowledgeable, skillful, communicative, productive, positive, team player*, kind of people. HR knows that, IT people know that, project managers know that, and productivity studies have borne that out for decades. In this book, we identified a number of roles and responsibilities, identified the required skills (Chap. 3), and strove to provide those skills through a combination of problem/issue analysis and solution patterns. It is also about the people the software is intended to serve, i.e., the *business people*, who try to provide value to customers while making money in the process, and the *end-customer*. We have been told, many times over, that we need to involve "the business" and the "users" in our software development projects to make sure that we address their needs – and that they use the software. We knew that that made sense, but we were not sure what we could have them do or review during our projects, beyond supplying the requirements at the very beginning and testing the software at the very end. The agile methods have been saying it too. But what possibly could I meet them about in the between while architects are architecting and developers are coding? It is the business rules! And because we are delivering rulesets incrementally, they will remain engaged throughout the project ... we are almost saying that the business rules approach is a *prerequisite* for the business-people-involvement aspect of agility.
- *It is about the process*. Naturally, we need to have in place systematic, reproducible processes to harness the people's knowledge, skills, and work towards achieving the desired outcome. *Process* does not contradict *agility*; in fact, we talk about *agile processes*! To borrow from Barry Boehm and Richard Turner's (2003) book title, finding the right dosage between *agility* and *discipline* is a *balancing act*. That is what we tried to with ABRD. ABRD is *disciplined* about creating opportunities for, and managing, communications between the various project stakeholders, in the various cycles, with greater frequency and intensity

during the rule harvesting (Chap. 3) and rule prototyping (Chap. 4) cycles. It is *agile* because it is incremental and iterative. It is also agile because of *what happens* during these interactive workshops.

- *It is about the technology.* Of course, technology matters. We have yet to get involved in a project that failed *because of* technology. However, technology can make your life easier. Technology is the medium within which the various solutions take shape. A good technology either provides the solution for you, out of the box, or provides the proper ingredients for you to implement the solution on your own. A BRMS that is missing some basic fundamental feature or that has an awkward API will have you divert a significant amount of resources just to implement the basic infrastructure.

18.2   Success – and Failure – Factors

In this section, we provide some parting advice regarding success factors, as well as project risks. Unsurprisingly, most have to do with *people*, including their *commitment*, *motivation*, *discipline*, and *skills*.

- *Management commitment.* If you are starting out with the business rules approach, management commitment is critical, as it is with any important transformation that you try to implement within the organization. From our experience, anyone manager or decision maker above you, working *against* the approach – or against you – can derail your project, even if decision makers above *them* are committed. It takes lots of political skill to make sure that *all issues* have *appropriate visibility* along the command chain so that lack of support – or outright hostility – gets addressed at the management level.

- *Explain the impact of rule automation.* Many rule projects consist of *automating* currently manual decision processes using a BRMS. You need to get the buy-in of the subject matter experts, from whom you will elicit the business rules. The SMEs will undoubtedly, and understandably, feel threatened by the project, and you need to address those concerns up-front.[1] This is as much a project management issue as it is an HR issue.

- *Know when to listen and when to lead.* The importance of listening to business needs cannot be overstated. Business analysis is as much as people's skill as it is a technical/process skill. That being said, you need to know when to *lead*. This is true for requirements, in general, and even more so with business rules. A case in point: you will often find that decades of *nonbusiness-oriented* implementation of *business rules* have had a corrupting influence on SMEs and business analysts, who can no longer think of terms of business qualities, business decisions, or business

---

[1] We had one customer whose rule harvesting efforts were derailed by noncooperative SMEs. While there was an element of work displacement involvement, almost caricatural project management was largely to blame.

terminology, but will speak in terms of arcane codes, weird processes, and byzantine terminology. It is OK to disagree with business – and show them a better way.

• *Do not let architects run your project.* Architecture is important; in fact four chapters of this book *are* about architecture. However, the business rules approach is not *just* another architectural style. Sure, treating business logic as data that can be packaged and deployed separately from the other code is valuable. But the business rules approach is about *much more* than that. We have worked with a customer that was an early adopter of the business rules approach, and that had a corporate business rules expertise center, and a great team of extremely competent architects and developers. In fact, some used to joke about their heavy IT focus, which served them well in other areas: "we are not a <product> company, but a software company that sells <product>". They spent lots of resources and ingenuity on tooling and infrastructure, but fairly little on business analysis. As far as we are concerned, they did not treat business rules as *business assets*, but considered them still as IT assets.

• *Remember the rules, you know, the if-then things?* This is a corollary of the previous point and manifests itself in many ways. We have seen customers simply *translate* business logic expressions from their legacy implementation language into rule languages of their BRMS – JRules in this case. Again, that is (almost) totally missing the point. In this case, the *business rules* are barely *rules*, in the production system sense (see Sect. 3.1), and not business oriented. They are not understandable by "normal" business people, they are highly procedural – as opposed to *declarative* – strongly coupled, and very hard to maintain. Another manifestation of this lack of emphasis on *the rules* is the task assignment within the project. As mentioned in Chap. 11, we have seen many customers that assign rule authoring to their most junior staff. The thinking goes "they are young: they can pick up a new [programming?] language in no time". That is unfortunate because learning a rule language is the easy part. Good rule authoring requires a deep understanding of the business logic and knowledge of the rule coding patterns (see Chap.9). A junior person is likely to lack both.

• *Do not let developers write the rules.* This is a tough one. One of the objects – and tenets – of the business rules approach is to empower business to take over the ownership and management of business rules. Part of that empowerment is rule authoring. In *practice*, business teams often lack the *resources* to take over rule authoring and maintenance, both in terms of headcount and in terms of skills. Thus, they more than willingly let IT handle the authoring and maintenance part.[2] While this is an acceptable transitional arrangement for the first project release, we should make sure that, *ultimately*, business takes over. This does not necessarily mean retraining barely computer-literate policy managers; it can also happen by moving IT people over to the business side. This results into a cleaner separation of responsibilities between business and IT and will pave the way for a gradual takeover of business rules by business.

---

[2]And handle the fallout, in case of project failure.

18.3   Where to from Here

We wish we had a crystal ball that could tell us where the technology is headed within the next decade and beyond. Failing that, we can at least project from the trends that we have seen emerge over the past decade:

- *It is about business empowerment.* IT, which had long been perceived as an enabling technology for business excellence, has become, of late, a bottleneck for business agility. The lag time between business decisions and their IT support has simply become intenable. A number of technologies of the past dozen or so years have aimed at *empowering* business to implement business changes directly. Whether we are talking about *business* rules or *business* process management, in both cases we are *exposing* business logic in a way that business can express, can understand, and ultimately, can implement. This changes a number of things about the way we do business and the way we do IT, and is key to better business – IT alignment. From a people and process point of view, business will continue its move to the front and center of IT development, with IT moving to a supporting role. From a technological point of view, it will take continued innovation to expose, out of the increasing complexity and overwhelming clunkery of IT systems, intuitive, unambiguous, and safe *business abstractions* that business can manipulate. The role of IT is then to provide the illusion of simplicity, with enough safeguards to ensure security. That is no small feat.
- *It is all in the data.* This overloaded motto means several things. Being able to express business logic as *data* is a key paradigm in empowering business. Lest we oversimplify, we would expect business (policy setters, rule makers) to think in terms of desired outcomes, while IT thinks in terms of procedures. In some fundamental way, a rule engine reads statements of desired outcomes, expressed as declarative business rules, and transforms them into a decision-making procedure. Similarly, a workflow engine reads a description of a workflow process, in terms of tasks and dependencies between tasks, and turns it into a process. We can also read "it is all in the data" in relation to analytics. Organizations have been capitalizing on production data to extract valuable business information, some of it in the form of business rules; we have to look at business rules under the broader perspective of decision management and integrate the analytics stream into the ABRD methodology.
- *It is all about the cloud.* We can think of the cloud as the ultimate dematerialization of enterprise IT infrastructure along the physically bound – dematerialized spectrum, starting with monolithic applications on the physically bound end of the spectrum, to distributed applications, to service-oriented applications, to cloud computing. In this book, we have talked about deploying rules to a *rule execution service*, but with the implicit assumption that that service is proprietary and internal to an organization. But how about BraaS, or business rules as a service? Actually, that has been happening for decades! FICO's credit scoring *is* business rules as a service. Banks, government agencies, retailers, and utilities

submit personal identification information for prospective customers and get a rule-driven credit report. In addition to this, one-shoe-fits-all credit report, FICO also develops *custom* credit reports for some of its corporate customers. An interesting feature of credit rating agencies (FICO, Equifax, Transunion, Experian, etc.) is that the data they use to compile those reports is based on raw data submitted by those same banks, government agencies, retailers, utilities, and so forth. Can this business model be replicated for mortgage underwriting, insurance policy underwriting, or claim processing? What are the implications on data privacy, competitive financial information, and proprietary business rules? Interesting questions to ponder.

Bibliography

This bibliography reflects the age we live in: we draw our information not only from traditional publications and media (books, professional, and academic journal articles), but *mostly* from information available on the web. Hence the different categories:

- *Books.* These are good old paper books.
- *Articles and papers.* These include professional, trade, or academic publications.
- *Web sites.* Here we grouped web-bound organized sources of information, including blogs, conference web sites, technologies (e.g., WS-BPEL, EPF, J2EE, etc.), trade or standards organizations (e.g., OMG, the Business Rules Group), and on-line, or mixed-media (paper and on-line) publications.
- *Documents.* Although these are mostly available on the web, they do not represent elaborate sources of information like the many portals we find under web sites.
- *Tools.* We list some of the tools that are relevant to the book.

Books

- Kent Beck, *Test-Driven Development by Example*, Addison Wesley, 2003
- Barry Boehm and Richard Turner, *Balancing Agility and Discipline: A Guide for the Perplexed*, Addison-Wesley (2003)
- Thomas Erl, *Service-Oriented Architecture: Concepts, Technology & Design* Prentice Hall/PearsonPTR (2005). ISBN 0-131-85858-0
- Thomas Erl, *SOA Patterns*, Prentice-Hall (2009) ISBN 0136135161
- Charles Forgy, "On the efficient implementation of production systems". Ph.D. Thesis, Carnegie-Mellon University, 1979
- Martin Fowler, *Patterns of Enterprise Application Architecture*, Addison Wesley, 2002, ISBN 0321127420)
- Erich Gamma, Richard Helm, Ralph Johnson, and John Vlissides, *Design Patterns: Elements of Reusable Design*, published by Addison-Wesley, 1994
- Barbara von Halle, *Business Rules Applied*, John Wiley & Sons, 2001, ISBN 0-471-41293-7
- Gregor Hohpe and Bobby Woolf's book *Enterprise Integration Patterns* (Addison Wesley, 2003, ISBN 0321200683)
- Ivar Jacobson, Grady Booch and James Rumbaugh, *The Unified Software Development Process*, Addison-Wesley (1999). ISBN 0-201-57169-2
- Mike Keith and Merrick Schincariol, *Pro JPA 2: Mastering the Java™ Persistence API (Expert's Voice in Java Technology)*, Apress (2009)
- Hafedh Mili, Ali Mili, Sherif Yacoub, and Edward Addy, Reuse-Based Software Engineering: Techniques, organizations, and controls, John Wiley & Sons, 2002, ISBN 0-471-39819-5

J. Boyer and H. Mili, *Agile Business Rule Development*,
DOI 10.1007/978 3-642-19041-4, © Springer-Verlag Berlin Heidelberg 2011

- Tony Morgan, Business Rules and Information Systems: Aligning IT with Business Goals, Addison-Wesley, 2002, ISBN 0-201-74391-4
- Ronald G. Ross, Principles of the Business Rules Approach, Addison Wesley, 2003, ISBN 0-201-78893-4
- Naeem Siddiqui, *Credit Risk Scorecards: Developing and Implementing Intelligent Credit Scoring* by John Wiley & Sons (2006), ISBN 9780471754510
- James Taylor, and Neil Raden, *Smart Enough Systems: How to Deliver Competitive Advantage by Automating Hidden Decisions,* Prentice Hall (2007)

Articles and Papers (Professional Journals, Trade Magazines, etc.)

- Barbara von Halle, "What Exactly Are Business Rules", in *The Business Rule Revolution: Running Business the Right Way*, von Halle & L. Goldberg eds, Happy About Info, 2006, ISBN 1-600005-013-1
- Randall Davis & Jonathan J. King, "The Origin of Rule-Based Systems in AI", chapter 2 in Rule-Based Expert Systems: The MYCIN Experiments of the Stanford Heuristic Programming Project, eds B. Buchanan & E. Shorliffe, Addison-Wesley, 1984, pp. 20–52
- Alasdair Urquhart, "Emil Post", in Handbook of the History of Logic, vol 5: Logic from Russell to Church, Dov M. Gabbay and John Woods Eds, pp. 429–478
- Allen Newell, 1973, "Production systems: Models of control structures". In Visual Information Processing, ed. W. G. Chase, pp. 463–526. New York: Academic Press.
- Michael P. Papazoglou, Paolo Traverso, Schahram Dustdar, Frank Leymann, "Service-Oriented Computing: State of the Art and Research Challenges", IEEE Computer, nov. 2007, pp. 38–45
- Michael Huhns & Munindar P. Singh, "Service-Oriented Computing: Key Concepts and Principles", IEEE Internet Computing, Jan/Feb 2005, pp. 75–81
- Olaf Zimmermann, Pal Krogdahl & Clive Gee, "Elements of Service-Oriented Analysis and Design", http://www.ibm.com/developerworks/webservices/library/ws-soad1/
- Kyo C. Kang, Sholom G. Cohen, James A. Hess, William E. Novak, A.Spencer Peterson, Feature-Oriented Domain Analysis (FODA) – Feasibility Study, CMU/SEI-90-TR-21, Software Engineering Institute, Nov, 1990

Web Sites

- Blogs: there are too many, high quality, informative blogs on business rules. Here we list the ones we referenced in specific parts of the book:
  - Pierre Berlandier explores different alternatives for structuring ruleset which can impact both performance and management. See http://www.ibm.com/developerworks/websphere/library/techarticles/1003_berlandier/ 1003_berlandier.html
  - Eric Charpentier reported in his blog at http://www.primatek.ca/blog/2009/11/01/business-rules-governance-and-management-part-iv-stakeholders/
  - John D McGregor at http://www.cs.clemson.edu/~johnmc/joop/col3/column3.html details the component testing, needs, and approach
  - James Taylor on Everything Decision Management at http://jtonedm.com/
- Conferences: there are *many many academic* conferences on a variety of areas related to business rules, including the main AI conferences (AAAI, IJCAI, ICTAI, etc), that would be too numerous to mention. Here we simply list the two main indutrial conferences on *business rules*:

- The *business rules forum* (http://www.businessrulesforum.com) is an annual conference for people interested in the business rules approach and is a good opportunity for learning about new product features and cutting-edge thinking
- Rule Fest (http://www.rulefest.org)
- Technologies
  - ABRD is an Eclipse Process Framework practice plugin readers may find at http://www.eclipse.org/epf and within the practice library at http://www.eclipse.org/epf/downloads/praclib/praclib_downloads.php
  - BPEL-WS http://www.oasis-open.org/committees/tc_home.php?wg_abbrev=wsbpel
  - Business Process Modeling Notation, at http://www.bpmn.org
  - DAO (Sun Core J2EE Patterns - Data Access Object), at http://java.sun.com/blueprints/corej2eepatterns/Patterns/DataAccessObject.html
  - *Eclipse Process Framework* (http://www.eclipse.org/epf)
  - IBM WebSphere ILOG JRules product documentation can be found at http://publib.boulder.ibm.com/infocenter/brjrules/v7r1/index.jsp
  - The java architecture for XML binding (JAXB) specification and documentation is at http://www.oracle.com/technetwork/articles/javase/index-140168.html
  - Java Connector Architecture, http://java.sun.com/j2ee/connector/
  - Java 2 Enterprise Edition (J2EE), http://java.sun.com/j2ee/overview.html
  - Java Management Extensions (JMX) at http://java.sun.com/javase/technologies/core/mntr-mgmt/javamanagement/
  - Java Persistence API (JSR 317), http://www.jcp.org/en/jsr/detail?id=317
  - Java Runtime API for Rule Engines (JSR 94) specification `http://jcp.org/about Java/communityprocess/review/jsr094/index.html`
  - The latest of the Java Thread API is documentated at http://download-llnw.oracle.com/javase/6/docs/api/
  - OpenUp http://epf.eclipse.org/wikis/openup/
  - Object pooling, Apache project for Commons pool at http://commons.apache.org/pool/
  - Resource Description Framework (RDF): http://www.w3.org/TR/2004/REC-owl-features-20040210/#ref-rdf-schema
  - Rule Interchange Format http://www.w3.org/blog/SW/2010/06/22/w3c_rif_recommendation_published
  - SID, a reference model for telecom service providers and vendors, can be downloaded from the web site of the *tele-management forum*, at http://www.tmforum.org/InformationFramework/1684/home.html
  - The Service Component Architecture (SCA):
    - The specification is available at http://www.ibm.com/developerworks/library/specification/ws-sca/
    - A forurm is hosted by the *Open Service Oriented Architecture collaboration* (OSOA), at http://www.osoa.org/display/main/service+component+architecture+home
    - Apache Tuscany open source implementation of the SCA specification at http://tuscany.apache.org/
  - Service Data Objects:
    - Specification at http://www.osoa.org/display/main/service+data+objects+home
    - SDO Apache tuscany project in http://tuscany.apache.org/sdo-overview.html
  - Unified Process (UP): http://en.wikipedia.org/wiki/Unified_Process
  - Web Ontology Language (OWL) http://www.w3.org/2004/OWL/
  - Work Managener for Application Servers (JSR-237), details at http://jcp.org/en/jsr/detail?id=237
- Trade/industry/standard organizations
  - The Business Rule Group web site: http://www.businessrulesgroup.org/defnbrg.shtml

- MISMO is a "technology standards development body for the residential and commercial real estate finance industries, ... wholly owned subsidiary of the Mortgage Bankers Association," http://www.mismo.org
- The Object Management Group (http://www.omg.org) has a number of active standards related to business rules, a number of which are based on (more readable) submissions of the business rules group
- On-line and mixed-media publications
  - http://intelligent-enterprise.informationweek.com
  - http://www.information-management.com/channels/decision_management.html
  - http://www.kmworld.com
  - http://www.bptrends.com
  - InfoWorld publishes, with some regularity, the results of some academic benchmarks using the latest versions of the best known commercial and open-source engines (http://www.infoworld.com)

Documents (standards, web documents, etc.)

- OMG, *Semantics of Business Vocabulary and Business Rules,* SBVR v1.0, January 2008
- The ACORD data model can be found at http://www.acord.org
- The Business Rules, Group, *The Business Motivation Model: Business Governance in a Volatile World*, release 1.3, September 2007
- *Withholding of Tax on Nonresident Aliens and Foreign Entities*, Publication 515 (rev. Aril 2008), Department of the Treasury, Internal Revenue Service
- *Test-driven development:* http://en.wikipedia.org/wiki/Test-driven_development
- Semantics of Business Vocabulary and Business Rules (SBVR), v1.0 http://www.omg.org/spec/SBVR/1.0/PDF
- *Business Motivation Model V 1.0,* Object Management Group
- The Business Rules Group, "Defining business rules – What are they really?", http://www.businessrulesgroup.org/first_paper/br01c3.htm
- For an introductory definition of *finite state machines*, check http://en.wikipedia.org/wiki/Finite-state_machine
- A good introduction to the RETE network that explores more advanced concepts like the handling of ORs and negations. See http://en.wikipedia.org/wiki/Rete_algorithm
- Adaptive Object Model pattern, by Joe Yoder, see http://adaptiveobjectmodel.com/
- Introduction to boolean algebra:
  - http://en.wikipedia.org/wiki/Introduction_to_Boolean_algebra
  - http://www.internettutorials.net/boolean.asp.
- The GOF *Command* pattern is included in the GOF book, but alo explained in http://en.wikipedia.org/wiki/Command_pattern

Tools

In this section, we list the tools that we either referred to in the book or that are relevant. In particular, we listed *some* of the commercial BRMSs (Blaze Advisor, PegaRules , Corticon) and *some* open source/free ones (DROOLS, JESS). There are many more that we did not list. This list is given for illustration purposes only. We also listed other tools that were referred to in the book, including Junit, and some early BRMS tools (see Chap. 7).

- Blaze Advisor, by FICO (http://www.fico.com/en/Products/DMTools/Pages/FICO-Blaze-Advisor-System.aspx)
- Corticon, http://www.corticon.com/
- DROOLS, the Jboss open source BRMS, http://jboss.org/drools/
- JESS, an open-source Java Expert System Shell, from Sandia National Laboratories, at http://herzberg.ca.sandia.gov/jess/
- IBM WebSphere ILOG JRules (or JRules, in short), presented in this book, http://www-01.ibm.com/software/websphere/products/business-rule-management/
- JUnit, the unit testing framework mentioned many times in the book, is available at http://www.junit.org/
- PegaRules, by Pega Systems, at http://www.pega.com/products/decision-management/business-rules
- *International Council on Systems Engineering* maintains a survey of requirements management tools (http://www.incose.org/productspubs/products/rmsurvey.aspx)
- BRS RuleTrack is a product of Business Rule Solutions, http://www.BRSolutions.com
- RuleXpress is a product of RuleArts, check http://www.RuleArts.com
- Versata, http://www.versata.com

Index

CPSIA information can be obtained at www.ICGtesting.com
Printed in the USA
LVOW01*1055160314

377605LV00010B/136/P